ACCOUNTING

THEORY and ANALYSIS

TEXT CASES AND READINGS

Seventh Edition

Richard G. Schroeder
University of North Carolina at Charlotte

Myrtle W. Clark
University of Kentucky

Jack M. Cathey
University of North Carolina at Charlotte

John Wiley & Sons, Inc.
New York · Chichester · Weinheim · Brisbane · Toronto · Singapore

Acquisitions Editor	Mark Bonadeo
Marketing Manager	Clancy Marshall
Senior Production Editor	Patricia McFadden
Senior Designer	Dawn Stanley
Production Management Services	Hermitage Publishing Services

This book was set in 9.5/11 Meridien by Hermitage Publishing Services and printed and bound by Courier Westford. The cover was printed by Phoenix Color.

This book is printed on acid-free paper. ∞

ISBN 0-471-379549

Printed in the United States of America

10 9 8 7 6 5 4 3

Preface

Accounting education has experienced many dramatic changes over the life of this accounting theory text. The publication of the Seventh Edition represents over 20 years of evolution. At its inception, much of what was then considered theory was in reality rule memorization. In recent years, the impact of globalization of the world economy has impacted the skills necessary to be a successful accountant and has caused accounting educators to develop new methods of communicating accounting education. Emphasis is now being given to the incorporation of ethics into the curriculum, the analysis of a company's quality of earning and sustainable income, the use of the World Wide Web as a source of information, and increased emphasis on the international dimension of accounting, the development of critical thinking skills, the development of communication skills, and the use of group projects to develop cooperative skills.

This edition of the text is a further extension of the refocusing of the material to suit the needs of accounting professionals in the twenty-first century. Among the changes in this edition that were designed to accomplish this objective are:

- The expanded use of the World Wide Web by including articles, cases, and updates on the book's web page.
- The inclusion of new material to emphasize the financial analysis of the major topics.
- Discussion of the Business Reporting Research Project in Chapter 1.
- Discussion of fundamental analysis in Chapter 2.
- Discussion of the concept of earning quality in Chapter 3.
- Discussion of the value of corporate earnings in Chapter 4.
- Now included in Chapter 6 is a discussion of the International Accounting Standards Committee's "Framework for the Preparation and Presentation of Financial Statements", a discussion of the IASC's proposed restructuring, a discussion of the FASB's report "International Accounting Standard Setting: A Vision for the Future," and the G4 + 1.
- Updating of the coverage of the 40 International Accounting Standards in each of the appropriate text chapters including the updating of the FASB's evaluation of each of these standards.
- Updating the coverage of the Financial Accounting Standards Board's "Statement of Financial Accounting Standards".

- Addition of new cases to the assignment material including financial analysis cases and cases involving the use of the World Wide Web.
- Inclusion of classroom debate topics to the assignment material in each chapter.

As with earlier editions, each chapter begins with a discussion of the relevant theoretical issues associated with each chapter topic. Next, in this edition, we have incorporated financial analysis of the chapter material. Several readings have been added on the text's web page that address a controversial or confusing issue contained in the chapter. These cases are designed to improve student critical thinking skills, and may be used as group projects. We have also included a financial analysis case and one or two "Room for Debate" cases in each chapter. Finally, each chapter contains an extensive bibliography.

The World Wide Web cases frequently require the student to address questions that involve actual company financial statements. The financial statements of many companies are available through the SEC Edgar form pick page that is found at: www.sec.gov/edaux/formlynx.htm. It contains reports such as forms 10-K and 8-K filed electronically with the SEC by public companies. Many of these forms contain annual reports, including financial statements and the footnote disclosures thereto.

The publication of this text would not be possible without the assistance of many individuals. We are extremely indebted to our colleagues whose comments and criticisms have contributed to the development of the Seventh Edition including Howard Felt, Temple University; Marge O'Reilly-Allen, Rider University; Allen Bizzell, Southwest Texas State University; Larry Watkins, Northern Arizona State University, and Michael Welker, Drexel University. We would also like to single out for special thanks our editor Mark Bonadeo who patiently guided us through a major change of focus for this edition. We are also indebted to our copy editor Betty Pessagno, Patricia McFadden of John Wiley & Sons, and to the staff at Hermitage Publishing Services for their work on this project.

Contents

10 LONG-TERM LIABILITIES   **304**

The Definition of Liabilities, Recognition and Measurement
of Liabilities, Debt versus Equity, Trouble Debt Restructuring,
Financial Analysis of Long-Term Debt, International
Accounting Standards

11 ACCOUNTING FOR INCOME TAXES   **350**

Historical Perspective, The Income Tax Allocation Issue,
Permanent and Temporary Differences, Alternative
Interperiod Tax Allocation Methods, SFAS No 109, Financial
Analysis of Income Taxes, International Accounting
Standards

12 LEASES   **384**

Criteria for Classifying Leases, Accounting and Reporting by
Lessees Under SFAS No 13, Accounting for Loan Origination
Fees and Costs, Financial Analysis of Leases, International
Accounting Standards

13 PENSIONS AND OTHER POSTRETIREMENT BENEFITS   **413**

Historical Perspective, Accounting for the Pension Fund, The
Employee Retirement Income Security Act, Other
Postretirement Benefits, Financial Analysis of Retirement
Benefits, International Accounting Standards

14 EQUITY   **442**

Theories of Equity, Definition of Equity, Recording Equity,
Financial Analysis of Equity, International Accounting
Standards

The

Development of

Accounting

Theory

In its simplest form theory may be just a belief, but in order for a theory to be useful it must have wide acceptance. Webster defines theory as "a systematic statement of principles" and as "a formulation of apparent relationships or underlying principles of certain observed phenomena which has been verified to some degree."[1] The objective of theory is to explain and predict. Consequently, one of the basic goals of the theory of a particular discipline is to have a well-defined body of knowledge that has been systematically accumulated, organized, and verified well enough to provide a frame of reference for future actions.

Theories may be described as normative or positive. *Normative theories* explain what should be, whereas *positive theories* explain what is. Ideally, there should be no such distinction because a well-developed and complete theory encompasses both what should be and what is.

The goal of accounting theory is to provide a set of principles and relationships that provide an explanation for observed practices and predict unobserved practices. That is, accounting theory should be able to explain why business organizations elect certain accounting methods over other alternatives and predict the attributes of firms that elect various accounting methods. Accounting theory should also be verifiable through accounting research.

The development of a general theory of accounting is important because of the role accounting plays in our economic society. We live in a capitalistic society, which is characterized by a self-regulated market that operates through the forces of supply and demand. Goods and services are available for purchase in markets, and individuals are free to enter or exit

[1] *Webster's New Universal Unabridged Dictionary,* 2nd ed. (New York: Simon & Schuster, 1983).

1

the market to pursue their economic goals. All societies are constrained by scarce resources that limit the attainment of all individual or group economic goals. The role of accounting in our society is to report how organizations utilize scarce resources and to report on the status of resources and claims to resources.

As discussed in more detail in Chapter 2, there are various "theories of accounting", including the fundamental analysis model, the efficient markets hypothesis, the capital asset pricing model, the human information processing model, positive accounting theory, and the critical perspective model. These often competing theories exist because accounting theory is still in its developmental stage.

Accounting research is needed to attain a more general theory of accounting and in this regard the various theories of accounting that have been posited must be subjected to verification. A critical question concerns the usefulness of accounting data to users. That is, does the use of a theory help individual decision makers make more correct decisions? Various suggestions on the empirical testing of accounting theories have been offered.[2] As theories are tested and either confirmed or discarded, we will move closer to a general theory of accounting.

The goal of this text is to provide a user perspective on accounting theory. To this end, we first review the development of accounting theory in an effort to illustrate how investor needs have been perceived over time. Next we review the current status of accounting theory with an emphasis on how investors and potential investors use accounting and other financial information. Finally, we illustrate current disclosure requirements for various financial statement items and show how various companies are complying with these disclosure requirements.

The Early History of Accounting

Accounting records dating back several thousand years have been found in various parts of the world. These records indicate that at all levels of development people desire information about their efforts and accomplishments. For example, the Zenon papyri, which were discovered in 1915, contain information about the construction projects, agricultural activities, and business operations of the private estate of Apollonius for a period of about 30 years during the third century B.C.

According to Hain, "The Zenon papyri give evidence of a surprisingly elaborate accounting system which had been used in Greece since the fifth century B.C. and which, in the wake of Greek trade or conquest, gradually spread throughout the Eastern Mediterranean and Middle East."[3] Zenon's accounting system contained provisions for responsibility accounting, a written record of all transactions, a personal account for wages paid to employ-

---

[2] See, for example, Robert Sterling, "On Theory Structure and Verification," *The Accounting Review* (July 1970), pp. 444–457.

[3] H. P. Hain, "Accounting Control in the Zenon Papyri," *The Accounting Review* (October 1966), p. 699.

ees, inventory records, and a record of asset acquisitions and disposals. In addition, there is evidence that all the accounts were audited.[4]

Later, the Romans kept elaborate records, but since they expressed numbers through letters of the alphabet, they were not able to develop any structured system of accounting. It was not until the Renaissance, approximately 1300–1500, when the Italians were vigorously pursuing trade and commerce, that the need to keep accurate records arose. Italian merchants borrowed the Arabic numeral system and the basis of arithmetic, and an evolving trend toward the double-entry bookkeeping system we now use developed.

In 1494 an Italian monk, Fra Luca Pacioli, wrote a book on arithmetic that included a description of double-entry bookkeeping. Pacioli's work, *Summa de Arithmetica Geometria Proportioni et Proportionalita,* did not fully describe double-entry bookkeeping; rather, it formalized the practices and ideas that had been evolving over the years. Double-entry bookkeeping enabled business organizations to keep complete records of transactions and ultimately resulted in the ability to prepare financial statements.

Statements of profit and loss and statements of balances emerged in about 1600.[5] Initially, the primary motive for separate financial statements was to obtain information regarding capital. Consequently, balance sheet data were stressed and refined in various ways, while expense and income data were viewed as incidental.[6]

As ongoing business organizations replaced isolated ventures, it became necessary to develop accounting records and reports that reflected a continuing investment of capital employed in various ways and to periodically summarize the results of activities. By the 19th century, bookkeeping expanded into accounting, and the concept that the owner's original contribution, plus or minus profits or losses, indicated net worth emerged. However, profit was considered an increase in assets from any source, as the concepts of cost and income were yet to be developed.

Another factor that influenced the development of accounting during the 19th century was the evolution of joint ventures into business corporations in England. The fact that many individuals, external to the business, needed information about the corporation's activities created the necessity for periodic reports. In addition, the emerging existence of corporations created the need to distinguish between capital and income.

The statutory establishment of corporations in England in 1845 stimulated the development of accounting standards, and laws were subsequently passed that were designed to safeguard shareholders against improper actions by corporate officers. Dividends were required to be paid from profits, and accounts were required to be kept and audited by persons other than the directors. However, initially anyone could claim to be an accountant, for there were no organized professions or standards of qualifications.

[4] Ibid., pp. 700–701.

[5] A. C. Littleton, *Accounting Evolution to 1900* (New York: AICPA, 1933).

[6] John L. Cary, *The Rise of the Accounting Profession* (New York: AICPA, 1969), p. 5.

The Industrial Revolution and the succession of Companies Acts in England also served to increase the need for professional standards and accountants. In the later part of the 19th century, the Industrial Revolution arrived in the United States, and with it came the need for more formal accounting procedures and standards. This period was also characterized by widespread speculation in the securities markets, watered stocks, and large monopolies that controlled segments of the U.S. economy.

In the 19th century the progressive movement was established in the United States, and in 1898 the Industrial Commission was formed to investigate and report on questions relating to immigration, labor, agriculture, manufacturing, and business. Although no accountants were either on the Commission or used by the Commission, a preliminary report issued in 1900 suggested that an independent public accounting profession should be established in order to curtail observed corporate abuses.

Although most accountants did not necessarily subscribe to the desirability of the progressive reforms, the progressive movement conferred specific social obligations on accountants.[7] As a consequence, accountants generally came to accept three general levels of progressiveness: (1) a fundamental faith in democracy, a concern for morality and justice, and a broad acceptance of the efficiency of education as a major tool in social amelioration; (2) an increased awareness of the social obligation of all segments of society and introduction of the idea of the public accountability of business and political leaders; and (3) an acceptance of pragmatism as the most relevant operative philosophy of the day.[8]

The major concern of accounting during the early 1900s was the development of a theory that could cope with corporate abuses that were occurring at that time, and capital maintenance emerged as a concept. This concept evolved from maintaining invested capital intact to maintaining the physical productive capacity of the firm to maintaining real capital. In essence, this last view of capital maintenance was an extension of the economic concept of income (see Chapter 3) that there could be no increase in wealth unless the stockholder or the firm were better off at the end of the period than at the beginning.

During the period 1900–1915, the concept of income determination was not well developed. There was, however, a debate over which financial statement should be viewed as more important, the balance sheet or the income statement. Implicit in this debate was the view that either the balance sheet or the income statement must be viewed as fundamental and the other residual, and that relevant values could not be disclosed in both statements.

The 1904 International Congress of Accountants marked the initial development of the organized accounting profession in the United States, although there had been earlier attempts to organize and several states had state societies. At this meeting, the American Association of Public Accoun-

[7] Gary John Previts and Barbara Dubis Merino, *A History of Accounting in America* (New York: Ronald Press, 1979), p. 136.

[8] Richard Hofstadter, *Social Darwinism in American Thought* (Philadelphia: University of Pennsylvania Press, 1944).

tants was formed as the professional organization of accountants in the United States. In 1916, after a decade of bitter interfactional disputes, this group was reorganized into the American Institute of Accountants (AIA).

The American Association of the University Instructors in Accounting was also formed in 1916. Initially, this group focused on matters of curriculum development, and it was not until much later that it attempted to become involved in the development of accounting theory.

World War I changed the public's attitude toward the business sector. Many people believed that the successful completion of the war could at least partially be attributed to the ingenuity of American business. As a consequence, the public perceived that business had reformed and that external regulation was no longer necessary. The accountant's role changed from protector of third parties to protector of business interests.

Critics of accounting practice during the 1920s suggested that accountants abdicated the stewardship role, placed too much emphasis on the needs of management, and permitted too much flexibility in financial reporting. During this time financial statements were viewed as the representations of management, and accountants did not have the ability to require businesses to use accounting principles they did not wish to employ.

The result of this attitude is well known. In 1929 the stock market crashed and the Great Depression ensued. Although accountants were not initially blamed for these events, the possibility of governmental intervention in the corporate sector loomed.

Accounting in the United States Since 1930

One of the first attempts to improve accounting began shortly after the inception of the Great Depression with a series of meetings between representatives of the New York Stock Exchange (NYSE) and the American Institute of Accountants. The purpose of these meetings was to discuss problems pertaining to the interests of investors, the NYSE, and accountants in the preparation of external financial statements.

Similarly, in 1935 the American Association of University Instructors in Accounting changed its name to the American Accounting Association (AAA) and announced its intention to expand its activities in the research and development of accounting principles and standards. The first result of these expanded activities was the publication, in 1936, of a brief report cautiously titled "A Tentative Statement of Accounting Principles Underlying Corporate Financial Statements." The four-and-one-half-page document summarized the significant concepts underlying financial statements at that time.

The cooperative efforts between the members of the NYSE and the AIA were well received. However, the post–Depression atmosphere in the United States was characterized by regulation. There was even legislation introduced that would have required auditors to be licensed by the federal government after passing a civil service examination.

Two of the most important pieces of legislation passed at this time were the Securities Act of 1933 and the Securities Exchange Act of 1934, which established the Securities and Exchange Commission (SEC). The SEC was created to administer various securities acts. Under powers provided by Congress, the SEC was given the authority to prescribe accounting principles and reporting practices. Nevertheless, because the SEC has acted as an overseer and allowed the private sector to develop accounting principles, this authority has seldom been used. However, the SEC has exerted pressure on the accounting profession and has been especially interested in narrowing areas of difference in accounting practice. (The role of the SEC is discussed in more detail in Chapter 16.)

By 1937 the prevailing view was that if accountants did not come up with answers to issues the SEC would. The profession was also convinced that it did not have the time needed to develop a theoretical framework of accounting. As a result, the AIA agreed to publish the study by Sanders, Hatfield, and Moore titled *A Statement of Accounting Principles.* The publication of this work was quite controversial in that it was simply a survey of existing practice that was seen as telling practicing accountants, "do what you think is best." Some accountants also used the study as an authoritative source that justified current practice.

In 1937 the AIA merged with the American Society of Certified Public Accountants, and a new, larger organization later named the American Institute of Certified Public Accountants, (AICPA) was formed. This organization has had increasing influence over the development of accounting theory.

Over the years, the AICPA established several committees and boards to deal with the need to further develop accounting principles. The first was the Committee on Accounting Procedure (CAP). It was followed by the Accounting Principles Board (APB), which was replaced by the Financial Accounting Standards Board (FASB). Each of these bodies has issued pronouncements on accounting issues, which have become the primary source of generally accepted accounting principles that guide accounting practice today.

Committee on Accounting Procedure

Professional accountants became more actively involved in the development of accounting principles following the meetings between members of the New York Stock Exchange and the AICPA and the controversy surrounding the publication of the Sanders, Hatfield, and Moore study. In 1938 the AICPA's Committee on Accounting Procedure was formed. This committee had the authority to issue pronouncements on matters of accounting practice and procedure in order to establish generally accepted practices. The works of the committee were published in the form of *Accounting Research Bulletins (ARBs);* however, these pronouncements did not dictate mandatory practice and received authority only from their general acceptance.

The *ARBs* were consolidated in 1953 into *Accounting Terminology Bulletin No. 1,* "Review and Resume"[9] and *ARB No. 43.*[10] From 1953 until 1959 *ARBs*

[9] *Accounting Terminology Bulletin No. 1,* "Review and Resume" (New York: AICPA, 1953).

[10] *Accounting Research Bulletin No. 43,* "Restatement and Revision of Accounting Research Bulletins" (New York: AICPA, 1953).

No. 44 through *No. 51* were published. The recommendations of these bulletins, which have not been superseded, are presented throughout this text where the specific topics covered by the *ARBs* are discussed.

Accounting Principles Board

By 1959 the methods of formulating accounting principles were being criticized, and accountants and financial statement users sought wider representation in the development of accounting principles. The AICPA responded by forming the Accounting Principles Board (APB). The objectives of this body were to advance the written expression of generally accepted accounting principles, to narrow areas of difference in appropriate practice, and to discuss unsettled and controversial issues. The APB was comprised of 17 to 21 members who were selected primarily from the accounting profession but also included individuals from industry, government, and academia.

Initially, the pronouncements of the APB that were termed "Opinions" were not mandatory practice; however, the issuance of *APB Opinion No. 2*[11] and a subsequent partial retraction contained in *APB Opinion No. 4*[12] highlighted the need for more authority. This controversy was due to differences in accounting for the investment tax credit. In 1961 Congress passed the investment tax credit. This legislation provided for a direct tax reduction based on a percentage of the cost of a qualified investment. The APB, after a review of the accounting requirements of this legislation, issued *APB Opinion No. 2*, which stated that this tax reduction amounted to a cost reduction and that the effects of this cost reduction should be amortized over the useful life of the asset acquired. Nevertheless, several large public accounting firms decided to report the results of the investment tax credit only in the period in which it occurred. The APB was thus faced with a serious threat to its authority.

The lack of general acceptance of *APB Opinion No. 2* resulted in the APB partially retreating from its previous position. Though reaffirming the previous decision as being the proper and most appropriate treatment, *APB Opinion No. 4* approved the use of either of the two methods.

The lack of support for some of the APB's pronouncements and concern over the formulation and acceptance of "generally accepted accounting principles" caused the Council of the American Institute of Certified Public Accountants to adopt Rule 203 of the Code of Professional Ethics.[13] This rule requires departures from accounting principles published in *APB Opinions* or *Accounting Research Bulletins* (or subsequently *FASB Statements*) to be disclosed in footnotes to financial statements or in independent auditors' reports when the effects of such departures are material. This action has had the effect of requiring companies and public accountants who deviate from the reporting

---

[11] *APB Opinion No. 2*, "Accounting for the 'Investment Credit'" (New York: AICPA, 1962).

[12] *Accounting Principles Board Opinion No. 4*, "Accounting for the 'Investment Credit'" (New York: AICPA, 1964).

[13] The AICPA's Professional Code of Ethics is discussed in more detail in Chapter 16.

requirements contained in *FASB Statements, APB Opinions,* and *Accounting Research Bulletins* to justify such departures.

In addition to the difficulties associated with passage of *APB Opinions No. 2* and *No. 4,* the APB encountered other problems. The members of the APB were, in effect, volunteers. These individuals had full-time responsibilities to their employers; therefore, the performance of their duties on the APB became secondary. By the late 1960s, criticism of the development of accounting principles again arose. This criticism centered on the following factors.

1. **The independence of the members of the APB.** The individuals serving on the board had full-time responsibilities elsewhere that might have an impact on their views of certain issues.
2. **The structure of the board.** The largest eight public accounting firms (at that time) were automatically awarded one member, and there were usually five or six other public accountants on the APB.
3. **Response time.** The emerging accounting problems were not being investigated and solved quickly enough by the part-time members.

The Financial Accounting Standards Board

As a result of the growing criticism of the APB, the board of directors of the AICPA appointed two committees in 1971. The Wheat Committee, named after its chairman, Francis Wheat, was to study how financial accounting principles should be established. The Trueblood Committee, named after its chairman, Robert Trueblood, was asked to determine the objectives of financial statements.

The Wheat Committee issued its report in 1972 with a recommendation that the APB be abolished and the Financial Accounting Standards Board (FASB) be created. This new board was composed of representatives from various organizations, in contrast to the APB, whose members were all from the AICPA. The members of the FASB were also to be paid and were to work full time, unlike the APB members, who served part time and were not paid.

The Trueblood Committee, formally known as the Study Group on Objectives of Financial Statements, issued its report in 1973 after substantial debate and with considerably more tentativeness in its recommendations about objectives than the Wheat Committee had with respect to the establishment of principles. The study group requested that its report be regarded as an initial step in developing objectives and that significant efforts should be made to continue progress on the refinement and improvement of accounting standards and practices. The objectives enumerated by the Trueblood Committee later became the basis for *Statement of Financial Accounting Concepts No. 1* (discussed later in the chapter).

The AICPA quickly adopted the Wheat Committee recommendations, and the FASB became the official body charged with issuing accounting standards. The structure of the FASB is as follows. A board of trustees nominated by eight organizations whose members have special knowledge and interest in financial reporting is selected. The eight organizations selecting the electors are the American Accounting Association, the AICPA, the Association for Investment Management and Research, the Financial Executives Institute, the Government Finance Officers Association, the Institute of Management Accountants, the National Association of State Auditors, Comptrollers, and Treasurers, and the Security Industry Association.

The board that governs the FASB is the Financial Accounting Foundation (FAF). There are 15 trustees of the FAF. The FAF appoints the Financial Accounting Standards Advisory Council (FASAC), which advises the FASB on major policy issues, the selection of task forces, and the agenda of topics. The number of members on the FASAC varies from year to year. The bylaws call for at least 20 members to be appointed. However, the actual number of members has grown to about 30 in recent years to obtain representation from a wider group of interested parties.

The FAF is also responsible for appointing the seven members of the FASB and raising the funds to operate the FASB. The FAF currently collects in excess of $11 million a year to support the activities of the FASB. Figure 1.1 illustrates the current structures of the FASB.

Both the FAF and the FASB have a broader representation of the total profession than did the APB; however, the majority of members are usually CPAs from public practice. The structure of the Financial Accounting Foundation has recently come under scrutiny by the SEC. In 1996, Arthur Levitt, the chairman of the SEC, voiced concern that the FAF's public interest objec-

FIGURE 1.1. *Structure of the FASB*

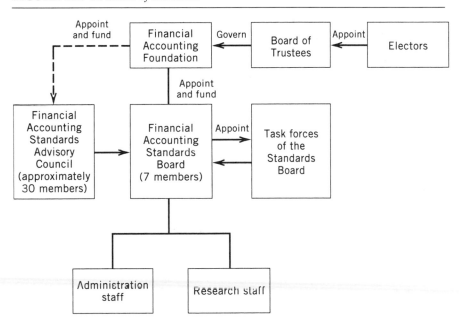

tives were at risk. He suggested that the FAF be reorganized so that the majority of its members would be individuals with strong public service backgrounds who are better able to represent the public free of any conflict of interest. He went on to suggest that the SEC should approve the appointments to the FAF.[14] To date there has been no change in the method of appointing FAF members, and changes in the structure of either the FAF or the FASB are likely to be evolutionary.

At the present time, the FASB is still the body officially designated by the AICPA as having the authority to issue standards for financial accounting. Thus, throughout this book pronouncements of the FASB and APB will be presented as generally accepted accounting principles (GAAP). (One of the first acts of the FASB was to sanction all actions of the APB until such time as they could be reviewed or revised. The APB had done likewise for actions of the CAP. Thus, at this point, the FASB has accepted all currently outstanding pronouncements of both the CAP and the APB.) This book makes frequent references to the APB because much of what is presented originated with that group. The reader should keep in mind that the FASB has adopted those pronouncements.

The Mission of the FASB

The FASB's mission is to establish and improve standards of financial accounting and reporting for the guidance and education of the public, including issuers, auditors, and users of financial information.

In attempting to accomplish this mission, the FASB seeks to:

1. Improve the usefulness of financial reporting by focusing on the primary characteristics of relevance and reliability and on the qualities of comparability and consistency (discussed later in the chapter).

2. Keep standards current to reflect changes in methods of doing business and changes in the economic environment.

3. Consider promptly any significant areas of deficiency in financial reporting that might be improved through the standard-setting process.

4. Promote the international comparability of accounting standards concurrent with improving the quality of financial reporting.

5. Improve the common understanding of the nature and purposes of information contained in financial reports.

The FASB develops broad accounting concepts as well as standards for financial reporting. It also provides guidance on the implementation of standards.

Types of Pronouncements

Originally, the FASB issued two types of pronouncements, *Statements* and *Interpretations.* Subsequently, the FASB established two new series of releases entitled (1) *Statements of Financial Accounting Concepts (SFACs)* and (2) *Technical Bulletins. SFACs* are intended to establish the objectives and concepts that the FASB will use in developing standards of financial accounting and reporting.

---

[14] R. Abelson, "Accounting Group to Meet with SEC in Rules Debate," *New York Times,* May 5, 1996, p. D5.

To date, the FASB has issued seven *Statements of Financial Concepts,* as discussed later in this chapter.

SFACs differ from *Statements of Financial Accounting Standards* in that they do not establish GAAP. Similarly, they are not intended to invoke Rule 203 of the Rules of Conduct of the Code of Professional Ethics. It is anticipated that the major beneficiary of these *SFACs* will be the FASB itself. However, knowledge of the objectives and concepts the board uses should enable financial statement users to better understand the content and limitations of financial accounting information.

Technical Bulletins are strictly interpretive in nature and do not establish new standards or amend existing standards. They are intended to provide guidance on financial accounting and reporting problems on a timely basis.

In summary, the FASB now issues four types of pronouncements.

1. **Statements of Financial Accounting Concepts**—releases designed to establish the fundamentals on which financial accounting standards are based. They do not create GAAP and are issued to (1) guide the FASB in setting standards, (2) guide practicing accountants in dealing with unresolved issues, and (3) help educate nonaccountants.

2. **Statements of Financial Accounting Standards**—releases indicating required accounting methods and procedures for specific accounting issues. SFASs officially create GAAP.

3. **Interpretations**—*modifications or extensions of issues related to previously issued FASB Statements—APB Opinions,* or *Accounting Research Bulletins.* The purpose of Interpretations is to clarify, explain, or elaborate on existing *SFASs, APB Opinions,* or *ARBs.* They require the support of a majority of the members of the FASB, and they also create GAAP.

4. **Technical Bulletins**—guidance on accounting and reporting problems issued by the staff of the FASB. *Technical Bulletins* do not officially create GAAP and are used mainly to assist in dealing with implementation problems.

Emerging Issues

The FASB has been criticized for failing to provide timely guidance on emerging implementation and practice problems. During 1984 the FASB responded to this criticism by (1) establishing a task force to assist in identifying issues and problems that might require action, the Emerging Issues Task Force (EITF), and (2) expanding the scope of the *FASB Technical Bulletins* in an effort to offer quicker guidance on a wider variety of issues.

The EITF was formed in response to two conflicting issues. On the one hand, accountants are faced with a variety of issues that are not fully addressed in accounting pronouncements such as interest rate swaps or new financial instruments. These and other new issues need immediate resolution. On the other hand, many accountants maintain that the ever-increasing body of professional pronouncements has created a standards overload problem (discussed in more detail below). The FASB established the EITF in an attempt to simultaneously address both issues. The goal of the EITF is to provide timely guidance on new issues while limiting the number of issues whose resolutions require formal pronouncements by the FASB.

All the members of the task force occupy positions that make them aware of emerging issues. The current members include the directors of accounting and auditing from the largest CPA firms, representatives from smaller CPA firms, and the FASB's Director of Research, who serves as chairman. It is also expected that the chief accountant of the SEC will attend the meetings of the task force and participate in the deliberations.

The EITF discusses current accounting issues that are not specifically addressed by current authoritative pronouncements and advises the FASB staff on whether an issue requires FASB action. Emerging issues arise because of new types of transactions, variations in accounting for existing types of transactions, new types of securities, and new products and services. They frequently involve a company's desire to achieve "off-balance sheet" financing or "off-income statement" accounting.

Issues may come to the EITF from a variety of sources. Many are raised by members of the task force themselves; others come from questions asked by auditors. Occasionally, an issue may arise because of a question from the SEC or another federal agency. An issue summary is prepared and provides the basis for each issue brought before the EITF. Issue summaries generally include a discussion of the issue, alternate approaches to the resolution of the issue, available references pertaining to the issue, and examples of the transaction in question. An issue summary is not an authoritative pronouncement—it merely represents the views of the EITF members at that time.

The task force attempts to arrive at a consensus on each issue. A consensus is defined as 13 of the 15 voting members. A consensus results in the establishment of a GAAP as described in paragraph 5, level (C) of *SAS No. 69*, discussed later in the chapter.

Standards Overload

In recent years, the FASB, the Securities and Exchange Commission, and the American Institute of Certified Public Accountants have been criticized for imposing too many accounting standards on the business community. This *standards overload* problem has been particularly burdensome for small businesses that do not have the necessary economic resources to research and apply all the pronouncements issued by these authoritative bodies. Those who contend that there is a standards overload problem base their arguments on two allegations:

1. Not all GAAP requirements are relevant to small business financial reporting needs.
2. Even when they are relevant, they frequently violate the pervasive cost-benefit constraint (discussed later in the chapter).

Critics of the standard-setting process for small businesses also assert that GAAP was developed primarily to serve the needs of the securities market. Many small businesses do not raise capital in these markets; therefore, it is contended that GAAP was not developed with small business needs in mind.

Some of the consequences of the standards overload problem to small business are as follows:

1. If a small business omits a GAAP requirement from audited financial statements, a qualified or adverse opinion may be rendered.
2. The cost of complying with GAAP requirements may cause a small business to forgo the development of other, more relevant information.
3. Small CPA firms that audit smaller companies must keep up to date on all the same requirements as large international firms, but cannot afford the specialists that are available on a centralized basis in the large firms.

Many accountants have argued for differential disclosure standards as a solution to the standards overload problem. That is, standards might be divided into two groups. One group would apply to businesses regardless of size. The second group would apply selectively only to large businesses, small businesses, or particular industries. For example, the disclosure of significant accounting policies would pertain to all businesses, whereas a differential disclosure such as earnings per share would be applicable only to large businesses.

The FASB and various other organizations have studied but have not reached a consensus. A special committee of the AICPA favored differential measurement.[15] However, the FASB has generally taken the position that financial statement users might be confused by two measures used to describe or disclose the same economic event. In addition, bankers (a major source of capital for small businesses) and financial analysts have fairly consistently criticized differential measurement as a solution to the standards overload problem.[16]

Standard Setting as a Political Process
A highly influential academic accountant has stated that accounting standards are as much a product of political action as they are of careful logic or empirical findings.[17] This phenomenon exists because a variety of parties are interested in and affected by the development of accounting standards. Various users of accounting information have found that the best way to influence the formulation of accounting standards is to attempt to influence the standard setters. Consequently, the FASB has come under a great deal of pressure to develop or amend standards so as to benefit a particular user group. In some cases this effort has been successful as in the Business Roundtable's efforts to increase the required consensus for passage of a SFAS from a simple majority to five of the seven members of the FASB.

The growth of these pressures is not surprising considering the fact that many accounting standards have significant economic consequences. *Eco-*

---

[15] Special Committee on Accounting Standards Overload, *Report on the Special Committee on Accounting Standards Overload* (New York: AICPA, 1983).

[16] "The FASB's Second Decade," *Journal of Accountancy* (November 1983), p. 95.

[17] Charles T. Horngren, "The Marketing of Accounting Standards," *Journal of Accountancy* (October 1973), p. 61.

nomic consequences refers to the impact of accounting reports on various segments of our economic society. Consider the release of *FASB Statement No. 106* on Other Post Retirement Benefits. This pronouncement requires many companies to change from a pay-as-you-go basis to an accrual basis for health care and other benefits that companies provide to retirees and their dependents. The accrual basis requires companies to measure their obligation to provide future services and accrue these costs during the years employees provide service. The result of *SFAS No. 106* was that many companies simply ceased providing such benefits to their employees, at a large social cost.

The impact on our economic society from *SFAS No. 106* serves to illustrate the need for the FASB to fully consider both the necessity to further develop sound reporting practices and the possible economic consequences of a proposed standard. Accounting standard setting does not exist in a vacuum. It cannot be completely insulated from political pressures, nor can it avoid carefully evaluating the possible ramifications of standard setting.

The Evolution of the Phrase "Generally Accepted Accounting Principles"

One result of the meetings between the AICPA and members of the NYSE discussed earlier was a revision in the wording of the certificate issued by CPAs. The opinion paragraph formerly stated that the financial statements had been examined and were accurate. The terminology was changed to say that the statements are "fairly presented in accordance with generally accepted accounting principles." This expression is now interpreted as encompassing the conventions, rules, and procedures that are necessary to explain accepted accounting practice at a given time. Therefore, financial statements are fair only to the extent that the principles are fair and the statements comply with the principles.

The expression *generally accepted accounting principles* (GAAP) has thus come to play a significant role in the accounting profession. The precise meaning of the term, however, has evolved rather slowly. In addition to official pronouncements promulgated by authoritative organizations, another method of developing GAAP is to determine whether other accountants are using the particular practice in question. There is no need for complete uniformity; rather, when faced with a particular transaction, the accountant is to review the literature and current practice to determine if a treatment similar to the one proposed is being used. For example, if many accountants are using sum-of-year's-digits (SYD) depreciation for assets, this method becomes a GAAP. In the theoretical sense, depreciation may not even be a principle; however, according to current accounting theory formation, if many accountants are using SYD, it becomes a GAAP.

The APB further defined GAAP to

> incorporate the consensus at any time as to which economic resources and obligations should be recorded as assets and liabilities, which changes in them should be recorded, when these changes should be recorded, how the recorded assets and liabilities and changes in them should be measured, what information should be dis-

closed and how it should be disclosed, and which financial statements should be prepared.[18]

This statement did not mean that a GAAP was to be based on what was most appropriate or reasonable in a given situation but that the practice represented consensus; consequently, the APB adopted a positive approach to the development of accounting theory. However, even this definition lacked clarity, since a variety of practices may exist despite a consensus in favor of one or the other. For example, such variation occurs in inventory and depreciation methods.

In 1975 the Auditing Standards Executive Committee of the AICPA issued *Statement on Auditing Standards (SAS) No. 5* with the purpose of explaining more precisely the meaning of the phrase "present fairly ... in conformity with generally accepted accounting principles" as used in the report of independent auditors. According to the committee, the auditor's opinion on the fairness of an entity's financial statements in conformity with GAAP should be based on the judgment as to whether

> *(a) the accounting principles selected and applied have general acceptance; (b) the accounting principles are appropriate in the circumstances; (c) the financial statements, including the related notes, are informative of matters that may affect their use, understanding, and interpretation; (d) the information presented in the financial statements is classified and summarized in a reasonable manner, that is, neither too detailed nor too condensed; and (e) the financial statements reflect the underlying events and transactions in a manner that presents the financial position, results of operations, and changes in financial position stated within a range of acceptable limits, that is, limits that are reasonable and practicable to attain in financial statements.*[19]

A GAAP thus serves to provide the auditor with a framework for making judgments about the fairness of financial statements on the basis of some uniform standard.

The most precise criterion that has been established for determining whether a practice has gained the stature of a GAAP was originally developed by the AICPA and NYSE committee. Those principles having "substantial authoritative support" were to be classified as GAAP. The meaning of the term was not specifically defined at that time, and no single source exists for all established accounting principles. However, Rule 203 of the AICPA Code of Professional Ethics requires compliance with accounting principles promulgated by the body designated by the Council of the Institute to establish such principles, except in unusual circumstances. (Currently, that body is the FASB).

Later, *SAS No. 5* was amended by *SAS No. 43*. This amendment classified the order of priority that an auditor should follow in determining whether an

[18] *APB Statement No. 4,* "Basic Concepts and Accounting Principles Underlying Financial Statements of Business Enterprises" (New York: AICPA, 1970), par. 27.

[19] *Statement on Auditing Standards No. 5,* "The Meaning of 'Present Fairly in Conformity with Generally Accepted Accounting Principles' in the Independent Auditor's Report" (New York: AICPA, 1975), par. 4.

accounting principle is generally accepted. Also, it added to the sources of established accounting principles certain types of pronouncements that did not exist when *SAS No. 5* was issued. This release noted that the determination that a particular accounting principle is generally accepted may be difficult because no single source exists for all such principles.

SAS No. 43 was further amended by *SAS No. 69*, whose stated purpose was to explain the meaning of the phrase "present fairly ... in conformance with generally accepted accounting principles" in the independent auditor's report.[20] *SAS No. 69* again noted that the determination of the general acceptance of a particular accounting principle is difficult because no single reference source exists for all such principles. Section AU of the *Codification of Statements of Auditing Standards* describes the following hierarchy of GAAP:

Level A   FASB Statements
           FASB Interpretations
           SEC Rules and Interpretive Releases
           Accounting Principles Board Opinions (Unless amended)
           Accounting Research Bulletins (Unless amended)
Level B   FASB Technical Bulletins
           AICPA Industry Audit Guides that have been reviewed by the FASB
Level C   AcSEC Practice Bulletins that have been reviewed by the FASB
           Consensuses reached by the EITF
Level D   AICPA Accounting Interpretations (No longer issued)
           FASB Implementation Guides
           Other widely recognized or prevalent accounting practices

In this chapter and throughout much of the book, special attention is given to the pronouncements referred to in Rule 203 of the AICPA Code of Professional Ethics. The reason for this special attention is apparent: Practicing CPAs have an ethical obligation to consider such pronouncements as the primary source of generally accepted accounting principles in their exercise of judgment as to the fairness of financial statements. Opposing views as well as alternative treatments are considered in the text narrative and in the articles contained on the text's website; however, the reader should keep in mind that the development of GAAP has been narrowly defined by the AICPA.

Despite the continuing effort to narrow the scope of GAAP, critics maintain that management is allowed too much leeway in the selection of the accounting procedures used in corporate financial reports. These criticisms revolve around two issues that are elaborated on later in the text: (1) Executive compensation is frequently tied to reported earnings, so management is inclined to adopt accounting principles that increase current revenues and decrease current expenses and (2) the value of a firm in the marketplace is determined by its stock price. This value is highly influenced by financial

---

[20] *Statement on Auditing Standards No. 69*, "The Meaning of 'Present Fairly in Conformity with Generally Accepted Accounting Principles' in the Independent Auditor's Report" (New York, 1993), par. 1.

analysts' quarterly earnings estimates. Managers are fearful that failing to meet these earnings estimates will trigger a selloff of the company's stock and a resultant decline in the value of the firm.

Recently, SEC Chairman Levitt noted these issues and indicated his belief that financial reports were descending "into the grey area between illegitimacy and outright fraud." As a consequence, the SEC has set up an earnings management task force to uncover accounting distortions. Some companies have already voluntarily agreed to restructure their financial statements as a result of this new effort by the SEC. For example, SunTrust Bank, Inc. of Atlanta, though not accused of any wrongdoing, agreed to a three-year restructuring of earnings for the period ended December 31, 1996.[21]

Authority

Neither the AICPA nor any of its committees or boards has any legal authority. In order to be a member of the AICPA, it is necessary to be a certified public accountant, but it is not necessary to be a member in order to be a CPA. The designation CPA and the license to practice are both granted by the individual states. Therefore, a CPA can become a member of the AICPA if he or she so chooses; in fact, a majority of practicing CPAs are members.

Under these circumstances, when official statements are issued, those CPAs who are not members of the AICPA can simply choose to ignore the position taken in the statements. Those who are members can also assert that they are following other substantial authoritative support, and the AICPA can do little in the way of penalty. The individual state boards of accountancy, on the other hand, may suspend a CPA's license for a variety of reasons, and that is indeed a significant penalty. The state boards, however, have played virtually no part in developing or establishing accounting principles.

The fact that acceptance and compliance by CPAs with the pronouncements of the APB and the FASB are voluntary, not legally mandatory, is most important to an understanding of the structure of accounting principles that is presented in this text, since the present volume draws primarily on those pronouncements. In contrast to the APB and FASB pronouncements, those companies that report to the SEC *must* comply with the numerous legal requirements issued by the Securities and Exchange Commission (SEC).

The Conceptual Framework Project

The Conceptual Framework Project represents an attempt by the FASB to develop concepts useful in guiding the board in establishing standards and in providing a frame of reference for resolving accounting issues. Over the years this project first attempted to develop principles or broad qualitative standards to permit the making of systematic rational choices among alternative methods of financial reporting. Subsequently, the project focused on how

---

[21] E. McDonald, "SEC's Levitt Pushes Harder for Changes in Fiscal Reporting and Some Cry Foul," *The Wall Street Journal*, November 17, 1998, p. A2.

these overall objectives could be achieved. The FASB has stated that it intends the Conceptual Framework Project to be viewed not as a package of solutions to problems but rather as a common basis for identifying and discussing issues, for asking relevant questions, and for suggesting avenues for research. The Conceptual Framework Project has resulted in the issuance of seven statements of *Financial Accounting Concepts: No. 1:* "Objectives of Financial Reporting by Business Enterprises"; *No. 2:* "Qualitative Characteristics of Accounting Information"; *No. 3:* "Elements of Financial Statements of Business Enterprises"; *No. 4:* "Objectives of Financial Reporting by Nonbusiness Organizations" (because the focus of this text is financial accounting, *SFAC No. 4* will not be discussed here); *No. 5:* "Recognition and Measurement in Financial Statements of Business Enterprises"; *No. 6:* "Elements of Financial Statements" (*SFAC No. 6* replaced *SFAC No. 3*); and *No. 7:* "Using Cash Flow Information and Present Value in Accounting Measurements."

SFAC Nos. 1 and 2 can be described as the goals to guide practice and indicate how these goals are useful in making qualitative decisions about what to report. Specifically, *SFAC No. 1* defines the primary objective of financial reporting as usefulness. *SFAC No. 2* describes how financial statements can be useful in qualitative terms. *SFAC No. 5* explains that *SFAC Nos. 1* and 2 provide the guidelines for accountants to be able to recognize and measure accounting information. In addition, *SFAC No. 5* describes measurability and states that an item must also meet the definition of an element provided in *SFAC No. 6* to be measurable. *SFAC No. 7* provides a framework for using future cash flows and present value as the basis for accounting measurements. The Conceptual Framework Project is discussed in further detail in the following paragraphs.

Statement of Financial Accounting Concepts No. 1: "Objectives of Financial Reporting by Business Enterprises"

The foundation for *SFAC No. 1* was the work of the Trueblood Committee on the objectives of financial statements; consequently, it is an attempt to establish normative accounting theory. *SFAC No. 1* points out that external financial reporting by business enterprises is not an end in itself. Rather, it is a source of useful information furnished by management to financial statement users who can obtain this information in no other way. *SFAC No. 1* established that the overall objective of financial reporting is to give users a basis for choosing among alternative uses of scarce resources. Although this objective may seem self-explanatory, it is important because it established that user needs are more important than auditor needs in the development of accounting standards. Consequently, effective financial reporting must meet several broad objectives. It must enable current and potential investors, creditors, and other users to

1. Make investment and credit decisions.
2. Assess cash flow prospects.
3. Report enterprise resources, claims to those resources, and changes in them.
4. Report economic resources, obligations, and owners' equity.
5. Report enterprise performance and earnings.

6. Evaluate liquidity, solvency, and flow of funds.

7 Evaluate management stewardship and performance.

8. Explain and interpret financial information.

Following on the basic objective, *SFAC No. 1* went on to state that the FASB intends that these broad objectives will act as guidelines for evaluating the usefulness of new and existing GAAP to users making investment and credit decisions. This goal will help facilitate the efficient use of scarce resources and the operation of capital markets.

Statement of Financial Accounting Concepts No. 2: "Qualitative Characteristics of Accounting Information"

This statement bridges the gap between *Statement of Concepts No. 1* and subsequent statements, covering the elements of financial statements and their recognition, measurement, and disclosure. It addresses the question: What characteristics of accounting information make it useful? Later statements are intended to be concerned with how the purposes of financial accounting are to be attained.

SFAC No. 2 notes that accounting choices are made on at least two levels. First, the FASB or other agencies have the power to require businesses to report in some particular way or to prohibit a method that might be considered undesirable. Second, the reporting enterprise makes accounting choices between alternatives. *SFAC No. 2* attempts to identify and define the qualities that make accounting information useful by developing a number of generalizations or guidelines for making accounting choices on both levels.

The statement indicates that the primary criterion of choice between two alternative accounting methods involves asking which method produces the better, that is, the more useful, information. If the answer to that question is clear, it then becomes necessary to ask whether the value of the better information significantly exceeds that of the inferior information to justify any extra cost (cost-benefit analysis). If a satisfactory answer is given, the choice between alternatives should be clear. The qualities that distinguish better (or more useful) information from inferior (less useful) are primarily the qualities of relevance and reliability (discussed later).

Figure 1.2 illustrates the Hierarchy of Accounting Qualities discussed by *SFAC No. 2* in reviewing the characteristics of accounting information.

From Figure 1.2 we can see that the characteristics of information that make it a desirable commodity are viewed as a hierarchy of qualities, with usefulness for decision making being the most important quality. However, the hierarchy does not distinguish between the primary qualities and other qualities, nor does it assign priority among qualities. In the following paragraphs we discuss each of the hierarchical levels in detail.

Decision Makers and Their Characteristics

Each decision maker judges what accounting information is useful, and that judgment is influenced by such factors as the decision to be made, the methods of decision making to be used, the information already possessed or obtained from other sources, and the decision maker's capacity to process the informa-

FIGURE 1.2. *A Hierarchy of Accounting Qualities*

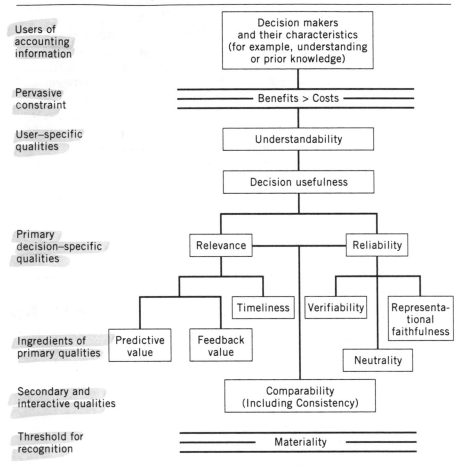

tion. These characteristics indicate that generally managers and owners of small or closely held enterprises may find some external financial reporting information less useful than do stockholders of large publicly held enterprises.[22]

Cost-Benefit Constraint

Unless the benefits to be derived from a commodity or service exceed the costs associated with providing it, it will not be sought after. However, financial information differs from other commodities in that the costs of providing

---

[22] The FASB's Exposure Draft, "Financial Statements and Other Means of Financial Reporting" expands on the conclusion This release examines the issues of what information should be provided, who should provide it, and where it should be presented. In addition, it examines the question: Should GAAP be the same for all companies regardless of size? As noted earlier, the FASB has not issued a final statement that addresses this question.

financial information initially fall on preparers, whereas the benefits accrue to both preparers and users. Ultimately, a standard-setting body must do its best to meet the needs of society as a whole when it promulgates a standard that sacrifices one of those qualities for the other, and it must constantly be aware of the relationship of costs and benefits.

Understandability

Understandability of information is governed by a combination of user characteristics and characteristics inherent in the information. It serves as a "link" between decision makers and accounting information. To meet the *SFAC No. 1* criterion of usefulness, the decision maker must explicitly understand the information. Understandability can be classified as relating to particular decision makers (Does the decision maker speak that language?) or relating to classes of decision makers (Is the disclosure intelligible to the audience for which it is intended?).

Decision Usefulness

According to *SFAC No. 1*, financial information is intended to be useful to decision makers. *SFAC No. 1* established that relevance and reliability are the two primary qualities that make accounting information useful for decision making. Subject to constraints imposed by cost and materiality, increased relevance and increased reliability are the characteristics that make information a more desirable commodity—that is, one useful in making decisions. If either of those qualities is completely missing, the information will not be useful. Although, ideally, the choice of an accounting alternative should produce information that is both more reliable and more relevant, it may be necessary to sacrifice some of one quality for a gain in another.

Relevance

Relevant accounting information can make a difference in a decision by helping users to form predictions about the outcomes of past, present, and future events or to confirm or correct prior expectations. Relevant information has predictive value, feedback value, and timeliness.

Predictive Value and Feedback Value

Information can make a difference to decisions by improving decision makers' capacities to predict or by confirming or correcting their earlier expectations. Usually, information does both at once because knowledge about the outcome of actions already taken will generally improve decision makers' abilities to predict the results of similar future actions.

Timeliness

Having information available to decision makers before it loses its capacity to influence decisions is an ancillary aspect of relevance. If information is not available when it is needed or it becomes available so long after the reported events that it has no value for future action, it lacks relevance and is of little or no use. While timeliness alone cannot make information relevant, a lack of timeliness can rob information of relevance it might otherwise have had.

Reliability

The reliability of a measure rests on the faithfulness with which it represents what it purports to represent, coupled with an assurance for the user that it has that representational quality. To be useful, information must be both reliable and relevant. Degrees of reliability must be recognized. It is hardly ever a question of black and white, but rather of more or less reliability. Reliability rests on the extent to which the accounting description or measurement is verifiable and representationally faithful. Neutrality of information also interacts with those two components of reliability to affect the usefulness of the information.

Verifiability

Verifiability may be demonstrated by securing a high degree of consensus among independent measures using the same measurement methods. Representational faithfulness, on the other hand, refers to the correspondence or agreement between the accounting numbers and the resources or events those numbers purport to represent. A high degree of correspondence, however, does not guarantee that an accounting measurement will be relevant to the user's needs if the resources or events represented by the measurement are inappropriate to the purpose at hand.

Representational Faithfulness

This quality is the correspondence or agreement between a measure and the phenomenon it purports to represent. Sometimes information may be unreliable because of simple misrepresentation. For example, receivables may misrepresent large sums as collectible that are actually uncollectible. Social scientists have defined this concept as validity.

Neutrality

In formulating or implementing standards, the primary concern should be the relevance and reliability of the information that results, not the effect that the new rule may have on a particular interest. A neutral choice between accounting alternatives is free from bias toward a predetermined result. The objectives of financial reporting serve many different information users, who have diverse interests, and no one, predetermined result is likely to suit all interests.

Comparability and Consistency

The usefulness of information about a particular enterprise increases greatly if it can be compared with similar information about other enterprises and with similar information about the same enterprise for some other period or point in time. Comparability between enterprises and consistency in the application of methods over time increase the informational value of comparisons of relative economic opportunities or performance. The significance of information, especially quantitative information, depends to a great extent on the user's ability to relate it to some benchmark.

Materiality Constraint

Materiality is a pervasive concept that relates to the qualitative characteristics, especially relevance and reliability. Both materiality and relevance are defined in terms of what influences or makes a difference to a decision maker, but the two terms can be distinguished. A decision not to disclose certain information may be made, say, because investors have no need for that kind of information (it is not relevant) or because the amounts involved are too small to make a difference (they are not material). Magnitude by itself, without regard to the nature of the item and the circumstances in which the judgment has to be made, will not generally be a sufficient basis for a materiality judgment. The FASB's present position is that no general standards of materiality can be formulated to take into account all the considerations that enter into an experienced human judgment. Quantitative materiality criteria may be given by the board in specific standards in the future, as in the past, as appropriate. See Chapter 2 for a further discussion of materiality.

Statement of Financial Accounting Concepts No. 5: "Recognition and Measurement in Financial Statements of Business Enterprises"

SFAC No. 5 (discussed in more detail in Chapter 4) sets forth recognition criteria and guidance on what information should be incorporated into financial statements and when this information should be reported. This release indicates that a full set of financial statements for a period should disclose financial position at the end of a period, earnings for the period, comprehensive income for the period, cash flows during the period, and investments by and distributions to owners during the period. The statement also notes that recognition and measurement in financial statements are subject to a cost-benefit constraint and a materiality threshold.

Although *SFAC No. 5* did not suggest any radical changes in the then current structure and content of financial statements, it did provide the impetus for the change to a statement of cash flows from the statement of changes in financial position that was previously required. In addition, the scope of the measurement of the operating results of business enterprises was broadened by the definition of comprehensive income.

The future development of accounting theory will use the concepts defined in *SFAC No. 5* as operational guidelines. They should serve as broad boundaries in the development of responses to controversial accounting issues.

Statement of Financial Accounting Concepts No. 6: "The Elements of Financial Statements"

SFAC No. 6 (discussed in more detail in Chapters 4 and 5 defines the 10 elements of financial statements that are used to measure the performance and position of economic entities. These 10 elements—assets, liabilities, equity, investments by owners, distributions to owners, comprehensive income, revenues, expenses, gains, and losses—represent the building blocks used to construct financial statements. The definitions of the elements can be used to determine the content of financial statements. If an item does not meet all of the characteristics of an element, it should not be included in the financial statements.

Statement of Accounting Concepts No. 7: "Using Cash Flow Information and Present Value in Accounting Measurements"

SFAC No. 7 (discussed in more detail in Chapter 5) provides guidance on the use of present value for initial measurement and fresh start measurements and on amortization techniques that are based on future cash flows. This release states that the objective of present value is to estimate fair value. It sets forth five components of present value measurement and describes general principles that govern the application of present value in the measurement of assets and liabilities. In addition, the statement suggests that changes in the original estimated future cash flows be captured either by a change in the interest amortization schedule or by a fresh start measurement of the asset or liability. The Board prefers that these changes in estimate be reported under the catch-up approach.

The Business Reporting Research Project

In 1994 the AICPA's Special Committee on Financial Reporting issued a report titled *Improving Business Reporting—A Customer Focus: Meeting the Information Needs of Investors and Creditors.* This report recommended expanding the types of information disclosed by companies and developed a model of business reporting that the committee believed users need to value and assess the risk of their investments. The model was comprised of the following 10 elements:

1. Financial statements and related disclosures.
2. High-level operating data and performance measurements that management uses to manage its business.
3. Reasons for changes in the financial, operating, and performance-related data and the identity and past effect of key trends.
4. A description of opportunities and risks, including those resulting from key trends.
5. Management's plans, including critical success factors.
6. Comparison of actual business performance to previously disclosed opportunities, risks, and management's plans.
7. Information about directors, management, compensation, major shareholders, and transactions and relationships among related parties.
8. Broad objectives and strategies of the company.
9. Scope and description of the business and properties.
10. Impact of industry structure on the company.

In response to this report and one by the Association for Investment Management and Research that reported on financial analysts' views on the state of financial reporting, the FASB issued an invitation to comment in 1996. The question addressed by this invitation to comment was: "Should the FASB broaden its activities beyond financial statements and related disclosures to also address the types of information that would be included in a more comprehensive business reporting model?"

The results of the invitation to comment were mixed; nevertheless, the FASB decided to undertake a research project on business reporting. The business Reporting Research Project consists of a Steering Committee and seven Working Groups. The Steering Committee provides guidance to the Working Groups and is responsible for achieving the following objectives of the project:

1. Develop recommendations for the voluntary and broad disclosure of certain types of business information for all or selected industries that users of business reporting find helpful in making their investment decisions.
2. Develop recommendations for ways to coordinate generally accepted accounting principles and SEC disclosure requirements to reduce redundancies.
3. Study present systems for the electronic delivery of business information and consider the implications of technology for business reporting in the future.

The seven Working Groups are responsible for the basic research and fact-finding for the project. Some are identifying present practices for the voluntary disclosure of business information in specific industries not presently required by GAAP. Other Working Groups are considering ways to coordinate GAAP and SEC disclosure requirements to eliminate redundancies and are studying present systems for the electronic distribution of information.

The Working Groups will make recommendations to the Steering Committee. Subsequently, the Steering Committee will consider the findings and publish recommendations for the voluntary disclosure of business information. At the present time, it is expected that these disclosures will be encouraged but not be made mandatory. The FASB expects market forces to broaden the number of companies providing these disclosures.

It is expected that the project will be completed in 2001. A summary of its recommendations will be posted on the website for this text.

The Role of Ethics in Accounting

Ethics are concerned with the types of behavior society considers right and wrong. Accounting ethics incorporate social standards of behavior as well as behavioral standards that relate specifically to the profession. The environment of public accounting has become ethically complex. The accountants' Code of Professional Ethics developed by the AICPA has been evolving for a number of years, and as business transactions have become more and more complex, ethical issues have also become more complex.

The public accountant has a Ralph Nader-type overseer role in our society. This role was described by former Chief Justice of the Supreme Court Warren Burger as follows:

> *Corporate financial statements are one of the primary sources of information available to guide the decisions of the investing public. In an effort to control the*

accuracy of their financial data available to investors in the securities markets, various provisions of the federal securities laws require publicly held corporations to file their financial statements with the Securities and Exchange Commission. Commission regulations stipulate that these financial reports must be audited by an independent certified public accountant....

By certifying the public reports that collectively depict a corporation's financial status, the independent accountant assumes a public responsibility transcending any employment relationship with the client. The independent public accountant performing this special function owes ultimate allegiance to the corporation's creditors and stockholders as well as the investing public. This "public watchdog" function demands that the accountant maintain total independence from the client at all times and requires complete fidelity to the public trust.

The SEC requires the filing of audited financial statements in order to obviate the fear of loss from reliance on inaccurate information, thereby encouraging public investment in the nation's industries. It is, therefore, not enough that financial statements be accurate; the public must perceive them as being accurate. Public faith in the reliability of a corporation's financial statements depends upon the public perception of an outside auditor as an independent professional.[23]

Justice Burger outlined the very important role accountants play in our society. This role requires highly ethical conduct at all times. The role of ethics in accounting is discussed in more detail in Chapter 16.

International Accounting Standards

A truly global economy emerged during the 1990s, with many U.S. companies generating significant amounts of revenue and profits in foreign markets. For example, in 1999 over 50% of Procter and Gamble's revenues were earned outside the United States, as illustrated in Table 1.1.

Multinational companies, such as Procter and Gamble, are faced with decisions on the allocation of resources to their most efficient uses. These allocations cannot be accomplished without accurate and reliable financial information. Companies seeking capital or investment opportunities across national boundaries face cost and time issues. Capital-seeking firms must reconcile their financial statements to the accounting rules of the nation in which they are seeking capital, and investors must identify foreign reporting differences. The increasingly global economy requires that this process be simplified. Thus, there is a push to harmonize international accounting standards.

The International Accounting Standards Committee (IASC) is an independent private-sector body that was formed in 1973 to achieve this purpose. Its objectives are:

a. To formulate and publish in the public interest accounting standards to be observed in the presentation of financial statements and to promote their worldwide acceptance and observance.

[23] *U.S. vs. Arthur Young and Co. et al.*, U.S. Supreme Court No. 8206871 U.S.L.W. 4355 (U.S. Mar. 21, 1984), 1.

TABLE 1.1 *Procter and Gamble Segment Information*

	Year	North America	Europe, Middle East, and Africa	Asia	Latin America	Corporate & Other	Total
Net Sales	1999	$18,997	$11,878	$3,648	$2,825	$797	$38,125
	1998	18,456	11,835	3,453	2,640	770	37,154
	1997	17,625	11,587	3,573	2,306	673	35,764
Net Earnings	1999	2,710	1,214	279	318	(758)	3,763
	1998	2,474	1,092	174	274	(234)	3,780
	1997	2,253	956	275	256	(325)	3,415

b. To work generally for the improvement and harmonization of regulations, accounting standards, and procedures relating to the presentation of financial statements.[24]

These objectives have resulted in attempts to coordinate and harmonize the activities of the many countries and agencies engaged in setting accounting standards. The IASC standards also provide a useful starting point for developing countries wishing to establish accounting standards.

The IASC has also developed a conceptual framework termed the Framework for the Preparation and Presentation of Financial Statements. The conclusions articulated in this release are similar to those contained in the FASB's Conceptual Framework Project. That is, the objective of financial statements is to provide useful information to a wide range of users for decision-making purposes. The information provided should contain the qualitative characteristics of relevance, reliability, comparability, and understandability.

To date, the IASC has issued 40 Statements of Accounting Standards (IASs), but since it does not have any enforcement authority the IASC must rely on the "best endeavors" of its members. Neither the Financial Accounting Standards Board nor the Securities and Exchange Commission is a member of the IASC, so its standards do not have authority in the United States. Nevertheless, the emergence of multinational corporations has resulted in a need for the increased harmonization of worldwide accounting standards. The role of the IASC is discussed in more detail in Chapter 6, and the IASC standards are reviewed throughout this text in the chapters dealing with the issued addressed by each IAS. Additionally, the FASB staff has reviewed most of the IASC and these reviews are summarized in the appropriate chapters.

Summary

Accounting activities have been conducted for many hundreds of years, but a general theory of accounting that has universal acceptance has not been

---

[24] *International Accounting Standards* 1996, International Accounting Standards Committee, London, United Kingdom, p. 7.

developed. The factors that have given rise to the need for accounting have included mercantilism, which created the need to account for ventures; the Industrial Revolution, which introduced the need to report to external stockholders; and the Great Depression, which highlighted the need for stricter accounting standards.

The AICPA and its various subgroups continue to be active in the development of accounting principles. In addition, the practices of the accounting profession, the actions of the Securities and Exchange Commission, and the opinions of the academic community influence the development of accounting principles and theory.

The term "generally accepted accounting principles" has become significant in accounting practice. In general, it refers to a consensus within the profession that a given principle is generally accepted as being appropriate to the circumstances in which it is used. Although there are several possible sources for statements of accounting principles, the most authoritative is the FASB and its predecessors, the APB and the CAP. The theoretical framework of accounting has been studied by both the APB and the FASB. The FASB's conclusions are contained in the Conceptual Framework Project.

In the readings contained on the text's website for Chapter 1, the development and current status of the accounting profession is examined further.

Cases

• Case 1-1 Sources of GAAP

Rule 203 of the AICPA Code of Professional Ethics requires compliance with accounting principles, and *Statement of Auditing Standards No. 69* classified the order of priority an auditor should follow in determining whether an accounting principle is generally accepted.

Required:
List and discuss the sources of generally accepted accounting principles.

• Case 1-2 SFAS No. 2

The Financial Accounting Standards Board (FASB) has been working on a conceptual framework for financial accounting and reporting. The FASB has issued seven *Statements of Financial Accounting Concepts*. These statements are intended to set forth objectives and fundamentals that will be the basis for developing financial accounting and reporting standards. The objectives identify the goals and purposes of financial reporting. The fundamentals are the underlying concepts of financial accounting—concepts that guide the selection of transactions, events, and circumstances to be accounted for; their recognition and measurement; and the means of summarizing and communicating them to interested parties.

The purpose of *Statement of Financial Accounting Concepts No. 2*, "Qualitative Characteristics of Accounting Information," is to examine the characteristics that make accounting information useful. The characteristics or qualities of information discussed in *SFAC No. 2* are the ingredients that make information useful and the qualities to be sought when accounting choices are made.

Required:
a. Identify and discuss the benefits that can be expected to be derived from the FASB's conceptual framework study.
b. What is the most important quality for accounting information as identified in *Statement of Financial Accounting Concepts No. 2?* Explain why it is the most important.
c. *Statement of Financial Accounting Concepts No. 2* describes a number of key characteristics or qualities for accounting information. Briefly discuss the importance of any three of these qualities for financial reporting purposes. (CMA adapted)

• Case 1-3 Accounting Ethics

When the FASB issues new standards, the implementation date is usually 12 months from date of issuance, with early implementation encouraged. Becky Hoger, controller, discusses with her financial vice-president the need for early implementation of a standard that would result in a fairer presentation of the company's financial condition and earnings. When the financial vice-president determines that early implementation of the standard will adversely affect the reported net income for the year, he discourages Becky from implementing the standard until it is required.

Required:
a. What, if any, is the ethical issue involved in this case?
b. Is the financial vice-president acting improperly or immorally?
c. What does Hoger have to gain by advocacy of early implementation?
d. Who might be affected by the decision against early implementation? (CMA adapted)

• Case 1-4 Politicalization of Accounting Standards

Some accountants have said that politicalization in the development and acceptance of generally accepted accounting principles (i.e., standard setting) is taking place. Some use the term *politicalization* in a narrow sense to mean the influence by governmental agencies, particularly the Securities and Exchange Commission, on the development of generally accepted accounting principles. Others use it more broadly to mean the compromising that takes place in bodies responsible for developing these principles because of the influence and pressure of interested groups (SEC, American Accounting Association, businesses through their various organizations, Institute of Management Accountants, financial analysts, bankers, lawyers, etc.).

Required:
a. The Committee on Accounting Procedure of the AICPA was established in the mid-to late 1930s and functioned until 1959, at which time the Accounting Principles Board came into existence. In 1973, the Financial Accounting Standards Board was formed, and the APB went out of existence. Do the reasons these groups were formed, their methods of operation while in existence, and the reasons for the demise of the first two indicate an increasing politicalization (as the term is used in the broad sense) of accounting standard setting? Explain your answer by indicating how the CAP, APB, and FASB operated or operate. Cite specific developments that tend to support your answer.
b. What arguments can be raised to support the "politicalization" of accounting standard setting?
c. What arguments can be raised against the "politicalization" of accounting standard setting? (CMA adapted)

• Case 1-5 The FASB

The Financial Accounting Standards Board (FASB) is the official body charged with issuing accounting standards.

Required:
a. Discuss the structure of the FASB.
b. How are the Financial Accounting Foundation members nominated?
c. Discuss the types of pronouncements issued by the FASB.

• Case 1-6 The Theoretical Foundation of Accounting Principles

During the past several years, the Financial Accounting Standards Board has attempted to strengthen the theoretical foundation for the development of accounting principles. Two of the most important results of this attempt are the Conceptual Framework Project and the Emerging Issues Task Force. During this same period, the FASB has been criticized for imposing too many standards on the financial reporting process, the so-called standards overload problem.

Required:
a. Discuss the goals and objectives of
    i. The Conceptual Framework Project
    ii. The Emerging Issues Task Force
b. Discuss the standards overload problem.

• Case 1-7 Generally Accepted Accounting Principles

At the completion of the Darby Department Store audit, the president asks about the meaning of the phrase "in conformity with generally accepted accounting principles" that appears in your audit report on the management's financial statements. He observes that the meaning of the phrase must include more than what he thinks of as "principles."

Required:
a. Explain the meaning of the term "accounting principles" as used in the audit report. (Do not in this part discuss the significance of "generally accepted.")
b. The president wants to know how you determine whether or not an accounting principle is generally accepted. Discuss the sources of evidence for determining whether an accounting principle has substantial authoritative support. Do not merely list the titles of publications.
c. The president believes that diversity in accounting practice will always exist among independent entities despite continual improvements in comparability. Discuss the arguments that support his belief.

• Case 1-8 The Evolution of the Accounting Profession

The 19th century witnessed the evolution of joint ventures into business corporations.

Required:
Discuss how the emergence and growth of the corporate form of business affected perceptions regarding the role of the accounting profession in financial reporting in England and the United States.

• Case 1-9 Comparability and Representational Faithfulness

The FASB has issued *SFAS No. 115,* "Accounting for Certain Investments in Debt and Equity Securities." The Scope section of the pronouncement states that its provisions do not apply to enterprises whose specialized accounting practices include accounting for these investments at market value or fair value.

The result of the scope limitation is that some enterprises will be using the specialized practices and others will be using the practices required by the pronouncement. Thus, the financial statements will be different. The presentation of stockholders' equity will be different. Also, those companies that use the specialized accounting practices will recognize more unrealized gains and losses in the income statements than those companies that will account for the same types of investments under *SFAS No. 115.*

Required:
a. Discuss the qualitative characteristic of comparability. What is its purpose?
b. Does the scope limitation of *SFAS No. 115* affect comparability? Explain. (You do not need to know or describe the specifics of the pronouncement to discuss this issue.)
c. Discuss the concept of representational faithfulness. If financial statements differ under different accounting representations, how can each

company say that their financial statements fairly represent the underlying economic phenomenon which they purport to represent? Discuss.

• Case 1-10 Verifiability and Neutrality

Marcy Corporation purchased a machine, a depreciable asset, for $100,000. Accounting for depreciable assets involves estimating useful life and salvage value and selecting a depreciation method.

Required:
a. Longer depreciable lives and higher salvage values result in lower depreciation charges. How can the selection of useful life and salvage value affect the financial statements? Discuss.
b. Explain the concept of verifiability. Would the useful life and/or amount of salvage value selected be verifiable? Discuss.
c. Explain the concept of neutrality. Selection of the straight-line method over an accelerated method would result in lower depreciation charges in earlier years. Would the selection of straight-line over an accelerated method be neutral? Explain. Would it be ethical? Explain.

• Case 1-11 Decision Usefulness and Relevance

Traditional accounting practice relies on the historical cost principle. For example, fixed assets (property, plant, and equipment) are reported at book value in the balance sheet, that is, at the cost to acquire them less accumulated depreciation. However, the fair value of these assets could be more or less than the reported book value.

Required:
a. Describe the concepts of decision usefulness and relevance.
b. If you were going to buy a company and were seeking information on which to base your decision to purchase, would you prefer that the assets be measured using historical cost or fair value? Why?
c. Do you believe that historical cost is relevant? Explain.

Room for Debate

• Issue 1

Roper Corporation purchased 100 storage boxes for the office. The boxes cost $15 each and should last at least 10 years.

Team Debate:

Team 1:   Argue for the capitalization of the boxes. Your arguments should be grounded on the Conceptual Framework, emphasizing the Objectives of Financial Reporting and the qualitative characteristics of accounting information.

Team 2: Argue against the capitalization of the boxes. Your arguments should be grounded on the Conceptual Framework, emphasizing the Objectives of Financial Reporting and the qualitative characteristics of accounting information.

Recommended Additional Readings

Agrawal, Surenda P. "On the Conceptual Framework of Accounting." *Journal of Accounting Literature* (1987), pp. 165–175.

Beresford, Dennis R. "The Balancing Act in Setting Accounting Standards." *Accounting Horizons* (March 1988), pp. 1–7.

Daley, Lane A., and Terry Tranter. "Limitations on the Value of the Conceptual Framework in Evaluating Extant Accounting Standards." *Accounting Horizons* (March 1990), pp. 15–24.

Depree, Chauncey M., Jr. "Testing and Evaluating a Conceptual Framework of Accounting." *Abacus* (1989), pp. 61–73.

Fogerty, Timothy, J. Mohamed, E. A. Hussein, and J. Edward Ketz. "Political Aspects of Financial Accounting Standard Setting in the USA." *Accounting, Auditing and Accountability*" (Winter 1994), pp. 24–46.

Gerborth, Dale L. "The Conceptual Framework: Not Definitions, But Professional Values." *Accounting Horizons* (September 1987), pp. 1–8.

Hagood, Nanette, and Ray G. Stephens. "A Guide to Standard Setting Bodies." *The Ohio CPA Journal* (August 1995), pp. 44–48.

Harding, Noel, and Jill McKinnon. "User Involvement in the Standard Setting Process: A Research Note on the Congruence of Accountant and User Perceptions of Decision Usefulness." *Accounting, Organizations and Society* (January 1997), pp. 55–67.

Hudack, Lawrence R., and John R. McCallister. "An Investigation of the FASB's Application of Its Decision Usefulness Criteria." *Accounting Horizons* (September 1994), pp. 1–8.

Miller, Paul B.W. "The Conceptual Framework: Myths and Realities." *Journal of Accountancy* (March 1985), pp. 62–71.

Sanders, Thomas Henry, Henry Rand Hatfield, and Underhill Moore. A Statement of Accounting Principles (1939). New York: American Institute of Certified Public Accountants, Haskens and Sells Foundation, Inc.

Solomons, David. "The FASB's Conceptual Framework: An Evaluation." *Journal of Accountancy* (June 1986), pp. 114–125.

Solomons, David. "The Politicization of Accounting." *Journal of Accountancy* (January 1978), pp. 65–72.

Zeff, Stephen A., "The Rise of Economic Consequences." *Journal of Accountancy* (June 1978), pp. 56–63.

Bibliography

American Accounting Association, Committee on Concepts and Standards for External Financial Reports. *Statements on Accounting Theory and Theory Acceptance*, 1977.

American Accounting Association, Committee to Prepare a Statement of Basic Accounting Theory. *A Statement of Basic Accounting Theory*. Sarasota, FL: American Accounting Association, 1966.

Barlev, Benzion. "On the Measurement of Materiality." *Accounting and Business Research* (Summer 1972), pp. 194–197.

Beaver, William H. "What Should Be the FASB's Objectives?" *Journal of Accountancy* (August 1963), pp. 49–56.

Beresford, Dennis R. "What Is the FASB's Role, and How Is it Performing?" *Financial Executive* (September/October 1988), pp. 20–26.

Bernstein, Leopold A. "The Concept of Materiality." *The Accounting Review* 42 (January 1967), pp. 86–95.

Carey, John L. *The Rise of the Accounting Profession,* Vol. 1. New York: American Institute of Certified Public Accountants, 1969.

Carey, John L. *The Rise of the Accounting Profession,* Vol. 2. New York: American Institute of Certified Public Accountants, 1970.

Chambers, Raymond J. "Accounting Principles or Accounting Policies?" *Journal of Accountancy,* (May 1973), pp. 48–53.

Chatfield, Michael. *A History of Accounting Thought,* rev. ed. Huntington, NY: Robert E. Krieger Publishing Co., 1977.

Defliese, Philip L. "The Search for a New Conceptual Framework of Accounting." *Journal of Accountancy* (July 1977), pp. 59–67.

Deinzer, Harvey T. *Development of Accounting Thought.* New York: Holt, Rinehart & Winston, 1965, Chapters 8 and 9.

Frishkoff, Paul. "An Empirical Investigation of the Concept of Materiality in Accounting." *Empirical Research in Accounting: Selected Studies* (1970), pp. 116–129.

Gellein, Oscar S. "Good Financial Reporting." *The CPA Journal* (November 1983), pp. 39–45.

Glazer, Alan S., and Henry R. Jaenicke. "The Conceptual Framework, Museum Collections, and User Oriented Financial Statements," *Accounting Horizons* (December 1991), pp. 28–43.

Hatfield, Henry Rand. "An Historical Defense of Bookkeeping." *Journal of Accountancy* (April 1924), pp. 241–253.

Hertz, Ronald S. "Standards Overload—A Euphemism." *The CPA Journal* (October 1983), pp. 24–33.

Hines, Ruth D. "The FASBs Conceptual Framework, Financial Accounting and the Maintenance of the Social World." *Accounting, Organizations and Society* (1991), pp. 313–332.

Holder, William, and Kimberly Eudy. "A Framework for Building an Accounting Constitution." *Journal of Accounting Auditing and Finance* (Winter 1982), pp. 111–125.

Horngren, Charles T. "Accounting Principles: Private or Public Sector?" *Journal of Accountancy* (May 1972), pp. 37–41.

Ijiri, Yugi. *Theory of Accounting Measurement.* Sarasota, FL: American Accounting Association, 1975.

Larson, Rholan E., and Thomas P. Kelley. "Differential Measurement in Accounting Standards: The Concept Makes Sense." *Journal of Accountancy* (November 1984), pp. 78–86.

Lee, Bernard Z., Rholan E. Larson, and Philip B. Chenok. "Issues Confronting the Accounting Profession." *Journal of Accountancy* (November 1983), pp. 78–85.

Littleton, A. C. *Accounting Evolution to 1900.* New York: AICPA, 1933.

May, Robert G., and Gary L. Sundem. "Research for Accounting Policy: An Overview." *The Accounting Review* (October 1976), pp. 747–763.

Meyer, Philip E. "A Framework for Understanding 'Substance over Form' in Accounting." *The Accounting Review* (January 1976), pp. 80–89.

Miller, Paul B. W. "A New View of Comparability." *Journal of Accountancy* (August 1978), pp. 70–78.

Mosso, David. "Standards Overload—No Simple Solution." *The CPA Journal* (October 1983), pp. 12–22.

Murray, Dennis, and Raymond Johnson. "Differential GAAP and the FASB's Conceptual Framework." *Journal of Accounting Auditing and Finance* (Fall 1983), pp. 4–15.

Paton, W. A., and A. C. Littleton. *An Introduction to Corporate Accounting Standards.* Sarasota, FL: American Accounting Association, 1940.

Paton, William Andrew. *Accounting Theory.* Houston: Scholars Book Co., 1972 (originally published, New York: Ronald Press, 1922).

Pattillo, James W. *The Concept of Materiality in Financial Reporting.* New York: Financial Executives Research Foundation, 1976.

Previts, Gary John. "The SEC and Its Chief Accountants: Historical Impressions." *Journal of Accountancy* (August 1978), pp. 83–91.

Previts, Gary John, and Barbara Dubis Merino. *A History of Accounting in America.* New York: Ronald Press, 1979.

Richardson, Frederick M. "Standards Overload: A Case for Accountant Judgment." *The CPA Journal* (October 1986), pp. 44–52.

Ronen, Joshua, and Michael Schiff. "The Setting of Financial Accounting Standards—Private or Public? *Journal of Accountancy* (January 1978), pp. 66–73.

Snavely, H. Jim. "Needed: An Accounting Constitution." *Management Accounting* (May 1987), pp. 43–47.

Sorter, George H., and Martin S. Gans. "Opportunities and Implications of the Report on Objectives of Financial Statements." *Studies on Financial Accounting Objectives: 1974.* Supplement to Vol. 12 of the *Journal of Accounting Research,* pp. 1–12.

Sprouse, Robert T. "The Importance of Earnings in the Conceptual Framework." *Journal of Accountancy* (January 1978), pp. 64–71.

Sprouse, Robert T. "Prospects for Progress in Financial Reporting." *Financial Analysts Journal* (September–October 1979), pp. 56–60.

Stanga, Keith G., and Jan R. Williams. "The FASB's Objectives of Financial Reporting." *The CPA Journal* (May 1979), pp. 30–34.

Sterling, Robert R. "Conservatism: The Fundamental Principle of Valuation in Traditional Accounting." *Abacus* (December 1967), pp. 109–132.

Sterling, Robert R. "Decision Oriented Financial Accounting." *Accounting and Business Research* (Summer 1972), pp. 198–208.

Sterling, Robert R. "The Going Concern: An Examination." *The Accounting Review* (July 1968), pp. 481–502.

Sterling, Robert R. "A Test of the Uniformity Hypothesis." *Abacus* (September 1969), pp. 37–47.

Tippet, M. "The Axioms of Accounting Measurement." *Accounting and Business Research* (Autumn 1978), pp. 266–278.

Zeff, Stephen A. "Some Junctures in the Evolution of the Process of Establishing Accounting Principles in the U.S.A.: 1917–1972." *The Accounting Review* (July 1984), pp. 447–468.

Zell, Gary A. "The Relationship Between the SEC and the FASB." *The Ohio CPA Journal* (Spring 1982), pp. 81–83.

Research Methodology
and Theories on the
Uses of Accounting
Information

To have a science is to have recognized a domain and a set of phenomena in that domain, and next to have defined a theory whose inputs and outputs are descriptions of phenomena (the first are observations, the second are predictions), whose terms describe the underlying reality of the domain.[1] In Chapter 1, the FASB's Conceptual Framework Project was introduced as the state-of-the-art theory of accounting. However, this theory does not explain how accounting information is used because very little predictive behavior is explained by existing accounting theory. Over the years, accountants have done a great deal of theorizing providing new insights and various ways of looking at accounting and its outcomes. A distinction can be made between theorizing and theory construction. Theorizing is the first step to theory construction, but it is frequently lacking because its results are untested or untestable value judgments.[2]

In the following pages we first introduce several research methods that might be used to develop theories of accounting and its uses. Next we discuss the use of accounting information by investors, and a number of theories on the outcomes of the use of accounting information, including fundamental analysis, the efficient market hypothesis, the capital asset pricing model, agency theory, human information processing, and critical perspective research.

---

[1] Peter Caws, "Accounting Research—Science or Methodology," in Robert R. Sterling (ed.), *Research Methodology in Accounting* (Lawrence, KS: Scholars Book Company, 1972), p. 71.

[2] Edwin H. Caplan, "Accounting Research as an Information Source for Theory Construction," in Robert R. Sterling (ed.), *Research Methodology in Accounting* (Lawrence, KS: Scholars Book Company, 1972), p. 46.

None of these theories is completely accepted; consequently, each of them is somewhere along the path between theorizing and theory.

Research Methodology

Accounting theory can be developed by using several research methodologies. Among the more commonly identified methodologies are (1) the deductive approach, (2) the inductive approach, (3) the pragmatic approach, (4) the ethical approach, and (5) the behavioral approach. In this section we briefly describe each of these research approaches. In addition, we present the scientific method of inquiry, which is essentially a combination of deductive and inductive reasoning, as a guide to research in accounting theory development.

Deductive Approach

The deductive approach to the development of theory begins with the establishment of objectives. Once the objectives have been identified, certain key definitions and assumptions must be stated. The researcher must then develop a logical structure for accomplishing the objectives, based on the definitions and assumptions. This methodology is often described as "going from the general to the specific." If accounting theory is to be developed using the deductive approach, the researcher must develop a structure that includes the objectives of accounting, the environment in which accounting is operating, the definitions and assumptions of the system, and the procedures and practices, all of which follow a logical pattern.

The deductive approach is essentially a mental or "armchair" type of research. The validity of any accounting theory developed through this process is highly dependent on the researcher's ability to identify correctly and relate the various components of the accounting process in a logical manner. To the extent that the researcher is in error as to the objectives, the environment, or the ability of the procedures to accomplish the objectives, the conclusions reached will also be in error.

Inductive Approach

The inductive approach to research emphasizes making observations and drawing conclusions from those observations. Thus, this method is described as "going from the specific to the general" because the researcher generalizes about the universe on the basis of limited observations of specific situations.

Accounting Principles Board Statement No. 4 is an example of inductive research.[3] The "generally accepted accounting principles" described in the statement were based primarily on observation of current practice. In addition, the APB acknowledged that the then current principles had not been derived from the environment, objectives, and basic features of financial accounting. Thus, the study was essentially inductive in approach.

---

[3] This statement was an attempt by the APB to develop a theory of accounting.

Pragmatic Approach

The pragmatic approach to theory development is based on the concept of utility or usefulness. Once the problem has been identified, the researcher attempts to find a utilitarian solution, that is, one that will resolve the problem. This does not suggest that the optimum solution has been found or that the solution will accomplish some stated objective. (Actually, the only objective may be to find a "workable" solution to a problem.) Thus, any answers obtained through the pragmatic approach should be viewed as tentative solutions to problems.

Unfortunately in accounting, most of the current principles and practices have resulted from the pragmatic approach, and the solutions have been adopted as "generally accepted accounting principles" rather than as an expedient resolution to a problem. As noted in Chapter 1, the Sanders, Hatfield, and Moore study, *A Statement of Accounting Principles*, was a pragmatic approach to theory construction. Unfortunately, much subsequent theory development also used this approach. As a result, the accounting profession must frequently admit that a certain practice is followed merely because "that is the way we have always done it," a most unsatisfactory reason, particularly when such questions arise in legal suits.

Scientific Method of Inquiry

The scientific method of inquiry, as the name suggests, was developed for the natural and physical sciences and not specifically for social sciences such as accounting. There are some clear limitations on the application of this research methodology to accounting; for example, the influence of people and the economic environment make it impossible to hold the variables constant. Nevertheless, an understanding of the scientific method can provide useful insights as to how research should be conducted.

Conducting research by the scientific method involves five major steps, which may also have several substeps.

1. Identify and state the problem to be studied.
2. State the hypotheses to be tested.
3. Collect the data that seem necessary for testing the hypotheses.
4. Analyze and evaluate the data in relation to the hypotheses.
5. Draw a tentative conclusion.

Although the steps are listed sequentially, there is considerable back-and-forth movement between the steps. For example, at the point of stating the hypotheses, it may be necessary to go back to step 1 and state the problem more precisely. Again, when collecting data, it may be necessary to clarify the problem or the hypotheses, or both. This back-and-forth motion continues throughout the process and is a major factor in the strength of the scientific method.

The back-and-forth movement involved in the scientific method also suggests why it is difficult to do purely deductive or inductive research. Once the problem has been identified, the statement of hypotheses is primarily a deductive process, but the researcher must have previously made some observations in order to formulate expectations. The collection of data is primarily an inductive process, but determining what to observe and which data to collect will be influenced by the hypotheses. Thus, the researcher may, at any given moment, emphasize induction or deduction, but each is influenced by the other and the emphasis is continually shifting so that the two approaches are coordinate aspects of one method.

Unfortunately, the scientific method of inquiry has received only limited attention in accounting research. Those procedures found to have "utility" have become generally accepted regardless of whether they were tested for any relevance to a particular hypothesis.

Other Research Approaches

Various writers have also discussed the ethical and behavioral approaches to research as being applicable to the development of accounting theory. Others view these approaches as supportive rather than as specific methods for research; that is, they can, and should, influence the researcher's attitude but cannot by themselves lead to tightly reasoned conclusions.

The ethical approach, which is attributed to DR Scott,[4] emphasizes the concepts of truth, justice, and fairness. No one would argue with these concepts as guides to actions by the researcher, but there is always the question of fair to whom, for what purpose, and under what circumstances. Because of questions such as these, this approach may be difficult to use in the development of accounting theory, but it has gained renewed stature as a result of the emergence of a new school of accounting theory development termed "critical perspective" research discussed later in the chapter.

Accounting is recognized as a practice whose consequences are mediated by the human and social contexts in which it operates and the ways in which it intersects with other organizational and social phenomena. As a consequence, both the behavioral and the economic functioning of accounting are now of interest, and questions are being asked about how accounting information is actually used and how it sometimes seems to generate seemingly undesirable and often unanticipated consequences.[5] From this realization has come a new school of accounting research and theory development termed *behavioral accounting research (BAR)*. BAR is the study of the behavior of accountants or the behavior of nonaccountants as they are influenced by accounting functions and reports[6] and is based on research activities in the

[4] DR Scott, "The Basis for Accounting Principles," *The Accounting Review* (December 1941), pp. 341–349.

[5] Anthony M. Hopwood, "Behavioral Accounting in Retrospect and Prospect," *Behavioral Research in Accounting* (1989), p. 2.

[6] Thomas R. Hofstedt and James C. Kinnard, "A Strategy for Behavioral Accounting Research," *The Accounting Review* (January 1970), p. 43.

behavioral sciences. Since the purpose of accounting is to provide information for decision makers, it seems appropriate to be concerned with how preparers and users react to information. BAR has been seen as studying relevant issues but as not having the impact on practice that it should, given the importance of these issues.[7]

The Outcomes of Providing Accounting Information

The development of a theory of accounting will not solve all of the needs of the users of accounting information. Theories must also be developed that predict market reactions to accounting information and how users react to accounting data. In the following section we describe the use of accounting and other information by individuals, and present several theories on how users react to accounting data.

Fundamental Analysis

In Chapter 1 we noted that the FASB has indicated that the one goal of providing accounting information is to provide investors with relevant and reliable information so that they can make informed investment decisions. Individual investors make the following investment decisions:

Buy—A potential investor decides to purchase a particular security on the basis of available information.

Hold—An actual investor decides to retain a particular security on the basis of available information.

Sell—An actual investor decides to dispose of a particular security on the basis of available information.

Individual investors use all available financial information to assist in acquiring or disposing of the securities contained in their investment portfolios that are consistent with their risk preferences and the expected returns offered by their investments. The decision process utilized by individual investors is termed fundamental analysis. *Fundamental analysis* is an attempt to identify individual securities that are mispriced by reviewing all available financial information. These data are then used to estimate the amount and timing of future cash flows offered by investment opportunities, and incorporate the associated degree of risk to arrive at an expected share price for a security. This discounted share price is then compared to the current market price of the security, thereby allowing the investor to make buy-hold-sell decisions.

Investment analysis may be performed by investors themselves or by security analysts. Security analysts are individuals who, because of their training and experience, are able to process and disseminate financial information more accurately and economically than are individual investors. Security analysts and individual investors use published financial statements;

---

[7] Edwin H. Caplan, "Behavioral Accounting—A Personal View," *Behavioral Research in Accounting* (1989), p. 115.

quarterly earnings reports; and the information contained in the Management Discussion and Analysis section of the annual report, particularly those sections containing forward-looking information and the company's future plans. Upon review of these information sources, security analysts frequently make their own quarterly earnings estimates for the most widely held companies. Subsequently, as company quarterly information is released, security analysts comment on the company's performance and may make buy-hold-sell recommendations. As discussed in Chapter 3, security analysts' estimations and recommendations may impact the market price of a company's stock. For example, on April 17, 2000, IBM released a quarterly earnings report after the stock market had closed that indicated its first quarter performance was better than anticipated. Nevertheless, the company's stock dropped $6.50 from $111.50 to $105 because several security analysts lowered their ratings on the stock based on IBM's lowered revenue expectations for the second quarter of 2000. The decline in the value of IBM's stock was probably influenced by the fact that the overall stock market also declined on April 18, 2000, but this example illustrates how investor perceptions of future expectations can impact stock prices.

One school of thought, termed the *efficient market hypothesis,* holds that fundamental analysis is not a useful investment decision tool because a stock's current price reflects the market's consensus of its value. As a result, individual investors are not able to identify mispriced securities. The effect of market forces on the price of securities and the efficient market hypothesis are discussed in the following sections.

The Efficient Market Hypothesis

Economists have argued for many years that in a free market economy with perfect competition, price is determined by (1) the availability of the product (supply) and (2) the desire to possess that product (demand). According to this theory, the price of the particular product is then determined by a consensus in the marketplace. This process is generally represented by the following diagram.

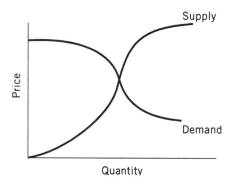

Economists also argue that this model is not completely operational in the marketplace because the following assumptions about the perfectly competitive market are routinely violated by the nature of our economic system.

1. All economic units possess complete knowledge of the economy.
2. All goods and services in the economy are completely mobile and can be easily shifted within the economy.
3. Each buyer and seller must be so small in relation to the total supply and demand that neither has an influence on the price or demand in total.
4. There are no artificial restrictions placed on demand, supply, or prices of goods and services.

The best example of the supply and demand model may be in the securities market, particularly when we consider that stock exchanges provide a relatively efficient distribution system and that information concerning securities is available through many different outlets. Examples of these information sources are

1. Published financial statements from the companies.
2. Quarterly earnings reports released by the corporation through the news media.
3. Reports of management changes released through the news media.
4. Competitor financial information released through financial reports or the news media.
5. Contract awardings announced by the government or private firms.
6. Information disseminated to stockholders at annual stockholders' meetings.

According to the supply and demand model, price is determined by the consensus of purchasers' knowledge of relevant information about the product. This model has been refined in the securities market to become known as the efficient market hypothesis (EMH). The issues addressed by the EMH are (1) what information about a company is of value to investors and (2) does the form of the disclosure of various types of corporate information have impact on the understandability of that information?

The market for securities can be described as efficient if it reflects all available information and reacts instantaneously to new information. Discussions of the EMH in academic literature have varied in the definition of all available information and have resulted in three separate forms of the efficient market hypothesis: the *weak form*, the *semistrong form*, and the *strong form*. The efficient market hypothesis holds that an investor cannot make an *excess return* (a return above what should be expected for a group of securities, given market conditions and the risk associated with the securities) by knowledge of particular pieces of information. The three forms of the EMH differ with respect to their definitions of available information.

Weak Form

The weak form of the EMH is essentially an extension of the random walk theory expressed in the financial management literature. According to this theory, the historical price of a stock provides an unbiased estimate of the future price of that stock, and several studies have supported this argument.[8] However, the argument that stock prices are random does not mean that fluctuation takes place without cause or reason. On the contrary, it suggests that price changes take place because of investor knowledge about perceived earnings potential or alternative investment opportunities.

According to the weak form of the EMH, an investor cannot make excess returns on the basis of simple knowledge of past prices. For example, suppose a certain group of securities with a known risk yields an average return on investment of 10 percent (this average is composed of returns above and below that figure). According to the weak form of the EMH, the stock market incorporates all information on past prices into the determination of the current price. Therefore, the charting of the trends of security prices provides no additional information for the investor. If this form of the EMH is correct, an investor could do just as well by randomly selecting a portfolio of securities as he or she could by charting the past prices of securities and selecting the portfolio on that basis. (It is important to note here that the EMH is based on a portfolio of securities and average returns on investments, not on individual purchases of securities.) The implication of this form of the EMH is that some of the information provided by security analysts is useless. That is, security analysts have correctly maintained that trends in prices are good indicators of future prices. However, knowledge of this information will not aid an investor because, as we have said, it has already been incorporated into the price determination process in the marketplace.

Semistrong Form

The difference between the weak, semistrong, and strong forms of the EMH lies in the amount of information assumed to be incorporated into the determination of security prices. Under the semistrong form of the EMH, all publicly available information including past stock prices is assumed to be important in determining security prices. In other words, if this form of the EMH is correct, no investor can make an excess return by use of publicly available information because this information has already been considered by the marketplace in establishing security prices. The implication of this form of the EMH for accountants is that footnote disclosure is just as relevant as information in the body of financial statements. In addition, it suggests that the accounting procedures adopted by a particular organization will have no effect if an investor can convert to the desired method. The results of studies on this form of the EMH have been generally supportive.

Strong Form

According to the strong form of the EMH, all information, including security price trends, publicly available information, and insider information, is impounded into security prices in such a way as to leave no opportunity for excess returns. The implications of this form of the EMH for accountants is that the marketplace will consider all information available, whether external or internal. That is, as soon as anyone in a corporation knows a piece of information, that information is immediately incorporated into determining

---

[8] See, for example, E. Fama, "The Behavior of Stock Market Prices," *Journal of Business* (January 1965), pp. 285–299.

a security's price in the market. In effect, this form says that published accounting information is no more valuable than any other type of available information, whether or not publicly available.

Most of the evidence testing this form of the EMH suggests that it is not valid. However, one study of mutual funds, whose managers are more likely to have insider information, indicated that such funds did no better than an individual investor could expect to do if he or she had purchased a diversified portfolio with similar risk. In fact, many did worse than randomly selected portfolios would have done.[9] This study tends to support the strong form of the EMH.

The efficient market hypothesis presents an interesting research challenge for accountants. Research strategies must continue to be designed to test each of the EMH forms so that more solid conclusions can be drawn. The EMH is important to accountants because it provides evidence on the manner in which information about business enterprises is incorporated into the price of corporate securities, and research of this nature will allow investor-oriented accounting principles to be developed.

The Implications of Efficient Market Research

The efficient market hypothesis has implications for the development of accounting theory. Some critics of accounting have argued that the lack of uniformity in accounting principles has allowed corporate managers to manipulate earnings and mislead investors.[10] This argument is based on the assumption that accounting reports are the only source of information on a business organization. The results of EMH research suggest that stock prices are not determined solely by accounting reports. This conclusion has led researchers to investigate how accounting earnings are related to stock prices.

The results of these investigations imply that accounting earnings are correlated with security returns. Other accounting research relies on research findings that support the EMH to test market perceptions of accounting numbers and financial disclosures. This research is based on the premise that an efficient market implies that the market price of a firm's shares reflects the consensus of investors regarding the value of the firm. Thus, if accounting information or other financial disclosures reflect items that affect firm value, then they should be reflected in the firms's security price.[11]

---

[9] See, for example, J. Williamson, "Measuring Mutual Fund Performance," *Financial Analyst's Journal* (November–December 1972), pp. 78–84.

[10] Raymond J. Ball and Philip R. Brown, "An Empirical Evaluation of Accounting Income Numbers," *Journal of Accounting Research* (Autumn 1968), pp. 159–178.

[11] Examples of this type of research include G. Peter Wilson, "The Incremental Information Content of the Accrual and Funds Components of Earnings after Controlling for Earnings," *The Accounting Review* (April 1987), pp. 293–321; Thomas L. Stober, "The Incremental Information Content of Financial Statement Disclosures: The Case of LIFO Inventory Liquidations," *Journal of Accounting Research* (Supplement 1986), pp. 138–160; and Bruce Bublitz and Michael Ettredge, "The Information in Discretionary Outlays: Advertising, Research, and Development," *The Accounting Review* (January 1989), pp. 108–124.

The Capital Asset Pricing Model

As indicated earlier in the chapter, investors often wish to use accounting information in an attempt to minimize risk and maximize returns. It is generally assumed that rational individual investors are risk aversive. Consequently, more risky investments must offer higher rates of return in order to attract investors. From an accounting standpoint, this means investors need information on both expected risks and returns. The capital asset pricing model (CAPM) is an attempt to deal with both risks and returns. The actual rate of return to an investor from buying a common stock and holding it for a period of time is calculated by adding the dividends to the increase (or decrease) in value of the security during the holding period and dividing this amount by the purchase price of the security or

$$\frac{\text{dividends} + \text{increase (or} - \text{decrease) in value}}{\text{purchase price}}$$

Since stock prices fluctuate in response to changes in investor expectations about the firm's future cash flows, common stocks are considered risky investments. In contrast, U.S. Treasury Bills are not considered risky investments because the expected and stated rates of return are equal (assuming the T-Bill is held to maturity). Risk is defined as the possibility that actual returns will deviate from expected returns, and the amount of potential fluctuation determines the degree of risk.

A basic assumption of the CAPM is that risky stocks can be combined into a portfolio that is less risky than any of the individual common stocks that make up that portfolio. This diversification attempts to match the common stocks of companies in such a manner that environmental forces causing a poor performance by one company will simultaneously cause a good performance by another, for example, purchasing the common stock of an oil company and an airline company. Although such negative relationships are rare in our society, diversification will reduce risk.

Types of Risk

Some risk is peculiar to the common stock of a particular company. For example, the value of a company's stock may decline when the company loses a major customer such as occurred when the Ford Motor Company lost Hertz as a purchaser of rental cars. On the other hand, overall environmental forces cause fluctuations in the stock market that have impact on all stock prices, such as the oil crisis in 1974.

These two types of risk are termed unsystematic risk and systematic risk. *Unsystematic risk* is that portion of risk peculiar to a company that can be diversified away. *Systematic risk* is the nondiversifiable portion that is related to overall movements in the stock market and is consequently unavoidable. Earlier in the chapter, we indicated that the EMH suggests that investors cannot discover under- or overvalued securities because the market consensus will quickly incorporate all available information into a firm's stock price. However, financial information about a firm can help determine the amount of systematic risk associated with a particular stock.

As securities are added to a portfolio, unsystematic risk is reduced. Empirical research has demonstrated that unsystematic risk is virtually eliminated in portfolios of 30 to 40 randomly selected stocks. However, if a portfolio contains many common stocks in the same or related industries, a much larger number of stocks must be acquired because the rate of returns on such stocks are positively correlated and will tend to increase or decrease in the same direction. The CAPM also assumes that investors are risk aversive; consequently, investors will demand additional returns for taking additional risks. As a result, high-risk securities must be priced to yield higher expected returns than lower risk securities in the marketplace.

A simple equation can be formulated to express the relationship between risk and return. This equation uses the risk-free return (the Treasury Bill rate) as its foundation and is stated

$$R_s = R_f + R_p$$

where

R_s = the expected return on a given risky security

R_f = the risk-free rate

R_p = the risk premium

Since investors can eliminate the risk associated with acquiring a particular company's common stock by purchasing diversified portfolios, they are not compensated for bearing unsystematic risk. And since well-diversified investors are exposed only to systematic risk, investors using the CAPM as the basis for acquiring their portfolios will be subject only to systematic risk. Consequently, the only relevant risk is systematic risk, and investors will be rewarded with higher expected returns for bearing market-related risk that will not be affected by company-specific risk.

The measure of the parallel relationship of a particular common stock with the overall trend in the stock market is termed beta (β). β may be viewed as a gauge of a particular stock's volatility to the total stock market.

A stock with a β of 1.00 has a perfect relationship to the performance of the overall market as measured by a market index such as the Dow-Jones Industrials or the Standard and Poor's 500-stock index. Stocks with a β of greater than 1.00 tend to rise and fall by a greater percentage than the market, whereas stocks with a β of less than 1.00 are less likely to rise and fall than the general market index over the selected period of analysis. Therefore β can be viewed as a particular stock's sensitivity to market changes and as a measure of systematic risk.

The previously stated equation can be restated to incorporate β. Recall that we stated the risk-return equation as

$$R_s = R_f + R_p$$

Restating this equation to incorporate β results in

$$R_s = R_f + P_s(R_m - R_f)$$

where

R_s = the stock's expected return

R_f = the risk-free rate

R_m = the expected return on the stock market as a whole

P_s = the stock's beta, which is calculated over some historical period

The final component of the CAPM concerns how the risk-expected return relationship and securities prices are related. As indicated above, the expected return on a security equals the risk-free rate plus a risk premium. In the competitive and efficient financial markets assumed by the CAPM, no security will be able to sell at low prices to yield more than its appropriate return, nor will a security be able to sell at higher than market price and offer a low return. Consequently, the CAPM holds that a security's price will not be impacted by unsystematic risk, and securities offering relatively higher risk (higher βs) will be priced relatively lower than securities offering relatively lower risk.

A major concern over the use of the CAPM is the relationship of past and future βs. That is, can past βs be used to predict future risk and return relationships? Much of this concern has now been alleviated because empirical research has supported the contention that past βs are good predictors of future stock prices.

The CAPM has also been criticized for contributing to the United States' competitiveness problem. According to critics, U.S. corporate managers using the CAPM are forced into making safe investments with predictable short-term returns instead of investing for the long term. This is particularly true when companies with higher βs attempt to invest in new ventures. Since a high β is seen as evidence of a risky investment, these companies are forced to accept only new projects that promise high rates of return. As a result, researchers have been attempting to develop new models that view the markets as complex and evolving systems that will enable business managers to adopt a more long-range viewpoint.

The CAPM is relevant for accounting theory development because researchers have used it to test hypotheses that rely on the efficient market hypothesis described earlier. For example, researchers have estimated the expected returns of firms using CAPM to discern whether the release of accounting information has information content. The expected returns are compared to actual returns, and the residuals (the differences between expected and actual returns) are examined to see if there is a market reaction to the information release. This approach could be used to see if a new FASB pronouncement provides information that was not previously reflected in security prices.

Normative and Positive Theory

Financial accounting theory attempts to specify which events to record, how the recorded data should be manipulated, and the manner in which the data should be presented. As discussed earlier, accounting theory has developed pragmatically. That is, if a practice or method has been used to satisfy a particular reporting need in the past by a large number of accountants, its continued use is acceptable. As noted in Chapter 1, few attempts to develop a comprehensive theory of accounting were made prior to World War II. Since that time, there has been an increasing demand for a theory of accounting. In the last two decades the efforts to satisfy this demand have permeated accounting literature. These efforts rely heavily on theories developed in mathematics, economics, and finance.

Recall from Chapter 1 that there are two basic types of theory: positive and normative. Positive theories attempt to explain observed phenomena. The extreme diversity of accounting practices and application has made development of a comprehensive description of accounting difficult. Concurrently, to become a theory, description must have explanatory value. For example, not only must the use of historical cost be observed, but that use must also be explained.

Normative theories are based on sets of goals, but there is no set of goals that is universally accepted by accountants. Normative accounting theories are usually acceptable only to those individuals who agree with the assumptions on which they are based. Nevertheless, most accounting theories are normative because they are based on some particular objectives of financial reporting.

Agency Theory

Attempts to describe financial statements and the accounting theories from which they originate, as well as to explain their development based on the economic theories of prices, agency, public choice, and economic regulation, have been grouped under the term *agency theory*. Agency theory attempts to offer a consistent and relatively complete explanation for accounting practices and standards. This research takes the EMH as given and views accounting as the supplier of information to the capital markets.

The basic assumption of agency theory is that individuals maximize their own expected utilities and are resourceful and innovative in doing so. Therefore, the issue raised by agency theory is as follows: What is a particular individual's expected benefit from a particular course of action? That is, how might a manager or stockholder benefit from a corporate decision?

An *agency* is defined as a relationship by consent between two parties, whereby one party (agent) agrees to act on behalf of the other party (principal). For example, the relationship between shareholders and managers of a corporation is an agency relationship, as is the relationship between managers and auditors and, to a greater or lesser degree, that between auditors and shareholders.

An agency relationship exists between shareholders and managers because the owners don't have the training or expertise to manage the firm themselves, have other occupations, and are scattered around the country and world. Consequently, the stockholders must employ someone to represent them. These employees are agents who are entrusted with making decisions in the shareholders' best interests. However, the shareholders cannot observe all of the actions and decisions made by the agents, so a threat exists that the agents will act to maximize their own wealth rather than that of the stockholders. This is the major agency theory issue—the challenge of insuring that the manager/agent operates on behalf of the shareholders and maximizes their wealth rather than his/her own.

Inherent in agency theory is the assumption that a conflict of interest exists between the owners of a firm (shareholders) and the managers. This conflict of interest arises from the possibility that managers are maximizing their own utility, whereas shareholders desire to maximize their own profits. The conflict develops when decisions made by managers to maximize their own utility do not maximize shareholder wealth. For example, a manager may choose accounting alternatives that increase accounting earnings when a management compensation scheme is tied to those earnings.

Agency relationships involve costs to the principals. The costs of an agency relationship have been defined as the sum of (1) monitoring expenditures by the principal, (2) bonding expenditures by the agent, and (3) the residual loss.[12] Watts explains these concepts as follows.

> *Monitoring expenditures are expenditures by the principal to "control" the agent's behavior (e.g., costs of measuring and observing the agent's behavior, costs of establishing compensation policies, etc.). The agent has incentives to make expenditures to guarantee that he will not take certain actions to harm the principal's interest or that he will compensate the principal if he does. These are bonding costs. Finally, even with monitoring and bonding expenditures, the actions taken by the agent will differ from the actions the principal would take himself … the wealth effect of this divergence in actions [is defined] as "residual loss."[13]*

Examples of monitoring costs are external and internal auditors, the Securities and Exchange Commission, capital markets including underwriters and lenders, boards of directors, and dividend payments. Examples, of bonding costs include managerial compensation, including stock options and bonuses, and the threat of a takeover if mismanagement causes a reduction in stock prices.

Since agency theory holds that all individuals will act to maximize their own utility, managers and shareholders would be expected to incur bonding and monitoring costs as long as those costs are less than the reduction in the residual loss. For instance, a management compensation plan that ties management wealth to shareholder wealth will reduce the agency cost of equity, or a bond covenant that restricts dividend payments will reduce the agency costs of debt. Examples of this last type of costs were included in corporate charters as early as the 1600s. According to agency theory, in an unregulated economy, the preparation of financial statements will be determined by the effect of such statements on agency costs. That is, financial statements would tend to be presented more often by companies with many bond covenants (e.g., restrictions on dividends or relatively more outside debt). Similarly, the greater the value of a company's fixed assets, the more likely a charge for

---

[12] M. Johnson and W. H. Meckling, "Theory of the Firm: Managerial Behavior, Agency Costs and Ownership Structures," *Journal of Financial Economics* (October 1976), p. 308.

[13] L. Watts, "Corporate Financial Statements, a Product of the Market and Political Processes," *Australian Journal of Management* (September 1977), p. 131.

maintenance, repair, or depreciation will be included in the financial statements. The conclusion drawn by agency theory is that multiple methods of accounting for similar circumstances have developed from the desires of various individuals, such as managers, shareholders, and bondholders, to minimize agency costs.

Since private-sector regulations and federal legislation help to determine the items disclosed in financial statements, the effects of regulation and the political process must be added to the results of agency relationships. However, the regulation process is affected by external pressures. Groups of individuals may have incentives to band together to cause the government to transfer wealth, as in farm subsidies. The justification for these transfers is that they are "in the public interest." In addition, elected officials and special interest groups may use the so-called high profits of corporations to create crises, which are solved by wealth transfers "in the public interest." A prime example is the "windfall profits" tax enacted at the time of the 1974 oil crisis.

The larger a corporation is, the more susceptible it is to political scrutiny and subsequent wealth transfers. Therefore, the larger a company is, the more likely it is to choose accounting alternatives that minimize net income. Conversely, small companies often have incentives to show greater net income in order to increase borrowing potential and available capital. Agency theory holds that these varying desires are a reason for the diversity of acceptable accounting practices.

Agency theory also attributes the preponderance of normative theories of accounting to impact on the political processes. When a crisis develops, elected officials base their positions on "public interest" arguments. These positions are frequently grounded in the notion that the problem is caused by an inefficiency in the market that can only be remedied by government intervention. Elected officials then seek justification of their position in the form of normative theories supporting that position. They also tend to look for theories prescribing accounting procedures that should be used to increase the information available to investors or make the market more efficient.

The advocates of agency theory maintain that it helps to explain financial statements and the absence of a comprehensive theory of accounting. However, the basic assumption that everyone acts to maximize his or her own expected utility causes this theory to be politically and socially unacceptable. Agency theory advocates maintain that this is true regardless of how logically sound the theory may be, or even how well it may stand up to empirical testing. For example, if an elected official supported a theory that explained her or his actions as those that maximize her or his own utility, rather than the public good, the official would not be maximizing her or his own utility.

Agency theory may help to explain the lack of a comprehensive accounting theory. It implies that a framework of accounting theory cannot be developed because of the diverse interests involved in financial reporting. However, there is an even more basic reason why agency theory will have limited direct impact on financial accounting. Agency theory is a descriptive theory in that it helps to explain why a diversity of accounting practices exists. Therefore, even if subsequent testing supports this theory, it will *not* identify the correct accounting procedures to be used in various circumstances, and thus accounting practice will not be changed.

Human Information Processing

The annual reports of large corporations provide investors with vast amounts of information. These reports may include a balance sheet, an income statement, a statement of cash flows, numerous footnotes to the financial statements, a five-year summary of operations, a description of the various activities of the corporation, a message to the stockholders from the top management of the corporation, a discussion and analysis by management of the annual operations and the company's plans for the future, and the report of the company's independent certified public accountant.

The disclosure of all this information is intended to aid investors and potential investors in making buy-hold-sell decisions about the company's securities. Studies attempting to assess an individual's ability to use information have been broadly classified under the title *human information processing* (HIP) research. The issue addressed by these studies is, How do individuals utilize available information? Consequently, HIP research can be used to determine how individual investors make decisions.

In general, HIP research has indicated that individuals have a very limited ability to process large amounts of information.[14] This finding has three main consequences. In summary, individuals use a selective, stepwise information processing system.

1. An individual's perception of information is quite selective. That is, since individuals are capable of comprehending only a small part of their environment, their anticipation of what they expect to perceive about a particular situation will determine to a large extent what they do perceive.

2. Since individuals make decisions on the basis of a small part of the total information available, they do not have the capacity to make optimal decisions.

3. Since individuals are incapable of integrating a great deal of information, they process information in a sequential fashion.

In summary, this system has limited capacity, and uncertainty is frequently ignored.[15] These findings may have far-reaching disclosure implications for accountants. The current trend of the FASB and SEC is to require the disclosure of more and more information. But if the tentative conclusions of the HIP research are correct, these additional disclosures may have an effect opposite to what was intended. That is, the goal of the FASB and SEC is to provide all

[14] See, for example, R. Libby and B. Lewis. "Human Information Processing Research in Accounting: The State of the Art" *Accounting Organizations and Society,* Vol. 2, No. 3 (1977), pp. 245–268.

[15] For a more thorough discussion, see R. M. Hogarth, "Process Tracing in Clinical Judgments," *Behavioral Science* (September 1974), pp. 298–313.

relevant information so that individuals may make informed decisions about the company. However, the annual reports may already contain more information than can be adequately and efficiently processed by individuals.

Research is needed to determine how the selective processing of information by individuals is processed into the marketplace consensus described by the efficient market hypothesis and to determine the most relevant information to include in corporate annual reports. Once these goals have been accomplished, accountants will have taken a large step in determining what information to disclose about accounting entities.

Critical Perspective Research

Our discussion of fundamental analysis EMH, CAPM, agency theory, and HIP included references to research studies that attempted to test the hypotheses on which these theories were built. Such testing carries an assumption that knowledge of facts can be gained by observation, and accounting research is completely objective. Critical perspective research rejects the view that knowledge of accounting is grounded in objective principles. Rather, researchers adopting this viewpoint share a belief in the indeterminacy of knowledge claims. This indeterminacy view rejects the notion that knowledge is externally grounded and is only revealed through systems of rules that are superior to other ways of understanding phenomena. Critical perspective researchers attempt to interpret the history of accounting as a complex web of economic, political, and accidental co-occurrences.[16] They have also argued that accountants have been unduly influenced by one particular viewpoint in economics (utility-based, marginalist economics). This economic viewpoint holds that business organizations trade in markets that form part of a society's economy. Profit is the result of these activities and is indicative of the organization's efficiency in using society's scarce resources. In addition, these researchers maintain that accountants have also taken as given the current institutional framework of government, markets, prices, and organizational forms,[17] with the result that accounting serves to aid certain interest groups in society to the detriment of other interest groups.[18]

Critical perspective research views mainstream accounting research as being based on the view that there is a world of objective reality that exists independently of human beings, has a determinable nature, and can be observed and known through research. Consequently, individuals are not seen as makers of their social reality; instead, they are viewed as possessing

---

[16] C. Edward Arrington and Jere R. Francis, "Letting the Chat Out of the Bag: Deconstruction, Privilege and Accounting Research," *Accounting, Organizations and Society* (1989), p. 1.

[17] Wai Fong Chau, "Radical Development in Accounting Thought," *The Accounting Review* (October 1986), p. 610.

[18] Anthony M. Tinker, Barbara D. Merino, and Marilyn D. Neimark, "The Normative Origins of Positive Theories, Ideology and Accounting Thought," *Accounting Organizations and Society* (1982), p. 167.

attributes that can be objectively described (i.e., leadership styles or personalities). The critical perspectivists maintain that mainstream accounting research equates normative and positive theory. That is, what is and what ought to be are the same. They also maintain that mainstream accounting research theories are put forth as attempts to discover an objective reality, and there is an expressed or implied belief that the observed phenomena are not impacted by the research methodology. In summary, this branch of accounting theory, mainstream accounting research, is based on a belief in empirical testability.

In contrast, critical perspective research is concerned with the ways societies, and the institutions that make them up, have emerged and can be understood.[19] Research from this viewpoint has been claimed to be based on three assumptions:

1. Society has the potential to be what it is not.
2. Conscious human action is capable of molding the social world to be something different or better.
3. No. 2 can be promoted by using critical theory.[20]

Using these assumptions, critical theory attempts to view organizations in both an historic and a societal context. It seeks to detect any hidden meanings that reside in these contexts, and it is concerned with the power of multinational corporations and the resultant distributions of benefits and costs to societies. Critical theory also does not accept the belief of mainstream accounting theories that organizations survive because they are maximally efficient; rather, it maintains that the methods of research are biased in favor of achieving that conclusion.[21]

Critical perspective accounting researchers have been criticized as wanting to change society and of making accounting only incidental to that desire. The contrasting viewpoints of the mainstream and critical perspective schools of accounting research are further illustrated in the readings contained on the webpage for Chapter 2.

The Relationship Among Research, Education, and Practice

Research is necessary for effective theory development. In most professional disciplines, when research indicates that a preferable method has been found to handle a particular situation, the new method is taught to students, who then implement the method as they enter their profession. That is, research results in education that influences practice. For example, physicians once believed that patients undergoing major surgery needed long periods of bed-

[19] Richard C. Laughlin, "Accounting Systems in Organizational Contexts: A Case for Critical Theory," *Accounting, Organizations and Society* (1987), p. 482.

[20] Ibid., p. 483.

[21] Walter R. Nord, "Toward an Optimal Dialectical Perspective: Comments and Extensions on Neimark and Tinker," *Accounting, Organizations and Society* (1986), p. 398.

rest for effective recovery. However, subsequent research indicated that immediate activity and exercise improved recovery rates. Consequently, it is now common practice for doctors to encourage their surgery patients to begin walking and exercising as soon as it is feasible.

The accounting profession has been criticized for not following this model.[22] In fact, prior to the FASB's development of the Conceptual Framework, research and normative theory had little impact on accounting education. During this period, students were taught current accounting practice as the desired state of affairs, and theoretically preferred methods were almost never discussed in accounting classrooms. As a result, the use of historical cost accounting received little criticism from accounting educators since it was the accepted method of practice, even though it has little relevance to current decision making. Think about where the medical profession might be today if it had adopted a similar policy—doctors might still be using the practice of bloodletting to cure diseases.

The development of the Conceptual Framework and the refinements of the various theories on the outcomes of accounting are serving to elevate the relationship of research, education, and practice to a more desirable state. For example, historical cost accounting is now being openly referred to in a disparaging manner as "once upon a time accounting";[23] *SFAS No. 115* now requires certain marketable securities to be valued at their market values (see Chapters 7 and 8); and new schools of thought, such as the critical perspective theorists, are forcing both educators and practitioners to rethink previously unquestioned practices. However, additional progress is still needed. Traditions are difficult to overcome, and accountants as a group are not known to advocate a great deal of rapid change.

Summary

Several research approaches are available to assist in developing theories of accounting and its uses. The deductive approach requires the establishment of objectives and then proceeding to specific practices. The inductive approach involves making observations and drawing conclusions from those observations. The pragmatic approach identifies problems and reaches utilitarian solutions. The scientific approach involves testing hypotheses and proposed solutions. The ethical approach emphasizes the concepts of truth, justice, and fairness. Finally, behavioral accounting research studies how individuals are influenced by accounting functions and reports.

Several theories on the outcomes of accounting issues were presented. Fundamental analysis attempts to allow individual investors to discover mispriced securities. Efficient market research studies what information is of value to investors and the impact forms of disclosure have on the value of information. Agency theory studies how individuals benefit from particular

---

[22] See, for example, Robert R. Sterling, "Accounting Research, Education and Practice," *Journal of Accountancy* (September 1973), pp. 44–52.

[23] Richard C. Breeden, Chairman of the SEC, in testimony before the United States Senate Committee on Banking, Housing, and Urban Affairs, September 1990.

courses of action. The capital asset pricing model attempts to explain how investors can minimize risk and maximize returns. Human information processing research studies how individuals use and process information. Finally, critical perspective research questions some of the assumptions about economics that accountants have taken as given.

In the readings contained on the webpage, the outcomes of providing accounting information are examined in more detail.

Cases

• Case 2-1 Behavioral Accounting Research

One goal of behavioral accounting research is to assess the effect of accounting numbers and presentations on decision making.

Required:
Design a case with alternative presentations of the same material or alternative numbers to be used to assess the impact of information on decision making. (*Hint:* You may wish to consult Robert Ashton, "Integrating Research and Teaching in Auditing: Fifteen Cases on Audit Judgement and Decision Making," *The Accounting Review* (January 1984), pp. 78–97, to help you develop a case.)

• Case 2-2 Contrasting Views of Profit

Critical perspective theorists maintain that accountants have almost uniformly adopted the marginal economics viewpoint of income and have not considered other views of income. Another view of the nature of income is termed the classical political economy.

Required:
Compare and contrast these two views of income. Can accounting adopt a different view as to income and maintain its important role in our society? (*Hint:* In addition to the articles by Solomons and Tinker contained on the webpage for this chapter, a good starting point is presented in Anthony M. Tinker's "Toward a Political Economy of Accounting: An Illustration of the Cambridge Controversies," *Accounting, Organizations and Society,* Vol. 5, No. 1 (1980), pp. 147–160).

• Case 2-3 Capital Asset Pricing Model

The capital asset pricing model illustrates how risk is incorporated into user decision models.

Required:
Discuss the capital asset pricing model, including systematic and unsystematic risk, beta, the relationship between risk, and return, how to avoid risk, and the relationship of beta to stock prices.

• Case 2-4 Supply and Demand

The efficient market hypothesis is an extension of the supply and demand model.

Required:
a. Discuss the assumptions of the supply and demand model inherent in the efficient market hypothesis.
b. Why is the securities market viewed as a good example of the supply and demand model?
c. Discuss the three forms of the efficient market hypothesis.

• Case 2-5 Research Methodology

Various research methodologies are available with which to study the development of accounting theory.

Required:
Discuss the deductive, inductive, and pragmatic research methods. Include in your discussion examples of accounting research that used each method.

• Case 2-6 Agency Theory

Agency theory provides an explanation for the development of accounting theory.

Required:
Discuss agency theory, including its basic assumptions, agency relationships, why the political process has impact on agency relationships, and why it does or does not explain accounting theory.

• Case 2-7 Human Information Processing

The study of the ability of individuals to interpret information is classified as human information processing research.

Required:
Discuss human information processing research. What is the general finding of this research? What are the consequences of this finding? What impact do these consequences have on accounting?

• Case 2-8 Critical Perspective Research

Critical perspective research views accounting in a somewhat different manner than traditional accounting research.

Required:
a. What is critical perspective research?
b. How does it differ from traditional accounting research?
c. What are the three assumptions of critical perspective research?

• Case 2-9 Economic Consequences

The FASB recently issued *SFAS No. 106*, "Employers' Accounting for Postre-tirement Benefits Other Than Pensions," and *SFAS No. 112*, "Employers' Accounting for Postemployment Benefits." These pronouncements require that companies change from accounting for benefits, such as health care, which are paid to former employees during retirement and between employ-ment and retirement postemployment benefits, on a pay-as-you-go basis to recognizing the expected cost of benefits during employment. As a result, companies must accrue and report expenses today, thereby reducing income and increasing liabilities.

Some have argued that these pronouncements will cause employers to reduce or eliminate postretirement and postemployment benefits. It is not necessary for you to know the particulars of implementing either *SFAS No. 106* or *SFAS No. 112* to address the issues described below.

Required:
a. Should financial reporting requirements affect management's decision-making process? Discuss. Should management reduce or eliminate postretirement or postemployment benefits simply because of the new pronouncement? Discuss.
b. Are there social costs associated with these pronouncements? Explain.
c. What would critical perspectives proponents say about the potential and/or actual impact of these pronouncements?
d. What would mainstream accounting proponents say about the potential and/or actual impact of these pronouncements?

• Case 2-10 Financial Statement Disclosure

Current accounting for leases requires that certain leases be capitalized. For capital leases, an asset and the associated liability are recorded. Whether or not the lease is capitalized, the cash flows are the same. The rental payments are set by contract and are paid over time at equally spaced intervals.

Required:
a. If one of the objectives of financial reporting is to enable investors, cred-itors, and other users to project future cash flows, what difference does it make whether we report the lease as a liability or simply describe its terms in footnotes? Discuss.
b. The efficient market hypothesis (EMH) states that all available informa-tion is impounded in security prices. In an efficient capital market, would it make a difference whether the lease is reported as a liability or simply described in footnotes? Explain.
c. When there are debt covenants that restrict a company's debt to equity ratio and when debt levels rise relative to equity, management may be motivated to structure leasing agreements so that they are not recorded as capital leases. Discuss this motivation in terms of agency theory.

Room for Debate

• Issue 1

According to the efficient market hypothesis (EMH), in an efficient market, the market price of a security instantaneously reflects all relevant information. It has been argued that by the time financial statements are issued, the market price of shares already reflects the information; hence, accounting information is not relevant.

Team debate:

Team 1:   Present arguments that, given the EMH, accounting information is relevant. Your arguments should address all three forms of the EMH.

Team 2:   Present arguments that, given the EMH, accounting information is irrelevant. Your arguments should address all three forms of the EMH.

• Issue 2

Proponents of critical perspectives research believe that mainstream accounting research relies on assumptions that are considered in a vacuum, which does not mirror reality.

Team debate:

Team 1:   Present arguments supporting critical perspectives research.

Team 2:   Present arguments supporting traditional, mainstream accounting research.

Recommended Additional Readings

Chau, Wai Fong. "Radical Development in Accounting Thought." *The Accounting Review* (October 1986), pp. 601–629.

Fama, Eugene, and Kenneth A. French. "The CAPM Is Wanted, Dead or Alive." *Journal of Finance* (December 1996), pp. 1947–1958.

Hopwood, Anthony M. "Behavioral Accounting in Retrospect and Prospect." *Behavioral Research in Accounting* (1989), pp. 1–22.

Jagannathan, Ravi, and Ellen R. McGrattan. "The CAPM Debate." *Federal Reserve Bank of Minneapolis Quarterly Review* (Fall 1995), pp. 2–17.

Libby, Robert, and Barry L. Lewis. "Human Information Processing Research in Accounting: The State of the Art." *Accounting, Organizations and Society,* Vol. 2. No. 3 (1977), pp. 246–268.

Sterling, Robert R. "Accounting Research, Education and Practice." *Journal of Accountancy* (September 1973), pp. 44–52.

Sterling, Robert R. "On Theory Construction and Verification." *The Accounting Review* (July 1970), pp. 444–457.

Wyatt, Arthur R. "Efficient Market Theory: Its Impact on Accounting." *Journal of Accountancy* (February 1983), pp. 56–65.

Bibliography

Abdel-Khalik, A. Rashad. "The Efficient Market Hypothesis and Accounting Data: A Point of View." *The Accounting Review* (October 1972), pp. 791–793.

American Accounting Association. "Report of the 1976–77 Committee on Human Information Processing." *Committee Reports,* Vol. 1978–2 (August 1977).

Arrington, C. Edward, and Jere R. Francis. "Letting the Chat Out of the Bag: Deconstruction, Privilege and Accounting Research." *Accounting, Organizations and Society* (1989), pp. 1–28.

Ashton, Robert. *Human Information Processing in Accounting.* Sarasota, FL: American Accounting Association, 1982.

Ball, Raymond J., and Philip R. Brown. "An Empirical Evaluation of Accounting Income Numbers." *Journal of Accounting Research* (Autumn 1968), pp. 159–178.

Beaver, William. "The Information Content of Annual Earnings Announcements." *Journal of Accounting Research, Selected Studies—Empirical Research in Accounting* (1968), pp. 67–92.

Bierman, Harold, Jr. "The Implications to Accounting of Efficient Markets and the Capital Asset Pricing Model." *The Accounting Review* (July 1974), pp. 557–562.

Caplan, Edwin H. "Behavioral Accounting—A Personal View." *Behavioral Research in Accounting* (1989), pp. 109–123.

Chambers, Anne E., and Stephen H. Penman. "Timeliness of Reporting and the Stock Price Reaction to Earnings Announcements." *Journal of Accounting Research* (Spring 1984), pp. 21–47.

Chambers, R. J. "Stock Market Prices and Accounting Research." *Abacus* (June 1974), pp. 39–54.

Christenson, Charles. "The Methodology of Positive Accounting." *The Accounting Review* (January 1983), pp. 1–22.

Demski, Joel S. "The General Impossibility of Normative Accounting Standards." *The Accounting Review* (October 1973), pp. 718–723.

Downers, David, and Thomas Dyckman. "A Critical Look at the Efficient Market Empirical Research Literature as It Relates to Accounting Information." *The Accounting Review* (April 1973), pp. 300–317.

Dyckman, Thomas R., David H. Downes, and Robert P. Magee. *Efficient Capital Markets and Accounting: A Critical Analysis.* Englewood Cliffs, NJ: Prentice-Hall, 1975.

Evans, John, and Stephen H. Archer. "Diversification and the Reduction of Dispersion: An Empirical Analysis." *Journal of Finance* (December 1968), pp. 761–767.

Frankfurter, George M., and Allan Young. "Financial Theory: Its Message to the Accountant." *Journal of Accounting, Auditing and Finance* (1983), pp. 314–324.

Friend, Irwin, and Marshall E. Blume. "Measurement of Portfolio Performance under Uncertainty." *American Economic Review* (September 1970), pp. 561–575.

Friend, Irwin, Randolph Westerfield, and Michael Granito. "New Evidence on the Capital Asset Pricing Model." *Journal of Finance* (June 1978), pp. 903–920.

Gonedes, Nicholas J. "Efficient Capital Market and External Accounting." *The Accounting Review* (January 1972), pp. 11–21.

Hines, Ruth. "Popper's Method of Falsification and Accounting Research." *The Accounting Review* (October 1988), pp. 657–662.

Hofstedt, Thomas R., and James C. Kinnard. "A Strategy for Behavioral Accounting Research." *The Accounting Review* (January 1970), pp. 38–54.

Hopper, Trevor, John Storey, and Hugh Willmott. "Accounting for Accounting: Toward the Development of the Dialectical View." *Accounting, Organizations and Society* (1987), pp. 437–456.

Laughlin, Richard C. "Accounting Systems in Organizational Contexts: A Case for Critical Theory." *Accounting, Organizations and Society* (1987), pp. 479–502.

Lehman, Cheryl, and Anthony Tinker. "The Real Cultural Significance of Accounts." *Accounting, Organizations and Society* (1989), pp. 503–522.

Libby, Robert. *Accounting and Human Information Processing Theory and Applications.* Englewood Cliffs, NJ: Prentice-Hall, 1981.

Mattessich, Richard. "Methodological Preconditions and Problems of a General Theory of Accounting." *The Accounting Review* (July 1972), pp. 469–487.

Mayer-Sommer, Alan P. "Understanding and Acceptance of the Efficient Market Hypothesis and Its Accounting Implications." *The Accounting Review* (January 1979), pp. 88–106.

Modigliani, Franco, and Gerald A. Pogue. "An Introduction to Risk and Return." *Financial Analysts Journal* (March–April 1974), pp. 68–80.

Nord, Walter R. "Toward an Optimal Dialectical Perspective: Comments and Extensions on Neimark and Tinker." *Accounting, Organizations and Society* (1986), pp. 398–402.

Roll, Richard. "A Critique of the Asset Pricing Theory's Tests." *Journal of Financial Economics* (March 1977), pp. 129–176.

Sharpe, William. "Capital Asset Prices: A Theory of Market Equilibrium under Conditions of Risk." *Journal of Finance* (September 1964), pp. 425–442.

Sterling, Robert R. (ed.). *Research Methodology in Accounting.* Lawrence, KS: Scholars Book Company, 1972.

Tinker, Anthony M. *Paper Profits,* New York: Praeger Publishers, 1985.

Tinker, Anthony M. "Toward a Political Economy of Accounting: An Empirical Illustration of the Cambridge Controversies." *Accounting, Organizations and Society* (1980), pp. 147–160.

Tinker, Anthony M., Barbara D. Merino, and Marilyn D. Neimark. "The Normative Origins of Positive Theories, Ideology and Accounting Thought." *Accounting Organizations and Society* (1982), pp. 167–200.

Tinker, Anthony M., and Marilyn Neimark. "The Struggle over Meaning in Accounting and Corporate Research: Comparative Evaluation of Conservative and Critical Historiography." *Accounting, Auditing and Accountability* (1988), pp. 55–74.

Tippet, Mark. "The Axioms of Accounting Measurement." *Accounting and Business Research* (Autumn 1978), pp. 266–278.

Watts, Ross, and Jerold L. Zimmerman. "The Demand for and the Supply of Accounting Theories: The Market for Excuses." *The Accounting Review* (April 1979), pp. 273–305.

Watts, Ross, and Jerold L. Zimmerman. *Positive Accounting Theory.* Englewood Cliffs, NJ: Prentice-Hall, 1986.

Watts, Ross, and Jerold L. Zimmerman. "Positive Accounting Theory: A Ten Year Perspective." *The Accounting Review* (January 1990), pp. 131–156.

Watts, Ross, and Jerold L. Zimmerman. "Toward a Positive Theory of Determination of Accounting Standards." *The Accounting Review* (January 1978), pp. 112–134.

Williamson, Paul. "The Logic of Positive Accounting Research." *Accounting, Organizations and Society* (1989), pp. 455–468.

Income Concepts

The primary objective of financial accounting is to provide information useful to investors in making predictions about enterprise performance. The emergence of income reporting as the primary source for investor decision making has been well documented,[1] and income reporting aids economic society in a variety of ways. For example, the Study Group on Business Income documented the need for the income concept in society, and Alexander discussed the following uses of income in this work.

1. Income is used as the basis of one of the principal forms of taxation.

2. Income is used in public reports as a measure of the success of a corporation's operations.

3. Income is used as a criterion for determining the availability of dividends.

4. Income is used by rate-regulating authorities for investigating whether those rates are fair and reasonable.

5. Income is used as a guide to trustees charged with distributing income to a life tenant while preserving the principal for a remainderman.

6. Income is used as a guide to management of an enterprise in the conduct of its affairs.[2]

---

[1] Clifford D. Brown, "The Emergence of Income Reporting: An Historical Study," M.S.U. Business Studies (East Lansing, MI: Division of Research, Graduate School of Business Administration, Michigan State University, 1971).

[2] Sidney S. Alexander, "Income Measurement in a Dynamic Economy," *Five Monographs on Business Income,* report by Study Group on Business Income (New York, 1950), p. 6.

Income determination is also important because a company's value is related to its current and future earnings. The FASB has indicated that the purpose of financial accounting is to provide information to financial statement users that will assist them in assessing the amount, timing, and uncertainty of future cash flows. However, the FASB has also asserted that information about corporate earnings provides a better indicator of performance than does cash flow information.[3]

During the past three decades, the relationship of accounting information to the value of the firm has been of interest to accounting researchers. In Chapter 2, the efficient markets hypothesis (EMH) was introduced. EMH holds that a company's stock price reflects market consensus expectations about a company's future earnings and cash flows while simultaneously incorporating information about the economy and competitor actions. The stock price changes in response to new information that is received periodically such as quarterly earnings information. As discussed in Chapter 2, the performance of many large companies is closely followed by financial analysts who provide quarterly earnings estimates. When actual quarterly earnings exceed the financial analysts' consensus estimates, a positive surprise earnings announcement occurs and a company's stock price increases *ceteris paribus*.[4] For a negative surprise the reverse is true. This issue may be further complicated by the existence of a whisper number for closely followed companies. The whisper number occurs when some financial analysts' estimates of a company's quarterly earnings differ from their original estimate as the reporting date approaches. The existence of a whisper number can cause additional positive or negative earnings announcement surprises and also have an impact on the company's stock price. For example, on January 18, 2000 Microsoft's share price rose to $116.50 in anticipation of the company's expected positive earnings surprise announcement the next day (its "whisper number"). However, when the earnings announcement was made on January 19, 2000, the value of Microsoft's shares dropped 8% to 107. Microsoft's actual earnings per share for the quarter were $0.44 as opposed to an estimate of $0.42, but analysts attributed much of the drop in price to Microsoft's inability to meet the whisper number of $0.49.[5] However, other factors that might have contributed to this decline were the company's ongoing problems with the U.S. Justice Department and management's expressed concern about the company's ability to meet future revenue expectations. This issue is particularly relevant for the discussions of materiality, earnings quality, and earnings management contained later in the chapter.

---

[3] *Statement of Financial Accounting Concepts No. 1,* Objectives of Business Reporting by Business Enterprises Business Enterprises" (Stamford, CT: Financial Accounting Standards Board, 1978).

[4] Assuming all other variables remain unchanged.

[5] In October 2000 the SEC released Regulation FD which prohibits the selective disclosure of material nonpublic information. According to this regulation, companies may no longer provide information to financial analysts without making the information freely available to all investors.

Despite the wide use of the income concept in our economy, there is a general lack of agreement as to the proper definition of income. This disagreement is most noticeable when the prevailing definitions used in the disciplines of economics and accounting are analyzed. Although there is general agreement that economics and accounting are related sciences and that both are concerned with the activities of business firms and deal with similar variables, there has been a lack of agreement between the two disciplines regarding the proper timing and measurement of income. As a consequence, a good deal of debate has occurred over the relative importance of the balance sheet and the income statement in determining income. Those who adopt the balance sheet viewpoint see income as the increase in net worth (net increase in asset values) that has occurred during a period—the economic approach. Those favoring the income statement approach view income as the result of certain activities that have taken place during a period. They also view the balance sheet as a list of items that remain after income has been determined by matching costs and revenues—the transactions approach. In order to attempt to reconcile these two viewpoints, the following questions will be addressed:

1. What is the nature of income?
2. When should income be reported?
3. Who are the recipients of income?

The Nature of Income

Income may take various forms; for example, Bedford noted that the literature usually discusses three basic concepts of income:

1. *Psychic income*, which refers to the satisfaction of human wants.
2. *Real income*, which refers to increases in economic wealth.
3. *Money income*, which refers to increases in the monetary valuation of resources.[6]

These three concepts are all important, yet each has both advantages and disadvantages. The measurement of psychic income is difficult because the human wants are not quantifiable and are satisfied on various levels as an individual gains real income.[7] Money income is easily measured but does not take into consideration changes in the value of the monetary unit. Economists generally agree that the objective of measuring income is to determine how much better off an entity has become during some period of time. Consequently, economists have focused on the determination of real income. The

---

[6] Norton M. Bedford, *Income Determination Theory: An Accounting Framework* (Reading, MA: Addison-Wesley Publishing Company, 1965), p. 20.

[7] See, for example, Abraham H. Maslow, *Motivation and Personality* (New York: Harper & Brothers, 1954), Chapter 5.

definition of the economic concept of income is usually credited to the economist J. R. Hicks, who stated:

> *The purpose of income calculation in practical affairs is to give people an indication of the amount which they can consume without impoverishing themselves. Following out this idea it would seem that we ought to define a man's income as the maximum value which he can consume during a week, and still expect to be as well off at the end of the week as he was at the beginning.*[8]

The Hicksian definition emphasizes individual income; however, the concept can also be used as the basis for determining business income by changing the word *consume* to *distribute*. Well-offness at the beginning and end of each accounting period would be the amount of net assets (assets minus liabilities) available to conduct the affairs of the business entity. Business income would be the change in net assets resulting from business activities during the accounting period. That is, business income would be the change in net assets during the accounting period, exclusive of investments by owners and distributions to owners. This concept of income determination, termed the *capital maintenance* concept by accountants, holds that no income should be recognized until capital (equity, or net assets) has been retained and costs recovered.

Capital Maintenance Concepts

The occurrence of income implies a return on invested capital. A return on invested capital occurs only after the amount invested has been maintained or recovered. Consequently, a concept of capital maintenance is critical to distinguishing between a *return of* and a *return on* invested capital, and thus, to the determination of income.

There are two primary concepts of capital maintenance: financial capital maintenance and physical capital maintenance. *Financial capital maintenance* occurs when the financial (money) amount of enterprise net assets at the end of the period exceeds the financial amount of net assets at the beginning of the period, excluding transactions with owners. This view is transactions based. It is the traditional view of capital maintenance employed by financial accountants.

Physical capital maintenance implies that a return on capital (income) occurs when the **physical** productive capacity of the enterprise at the end of the period exceeds its physical productive capacity at the beginning of the period, excluding transactions with owners. This concept implies that income is recognized only after providing for the physical replacement of operating assets.[9] Physical productive capacity at a point in time is equal to the current value of the net assets employed to generate earnings. *Current value* embodies expectations regarding the future earning power of the net assets.

The primary difference between physical capital maintenance and financial capital maintenance lies in the treatment of holding gains and losses. A holding

---

[8] J.R. Hicks, *Value and Capital* (Oxford: Claredon Press, 1946), p. 172.

[9] S. Davidson and R. L. Weil, "Inflation Accounting: The SEC Proposal for Replacement Cost Disclosures," *Financial Analyst Journal* (March/April 1976), pp. 58, 60.

gain or loss occurs when the value of a balance sheet item changes during an accounting period. For example, when land held by a company increases in value, a holding gain has occurred. Proponents of physical capital maintenance consider holding gains and losses as returns of capital and do not include them in income. Instead, holding gains and losses are treated as direct adjustments to equity. Conversely, under the financial capital maintenance concept, holding gains and losses are considered as returns on capital and are included in income.

Current Value Accounting

The concept of physical capital maintenance requires that all assets and liabilities be stated at their current values. The most common approaches to current-value measurement are (1) entry price or replacement cost, (2) exit value or selling price, and (3) discounted present value of expected future cash flows. Each of these approaches will be discussed briefly in order to demonstrate their strengths and weaknesses.

Entry Price or Replacement Cost

When productive capacity is measured using replacement cost, assets are stated at the cost to replace them with similar assets in similar condition. In order to maintain the entity's physical productive capacity, it must generate enough cash flows to provide for the physical replacement of operating assets. To determine income under this approach, revenues are matched against the current cost of replacing these assets. Consequently, income can be distributed to the owners without impairing the physical capacity to continue operating into the future.[10] As a result, the appropriateness of using the entry value approach relies on the accounting assumption of business continuity.

According to Edwards and Bell, current entry prices allow the assessment of managerial decisions to hold assets by segregating current value income (holding gains and losses) from current operating income.[11] Under the assumption that operations will continue, this dichotomy allows the long-run profitability of the enterprise to be assessed. The recurring and relatively controllable profits can be evaluated vis-à-vis those factors that affect operations over time but are beyond the control of management. Replacement cost provides a measure of the cost to replace the current operating capacity and, hence, a means of evaluating how much the firm can distribute to stockholders and still maintain its productive capacity.

---

[10] Experiments using entry price or replacement cost measurements were first attempted in the 1920s. Renewed interest in this approach to asset valuation and income determination was generated in the 1960s by E. O. Edwards and P. W. Bell, *Theory and Measurement of Business Income* (Berkeley: University of California Press, 1961, pp. 33–69, Robert T. Sprouse and Maurice Moonitz, "A Tentative Set of Broad Accounting Principles for Business Enterprises," *Accounting Research Study No. 3* (New York: AICPA, 1962), and a committee of the American Accounting Association, *A Statement of Basic Accounting Theory* (Evanston, IL: AAA, 1966), among others.

[11] Edwards and Bell, op. cit., p. 73.

Nevertheless, numerous measurement problems are encountered in determining replacement cost values. That is, the firm may be able to determine precisely the replacement cost for inventories and certain other assets; for many assets, however, especially the physical plant, there may not be a ready market from which to acquire replacement assets. In such cases, the firm may have to get the assets appraised in order to arrive at an approximation of their current replacement values.

An alternative approach to approximate replacement cost is to use a specific purchasing power index. A specific price index is designed to measure what has happened to the prices of a specific segment of the economy, for example, capital equipment used in a particular industry, such as steel or mining. Application of a specific purchasing power index should provide a reasonable approximation of replacement cost as long as the price of the asset being measured moves in a manner similar to similar assets in the industry.

Finally, the relevance of entry values has been questioned. Sterling argued that the entry value of unowned assets is relevant only when asset purchases are contemplated. For owned assets, entry value is irrelevant to what could be realized upon sale of those assets and to their purchase since they are already owned.[12] Moreover, the current replacement cost of a company's assets does not measure the capacity, on the basis of present holdings, to make decisions to buy, hold, or sell in the market place.[13] In short, the contention is that it does not disclose the entity's ability to adapt to present decision alternatives.

Exit Value or Selling Price
Another approach to determining current value is exit value or selling price.[14] This valuation approach requires the assessment of each asset from a disposal point of view. That is, all assets—inventory, plant, equipment, and so on—are valued based on the selling price that would be realized if the firm chose to dispose of the assets. In determining the cash equivalent exit price, it is presumed that the assets will be sold in an orderly manner rather than be subject to forced liquidation.

Because holding gains and losses receive immediate recognition, the exit price approach to valuation completely abandons the realization principle for the recognition of revenues. The critical event for earnings recognition purposes becomes the point of purchase rather than the point of sale.

Chambers and Sterling contend that exit prices have decision relevance. Accordingly, during each accounting period, management decides whether to hold, sell, or replace the assets. It is argued that the exit prices provide users with better information to evaluate liquidity and thus the ability of the enterprise to adapt to changing economic stimuli. Because management has the option of selling the asset, exit price provides a means of assessing downside

---

[12] Robert R. Sterling, *Toward a Science of Accounting* (Houston, TX: Scholars Book Co., 1979), p. 124.

[13] Chambers, Raymond S. *Accounting Evaluation and Economic Behavior* (Englewood Cliffs, NJ: Prentice Hall, 1966), p. 92.

[14] Exit price was first advocated by McNeal (1939).

risk. It measures the current sacrifice of holding the asset and thereby provides a guide for evaluating management's stewardship function.

Like entry prices, determining exit values also poses measurement problems. First, there is the basic problem of determining a selling price for those assets, such as property, plant, and equipment, for which there is no ready market. Second, the notion that exit price should be based on prices arising from sales in the normal course of business, rather than forced liquidation, may be feasible for assets such as inventory but may be impracticable, if not impossible, for the physical plant, since it would not be disposed of in the normal course of business.

One can argue that replacement costs are more relevant measures of the current value of fixed assets, whereas exit values are better measures of the current value of inventory items. Since management intends to use rather than sell fixed assets, their value in use is what it would cost to replace them. On the other hand, inventory is purchased for resale. Consequently, its value is directly related to its selling price to customers.

Finally, exit value or selling price is inconsistent with the concept of physical capital maintenance. Selling prices generate the cash inflows that must cover the expected cost of replacing operating assets before a return on capital can be distributed to owners. Exit value is a type of opportunity cost. It measures the sacrifice of holding an asset rather than the expected cost of replacing it. Moreover, physical capital maintenance is based on the concept of continuity, not liquidation.

Discounted Present Value

A third approach to the measurement of net asset value is discounted cash flow. According to this concept, the present value of the future cash flows expected to be received from an asset (or disbursed for a liability) is the relevant value of the asset (or liability) that should be disclosed in the balance sheet. Under this method, income is equal to the difference between the present value of the net assets at the end of the period and their present value at the beginning of the period, excluding the effects of investments by owners and distributions to owners. This measurement process is similar to the economic concept of income because discounted present value is perhaps the closest approximation of the actual value of the assets in use and hence may be viewed as an appropriate surrogate measure of *well-offness*.

A strong argument can be made for the concept of discounted cash flow. All assets are presumed to be acquired for the future service potential they provide to the firm. Furthermore, there is a presumption that the initial purchase price was paid because of a belief that the asset would generate sufficient revenue in the future to make its acquisition worthwhile. Thus, either implicitly or explicitly, the original cost was related to the present value of expected cash flows. It follows that the continued use of the asset implies that its value in use is related to expected future cash flows. Hence, the change in expected future cash flows and thus present value from one period to the next is decision relevant. Moreover, presumably the present value at the end of the period would approximate what the company would be willing to invest to purchase a similar asset and thereby maintain its physical operating capacity. Hence, the resulting income measurement is consistent with the physical capital maintenance concept of income.

Three major measurement problems are associated with the concept of discounted cash flow. First, the concept depends on an estimate of future cash flows by time periods. As a result, both the amounts of the cash flows to be generated in the future and the timing of those cash flows must be determined.

The second problem is selection of an appropriate discount rate. Since a dollar received in the future is not as valuable as a dollar received today, the expected future cash flows must be discounted to the present. Theoretically, the discount rate should be the internal rate of return on the asset. However, this rate can only be approximated because knowledge of the exact rate of return would require exact knowledge of the amounts and timing of future cash flows expected when the asset was purchased.

The third problem arises because a firm's assets are interrelated. Revenues are generated by the combined use of a company's resources. Therefore, even if the company's future cash flows and the appropriate discount rate could be precisely determined, it would not be practicable to determine exactly how much each asset contributed to those cash flows. As a result, the discounted present value of individual firm assets cannot be determined and summed to determine the present value of a company.

Use of present-value techniques to measure current value can be only as valid as the estimates of the amounts and timing of future cash flow and the appropriateness of the discount factor. To the extent that these estimates approximate reality, the measurement of the present value of future service potential is probably the most relevant measurement to disclose on the balance sheet. That is, this measurement is relevant in the sense that the balance sheet would provide information about the ability of the assets to produce income in the future.

Current Value and the Historical Accounting Model

Although the current accounting model relies heavily on historical cost, recent pronouncements and discussion memorandums issued by the FASB indicate a move toward providing more current value information. For example, *SFAS No. 33*, as amended, establishes guidelines for reporting supplementary current cost information for certain nonmonetary assets; *SFAS Nos. 114* and *115* require that investments in certain financial instruments be reported at fair value; and *SFAS Nos. 105* and *107* that companies disclose additional market value information. The FASB recently issued a summary of its fair value project that advocates using fair value to measure all financial assets and liabilities (see Chapter 8).

Income Recognition

In an attempt to overcome the measurement problems associated with using the economic concept of income, accountants have traditionally taken the position that a *transactions approach* should be used to account for assets, liabilities, revenues, and expenses. This approach relies on the presumption that the elements of financial statements should be reported when there is evidence of an outside exchange (or an "arm's length transaction"). Transactions-based accounting generally requires that reported income be the result of dealings with entities external to the reporting unit and gives rise to the realization principle. The *realization principle* holds that income should be recognized when the earnings process is complete or virtually complete and an exchange transaction has taken place. The exchange transaction is the basis of accountability and determines both the timing of revenue recognition and the amount of revenue to be recorded. The resulting financial statements are expressed in terms of financial capital (money) invested in net assets and a return on that investment to stockholders. Consequently, traditional, transactions-based accounting is consistent with the financial capital maintenance concept.

Transactions-based accounting contrasts with the economic concept of income in that accounting income is determined by measuring only the *recorded* net asset values, exclusive of capital and dividend transactions, during a period. The accounting concept of income generally does not attempt to place an expected value on the firm or to report on changes in the expected value of assets or liabilities.

Empirical research has indicated that accounting income is related to market-based measures of income such as stock returns, and security prices respond to the information content in financial statements.[15] Nevertheless, the transactions-based approach to income determination has been criticized for not reporting all relevant information about business entities. Those who favor a more liberal interpretation of the income concept argue that income should include all gains and losses in assets or liabilities held by an entity during a particular period.[16]

Edwards and Bell suggested that with only slight changes in present accounting procedures, four types of income can be isolated. These income measures are defined as (1) current operating profit—the excess of sales revenues over the current cost of inputs used in production and sold; (2) realizable cost savings—the increases in the prices of assets held during the period; (3) realized cost savings—the difference between historical costs and the current purchase price of goods sold; and (4) realized capital gains—the excess of sales proceeds over historical costs on the disposal of long-term assets. Edwards and Bell contended that these measures are better indications of well-offness and provide users more information to analyze enterprise results.[17]

Sprouse, in elaborating on the findings of *Accounting Research Study No. 3*, discussed the concept somewhat more narrowly:

Because ownership interests are constantly changing hands, we must strive for timely recognition of measurable change, and in so doing we must identify the nature of the

---

[15] Robert Ball and Philip Brown, "An Empirical Evaluation of Accounting Income Numbers," *Journal of Accounting Research* (Autumn 1968), pp. 159–178.

[16] The initial impetus for this broader measure of income is found in Edwards and Bell, op. cit. and Sprouse and Moonitz, op. cit.

[17] Edwards and Bell, op. cit., p. 111.

changes. As currently reported, income may well be composed of three elements, each of which has considerably different economic significance. Is the gross margin truly the result of operations—the difference between current selling prices of products and current costs of producing products, both measured in today's dollars? How much of the company's income is not the result of its operations but is the result of changes in the value of a significant asset, for example, a large supply of raw material, perhaps a warehouse full of sugar? Such changes are apt to be fortuitous and unpredictable and therefore need to be segregated, if financial statements are to be interpreted meaningfully and if rational investment decisions are to be based on income measurements. And how much of what is now reported as income is not income at all but is merely the spurious result of using a current unit of measurement for revenues and an obsolete unit measurement for costs—particularly depreciation?[18]

The major change advocated by both Edwards and Bell and *Accounting Research Study No. 3* is the reporting of unrealized gains or losses in the net assets of the entity during the period. As discussed earlier, these gains and losses are termed *holding gains and losses,* and proponents claim that reporting holding gains and losses would increase the information content of published financial statements. This argument focuses on two main points: (1) windfall gains and losses from holding specific assets and liabilities should be reported as they occur, and (2) changes in the measuring unit should be eliminated from the reporting process; that is, financial statements should be adjusted for the effects of inflation.

The effect on income of failing to record holding gains and losses is illustrated by the following example. Suppose two individuals, A and B, purchase adjoining 100-acre plots of land for $100,000 on January 1, 2000. Assume that the appraisal value of these plots of land rises to $150,000 on December 31, 2000, and that A sells his land on this date while B retains hers. Traditional accounting practice allows A to recognize a gain of $50,000, whereas B cannot record her gain because it has not been realized by an arm's length transaction. This difference occurs even though the economic substance of both events is essentially the same. This example illustrates the impact of the transactions approach to income determination.

Measurement

The reporting of business income assumes that all items of revenue and expense are capable of being measured. One requirement of measurement is that the object or event is capable of being ordered or ranked in respect to some property. Measurement is the assigning of numbers to objects or events according to rules. It is also a process of comparison in order to obtain more precise information to distinguish one alternative from another in a decision situation.

The accounting measuring unit in the United States is the dollar; however, the instability of the measuring unit causes major problems. For example, consider the room you are now in. If you were to measure its width in

---

[18] Robert T. Sprouse, "The Radically Different Principles of Accounting Research Study No. 3," *Journal of Accountancy* (May 1964), p. 66.

feet and inches today, next week, and next year, accurate measurements would give the same result each time. In contrast, the accounting measurement of sales each year will undoubtedly differ each year even if exactly the same number of units are sold. Much of this difference will be the result of changes in the value of the dollar.

Another factor that complicates accounting measurement is that arbitrary decisions must be made for periodic reporting purposes. Depreciation, depletion, and amortization are all examples of arbitrary and inexact measurement techniques that complicate the measurement process. Because changes in the measurement unit and arbitrary measurements caused by the necessity of periodic presentation persist, the users of accounting information should recognize the inherent limitations in the use of measurement techniques in accounting.

Accounting for Inflation

A primary cause of instability in the accounting measuring unit is the effect of inflationary or deflationary forces in the economy as a whole which have a general impact on the purchasing power of the dollar. Sweeney[19] proposed that to be meaningful, financial statement elements should be measured in common-sized dollars that reflect the same level of purchasing power so that they can be properly added together to get a valid result. These measurements are termed *general purchasing power adjustments.* They are not intended to measure the value of assets and liabilities; rather, they are intended to allow for assessing the effects of changes in the general price level. For example, holding receivables during an inflationary period means that when they are collected the dollars received are worth less than they would have been if the sales had been made for cash. The result is a purchasing power loss. General purchasing power adjustments would result in financial statements that would report gains and losses in purchasing power.

Inflation erodes the purchasing power of net monetary assets (receivables minus payables). Purchasing power losses negatively affect the value of the money capital invested in the firm's net assets. Income measured as the change in price-level-adjusted net assets from the beginning of the period to the end of the period, exclusive of transactions with owners, would reflect the erosion of the monetary capital investment and is therefore consistent with the financial capital maintenance concept of income determination. Proponents of inflation-adjusted financial statements contend that these adjustments are necessary if income is to measure the increase in the well-offness from one period to the next.[20]

Revenue Recognition and Realization

There has been a great deal of confusion in accounting literature over the precise meaning of the terms recognition and realization. *Recognition* is the

---

[19] Henry W. Sweeney, *Stabilized Accounting* (New York: Harper & Bros., 1930).

[20] *SFAS No. 33,* as amended by *SFAS Nos. 82* and *89,* encourages, but does not require, the disclosure of information on changing price on a voluntary basis.

formal process of recording a transaction or event, whereas *realization* is the process of converting noncash assets to cash or claims to cash. Transactions-based accounting recognizes and reports revenues that are realized or realizable. Hence, accounting recognition relies on the determination of when realization has occurred. Critics of the accounting process favor the economic concept of real income, whereby revenue is earned continuously over time. Accountants contend that it is not practical to record revenues on a continuous basis. Consequently, accountants must choose an appropriate point in time to record the occurrence of revenue. For a manufacturing company, several possibilities exist including the acquisition of raw materials, the production of the company's product, the sale of the product, the collection of cash, or the completion of after-sale activities such as product warranties.

In 1964, the American Accounting Association Committee on Realization recommended that the concept of realization could be improved if the following criteria were applied: (1) revenue must be capable of measurement, (2) the measurement must be verified by an external market transaction, and (3) the crucial event must have occurred.[21] The key element in these recommendations is the third criterion. The crucial-event test states that revenue should be realized on the completion of the most crucial task in the earning process. This test results in the recognition of revenue at various times for different business organizations.

The combined use of the crucial-event test and the transactions approach has resulted in accounting income that measures the difference between sales of the company's product (revenue) and costs incurred in the production and sale of that product (expenses). The FASB defines revenue as "inflows or other enhancements of assets of an entity or settlements of its liabilities (or a combination of both) during a period from delivering or producing goods, rendering services or other activities that constitute the entity's ongoing operations."[22]

Under current practice, revenue is usually recognized at the point of sale; however, the timing of recognition may be advanced or delayed by the nature of specific transactions. Generally, departures from recording revenue at the point of sale occur due to varying degrees of certainty. When a high degree of certainty is associated with realization, revenue recognition may precede the point of sale. Conversely, the greater the level of uncertainty associated with realization, the greater is the tendency to delay revenue recognition. The degree of certainty criterion results in revenue recognition at several different points in the production–sale cycle.

Revenue Recognized During the Production Process
When production of the company's product carries over into two or more periods, the allocation of revenue to the various accounting periods is considered essential for proper reporting. In such cases, a method of revenue

---

[21] American Accounting Association, 1964, Concepts and Standards Research Study Committee: "The Matching Concept," *The Accounting Review,* Vol. 40 (April 1965), p. 318.

[22] Statement of Financial Accounting Concepts No. 6, "Elements of Financial Statements of Business Enterprises" (Stamford, CT, 1985), par. 79.

recognition termed *percentage of completion* may be used. This method allocates revenue on the basis of the percentage of the expected total costs that were incurred in a particular accounting period. The percentage of completion method requires a known selling price and the ability to estimate reasonably the total costs of the product. It is used in accounting for long-term construction contracts such as roads, shipbuilding, and dams. Because the percentage of completion method recognizes income as it is earned, rather than waiting until the transaction has been completed, the concept of revenue recognition provides income measurements that are closer to the economic concept of income espoused by Hicks.

Revenue Recognized at the Completion of Production

When the company's product is to be sold at a determinable price on an organized market, revenue may be realized when the goods are ready for sale. The gold market formerly was an example of this method in that all gold mined was required to be sold to the government at a fixed price. Some farm products and commodities also meet these conditions. Revenue recognition at the completion of production is defended on the grounds that the event critical to the earnings process has occurred.

Revenue Recognized as Services Are Performed

The three steps involved in service contracts are: (1) order taking, (2) performance of services, and (3) collection of cash. These steps may all be performed in one accounting period or divided between periods. In service contracts, realization should generally be connected with the performance of services, and revenue should be recorded in relation to the degree of services performed. Realization should be tied to services performed because it is the most crucial decision. The signing of the contract results in a partially executory contract, and the collection of cash may precede or follow the performance of services.

Revenue Recognized as Cash Is Received

In certain circumstances, where the ultimate collectibility of the revenue is in doubt, recognition is delayed until cash payment is received. The installment method and the cash recovery method are examples of delaying revenue recognition until the receipt of cash. However, the APB states that revenue recognition should not be delayed unless ultimate collectibility is so seriously doubted that an appropriate allowance for the uncollectible amount cannot be estimated.

Revenue Recognized on the Occurrence of Some Event

In some instances, where binding contracts do not exist or rights to cancel are in evidence, the level of uncertainty may dictate that revenue recognition be delayed until the point of ratification or the passage of time. For example, some states have passed laws that allow door-to-door sales contracts to be voided within certain periods of time. In such cases, recognition should be delayed until that period has passed.

Special Recognition Circumstances

Some events do not fall into any of the above categories. Consequently, it may be necessary to establish new GAAPs to account for specific types of transactions. For example, the FASB specifically addressed revenue recognition criteria for franchisors and in situations where the right of return exists. In *SFAS No. 45*, "Accounting for Franchise Fee Revenue," the Board stated that franchise fee revenue (net of an appropriate provision for uncollectible accounts) should be recognized when all material services have been substantially performed by the franchisor. In most cases, the earliest point at which revenue may be recognized by franchisors will be the start of operations by the franchisee. In addition, the installment method may be used only when revenue is collected over an extended period of time and there is no reasonable basis for estimating its ultimate collectibility.

In *SFAS No. 48*, "Revenue Recognition When Right of Return Exists," the FASB stated that a seller should recognize revenue at the point of sale when a return privilege exists only when all the following conditions are met.

1. The selling price is fixed or determinable at the date of sale.
2. The buyer has paid or is obligated to pay the seller.
3. The buyer bears the risk of loss from theft or damage.
4. The buyer has economic substance apart from the seller.
5. The seller has no major obligations for future performance involving the resale of the product.
6. Future returns are reasonably estimable.

In the event these conditions are not met and revenue recognition is deferred, revenue should be recognized at the first point at which the return privilege has expired or any conditions are satisfied.

The preceding discussion illustrates that the timing of revenue recognition may differ substantially. The underlying rationale for this diversity is the existence of varying levels of certainty and thus the occurrence of critical events or activities in the earnings process. Unfortunately, there is no specific criterion by which accountants can make judgments as to the most appropriate moments of recognition. Thus, over the years, various precedents and conventions have provided support for the recognition of revenues at different times; the revenue recognition convention has taken on the meaning of a set of criteria to be used when certain circumstances are in evidence.

The lack of specific criteria to assist in determining when to record revenue can also lead to reporting abuses. McKesson Corporation recently acquired a medical software company, HBO and Co., for $12 billion. This acquisition was based on previously reported revenue and income amounts that indicated the new combined company would increase its profitability. A subsequent investigation of revenue recognition practices at HBO and Co. in 1999 revealed that the company had recognized revenue on sales contracts that were not final and had falsified contract data. For example, a $200,000 software upgrade was recorded as revenue, even though the customer had only agreed to consider buying it later. In addition, salespeople were encouraged to backdate contracts to include them in the previous quarter's earnings.

As a result of these findings, the merged company's earnings were reduced by $191 million over the previous three-year reporting period.[23]

SEC Staff Accounting Bulletin No. 101
The Securities and Exchange Commission has become increasingly interested in the issue of revenue recognition, and in December 1999 it issued *SAB No. 101*, which summarizes the SEC staff's views on applying generally accepted accounting principles to revenue recognition in financial statements. This document indicated that providing this guidance was due to the large number of revenue recognition issues that registrants encounter. Concern was also expressed that a large portion of financial reporting frauds involve overstating revenue as illustrated by the previous example. According to *SAB No. 101*, if a transaction is within the scope of specific authoritative literature that provides revenue recognition guidance (such as a lease transaction covered by *SFAS No. 13*), that literature should be applied. However, in the absence of authoritative literature addressing a specific arrangement or a specific industry, existing authoritative accounting standards as well as the broad revenue recognition criteria specified in the FASB's conceptual framework that contain basic guidelines for revenue recognition should be considered.

Based on these guidelines, *SAB No. 101* indicated that revenue should not be recognized until it is realized or realizable and earned according to the following criteria:

- Persuasive evidence of an arrangement exists.
- Delivery has occurred or services have been rendered.
- The seller's price to the buyer is fixed or determinable.
- Collectibility is reasonably assured; the seller's price to the buyer is fixed or determinable.

The publication of *SAB No. 101* has resulted in changed revenue recognition criteria for several companies. For example, USAIR modified its treatment of its sales of Dividend Miles to marketing partners such as Bank of America as disclosed in the following note to its 1999 financial statements.

> The Company will implement SAB 101 effective January 1, 2000. As a result, the Company will modify its revenue recognition policy for the sale of mileage credits, or Dividend Miles, sold to partners.
>
> The portion of proceeds from sales of Dividend Miles that represents the Company's obligation to provide future travel to Dividend Miles members will be deferred and recognized as a component of Passenger transportation revenues when the service is rendered. The remaining portion of the sales proceeds will continue to be recognized immediately as a component of Other operating revenues.
>
> The Company will recognize a cumulative effect of adopting SAB 101 as a change in accounting principle as of January 1, 2000. The cumulative effect of accounting change, net of applicable income taxes, is estimated to be $103 million.

---

[23] Elizabeth MacDonald, "SEC to Issue Stricter Accounting Rules," *Wall Street Journal*, August 11, 1999, p. A4.

Matching

In addition to the realization principle, the matching concept is of primary importance in the determination of accounting income because of the need for periodic reporting and the theoretical basis underlying the accrual concept of income. Normal accounting procedures are based on the premise that the business enterprise is a going concern and, as such, must provide periodic reports to investors in order for them to assess their investments. To be relevant, these reports are intended to apprise investors of the earnings that have accrued during the period. Because accounting earnings comprise revenues and expenses, accounting principles have evolved to establish when to recognize revenue and how to match revenues with costs. The process of associating revenues with cost is termed the *matching concept.*

Paton and Littleton described the matching concept as the association of effort and accomplishment.[24] Similarly, an American Accounting Association Committee investigating the matching concept recommended that costs should be related to revenues realized within a specific period on the basis of some correlation of these costs with the recognized revenues.[25]

Determining when costs are of no future benefit and should therefore be charged against revenue depends on the definitions of the terms *cost, expense,* and *loss.* These terms are defined as follows:

> **Cost**—*the amount given in consideration of goods received or to be received. Costs can be classified as unexpired (assets), which are applicable to the production of future revenues, and expired, those not applicable to the production of future revenues and thus deducted from revenues or retained earnings in the current period.[26]*
>
> **Expense**—*outflows or other using up of assets or incurrences of liabilities (or a combination of both) during a period from delivering or producing goods, rendering services, or carrying out other activities that constitute the entity's ongoing major or central operations.[27]*
>
> **Loss**—*decreases in equity (net assets) from peripheral or incidental transactions of an entity and from all other transactions and other events and circumstances affecting the entity during a period except those that result from expenses or distributions to owners.[28]*

In other words, expenses are revenue-producing cost expirations, whereas losses are non-revenue-producing cost expirations.

---

[24] A. Paton and A. C. Littleton, *An Introduction to Corporate Accounting Standards,* American Accounting Association Monograph No. 3 (AAA, 1940).

[25] American Accounting Association, 1964, Concepts and Standards Research Study Committee, op. cit., pp. 368–372.

[26] Committee on Terminology, AICPA, "Review and Resume," *Accounting Terminology Bulletin No. 4* (New York, 1953).

[27] FASB Statement of Concepts No. 6, op. cit., par. 80.

[28] Ibid., par. 81.

These definitions are illustrated as follows:

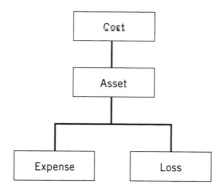

Thus, the accountant must determine the costs that have expired during the current period and whether or not these costs are revenue-producing or non-revenue-producing cost expirations. This determination is aided by separating expenses into product costs and period costs. Product costs are those cost expirations that can be directly associated with the company's product, such as direct material, direct labor, and direct factory overhead. In addition, it is common practice arbitrarily to assign some costs, such as indirect overhead, to the product even though a direct measure of association may be lacking. *Product costs* are charged to expense on the basis of the number of products sold. Period costs are those cost expirations that are more closely related to a period of time than to a product, such as administrative salaries. *Period costs* are charged to expense on the basis of the period of benefit. All losses are written off in the period in which their lack of future benefit is determined.

In summary, it can be seen that the recognition of accounting income is the result of the ability to measure inflows (revenues) and associated outflows (expenses). Where inflows or outflows are not measurable, the timing of income recognition is deferred. Consequently, accounting income is closely tied to past and present operations, and the traditional income statement indicates little in the way of future expectations. Accountants have generally taken the position that the best indicator of the future is past performance and that reporting anticipated gains involves an element of subjectivity in the calculation that could impair the usefulness of financial statements. In addition, the concepts of conservatism and materiality have played an important role in determining accounting income.

Conservatism

Sterling called *conservatism* the most influential principle of valuation in accounting.[29] Simply stated, conservatism holds that when you are in doubt,

---

[29] Robert R. Sterling, *Theory of the Measurement of Enterprise Income* (Lawrence: University of Kansas Press, 1970), p. 256.

choose the accounting alternative that will be least likely to overstate assets and income.

The principle of conservatism originally gained prominence as a partial offset to the eternal optimism of management and the tendency to overstate financial statements that characterized the first three decades of the 20th century. Conservatism was also seen as overriding the holding gains argument because many accountants believed that by placing the least favorable alternative valuation on the firm, the users of financial accounting information were less likely to be misled. In recent years, pressures for more reliable and relevant information have reduced the influence of this concept. Conservative financial statements are usually unfair to present stockholders and biased in favor of prospective stockholders because the net valuation of the firm does not include future expectations. As a consequence, the company's common stock will be priced at a relatively lower value in the marketplace.

Materiality

The concept of *materiality* has had a pervasive influence on all accounting activities despite the fact that no all-encompassing definition of the concept exists. Although materiality affects the measurement and disclosure of all information presented on the financial statements, it has its greatest impact on items of revenue and expense.

The concept has both qualitative and quantitative aspects. For example, the private-sector organizations empowered to develop GAAP have defined materiality both qualitatively and quantitatively. *Accounting Research Study No. 7* provided the following qualitative definition:

> *A statement, fact or item is material, if giving full consideration to the surrounding circumstances, as they exist at the time, it is of such a nature that its disclosure, or the method of treating it, would be likely to influence or to "make a difference" in the judgment and conduct of a reasonable person.*[30]

These organizations have also furnished quantitative definitions of materiality. For example, as quantitative requirements were established in *APB Opinion No. 18*, an investment of 20 percent or more in the voting stock of an investee is considered material. In *APB Opinion No. 15*, a reduction of less than 3 percent in the aggregate of earnings per share is not considered material. In addition, the FASB defined a reportable segment as one that constitutes 10 percent of revenues, operating profits, or assets. And most SFASs contain the following: "The provisions of this Statement need not be applied to immaterial items."[31]

---

[30] Paul Grady, "Inventory of Generally Accepted Accounting Principles for Business Enterprises," *Accounting Research Study No. 7*, (New York: AICPA, 1965), p. 40.

[31] See, for example, *Statement of Financial Accounting Standards No. 42*, "Determining Materiality for Capitalization of Interest Cost" (Stamford, CT: FASB, November 1980), p. 3.

In *Statement of Financial Accounting Concepts No. 2*, the FASB made the following statement regarding materiality.

Those who make accounting decisions and those who make judgments as auditors continually confront the need to make judgments about materiality. Materiality judgments are primarily quantitative in nature. They pose the question: Is this item large enough for users of the information to be influenced by it? However, the answer to that question will usually be affected by the nature of the item; items too small to be thought material if they result from routine transactions may be considered material if they arise in abnormal circumstances.[32]

SFAC No. 2 went on to define materiality judgments as "screens" or thresholds. That is, is an item (error or omission) large enough to pass through the threshold that separates material from immaterial items? The more important the item, the finer is the screen that will exist.

The following items are cited as examples:

1. An accounting change in circumstances that puts an enterprise in danger of being in breach of covenant regarding its financial condition may justify a lower materiality threshold than if its position were stronger.

2. A failure to disclose separately a nonrecurrent item of revenue may be material at a lower threshold than would be the case if the revenue turns a loss into a profit or reverses the earnings trend from a downward to an upward trend.

3. A misclassification of assets that would not be material in amount if it affected two categories of plant or equipment might be material if it changed the classification between a noncurrent and a current asset category.

4. Amounts too small to warrant disclosure or correction in normal circumstances may be considered material if they arise from abnormal or unusual transactions or events.[33]

Other organizations have also attempted to define materiality. The American Accounting Association contributed both quantitative and qualitative guidelines.

Materiality, as used in accounting, may be described as a state of relative importance. Materiality is not, however, entirely dependent upon relative size. Importance may depend on either quantitative or qualitative characteristics, often upon a combination of both. Factors indicative of materiality may be classified as follows:

1. Characteristics having primarily quantitative significance:

  a. the magnitude of the item (either smaller or larger) relative to normal expectation

---

[32] *Statement of Financial Accounting Concepts No. 2*, "Qualitative Characteristics of Accounting Information" (Stamford, CT: FASB, May 1980), par. 123.

[33] Ibid., par. 128.

   b. *the magnitude of the item relative to similar or related items (relative to total of its class, earnings for the period, etc.)*

2. *Characteristics having primarily qualitative significance:*

   a. *the inherent importance of the action, activity, or condition reflected (unusual, unexpected, improper, in violation of contract or statute, etc.)*

   b. *the inherent importance of the item as an indicator of the probable course of future events (suggestive of a change in business practices, etc.)*[34]

The Securities and Exchange Commission (SEC) used a qualitative definition in Rule 1.02 of Regulation S-X,

The term "material" when used to qualify a requirement for the furnishing of information as to any subject limits the information required to those matters about which an average prudent investor ought reasonably to be informed.[35]

The SEC has recently renewed its interest in the concept of materiality. A recently published Staff Accounting Bulletin indicated that companies should not rely exclusively on quantitative measures to determine whether an item is material. Over the recent past, items that constituted less than 3 to 5 percent of a company's reported earnings were frequently considered immaterial. The present SEC position is that this percentage test is acceptable for an initial assessment but companies should also consider whether a reasonable investor would consider the item important. In addition, companies are prohibited from declining to report items in order to meet quarterly earnings estimates, convert a loss to a profit, preserve an earnings trend, increase management compensation, or hide an illegal transaction.

Earnings Quality

Recall from Chapter 1 that the FASB has concluded that relevant information about an entity should provide predictive ability. A major purpose of income reporting is to allow investors to predict future cash flows. Despite the evidence that accounting earnings are good indicators of stock returns, use of the transactions approach to income determination along with the principle of conservatism and the materiality constraint have led security analysts to the conclusion that economic income, rather than accounting income, is a better predictor of future cash flows. Consequently, these individuals have suggested assessing the quality of earnings to predict future cash flows. *Earnings quality* is defined as the degree of correlation between a company's

---

[34] American Accounting Association, Committee on Concepts and Standards Underlying Corporate Financial Statements, *Accounting and Reporting Standards for Corporate Financial Statements and Preceding Statements and Supplements*, "Standards of Disclosure for Published Financial Reports: Supplementary Statement No. 8" (Columbus, OH: American Accounting Association, 1957), p. 49.

[35] Securities and Exchange Commission Regulation S-X Rule 1.02.

accounting income and its economic income. Several techniques may be used to assess earnings quality, including:

1. Compare the accounting principles employed by the company with those generally used in the industry and by the competition. Do the principles used by the company inflate earnings?

2. Review recent changes in accounting principles and changes in estimates to determine if they inflate earnings.

3. Determine if discretionary expenditures, such as advertising, have been postponed by comparing them to those of previous periods.

4. Attempt to assess whether some expenses, such as warranty expense, are not reflected on the income statement.

5. Determine the replacement cost of inventories and other assets. Assess whether the company generates sufficient cash flow to replace its assets.

6. Review the notes to financial statements to determine if loss contingencies exist that might reduce future earnings and cash flows.

7. Review the relationship between sales and receivables to determine if receivables are increasing more rapidly than sales.

8. Review the management discussion and analysis section of the annual report and the auditor's opinion to determine management's opinion of the company's future and to identify any major accounting issues.

These techniques can help determine whether a company's financial statements have not adequately captured the economic substance of the company's operations. Lev and Thiagarajan found that quality-adjusted earnings for nonsustainable gains and losses provided a better explanation of changes in stock prices than did reported income.[36] Consequently, investors should attempt to adjust the financial statements to reflect economic reality.

There is evidence that investors are becoming more interested in the quality of earnings issue. In late 1999, the stock prices of American Express, Pitney Bowes, and Tyco International were negatively impacted after the companies reported nonsustainable gains as a portion of their quarterly reports that the market apparently viewed as an effort to attain earnings expectations.[37] In previous years, investors frequently ignored the components of the reported quarterly income numbers as long as income estimates were met. However, it now appears that the market is looking at the components of the income number more skeptically.

---

[36] B. Lev and R. Thiagarajan, "Fundamental Information Analysis," *Journal of Accounting Research* (Autumn 1991), pp. 190–215.

[37] Susan Pulliam, "Earnings Management Spurs Selloffs Now," *Wall Street Journal,* October 29, 1999, pp. C1, C2.

The SEC has also expressed interest in this issue. Specifically, it has adopted rules that will allow it to consider what might have prompted companies to make or fail to make adjustments to its financial statements. These concerns arise from the fact that missing expected earnings estimates by even a small amount often has a large impact on a company's share price. Consequently, the guidelines indicate that if a company expects an item to have a significant negative impact on its stock price, it must be reported.[38]

Another aspect of the quality of earnings issue is earnings management. *Earnings management* is the attempt by corporate officers to influence short-term reported income. A recent study found that earnings management occurs for a variety of reasons, including influencing the stock market, increasing management compensation, reducing the likelihood of violating lending agreements, and avoiding intervention by government regulators.[39] It is believed that managers may attempt to manage earnings because they believe investors are influenced by reported earnings. Earnings management techniques include advancing or postponing production and investment decisions, the strategic timing of revenue and expense recognition, and the choice of accounting techniques (including the early adoption of new accounting standards). In most cases, earnings management techniques are designed to improve reported income effects and to lower the company's cost of capital. On the other hand, management may take the opportunity to report more bad news in periods when performance is low in a move to increase future profits. This approach to earnings management is referred to as the "big bath theory." An alternative argument is that management may choose to take large write-offs in periods when their performance is otherwise extremely positive.

The effort to manage earnings may be irrelevant in light of efficient market research. The general findings of this research indicate that the market is not deceived by the manipulation of accounting numbers. Alternately, if compensation is tied to earnings, there may be utility maximization reasons why managers attempt to manage earnings. Such explanations are tied to agency theory (discussed in Chapter 2).

Income Recipients

In addition to the questions concerning the nature and reporting of income, there is the corollary query: Who are the recipients of income? This question involves determining the proper recipients of income and the proper reporting procedures to incorporate under each of the various alternatives. Hendriksen has suggested that net income may be presented under the following concepts: value added, enterprise net income, net income to investors, net

---

[38] Elizabeth MacDonald, "Accounting Gets Two Sided Overhaul," *Wall Street Journal,* September 9, 1999, p. A16.

[39] Paul M. Healy and James Wahlen, "A Review of the Earnings Management Literature and Its Implications for Standard Setting," *Accounting Horizons* (December 1999), pp. 366–383.

income to stockholders, and net income to residual equity holders.[40] The determination of the net income figure to be reported in each instance turns on the question of whether deductions from revenue are to be viewed as expenses or as income distributions. The question of income determination can, therefore, also turn on whether a particular distribution is termed a distribution of earnings or an external expense.

Value-Added Concept of Income

The economic concept views income as the current market price (including holding gains) of the company's product less the external cost of goods and services associated with acquiring the product. If the enterprise is thus viewed in the broad social sense, individuals other than owners or creditors may have claims against this income. For example, employees and the government may also be viewed as the recipients of income.

The value-added concept of income may be defined as the net amount of the increase in the market price of a product attributable to each enterprise. It indicates the total amount of income that can be divided among the various interested parties. In recent years, this income concept has gained increased attention because of an alternative method of taxation termed the value-added tax.

Enterprise Net Income

The modern corporation generally has two main activities: operations and financing. Enterprise net income is determined from the operations aspect only, and all financing activities and other payments necessitated by operations are regarded as return on investment rather than as expenses. Enterprise net income is consistent with the entity concept, which views the company as independent of and unaffected by the source of capital financing (see Chapter 14 for a further discussion of the entity theory). Moreover, income tax paid by the company is based on enterprise net income and is viewed as a distribution of income to the government. Thus, stockholders, bondholders, and the government are viewed as the recipients of income. Under this concept, revenue less all expenses, exclusive of interest and income taxes, provides the net income figure. A major criticism of this concept is the inclusion of the government as an income recipient while excluding employees.

Net Income to Investors

The concept of net income to investors is also consistent with the entity theory. It is based on the view of the accounting equation, which states that assets equal equities. According to this concept, both long-term debtholders and stockholders are viewed as investors in the firm, and income would be reported as revenue less all expenses except interest. The difference between

---

[40] Eldon S. Hendriksen, *Accounting Theory,* 4th ed. (Homewood, IL: Richard D. Irwin, 1982), pp. 163–167.

the enterprise net income and net income to investors concepts is the treatment of taxes. Under the net income to investors concept, the government is not viewed as an income recipient and taxes are treated as expenses. The major premise of this concept of income is that the method of obtaining investment funds should not have an impact on income determination.

Net Income to Shareholders

The owners of the enterprise are usually viewed as the proper recipients of income. Accordingly, the net income to shareholders concept is based on the proprietary view of the accounting equation that states assets minus liabilities equals proprietorship (see Chapter 14 for a discussion of the proprietary theory). This view sees income as accruing to both preferred and common stockholders and net income as determined by subtracting all expenses from revenue.

Net Income to Residual Equity Holders

The recent emphasis on earnings per share computations is an outgrowth of the concept of net income to residual equity holders. The income available to common stockholders is viewed as the single most important figure under this concept, and, in addition to all expenses, preferred dividends are deducted from revenue in arriving at a net income figure. This concept of income is consistent with recent finance theory, which models earnings in terms of its effect on firm value and common stock. These models are based on the fact that earnings to stockholders are a function of how well firm resources are managed, while other capital sources such as bonds are generally riskless because the income stream is guaranteed for a going concern and is not dependent on the success of the enterprise. Figure 3.1 summarizes the nature of income under each of the preceding assumptions.

Although net income to shareholders is the income concept used in published financial reports, it should be noted that each of these income figures has usefulness in certain circumstances. The value-added concept is used in

FIGURE 3.1. *Summary of Various Net Income Concepts*

Current market price of the product
Less: Cost of goods produced and other external expenses
           = *Value-added income*
               Less: Unrealized holding gains and payments to employees
           = *Enterprise net income*
               Less: Income taxes
           = *Net income to investors*
               Less: Interest charges
           = *Net income to shareholders*
               Less: Preferred dividends
           = *Net income to residual equity holders*

---

determining the gross national product; the enterprise net income and net income to investors concepts are useful in determining the profitability of a firm exclusive of financing activities; and the residual equity concept forms the basis of earnings per-share computations. The income concept that is most useful will be determined by the goals of the various groups of users.

Summary

Economic income is the result of two factors: (1) the sale of the company's product (*realized income*) and (2) increases or decreases in retained net assets (*realizable income,* that is, holding gains). Complete reporting of income would require including both of these factors; however, limitations in techniques and objective evidence constrain the income reporting process. The timing of income reporting has been constrained by the accounting convention of *realization.* This convention requires that a transaction with an outsider take place, or that there be evidence that such a transaction will soon take place, before revenue is recognized. The timing of revenue recognition may vary with different types of transactions. Accountants have also placed emphasis on the proper matching of cost expiration with the revenue recognized during a particular accounting period in determining periodic income.

Another variation in the income concept is that different groups can be viewed as income recipients. The expenses deducted from revenue in reporting income vary with these different assumptions as to the income recipients. There is no one "correct" view of income recipients. Rather, different segments of the economy use various income recipient assumptions for different purposes.

In the readings contained on the webpage for this chapter, income determination is further examined.

Cases

• Case 3-1 Income Smoothing

One reason accounting earnings may not be a realistic measure of economic income is the incentive and ability of business managers to manipulate reported profits for their own benefit. This may be particularly true when their company has an incentive compensation plan that is linked to reported net income. The manipulation of earnings is termed *earnings management* and frequently involves income smoothing. Income smoothing has been defined as the dampening of fluctuations about some level of earnings that is considered normal for the company. Research has indicated that income smoothing occurs because business managers have a preference for a stable rather than a volatile earnings trend.

Required:
a. Why do business managers prefer stable earnings trends?
b. Discuss several methods business managers might use to smooth earnings.

• Case 3-2 Earnings Quality

Economic income is considered to be a better predictor of future cash flows than accounting income. A technique used by security analysts to determine the degree of correlation between a firm's accounting earnings and its true economic income is quality of earnings assessment.

Required:
a. Discuss measures that may be used to assess the quality of a firm's reported earnings.
b. Obtain an annual report for a large corporation and perform a quality of earnings assessment.

• Case 3-3 Revenue Recognition

A business enterprise's earning of revenue is recognized for accounting purposes when the transaction is recorded. In some situations, revenue is recognized approximately as it is earned in the economic sense. In other situations, accountants have developed guidelines for recognizing revenue by other criteria, for example, at the point of sale.

Required:
a. Ignore income taxes.
    i. Explain and justify why revenue is often recognized as earned at the time of sale.
    ii. Explain in what situations it would be appropriate to recognize revenue as the productive activity takes place.
    iii. At what times, other than those included in (i) and (ii), may it be appropriate to recognize revenue? Explain.
    iv. Income measurements can be divided into different income concepts classified by income recipients. The income concepts in the following table are tailored to the listed categories of income recipients.

Income Concepts	Income Recipients
1. Net income to residual equity holders	Common stockholders
2. Net income to investors	Stockholders and long-term debt holders
3. Value-added income	All employees, stockholders, governments, and some creditors

b. For each of the concepts listed in the table, explain in separately numbered paragraphs what major categories of revenue, expense, and other items would be included in the determination of income.

• Case 3-4 Revenue Recognition

Bonanza Trading Stamps, Inc., was formed early this year to sell trading stamps throughout the Southwest to retailers who distribute the stamps gratuitously to their customers. Books for accumulating the stamps and catalogs illustrating the merchandise for which the stamps may be exchanged are given free to retailers for distribution to stamp recipients. Centers with inventories of merchandise premiums have been established for redemption of the stamps. Retailers may not return unused stamps to Bonanza.

The following schedule expresses Bonanza's expectations as to the percentages of a normal month's activity that will be attained. For this purpose, a *normal month's activity* is defined as the level of operations expected when expansion of activities ceases or tapers off to a stable rate. The company expects that this level will be attained in the third year and that sales of stamps will average $2 million per month throughout the third year.

Month	Actual Stamp Sales Percentage	Merchandise Premium Purchases Percentage	Stamp Redemptions Percentage
6	30%	40%	10%
12	60	60	45
18	80	80	70
24	90	90	80
30	100	100	95

Required:
a. Discuss the factors to be considered in determining when revenue should be recognized in measuring the income of a business enterprise.
b. Discuss the accounting alternatives that should be considered by Bonanza Trading Stamps, Inc., for the recognition of its revenues and related expenses.
c. For each accounting alternative discussed in (b) above, give balance sheet accounts that should be used and indicate how each should be classified.

• Case 3-5 Cost, Expense, and Loss

You are requested to deliver your auditor's report personally to the board of directors of Sebal Manufacturing Corporation and answer questions posed about the financial statements. While reading the statements, one director asks, "What are the precise meanings of the terms cost, expense, and loss? These terms sometimes seem to identify similar items and other times seem to identify dissimilar items."

Required:
a. Explain the meanings of the terms (1) *cost,* (2) *expense,* and (3) *loss* as used for financial reporting in conformity with generally accepted accounting principles. In your explanation discuss the distinguishing characteristics of the terms and their similarities and interrelationships.
b. Classify each of the following items as a cost, expense, loss, or other category, and explain how the classification of each item may change:
   i. Cost of goods sold
   ii. Bad debts expense

    iii. Depreciation expense for plant machinery

    iv. Organization costs

    v. Spoiled goods

c. The terms *period cost* and *product cost* are sometimes used to describe certain items in financial statements. Define these terms and distinguish between them. To what types of items does each apply?

• Case 3-6 Revenue Recognition

Revenue is usually recognized at the point of sale. Under special circumstances, however, bases other than the point of sale are used for the timing of revenue recognition.

Required:

a. Why is the point of sale generally used as the basis for the timing of revenue recognition?

b. Disregarding the special circumstances when bases other than the point of sale are used, discuss the merits of each of the following objections to the sales basis of revenue recognition:

    i. It is too conservative because revenue is earned throughout the entire process of production.

    ii. It is not conservative enough because accounts receivable do not represent disposable funds, sales returns and allowances may be made, and collection and bad debt expenses may be incurred in a later period.

c. Revenue may also be recognized (1) during production and (2) when cash is received. For each of these two bases of timing revenue recognition, give an example of the circumstances in which it is properly used and discuss the accounting merits of its use in lieu of the sales basis.

• Case 3-7 Presentation of Financial Statement Information

The FASB has issued *Statement of Financial Accounting Concepts No. 5,* "Recognition and Measurement in Financial Statements of Business Enterprises." In general, this statement attempts to set recognition criteria and guidance for what information should be incorporated into financial statements and when this information should be reported.

Required:

According to *SFAC No. 5,* five general categories of information should be provided by a full set of financial statements. List and discuss these five categories of information.

• Case 3-8 Matching Concept

The accounting profession has employed the matching concept to determine what to report in the income statement and to determine how to measure items reported in the income statement. This concept implies that expenses should be measured directly and thus balance sheet measures are residuals. The matching concept is therefore an income statement approach to the measurement and reporting of revenues and expenses.

SFAC No. 5 defined earnings as the change in net assets exclusive of investments by owners and distributions to owners, a capital maintenance concept of earnings measurement. Under this concept, asset and liabilities would be measured directly, and changes to them would flow through the income statement. Thus, the *SFAC No. 5* definition of earnings represents a balance sheet approach to the measurement and report of revenues and expenses.

Required:
a. Describe and discuss the matching concept and its importance to income reporting.
b. Give specific examples of how the matching concept is used in practice.
c. Describe and discuss the balance sheet approach and its importance to income reporting.
d. Give specific examples of how balance sheet measurements affect the measurement and reporting of earnings.

• Case 3-9 The Concept of Conservatism

The concept of conservatism has been influential in the development of accounting theory and practice. A major effect of conservatism is that accountants tend to recognize losses but not gains. For example, when the value of an asset is impaired, it is written down to fair value and an unrealized loss is recognized in the income statement. However, when the asset's value appreciates, its value is not written up to fair value. (An exception is current accounting for investments in securities having readily determinable fair values.) That is, accountants tend to recognize holding losses but not holding gains.

Required:
a. Define conservatism.
b. Why do you believe conservatism has affected financial reporting? Explain.
c. Do you believe that financial statements which recognize losses but not gains provide information that is relevant and representationally faithful? Explain.
d. Do you believe that the concept of conservatism is consistent with the physical capital maintenance concept? Explain.
e. Do you believe that the concept of conservatism is consistent with the financial capital maintenance concept? Explain.

Room for Debate

• Issue 1

SFAC No. 5 states that the concept of capital maintenance is critical in distinguishing an enterprise's return on investment from return of its investment.

Two concepts of capital maintenance are discussed—physical capital maintenance and financial capital maintenance.

Team debate:

Team 1: Present arguments in favor of the physical capital maintenance concept.

Team 2: Present arguments in favor of the financial capital maintenance concept.

• Issue 2

Economists and accountants agree that the concept of income is vitally important. However, the two disciplines disagree on what income is and how it should be measured.

Team debate:

Team 1: Present arguments in favor of the economist's view of the concept of income.

Team 2: Present arguments in favor of the accountant's view of the concept of income.

Recommended Additional Readings

Barlev, Benzion, and Haim Levy. "On the Variability of Accounting Income Numbers." *Journal of Accounting Research* (Autumn 1979), pp. 305–315.

Barton, A. D. "Expectations and Achievements in Income Theory." *The Accounting Review* (October 1974), pp. 664–681.

Beaver, William H., and Joel S. Demski. "The Nature of Income Measurement." *The Accounting Review* (January 1979), pp. 38–46.

Bedford, Norton M. *Income Determination Theory: An Accounting Framework*. Reading, MA: Addison-Wesley, 1965.

Boulding, K. E. "Economics and Accounting: The Uncongenial Twins." In W. T. Baxter and Sidney Davidson, eds., *Studies in Accounting Theory*. Homewood, IL: Richard D. Irwin, 1962.

Gellein, Oscar S. "Periodic Earnings: Income or Indicator?" *Accounting Horizons* (June 1987), pp. 59–64.

Healy, Paul M., and James Wahlen. "A Review of the Earnings Management Literature and Its Implications for Standard Setting." *Accounting Horizons* (December 1999), pp. 366–383.

Mitchell, Bert N. "A Comparison of Accounting and Economic Concepts of Business Income." *The New York CPA* (October 1967), pp. 762–772.

Shwayder, Keith. "A Critique of Economic Income as an Accounting Concept." *Abacus* (August 1967), pp. 23–35.

Solomons, David. "Economic and Accounting Concepts of Income." *The Accounting Review* (July 1961), pp. 374–383.

Sprouse, Robert T. "The Importance of Earnings in the Conceptual Framework." *Journal of Accountancy* (January 1978), pp. 64–71.

Bibliography

Accounting for Extraordinary Gains and Losses. New York: Ronald Press Co., 1967, particularly Chapters 1, 2, and 3, and Appendix B.

Alexander, Sidney S. "Income Measurement in a Dynamic Economy." Revised by David Solomons and reprinted in W. T. Baxter and Sidney Davidson (eds.), *Studies in Accounting Theory*. Homewood, IL: Richard D. Irwin, 1962, pp. 126–200.

American Accounting Association, Committee on External Reporting. "An Evaluation of External Reporting Practices." *The Accounting Review*. Supplement to Vol. 44 (1969), pp. 79–123.

American Accounting Association, 1964, Concepts and Standards Research Study Committee. "The Realization Concept." *The Accounting Review* (April 1965), pp. 312–322.

American Accounting Association, 1964, Concepts and Standards Research Committee. "The Matching Concept." *The Accounting Review* (April 1965), pp. 368–372.

American Accounting Association, 1972–73, Committee on Concepts and Standards—External Reporting. *The Accounting Review*. Supplement to Vol. 49 (1974), pp. 203–222.

Anderson, James A. *A Comparative Analysis of Selected Income Measurement Theories in Financial Accounting*. Sarasota, FL: American Accounting Association, 1976.

Bedford, Norton M. "Income Concept Complex: Expansion or Decline." In Robert R. Sterling (ed.), *Asset Valuation and Income Determination*. Lawrence, KS: Scholars Book Co., 1971, pp. 135–144.

Chambers, R. J. "Edwards and Bell on Income Measurement in Retrospect." *Abacus* (1982), pp. 3–39.

Chambers, Raymond J. *Accounting, Evaluation and Economic Behavior*. Englewood Cliffs, NJ: Prentice-Hall, 1966.

Devine, Carl Thomas. "Loss Recognition." In Sidney Davidson, David Green, Jr., Charles T. Horngren, and George H. Sorter, eds., *An Income Approach to Accounting Theory*. Englewood Cliffs, NJ: Prentice-Hall, 1964, pp. 162–172 (originally published in *Accounting Research* [October 1955], pp. 310–320.

Edwards, Edgar O., and Phillip W. Bell. *The Theory and Measurement of Business Income*. Berkeley and Los Angeles: University of California Press, 1961.

Fess, Philip E., and William L. Ferrara. "The Period Cost Concept for Income Measurement—Can It Be Defended?" *The Accounting Review* (October 1961), pp. 598–602.

Graese, Clifford E., and Joseph R. Demario. "Revenue Recognition for Long Term Contracts." *Journal of Accountancy* (December 1976), pp. 53–59.

Hepworth, Samuel R. "Smoothing Periodic Income." *The Accounting Review* (January 1953), pp. 32–39.

Horngren, Charles T. "How Should We Interpret the Realization Concept?" *The Accounting Review* (April 1965), pp. 323–333.

Hylton, Delmer P. "On Matching Revenue with Expense." *The Accounting Review* (October 1965), pp. 824–828.

Jarrett, Jeffrey F. "Principle of Matching and Realization as Estimation Problems." *Journal of Accounting Research* (Autumn 1971), pp. 378–382.

Mobley, Sybil C. "The Concept of Realization: A Useful Device." *The Accounting Review* (April 1966), pp. 292–296.

Ohlson, James A. "On the Nature of Income Measurement: The Basic Results." *Contemporary Accounting Research* (Fall 1987), pp. 1–15.

Petri, Enrico. "Income Reporting and APB Opinion No. 18." *Management Accounting* (December 1974), pp. 49–52.

Shwayder, Keith. "A Critique of Economic Income as an Accounting Concept." *Abacus* (August 1967), pp. 23–35.

Shwayder, Keith. "The Capital Maintenance Rule and the Net Asset Valuation Rule." *The Accounting Review* (April 1969), pp. 304–316.

Solomons, David. "Economic and Accounting Concepts of Income." *The Accounting Review* (July 1961), pp. 374–383.

Spiller, Earl A., Jr. "The Revenue Postulate—Recognition or Realization." *N.A.A. Bulletin* (February 1962), pp. 41–47.

Sprouse, Robert T. "The Importance of Earnings in the Conceptual Framework." *Journal of Accountancy* (January 1978), pp. 64–71.

Sterling, Robert R. *Theory of the Measurement of Enterprise Income.* Lawrence: University Press of Kansas, 1970.

Storey, Reed K. "Revenue Realization, Going Concern and Measurement of Income." *The Accounting Review* (April 1959), pp. 232–238.

Thomas, Arthur L. *Revenue Recognition.* Michigan Business Reports No. 49. Ann Arbor: Bureau of Business Research, Graduate School of Business Administration, University of Michigan, 1966.

Tiller, Mikel G., and Jan R. Williams. "Revenue Recognition under New FASB Statements." *The CPA Journal* (January 1982), pp. 43–47.

Tucker, Marvin W. "Probabilistic Aspects of Revenue Recognition, Conventional and Innovational." *Australian Accountant* (May 1973), pp. 198–202.

Walker, Lauren M., Gerhard G. Mueller, and Fauzi G. Dimian. "Significant Events in the Development of the Realization Concept in the U.S." *Accountants Magazine* [Scotland] (August 1970), pp. 357–360.

Windal, Floyd W. "The Accounting Concept of Realization." *The Accounting Review* (April 1961), pp. 249–258.

Financial Statements I: The Income Statement

The current financial reporting environment in the United States consists of various groups who are affected by and have a stake in the financial reporting requirements of the FASB and the SEC. These groups include investors, creditors, security analysts, regulators, management, and auditors. Investors in equity securities are the central focus of the financial reporting environment. Investment involves foregoing current uses of resources for ownership interests in companies. These ownership interests are claims to uncertain future cash flows. Consequently, investment involves giving up current resources for future, uncertain resources; and investors require information that will assist in assessing future cash flows from securities.

The Economic Consequences of Financial Reporting

In Chapter 1, we introduced the concept of economic consequences. Income measurement and financial reporting also involve economic consequences, including:

1. Financial information can affect the distribution of wealth among investors. More informed investors, or investors employing security analysts, may be able to increase their wealth at the expense of less informed investors.
2. Financial information can affect the level of risk accepted by a firm. As discussed in Chapter 2, focusing on short-term, less risky projects may have long-term detrimental effects.
3. Financial information can affect the rate of capital formation in the economy and result in a reallocation of wealth between consumption and investment within the economy.

4. Financial information can affect how investment is allocated among firms.

Since these economic consequences may affect different users of information differently, the selection of financial reporting methods by the FASB and the SEC involves trade-offs. Future deliberations of accounting standards should consider these economic consequences.

Income Statement Elements

The FASB's *Statement of Financial Accounting Concepts (SFAC) No. 1* indicates that the primary purpose of financial reporting is to provide information about a company's performance provided by measures of earnings. The income statement is of primary importance in this endeavor because of its predictive value, a qualitative characteristic defined in *SFAC No. 2.* Income reporting also has value as a measure of future cash flows, as a measure of management efficiency, and as a guide to the accomplishment of managerial objectives.

The emphasis on corporate income reporting as the vehicle for relaying performance assessments to investors has caused a continuing dialogue among accountants about the proper identification of revenues, gains, expenses, and losses. These financial statement elements are defined in *SFAC No. 6* as follows:

Revenues. Inflows or other enhancements of assets of an entity or settlement of its liabilities (or a combination of both) during a period from delivering or producing goods, rendering services, or other activities that constitute the entity's ongoing major or central operations.

Gains. Increases in net assets from peripheral or incidental transactions of an entity and from all other transactions and other events and circumstances affecting the entity during a period except those that result from revenues or investments by owners.

Expenses. Outflows or other using up of assets or incurrences of liabilities (or a combination of both) during a period from delivering or producing goods, rendering services, or carrying out other activities that constitute the entity's ongoing major or central operations.

Losses. Decreases in net assets from peripheral or incidental transactions of an entity and from all other transactions and other events and circumstances affecting the entity during a period except from expenses or distributions to owners.[1]

Notice that each of these terms is defined as changes in assets and/or liabilities. This represents a change in emphasis by the FASB from previous definitions provided by the APB that stressed inflows and outflows. Consequently, current recognition and measurement criteria for revenues, expenses, gains, and losses are more closely associated with asset and liability valuation issues, and the balance sheet is becoming more than a place to store residual values

---

[1] *Statement of Financial Accounting Concepts No. 6,* "Elements of Financial Statements" (Stamford, CT: FASB, 1985), pars. 79–88.

in the income determination process. As we shall see in subsequent chapters, this changing emphasis is apparent in the accounting treatment specified by the FASB for a variety of issues.

Differences between the changes in assets and/or liabilities, and inflows and outflows definitions of income include:

1. *The changes in assets and or liabilities method determines earnings as a measure of change in net economic resources for a period, whereas the inflows and outflows definition views income as a measure of effectiveness.*

2. *The changes in assets and/or liabilities method depends on the definition of assets and liabilities to define earnings, whereas the inflows and outflows method depends on definitions of revenues and expenses and matching them to determine income.*

3. *The inflow and outflow method results in the creation of deferred charges, deferred credits, and reserves when measuring periodic income; the changes in assets and/or liabilities method recognizes deferred items only when they are economic resources or obligations.*

4. *Both methods agree that because investors look to financial statements to provide information from which they can extrapolate future resource flows, the income statement is more useful to investors than is the balance sheet.*

5. *The changes in assets and/or liabilities method limits the population from which the elements of financial statements can be selected to net economic resources and to the transactions and events that change measurable attributes of those net resources. Under the inflow and outflow method, revenues and expenses may include items necessary to match costs with revenues, even if they do not represent changes in net resources.*[2]

An important distinction between revenues and gains and expenses and losses is whether or not they are associated with ongoing operations. Over the years, this distinction has generated questions concerning the nature of income reporting desired by various financial statement users. Historically, two viewpoints have dominated this dialogue and have been termed the *current operating performance concept* and the *all-inclusive concept* of income reporting. These viewpoints are summarized in the following paragraphs.

Statement Format

The proponents of the *current operating performance* concept of income base their arguments on the belief that only changes and events controllable by management that result from current period decisions should be included in income. Consequently, normal and recurring items should constitute the principal measure of enterprise performance. That is, net income should reflect the day-to-day, profit-directed activities of the enterprise, and the inclusion of other items of profit or loss distorts the meaning of the term *net income*.

[2] T. E. Robinson, "The Time Has Come to Report Comprehensive Income," *Accounting Horizons* (June 1991), p. 110.

On the other hand, advocates of the *all-inclusive* concept of income hold that net income should reflect all items that affected the net increase or decrease in stockholders' equity during the period, with the exception of capital transactions. Specifically, these individuals believe that the total net income for the life of an enterprise should be determinable by summing the periodic net income figures.

The underlying assumption behind this controversy is that the method used to present financial information is important. That is, both viewpoints agree on the information to be presented but disagree on where to disclose types of revenue, expenses, gains, and losses. As discussed in Chapters 2 and 3, research has tended to indicate that investors are not influenced by the format of financial statements if the statements disclose the same information. So, perhaps, the concern over statement format is unwarranted. The FASB's view of this issue has evolved over time.

APB Opinion No. 9

One of the first issues the APB studied was what to include in net income. An APB study revealed that business managers were exercising a great deal of discretion in determining which revenues and expenses, and gains and losses, to include on the income statement or on the retained earnings statement. The lack of formal guidelines concerning adjustments to retained earnings resulted in the placement of most items of revenue or gain on the income statement, whereas many expense and loss items that were only remotely related to previous periods were treated as adjustments to retained earnings.

The APB's study of these reporting abuses and its general review of the overall nature of income resulted in the release of *APB Opinion No. 9*, "Reporting the Results of Operations." This opinion took a middle position between the current operating performance and all-inclusive concepts by stating that net income should reflect all items of profit and loss recognized during the period, with the exception of prior period adjustments. In addition, the prescribed statement format included two income figures: net income from operations and net income from operations plus extraordinary items. This pronouncement required business managers and accountants to determine whether revenues and expenses, and gains and losses, were properly classified as normal recurring items, extraordinary items, or prior period adjustments according to established criteria. In general, the provisions of *APB Opinion No. 9* specified that all items were to be considered normal and recurring unless they met the stated requirements for classification as either extraordinary items or prior period adjustments (discussed later in the chapter).

The separation of the income statement into net income from operations and net income after extraordinary items allowed for the disclosure of most items of revenue and expense, or gains and losses, on the income statement during any period. It also allowed financial statement users to evaluate the results of normal operations or total income according to their needs.

The FASB noted in *SFAC No. 5* that the all-inclusive income statement is intended to avoid discretionary omissions from the income statement, even though "inclusion of unusual or non-recurring gains or losses might reduce the usefulness of an income statement for one year for predictive purposes."[3] The FASB has also stated that because the effects of an entity's activities vary in terms of stability, risks, and predictability, there is a need for information about the various components of income. In the following paragraphs, we examine the elements of the income statement, introduce the accounting principles currently being used in measuring these elements, and discuss how they are disclosed on Kroll-O'Gara's income statement illustrated in Figure. 4.1.

The Kroll-O'Gara Company, an Ohio corporation, is a leading global provider of a broad range of specialized products and services designed to provide solutions to a variety of security needs. The company has several divisions that engage in different activities. The Security Products and Services Group markets ballistic and blast-protected vehicles and security services; the Investigations and Intelligence Group offers business intelligence and investigation services; the Voice and Data Communications Group, secure satellite communication equipment and satellite navigation systems; and the Information Security Group, information and computer security services, including network and system security review and repair. The company's income statement discloses the aggregate financial results of these activities,[4] incorporates all the components of income defined by the APB and FASB in various Opinions and Statements, and includes comparative information for 1998, 1997, and 1996. The Securities and Exchange Commission requires all companies to provide three-year comparative income statements and two-year comparative balance sheets. Consequently, most publicly held companies such as Kroll-O'Gara also provide similar data in their annual reports. The components of the traditional income statement exclusive of the elements of other comprehensive income are discussed in the following paragraphs. The elements of other comprehensive income are discussed later in the chapter.

Income from Continuing Operations

The amounts disclosed to arrive at income from continuing operations are the company's normal and recurring revenues and expenses. The resulting income figure represents the amount that is expected to recur in the future or the company's *sustainable income*. This is the amount investors should use as a starting point to predict future earnings. In addition, the amount of income tax disclosed in this section of the income statement is the amount the company would have earned if no nonrecurring income items had been incurred. The amounts of income from continuing operations and the calculated amount of tax attributable to that income for Kroll-O'Gara Company for 1998 are $20,555,370 and $7,466,464, respectively. Notice that the company also

---

[3] *Statement of Financial Accounting Concepts No. 5*, "Recognition and Measurement in Financial Statements of Business Enterprises" (Stamford, CT: Financial Accounting Standards Board, 1984), par. 35.

[4] Summary segmental performance information is required to be disclosed as under *SFAS No. 14*, as discussed in Chapter 15.

FIGURE 4.1 *The Kroll-O'Gara Company Consolidated Statements of Operations for the Years Ended December 31, 1996, 1997, and 1998*

	1996	1997	1998
NET SALES	$164,918,313	$206,102,605	$264,844,847
COST OF SALES	117,298,266	139,765,613	173,317,466
Gross profit	47,620,047	66,336,992	91,527,381
OPERATING EXPENSES:			
Selling and marketing	10,401,530	15,054,990	21,956,479
General and administrative	27,310,521	32,590,832	39,817,057
Asset impairment	124,531	—	—
Merger-related costs	—	7,204,926	5,339,358
Operating expenses	37,836,582	54,850,748	67,112,894
Operating Income	9,783,465	11,486,244	24,414,487
OTHER INCOME (EXPENSE):			
Interest expense	(3,260,945)	(5,092,372)	(4,481,823)
Interest income	41,260	79,438	1,181,579
Other, net	344,398	(411,576)	(558,873)
Income from continuing operations before minority interest, provision for income taxes, extraordinary item, and cumulative effect of change in accounting principle	6,908,178	6,061,734	20,555,370
Minority interest	—	(156,223)	—
Income from continuing operations before provision for income taxes, extraordinary item, and cumulative effect of change in accounting principle	6,908,178	5,905,511	20,555,370
Provision for income taxes	365,547	3,304,993	7,466,464
Income from continuing operations before extraordinary item and cumulative effect of change in accounting principle	6,542,631	2,600,518	13,088,906
Discontinued operations			
Loss from operations of discontinued clinical business, net of tax benefit of $257,904	(500,636)		
Loss on disposal of clinical business, net of tax benefit of $489,420	(773,580)		
Income before extraordinary item and cumulative effect of change in accounting principle	5,268,415	2,600,518	13,088,906
Extraordinary loss, net of applicable tax benefit of $129,250	—	(193,875)	—
Income before cumulative effect of change in accounting principle	5,268,415	2,406,643	13,088,906
Cumulative effect of change in accounting principle, net of applicable tax benefit of $240,000	—	(360,000)	—
Net Income	$ 5,268,415	$ 2,046,643	$ 13,088,906
Earnings per share			
Basic	$ 0.45	$ 0.15	$ 0.71
Diluted	$ 0.42	$ 0.14	$ 0.69

discloses minority interest as a special line item in calculating income from continuing operations.[5]

Three nonrecurring items of income may also be incurred by a company. These items, in the order they are to be disclosed if present, are: discontinued operations, extraordinary items and change in accounting principle. Each of these items is disclosed net of its tax effects in order to match its income and tax effects.

Discontinued Operations

Study of the results of the application of *APB Opinion No. 9* by various entities disclosed some reporting abuses. For example, some companies were reporting the results of the disposal of segment assets as extraordinary while including the revenue from these segments during the disposal period as ordinary income. In its *Opinion No. 30*, the APB concluded that additional criteria were necessary to identify disposed segments of a business. This release requires the separate presentation of (1) the results of operations prior to the measurement date, and (2) gain or loss on the sale of assets for disposed segments, including any operating gains or losses during the disposal period. This information was seen as necessary to users in order to evaluate the past and expected future operations of a particular business entity. The total gain or loss is determined by *summing any gains or losses on disposal of segment assets, and gains or losses incurred by the operations of the disposed segment* during the period of disposal. The APB provided the following definitions to help determine when and how to report a disposal of a segment of a business.

> *Segment of a Business* A component of an entity whose activities represent a separate major line of business or class of customers. A segment may be a division, department, or joint venture, providing its operations can be clearly distinguished physically and operationally. If the component is truly a segment, it should be possible to recast the financial statements to segregate its operations. If its operations cannot be segregated, the presumption is that the component is not a segment.

> *Measurement Date* The date on which management commits itself to a formal plan of disposal. This plan should include identification of the assets, method of disposal, period of disposal, estimated results of operations from the measurement date to the disposal date, and estimated proceeds from disposal.

> *Disposal Date* The date of sale or the date operations cease.

The accounting treatment for the disposal of a segment of a business is influenced by whether a gain or a loss is anticipated on the measurement date.[6] Under current GAAP, the expected total gain or loss is determined by

---

[5] Minority interest is the outside interest in a consolidated subsidiary company. This issue is discussed in depth in Chapter 15.

[6] This issue is currently under study by the FASB, and it is anticipated that *Opinion No. 30* will be amended to require the recognition of all gains and losses when they are realized. This issue will be updated on the text's webpage.

comparing the expected net realizable value of the segment assets to the book value of those same assets, less the expenses connected with disposal. Any expected gains or losses on operations of the segment during the period of disposal are then added or subtracted to arrive at the expected total gain or loss. If a loss is expected, the loss is recorded on the measurement date, whereas net gains are recognized when realized (ordinarily this will be the disposal date). This accounting treatment is in accordance with the general principle of conservatism discussed earlier in Chapter 3.

The discontinued operation disclosed by the Kroll-O'Gara Company related to a previous acquisition of a company specializing in forensic and clinical testing and analysis. The Kroll-O'Gara Company had intended to sell the clinical portion of this acquisition, but negotiations with several potential buyers were unsuccessful. The clinical operations were discontinued in the fourth quarter of 1996 at a net after-tax loss of $1,274,216.

Extraordinary Items

Extraordinary items were originally defined in *APB Opinion No. 9* as events and transactions of material effect that would not be expected to recur frequently and that would not be considered as recurring factors in any evaluation of the ordinary operating processes of the business.[7] This release also provided the following examples of these events and transactions: gains or losses from the sale or abandonment of a plant or a significant segment of the business; gains or losses from the sale of an investment not held for resale; the write-off of goodwill owing to unusual events during the period; the condemnation or expropriation of properties; and major devaluations of currencies in a foreign country in which the company was operating.

The usefulness of the then prevailing definition of extraordinary items came under review in 1973, and the APB concluded that similar items of revenues and expenses were not being classified in the same manner across the spectrum of business enterprises. The Board also concluded that business enterprises were not interpreting *APB Opinion No. 9* in a similar manner and decided that more specific criteria were needed to ensure a more uniform interpretation of its provisions. In *APB Opinion No. 30,* "Reporting the Results of Operations," extraordinary items were defined as events and transactions that are distinguished by both their unusual nature and their infrequency of occurrence. These characteristics were defined as follows.

> **Unusual nature**—*the event or transaction should possess a high degree of abnormality and be unrelated or only incidentally related to ordinary activities.*

> **Infrequency of occurrence**—*the event or transaction would not reasonably be expected to recur in the foreseeable future.[8]*

In *APB Opinion No. 30* several types of transactions were defined as not meeting these criteria. These included write-downs and write-offs of receiv-

---

[7] *APB Opinion No. 9,* "Reporting the Results of Operations" (New York: American Institute of Certified Public Accountants, 1966).

[8] *Accounting Principles Board Opinion No. 30,* "Reporting the Results of Operations" (New York: American Institute of Certified Public Accountants, 1973), par. 20.

ables, inventories, equipment leased to others, deferred research and development costs, or other intangible assets; gains or losses in foreign currency transactions or devaluations; gains or losses on disposals of segments of a business; other gains or losses on the sale or abandonment of property, plant, and equipment used in business; effects of strikes; and adjustments of accruals on long term contracts. The position expressed by the APB in *Opinion No. 30* was, therefore, somewhat of a reversal in philosophy; some items previously defined as extraordinary in *APB Opinion No. 9* were now specifically excluded from that classification. The result of *APB Opinion No. 30* was the retention of the extraordinary item classification on the income statement. However, the number of revenue and expense items allowed to be reported as extraordinary was significantly reduced. The extraordinary item reported on the Kroll-O'Gara Company's income statement is due to a refinancing agreement for a revolving line of credit that resulted in a one-time after-tax charge against net income of $193,875.

The separation of extraordinary items from other items on the income statement does not result in a separation of recurring from nonrecurring items. That is, an item that is infrequent but not unusual is classified as nonoperating income in the other gains and losses section of the income statement. Research has indicated that this requirement is not consistent with the FASB's predictive ability criterion. The classification of nonrecurring items tends to increase the variability of earnings per share before extraordinary items and to decrease the predictive ability of earnings.[9] If this evidence is proven correct, the FASB should consider revising income statement reporting practices so that they provide increased predictive ability when nonrecurring items are in evidence. One possible method of achieving this result might be to require footnote disclosure of the effect of nonrecurring items on income and earnings per share.

Accounting Changes

The accounting standard of consistency indicates that similar transactions should be recorded and reported in the same manner each year. That is, management should choose the set of accounting practices that best satisfies the needs of the reporting unit and continue to use those practices each year. However, individual entities may occasionally find that reporting is improved by changing the methods and procedures previously used or that changes in reporting may be dictated by the FASB or the SEC. Even though the results of efficient market research indicate that changes in income due to changed accounting methods do not affect stock prices, when changes in reporting practices occur, the comparability of financial statements between periods is impaired. The accounting standard of disclosure dictates that the effect of these changes should be reported. The major question surrounding changes

[9] A. B. Cameron and L. Stephens, "The Treatment of Non-Recurring Items in the Income Statement and Their Consistency with the FASB Concept Statements," *Abacus* (September 1991), pp. 81–96.

in accounting practices is the proper method to use in disclosing them. That is, should previously issued financial statements be changed to reflect the new method or procedure?

The APB studied this problem and issued its findings in *APB Opinion No. 20,* "Accounting Changes." This release identified three types of accounting changes, discussed the general question of errors in the preparation of financial statements, and defined these changes and errors as follows.

1. **Change in an accounting principle.** *This type of change occurs when an entity adopts a generally accepted accounting principle that differs from one previously used for reporting purposes. Examples of such changes are a change from Lifo to Fifo inventory pricing or a change in depreciation methods.*

2. **Change in an accounting estimate.** *These changes result from the necessary consequences of periodic presentation. That is, financial statement presentation requires estimation of future events, and such estimates are subject to periodic review. Examples of such changes are the life of depreciable assets and the estimated collectibility of receivables.*

3. **Change in a reporting entity.** *Changes of this type are caused by changes in reporting units, which may be the result of consolidations, changes in specific subsidiaries, or a change in the number of companies consolidated.*

4. **Errors.** *Errors are not viewed as accounting changes: rather they are the result of mistakes or oversights such as the use of incorrect accounting methods or mathematical miscalculations.*[10]

The Board then went on to specify the accounting treatment required to satisfy disclosure requirements in each instance. The basic question was the advisability of retroactive presentation. The following paragraphs summarize the board's recommendations.

Change in an Accounting Principle

When an accounting principle is changed, it should be treated currently. That is, the corporation should present its previously issued financial statements as they were before the change occurred, with the cumulative prior effects of the change shown as a component of net income for the period in which the change occurred. This requirement necessitates determining the yearly changes in net income of all prior periods attributable to changing from one GAAP to another. For example, if a company changed from straight-line to sum-of-year's-digits depreciation, the cumulative effect of this change on all years prior to the change must be calculated and disclosed (net of tax) as a separate figure between extraordinary items and net income. This total amount of change in income (net of tax) is then disclosed as a separate figure between extraordinary items and net income. In addition, per-share data for all comparative statements should include the results of the change as if the change had been consistently applied. This requirement results in the disclosure of additional pro-forma per-share figures for each period presented in which the change affected net income.

---

[10] *APB Opinion No. 20,* "Accounting Changes" (New York: AICPA, 1971).

The general conclusion of *APB Opinion No. 20* was that previously issued financial statements need not be revised for changes in accounting principles. However, exceptions were noted for situations deemed to be of such importance that they required retroactive presentation in the financial statements of all prior periods presented. Specifically, retroactive presentation is required for (1) a change from LIFO inventory valuation to any other method, (2) any change in the method of accounting for long-term construction contracts, and (3) a change to or from the full-cost method in the extractive industries. In each of these cases, the previous income statements must be recast to reflect the adoption of the new principle, and no additional pro-forma figures need to be disclosed.

Since it is typically not practicable to compute the cumulative effect of a change to LIFO, changes to LIFO from any other inventory method should be treated prospectively. That is, no restatement of previous financial statements is made, and no cumulative effect is reported. In these cases, the ending inventory costed under the old method becomes the beginning LIFO inventory.

Cumulative effect type treatment, with accompanying pro formas and retroactively recasting prior financial statements to reflect the use of a new method, is intended to fulfill the qualitative characteristic of comparability. These provisions allow users to compare company performance from one period to the next in order to detect trends so that projections of future cash flows can be made and firm value thereby determined. The one exception, a change in LIFO, requires additional disclosure of the effect of this accounting change on current period earnings. The user can then adjust current period earnings so that comparisons with prior periods can be made.

The change in accounting principle reported by the Kroll-O'Gara Company was the result of a decision to comply with a recommendation by the FASB's Emerging Issues Task Force. As a result, costs previously capitalized in connection with business processing reengineering activities relating to information technology were charged to expense in the fourth quarter of 1997, resulting in an after-tax loss of $360,000.

Change in Estimates

Estimated changes are handled prospectively. They require no adjustments to previously issued financial statements. These changes are accounted for in the period of the change, or if more than one period is affected, in both the period of the change and in the future. For example, assume that a company originally estimated that an asset would have a useful service life of 10 years, and after 3 years of service the total service life of the asset was estimated to be only 8 years. The remaining book value of the asset would be depreciated over the remaining useful life of 5 years. The effects of changes in estimates on operating income, extraordinary items, and the related per-share amounts must be disclosed in the year they occur. As with accounting changes to LIFO, the added disclosures should aid users in their judgments regarding comparability.

Change in Reporting Entities

Changes in reporting entities must be disclosed retroactively by restating all financial statements presented as if the new reporting unit had been in existence at the time the statements were first prepared. That is, previously issued statements are recast to reflect the results of a change in reporting entity. The financial statements should also indicate the nature of the change and the reason for the change. In addition, the effect of the change on operating income, net income, and the related per-share amounts must be disclosed for all comparative statements presented. A change in reporting entity may materially alter financial statements. For example, if a previously unconsolidated subsidiary is consolidated, the investment account is removed and the assets and liabilities of the subsidiary are added to those of the parent company. When this occurs, total assets, debt, and most financial ratios are typically affected. Without retroactive restatement for an accounting change in reporting entity, the investor would find it difficult, if not impossible, to compare company performance before and after the accounting change.

The 1999 edition of *Accounting Trends and Techniques* reported that 107 of the 600 companies it surveyed disclosed accounting changes. The types of changes and the number of companies reporting these changes are:[11]

Type of Change	*Number of Companies*
Software development costs	37
Start-up costs	29
Business process reengineering costs	10
Inventories	5
Depreciable lives	4
Impairment of long-lived assets	3
Reporting entity	2
Other	13

Errors

Errors are defined as prior period adjustments (discussed later in the chapter) in *SFAS No. 16*. In the period the error is discovered, the nature of the error and its effect on operating income, net income, and the related per-share amounts must be disclosed. In the event the prior period affected is reported for comparative purposes, the corrected information must be disclosed for the period in which it occurred. This requirement is a logical extension of retroactive treatment. To continue to report information, known to be incorrect, would purposefully mislead investors. By providing retroactive corrections, users can better assess the actual performance of the company over time.

The following are examples of errors:

1. A change from an accounting practice that is not generally acceptable to a practice that is generally acceptable.

2. Mathematical mistakes.

---

[11] American Institute of Certified Public Accountants, *Accounting Trends and Techniques* (New York: AICPA, 1999), p. 151.

3. The failure to accrue or defer revenues and expenses at the end of any accounting period.

4. The incorrect classification of costs and expenses.

Earnings per Share

Use of the income statement as the primary source of information by decision makers has resulted in a need to disclose the amount of earnings that accrue to different classes of investors. The amount of earnings accruing to holders of debt and preferred stock (termed senior securities) is generally fixed. Common stockholders are considered residual owners. Their claim to corporate profits is dependent on the levels of revenues and associated expenses. The income remaining after the distribution of interest and preferred dividends is available to common stockholders; it is the focus of accounting income determination. The amount of corporate income accruing to common stockholders is reported on the income statement on a per-share basis.

The basic calculation of earnings per share (EPS) is relatively easy. The net income available to common stockholders, after deducting required payments to senior security holders, is divided by the weighted average number of common shares outstanding during the accounting period. However, reporting basic EPS was considered insufficient to meet investor needs because of the potential impact on EPS of a wide variety of securities issued by corporations. For example, many companies have issued stock options, stock warrants, and convertible securities that can be converted into common stock at the option of the holders of the securities. In the event these types of securities are exchanged for common stock, they have the effect of reducing (diluting) the earnings accruing to preexisting stockholders. Increases in reported earnings may result in the holders of options, warrants, or convertibles exchanging their securities for common stock. Consequently, the effect of increases in earnings could be a decrease in reported EPS because the increase in common shares outstanding might be proportionately greater than the increase in net income.

The APB first discussed the ramifications of these issues in *Opinion No. 9* and developed the residual security and senior security concepts. This release stated

> *When more than one class of common stock is outstanding, or when an outstanding security has participation dividend rights, or when an outstanding security clearly derives a major portion of its value from its conversion rights or its common stock characteristics, such securities should be considered "residual securities" and not "senior securities" for purposes of computing earnings per share.*[12]

This provision of *APB Opinion No. 9* was only "strongly recommended" and not made mandatory, but the development of the concept formed the framework for *APB Opinion No. 15*, "Earnings per Share."[13] The latter opinion

---

[12] *APB Opinion No. 9*, op. cit., par. 23.

[13] *APB Opinion No. 15*, "Earnings per Share" (New York: AICPA, 1969).

noted the importance placed on per-share information by investors and the marketplace and concluded that a consistent method of computation was needed to make EPS amounts comparable across all segments of the business environment.

APB Opinion No. 15 made mandatory the presentation of EPS figures for income before extraordinary items and net income. This requirement was superseded by *SFAS No. 128*,[14] which requires that EPS figures[15] for income from continuing operations and net income be presented on the face of the income statement. In addition, EPS figures for discontinued operations, extraordinary items, and cumulative effects of accounting change are to be disclosed.

Under the provisions of *APB Opinion No. 15,* a company had either a simple or complex capital structure. A *simple capital structure* was comprised solely of common stock or had other securities whose exercise or conversion would not in the aggregate dilute EPS by 3 percent or more.

Companies with *complex capital structures* were required to disclose dual EPS figures: (1) primary EPS and (2) fully diluted EPS. *Primary EPS* was intended to display the most likely dilutive effect of exercise or conversion on EPS. It included only the dilutive effects of common stock equivalents. *APB Opinion No. 15* described *common stock equivalents* as securities that are not, in form, common stock, but rather contain provisions that enable the holders of such securities to become common stockholders and to participate in any value appreciation of the common stock. For example, stock warrants, options, and rights were considered common stock equivalents because they exist solely to give the holder the right to acquire common stock. Dual presentation required that EPS be recast under the assumption that the exercise or conversion of potentially dilutive securities (common stock equivalents for primary EPS and all securities for fully dilutive EPS) had actually occurred.

The provisions of *APB Opinion No. 15* were criticized as being arbitrary, too complex, and illogical. Criticisms focused mainly on the requirements for determining whether a convertible security is a common stock equivalent. Under *APB Opinion No. 15* a convertible security was considered a common stock equivalent if, at issuance, its yield was less than two-thirds of the Aa corporate bond yield. This requirement did not reflect the likelihood of conversion in a dynamic securities market. As a result, changes in market prices subsequent to issuance, which may change the nature of convertibles from senior securities to securities that likely to be converted, were ignored. As a result, similar securities issued by different companies were likely to have been classified differently, for common stock equivalency purposes.

In addition, the need for dual presentation as required under *APB Opinion No. 15* was questioned. Companies with a complex capital structure were not required to report basic (undiluted) EPS. Critics argued that the extremes,

[14] *Statement of Financial Accounting Standards No. 128,* "Earnings per Share" (Stamford, CT: FASB, 1997).

[15] Firms with simple capital structures report basic EPS figures. All others report diluted EPS figures. Basic and diluted EPS are discussed later in the chapter.

no dilution to full dilution, were endpoints on a continuum of potential dilution and that both endpoints have information content. Moreover, many users contended that basic EPS would be more useful than primary EPS. Consistent with these views, a research study indicated that primary EPS seldom differs from fully diluted EPS.[16]

SFAS No. 128

In 1991, the FASB issued a plan to make financial statements more useful to investors and creditors by increasing the international comparability of financial information. Subsequently, the FASB undertook a project on the calculation and presentation of EPS information.[17] The International Accounting Standards Committee (IASC) had begun a similar project in 1989. Both projects were undertaken in response to the criticisms leveled at the complexity and arbitrariness of EPS calculations as described above. While the two bodies agreed to cooperate with each other in sharing information, each issued separate but similar statements: *IAS No. 33* and *SFAS No. 128*.

The FASB decided to replace primary EPS with basic EPS, citing the following reasons:

1. Basic EPS and diluted EPS data would give users the most factually supportable range of EPS possibilities.

2. Use of a common international EPS statistic is important due to database-oriented financial analysis and the internationalization of business and capital markets.

3. The notion of common stock equivalents does not operate effectively in practice.

4. The computation of primary EPS is complex and may not be well understood or consistently applied.

5. Presenting basic EPS would eliminate the criticisms about the arbitrary determination of whether a security is a common stock equivalent.[18]

SFAS No. 128 requires presentation of EPS by all companies that have issued common stock or other securities which upon exercise or conversion would result in the issuance of common stock when those securities are publicly traded.[19] Companies with simple capital structures are to report basic EPS figures. *SFAS No. 128* defines simple capital structures as those with only

---

[16] C. L. DeBerg and B. Murdock, "An Empirical Investigation of the Usefulness of Earnings per Share Information," *Journal of Accounting, Auditing and Finance* (Spring 1994), pp. 249–264.

[17] See *FASB Highlights*, "FASB's Plan for International Activities," January 1995, for the revised plan.

[18] *Statement of Financial Accounting Standards No. 128*, "Earnings per Share" (Stamford, CT: FASB, 1997), par. 89.

[19] *SFAS No. 128* also applies to companies that have filed or are in the process of filing with a regulatory agency to issue securities in a public market.

common stock outstanding.[20] All other companies are required to present basic and diluted EPS amounts.

Basic EPS   The objective of *basic EPS* is to measure a company's performance over the reporting period from the perspective of the common stockholder. Basic EPS is computed by dividing income available to common stockholders by the weighted average number of shares outstanding during the period. That is,

$$\text{Basic EPS} = \frac{\text{Net Income} - \text{Preferred Dividends}}{\text{Weighted Average Number of Shares Outstanding}}$$

Diluted EPS   The objective of *diluted EPS* is to measure a company's proforma performance over the reporting period from the perspective of the common stockholder as if the exercise or conversion of potentially dilutive securities had actually occurred. This presentation is consistent with the conceptual framework objective of providing information on an enterprise's financial performance which is useful in assessing the prospects of the enterprise. Basic EPS is historical. It reports what enterprise performance was during the period. Diluted EPS reveals what could happen to EPS if and when dilution occurs. Taken together, these two measures provide users with information to project historical information into the future and to adjust those projections for the effects of potential dilution.

The dilutive effects of *call options and warrants* are reflected in EPS by applying the treasury stock method. The dilutive effects of written *put options* that require the reporting entity to repurchase shares of its own stock are computed by applying the reverse treasury stock method. And the dilutive effects of convertible securities are computed by applying the if-converted method. Each of these methods is described below.

Securities whose exercise or conversion is antidilutive (exercise or conversion causes EPS to increase) are to be excluded from the computation of diluted EPS. Diluted EPS should report the maximum potential dilution. When there is more than one potentially dilutive security, the potential dilutive effect of individual securities is determined first by calculating earnings per incremental share. Securities are sequentially included in the calculation of diluted EPS. Those with the lowest earnings per incremental share are included first.

Call Options and Warrants   *Call options and warrants* give the holder the right to purchase shares of the company's stock for a predetermined option (exercise or strike) price. In the typical exercise of stock options and warrants, the holder receives shares of common stock in exchange for cash. The holders

---

[20] This definition eliminates the 3 percent materiality criterion of *APB Opinion No. 15.*

will exercise their options only when the market price of common stock exceeds the option price.[21]

Rather than making complex assumptions regarding how the company might utilize the cash proceeds[22] from presumed exercise of call options or warrants, the FASB requires the use of the *treasury stock method* to determine the dilutive effect on EPS. Under this approach, treasury shares are presumed to be purchased with the proceeds[23] at the average market price during the period. The difference between the number of shares assumed issued upon exercise of the options and the number of treasury shares is termed *incremental shares*. The incremental shares are added to the weighted average number of shares outstanding during the period to determine the dilutive effect of exercising the options or warrants.

Written Put Options *Written put options* and forward purchase contracts require the reporting entity to repurchase shares of its own stock at a predetermined price. These securities are dilutive when the exercise price is above the average market price during the period. Hence, their dilutive effect is computed using the *reverse treasury stock method.* This procedure is essentially the opposite of the treasury stock method we have described for call options and warrants.

Under the reverse treasury stock method, it is presumed that the company issues enough common shares at the average market price to generate enough cash to satisfy the contract. It is then assumed that the proceeds from the stock issuance are used to exercise the put (buy back the shares under contract). The incremental shares (the difference between the number of shares assumed issued and the number of shares that would be received when the put is exercised) are added to the denominator to calculate diluted EPS.

Convertible Securities *Convertible securities* are securities (usually bonds or preferred stock) that are convertible into other securities (usually common stock) at a predetermined exchange rate. To determine whether a convertible

---

[21] Alternatively, when the option price is higher than the market price of common shares, it would be illogical to presume that dilution would occur. In this case, the options, warrants, or rights are said to be antidilutive. Under *SFAS No. 128*, antidilution occurs when the option price exceeds the average market price during the period.

[22] For example, if it were assumed that the cash would be spent on operations, the company would have to project the impact of such an investment on revenues and expenses. This would require assumptions regarding such things as the price elasticity of the company's products and services and whether the present physical plant could accommodate the presumed expanded activities.

[23] The APB also required the treasury stock approach. As a safeguard against the potential impact that a large repurchase of treasury shares might have on the market price of common shares, the number of treasury shares was limited to 20 percent of the outstanding shares at the end of the period. Excess cash was presumed to have been spent to reduce debt or purchase U.S. government securities. *SFAS No. 128* imposes no limit on the number of treasury shares assumed repurchased. This is an example of one of the objectives of the pronouncement: to minimize the computational complexity and arbitrary assumptions of its predecessor, *APB Opinion No. 15.*

security is dilutive requires calculation of EPS as if conversion had occurred. The "as-if-converted" figure is then compared to EPS without conversion. If conversion would cause EPS to decline, the security is dilutive. If not, the security would be considered antidilutive, and the pro-forma effect of conversion would not be included in diluted EPS.

Under the *if-converted method,*

1. If the company has convertible preferred stock, the preferred dividend applicable to the convertible preferred stock is added back to the numerator. If the preferred stock had been converted, the preferred shares would not have been outstanding during the period and the preferred dividends would not have been paid. Hence, there would have been no convertible preferred stockholder claim to net income.

2. If the company has convertible debt, the interest expense applicable to the convertible debt net of its tax effect is added to the numerator. If the convertible debt had been converted, the interest would not have been paid to the creditors. At the same time, there would be no associated tax benefit. As a result, net income and hence income to common stockholders would have been higher by the amount of the interest expense saved minus its tax benefit.

3. The number of shares that would have been issued upon conversion of the convertible security is added to the denominator.

Contingently Issuable Shares   *Contingently issuable shares* are those shares whose issuance is contingent upon the satisfaction of certain conditions, such as attaining a certain level of income or market price of the common shares in the future. If all necessary conditions have not been met by the end of the reporting period, *SFAS No. 128* requires that contingently issuable shares be included in the computation of diluted EPS based on the number of shares that would be included, if any, if the reporting period were the end of the contingency period. For example, if the shares are issuable once a given level of net income is attained, the company must presume that the current level of earnings will continue until the end of the agreement. Under this presumption, if current earnings is at least as great as the target level of earnings, the contingently issuable shares must be included in diluted EPS if they are dilutive.

Earnings Per Share Illustration
The Kroll-O'Gara Company has a complex capital structure. Consequently, it discloses both basic and diluted earnings per share on its 1998 income statement of $0.71 and $0.69, respectively (Figure 4.1). The company discloses the earnings per share effects of other nonrecurring items of income in a footnote to its financial statements as follows:

> *Basic and diluted earnings per share based on income from continuing operations were $0.56 and $0.52, respectively, for the year ended December 31, 1996. The basic and diluted per share impact of the discontinued operations were $0.11 and $0.10, respectively. Basic and diluted earnings per share based on income from continuing operations before the extraordinary item and cumulative effect of*

change in accounting principle were $0.19 and $0.18, respectively, for the year ended December 31, 1997. The basic and diluted per share impact of the extraordinary item was $0.01 and the basic and diluted per share impact of the change in accounting principle were $0.03 and $0.02, respectively. During 1997, 66,000 warrants to purchase a total of 27,746 shares of common stock of the Company at $7.20 per warrant were outstanding but were not included in the computation of diluted earnings per share because the warrants' exercise price was greater than the average market price of the common shares. During 1998, 11,666 warrants to purchase an equivalent amount of shares of common stock of the Company at $25.69 per warrant were outstanding but were not included in the computation of diluted earnings per share because the warrants' exercise price was greater than the average market price of the common shares.

Usefulness of Earnings per Share

The overall objective of EPS data is to provide investors with an indication of (1) the value of the firm and (2) expected future dividends. A major theoretical issue surrounding the presentation of EPS is whether this information should be based on historical or forecasted information. Authoritative accounting bodies have generally taken the position that financial information should be based only on historical data; views formerly expressed by *APB Opinion No. 15* and currently by *SFAS No. 128* are consistent with this trend.

EPS has been termed a *summary indicator,* that is, a single item that communicates considerable information about an enterprise's performance or financial position. The continuing trend toward complexity in financial reporting has caused many financial statement users to utilize summary indicators. EPS is especially popular because it is thought to contain information useful in making predictions about future dividends and stock prices, and as a measure of management efficiency. However, investors' needs might be better satisfied with measures that predict future cash flows (such as current or pro-forma dividends per share). As discussed in Chapter 5, cash flow data itself may provide more relevant information to investors than earnings data utilizing accrual basis accounting income. Many accountants discourage the use of *summary indicators,* such as EPS. These individuals maintain that an understanding of a company's performance requires a more comprehensive analysis than is provided by a single ratio. This issue is discussed further in the readings contained on the text's webpage for Chapter 4.

Statement of Financial Accounting Concepts No. 5

In 1984 the FASB released its *Statement of Financial Accounting Concepts No. 5,* "Recognition and Measurement in Financial Statements of Business Enterprises." In this document the FASB attempted to broaden the scope of the measurements of the operating results of business enterprises by introducing the definition of comprehensive income as follows:

Comprehensive income is the change in equity (net assets) of an entity during a period from transactions and events and circumstances from non-owner sources.

> *It includes all changes in equity during a period except those resulting from investments by owners and distributions to owners.*[24]

This approach represents the FASB's attempt to tie together the Hicksian capital maintenance approach and the traditional accounting transactions approach to income measurement. Net income is defined as the maximum amount of a firm's resources that can be distributed to owners during a given period of time (exclusive of new owner investments) and still leave the business enterprise as well off at the end of that period as it was in the beginning. However, the FASB attempted to allay fears that the concept of comprehensive income was a radical shift toward using current value measurements by stating that the measurement of most assets and liabilities would not differ under the concept of comprehensive income. Yet recent FASB pronouncements, such as FASB *Statement of Financial Accounting Standards No. 115*, which requires the use of market values to measure investments in common stock, provide evidence that the FASB may be making a gradual shift toward current value accounting.

SFAC No. 5 did not suggest major changes in the current structure and content of financial statements. However, it did propose that a statement of cash flows should replace the previously required statement of changes in financial position and provided the impetus for this statement (discussed in Chapter 5). *SFAC No. 5* attempted to set forth recognition criteria and guidance on what information should be incorporated into financial statements, and when this information should be reported. According to *SFAC No. 5*, a full set of financial statements for a period should show

1. Financial position at the end of the period.
2. Earnings for the period.
3. Comprehensive income for the period.
4. Cash flows during the period.
5. Investments by and distributions to owners during the period.

The statement of financial position should provide information about an entity's assets, liabilities, and equity and their relationship to each other at a moment in time. It should also delineate the entity's resource structure—major classes and amounts of assets—and its financing structure—major classes and amounts of liabilities and equity. The statement of financial position is not intended to show the value of a business, but it should provide information to users wishing to make their own estimates of the enterprise's value.

Earnings is a measure of entity performance during a period. It measures the extent to which asset inflows (revenues and gains) exceed asset outflows. The concept of earnings provided in *SFAC No. 5* is similar to net income for a period determined under the transactions approach. It is expected that the

---

[24] *Statement of Financial Accounting Concepts No. 5*, "Recognition and Measurement in Financial Statements of Business Enterprises" (Stamford, CT: FASB, 1984), par. 39.

concept of earnings will continue to be subject to the process of gradual change that has characterized its development.

Comprehensive income is defined as a broad measure of the effects of transactions and other events on an entity. It comprises all recognized changes in equity of the entity during a period from transactions except those resulting from investments by owners and distributions to owners. The relationship between earnings and comprehensive income is illustrated as follows.

Revenues	Earnings
Less: Expenses	Plus or minus cumulative accounting adjustments
Plus: Gains	Plus or minus other nonowner changes in equity
Less: Losses	
= Earnings	= Comprehensive income

The statement of cash flows should directly or indirectly reflect an entity's cash receipts classified by major source and its cash payments classified by major uses during a period. The statement should include cash flow information about its operating, financing, and investing activities.

A statement of investments by and distributions to owners reflects an entity's capital transactions during a period. That is, it reflects the extent to which and in what ways the equity of the entity increased or decreased from transactions with owners.

The scope of *SFAC No. 5* and its relationship to other methods of reporting are illustrated in Figure 4.2.

In addition to the issue of comprehensive income, *SFAC No. 5* addresses certain measurement issues that are closely related to recognition. Accordingly, an item and information about it should meet four recognition criteria and should be recognized at the time these criteria are met (subject to the cost-benefit and materiality constraints).

1. **Definitions.** The item meets the definition of an element contained in *SFAC No. 6*.

2. **Measurability.** It has a relevant attribute, measurable with sufficient reliability.

3. **Relevance.** The information about the item is capable of making a difference in user decisions.

4. **Reliability.** The information is representationally faithful, verifiable, and neutral.

These recognition criteria are consistent with and in fact drawn from *SFAC Nos. 1, 2,* and *6. SFAC No. 5* goes on to provide guidance in applying the recognition criteria when enterprise earnings are affected by the recognition decision. This guidance is consistent with the doctrine of conservatism. That is, recognition of revenues and gains is based on the additional tests of their (1) being realized or realizable and (2) being earned before recognized as income. Guidance for recognizing expenses and losses is dependent on either consumption of benefit or loss of future benefit

FIGURE 4.2. *Relationship of* SFAC *No. 5 to Other Methods of Reporting (Source: Statement of* Financial Accounting Concepts No. 5, *"Recognition and Measurement in Financial Statements of Business Entertprises" (Stamford, CT: FASB, 1985), par. 8.)*

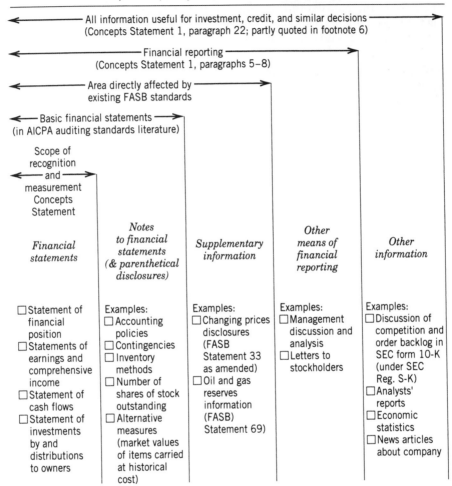

One of the major gaps in *SFAC No. 5* is its failure to define the term *earnings*.[25] Moreover, it does not resolve the current value/historical cost debate. This failure was apparently due to the board's position of accepting *decision usefulness* as the overriding objective of financial reporting.

[25] *Statement of Financial Accounting Concepts No. 5,* "Recognition and Measurement in Financial Statements of Business Enterprises" (Stamford, CT: Financial Accounting Standards Board, 1984), par. 39.

This document is disappointing to those who had hoped it would provide a formula or set of formulas from which solutions to specific accounting problems could be derived. In other words, some accountants and financial statement users would prefer a document that provides answers to questions about when, if at all, a specific event should be recognized and what amount best measures that event.

SFAS No. 130

Issues about income reporting have been characterized broadly in terms of a contrast between the current operating performance and the all-inclusive income concepts. Although the FASB generally has followed the all-inclusive income concept, occasionally it has made specific exceptions to that concept. Several accounting standards require that certain items that qualify as components of comprehensive income bypass the income statement. Other components are required to be disclosed in the notes. The rationale for this treatment is that the earnings process is incomplete. Examples of items currently not disclosed on the traditional income statement and reported elsewhere are as follows (the chapter in which these items are discussed is in parentheses):

a. Foreign currency translation adjustments (Chapter 15).
b. Gains and losses on foreign currency transactions that are designated as, and are effective as, economic hedges of a net investment in a foreign entity (Chapter 15).
c. Gains and losses on intercompany foreign currency transactions that are of a long-term-investment nature (that is, settlement is not planned or anticipated in the foreseeable future), when the entities to the transaction are consolidated, combined, or accounted for by the equity method in the reporting enterprise's financial statements (Chapter 15).
d. A change in the market value of a future contract that qualifies as a hedge of an asset reported at fair value unless earlier recognition of a gain or loss in income is required because high correlation has not occurred (Chapter 15).
e. The excess of the additional pension liability over unrecognized prior service cost (Chapter 13).
f. Unrealized holding gains and losses on available-for-sale securities (Chapter 7).
g. Unrealized holding gains and losses that result from a debt security being transferred into the available-for-sale category from the held-to-maturity category (Chapter 7).
h. Subsequent decreases (if not an other-than-temporary impairment) or increases in the fair value of available-for-sale securities previously written down as impaired (Chapter 7).

In 1996, the FASB initiated a project designed to require the disclosure of comprehensive income by business enterprises. This project was undertaken in response to a variety of concerns including: (1) The increasing use of off-balance sheet financing by companies, (2) the practice of reporting some items of comprehensive income directly in stockholders' equity, and (3) acknowledgment of the need to promote the international harmonization of accounting standards.

The issues considered in this project were organized under five general questions: (1) whether comprehensive income should be reported, (2) whether cumulative accounting adjustments should be included in comprehensive income, (3) how the components of comprehensive income should be classified for disclosure, (4) whether comprehensive income should be disclosed in one or two statements of financial performance, and (5) whether components of other comprehensive income should be displayed before or after their related tax effects.

Comprehensive income is defined as "the change in equity [net assets] of a business enterprise during a period from transactions and other events and circumstances from nonowner sources. It includes all changes in equity during a period except those resulting from investments by owners and distributions to owners." The term *comprehensive income* is used to describe the total of all components of comprehensive income, including net income. The Statement uses the term *other comprehensive income* to refer to revenues, expenses, gains, and losses included in comprehensive income but excluded from net income. The stated purpose of reporting comprehensive income is to report a measure of overall enterprise performance by disclosing all changes in equity of a business enterprise that result from recognized transactions and other economic events of the period other than transactions with owners in their capacity as owners.

The Statement requires the disclosure of comprehensive and discusses how to report and disclose comprehensive income and its components, including net income. However, it does not specify when to recognize or how to measure the items that make up comprehensive income. The FASB indicated that existing and future accounting standards will provide guidance on items that are to be included in comprehensive income and its components. When used with related disclosures and information in the other financial statements, the information provided by reporting comprehensive income should help investors, creditors, and others in assessing an enterprise's financial performance and the timing and magnitude of an enterprise's future cash flows.

In addressing what items should be included in comprehensive income, the main issue was whether the effects of certain accounting adjustments of earlier periods, such as the cumulative effects of changes in accounting principles, should be reported as part of comprehensive income. In reaching its conclusions, the FASB considered the definition of comprehensive income in *SFAC No. 5*, which indicates that the concept includes all recognized changes in equity (net assets), including cumulative accounting adjustments. The Board decided to follow that definition and, therefore, to include cumulative accounting adjustments as part of comprehensive income.

With respect to the components of comprehensive income, the standard requires companies to disclose an amount for net income, but that amount must be accorded equal prominence with the amount disclosed for comprehensive income. Net income and comprehensive income are identical for an enterprise that has no items of comprehensive income other than net income. The Statement does not change the classifications within net income. Those classifications, as discussed earlier, include income from continuing operations, discontinued operations, extraordinary items, and cumulative effects of changes in accounting principles. Items included in other comprehensive income are classified based on their nature. For example, under existing accounting standards, other comprehensive income may be separately classified into foreign currency items, minimum pension liability adjustments, and unrealized gains and losses on certain investments in debt and equity securities.

In reporting comprehensive income, companies are required to use a gross disclosure technique for classifications related to items of other comprehensive income other than minimum pension liability adjustments. For those classifications, reclassification adjustments must be disclosed separately from other changes in the balances of those items so that the total change is disclosed as two amounts. A net disclose technique for the classification related to minimum pension liability adjustments is required (see Chapter 13). For this classification, the reclassification adjustment must be combined with other changes in the balance of that item so that the total change is disclosed as a single amount.

When using the gross disclosure technique, reclassification adjustments may be disclosed in one of two ways. One way is as part of the classification of other comprehensive income to which those adjustments relate, such as within a classification for unrealized securities gains and losses. The other way is to disclose a separate classification consisting solely of reclassification adjustments in which all reclassification adjustments for a period are disclosed.

SFAS No. 130 allows for the reporting of comprehensive income in a financial statement that is displayed with the same prominence as other financial statements. This provision allows an enterprise to display the components of other comprehensive income below the total for net income in (1) an income statement, (2) a separate statement that begins with net income, or (3) a statement of changes in equity. However, regardless of the display format chosen, the total for comprehensive income is now required to be disclosed in the financial statements for fiscal years beginning after December 15, 1997.

The method of disclosing comprehensive income may be important to investors. A study by Hirst and Hopkins[26] indicated that financial analysts detected earnings management on selected items only when this information was presented in a separate statement of comprehensive income. Maines and McDaniel[27] found that the corporate performance evaluations of nonprofessional investors' (the general public) were affected by the method of presentation. They argue that, according to their results, nonprofessional investors will use comprehensive income information only if it

---

[26] D. Eric Hirst and Patrick Hopkins, "Comprehensive Income Reporting: Financial Analyst's Judgments," *Journal of Accounting Research* (1998 Supplement), pp. 47–75.

[27] Laureen A. Maines and Linda S. McDaniel, "Effects of Comprehensive-Income Characteristics on Nonprofessional Investor Judgments: The Roll of Financial-Statement Presentation Format," *The Accounting Review* (April 2000), pp. 179–207.

is included in a separate statement rather than as a component of stock-holders' equity. Taken together, these results provide evidence that the presentation format for comprehensive income may impact on decision making. These findings are consistent with the FASB's previous contention that the placement of comprehensive income provides a signal to investors about its importance.[28]

Finally, with respect to disclosing the tax effects, the Statement allows the components of other comprehensive income to be disclosed either (a) net of related tax effects or (b) before related tax effects with one amount shown for the aggregate income tax expense or benefit related to the total amount of other comprehensive income. Disclosure of the amount of income tax expense or benefit allocated to each component of other comprehensive income can be made either on the face of the statement in which those components are disclosed or in the notes to the financial statements.

The total of other comprehensive income, for elements not reported as part of traditional net income for a period, is required to be transferred to a separate component of equity in a statement of financial position at the end of an accounting period. A descriptive title such as *accumulated other comprehensive income* is to be used for that component of equity. A company must also disclose accumulated balances for each classification in that separate component of equity on the face of a statement of financial position, in a statement of changes in equity, or in notes accompanying the financial statements. Those classifications must correspond to classifications used for components of other comprehensive income in a statement of financial performance.

In 1998, 347 of the 600 companies surveyed in *Accounting Trends and Techniques* presented a financial statement reporting comprehensive income. Other survey companies disclosed comprehensive income items but did not present a financial statement reporting comprehensive income because their financial statements were for a fiscal year prior to the effective date of *SFAS No. 130*. Of the 347 survey companies reporting comprehensive income, 14 did so in a combined statement of income and comprehensive income; 61 in a separate statement of comprehensive income; and 272 in a statement of changes in stockholders' equity. If comprehensive income was reported in a separate statement, such a statement was most frequently presented on the same page as the statement of income.[29]

The overriding question regarding the disclosure of comprehensive income on corporate financial reports is as follows: Does this amount provide investors with additional information that allows for better predictions? The evidence so far is mixed. The previously cited study by Hirst and Hopkins[30] found that

---

[28] Financial Accounting Standards Board, "Exposure Draft-Reporting Comprehensive Income," 1996, pars. 50 & 63.

[29] American Institute of Certified Public Accountants, *Accounting Trends and Techniques* (New York: AICPA, 1999), p. 58.

[30] Hirst and Hopkins, op. cit.

FIGURE 4.3 *The Kroll-O'Gara Company Comprehensive Income as Disclosed in its Consolidated Statements of Shareholders' Equity for the Year Ended December 31, 1998*

	COMPREHENSIVE INCOME (LOSS)
Comprehensive income:	
Net income,	$13,088,906
Foreign currency translation adjustment, net of $764,000 tax benefit	(476,956)
Reclassification adjustment for gain on securities included in net income, net of $7,000 tax benefit	(10,469)
Other comprehensive income (loss)	(487,425)
Comprehensive income	$12,601,481

the presentation of comprehensive income influenced financial analysts' estimates of the value of a company engaged in earnings management. However, Dhaliwal, Subramanyam, and Trezevan[31] did not find that comprehensive income was associated with the market value of a firm's stock or that it was a better predictor of future cash slows than net income. Additional research is needed to further assess this relationship.

The Kroll-O'Gara Company has chosen to disclose comprehensive income, which encompasses net income, foreign currency translation adjustments, and unrealized holding gains of marketable securities in its consolidated statement of shareholders' equity as illustrated in Figure 4.3.[32]

The Value of Corporate Earnings

In Chapter 3 we noted that investors are interested in assessing the amount, timing, and uncertainty of future cash flows and that accounting earnings have been found to be more useful than cash flow information in making this assessment. Future cash flow and earnings assessments impact on the market price of a company's stock. Over the past three decades, accounting researchers have examined the relationship between corporate earnings and a company's stock prices. One measure that has been found useful in assessing this relationship is a company's price-earnings ratio (PE), which is calculated as

$$PE = \frac{\text{Current market price per share}}{\text{Earnings per share}}$$

[31] Dan Dhaliwal, K. R. Subramanyam, and Robert Trezevant, "Is Comprehensive Income to Net Income As a Measure of Firm Performance," *Journal of Accounting and Economics* (January 1999), pp. 43–67.

[32] The calculations of these two incomplete transactions are discussed in more detail in Chapters 15 and 7, respectively.

This ratio provides an earnings multiple at which a company's stock is currently trading. A firm's β or earnings volatility (as discussed in Chapter 2) will have an impact on its stock price. In addition, research has indicated that the components of earnings income from continuing operations, discontinued operations, extraordinary items, and earnings per share will also be incorporated into the determination of market prices.[33] That is, all things being equal, a firm reporting only income from continuing operations will be valued more highly than a firm with an equal amount of risk and the same earnings which reports one or more of the other components of income. This occurs because investors are most interested in a company's sustainable earnings, and investors view income components other than income from continuing operations as nonsustainable.

The price-earnings ratio for Kroll-O'Gara using the company's market price per share of $40 on December 31, 1998 was 56.33 and is calculated as

$$\frac{\text{Market Price per Share} \quad \$40.00}{\text{Basic Earnings per share} \quad \$\ 0.71}$$

A price-earnings ratio of this magnitude indicates that investors' perceptions of the future earnings potential for this company are very favorable because the average price-earnings ratio for large publicly traded companies during this period was about 25 times earnings.

Special Problems in Income Statement Presentation

Prior Period Adjustments

The test for classifying an item as a prior period adjustment (adjustment to retained earnings) was made quite rigid in *APB Opinion No. 9*. In order for events and transactions to be classified as prior period adjustments, they must have been

> (a) specifically identified and directly related to the business activities of particular prior periods, (b) not attributable to economic events occurring subsequent to the date of the financial statements for the prior period, (c) dependent primarily on determination by persons other than management, (d) not susceptible of reasonable estimation prior to such determination.[34]

At the time *Opinion No. 9* was issued, the APB took the position that prior period adjustments that are disclosed as increases or decreases in the beginning retained earnings balance should have been related to events of previous periods that were not susceptible to reasonable estimation at the time they occurred. In addition, since these amounts were material by definition, it would be expected

---

[33] Ram T.S. Ramakrishman and Jacob K. Thomas, "Valuation of Permanent, Transitory and Price Irrelevant Components of Reported Earnings," *Journal of Accounting Auditing and Finance* (Summer 1998), pp. 301–336.

[34] *APB Opinion No. 9*, op. cit., par. 23.

that the auditor's opinion would be at least qualified on the financial statements issued when the event or transaction took place. Examples of prior period adjustments under *APB Opinion No. 9* were settlements of income tax cases or other litigations. The category of errors was later added to this classification. Errors would, of course, not result in an opinion qualification because they would not be known to the auditors when the financial statements were released.

In 1976, the SEC released *Staff Accounting Bulletin No. 8,* which concluded that litigation is inevitably an economic event and that settlements of litigation constitute economic events of the period in which they occur. This conclusion created a discrepancy between generally accepted accounting principles and the reporting requirements for companies registered with the SEC. Prior to the release of *Staff Accounting Bulletin No. 8,* the FASB had undertaken a study of prior period adjustment reporting of 600 companies and also concluded that a clarification of the criteria outlined in *APB Opinion No. 9* was required.

Subsequently, the FASB issued *SFAS No. 16,* "Prior Period Adjustments," which indicated that the only items of profit and loss that should be reported as prior period adjustments were

a.   *Correction of an error in the financial statements of a prior period.*

b.   *Adjustments that result from the realization of income tax benefits of preacquisition operating loss carry-forwards of purchased subsidiaries.*[35]

This release put the FASB on the side of the all-inclusive concept of income. When considered in conjunction with *APB Opinion No. 30,* it ensures that almost all items of profit and loss that result from external transactions are reported as components of net income.

The restrictive criteria for classification of an item of revenue or expense to be categorized as a prior period adjustment has virtually eliminated their inclusion on financial statements. The 1999 edition of *Accounting Trends and Techniques* did not disclose a single company reporting a prior period adjustment. However, the 1996 Concurrent Computer Corporation financial statements disclosed the information contained in Figure 4.4.

> *The company has restated its consolidated statements for the year ended June 30, 1996. This action resulted from the identification of certain foreign assets that were disposed of in fiscal year 1996. The impact of these adjustments on the Company's financial results as originally reported is summarized below:*

Interim Financial Statements

Many companies issue financial statements for periods of less than a year and also release information on their periodic performance through various news media. The chief value of these statements is their timeliness. That is, investors need to be aware of any changes in the company's financial position as soon as possible. In addition, much of the information disclosed in interim financial statements enters into the analytical data used by the government to develop

---

[35] *Statement of Financial Accounting Standards No. 16,* "Prior Period Adjustments" (Stamford, CT: Financial Accounting Standards Board, 1977), par. 11.

**FIGURE 4.4 DOLLAR AMOUNT IN THOUSANDS EXCEPT PER
SHARE DATA**

	As Reported	As Restated
Other Non-recurring Charges	$ 1,700.00	$ 3,297.00
Net Loss	39,712.00	41,309.00
Net Loss Per Share	1.30	1.35
Accounts Receivable	27,948.00	27,807.00
Total Current Assets	55,654.00	55,313.00
Total Assets	80,214.00	80,073.00
Accumulated Deficit	76,740.00	78,337.00
Cumulative Translation Adjustment	798.00	(658.00)
Total Equity	7,068.00	6,927.00
Total Liabilities and Equity	80,214.00	80,073.00

information on the state of the economy, the need for monetary controls, or the need for modifications in the tax laws. Moreover, there is also evidence that interim reporting has an impact on stock prices, indicating that investors do use interim financial information. It is therefore important that interim information be as reliable as possible.

A wide variety of practices have existed with regard to the methods of reporting in these so-called interim periods. Thus, such things as seasonal fluctuations in revenues and the application of fixed costs to the various periods have a significant impact on the reported results for interim periods.

In 1973 the APB studied this problem and issued its conclusions in *APB Opinion No. 28*, "Interim Financial Reporting." In reviewing the general question, the Board noted that two views existed as to the principal objective of interim financial reporting.

1. *One view held that each interim period was a separate accounting period and that income should be determined in the same manner as for the annual period; thus revenues and expenses should be reported as they occur. (discrete view).*

2. *The other view held that interim periods were an integral part of the annual period; thus revenues and expenses might be allocated to various interim periods even though they occurred only in one period. (integral view).*[36]

In *APB Opinion No. 28* the Board noted that interim financial information was essential to provide timely data on the progress of the enterprise and that the usefulness of the data rests on its relationship to annual reports. Accordingly, it was determined that interim periods should be viewed as integral parts of the annual period and that the principles and practices followed in the annual period should be followed in the interim period. However, certain modifications were deemed necessary in order to provide a better relationship to the annual period.

[36] *Accounting Principles Board Opinion No. 28,* "Interim Financial Reporting" (New York: American Institute of Certified Public Accountants, 1973), par. 5.

It was also stated that the publicly traded companies that provide summary information for financial analysis should provide, at a minimum, certain information for the interim period in question and the same interim period for the previous year. These guidelines were intended to offset partially the reduction in detail from interim reports. Among the items to be disclosed are sales, earnings per share, seasonal revenues, disposal of a segment of a business, contingencies, and changes in accounting principles.

Subsequent to the issuance of *APB Opinion No. 28,* problems in reporting certain types of events became evident. These problems were concerned mainly with reporting the cumulative effect of an accounting change for changes in accounting principles during interim periods, and reporting accounting changes during the fourth quarter of a fiscal year by a company whose securities are publicly traded.

With respect to the cumulative adjustments required for interim changes in accounting principles, *APB Opinion No. 28* stated,

> *A change in accounting principle or practice adopted in an interim period that requires an adjustment for the cumulative effect of the change to the beginning of the current fiscal year should be reported in the interim period in a manner similar to that found in the annual report....The effect of the change from the beginning of the annual period to the period of change should be reported as a determinant of net income in the interim period in which the change is made.*[37]

Because of this requirement, the cumulative effect of the change on retained earnings at the beginning of the fiscal year was presented as a component of net income in the interim period in which the change was adopted. However, problems arose because reissued interim period balance sheets did not reflect the cumulative effect of the change on retained earnings, whereas reissued interim period income statements did reflect this effect.

On becoming aware of this inconsistency, the FASB reviewed the provisions of *APB Opinion No. 28* and issued *SFAS No. 3,* "Reporting Accounting Changes in Interim Financial Statements."[38] The provisions of this statement were to apply separately to changes other than changes to the LIFO inventory pricing method and fourth-quarter accounting changes made by publicly traded companies.

For all cumulative effect changes other than changes to LIFO, an accounting change made during the first interim period of the fiscal year should reflect the cumulative effect of the change on retained earnings in the net income of the first interim period. For changes in other than the first interim period, no cumulative effect of the change should be included in net income in the period of change. Rather, the new principle should be retroactively applied to all prior interim periods, and the cumulative effect of the change on retained earnings at the beginning of the year should be included in the net income for the first interim period. The statement also specifies certain

---

[37] Ibid., par. 27.

[38] *Statement of Financial Accounting Standards No. 3,* "Reporting Accounting Changes in Interim Financial Statements" (Stamford, CT: FASB, 1974).

disclosures as to the nature and justification for the change and its effect on continuing operations, net income, and per-share amounts.

Where changes to the LIFO method of inventory pricing have occurred, the cumulative effect of the change cannot ordinarily be calculated. Therefore, *SFAS No. 3* requires a paragraph explaining the reasons for omitting accounting for a cumulative effect and disclosure of the pro forma amounts for prior years.

With respect to fourth-quarter changes by publicly held companies, the provisions of *APB Opinion No. 28* require some of these organizations to disclose certain fourth-quarter information in footnotes. Information concerning the effects of an accounting change made during the fourth quarter was not explicitly identified as a part of this requirement. *SFAS No. 3* amended *APB Opinion No. 28* to require such disclosures.

International Accounting Standards

In addition to the release of *IAS No. 33* on earnings per share, the International Accounting Standards Committee has:

1. Defined performance and income in "Framework for the Preparation and Presentation of Financial Statements."
2. Discussed the objective of and the information to be presented on an income statement in *IAS No. 1*, "Presentation of Financial Statements."
3. Discussed the components of the income statement in *IAS No. 8*, "Net Profit or Loss for a Period, Fundamental Errors and Changes in Accounting Policies."
4. Defined concept of revenue in *IAS No. 18*, "Revenue."
5. Defined the minimum content of interim financial reports in *IAS No. 34*, "Interim Financial Reporting."
6. Discussed the required presentation and disclosure of a discontinued operation in *IAS No. 35*, "Discontinued Operations."

In discussing performance, the IASC noted that profit is used to measure performance or as the basis for other measures such as return on investment or earnings per share. The elements relating to the measurement of profit are income and expenses, but the measurements of income and expenses and ultimately profit are dependent on the concepts of capital and capital maintenance used by the enterprise in preparing its financial statements. The concepts of capital maintenance, physical capital maintenance, and financial capital maintenance were defined by the IASC much as they were defined earlier in this chapter.

IAS No. 1 requires an income statement that includes the following line items: revenue, the results of operations, finance costs, gains and losses from equity investments, tax expense, profits or losses from ordinary activities, minority interest, and net profit. In addition, expenses must be classified based on either their nature or function, and dividends declared for the period must be disclosed on a per-share basis. In contrast to U.S. GAAP, *IAS No. 1* does not require discontinued operations *(IAS No. 34)* or accounting changes (IAS No. 8) to be reported as separate components of income.

The FASB's review of *IAS No. 1* indicated that, although current GAAP does not require the disclosure of minimum line items on the income statement, generally U.S. companies already disclose information similar to what *IAS No. 1* requires. However, it was noted that the failure to separately disclose discontinued operations and accounting changes makes it difficult to compare IAS-based and U.S. GAAP-based income statements.

In *IAS No. 8*, the IASC defined the concepts of net profit or loss from ordinary activities, extraordinary items, accounting changes, and fundamental errors. Each of these income statement items was defined and is reported in a manner similar to U.S. GAAP with the exception of fundamental errors. The benchmark treatment for fundamental errors is the same as U.S. GAAP—an adjustment to the beginning balance of retained earnings. However, an allowed alternative treatment permits errors to be corrected by inclusion in net income with supplemental disclosure. The FASB staff analysis of *IAS No. 8* stated that the standard does not present a problem for making intercompany comparisons. However, concern was also expressed that the IASC's definition of errors allows for more discretion than is permissible under U.S. GAAP and alternative methods for correcting errors are allowed under *IAS No. 8*.[39]

In *IAS No. 18*, the IASC discussed the concept of revenue measurement. It indicated that revenue should be recognized when it is probable that future economic benefit will flow to the enterprise, should be measured at the fair value of the consideration received, and should be recognized from the sale of goods when all of the following conditions have been satisfied:

a. the enterprise has transferred to the buyer the significant risks and rewards of ownership of the goods;
b. the enterprise retains neither continuing managerial involvement to the degree usually associated with ownership nor effective control over the goods sold;
c. the amount of revenue can be measured reliably;
d. it is probable that the economic benefits associated with the transaction will flow to the enterprise; and
e. the costs incurred or to be incurred in respect of the transaction can be measured reliably.[40]

The concept of revenue has not been specifically addressed in any official pronouncements in the United States. In reviewing *IAS No. 18*, the FASB staff noted that approximately 75 documents provide guidance for revenue recognition in the United States.[41] The staff then went on to speculate that if a comprehensive document on revenue did exist, there would probably be

---

[39] Financial Accounting Standards Board, *The IASC-U.S. Comparison Project: A Report on the Similarities and Differences between IASC Standards and U.S. GAAP*, 2nd ed., Carrie Bloomer (ed.), (Norwalk, CT: Financial Accounting Standards Board, 1999), pp. 113–118.

[40] *International Accounting Standard No. 18*, "Revenue," International Accounting Standards Committee, 1993, par. 14.

[41] Financial Accounting Standards Board, *The IASC-U.S. Comparison Project*, p. 210.

different revenue recognition criteria because of the use of the term *probable future economic benefit* in the IASC's criteria for revenue recognition.[42]

In *IAS No. 34*, "Interim Financial Reporting," the IASC defined the minimum content of an interim financial report, provided presentation and measurement guidance, and defined the recognition and measurement principles to be followed in the presentation of interim financial reports. This release indicated that the decision to publish and the frequency of reporting are matters that are best left to be decided by national law.

The minimum content of an interim financial report was defined as a condensed balance sheet, condensed income statement, condensed statement of cash flows, condensed statement of changes in stockholders' equity, and all footnotes necessary to understand the financial statements. *IAS No. 34* requires companies to use the same accounting principles in interim financial reports that are used in the annual report and adopts the integral view of interim financial reports.

The FASB's analysis of *IAS No. 34* indicated that it is similar to *Opinion No. 28* in that both require the use of the same accounting principles in interim periods as are used in the annual period. Despite the fact that a few minor differences were noted, it was concluded that the information provided by enterprises applying either *IAS No. 34* or *Opinion No. 28* would be similar.[43]

Discontinued operations were defined in *IAS No. 35* as a relatively large component of an enterprise such as a business or a geographical segment (as defined in *IAS No. 14*) that the company is disposing of pursuant to a single plan. The required disclosure for these disposal includes:

a.   A description of the discontinued operation.
b.   The business or geographic segment in which it had previously been reported on the company's financial statements.
c.   The date the plan was announced.
d.   The expected completion date of the disposal.
e.   The carrying value of the assets and liabilities of the disposed segment.
f.   The revenues, expenses, taxes, and profits of the disposed segment.
g.   The gain or loss on the disposal and its related income tax effects.
h.   The cash flows attributed to the disposed segment.
i.   The contracted sales price and carrying value of the disposed assets.

Under *IAS No. 35*, a discontinued operation may occur when (a) management announces a plan of disposal or (b) when a binding sale of the disposed assets occurs. This differs from the *Opinion No. 28* criteria, which is management's commitment to a formal plan of disposal. In addition, the two statements differ as to the timing of recognition of the operating results during the disposal period in that *IAS No. 35* requires the results to be recognized as realized. (Under current U.S. GAAP, recognition is influenced by whether a gain or loss is expected.) As noted earlier, *IAS No. 35* does not require the gain or loss

---

[42] Ibid.
[43] Ibid., pp. 387–398.

on the disposal to be disclosed separately. This may make it more difficult for investors to determine sustainable income for those companies reporting under international accounting rules.

The FASB's review of *IAS No. 35* noted the differences from U.S. GAAP for revenue recognition and separate presentation. As a result, the Board indicated that companies following its provisions may not be readily comparable to those reporting under *APB Opinion No. 28.*[44]

Summary

There has been a great deal of discussion among accountants about the proper concept of income to use and the need for comparability among entities because various financial statement users have relied on the corporate net income figure. Since 1966, several pronouncements have had a major impact on preparing the income statement. These pronouncements affect the presentation of income from normal operations and other sources, EPS computations, changes in methods of presenting information, disposal of parts of the entity, and interim financial reports. In each case, the number of alternatives is narrowed in an attempt to improve comparability.

The extent to which these pronouncements have improved the understandability of corporate financial reports is not readily determinable. Only the most sophisticated users of financial statements are likely to be able to understand the differences between normal and abnormal events, the effects of accounting changes, or the relative merits of any number of earnings per share figures. Accounting is often criticized as being too simplistic in the establishment of its assumptions about the behavior of revenue and costs. However, attempting to provide comparability while maintaining some degree of flexibility to accommodate the reporting needs of various entities may lead to more confusion.

In the readings contained on the webpage for Chapter 4, the composition of the income statement is examined in more detail.

Cases

• Case 4-1 Income Recognition in the Motion Picture Industry

The motion picture industry has undergone significant changes during the past four decades. Originally, companies such as Paramount Pictures had to rely solely on domestic and foreign screenings of their movies for their revenues. The birth of the television industry in the 1950s resulted in opportunities for broadcasting rights to networks and individual stations. Moreover, the introduction of cable television in the 1970s opened up substantial new sources of revenue. In addition, the unsaturated demand for new films

---

[44] Ibid., pp. 399–412.

resulted in a market for "made for television" films. Finally, the invention of the video recorder opened yet another revenue source for these companies.

The production of a film involves four phases.

1. Acquisition of the story rights.
2. Preproduction, including script development, set design, cost selection, costume design, and selection of a filming location.
3. Actual filming.
4. Postproduction, including film editing, adding the musical score, and special effects.

Warmen Brothers Production Company has just finished the production of *Absence of Forethought,* a movie that is expected to be successfully distributed to all available markets.

Required:
a. What markets are available to Warmen Brothers for this film?
b. In what order would you suggest Warmen Brothers attempt to enter each market? Why?
c. How should revenues be recognized from each market?
d. How should costs be matched against these revenues?
e. What effect will your decisions have on Warmen Brothers' income statements for the years revenue is recognized?*

• Case 4-2 Extraordinary Charges

Goods Company is a major manufacturer of foodstuffs whose products are sold in grocery and convenience stores throughout the United States. The company's name is well known and respected because its products have been marketed nationally for over 50 years.

In April 2001 the company was forced to recall one of its major products. A total of 35 persons in Chicago were treated for severe intestinal pain, and eventually three people died from complications. All of the people had consumed Goods's product.

The product causing the problem was traced to one specific lot. Goods keeps samples from all lots of foodstuffs. After thorough testing, Goods and the legal authorities confirmed that the product had been tampered with after it had left the company's plant and was no longer under the company's control.

All of the product was recalled from the market—the only time a Goods product has been recalled nationally and the only time for reasons of tampering. Persons who still had the product in their homes, even though it was not from the affected lot, were encouraged to return the product for credit or refund. The company designed and implemented a media campaign to explain what had happened and what the company was doing to minimize

---

* *Note:* You may wish to consult *FASB Statement No. 53,* "Financial Reporting by Producers and Distributors of Motion Picture Films."

any chance of recurrence. Goods decided to continue the product with the same trade name and same wholesale price. However, the packaging was redesigned completely to be tamper resistant and safety sealed. This required the purchase and installation of new equipment.

The corporate accounting staff recommended that the costs associated with the tampered product be treated as an extraordinary charge on the 2001 financial statements. Corporate accounting was asked to identify the various costs that could be associated with the tampered product and related recall. These costs ($000 omitted) are as follows.

1.	Credits and refunds to stores and consumers	$30,000
2.	Insurance to cover lost sales and idle plant costs for possible future recalls	5,000
3.	Transportation costs and off-site warehousing of returned product	1,000
4.	Future security measures for other products	4,000
5.	Testing of returned product and inventory	700
6.	Destroying returned product and inventory	2,400
7.	Public relations program to reestablish brand credibility	4,200
8.	Communication program to inform customers, answer inquiries prepare press releases, and so on	1,600
9.	Higher cost arising from new packaging	700
10.	Investigation of possible involvement of employees, former employees, competitors, and the like	500
11.	Packaging redesign and testing	2,000
12.	Purchase and installation of new packaging equipment	6,000
13.	Legal costs for defense against liability suits	600
14.	Lost sales revenue due to recall	32,000

Goods's estimated earnings before income taxes and before consideration of any of the above items for the year ending December 31, 2001, are $230 million.

Required:
a. Goods Company plans to recognize the costs associated with the product tampering and recall as an extraordinary charge.
  i. Explain why Goods could classify this occurrence as an extraordinary charge.
  ii. Describe the placement and terminology used to present the extraordinary charge in the 2001 income statement.
b. Refer to the 14 cost items identified by the corporate accounting staff of Goods Company.
  i. Identify the cost items by number that should be included in the extraordinary charge for 2001.
  ii. For any item that is not included in the extraordinary charge, explain why it would not be included in the extraordinary charge.

(CMA adapted)

• Case 4-3 Income Statement Format

Over the years, accountants have advocated two types of income statements based on differing views of the concept of income. These types have been termed the *current operating performance* and *all-inclusive* concepts of income.

Required:
a. Discuss the general nature of these two concepts of income.
b. How would the following items be handled under each concept?
   i. Cost of goods sold
   ii. Selling expenses
   iii. Extraordinary items
   iv. Prior period adjustments

• Case 4-4 Accounting Changes

It is important in accounting theory to be able to distinguish the types of accounting changes.

Required:
a. If a public company desires to change from the sum-of-year's-digits depreciation method to the straight-line method for its fixed assets, what type of accounting change will this be? How would it be treated? Discuss the permissibility of this change.
b. When pro-forma disclosure is required for an accounting change, how are these pro-forma amounts determined?
c. If a public company obtained additional information about the service lives of some of its fixed assets that showed that the service lives previously used should be shortened, what type of accounting change would this be? Include in your discussion how the change should be reported in the income statement of the year of the change and what disclosures should be made in the financial statements or notes.
d. Changing specific subsidiaries comprising the group of companies for which consolidated financial statements are presented is an example of what type of accounting change, and what effect does it have on the consolidated income statements?

• Case 4-5 Earnings Per Share

Progresso Corporation, one of your new audit clients, has not reported earnings per share data in its annual reports to stockholders in the past. The president requested that you furnish information about the reporting of earnings per share data in the current year's annual report in accordance with generally accepted accounting principles.

Required:
a. Define the term *earnings per share* as it applies to a corporation with a capitalization structure composed of only one class of common stock and explain how earnings per share should be computed and how the information should be disclosed in the corporation's financial statements.

b. Explain the meanings of the terms *senior securities* and *residual securities*, which are often used in discussing earnings per share, and give examples of the types of items that each term includes.
c. Discuss the treatment, if any, that should be given to each of the following items in computing earnings per share of common stock for financial statement reporting.
    i.   The declaration of current dividends on cumulative preferred stock.
    ii. The acquisition of some of the corporation's outstanding common stock during the current fiscal year. The stock was classified as treasury stock.
    iii. A two-for-one stock split of common stock during the current fiscal year.
    iv. A provision created out of retained earnings for a contingent liability from a possible lawsuit.
    v.   Outstanding preferred stock issued at a premium with a par value liquidation right.
    vi. The exercise at a price below market value but above book value of a common stock option issued during the current year to officers of the corporation.
    vii. The replacement of a machine immediately before the close of the current year at a cost 20 percent above the original cost of the replaced machine. The new machine will perform the same function as the old machine which was sold for its book value.

• Case 4-6 Interim Reporting

The unaudited quarterly statements of income issued by many corporations to their stockholders are usually prepared on the same basis as annual statements, the statement for each quarter reflecting the transactions of that quarter.

Required:
a. Why do problems arise in using such quarterly statements to predict the income (before extraordinary items) for the year? Explain.
b. Discuss the ways in which quarterly income can be affected by the behavior of the costs recorded in a *repairs and maintenance of factory machinery account.*
c. Do such quarterly statements give management opportunities to manipulate the results of operations for a quarter? If so, explain or give an example.

• Case 4-7 Cost Allocation in Interim Financial Statements

The controller of Navar Corporation wants to issue to stockholders quarterly income statements that will be predictive of expected annual results. He proposes allocating all fixed costs for the year among quarters in proportion to the number of units expected to be sold in each quarter, stating that the annual income can then be predicted through use of the following equation:

annual income = quarterly income × 100%/percentage of
unit sales applicable to quarter

Navar expects the following activity for the year.

	Units	Average per Unit	Total (in $1,000s)
Sales revenue:			
First quarter	500,000	$2.00	$1,000
Second quarter	100,000	1.50	150
Third quarter	200,000	2.00	400
Fourth quarter	200,000	2.00	400
	1,000,000		
Costs to be incurred:			
Variable:			
Manufacturing		$0.70	700
Selling and administrative		0.25	250
		$0.95	950
Fixed:			
Manufacturing			380
Selling and administrative			220
			600
Income before income taxes			$ 400

Required:
Ignore income taxes in answering the following questions.
a. Assuming that Navar's activities do not vary from expectations, will the controller's plan achieve his objective? If not, how can it be modified to do so? Explain and give illustrative computations.
b. How should the effect of variations of actual activity from expected activity be treated in Navar's quarterly income statements?
c. What assumption has the controller made in regard to inventories? Discuss.

• Case 4-8 Accounting Changes

Accounting Principles Board Opinion No. 20 is concerned with accounting changes.

Required:
a. Define, discuss, and illustrate each of the following in such a way that one can be distinguished from the other:
    i. An accounting change

ii. A correction of an error in previously issued financial statements
b. Discuss the justification for a change in accounting principle.
c. Discuss the reporting (as required by *APB Opinion No. 20*) of a change from the LIFO method to another method of inventory pricing.

• Case 4-9 Identifying Accounting Changes

Sometimes a business entity may change its method of accounting for certain items. The change may be classified as a change in accounting principle, a change in accounting estimate, or a change in reporting entity. Listed below are three independent, unrelated sets of facts relating to accounting changes.

Situation 1
A company determined that the depreciable lives of its fixed assets were presently too long to fairly match the cost of the fixed assets with the revenue produced. The company decided at the beginning of the current year to reduce the depreciable lives of all its existing fixed assets by five years.

Situation 2
On December 31, 2000, Gary Company owned 51 percent of Allen Company, at which time Gary reported its investment using the cost method due to political uncertainties in the country in which Allen was located. On January 2, 2001, the management of Gary Company was satisfied that the political uncertainties were resolved and that the assets of the company were in no danger of nationalization. Accordingly, Gary will prepare consolidated financial statements for Gary and Allen for the year ended December 31, 2001.

Situation 3
A company decides in January 2001 to adopt the straight-line method of depreciation for plant equipment. This method will be used for new acquisitions as well as for previously acquired plant equipment for which depreciation had been provided on an accelerated basis.

Required:
For each of the preceding situations, provide the information indicated below. Complete your discussion of each situation before going on to the next situation.
a. Type of accounting change
b. Manner of reporting the change under current generally accepted accounting principles, including a discussion, where applicable, of how amounts are computed
c. Effects of the change on the statement of financial position and earnings statement
d. Footnote disclosures that would be necessary

• Case 4-10 Classification of Accounting Changes

Morgan Company grows various crops and then processes them for sale to retailers. Morgan has changed its depreciation method for its processing equipment from the double-declining balance method to the straight-line method effective January 1 of this year. This method has been determined to be preferable.

In the latter part of this year, a large portion of Morgan's crops was destroyed by a hailstorm. Morgan has incurred substantial costs in raising the crops that were destroyed. Severe damage from hailstorms is rare in the locality where the crops are grown.

Required:
a. How should Morgan report and calculate the effect of this change in accounting principle relative to the depreciation method in this year's income statement? Do not discuss earnings per share requirements.
b. Where should Morgan report the effects of the hailstorm in its income statement? Why?
c. How does the classification in the income statement of an extraordinary item differ from that of an operating item? Why? Do not discuss earnings per share requirements.

• Case 4-11 Treatment of Nonrecurring Items

David Company's statements of income for the year ended December 31, 2001 and December 31, 2000, are presented below. Additional facts are as follows:

On January 1, 2000 David Company changed its depreciation method for previously recorded plant machinery from the double-declining-balance method to the straight-line method. The effect of applying the straight-line method for the year of the change and the year after it is included in David Company's statements of income for the year ended December 31, 2001 and December 31, 2000 in "cost of goods sold."

The loss from operations of the discontinued Dex Division from January 1, 2001, to September 30, 2001 (the portion of the year prior to the measurement date), and from January 1, 2000, to December 31, 2000, is included in David Company's statements of income for the year ended December 31, 2001, and December 31, 2000, respectively, in "other, net."

David Company has a simple capital structure with only common stock outstanding, and the net income per share of common stock was based on the weighted average number of common shares outstanding during each year.

David Company common stock is listed on the New York Stock Exchange; it closed at $13 per share on December 31, 2001, and $15 per share on December 31, 2000.

Required:
Determine from the preceding additional facts whether the presentation of those facts in David Company's statements of income is appropriate. If the presentation is appropriate, discuss the theoretical rationale for the presentation. If the presentation is not appropriate, specify the appropriate presentation and discuss its theoretical rationale. Do not discuss disclosure requirements for the notes to the financial statements.

DAVID COMPANY
STATEMENTS OF INCOME

	Year Ended December 31	
	2000	2001
	(000 omitted)	
Net sales	$900,000	$750,000
Costs and expenses:		
Cost of goods sold	720,000	600,000
Selling, general and administrative expenses	112,000	90,000
Other, net	11,000	9,000
Total costs and expenses	843,000	699,000
Income from continuing operations before income taxes	57,000	51,000
Income taxes	23,000	24,000
Income from continuing operations	34,000	27,000
Loss on disposal of Dex Division, including provision of $1,500,000 for operating losses during phase-out period, less applicable income taxes of $8,000,000	8,000	—
Cumulative effect on prior years of change in depreciation method, less applicable income taxes of $1,500,000	—	3,000
Net income	$ 26,000	$ 30,000
Earnings per share of common stock:		
Income before cumulative effect of change in depreciation method	$ 2.60	$ 2.70
Cumulative effect on prior years of change in depreciation method, less applicable income taxes	—	.30
Net income	$ 2.60	$ 3.00

• Case 4-12 Comprehensive Income

Earnings defined in *SFAC No. 5* are consistent with the current operating performance concept of income. Comprehensive income is consistent with the all-inclusive concept of income.

Required:
a. Discuss the current operating performance concept of income.
b. Explain how earnings, as defined in *SFAC No. 5*, is consistent with the current operating performance concept of income.
c. Discuss the all-inclusive concept of income.

d. Explain how comprehensive income is consistent with the all-inclusive concept of income.

e. Explain how comprehensive income is consistent with the financial capital maintenance concept.

f. What additional changes in reporting practices would have to occur for financial reporting to be consistent with the physical capital maintenance concept? Have some similar changes already occurred? Give an example.

• Case 4-13 Earnings Per Share

The weak form of the efficient market hypothesis (EMH) discussed in Chapter 2 implies that a random walk model best describes the behavior of common stock prices. Accordingly, the most recent stock price is the best predictor of the future.

Under the treasury stock method, primary EPS and fully dilutive EPS utilize common stock prices to provide pro-forma information to investors so that they can make predictions about the future and thereby evaluate the firm.

Required:

a. Describe how diluted EPS utilizes stock prices to provide pro forma information.

b. Describe how diluted EPS differs from basic EPS.

c. Which form of EPS (primary or fully diluted) provides pro forma information that is most consistent with the objectives of financial reporting discussed in *SFAC No. 1?*

Room for Debate

• Issue 1

The FASB proposes that financial statements report comprehensive income.

Team Debate:

Team 1   Defend comprehensive income. Your defense should relate to the conceptual framework and to the concept of capital maintenance where appropriate.

Team 2   Oppose comprehensive income. Your opposition should relate to the conceptual framework and to the concept of capital maintenance where appropriate.

Recommended Additional Readings

Bernstein, Leopold A. "Extraordinary Gains and Losses—Their Significance to the Financial Analyst." *Financial Analysts Journal* (November–December 1972), pp. 49–52, 88–90.

Campbell, Linda. "How Companies Are Complying with Comprehensive Income Disclosure Requirements." *Ohio CPA Journal* (January–March 1999), pp. 13–19.

Coughlan, John W. "Anomalies in Calculating Earnings Per Share." *Accounting Horizons* (December 1988), pp. 80–88.

Cushing, Barry E. "Accounting Changes: The Impact of APB Opinion No. 20." *Journal of Accountancy* (November 1974), pp. 54–62.

DeBerg, Curtis L., and Brock Murdoch. "An Empirical Investigation of the Usefulness of Earnings per Share Information." *Journal of Accounting, Auditing and Finance* (Spring 1994), pp. 249–264.

Dhaliwal, Dan, K. R. Subramanyam, and Robert Trezevant. "Is Comprehensive Income to Net Income As a Measure of Firm Performance?" *Journal of Accounting and Economics* (January 1999), pp. 43–67.

Dudley, Lola Woodard. "A Critical Look at EPS." *Journal of Accountancy* (August 1985), pp. 102–111.

Hirst, D. Eric, and Patrick Hopkins. "Comprehensive Income Reporting: Financial Analyst's Judgments." *Journal of Accounting Research* (1998 Supplement), pp. 47–75.

Jaenicke, Henry R., and Joseph Rascoff. "Segment Disposition: Implementing APB Opinion No. 30." *Journal of Accountancy* (April 1974), pp. 63–69.

Luecke, Randall W., and David Meeling. "How Companies Report Income." *Journal of Accountancy* (May 1998), pp. 45–52.

Nurnberg, Hugo. "Annual and Interim Financial Reporting of Changes in Accounting Estimates." *Accounting Horizons* (September 1988), pp. 15–25.

Pincus, Morton, and Charles Wasley. "The Incidence of Accounting Changes and Characteristics of Firms Making Accounting Changes," *Accounting Horizons* (June 1994), pp. 1–24.

Ramakrishman, Ram T. S., and Jacob K. Thomas. "Valuation of Permanent, Transitory and Price Irrelevant Components of Reported Earnings." *Journal of Accounting Auditing and Finance* (Summer 1998), pp. 301–336.

Rapaccioli, Donna, and Allen Schiff. "Reporting Sales of Segments under APB Opinion No. 30." *Accounting Horizons* (December 1991), pp. 53–68.

Schmidt, Richard J. "The Impact of Reporting Comprehensive Income." *Ohio CPA Journal* (January–March 1999), pp. 50–52.

Smith, Pamela, and Cherri L. Reither. "Comprehensive Income and the Effects of Reporting It." *Financial Analysts Journal* (November–December 1996), pp. 14–19.

Stanko, Brian B., and Thomas L Zeller. "The ABCs of EPS." *Business and Economic Review* (April–June 1998), pp. 21–26.

Bibliography

Barton, M. Frank, William B. Carper, and Thomas S. O'Conner. "Chartered Financial Analysts Speak Out in the Need and Information Content of Interim Financial Reports." *The Ohio CPA* (Winter 1979), pp. 28–32.

Beresford, Dennis R. "Understanding the New Rules for Interim Financial Reporting." *The Ohio CPA* (Winter 1975), pp. 27–35.

Beresford, Dennis R., and Earl J. Elbert. "Reporting Discontinued Operations." *The Ohio CPA* (Spring 1974), pp. 56–65.

Bernstein, Leopold A. "Reporting the Results of Operations—A Reassessment of APB Opinion No. 9." *Journal of Accountancy* (July 1970), pp. 57–61.

Bows, Albert J., Jr., and Arthur R. Wyatt. "Improving Interim Financial Reporting." *Journal of Accountancy* (October 1973), pp. 54–59.

Boyer, Patricia A., and Charles H. Gibson. "How about Earnings per Share?" *The CPA Journal* (February 1979), pp. 36–41.

Brown, Lawrence D. "Accounting Changes and the Accuracy of Analysts' Earnings Forecasts." *Journal of Accounting Research* (Autumn 1983), pp. 432–443.

Curry, Dudley W. "Opinion 15 vs. a Comprehensive Financial Reporting Method for Convertible Debt." *The Accounting Review* (July 1971), pp. 495–503.

Deming, John R. "New Guidelines for Extraordinary Items." *The CPA Journal* (February 1974), pp. 21–26.

Eisenman, Seymour, Murray S. Akresh, and Charles Snow. "Reporting Unusual Events in Income Statements." *The CPA Journal* (June 1979), pp. 23–27.

Gibson, Charles H., and John Daniel Williams. "Should Common Stock Equivalents Be Considered in Earnings per Share?" *The CPA Journal* (March 1973), pp. 209–213.

Greipel, Rudolph C. "Review of APB Opinion No. 20—Accounting Changes." *The CPA Journal* (January 1972), pp. 17–24.

Hopwood, William S., and James C. McKeown. "The Incremental Informational Content of Interim Expenses over Interim Sales." *Journal of Accounting Research* (Spring 1985), pp. 161–174.

Kahn, Nathan, and Allen Schiff. "Tangible Equity Changes and the Evolution of the FASB's Definition of Income." *Journal of Accounting Auditing and Finance* (Fall 1985), pp. 40–49.

Knutson, Peter H. "Income Distribution: The Key to Earnings per Share." *The Accounting Review* (January 1970), pp. 55–58.

Koons, Robert L. "Changes in Interim Reports Are Coming." *Financial Executive* (July 1978), pp. 48–54.

Lambert, Richard A. "Income Smoothing as Rational Equilibrium Behavior." *The Accounting Review* (October 1984), pp. 604–618.

Matulich, Serge, Loren A. Nikolai, and Steven K. Olson. "Earnings per Share: A Flowchart Approach to Teaching Concepts and Procedures." *The Accounting Review* (January 1977), pp. 233–247.

Mautz, R. David Jr. and Thomas J. Hogan. "Earnings per Share Reporting: Time for an Overhaul." *Accounting Horizons* (September 1989), pp. 21–27.

Miller, Jerry D. "Accounting for Warrants and Convertible Bonds." *Management Accounting* (January 1973), pp. 26–28.

Miller, Rene A. "Interim Financial Accounting and Reporting—Review of APB Opinion No. 28." *The CPA Journal* (September 1973), pp. 755–761.

Nichols, Donald R. "The Never-to-Recur Unusual Item—A Critique of APB Opinion No. 30." *The CPA Journal* (March 1974), pp. 45–48.

Pacter, Paul A. "APB Opinion No. 15: Some Basic Examples." *The New York Certified Public Accountant* (August 1970), pp. 638–646.

Rhodes, Lola, and H. J. Snavely. "Convertible Bonds and Earnings per Share." *The CPA Journal* (December 1973), pp. 1116–1119.

Ricks, William E., and John S. Hughes. "Market Reactions to a Non-Discretionary Accounting Change: The Case of Long-Term Investments." *The Accounting Review* (January 1985), pp. 33–52.

Savage, Linda, and Joel Siegel. "Disposal of a Segment of a Business." *The CPA Journal* (September 1978), pp. 32–37.

Schiff, Michael. *Accounting Reporting Problems—Interim Financial Statement.* New York: Financial Executives Research Foundation, 1978.

Werner, G. Frank, and Jerry J. Weygandt. "Convertible Debt and Earnings per Share: Pragmatism vs. Good Theory." *The Accounting Review* (April 1970), pp. 280–289.

Financial
Statements II: The
Balance Sheet and
the Statement
of Cash Flows

Financial reports can be divided into two categories. The first category discloses the results of the flow of resources over time and includes the income statement, the statement of retained earnings, and the statement of cash flows. The second category summarizes the status of resources at a particular point in time.

These two categories suggest an important distinction in measurement emphasis between *flows* and *stocks*. Flows are productive services that must be measured over some period of time, whereas stocks are resources that are measured at a particular point in time. In recent years the matching concept emphasizes flows. This emphasis results in the direct measurement of flows and reporting stocks as residuals of the matching process. Alternatively, defining earnings as the change in net assets from non-owner transactions implies that stocks should be measured directly making flows the residuals. Recent pronouncements of the FASB are consistent with the latter measurement approach indicating a shift in emphasis from an income statement to an asset/liability, or balance sheet approach, to the measurement of net income.

Accounting is the means by which management reports to various users of financial information. Evaluation of a business enterprise's financial position is an important factor in satisfying the needs of creditors, stockholders, management, the government, and other interested parties. Management attempts to satisfy these needs by presenting information on the company's resources, obligations, and equities at periodic intervals.

In this chapter we first describe the balance sheet and the measurement techniques currently used to disclose assets, liabilities, and equity; illustrate the disclosure of financial statement elements on Kroll-O'Gara Company's balance sheet; and discuss how to evaluate a company's financial position. In so doing, we do not presume that current stock measurement techniques provide enough relevant information to the users of financial statements. Rather, we believe a thorough examination of these techniques will disclose their inherent limitations. Later in the chapter, we discuss the evolution of the third major financial statement from the statement of changes in financial position to the statement of cash flows, illustrate the disclosure of cash flow information on Kroll-O'Gara Company's statement of cash flows, and discuss how investors can use this information to evaluate a company's performance.

The Balance Sheet

The balance sheet should disclose a company's wealth at a point in time. *Wealth* is defined as the present value of all resources less the present value of all obligations. However, as noted earlier, the use of present value measurement techniques in accounting is limited, and a variety of methods are currently being used to measure changes in the individual components of the balance sheet. These measurement techniques can be summarized as past oriented—historical; current oriented—replacement amounts; and future oriented—expected amounts.

Over the years, accounting theorists have debated the respective merits of these measurement techniques. Those favoring historical cost base their argument on the premise that cost is objective and verifiable. Historical cost is not based on subjective estimations; rather, it is the result of the value buyers and sellers have agreed to in an "arm's-length" transaction. Some accounting theorists have even suggested that historical cost actually represents the present value of expected future cash flows at the time the exchange takes place. It is also argued that accountants serve a stewardship role, and because cost measures the actual resources exchanged, it is relevant to readers of financial statements. Opponents of historical cost maintain that values may change over time and, consequently, that historical cost can lose its relevance as a valuation base.

Those favoring current cost measurement hold that this value reflects current conditions, and, therefore, represents the current value to the firm. Opponents point out that current values may not be available for all balance sheet elements and that recording current values on the balance sheet would result in recording unrealized gain and losses on the income statement.

Those favoring expected future values maintain that this valuation procedure approximates the economic concept of income and is, therefore, the most relevant value to the users of financial statements. Critics of expected future value point out (as noted in Chapter 3) that the future cash flows associated with the elements of the balance sheet are difficult to estimate, the timing of these cash flows is uncertain, and an appropriate discount rate is difficult to ascertain.

In the following paragraphs we look more closely at the measurement techniques actually used to value the balance sheet elements. This review will reveal that no single measurement basis is used for all of the elements; rather, a variety of measurement techniques are currently acceptable, depending on the circumstances and available information.

Balance Sheet Elements

FASB Statement of Concepts No. 6 defined the elements of the balance sheet as:

> **Assets** *Assets are probable future economic benefits obtained or controlled by a particular entity as a result of past transactions or events. An asset has three essential characteristics: (1) it embodies a probable future benefit that involves a capacity, singly or in combination with other assets, to contribute directly or indirectly to future net cash inflows; (2) a particular enterprise can obtain the benefit and control others' access to it; and (3) the transaction or other event giving rise to the enterprise's right to or control of the benefit has already occurred.*

> **Liabilities** *Liabilities are probable future sacrifices of economic benefits arising from present obligations of a particular entity to transfer assets or provide services to other entities in the future as a result of past transactions or events. A liability has three essential characteristics: (1) it embodies a present duty or responsibility to one or more other entities that entails settlement by probable future transfer or use of assets at a specified or determinable date, on occurrence of a specified event, or on demand; (2) the duty or responsibility obligates a particular enterprise, leaving it little or no discretion to avoid the future sacrifice; and (3) the transaction or other event obligating the enterprise has already happened.*

> **Equity** *Equity is the residual interest in the assets of an entity that remains after deducting its liabilities. In a business enterprise, the equity is the ownership interest. Equity in a business enterprise stems from ownership rights (or the equivalent). It involves a relation between an enterprise and its owners as owners rather than as employees, suppliers, customers, lenders, or in some other nonowner role.*[1]

These definitions form the basis of the FASB's asset-liability approach to the measurement of stocks and flows that is prevalent in many subsequent standards. They represent a departure from previous definitions that viewed the balance sheet as a statement of residual amounts whose values were frequently arrived at through income determination. For example, consider the definitions of assets and liabilities presented by the APB in *Statement No. 4:*

> *(Assets are) economic resources of an enterprise that are recognized and measured in conformity with generally accepted accounting principles including certain deferred charges that are not resources.*[2]

> *(Liabilities are) economic obligations of an enterprise that are recognized and measured in conformity with generally accepted accounting principles.*[3]

That is, deferred charges, which result from unexpired costs not charged to expense, are assets, and liabilities are created because of the necessity to record debits.

Even with their limitations, the APB definitions were believed to be significant improvements over previous definitions when they were released.

---

[1] *Financial Accounting Standards Board Statement of Concepts No. 6,* "Elements of Financial Statements of Business Enterprises" (Stamford, CT: FASB, 1985), pars. 25, 26, 35, 36, and 49.

[2] *Accounting Principles Board Statement No. 4,* "Basic Concepts and Accounting Principles Underlying Financial Statements of Business Enterprises" (AICPA, 1970), par. 132.

[3] Ibid., par. 132.

Prior to that time, assets had been defined as debit balances carried forward when the books were closed, and liabilities as credit balances carried forward, except those representing owners' equity.[4]

The preceding *SFAC No. 6* definitions should be examined carefully. They assert that assets are economic resources of an enterprise and that liabilities are economic obligations of an enterprise. These statements probably correspond to most users' understanding of the terms *assets* and *liabilities*, and, therefore, they are not likely to be misunderstood. However, in order to properly understand the numbers presented on a balance sheet, the user must be aware of the recognition and measurement procedures associated with generally accepted accounting principles. These procedures are a combination of past, present, and future measurement techniques.

In addition, it has been considered more informative to provide subclassifications for each of these balance sheet elements. This classification scheme makes information more easily accessible to the various interested user groups and allows for more rapid identification of specific types of information for decision making. In general, the following classification scheme may be viewed as representative of the typical balance sheet presentation.

Assets
Current assets
Investments
Property, plant, and equipment
Intangible assets
Other assets

Liabilities and Stockholders' Equity
Current liabilities
Long-term liabilities
Other liabilities
Stockholders' equity
Capital stock
Additional paid-in capital
Retained earnings

In the following paragraphs we examine each of the elements of the balance sheet, introduce the accounting principles currently being used in measuring these elements, and discuss how they are disclosed on Kroll-O'Gara's balance sheet illustrated on page 144. The measurement issues for each of the balance sheet elements are discussed in greater depth in subsequent chapters.

Assets

Current Assets The Committee on Accounting Procedure has supplied the most commonly encountered definition of current assets. This definition may be summarized as follows: current assets are those assets that may *reasonably be expected* to be realized in cash or sold or consumed during the normal operat-

---

[4] *Accounting Terminology Bulletin No. 1*, "Review and Resume" (AICPA, 1953), pars. 26–27.

ing cycle of the business or one year, whichever is longer. The *operating cycle* is defined as the average time it takes to acquire materials, produce the product, sell the product, and collect the proceeds from customers.[5] Current assets are presented on the balance sheet in order of their liquidity and generally include the following items: cash, cash equivalents, temporary investments, receivables, inventories, and prepaid expenses. Nevertheless, special problems are connected with the valuation procedure for most of these items.

Companies are now required to determine whether temporary investment in debt and equity securities have a readily determinable fair value. If they do not, they are accounted for under the cost method. For those securities that have readily determinable fair values, companies must classify them as trading securities, available-for-sale securities, or in the case of debt, held-to-maturity securities. Trading securities and available-for-sale securities are reported at fair value. Unrealized gains and losses for trading securities are reported in earnings, while unrealized gains and losses for available-for-sale securities are reported as other comprehensive income. Debt securities for which management has a positive intent to hold-to-maturity, which are currently classified as temporary, are carried in the balance sheet at amortized cost. Amortized cost implies that premiums or discounts, which arose when the purchase price of the debt security differed from face value, are being amortized over the remaining life of the security. For those debt securities having short terms, for example, U.S. treasuries, amortization of premiums, and discounts are generally ignored for materiality reasons.

Receivables are generally recorded at amounts that approximate the expected present value of those items, since they are to be consumed in a short period of time. Generally accepted accounting principles dictate that items should not be valued at an amount in excess of their current value. It is considered appropriate to value receivables at their recorded amount less an amount deemed to be uncollectible, or their *expected net realizable value.*

Inventories and prepaid expenses present some additional valuation issues. With the emphasis on net income reporting, the inventory valuation process has become secondary to the matching of expired inventory costs to sales. The use of any of the acceptable inventory flow assumption techniques (e.g., LIFO, FIFO, weighted average discussed in Chapter 7) prescribes the amount that remains on the balance sheet, and it is likely that each of these flow assumptions will result in different inventory valuations in fluctuating market conditions. In addition, the accounting convention of conservatism requires that a lower of cost or market valuation be used for inventories. In any case, the financial statement user should interpret the inventory figure as being less than its estimated selling price.

Prepaid items are valued at historical cost, with an appropriate amount being charged to expense each year until they are consumed. Prepaid expenses are included under the current asset section because it is argued that if these items had not been paid in advance, they would require the use of current funds.

---

[5] *Accounting Research Bulletin No. 43*, "Restatement and Revision of Accounting Research Bulletins" (AICPA, 1953), Chapter 3, par. 5.

FIGURE 5.1 *The Kroll-O'Gara Company Consolidated Balance Sheets as of December 31, 1997 and 1998*

	1997	1998
ASSETS		
CURRENT ASSETS:		
Cash and cash equivalents	$ 9,765,422	$ 12,862,928
Marketable securities	22,969	13,285,322
Trade accounts receivable, net of allowance for doubtful accounts of approximately $3,100,064 and $3,769,624 in 1997 and 1998, respectively	40,796,471	55,570,815
Unbilled revenues	3,081,481	7,766,015
Related party receivables	939,894	2,720,464
Costs and estimated earnings in excess of billings on uncompleted contracts	12,078,464	26,408,097
Inventories	19,562,899	22,397,939
Prepaid expenses and other	6,786,288	7,794,242
Deferred tax asset	572,697	—
Total current assets	93,606,585	148,805,822
PROPERTY, PLANT, AND EQUIPMENT,		
Land	1,831,042	1,856,003
Buildings and improvements	8,100,454	8,271,967
Leasehold improvements	5,242,607	6,290,089
Furniture and fixtures	4,752,974	5,950,409
Machinery and equipment	13,500,247	18,351,528
Construction-in-progress	1,037,528	2,860,011
	34,464,852	43,580,007
Less—accumulated depreciation	(16,904,830)	(19,686,536)
	17,560,022	23,893,471
DATABASES, net of accumulated amortization of $19,505,625 and $22,788,857 in 1997 and 1998, respectively	8,335,211	9,238,903
COSTS IN EXCESS OF ASSETS ACQUIRED AND OTHER INTANGIBLE ASSETS, net of accumulated amortization of $1,691,307 and $4,213,426 in 1997 and 1998 respectively	26,651,017	60,938,886
OTHER ASSETS	4,331,645	6,078,977
	39,317,873	76,256,766
Total Assets	$150,484,480	$248,956,059

	1997	1998
LIABILITIES AND SHAREHOLDERS' EQUITY		
CURRENT LIABILITIES:		
Revolving lines of credit	$ 559,112	$ —
Current portion of long-term debt	4,038,080	1,965,752
Trade accounts payable	32,328,154	35,553,818
Related party payable	1,184,439	341,358
Billings in excess of costs and estimated earnings on uncompleted contracts	320,662	182,656
Accrued liabilities	15,212,260	22,013,571
Income taxes currently payable	845,753	617,942
Deferred income taxes	—	895,108
Customer deposits	3,839,770	3,865,219
Total current liabilities	58,328,230	65,435,424
OTHER LONG-TERM LIABILITIES	1,532,730	1,542,588
DEFERRED INCOME TAXES	2,514,606	1,625,363
LONG-TERM DEBT, net of current portion	49,641,484	39,257,245
Total liabilities	112,017,050	107,860,620
COMMITMENTS AND CONTINGENCIES		
SHAREHOLDERS' EQUITY		
Preferred stock, $.01 par value, 1,000,000 shares authorized; none issued	—	—
Common stock, $.01 par value, 50,000,000 shares authorized, 14,795,244 and 20,685,629 shares issued and outstanding in 1997 and 1998, respectively	147,952	206,856
Additional paid-in-capital	58,912,209	149,993,769
Retained deficit	(20,208,821)	(7,119,915)
Deferred compensation	—	(1,113,936)
Accumulated other comprehensive income (loss)	(383,910)	(871,335)
Total shareholders' Equity	38,467,430	141,095,439
Total liabilities and stockholders' equity	$150,484,480	$248,956,059

However, the same argument might be made for other assets, and the fact that the lives of many prepaid items encompass several accounting periods does not enhance the logic of the argument. It should be noted that prepaid items are not usually material, and perhaps that is where the argument loses its significance.

As can be seen from the previous discussion, two problems arise when we attempt to classify an asset as current: (1) the period of time over which it is to be consumed and (2) the proper valuation technique. In many cases historical precedent rather than accounting theory has dictated the inclusion of items as current assets. The valuation procedures associated with each of the items may in themselves be appropriate, but when all items are summed to arrive at a figure termed total current assets, it is difficult to interpret the result. This total approximates the minimum amount of cash that could be collected during the next fiscal period, but leaves to the user's imagination the actual amount expected to be realized. The issues associated with the valuation of current assets and current liabilities (i.e., working capital) are explored more fully in the next chapter.

Kroll-O'Gara Company's 1998 balance sheet discloses total current assets of $148,805,822 and contains all of the above current assets. In addition, the company's current asset section contains costs in excess of billings that are related to its revenue recognition procedures for long-term construction contracts, and a deferred tax asset that arises from a timing difference between its income tax expense and income tax payable (discussed in Chapter 11).

Investments Investments may be divided into three categories.

1. Securities acquired for specific purposes, such as using idle funds for long periods or exercising influence on the operations of another company.

2. Assets not currently in use by the business organization, such as land held for a future building site.

3. Special funds to be used for special purposes in the future, such as sinking funds.

The primary factor used in deciding which items to include under the investments caption is *managerial intent.* For example, an organization may own two identical blocks of common stock in another company, but one block may be classified as a current asset because it is anticipated that these shares will be disposed of in the current period, whereas the other block may be classified as an investment because the intention is to retain it for a longer period.

Equity securities acquired to influence the operations of other companies are required to be accounted for by the equity method. This treatment adjusts historical cost for income of the investee and dividends received. As with temporary investments, all other investments in equity securities are accounted for under the cost method when there is no readily determinable fair value for these securities. Those equity securities that have readily determinable fair values and debt securities that are not classified as held-to-maturity are considered available-for-sale. Long-term available-for-sale securities are treated in the same manner as temporary securities similarly classified. That is, these securities are reported at fair value and unrealized gains and losses are recognized in stockholders' equity as a component of accumulated other comprehensive income. Debt securities classified as held-to-maturity— that is, those debt securities that management has positive intent to hold to maturity—are reported at amortized cost. Kroll-O'Gara Company's 1998 balance sheet does not contain any long-term investments.

Property, Plant, and Equipment and Intangibles Although property, plant, and equipment and intangibles are physically dissimilar assets, the valuation procedures associated with them are similar. Except for land, the cost of these assets is allocated to the various accounting periods benefiting from their use. In the case of property, plant, and equipment, the carrying value is disclosed as the difference between cost and accumulated depreciation. However, intangible assets are generally disclosed at the net amount of their cost less amortization.

These valuation procedures are again the result of the emphasis on income reporting. Various methods of depreciation and amortization are available, but there is no attempt to disclose the current value of long-term assets or the expected future cash flows from holding these assets on the financial statements. The emphasis rather is on a proper matching of revenues and expenses, with asset valuation being the residual effect of this process.

Kroll-O'Gara Company's 1998 balance sheet discloses total property, plant, and equipment of $43,580,007 and accumulated depreciation of $19,686,536 to arrive at a book value of $23,893,471. The net amount of intangibles disclosed by the company is $60,938,886. In addition, the company's balance sheet contains the asset databases[6] in the net amount of $9,238,903.

Other Assets The preceding asset category captions usually will allow for the disclosure of all assets, but some corporations include a final category termed "other assets." Items such as fixed assets held for resale or long-term receivables may be included under this category. The valuation of these items is generally their carrying value on the balance sheet at the time they were originally recorded in the other assets category. Since the amounts associated with these items are usually immaterial, it is unlikely that any alternative valuation procedure would result in a significantly different carrying value. Kroll-O'Gara's Company's 1998 balance sheet discloses other assets of 6,078,977.

Asset Valuation The preceding discussion shows that many different measurement techniques are used when valuing assets on the typical balance sheet. Under almost any measurement scheme devised, it is common practice to add and subtract only like items measured in the same manner. However, the measurement of assets on the balance sheet takes an unusual form when we consider that sums are derived for subclassifications as well as total assets.

Consider the following measurement bases that are included in a typical balance sheet presentation of assets:

Asset	*Measurement Basis*
Cash	Current value
Accounts receivable	Expected future value
Marketable securities	Fair value or amortized cost
Inventory	Current or past value
Investments	Fair value or amortized cost
Property, plant, and equipment	Past value adjusted for depreciation

Summing these items is much like adding apples and oranges, and investors need to be aware of these differences when using the balance sheet to evaluate a company's financial position. If assets are truly the firm's eco-

---

[6] In footnote 2 (g) databases are defined as follows: Databases are capitalized costs incurred to obtain information from third-party providers. The company relies on this information to create and maintain its proprietary and nonproprietary databases. Because of the continuing accessibility of the information and its usefulness to future investigative procedures, the cost of acquiring the information is capitalized and amortized over a five-year period.

nomic resources, it seems plausible to conclude that the totals on the statements should reflect somewhat more than values arrived at by convention. Presentation of information on the expected future benefits to be derived from holding these items would better satisfy user needs.

Liabilities

Current Liabilities Current liabilities have been defined as "obligations whose liquidation is reasonably expected to require the use of existing resources properly classified as current assets or the creation of other current liabilities."[7] Notice that, although the operating cycle is not explicitly discussed in this definition, it is implied because the definition of current liabilities depends on the definition of current assets. Examples of current liabilities are short-term payables, the currently maturing portion of long-term debt, income taxes payable returnable deposits, and accrued liabilities.

Current liabilities are usually measured at liquidation value because their period of existence is relatively short and the satisfaction of these obligations generally involves the payment of cash. Since current liabilities usually require the use of current funds, it might be considered justifiable to offset them against current assets. However, the principle of disclosure requires that they be shown separately unless a specific right of offset exists. *APB Opinion No. 10* emphasized this point in stating: "It is a general principle of accounting that offsetting of assets and liabilities in the balance sheet is improper except where a right of offset exists."[8] Kroll-O'Gara Company's 1998 balance sheet includes all of the typical items and discloses total current liabilities of $65,435,424.

Long-Term and Other Liabilities Long-term liabilities are those obligations that will not require the use of current assets within the current year or operating cycle. In general, these obligations take the form of bonds, notes, and mortgages and are originally valued at the amount of consideration received by the entity incurring the obligation. A problem exists, however, when this consideration is different from the amount to be repaid. Generally accepted accounting principles dictate that premiums or discounts on long-term obligations should be written off over the life of the obligation to properly reflect the effective interest rate on the debt. In such cases, the conventions of realization and matching dictate the balance sheet presentation of long-term liabilities. This is an example of the use of discounted cash flow techniques to measure a balance sheet element.

The long-term liability section also may include long-term prepayments on contracts, deferred income taxes, and, in some cases, contingent liabilities, each of which has an associated measurement problem. Deferred revenues are measured at their historical cost and are retained at that amount until the situation that caused them to be recorded has reversed. Those reversals are

---

[7] Ibid., Chapter 3, par. 7.

[8] *Accounting Principles Board Opinion No. 10,* "Omnibus Opinion—1966" (New York: AICPA, 1966).

dictated by the conventions of realization and matching. Contingent liabilities, when they are actually recorded on the books, are measured as the best approximation of a future loss that the entity believes is forthcoming on the basis of the convention of conservatism. Kroll-O'Gara Company's 1998 balance sheet discloses three long-term liabilities: long-term debt—$39,257,245; deferred income taxes—$1,625,363; and other long-term liabilities—$1,542,588. The company's balance sheet also contains the caption commitments and contingencies, but no dollar amounts are included. (This issue is discussed in more depth in Chapter 10.)

Liability Valuation As with assets, liabilities are measured by a number of different procedures. Most current liabilities are measured by the amount of resources that it will ultimately take to cancel the obligation and ignore the time value of money. Long-term liabilities, on the other hand, are frequently measured by the present value of future payments discounted at the yield rate at the date of issue. In all cases, liability valuations are not changed to reflect current changes in the market rates of interest. Failure to consider the current market interest rates may cause the financial statements to be biased in favor of current creditors, particularly when many obligations are of a long-term nature.

Equity

State laws and corporate articles of incorporation make generalizations about the equity section of the balance sheet somewhat difficult. However, certain practices have become widespread enough to discuss several standards of reporting.

Common Stock Common stock is measured at historical cost. Initially, most corporations designate a par or stated value for their stock, and as each share of common stock is sold, an amount equal to the par or stated value is reported in the common stock section of the balance sheet. Any differences between selling price and par value are then reported under the caption "additional paid-in capital." These captions have no particular accounting significance except perhaps to determine an average issue price of common stock if such a computation seems meaningful. Kroll-O'Gara's Company's 1998 balance sheet discloses total common stock of $206,856 and additional paid-in capital of $149,993,769. The par value of the company's common stock is $0.01 per share.

Preferred Stock Many companies also issue other classes of stock termed "preferred." These shares generally have preference as to dividends, and a stated amount of dividends must be paid to preferred shareholders before any dividends can be paid to the common stockholders. The measurement basis of preferred stock is similar to that of common stock, with amounts divided between the par value of the shares and additional paid-in capital. Thus, the reported balance sheet amounts also represent historical cost. Kroll-O'Gara's Company's 1998 balance sheet indicates that the company has 1 million shares of authorized preferred stock; however, none of these shares had been issued on the balance sheet date.

Retained Earnings and Other Comprehensive Income Ownership interest in a corporation may be defined as the residual interest in the company's assets after the liabilities have been deducted. The recorded amount of retained earnings and other comprehensive income is associated with the measurement techniques used in recording specific assets and liabilities. However, this amount should not be confused with any attempt to measure the owners' current value interest in the firm. Consequently, the measurement of retained earnings and other comprehensive income is dependent on the measurement of revenues and cost expirations over the life of the firm.

Most states require that dividends not exceed the balance of retained earnings, and stockholders may wish to have extra dividends distributed when the retained earnings balance becomes relatively large. However, individual entities may have various long-range plans and commitments that do not allow for current distribution of dividends, and firms may provide for the dissemination of this information through an appropriation of retained earnings. This appropriation is termed a *reserve* and is measured by the sum of retained earnings set aside for the stated purpose. It should be emphasized that reserves and earnings appropriations do not provide the cash to finance such projects and is only presented to show managerial intent. This intent might just as easily be disclosed through a footnote.

The measurement of equity can be said to be based primarily on the measurement of specific assets and liabilities. The transfer of assets to expense and the cancellation of liabilities determine the measurement of changes in equity. As such, equity does not have a measurement criterion other than a residual valuation.

Kroll-O'Gara's Company's 1998 balance sheet disclosed a retained earnings deficit (accumulated net losses) of $7,119,915. The total of its other comprehensive income was a $871,335 accumulated loss. This amount reflects the restated total of all items of other comprehensive income for all prior years as required by *SFAS No. 130* (discussed in Chapter 4). It is interesting to note that while the company's retained earnings deficit was substantially reduced in 1998, the total other comprehensive income loss increased. This was mainly attributable to a foreign currency loss the company experienced in 1998.

Evaluating a Company's Financial Position

Investors and security analysts monitor company performance by using financial ratios. Financial ratios evaluate the relationship between financial statement elements and are most useful when compared to previous years' results, benchmarks, industry averages, or competitor companies. The return on assets (ROA) ratio measures the percentage return on the asset employed by a company and is computed as:

$$\text{ROA} = \frac{\text{Net operating profit after taxes}}{\text{Average total assets}^9}$$

[9] Computed current year total assets + previous year total assets/2.

Kroll-O'Gara Company's ROA for 1998 and 1997 are computed as:

1998	**1997**
$= \dfrac{\$13,088,906^{10}}{(\$248,956,059 + 150,484,480)/2}$	$\dfrac{\$2,406,643^{10}}{(\$150,484,480 + 106,016,255)/2^{11}}$
$= 6.6\%$	$= 1.88\%$

The comparative analysis indicates that Kroll-O'Gara Company's performance improved over the two-year period.

In recent years, financial analysts have suggested that adjustments should be made to both the numerator and denominator of the ROA ratio to improve its use in evaluating profitability. The adjustments suggested include the following.

1. Determination of sustainable income by removing nonrecurring items from the net operating profit.

2. Elimination of interest expense after tax to improve interfirm comparability by removing the impact of capital structure on the ratio.

3. Adjustments that incorporate the effects of off balance sheet financing (discussed in Chapter 10).

For example, the impact of capital structure could be eliminated from Kroll-O'Gara's 1998 return on assets ratio by increasing the numerator by the after-tax effect of the amount of interest expense incurred or $2,868,367.[12] Making this adjustment increases Kroll-O'Gara Company's ROA to 8.0 percent. In calculating the return on assets ratio for 1997, in addition to removing the effects of capital structure, the company's net income would be increased by the after-tax loss of $193,875 to reflect the effects of the change in accounting principal reported in 1997.

A company can improve its return on assets ratio by increasing either its profit margin or its asset utilization rate. A company's profit margin (PM) is calculated as:

$$\text{PM} = \frac{\text{Net operating profit after taxes}}{\text{Net Sales}}$$

Kroll-O'Gara Company's PM after eliminating the impact of capital structure for 1998 is calculated as:

---

[10] From the Statement of Operations contained in Chapter 4 and the company's Form 10-K contained on the text's webpage.

[11] 1997 total assets obtained from the company's 1997 10-K report.

[12] $4,481,822 × (1 − 0.36). The company's average tax rate can be approximated by dividing its income tax expense by income from continuing operations, or $7,466,464/$20,555,370.

$$= \frac{\$13,088,906 + 2,868,367}{\$264,844,847}$$

$$= 6.0\%$$

A company's asset utilization rate (AUR) is evaluated by calculating its asset turnover ratio as follows:

$$ATR = \frac{Net\ Sales}{Average\ total\ assets}$$

For Kroll-O'Gara Company, the 1998 AUR is calculated as:

$$= \frac{\$264,844,847}{(\$248,956,059 + 150,484,480)/2}$$

$$= 1.33$$

Notice that these two ratios are actually components of the return on assets ratio as indicated by the following:

$$\frac{Net\ operating\ profit\ after\ taxes}{Net\ Sales} \times \frac{Net\ Sales}{Average\ total\ assets}$$

Eliminating net sales from both the numerator and denominator leaves:

$$\frac{Net\ operating\ profit}{Average\ total\ assets}$$

The return on assets, profit margin, and asset turnover ratios are best used in conjunction with some basis of comparability. One popular method of analysis is to compare a company's ratios with industry averages. These industry averages are available from several sources such as Standard and Poor's *Industry Surveys*. This comparison asks the question: Is the company's performance better than that of the industry as a whole? Unfortunately, Kroll-O'Gara is a unique company offering specialized services and does not fit into common industry groupings. Other companies such as Ford Motor Company, which is an automobile manufacturer, or IBM, which is a computer manufacturer and services company, fit more easily into common industry groupings.

Another method of analysis is to compare a company's results with those of a competitor. Burns International Service Company is a competitor of Kroll-O'Gara Company. Following is a ratio comparison of the two companies:

	Kroll-O'Gara	*Burns International*
Return on assets	8.0%	11.5%
Profit margin	6.0%	2.5%
Asset turnover	1.33	4.6

This analysis indicates that Kroll-O'Gara Company's 1998 return on assets was somewhat less than Burns International's. This disadvantage is due to Burns's ability to generate a much higher asset turnover ratio even though its profit margin was somewhat lower.

One final method of analysis that might be used is to compare the return on assets ratio with an established benchmark. Investing in corporate stocks carries an associated degree of risk that varies by company. That is, a company may be unprofitable and go out of business, resulting in a loss of the amount originally invested. Consequently, investors wish to be compensated for assuming risk. The risk-free rate of return benchmark is the yield (or actual interest rate) on long-term government securities.[13] During 1998 the average interest rate on long-term government securities was approximately 6.5 percent. Kroll-O'Gara's return on assets indicates that during 1998 investors were compensated an additional 1.5 percent for assuming the risk associated with the company's stock. As indicated in Chapter 2, a company's risk is determined by its β. During 1998 Kroll-O'Gara Company's β was approximately 1.2. A β of this magnitude indicates that a moderate amount of systematic risk was associated with investing in the company. We also know from Chapter 4 that at the end of 1998, the company's stock was selling at about 56 times earnings. Taken together, these results indicate that during 1998 Kroll-O'Gara Company was earning a return on assets that was slightly above the current risk-free rate, the risk associated with the company was relatively low, but investor perceptions of the future outlook for the company were quite favorable.

The Statement of Cash Flows

Evolution of the Statement of Cash Flows

Prior to 1971, the income statement and the balance sheet were the only financial statements required under generally accepted accounting principles. However, many large firms were including additional financial statements to disclose relevant information needed to make economic decisions. These disclosures were in response to investors, creditors, and others who voiced the desire to receive information on the financing and investing activities of business organizations. One of the additional financial statements that was prepared in response to this need was termed the *funds statement.* This statement reported on the resources provided and the uses to which these resources were put during the reporting period.

Funds statements were not uniformly prepared initially, and the method of reporting sources and application of resources depended on the concept of funds preferred by the reporting entity. In general, the concepts of funds used can be categorized as (1) cash, (2) working capital, and (3) all financial

---

[13] The return on assets ratio is an overall measure of firm performance that can be used by all investors. Additional ratios that are used by various investor groups are discussed in subsequent chapters.

resources, although other concepts of funds such as quick assets or net monetary assets may also have been encountered.

Statements using the cash concept of funds summarize all material changes in the cash balance. These funds statements become, in effect, statements of cash receipts and disbursements, and they report the impact of these receipts and disbursements on all other accounts.

Under the working capital definition of funds, all material transactions that result in a change in working capital are reported (working capital being defined as current assets minus current liabilities). When using this concept, *funds* is defined as the amount of increases or decreases in cash, receivables, inventories, payables, and other current items.

Finally, if the all-financial-resources concept is used, the entity reports on the effect of all transactions with outsiders. This concept of funds must be used in conjunction with another concept of funds (e.g., cash, working capital) and includes all items that affect the financing and investing activities of the enterprise. An example of an all-financial-resources transaction that would not appear on a traditional statement prepared using the cash or working capital concepts is the purchase of assets by issuing stock. The advantage of the all-financial-resources concept is its inclusion of all transactions that are important items in the financial administration of the entity.

APB Opinions No. 3 and No. 19

In 1963 the APB noted the increased attention that had been given to flow of funds analysis and issued *Opinion No. 3*. This release suggested that funds statements should be presented as supplemental information in financial reports but did not make such disclosures mandatory.[14] In *APB Opinion No. 3* the board also suggested that the title of the statement be as descriptive as possible.

By 1971 the APB had noted that regulatory agencies were requiring the preparation of funds statements and that a number of companies were voluntarily disclosing funds statements in their annual reports. As a result, the Board issued *APB Opinion No. 19*, which stated that information usually contained on the funds statement was essential to financial statement users and that such a statement should be presented each time a balance sheet and an income statement were prepared. In addition, the Board stated that the funds statement should be prepared in accordance with the all-financial-resources concept and that the statement should be titled "Statement of Changes in Financial Position."[15]

The Board went on to prescribe the format of the statement as follows.

1. *The statement may be prepared in such a manner as to express the financial position in terms of cash, cash and temporary assets, quick assets, or working*

---

[14] *APB Opinion No. 3*, "The Statement of Source and Application of Funds" (New York: AICPA, 1963).

[15] *APB Opinion No. 19*, "Reporting Changes in Financial Position" (New York: AICPA, 1971).

capital so long as it utilizes the all-financial-resources concept and gives the most useful portrayal of the financing and investing activities of the entity.

2. In each case the statement should disclose the net change in the cash, cash and temporary investments, quick assets or working capital, depending on the form of presentation.

3. The statement should disclose outlays for long-term assets, net proceeds from the sale of long-term assets, conversion of long-term debt or preferred stock to common stocks, issuances and repayments of debts, issuances or repurchases of capital stock and dividends.[16]

The statement of changes in financial position was designed to enable financial statement users to answer such questions as

1. Where did the profits go?
2. Why weren't dividends larger?
3. How was it possible to distribute dividends in the presence of a loss?
4. Why are current assets down when there was a profit?
5. Why is extra financing required?
6. How was the expansion financed?
7. Where did the funds from the sale of securities go?
8. How was the debt retirement accomplished?
9. How was the increase in working capital financed?

Although definitive answers to these questions are not readily obtainable from a casual inspection of the statement, usual practice was to elaborate on the presentation in the footnotes. In addition, comparative analyses covering several years of operations enable the user to obtain useful information on past methods and practices and the contribution of funds derived from operations to the growth of the company.

The statement of changes in financial position was designed to report on the company's financial operations and to disclose the results of the company's financial management policies. It was also designed to improve the predictive decision-making ability of users.

Cash Flow Information

The cash inflows and outflows of a business are of primary importance to investors and creditors. The presentation of cash flow information by a business enterprise should enable investors to (1) predict the amount of cash that is likely to be distributed as dividends or interest in the future and (2) evaluate the potential risk of a given investment.

The FASB has emphasized the importance of cash flow information in its deliberations. *SFAC No. 1* states that effective financial reporting must enable investors, creditors, and other users to (1) assess cash flow prospects and (2) evaluate liquidity, solvency, and flow of funds.

[16] Ibid.

The presentation of cash flow data is necessary to evaluate a firm's liquidity, solvency, and financial flexibility. *Liquidity* is the firm's ability to convert an asset to cash or to pay a current liability. It is referred to as the "nearness to cash" of an entity's economic resources and obligations. Liquidity information is important to users in evaluating the timing of future cash flows; it is also necessary to evaluate solvency and financial flexibility.

Solvency refers to a firm's ability to obtain cash for business operations. Specifically, it refers to a firm's ability to pay its debts as they become due. Solvency is necessary for a firm to be considered a "going concern." Insolvency may result in liquidation and losses to owners and creditors. In addition, the threat of insolvency may cause the capital markets to react by increasing the cost of capital in the future; that is, the amount of risk is increased.

Financial flexibility is the firm's ability to use its financial resources to adapt to change. It is the firm's ability to take advantage of new investment opportunities or to react quickly to a "crisis" situation. Financial flexibility comes in part from quick access to the company's liquid assets. However, liquidity is only one part of financial flexibility. Financial flexibility also stems from a firm's ability to generate cash from its operations, contributed capital, or sale of economic resources without disrupting continuing operations.

The presentation of cash flow data is intended to enable investors to make rational decisions by providing them with useful information. The FASB, in *SFAC No. 2*, identified *relevance* and *reliability* as the primary ingredients that make accounting information useful. A statement of cash flows undoubtedly allows for the presentation of more useful information to investors and creditors because it enables users to be able to predict the probability of future returns and evaluate risk.

In 1987 the FASB issued *SFAS No. 95*, "Statement of Cash Flows." This statement established standards for cash flow reporting and superseded *APB Opinion No. 19*, "Reporting Changes in Financial Position." As a result, all business enterprises are now required to present a statement of cash flows in place of the statement of changes in financial position as part of the full set of financial statements.

Historical Perspective

The format required by *SFAS No. 95* for presentation of the statement of cash flows evolved over a number of years. In 1980 the FASB issued a discussion memorandum entitled *Reporting Funds Flows, Liquidity and Financial Flexibility* as a part of the conceptual framework project. The major questions raised in this discussion memorandum included:

1. Which concept of funds should be adopted?
2. How should transactions not having a direct impact on funds be reported?
3. Which of the various approaches should be used for presenting funds flow information?
4. How should information about funds flow from operations be presented?

5. Should funds flow information be separated into outflows for (a) maintenance of operating capacity, (b) expansion of operating capacity, and (c) nonoperating purposes?

Later, in 1981, the FASB issued an exposure draft entitled *Reporting Income, Cash Flows, and Financial Position of Business Enterprises*. This exposure draft concluded that funds flow reporting should focus on cash rather than working capital. However, a final statement was not issued during this time, and the FASB decided to consider the subject of cash flow reporting in connection with a study of recognition and measurement concepts.

In 1984 the FASB issued *SFAC No. 5*, "Recognition and Measurement in Financial Statements of Business Enterprises." Included in this statement is the conclusion that a cash flow statement should be part of a full set of financial statements. Concurrently, the Financial Executives Institute was reviewing the issue of cash flow reporting. In 1984 this organization published *The Funds Statement: Structure and Use*, a study that pointed out several areas of diversity inherent in the Statement of Changes in Financial Position. For example, *APB Opinion No. 19* allowed different definitions of funds, different definitions of cash and cash flow from operations, and different forms of presentation of the statement of changes in financial position.

During 1985 and 1986, the FASB organized a task force on cash flow reporting and issued an exposure draft that proposed standards for cash flow reporting. The FASB was concerned that the divergence in practice affected the understandability and usefulness of the information presented to investors, creditors, and other users of financial statements. In addition, some financial statement users were contending that accrual accounting had resulted in net income not reflecting the underlying cash flows of business enterprises. That is, too many arbitrary allocation procedures, such as deferred taxes and depreciation, resulted in a net income figure that was not necessarily related to the earning power of an enterprise. As a result, *SFAS No. 95* was issued in 1987.

Purposes of the Statement of Cash Flows

The primary purpose of the statement of cash flows is to provide relevant information about the cash receipts and cash payments of an enterprise during a period. This purpose is consistent with the objectives and concepts delineated in *SFAC Nos. 1* and *5*.

SFAC No. 1 stressed that financial reporting should provide information to help present and potential investors assess the amount, timing, and uncertainty of prospective cash receipts from interest, dividends, sale of securities, and proceeds from loans. These cash flows are seen as important because they may affect an enterprise's liquidity and solvency. *SFAC No. 5* indicated that a full set of financial statements should show cash flows for the period. *SFAC No. 5* also described the usefulness of cash flow reporting in assessing an entity's liquidity, financial flexibility, profitability, and risk.

These objectives and concepts delineated in *SFAC Nos. 1* and *5* led the FASB to conclude that the statement of cash flows should replace the statement of changes in financial position as a required financial statement. The statement of cash flows is intended to help investors, creditors, and others assess future cash flows, provide feedback about actual cash flows, evaluate the availability of cash for dividends and investments, as well as the enterprise's ability to finance growth from internal sources, and identify the reasons for differences between net income and net cash flows. An additional reason for the focus on cash rather than working capital is the questionable usefulness of working capital in evaluating liquidity. That is, a positive working capital balance does not necessarily indicate liquidity, and a negative working capital balance may not indicate a lack of liquidity. More information is needed on receivable and inventory financing to evaluate the overall liquidity of a business enterprise.

Statement Format

The statement of cash flows reports changes during an accounting period in cash and cash equivalents from the following activities:

1. Cash flows from operating activities.
2. Cash flows from investing activities.
3. Cash flows from financing activities.

Cash equivalents are defined as highly liquid investments that are both readily convertible to known amounts of cash and so near to maturity that they present insignificant risk changes in value because of changes in interest rates. In general, only investments with original maturities of three months from the date of purchase will qualify as cash equivalents. Kroll-O'Gara Company's statement of cash flows is presented in Figure 5.2 on page 160–161. This figure shows that during 1998 the company's activities resulted in a net increase in cash of $2,991,457.

Cash Flows from Operating Activities

Cash flows from operating activities are generally the cash effect from transactions that enter into the determination of net income exclusive of financing and investing activities. Among the cash inflows from operations are the following:

1. Receipts from sales of goods and services and collections on accounts or notes from customers.
2. Receipts of interest and dividends.
3. All the receipts that are not the result of transactions defined as investing or financing activities. Examples of such transactions are amounts received to settle lawsuits or insurance settlements.

Cash outflows from operations include:

1. Cash payments to acquire materials for manufacture or goods for resale, and cash payments to reduce payables and notes to creditors.

2. Cash payments to other suppliers and employees.

3. Cash payments to governments for taxes, duties, fines, and fees or penalties.

4. Cash payments to lenders and creditors for interest.

5. All other payments that are not the result of transactions defined as investing or financing activities. Examples of such transactions are payments to settle lawsuits and cash contributions to charities.

6. The cash flows from the purchase and sale of debt and equity securities classified as trading securities under the provisions of *SFAS No. 115*.

SFAS No. 95 encouraged companies to report operating activities by reporting major classes of gross cash receipts, major classes of gross cash payments, and the difference between them—the net cash flow from operating activities. Reporting gross cash receipts and payments is termed the *direct method,* and includes reporting the following classes of operating cash receipts and payments:

1. Cash collected from customers.

2. Interest and dividends received.

3. Other operating cash receipts.

4. Cash paid to employees and other suppliers of goods and services.

5. Interest paid.

6. Income taxes paid.

7. Other operating cash payments.

One criticism of the computation of cash flows from operating activities is the treatment of dividends and interest received and interest paid. This treatment separates investment returns and interest payments from the sources of these activities, the purchase and sale of investments which are disclosed as investing activities, and the sale and retirement of debt which are disclosed as financing activities. This issue is discussed in greater depth in an article by Hugo Nurnburg and James Largay III presented on the text's webpage for Chapter 5.

A company that chooses not to use the direct method for reporting operating cash flow information must report the same amount of operating cash flow by adjusting net income to reconcile it with operating cash flow. This method of reporting is termed the *indirect method.* The required adjustments include the effect of past deferrals of operating cash receipts and payments; accruals of expected operating cash receipts and payments; and the effect of items related to investing and financing activities such as depreciation, amortization of goodwill, and gains or losses on the sale of property, plant, and equipment.

A company that uses the direct method must reconcile net income to net cash flow from operating activities in a separate schedule. If the indirect method is used, the reconciliation is reported within the statement of cash flows. Consequently, it is sometimes referred to as the *reconciliation method.*

FIGURE 5.2 *The Kroll-O'Gara Company Consolidated Statements of Cash Flows for the Years Ended December 31, 1996, 1997, and 1998*

	1996	1997	1998
CASH FLOWS FROM OPERATING ACTIVITIES:			
Net income	$5,268,415	$2,046,64	$13,088,906
Adjustments to reconcile net income to net cash provided by (used in) operating activities—			
Depreciation and amortization	5,248,788	6,519,454	8,598,827
Bad debt expense	8,555,063	2,083,080	2,513,506
Shareholder stock compensation.	930,846	1,356,280	—
Loss on write-off of notes receivable	—	35,434	—
Share in net income of joint ventures	(19,224)	(121,650)	—
Gain on sale of marketable securities	(108,646)	(14,503)	(10,469)
Asset impairment	174,531	—	—
Disposal of clinical business	1,263,000	—	—
Noncash compensation expense	—	—	78,160
Change in assets and liabilities, net of effects of acquisitions			
Receivables—trade and unbilled	(7,191,858)	(9,974,669)	(13,253,384)
Costs and estimated earnings in excess of billings on uncompleted contracts	(7,626,473)	3,499,084	(14,329,633)
Inventories, prepaid expenses and other assets	(3,274,443)	(7,184,407)	(4,089,617)
Accounts payable and income taxes currently payable	1,539,236	8,101,505	901,853
Billings in excess of costs and estimated earnings on uncompleted contracts	(375,640)	(1,009,740)	(138,006)
Amounts due to/from related parties	(294,471)	443,290	(2,623,651)
Deferred Taxes	(1,150,316)	(156,892)	(725,135)
Accrued liabilities, long-term liabilities and customer deposits	5,016,351	571,909	(2,446,382)
Net cash provided by (used in) operating activities	7,955,159	6,194,818	(12,435,025)
CASH FLOWS FROM INVESTING ACTIVITIES:			
Purchases of property, plant and equipment, net	(3,473,979)	(5,521,131)	(6,947,155)
Additions to databases	(3,250,360)	(3,856,914)	(4,186,924)
Decrease in notes receivable— shareholder	233,253	—	—
Acquisitions, net of cash acquired	(2,139,123)	(10,710,128)	(18,462,000)
Sales (purchases) of marketable securities, net	200,313	35,424	(13,262,353)
Other	(66,711)	266,004	—
Net cash used in investing activities	(8,496,607)	(19,786,745)	(42,858,432)

FIGURE 5.2 *(Continued)*

	1996	1997	1998
CASH FLOWS FROM FINANCING ACTIVITIES:			
Loan financing fees	—	(723,727)	—
Net repayments under revolving lines of credit	(252,818)	(9,376,835)	(559,112)
Proceeds from debt	179,569	44,902,987	284,857
Payments of long-term debt	(5,832,603)	(10,042,503)	(13,662,425)
Proceeds from notes payable— shareholder	2,000,000	500,000	—
Repayment of notes payable— shareholder	(803,745)	(7,238,766)	—
Net proceeds from issuances of common stock	14,871,817	—	68,336,923
Purchase and retirement of stock	—	(2,695,824)	—
Foreign currency translation	(46,187)	(160,462)	(593,494)
Distributions to shareholders, including preferred dividends	(9,230,000)	—	—
Proceeds from exercise of stock options and warrants	445	2,776,466	4,478,145
Net cash provided by financing activities	886,478	17,941,336	58,284,914
NET INCREASE IN CASH AND CASH EQUIVALENTS	345,030	4,349,409	2,991,457
Effects of foreign currency exchange rates on cash and cash equivalents	34,032	(75,931)	106,049
CASH AND CASH EQUIVALENTS, beginning of year	5,112,882	5,491,944	9,765,422
CASH AND CASH EQUIVALENTS, end of year	$5,491,944	$ 9,765,422	$ 12,862,928

The operating section of Kroll-O'Gara's Company's 1998 statement of cash flows is prepared by using the indirect method and discloses that operating activities resulted in a use of cash of $12,435,025.

Cash Flow from Investing Activities
Investing activities include making and collecting loans; acquiring and disposing of debt or equity securities of other companies classified as available-for-sale or held-to-maturity securities under the provisions of *SFAS No. 115;* and acquiring and disposing of property, plant, and equipment, and other productive resources. Examples of cash inflows from investing activities are:

1. Receipts from the collection or sales of loans made to other entities.

2. Receipts from the collection or sale of other companies' debt instruments.

3. Receipts from the sales of other companies' equity instruments.

4. Receipts from the sales of property, plant, and equipment and other productive assets.

Examples of cash outflows from investing activities are

1. Disbursement for loans made by the enterprise to other entities.
2. Payments to acquire other companies' debt instruments.
3. Payments to acquire other companies' equity instruments.
4. Payments to acquire property, plant, and equipment and other productive assets.

The investing section of Kroll-O'Gara's Company's 1998 statement of cash flows indicates that investing activities resulted in a use of cash of $42,858,432.

Cash Flows from Financing Activities

Financing activities result from obtaining resources from owners, providing owners with a return of and a return on their investment, borrowing money and repaying the amount borrowed, and obtaining and paying for other resources from long-term creditors. Cash inflows from financing activities include

1. Proceeds from issuing equity instruments.
2. Proceeds from issuing debt instruments or other short- or long-term borrowings.

Cash outflows from financing activities include

1. Payments of dividends or other distributions to owners.
2. Repayments of amounts borrowed.

Although loans to or investments in other companies are classified as investing activities and repayments of amounts borrowed are classified as a financing activity, cash receipts from dividends and interest and cash payments for interest are classified as operating activities. The financing section of Kroll-O'Gara's Company's 1998 statement of cash flows indicates that the total increase in cash experienced by the company was due to cash provided from financing activities of $58,284,914. This increase was mainly attributable to the sale of common stock for $68,336,923.

Financial Analysis of Cash Flow Information

A major objective of accounting is to present data that allows investors and creditors to predict the amount of cash that will be distributed in the form of dividends and interest, and to allow an evaluation of risk. Net income is the result of changes in assets and liabilities, some cash, some current, and some noncurrent; consequently, it cannot be equated with a change in cash. The statement of cash flows discloses the effects of earnings activities on cash resources, how assets were acquired, and how they were financed. The ability of an enterprise to generate cash from operations is an important indicator of its financial health and the degree of risk associated with investing in the firm.

The investors and creditors of a firm anticipate a return that is at least equal to the market rate of interest for investments with equal risk. Or, stated differently, investors expect to receive a discounted present value of future cash flows that is equal to or greater than their original investment. The past cash flows from a firm are the best available basis for forecasting future cash flows.

The FASB stressed the importance of cash flows to investors when it stated:

financial reporting should provide information to help investors, creditors, and others assess the amounts, timing and uncertainty of prospective cash inflow to the related enterprise.[17]

The ability to predict returns to investors and creditors is somewhat complex because management may decide to use cash in a variety of manners, and the uses of cash are interrelated. For example, available cash may be reinvested in assets, or used to expand facilities and markets, retire debt and equity, or pay dividends. Accounting researchers are interested in determining the relationship between accounting information and decision making. Empirical research has indicated that cash flow data has incremental information content over accrual earnings data and that cash flow data is superior to changes in working capital information.[18] These findings support the FASB's position on the disclosure of cash flow data because they provide evidence that such information may result in better decisions. They also indicate that even given the uncertainties surrounding the alternate uses of available cash by firms, knowledge of past cash flow information allows investors and creditors to make better predictions of future cash flows and assessments of risk.

One method of analyzing a company's statement of cash flows is to determine the amount of annual financing needed to sustain annual activities. A company's *free cash flow* is the total amount of cash generated from all internal sources. A positive free cash flow amount indicates that the company has been able to generate sufficient cash internally to maintain its current level of operations. A negative amount indicates that the company found or will find it necessary to acquire funds from external financing sources to maintain operations. Free cash flow is calculated net cash provided (used) from operating activities +/− net cash provided (used) from investing activities. Kroll-O'Gara Company's free cash flows for 1998 and 1997 are calculated as

$$(\$12,435,025) + (\$42,858,432) = (\$55,293,457), \text{ and}$$
$$\$6,194,818 - 19,786,745 = (\$13,591,927).$$

---

[17] *Statement of Financial Accounting Concepts No. 1*, "Objectives of Financial Reporting by Business Enterprises" (New York: FASB, 1978), par. 37.

[18] Robert M. Bowen, David Burgstahler, and Lane A. Daley, "The Incremental Information Content of Accruals Versus Cash Flows," *The Accounting Review* (October 1987), pp. 723–747.

Consequently, the company found it necessary to obtain funds from external sources to maintain operations during both 1998 and 1997. As indicated in the financing section of its statement of cash flows, the major source of this external funding for 1998 was the sale of common stock for $68,336,923, whereas in 1997 the company issued debt in the amount of $44,902,987.

Development Stage Enterprises

A company in the development stage is a new organization attempting to become a going concern. Consequently, some of the company's expenditures may be considered investments in the future, and some of the reporting principles may be altered during the development period. Many companies in the development stage are faced with financing problems, and the use of generally accepted accounting principles may in themselves compound these financing problems. That is, reporting all start-up costs as expenses during the first years of operations will cause reported income to be reduced and thereby make it more difficult for the company to obtain investment funds.

The proper reporting procedures to use in accounting for development stage enterprises have been discussed for many years. The basic question in these discussions has been: Should generally accepted accounting principles differ for an organization just beginning operations? In 1975 the FASB undertook a study of this question and issued *SFAS No. 7*, "Accounting and Reporting by Development Stage Enterprises."[19] This release specifies guidelines for the identification of a development stage enterprise and for the procedures to be used to record and report on the activities of these types of organizations.

The Board noted that the activities of a development stage enterprise typically would be devoted to financial planning, raising capital, exploring for natural resources, developing natural resources, research and development, acquiring assets, recruiting and training personnel, developing markets, and beginning production. Thus, the FASB defined development stage enterprises as those devoting substantially all their efforts to establishing a new business and required that either of the following conditions be met:

1. Planned principal operations have not commenced.
2. Planned principal operations have commenced, but no significant revenue has been received.[20]

The FASB reached the conclusion that generally accepted accounting principles should apply to development stage enterprises and that GAAP should govern the recognition of revenue and the determination of whether a cost should be charged to expense or capitalized. That is, reporting on the activities of a development stage enterprise should not differ from any other type of organization. However, the FASB did state that certain additional information should be disclosed for development stage enterprises:

[19] *Statement of Financial Accounting Standards No. 7*, "Accounting and Reporting by Development Stage Enterprises" (Stamford, CT: FASB, 1975).

[20] Ibid., par. 8.

a. A balance sheet, including any cumulative net losses reported with a descriptive caption such as "deficit accumulated during the development stage" in the stockholders' equity section.

b. An income statement, showing amounts of revenue and expenses for each period covered by the income statement and, in addition, cumulative amounts from the enterprise's inception.

c. A statement of … (cash flows), showing the sources and uses of … (cash) for each period for which an income statement is presented and, in addition, cumulative amounts from the enterprise's inception.

d. A statement of stockholders' equity showing from the enterprise's inception:
    1. For each instance, the date and number of shares of stock, warrants, rights or other equity securities issued for cash and for other consideration.
    2. For each issuance, the dollar amounts (per share or other equity unit in total) assigned to the consideration received for shares of stock, warrants, rights, or other equity securities. Dollar amounts shall be assigned to any noncash consideration received.
    3. For each issuance involving noncash consideration, the nature of the noncash consideration and the basis for assigning amounts.[21]

The conclusions reached in *SFAS No. 7* indicate that the board believed that additional standards of disclosure for development stage enterprises would alleviate the accounting and reporting problems faced by these companies. This belief indicated that the FASB was retaining the emphasis on interfirm comparability initiated by the APB. That is, similar situations should be reported in a similar manner by all companies. It also provided additional evidence that the FASB believed that GAAP should be the same for all business organizations regardless of their special needs or particular environment.

International Accounting Standards

The International Accounting Standards Committee has:

1. Discussed the Statement of Financial Position and the various measurement bases used in financial statements, and defined assets, liabilities, and equity in its "Framework for the Preparation and Presentation of Financial Statements."
2. Discussed the information to be disclosed on the balance sheet and statement of cash flows in *IAS No. 1*.
3. Discussed the presentation of the statement of cash flows in *IAS No. 7*.

In discussing the statement of financial position in "Preparation and Presentation of Financial Statements," the IASC indicated that economic decisions that are taken by users of financial statements require an evaluation of

---

[21] Ibid., par. 11.

an enterprise's ability to generate cash. Consequently, the financial position of an enterprise is affected by the economic resources it controls, its financial structure, its liquidity and solvency, and its capacity to adapt to changes in the environment in which it operates. Information about the economic resources controlled by the enterprise and its capacity in the past to modify these resources is useful in predicting the ability of the enterprise to generate cash in the future.[22] The measurement bases used in the elements of financial statements included historical cost, current cost, realizable (settlement) value, and present value. The IASC also indicated that the most commonly used measurement basis is historical cost. The definitions of assets, liabilities, and equity are similar to those contained is *SFAC No. 6* and embody the concepts of resources, present obligations, and residual interest, respectively.

The IASC's overall considerations for preparing the financial statement contained in *IAS No. 1*, "Presentation of Financial Statements," were discussed in Chapter 4. The recommended disclosures for the balance sheet are similar to those required under U.S. GAAP. However, the IASC has taken the position that each enterprise can determine, based on the nature of its operations, whether or not to present current assets and current liabilities as separate classifications. *IAS No. 1* does require that assets and liabilities be presented in order of their liquidity, even if a classified balance sheet is not presented. In addition, the IASC recognizes that there are differences in the nature and function of assets, liabilities, and equity that are so fundamental that they should be presented on the face of the balance sheet. At a minimum, the following categories are to be disclosed:

Intangible assets
Tangible assets
Financial assets
Receivables
Inventories
Cash and cash equivalents
Payables
Interest-bearing liabilities
Provisions
Equity capital and reserves
Minority interest

Additional line items are to be presented based on materiality and the nature and function of each item. Monetary and nonmonetary items are to be presented separately, as well as operating and financial items and balances with other affiliated enterprises. A discussion of the FASB's staff review of *IAS No. 1* is contained in Chapter 4. This document did not specify any significant differences between FASB and IASC standards specifically relating to the balance sheet or statement of cash flows.

---

[22] "Preparation and Presentation of Financial Statements," International Accounting Standards Committee, pars. 15–16.

In *IAS No. 7*, "Cash Flow Statements," the IASC outlined the required disclosures and presentation for the statement of cash flows. As with U.S. GAAP, the statement reports cash flows from operating, investing, and financing activities. In addition, cash flows from operating activities may be reported by using either the direct or indirect method, but the IASC stated a preference for the direct method. Cash flows from extraordinary items are required to be disclosed separately as operating, investing, or financing activities under *IAS No. 7*. Also, the aggregate cash flow arising from the acquisition or disposal of subsidiaries is required to be presented separately and disclosed as an investing activity under the provisions of *IAS No. 7*. In reviewing *IAS No. 7*, the FASB staff noted that although *IAS No. 7* and *SFAS No. 95* are very similar, some differences in disclosure requirement and requirements for classifying items and definitions are in evidence. The most significant of these differences is that *IAS No. 7* allows for interest and dividends received and paid to be classified as either operating or inventing and financing, respectively. Because of these differences, users must understand how supplemental disclosures may help to reconcile these differences; however, in some cases that may not be possible because of differing disclosure requirements.[23]

Summary

The measurement techniques currently being used for assigning values to balance sheet items have been criticized for failing to give enough relevant information to financial statement users. A review of balance sheet disclosure procedures indicates that most valuations are the result of the residual effect of the emphasis on net income reporting. Consequently, they make little contribution to the users' ability to predict the future.

Partially in response to a need, the statement, now titled the statement of cash flows, has become the third major financial statement. This requirement has evolved over time from an original emphasis on changes in working capital to the current emphasis on cash flows.

Standards of accounting and reporting for development stage enterprises are also discussed in this chapter. In *SFAS No. 7*, the FASB set out guidelines for defining development stage enterprises and for reporting on their activities. The FASB retained the view that GAAP should be the same for all organizations but did allow the reporting of additional information for development stage organizations.

In the readings contained on the text's webpage for this chapter, some additional issues associated with the freelance sheet and statement of cash flows are addressed.

---

[23] Financial Accounting Standards Board, *The IASC-U.S. Comparison Project: A Report on the Similarities and Differences between IASC Standards and U.S. GAAP*, Carrie Bloom, ed., 2nd ed. (Norwalk, CT: Financial Accounting Standards Board, 1999), pp. 99–109.

Cases

• Case 5-1 Alternate Financial Statement Treatments

The financial statement on the next page was prepared by employees of your client, Linus Construction Company. The statement is not accompanied by footnotes, but you have discovered the following:

a. The average completion period for the company's jobs is 18 months. The company's method of journalizing contract transactions is summarized in the following pro-forma entries:

LINUS CONSTRUCTION COMPANY
Statement of Financial Position
October 31, 2001

Current assets:			
Cash		$ 182,200	
Accounts receivable (less allowance of $15,000 for doubtful accounts)		220,700	
Materials, supplies, labor, and overhead charged to construction		2,026,000	
Materials and supplies not charged to construction		288,000	
Deposits made to secure performance of contracts		360,000	$3,076,900
Less Current Liabilities:			
Accounts payable to subcontractors		$ 141,100	
Payable for materials and supplies		65,300	
Accrued payroll		8,260	
Accrued interest on mortgage note		12,000	
Estimated taxes payable		66,000	292,660
Net working capital			$2,784,240
Property Plant and Equipment (at cost):			

	Cost	Depreciation	Value
Land and buildings	$ 983,300	$310,000	$ 673,300
Machinery and equipment	905,000	338,000	567,000
Payments made on leased equipment	230,700	230,699	1
	$2,119,000	$878,699	$1,240,301

Deferred charges:			
Prepaid taxes and other expenses		$ 11,700	
Points charged on mortgage note		10,800	22,500
Total net working capital and noncurrent assets			4,047,041
Less Deferred Liabilities:			
Mortgage note payable		$ 300,000	
Unearned revenue on work in progress		1,898,000	2,198,000
Total Net Assets			$1,849,041
Stockholders' Equity:			
6% preferred stock at par value		$ 400,000	
Common stock at par value		800,000	
Paid-in surplus		210,000	
Retained earnings		483,641	
Treasury stock at cost (370 shares)		(44,600)	
Total Stockholders' Equity			$1,849,041

b. Linus both owns and leases equipment used on construction jobs. Typically, its equipment lease contracts provide that Linus may return the equipment on completion of a job or may apply all rentals in full toward purchase of the equipment. About 70 percent of lease rental payments made in the past have been applied to the purchase of equipment. While leased equipment is in use, rents are charged to the account *payments made on leased equipment* (except for $1 balance) and to jobs on which the equipment has been used. In the event of purchase, the balance in the *payments made on leased equipment* account is transferred to the *machinery and equipment* account, and the depreciation and other related accounts are corrected.

c. Management is unable to develop dependable estimates of costs to complete contracts in progress.

Required:
a. Identify the weaknesses in the financial statement.
b. For each item identified in part (a), indicate the preferable treatment and explain why the treatment is preferable.

• Case 5-2 The Use of Current Value

The argument among accountants and financial statement users over the proper valuation procedures for assets and liabilities has resulted in the release of *SFAS No. 115*. The statement requires current value disclosures for all investments. The chairman of the Securities and Exchange Commission termed historical cost valuations "once upon a time accounting." Historical cost accounting also has been criticized as contributing to the Savings and Loan crisis in the 1980s. During that period, these financial institutions continued to value assets at historical cost when they were billions of dollars overvalued. Critics of current value accounting point out that objective market values for many assets are not available, current values cannot be used for tax purposes, using current values can cause earnings volatility, and management could use current value to "manage earnings."

Required:
a. Determine how current values might be determined for investments, land, buildings, equipment, patents, copyrights, trademarks, and franchises.
b. How might the use of current values in the accounting records cause earnings volatility?
c. Discuss how management might manage earnings using current cost data.

• Case 5-3 Analysis of a Statement of Cash Flows

Obtain a copy of a large corporation's annual report and refer to the statement of cash flows.

Required:
a. Did the company use the direct method or the indirect method of disclosing cash flows?
b. Comment on the relationship between cash flows from operations and net income for the year of the statement and the previous year.

c. What were the most significant sources of cash from operating activities during the period covered by the statement? What percentage of total cash inflows do these sources represent? Answer the same question for the previous period.

d. Was the cash from operations more than or less than dividends during the period covered by the statement and the previous period?

e. What were the firm's major investing activities during the period covered by the statement and the previous period? Were cash flows from operations more or less than cash flows from investing activities for the company in question?

f. What were the most significant cash flows from financing activities during the year of the statement and the previous year?

g. Review the management discussion and analysis sections of the financial statements to determine if any additional information is available concerning the company's investment or financing strategy.

• Case 5-4 Measurement Techniques

The measurement of assets and liabilities on the balance sheet is frequently a secondary goal to income determination. As a result, various measurement techniques are used to disclose assets and liabilities.

Required:
Discuss the various measurement techniques used on the balance sheet to disclose assets and liabilities.

• Case 5-5 The Statement of Cash Flows

Presenting information on cash flows has become an important part of financial reporting.

Required:
a. What goals are attempted to be accomplished by the presentation of cash flow information to investors?
b. Discuss the following terms as they relate to the presentation of cash flow information.
   i. Liquidity.
   ii. Solvency.
   iii. Financial flexibility.

• Case 5-6 The Usefulness of the Balance Sheet

The recent emphasis on capital maintenance concepts of income as seen in the FASB's support for "comprehensive income" implies that balance sheet measurement should determine measures of income. That is, accrual accounting is to focus on measurements in the balance sheet, and because financial statements are articulated, measurements in the income statement are residual in nature.

Required:
a. Do you believe that this focus implies that the balance sheet is more important than the income statement? Explain.
b. How is the balance sheet useful to investors? Discuss.
c. What is meant by the phrase "financial statements are articulated"?
d. Which measurements currently reported in balance sheets are consistent with the physical capital maintenance concept? Give examples.
e. Which measurements currently reported in balance sheets are not consistent with the physical capital maintenance concept? Give examples.

• Case 5-7 Alternative Treatments of Items of the Statement of Cash Flows

The statement of cash flows is intended to provide information about the investing, financing, and operating activities of an enterprise during an accounting period. In a statement of cash flows, cash inflows and outflows for interest expense, interest revenue, and dividend revenue and payments to the government are considered operating activities.

Required:
a. Do you believe that cash inflows and outflows associated with nonoperating items, such as interest expense, interest revenue, and dividend revenue should be separated from operating cash flows? Explain.
b. Do you believe that the cash flows from investing activities should include not only the return of investment, but also the return on investment, that is, the interest and dividend revenue? Explain.
c. Do you believe that the cash flows from the sale of an investment should also include the tax effect of the sale? Explain. Do you believe that cash flows from sales of investments should be net of their tax effects, or do you believe that the tax effect should remain an operating activity because it is a part of "payments to the government"? Explain.

• Case 5-8 Evolution of the Statement of Cash Flows

Statement of Financial Accounting Concepts requires companies to prepare a Statement of Cash Flows.

Required:
Describe how the Conceptual Framework eventually led to the requirement that companies issue statements of cash flows.

Room for Debate

• Issue 1

According to *SFAC No. 1*, financial statements should provide information that is useful for investor decision making. Paragraph 37 of *SFAS No. 1* states that financial reporting should provide information to help users assess the amounts, timing, and uncertainty of prospective cash flows. Paragraph 43 of *SFAC No. 1* states that the primary focus of financial reporting is information about an enterprise's performance provided by measures of earnings and its components.

Team Debate:

Team 1: Present arguments that the statement of cash flows, not the income statement, is the most important financial statement to prospective investors.

Team 2: Present arguments that the income statement, not the statement of cash flows, is the most important financial statement to prospective investors.

Recommended Additional Readings

American Accounting Association Financial Accounting Standards Committee. "Response to FASB Exposure Draft: Proposed Statement of Financial Accounting Concepts—Using Cash Flow Information in Accounting Measurements." *Accounting Horizons* (September 1998), pp. 304–312.

Bahnson, Paul R., Paul B. W. Miller, and Bruce P. Budge. "Nonarticulation in Cash Flow Statements and Implications for Education, Research and Practice." *Accounting Horizons* (December 1996), pp. 1–15.

Bierman, Harold, Jr. "Measurement and Accounting." *The Accounting Review* (July 1963), pp. 501–507.

Cotter, Julie. "Accrual and Cash Flow Accounting Models: A Comparison of the Value Relevance and Timeliness of Their Components." *Accounting and Finance* (November 1996), pp. 127–150.

Francis, Jennifer. "Have Financial Statements Lost Their Relevance?" *Journal of Accounting Research* (Autumn 1999), pp. 319–353.

Gallager, George W. "A Framework for Financial Statement Analysis Part 1: Return on Asset Performance." *Business Credit* (February 2000), pp. 40–43.

Ijiri, Yuri. "Cash-Flow Accounting and Its Structure." *Journal of Accounting, Auditing and Finance* (Summer 1978), pp. 331–348.

Johnson, Brent E. "The Ascent of the Cash Flow Statement." *Journal of Accounting Education* (Fall 1994), pp. 375–383.

Jones, Stewart. "The Decision Relevance of Cash-Flow Information." *Abacus* (September 1998), pp. 204–230.

Ketz, J. Edward, and James A. Largay III. "Reporting Income and Cash Flows from Operations." *Accounting Horizons* (June 1987), pp. 9–17.

Kirk, Donald J. "On Future Events: When Incorporated into Today's Measurements?" *Accounting Horizons* (June 1990), pp. 86–92.

Krishnan, Gopal V. "The Predictive Ability of Direct Method Cash Flow Information." *Journal of Business Finance and Accounting* (January/March 2000), pp. 215–245.

Mills, John. "The Power of Cash Flow Ratios." *Journal of Accountancy* (October 1998), pp. 53–59.

Nurnberg, Hugo, and James A. Largay. "More Concerns over Cash Flow Reporting under FASB Statement No. 95." *Accounting Horizons* (December 1996), pp. 123–136.

Salamon, Gerald L. "Cash Recovery Rates and Measures of Firm Profitability." *The Accounting Review* (April 1982), pp. 292–302.

Sorter, George H., and Monroe Ingberman. "The Implicit Criteria for the Recognition, Quantification and Reporting of Accounting Events." *Journal of Accounting Auditing and Finance,* Vol. 2 (1987), pp. 99–116.

Stabus, George J. "Measurement of Assets and Liabilities." *Accounting and Business Research* (Autumn 1963), pp. 243–262.

Trenholm, Barbara, and Francisco Arcelus. "Accounting Valuation Methods: Structuring an Unstructured Problem." *Accounting Horizons* (September 1989), pp. 82–89.

Bibliography

American Accounting Association Committee on Accounting Valuation Bases. "Report of the Committee on Accounting Valuation Bases." *The Accounting Review,* Supplement to Vol. 47 (1972), pp. 535–573.

American Accounting Association. "Report of the Committee on Foundations of Accounting Measurement." *The Accounting Review.* Supplement to Vol. 46 (1979), pp. 36–45.

Ashton, Robert H. "Objectivity of Accounting Measures: A Multirule-Multimeasurer Approach." *The Accounting Review* (July 1977), pp. 567–575.

Braiotta, Louis, Jr. "Cash Basis Statement of Changes." *The CPA Journal* (August 1984), pp. 34–40.

Crooch, G. Michael, and Bruce E. Collier. "Reporting Guidelines for Companies in a State of Development." *The CPA Journal* (July 1973), pp. 579–584.

Fadel, Hisham, and John M. Parkinson. "Liquidity Evaluation by Means of Ratio Analysis." *Accounting and Business Research* (Spring 1978), pp. 101–107.

Heath, Loyd C. *Financial Reporting and the Evaluation of Solvency.* New York: American Institute of Certified Public Accountants, 1978.

Heath, Loyd C. "Let's Scrap the 'Funds' Statement." *Journal of Accountancy* (October 1978), pp. 94–103.

Heath, Loyd C., and Paul Rosenfield. "Solvency: The Forgotten Half of Financial Reporting." *Journal of Accountancy* (January 1979), pp. 48–54.

Jaedicke, Robert K., and Robert T. Sprouse. *Accounting Flows: Income, Funds, and Cash.* Englewood Cliffs, NJ: Prentice-Hall, 1965.

Largay, James A., III, Edward P. Swanson, and Max Block. "The 'Funds' Statement: Should It Be Scrapped, Retained or Revitalized?" *Journal of Accountancy* (December 1979), pp. 88–97.

Lemke, Kenneth W. "The Evaluation of Liquidity: An Analytical Study." *Journal of Accounting Research* (Spring 1970), pp. 47–77.

Mason, Perry. *Cash Flow Analysis and the Funds Statement.* New York: American Institute of Certified Public Accountants, 1961.

Moonitz, Maurice. "Reporting on the Flow of Funds." *The Accounting Review* (July 1956), pp. 378–385.

Nurnberg, Hugo. "APB Opinion No. 19—Pro and Con." *Financial Executive* (December 1972), pp. 58–60, 62, 64, 66, 68, 70.

"Report of the Committee on Accounting Valuation Bases." *The Accounting Review.* Supplement to Vol. 47 (1972), esp. pp. 556–568.

"Report of the Committee on Foundations of Accounting Measurements." *The Accounting Review,* Supplement to Vol. 46 (1971), pp. 3–48.

Spiller, Earl A., and Robert L. Virgil. "Effectiveness of APB #19 in Improving Funds Reporting." *Journal of Accounting Research* (Spring 1974), pp. 112–133.

Sprouse, Robert T. "Balance Sheet—Embodiment of the Most Fundamental Elements of Accounting Theory." *Foundations of Accounting Theory.* Gainesville: University of Florida Press, 1971, pp. 90–104.

Staubus, George J. "An Induced Theory of Accounting Measurement." *The Accounting Review* (January 1985), pp. 53–75.

Staubus, George J. "The Market Stimulation Theory of Accounting Measurement." *Accounting and Business Research* (Spring 1986), pp. 117–132.

Swanson, Edward P., and Richard Vangermeersch. "Statement of Financing and Investing Activities." *The CPA Journal* (November 1981), pp. 32, 34–36, 38–40.

Tippett, Mark. "The Axioms of Accounting Measurement." *Accounting and Business Research* (Autumn 1978), pp. 266–278.

Walker, R. G. "Asset Classification and Asset Valuation." *Accounting and Business Research* (Autumn 1974), pp. 286–296.

International

Accounting

Financial accounting is influenced by the environment in which it operates. Nations have different histories, values, cultures, and political and economic systems, and they are also in various stages of economic development. These national influences interact with each other and, in turn, influence the development and application of financial accounting practices and reporting procedures. Multinational corporations operating in many different countries, such as Procter and Gamble, earn more than half of their revenues outside of the United States (see Table 1.1 on page 27). Because of the above-mentioned national differences, the financial accounting standards that are applied to the accounting data reported by these multinational companies often vary significantly from country to country.

Companies prepare financial reports that are directed toward their primary users. In the past, most users were residents of the same country as the corporation issuing the financial statements. However, the emergence of multinational corporations and organizations such as the European Union (EU), the General Agreement on Tariffs and Trade (GATT), and the North American Free Trade Agreement (NAFTA) has made transnational financial reporting more commonplace. Transnational financial reporting requires users to understand the accounting practices employed by the company, the language of the country in which the company resides, and the currency used by the corporation to prepare its financial statements. If investors and creditors cannot obtain understandable financial information about companies that operate in foreign countries, they are not likely to invest in or lend money to these companies. As a result, there is a move to harmonize accounting standards among countries.

One of the major problems currently facing U.S. corporations is their ability to compete in a global economy with transnational financial reporting.

In the following sections we present several issues that must be addressed by multinational corporations.

International Business Accounting Issues

A company's first exposure to international accounting frequently occurs as a result of a purchase or sale of an item of merchandise with a foreign entity. Dealing with foreign companies presents some unique problems. First, there is the possibility of exchange gains and losses (discussed in more detail in Chapter 15) between the time an order is given or received and the time of payment. That is, changes in the relative values of currencies give rise to exchange gains and losses. Also, it is difficult to obtain international credit information, and evaluating the company's liquidity and solvency from its financial statements may be complicated by the use of a different language and/or different accounting principles.

As a company's foreign trade increases, it may be necessary to create an international division. It may also become necessary to develop international accounting expertise. Finally, the company may decide to attempt to raise capital in foreign markets. If so, the company will be required to prepare its financial statements in a manner that is acceptable to the appropriate foreign stock exchange. In many cases, statements prepared in accordance with U.S. GAAP are not acceptable for inclusion in listing documents of foreign exchanges, but in others such as those in Canada, Japan, and Hong Kong they are acceptable.[1]

The Development of Accounting Systems

The culture of a country has an impact on both its business practices and its accounting procedures. Hofstede provided a widely accepted definition of culture as "the collective programming of the mind that distinguishes one category of people from another."[2] He later categorized eight separate cultures: Occidental, Muslim, Japanese, Hindu, Confucian, Slavic, African, and Latin American. However, the classification of accounting practices simply by culture is too simplistic because many nations contain more than one of these cultural groups and many countries' accounting systems were developed during previous colonial relationships.

The level of development of a country's accounting system is also impacted by environmental forces such as overall level of education, type of political system, type of legal system, and extent of economic development. For example, the development of accounting standards in the United States was affected by the Industrial Revolution and the need to obtain private sources of capital. Consequently, financial accounting information was neces-

---

[1] John D. Gould, John P. McAllister, and Larry L. Orsini, "Raising Capital Overseas," *Journal of Accountancy* (February 1997), pp. 33–37.

[2] G. Hofstede, "The Cultural Relativity of Organizational Practices and Theories," *Journal of International Business Studies* (Fall 1983), pp. 25, 25–89.

sary to provide investors and creditors with information on profitability and stewardship. On the other hand, accounting standards in Russia are not well developed. Originally, the Russian economy was centrally planned and as a result required uniform accounting standards. As an emerging market economy country, these accounting standards are no longer useful, and new standards must be developed. The impact of various environmental factors on the development of accounting standards is discussed in the following paragraphs.

Level of Education

In general, there is a direct correlation between the level of education obtained by a country's citizens and the development of the financial accounting reporting practices in that country. The characteristics composing these environmental factors include (1) the degree of literacy in a country; (2) the percentage of the population that has completed grade school, high school, and college; (3) the orientation of the educational system (vocational, professional, etc.); and (4) the appropriateness of the educational system to the country's economic and social needs. Countries with better educated populations are associated with more advanced financial accounting systems.

Political System

The type of political system (socialist, democratic, totalitarian, etc.) can influence the development of accounting standards and procedures. The accounting system in a country with a centrally controlled economy will be different from the accounting system in a market-oriented economy. For example, companies in a socialist country may be required to provide information on social impact and cost-benefit analysis in addition to information on profitability and financial position.

Legal System

The extent to which a country's laws determine accounting practice influences the strengths of that country's accounting profession. When governments prescribe accounting practices and procedures, the authority of the accounting profession is usually weak, whereas the nonlegalistic establishment of accounting policies by professional organizations is a characteristic of common-law countries.

Economic Development

The level of a country's economic development influences both the development and application of its accounting reporting practices. Countries with low levels of economic development will have relatively less need for a sophisticated accounting system than countries with high levels of economic development.

Table 6.1 lists some potential social, cultural, political, and legal influences on the development of national financial reporting standards and practices.

TABLE 6.1 *Influences on the Development of Financial Reporting*

Type of economy	Agricultural
	Resource based
	Tourist based
	Manufacturing
Legal system	Codified
	Common law
Political system	Democratic
	Totalitarian
Nature of business ownership	Private enterprise
	Socialist
	Communist
Size and complexity of business firms	Conglomerates
	Sole traders
Social climate	Consumerism
	Laissez-faire
Stability of currency	
Sophistication of management	
Sophistication of financial community	
Existence of accounting legislation	
Growth pattern of the economy	Growing
	Stable
	Declining
Education system	

Current Accounting Practice

The classification of accounting practices into groupings has been attempted since the late 1960s. The initial grouping scheme was developed by Gerhard Mueller,[3] who classified country accounting practices based on the impact of differing business environments, as follows:

1. United States/Canada/The Netherlands

2. British Commonwealth (excluding Canada)

3. Germany/Japan

4. Continental Europe (excluding Germany, the Netherlands, and Scandinavia)

5. Scandinavia

6. Israel/Mexico

7. South America

8. Developing nations of the Near and Far East

[3] Gerhard G. Mueller, "Accounting Principles Generally Accepted in the United States versus Those Generally Accepted Elsewhere," *International Journal of Accounting* (Spring 1968), pp. 91–103.

9. Africa (excluding South Africa)

10. Communistic

Later, a committee of the American Accounting Association asserted that accounting practices throughout the world could be categorized according to spheres of influence.[4] This committee indicated that the following five zones of influence were discernible:

1. British

2. Franco-Spanish-Portuguese

3. Germanic-Dutch

4. United States

5. Communistic

Recent agreements such as the EU, GATT, NAFTA, and the changing economic systems in Eastern Europe have modified spheres of influence and resulted in the following groupings:

United States

Financial accounting standards for this grouping have been developed primarily in the private sector, and the result has been a relatively restrictive set of accounting standards. The United States' sphere of influence includes Canada, Mexico, Venezuela, and Central America. The passage of NAFTA will undoubtedly result in greater standardization of accounting principles among these countries.

United Kingdom/The Netherlands

This grouping closely resembles the U.S. group; however, it is characterized by relatively less restrictive accounting standards. In addition to the United Kingdom and The Netherlands, the countries included under this grouping are Ireland, Israel, and the former English colonies of India, Australia, New Zealand, South Africa, and Hong Kong. (Hong Kong became a part of China on July 1, 1997. How its accounting standards will be affected by this change is unknown at this time.)

Continental/Japan

The companies in this grouping rely on banks to supply most of their capital needs; consequently, conservative accounting practices have been developed. The countries in this group include most of Western Europe and Japan.

South America

These countries share a common language (except for Brazil) and cultural heritage. In addition, financial reporting within this group generally incorporates information on the impact of inflation. All South American countries except Venezuela, which follows U.S. GAAP, are included in this group.

[4] American Accounting Association, "Report of the American Accounting Association Committee on International Operations and Education 1975–1976," *Accounting Review* (Supplement), (1977), pp. 65–101.

Third World

This very loose grouping of countries shares a need to develop accounting standards for emerging economies. Many of these countries were formerly colonies of European countries and are now developing accounting standards to meet the needs of their economic systems. The countries included in this group are most of Africa (except South Africa) and many Far Eastern countries.

Changing Economies

The political upheaval in Eastern Europe in the late 1980s resulted in the need to develop different accounting standards and practices to meet the needs of changing economic systems. These countries are in the process of changing their accounting practices from centralized planning to market economies. They include almost all of the Eastern European countries that were under the USSR's sphere of influence prior to the disintegration of the Warsaw Pact.

Communist

The remaining communist countries use an accounting system that is designed to assist in central planning. The countries in this group are China, North Korea, and Cuba.

Specific accounting practices differ between countries as well as between groups. Table 6.2 illustrates some of the areas of difference among selected countries.

Preparation of Financial Statements for Foreign Users

A company issuing financial reports to users in foreign countries may take one of several different approaches in the preparation of its financial statements:

1. Send the same set of financial statements to all users (domestic or foreign).
2. Translate the financial statements sent to foreign users into the language of the foreign nation's users.
3. Translate the financial statements sent to foreign users into the foreign nation's language and currency.
4. Prepare two sets of financial statements, one using the home country language, currency, and accounting principles, and the second using the language, currency, and accounting principles of the foreign country's users.
5. Prepare one set of financial statements based on worldwide accepted accounting principles.

The International Accounting Standards Committee

The preparation of financial statements for foreign users under option five above is being increasingly advocated for transnational financial reporting. The International Accounting Standards Committee (IASC) was formed in 1973 to develop worldwide accounting standards. It is an independent private-sector body, whose objective is to achieve uniformity in accounting principles that are used for worldwide financial reporting. The original board members of the

TABLE 6.2 *Differences in Accounting Practice Between Selected Countries*

	Australia	Brazil	Britain	Canada	France	Germany	Japan	Netherlands
Requirements that make up GAAP	Company law and professional	Company law and professional	Company law and professional	Professional requirements	Primarily company law	Company law and professional	Company law and professional	Company law and professional
Companies required to have an audit	All	Public only	All large private	Public and large private	Public and large private	Public and large private	Public and large private	Public and large private
GAAP concerning leases	Similar to U.S.	None	Similar to U.S.	Similar to U.S.	Capitalization not allowed	Similar to U.S.	Similar to U.S.	Similar to U.S.
LIFO inventory	Not allowed	Not allowed	Not allowed	Permitted	Not allowed	Permitted	Permitted	Permitted
Research and development expenditures	May be capitalized	May be capitalized	Research capitalized, development expensed	May be capitalized	May be capitalized	Similar to U.S.	No GAAP	May be capitalized
Consolidated financial statements	Required	Required	Required	Required	Required for public companies	Required information for public companies	Supplemental	Required
Accounting for changing prices	No GAAP	No GAAP	Supplemental information permitted	Supplemental information required	No GAAP	Supplemental information permitted	No GAAP	No GAAP
Accounting for deferred taxes	Similar to U.S. (*APB Opinion No. 11*)	Not accounted for	Partial allocation	Similar to U.S. (*APB Opinion No. 11*)	Not accounted for	Similar to U.S. (*APB Opinion No. 11*)	Not accounted for	Similar to U.S. (*APB Opinion No. 11*)

Source: Adapted from Charles S. Dewhurst, "Accounting for International Operations," *CPA Journal* (January 1988), p. 81.

IASC were the accounting bodies of nine countries: Australia, Canada, France, Japan, Mexico, The Netherlands, the United Kingdom, the United States, and West Germany. Since 1983, the IASC's members have included all of the professional accounting bodies that are members of the International Federation of Accountants. This currently consists of 134 sponsoring organizations in 104 different countries. Most of these organizations are professional associations of licensed public accountants; consequently, the membership of the IASC is comprised of a more narrow range of organizations than the FASB.

The IASC's *Agreement and Constitution* gives it the authority to promulgate standards for the presentation of financial statements that are audited by its member organizations. The constitution of the IASC also establishes its role in promoting worldwide acceptance of IASC standards. This requirement had arisen because many countries did not have a program of developing accounting standards and because of the need to harmonize differences among national standards.[5] Many observers consider harmonization desirable because of the perceived need to increase the reliability of foreign financial statements. Improved decision making would occur because it would no longer be necessary to interpret foreign financial statements and because comparability would be improved.

Although many differences in worldwide financial reporting practices can be explained by environmental differences between countries, some cannot. The IASC is attempting to harmonize the differences that cannot be explained by environmental differences. The aim of the IASC is to formulate and publish accounting standards that are to be observed in the presentation of financial statements and to promote their worldwide acceptance and observance. The members of the IASC agree to support the standards and to use their best endeavors to ensure that published financial statements comply with the standards, to ensure that auditors enforce the standards, and to persuade governments, stock exchanges, and other bodies to back the standards.

The IASC's original intention was to avoid complex details and concentrate on basic standards. IASC standards also allow a range of practices. The standard-setting process of the IASC is similar to that followed by the FASB and includes the following steps:

1.   The Board sets up a Steering Committee.

2.   The Steering Committee identifies and reviews all of the accounting issues associated with the topic. The Steering Committee also considers the application of the IASC's Framework for the Preparation of Financial Statements (discussed later in the chapter) to the identified accounting issues. After completing this process, the Steering Committee submits a Point Outline to the Board.

3.   The Board prepares and submits comments to the Steering Committee on the Point Outline. After reviewing the Board's comments, the Steering

[5] J. A. Hepworth, "International Accounting Standards," *The Chartered Accountant in Australia* Vol. 48, no. 2 (August 1977) pp. 17–19.

Committee prepares and publishes a Draft Statement of Principles. This draft statement sets out the underlying accounting principles that will form the basis for preparing the Exposure Draft. It also describes the alternative solutions considered and the reasons for recommending their acceptance or rejection. Comments are then invited from interested parties.

4. The Steering Committee reviews the comments on the Draft Statement and prepares a final Statement of Principles that is submitted to the Board.

5. The Steering Committee prepares a draft Exposure Draft for approval by the Board. The Board must approve the publication of the Exposure Draft by a two-thirds majority. If approved, the Exposure Draft is published. A comment period of generally six months follows.

6. The Steering Committee reviews the comments and prepares a draft international Accounting Standard for review by the Board. The draft standard must be approved by at least a three-quarters majority. If approved, the Standard is published.

In contrast to standards issued by the FASB, International Accounting Standards (IASs) sometimes permit two accounting treatments for accounting transactions and events. In such cases, the preferable treatment is termed the *benchmark treatment,* whereas the other is termed the *alternative treatment.* Until recently, the IASC did not provide an explanation for the distinction between these two types of treatments. Recently, in the December 1995 issue of *IASC Insight,* it provided the following explanation:

> The Board has concluded that it should use the term "benchmark" instead of the proposed term "preferred" [as proposed in IAS No. 32] in those few cases where it continues to allow a choice of accounting treatment for like transactions and events. The term "benchmark" more closely reflects the Board's intention of identifying a point of reference when making its choice between alternatives.

Although this explanation implies that the IASC intends to reduce the choices available in its standards, elimination of the alternative treatment would decrease comparability with U.S. GAAP in those cases where the alternative rather than the benchmark treatment is similar to U.S. GAAP.

An additional difference in the standard-setting process is that the IASC currently does not issue interpretations of its standards and it prohibits IASC staff from giving advice on the meaning of its standards because of resource constraints. However, the IASC has received criticism for failing to issue interpretations. Critics note that regulators and professional bodies may and are developing procedures for interpreting standards which could detract from the effort to harmonize. The IASC established a system of issuing interpretations by studying:

1. The scope of the interpretation procedure—mature or emerging issues.

2. The nature of the body that provides the interpretations—the Board or a committee.

3. The process for issuing interpretations including questions such as: How are issues requiring interpretation identified? Do interpretations require Board approval? And should they be retroactive?

Subsequently a Standing Interpretations Committee was established that consists of twelve members from various countries. To date it has issued over 20 interpretations.

The Uses of International Accounting Standards

International accounting standards are used in a variety of ways. The IASC has noted that its standards are used[6]

1. As national requirements
2. As the basis for some or all national requirement
3. As an international benchmark for those counties that develop their own requirements
4. By regulatory authorities for domestic and foreign companies
5. By companies themselves

In addition, the International Organization of Securities Commissions (IOSCO) looks to the IASC to provide International Accounting Standards that can be used in multinational securities offerings. Currently, several stock exchanges in different countries require or allow issuers to prepare financial statements in accordance with International Accounting Standards.

The IASC has no enforcement authority and must rely on the "best endeavors" of its members. However, the influence of professional accounting bodies in the formation of accounting rules varies from country to country. In some countries, such as France and Germany, the strength and detail of company law leave little room for influence by accounting bodies. On the other hand, in the United Kingdom, Canada, and Australia accounting standards are actually set by the professional bodies that belong to the IASC. In the United States, the two bodies directly concerned with standard setting, the FASB and the SEC, are not members of the IASC.

The IASC's charter and actions do not accommodate national differences. That is, each nation has its own group of financial information users (owners, lenders, borrowers, employees, government, etc.), all of which operate within the cultural, social, legal, political, and economic environment. The users may also have different relative importance from nation to nation, creating variations in the role of financial accounting from nation to nation.

Several authors have reviewed the difficulty of achieving effective international harmonization. They have generally focused on the extent to which various IASC standards reflect a compromise between differing national requirements. Compromises may be significant for achieving effectiveness in enforcing standards because they reduce a standard's ability to narrow variation in national practices. In addition, compromises are generally made to accommodate these variations. As a result, the standards that form the reporting framework that results from compromises are likely to result in the

---

[6] *International Accounting Standards 1996* (London: International Accounting standards Committee, 1996), p. 12.

adoption of the lowest common denominator of differing national practices. Such standards are likely to have very little effect on practices in those countries that already have comprehensive systems of accounting standards.

To date, the IASC has issued 41 IASs covering a variety of issues such as disclosure of accounting policies; cash flow statements; depreciation; information to be disclosed; the statement of changes in financial position, unusual items, prior period items and changes in accounting policies; research and development; income taxes; foreign exchange; business combinations; and related party disclosures. Each of these standards is discussed in this text in chapters covering the appropriate topic.

Current Issues

In the mid-1990s, the IASC entered into partnership with the IOSCO to work together to encourage stock exchanges throughout the world to accept financial statements prepared under IASC standards. In order to achieve this objective, the IASC was required to complete a comprehensive work program that generated new or revised IASs acceptable to the IOSCO. The IOSCO has indicated that the successful completion of the IASC's work program would result in the promulgation of a comprehensive core set of standards for cross-border listings. It will also allow the IOSCO to consider endorsing International Accounting Standards for listing purposes in all global capital markets. The IOSCO had already endorsed the IASC's: pronouncement on cash flow statements and has indicated that 14 other IASC standards require no improvement, provided that the other core standards are successfully completed. Among the issues addressed in the work program were financial instruments, income taxes, intangibles, segmental reporting, earnings per share, employee benefit costs, interim reporting, discontinued operations, contingencies, and leases. Originally, a target date of December 1999 was set for completing this program; however, in 1996, the IASC Board advanced this date to March 1999. The project is now complete, but the IOACO had not yet endorsed the core set of standards at the time this text was published. (Further developments can be found on the webpage for this text.)

Until recently, IASs promulgated by the IASC have been little more than a curiosity in the United States.[7] This perspective is likely to change because of such factors as the increasing emphasis to transnational reporting and the growth of the global stock market, and a recent proposal to allow foreign companies to list their securities on U.S. stock exchanges using IASC standards (discussed later in the chapter). Therefore, standard-setting bodies need to address the following issues.

1. Can international accounting standards be set voluntarily by organizations representing a broad set of sovereign nations?

2. What impact do differing economies and social settings in various countries have on standard setting?

---

[7] A. Wyatt, "Commentary: Arthur Wyatt on International Accounting Standards: A New Perspective," *Accounting Horizons* (September 1989), p. 105.

3. Can lessons be learned from other international world bodies with sovereign members having experience in bringing conflicting national laws into harmony?

4. Have the major political and economic questions involved in standard setting been examined sufficiently?

5. How can the roadblock of national restrictions be eliminated so that international accounting standards can be enforced?

An argument advanced to support the harmonization of international accounting standards is the growth of multinational corporations and the global stock market. Although U.S. companies seeking listings on foreign stock markets may use U.S. GAAP, many have decided to use the appropriate foreign GAAP or a dual presentation. The growth of international standards will go a long way toward alleviating this problem.

The harmonization of international accounting standards is not a universally accepted goal, with some individuals criticizing this goal of harmonization. These critics maintain that financial reporting must consider the extent to which existing practices reflect specific national environmental characteristics. For example, Zeff contends that the accounting principles peculiar to individual nations develop from the interaction of accounting practice and theory with social, political, and economic factors that are nation-specific.[8]

Others maintain that global capital markets are developing without global GAAP and that global GAAP is not likely to come about because (1) too many national groups have vested interests in maintaining their own standards that have developed from widely different perspectives and histories, and (2) no international body has the authority to issue harmonized accounting principles.[9]

Restructuring the IASC

The IASC completed its work program in 1998 and subsequently embarked on a new effort aimed to address the standard-setting issues outlined earlier. To this end, the IASC Board formed a Strategy Working Party to consider what IASC's strategy and structure should be to meet its new challenges. In December 1998 this group issued a Discussion Paper titled "Shaping the IASC for the Future," which set out its proposals for changing the IASC's structure. During early 1999 comments on the proposal were received and a final report was issued. In March 2000 the IASC Board unamiously approved a new constitution for restructuring the IASC. Following is a summary of the key points addressed in this document.

---

[8] S. A. Zeff, *Forging Accounting Principles in Five Countries: A History and Analysis of Trends* (Champaign, IL: Stripes, 1972).

[9] Richard K. Goeltz, "International Accounting Harmonization: The Impossible (and Unnecessary?) Dream," *Accounting Horizons* (March 1991), pp. 85–88.

Several factors have contributed to the need for new approaches to international standard setting, including:

1. A rapid growth in international capital markets, combined with an increase in cross-border listings and cross-border investment. These issues have led to efforts by securities regulators to develop a common "passport" for cross-border securities listings and to achieve greater comparability in financial reporting.
2. The efforts of global organizations (such as the World Trade Organization) and regional bodies (such as the European Union, NAFTA, MERCOSUR, and APEC) to dismantle barriers to international world trade.
3. A trend toward the internationalization of business regulation.
4. The increasing influence of international accounting standards on national accounting requirements and practice.
5. The acceleration of innovation in business transactions.
6. Users' increasing demand for new types of financial and other performance information.
7. New developments in the electronic distribution of financial and other performance information.
8. A growing need for relevant and reliable financial and other performance information both in countries in transition from planned economies to market economies and in developing and newly industrialized economies.

As a result, a demand has arisen for high-quality global accounting standards that provide transparency and comparability. Consequently, the IASC's role in the future is unlikely to be the same as it was in the past. In its early years, IASC acted mainly as a harmonizer—a body that selects an accounting treatment that already exists at the national level in some countries and then seeks worldwide acceptance of that treatment, perhaps with some modifications. Recently, it has begun to combine that role with the role of a catalyst— a coordinator of national initiatives and an initiator of new work at the national level. In the future, IASC's role as catalyst and initiator should become more prominent, and it is important for the IASC to focus objectives more precisely, as follows:

1. To develop international accounting standards that require high-quality, transparent, and comparable information that will help participants in capital markets and others to make economic decisions; and
2. To promote the use of international accounting standards by working with national standard setters.

The IASC, in partnership with national standard setters, should make every effort to accelerate convergence between national accounting standards and international accounting standards. The goal of this convergence is for enterprises in all countries to report high-quality, transparent, and comparable information that will help participants in capital markets and others to make economic decisions. To this end, the IASC should continue to use an agreed conceptual framework (the Framework for the Preparation and Presentation of Financial Statements discussed in the following section). IASC's short-term aim should be to effect the convergence of national accounting standards and international accounting standards around high-quality solutions. However, its aim in the longer term should be global uniformity—a single set of high-quality accounting standards for all listed and other economically significant business enterprises around the world.

The changes in IASC's environment mean that structural changes are needed so that IASC can anticipate the new challenges facing it and meet those challenges effectively. The following were identified as issues that need to be addressed:

1. **Partnership with national standard setters.** IASC should enter into a partnership with national standard setters so that IASC can work together with them to accelerate convergence between national standards and international accounting standards around solutions requiring high-quality, transparent, and comparable information that will help participants in capital markets and others to make economic decisions.

2. **Wider participation in the IASC Board.** A wider group of countries and organizations should take part in the IASC Board without diluting the quality of the Board's work.

3. **Appointment.** The process for appointments to the IASC Board and key IASC committees should be the responsibility of a variety of constituencies, while ensuring that those appointed are competent, independent, and objective.

In order to address these key issues, the following changes have been proposed:

1. The Steering Committees should be replaced by a Standards Development Committee, on which national standard setters would play a major role in developing international accounting standards for approval by the IASC Board. The Standards Development Committee would also be responsible for approving the publication of final SIC Interpretations prepared by the Standing Interpretations Committee.

2. The Standards Development Committee should be supported by a Standards Development Advisory Committee, which would act as a channel of communication with those national standard setters who are unable to participate directly in the Standards Development Committee because of its limited size.

3. The IASC Board should be expanded from 16 to 25 countries and organizations, without diluting the quality of the Board's work.

4. The current Advisory Council should be replaced by 12 Trustees (three appointed by the International Federation of Accountants, three by other international organizations, and six by the Trustees to represent the world "at large." The Trustees would appoint members of the Standards

Development Committee, the Board, and the Standing Interpretations Committee. The Trustees would also have responsibility for monitoring IASC's effectiveness and for financing the IASC's activities.

FASB Reaction

The Financial Accounting Foundation (FAF) and the Financial Accounting Standards Board (FASB) were among the organizations accepting the IASC's invitations to comment on the Discussion Paper. Their position was somewhat critical and included the following points.

Because of the IASC's current position as an international standard-setting organization, the need for restructuring the international accounting standard-setting structure and process provides the IASC with an opportunity to establish a quality international accounting standard setter that will be successful over the long term. The FAF and the FASB believe that the IASC restructuring process should result in a standard-setting structure and process that embodies the eight functions and five characteristics. The eight essential functions of a quality international standard setter are leadership, innovation, relevance, responsiveness, objectivity, acceptability and credibility, understandability, and accountability. The five essential characteristics of a quality international standard setter are an independent decision-making body, adequate due process, adequate, technically qualified staff, independent fundraising, and independent oversight.

The existing IASC structure and process do not adequately embody all of those functions and characteristics. To achieve that goal, the following areas addressed in the Discussion Paper should be modified or strengthened:

1. The Standards Development Committee (SDC) should be an autonomous and independent decision-making body; that is, the SDC should have full and final authority to set its own agenda and to approve exposure drafts and standards. Representatives on the SDC should be highly qualified, technically competent individuals who would be independent of outside affiliations and function to serve only the public interest. (That is, members of the SDC should serve full-time and should sever ties with employers.)

2. The IASC Board should enjoy a strong advisory role in the standard-setting process. That would ensure adequate geographic and functional input to the standard-setting process and maintain liaison between the SDC and the business and professional worlds. The IASC Board should work closely with the SDC but should have no authority to override SDC decisions. Representatives on the IASC Board should be technically conversant in accounting and financial reporting issues and should be selected based on their ability to make a contribution to the development of high-quality accounting standards.

3. The Board of Trustees should have the responsibilities of (1) appointing SDC and IASC Board members and reviewing and ratifying appointments and renewals of individual representatives that would serve on those bodies, (2) exercising oversight and evaluating the SDC and the

IASC Board, with power to effect changes not subject to approval by another body, such as the IASC Board or International Federation of Accountants (IFAC) membership, and (3) raising funds. Members of the Board of Trustees should be well-respected business and professional leaders from throughout the world, with the ability to devote sufficient time to carry out their responsibilities.

4. The staff of the IASC should initially be supplemented by staff at national level organizations. Independently, it should be large enough and qualified to support the administrative needs of the entire IASC organization, provide technical support for IASC projects, including leading IASC projects in areas that already are covered by national standards, support the IASC's Standing Interpretations Committee (SIC), monitor proposals by national standard setters and others for projects or interpretations, identify inconsistencies that might arise, and answer questions about existing IASC standards that would be provided by organizations participating on the SDC.

In addition, several areas must be strengthened and improved, including:

1. *Standards approval process.* The proposal that the IASC Board should have veto power over standards developed and approved by the SDC would undermine the autonomy and efficiency of the SDC and the resulting quality of the standards. It also would be a disincentive to participation. The SDC should have final authority to issue exposure drafts and standards. We suggest an alternative role for the IASC Board.

2. *Role and responsibilities of the Board of Trustees.* The description of the proposed Board of Trustees and its relationship with the IASC Board raises questions about the appointment of Trustees, the appointment process for IASC Board delegates, and the Trustees' ultimate role and authority to oversee the IASC structure and process. We believe that a more definite proposal for Trustee appointment is desirable. We also believe the Trustees should have a stronger role in appointing delegates to the IASC Board and have authority to review and effect changes to the IASC structure and process as necessary.

3. *Funding and other resources.* Suggested sources of funding and resources are not well defined, and the resource commitment of participants is difficult to gauge. The resources the SDC would require from national standard setters should be more clearly set forth. A detailed analysis and presentation of the actual (direct and indirect) costs anticipated should be prepared, and a plan for obtaining sources of funding should be identified.

4. *Other issues.* Certain other important areas are not fully addressed in the Discussion Paper, including composition and criteria for SDC and IASC Board membership, rotation of membership and permanent seats on the SDC, IASC Board, and Board of Trustees, and coordination of the various national due processes of the IASC staff. We disagree with the Discussion Paper's proposals in some of those areas, and we believe that the coverage of others is incomplete. Those areas must be more fully considered before the viability of the proposed structure and process can be evaluated fully.

In addition to addressing these areas, the FASB indicated that the IASC should articulate a long-range plan for achieving the ideal international accounting standard setting process and structure. It should acknowledge that its proposal is an initial step in the evolution of international accounting. These issues are addressed further in the FASB's position paper, "International Accounting Standards: A Vision for the Future," discussed later in the chapter.

International vs. National Accounting Standards

The development of a comprehensive set of IASs will also have an impact on the United States' securities markets. In February 2000, the Securities and Exchange Commission voted to ask U.S. companies to comment on whether it should allow foreign companies to list their securities on U.S. stock exchanges under international accounting rules. Currently, foreign companies seeking to list on a U.S. stock exchange must recast their financial statements to reflect current GAAP. This reconciliation is made by filing a Form 20-F with the SEC within six months of the company's fiscal year-end. At the present time, only about 1000 foreign companies currently list on U.S. stock exchanges because of the high cost involved in recasting their financial statements to U.S. GAAP. To date, the SEC has consistently taken the position that allowing foreign firms to list using other than U.S. GAAP will result in a loss of investor protection and result in a two-tiered disclosure system, one for domestic registrants and another for foreign registrants. Thus far, there has been little empirical evidence on which to evaluate the SEC's position. One recent study found mixed evidence in that the Form 20-F reconciliation was found to be value relevant and IAS and U.S. GAAP earnings amounts were valued differently by the marketplace. However, the study did not show that the market valued earnings per share amounts differently.[10]

The text's webpage for Chapter 6 contains excerpts from an Annual Report and a Form 20-F Reconciliation for Cadbury Schweppes. The company is a domestic company in the United Kingdom that markets and produces confectionaries, beverages, and other products for sale worldwide. Among its products are Dr Pepper, Schweppes, Canada Dry, A & W, and Squirt internationally, and Seven Up and Mott's beverages in the United States only. The company wishes to sell securities in the U.S. capital markets; consequently, it must prepare a Form 20-F reconciliation that adjusts its financial statements to comply with U.S. GAAP.

Footnote 31 to the financial statements contains a summary of the effects on profits and shareholders' equity due to the differences between U.K. and U.S. GAAP. This summary reveals that 1999 reported profits under GAAP were £594 million or £48 million less than those reported under U.K. GAAP, whereas total shareholders' equity increased by £924 million to

---

[10] Mary S. Harris and Karl A. Muller III, "The Market Valuation of IAS Versus US GAAP Accounting Measures Using Form 20-F Reconciliations," *Journal of Accounting and Economics* (1999), pp. 285–312.

£3,164 billion when the company's financial statements were adjusted to comply with U.S. GAAP.

The SEC is under increasing pressure to accept international accounting rules because worldwide investors need help in deciphering the financial statements of various companies using country-by-country accounting rules. The Cadbury Schweppes Form 20-F reconciliation illustrates the magnitude of this problem. It has also been reported that it took the German auto manufacturer Daimler-Benz AG years to convert its books to U.S. GAAP in order to complete its merger with Chrysler. The New York Stock Exchange, which would profit from additional foreign listings, supports the international effort. A recent study of eight multinational companies found that using the international rules discloses essentially the same financial results as is disclosed by the use of U.S. GAAP.[11]

Nevertheless, the SEC is unlikely to approve the use of international standards in the near future. Both former Treasury Secretary Robert Rubin and Federal Reserve Chairman Alan Greenspan have criticized current international accounting rules as poor accounting, and they have indicated that the financial difficulties experienced in Brazil and Russia in the late 1990s were partially attributable to poor accounting disclosure policies.[12] It is also difficult to envision that U.S. companies, which would still be held to the stricter U.S. GAAP, will approve less strict rules for foreign companies competing for the sources of capital available in the United States. Finally, the international rules do not have an enforcement mechanism similar to the U.S. Securities and Exchange Commission, and there is an increased likelihood that investors might be misled. This issue is still evolving and will be periodically updated on the text's webpage.

Framework for the Preparation and Presentation of Financial Statements

In 1989, the IASC issued its conceptual framework titled "Framework for the Preparation and Presentation of Financial Statements." The IASC indicated that the purpose of this pronouncement was to set out the concepts that underlie the preparation and presentation of financial statements for external users by

1. Assisting the IASC in developing future accounting standards.
2. Promoting harmonization of accounting standards.
3. Assisting national standard setters.
4. Assisting preparers in applying international standards.
5. Assisting auditors in forming an opinion as to whether financial statements conform to international standards.

---

[11] Ibid.

[12] Elizabeth MacDonald, "U.S. Firms Likely to Balk at SEC Move to Ease Listing of Foreign Companies," *Wall Street Journal,* February 18, 2000, pp. A3–4.

6. Assisting users in interpreting financial statements prepared in conformity with international standards.

7. Providing interested parties with information about the IASC's approach to the formation of international accounting standards.

The framework specifies:

1. The objective of financial statements.

2. The qualitative characteristics that determine the usefulness of information in financial statements.

3. The definition, recognition, and measurement of the elements from which financial statements are constructed.

4. The concepts of capital and capital maintenance.

The framework indicates that companies prepare general-purpose financial statements that are directed toward the information needs of a wide variety of users including investors, employees, lenders, suppliers and other trade creditors, customers, governments and their agencies, and the general public. The framework also indicates that, although the information needs of these users cannot be met solely by the presentation of financial statements, there are needs that are common to all users. In addition, since investors are the providers of risk capital to the enterprise, the preparation of financial statements that meet their needs will also satisfy most of the needs of other users.

The Objective of Financial Statements

The framework indicates that the objective of financial statements is to provide information about the financial position, performance, and changes in financial position of an enterprise that is useful to a wide range of users making economic decisions. It also indicates that financial statements prepared for this purpose will satisfy most user needs, but that they do not provide all information that may be needed to make economic decisions because they largely portray past information and do not provide nonfinancial information.

In its discussion of general-purpose financial statements, the framework indicated the following:

1. Users require an evaluation of an enterprise's ability to generate cash and the timing and certainty of this generation.

2. The financial position of an enterprise is affected by the economic resources it controls, its financial structure, its liquidity and solvency, and its capacity to adapt to changes in its environment.

3. Information on profitability is required to assess changes in the economic resources an enterprise controls in the future.

4. Information on the financial position of an enterprise is useful in assessing its investing, financing, and operating activities.

5. Information about financial position is contained in the balance sheet, and information about performance is contained in an income statement.

The framework also indicated that two underlying assumptions for the preparation of financial statements were the *accrual basis* and *going concern.*

Qualitative Characteristics

The framework describes qualitative characteristics as the attributes that make the information provided in financial statements useful. The following four principal qualitative characteristics were defined.

Understandability

Information should be provided so that individuals with a reasonable knowledge of business and economic activities and accounting and a willingness to study the information are capable of using it. Nevertheless, complex information should not be withheld because it is too difficult for some users to understand.

Relevance

Information is relevant when it influences the economic decisions of users by helping them to evaluate past, present, or future events or by confirming or correcting their past evaluations. Relevance is also affected by materiality.

Reliability

Information is reliable when it is free from material error and bias and when users can depend on it to represent faithfully that which it purports to represent. As a consequence, events should be accounted for and presented in accordance with their substance and economic reality, not merely their legal form.

Comparability

Users must be able to compare an enterprise's performance over time and to make comparisons with the performance of other enterprises.

The framework also recognized that timeliness and the balance between benefits and costs were constraints on providing both relevant and reliable information.

The Elements of Financial Statements

The framework stated that financial statements portray the financial effects of transactions and other events by grouping them into broad classes according to their economic characteristics. These characteristics are the elements of financial statements. It indicated that the elements directly related to the measurement of financial position in the balance sheet are assets, liabilities, and equity. These elements were defined as follows:

Asset: A resource controlled by an enterprise as a result of past events from which future economic benefits are expected to flow to the enterprise.

Liability: A present obligation of the enterprise arising from past events, the settlement of which is expected to result in an outflow from the enterprise of resources embodying economic benefits.

Equity: The residual interest in the assets of the enterprise after deducting all its liabilities.

the elements directly related to the measurement of performance in the income statement are income and expenses. These elements were defined as follows:

Income: Increases in economic benefits during the accounting period in the form of inflows or enhancement of assets or the decreases in liabilities that result in increases in equity, other than those relating to contributions from equity participants.

Expenses: Decreases in economic benefits during the accounting period in the form of outflows or depletions of assets or incurrences of liabilities that result in decreases in equity, other than those relating to contributions from equity participants.

The framework went on to indicate that recognition is the process of incorporating in the financial statements an item that meets the definition of an element and satisfies the following recognition criteria: (a) It is probable that any future economic benefit associated with the item will flow to or from the enterprise; and (b) the item has a cost or value that can be measured with reliability.

Finally, with respect to recognition, the framework defined *measurement* as the process of determining the monetary amounts at which the elements of the financial statements are to be recognized and carried. It also indicated that a variety of measurement bases are employed in financial statements, including historical cost, current cost, realizable value, and present value.

Concepts of Capital and Capital Maintenance

The final issue addressed in the framework were concepts of capital. Under the financial concept of capital, capital was defined as being synonymous with the net assets or equity of the enterprise. Under a physical concept of capital, capital is regarded as the productive capacity of the enterprise. The framework indicated that the selection of the appropriate concept of capital by an enterprise should be based on the needs of the user of its financial statements. As a consequence, a financial concept of capital should be adopted if users are concerned primarily with the maintenance of nominal invested capital or the purchasing power of invested capital. However, if the users' main concern is with the operating capacity of an enterprise, a physical concept of capital should be used. As a result, the following concepts of capital maintenance may be used:

Financial capital maintenance. Profit is earned only if the financial (or money) amount of net assets at the end of the period exceeds the net asset at the beginning of the period, excluding any distributions to or contributions from owners.

Physical capital maintenance. Profit is earned only if the physical productive capacity (or operating capacity) of the enterprise exceeds the physical productive capacity at the beginning of the period.

Finally, the framework noted that the selection of the measurement bases and concept of capital maintenance will determine the accounting model used in preparing financial statements. Also, since different accounting models differ with respect to relevance and reliability, management must seek a balance between these qualitative characteristics. At the current time, the IASC does not intend to prescribe a particular model other than for exceptional circumstances, such as for reporting in the currency of a hyperinflationary economy.

IAS No. 1

In *IAS No. 1*, "Presentation of Financial Statements," the IASC discussed the following considerations for preparing financial statements:

1. Fair presentation and compliance with IASC standards
2. Accounting policies
3. Going concern
4. Accrual basis of accounting
5. Consistency of presentation
6. Materiality and aggregation
7. Offsetting
8. Comparative information

The guidance for applying these considerations is somewhat less detailed than that provided by U.S. GAAP: however, in general it results in similar requirements.

In its review of *IAS No. 1*, the FASB staff noted that one possible area of difference was in the application of the concept of fair presentation. Although both standard-setting bodies allow for departures from standards when their application would result in misleading financial statements, the IASC approach was seen as allowing more flexibility in departing from standards. The FASB went on to note that such departures are almost nonexistent in the United States, whereas they are more common in other countries. Thus there is a greater possibility of a difference in the interpretation of fair presentation criteria for IASC reporting enterprises than for U.S. GAAP reporting enterprises.[13]

International Accounting Standard Setting: A Vision for the Future

In 1998, The FASB issued a report titled *International Accounting Standard Setting: A Vision for the Future.* The introduction to this report noted that the evolution of a global society carries with it many implications that in the past have been considered areas of national authority or responsibility. Financial

---

[13] Financial Accounting Standards Board, *The IASC-U.S. Comparison Project: A Report on the Similarities and Differences between IASC Standards and U.S. GAAP,* Carrie Bloom, ed., 2nd ed. (Norwalk, CT: Financial Accounting Standards Board, 1999), pp. 63–87.

reporting and standard setting are among these implications. The report goes on to discuss how the FASB's role may continue to evolve and how its structure and processes may change over time in response to the needs of the changing international environment within the context of the FASB's objective. Included in the report are (1) a discussion of the FASB's objective and related goals; (2) the FASB's vision of the international accounting system of the future; (3) a discussion of the characteristics of high-quality accounting standards; and (4) a discussion of the minimum fluctuations and characteristics of a quality international accounting standard setter.

The FASB describes *international standards* as a set of accounting standards that are internationally recognized as acceptable through, for example, endorsement by the relevant capital market authorities of individual nations and through acceptance by financial statement users. The FASB has concluded that whatever the ultimate function of international standards, their use will affect financial reporting in the United States, and, therefore, the FASB must participate in the process that leads to their development. The FASB's meaningful participation in the development of international standards is necessary in order to ensure that future international standards are of sufficient quality to be acceptable in the United States. In addition, the FASB believes that, for the long term, if the future international accounting system is to succeed and, ultimately, result in the use of a single set of high-quality accounting standards worldwide for both domestic and cross-border financial reporting, the establishment of a quality international accounting standard setter to coordinate and direct the process is key.

To this end, the FASB has stipulated two related goals:

1. To ensure that international accounting standards are of the highest quality, *high-quality* financial reporting is financial reporting that provides useful information for outside investors, creditors, and others who make similar decisions about the allocation of resources in the economy. The FASB has reached consensus that a set of high-quality international standards is desirable because their use would improve international comparability; reduce costs to financial statement users, preparers, auditors, and others; and, ultimately, optimize the efficiency of capital markets.

2. To accelerate the convergence of the accounting standards used in different nations. Convergence is both a goal and a process. The FASB describes the *goal of convergence* as different standard setters arriving at high-quality national or international standards on the same topic that are as similar as possible.

The FASB believes that sacrificing quality for convergence or focusing on arriving at consensus rather than the best possible solution in the circumstances does a disservice to the consumers of financial reporting, that is, financial statement users, and undermines the credibility and efficiency of global capital markets. Although it is difficult to define "high quality," the FASB believes that a number of attributes of high-quality accounting standards can be identified. A reasonably complete set of unbiased accounting standards that require relevant, reliable information that is useful for out-side investors, creditors, and others who make similar decisions would con-stitute a high-quality set of accounting standards. Each of those accounting standards should

1. Be consistent with the guidance provided by an underlying conceptual framework.
2. Avoid or minimize alternative accounting procedures, explicit or implicit, because comparability and consistency enhance the usefulness of infor-mation.
3. Be unambiguous and comprehensible so that the standard is under-standable by preparers and auditors who must apply the standard, by authorities who must enforce the standard, and by users who must deal with the information produced by the standard.
4. Be capable of rigorous interpretation and application so that similar events and transactions are accounted for similarly across time periods and among companies.

Overall, financial reporting under such standards should result in trans-parent information. *Transparent information* is sufficient in its content and readily comprehensible so as to provide a meaningful basis for economic decision making by financial statement users. Transparent information does not obscure information relevant to economic decision making. In that con-text, a set of high-quality accounting standards should result in accounting information that is irrelevant. *Relevant information* is capable of making a dif-ference in a decision by helping users to form judgments about the outcomes of past, present, and future events or to confirm or correct prior expectations. Such information also should be reliable, neutral, comparable, and consistent as defined by the FASB.

Reliable: Reliable information faithfully represents what it purports to represent, and that quality of representational faithfulness is verifiable using independent measures.

Neutral: Neutral information is not biased toward a predetermined result.

Comparable: Comparable information can be meaningfully compared with similar information about other enterprises. Information is comparable if similar transactions and events are accounted for similarly, and different transactions and events are accounted for differently.

Consistent: Consistent information can be meaningfully compared with similar information about the same enterprise for some other period or some other point in time.

A great deal of progress toward increasing international comparability and the quality of accounting standards can be made through the inde-pendent cooperative efforts of standard setters, but for the international accounting system of the future to be successful and efficient, a quality

International standard setter is needed. As such, it is important to have some guidelines for moving toward that goal. Establishment of such an organization may occur in any number of ways. For example, a structurally changed International Accounting Standards Committee (IASC) might succeed; a successor international organization might emerge and build on what the IASC has done, or the FASB might be modified to become more acceptable internationally. The characteristics this organization should possess are (1) an independent decision-making body, (2) adequate due process, (3) adequate staff, (4) independent fundraising, and (5) independent oversight.

The FASB believes it has a leadership role to play in the evolution of the international accounting system. That will require that a high and increasing level of resources be devoted to positioning the FASB as a strong influence on the establishment of a quality international accounting standard-setting organization. If a quality international accounting standard-setting structure and process emerges, the FASB's commitment and desire to participate in a meaningful way in the operations of that standard-setting organization may ultimately lead to structural and procedural changes to the FASB, a shift in the FASB's national role, and a substantial contribution of resources to the international standard-setting process. At the same time, the FASB believes it is important to maintain its program of improving U.S. national standards in order to meet the objective of high-quality accounting standards (whether national or international standards) in the United States.

G4 + 1

In 1988, the then chairman of the Financial Accounting Standards Board, Dennis Beresford, suggested that international standard setters should meet to discuss common interests. Subsequently, standard setters from approximately 40 countries met in 1993. However, it soon became apparent that the standard-setting process was too diverse across the spectrum of countries; consequently, a smaller group was formed. This group was called the G4 + 1 because it included standard setters from the United States, Canada, the United Kingdom, and Australia, with the IASC acting as an observer. Later, the group was expanded to include New Zealand. The G4 + 1 meets approximately four times a year to analyze and discuss financial reporting issues. Commencing in August 1998, the Group decided to produce a Communiqué after each meeting. The Group has also prepared a series of position papers and special reports to promote discussion of issues that may lead standard setters to develop new and improved accounting standards. However, its positions are not binding on the organizations which the members of the G4 + 1 represent. Among the issues it has deliberated are stock-based compensation, the equity method of accounting, and financial instruments. The activities of the G4 + 1 are discussed in more detail in the readings by Dennis Beresford and Stephen Zeff contained on the webpage for Chapter 6.

The Financial Statement Impact of International Accounting Standards

In 1996 the FASB released the results of a project whose objective was to analyze the financial statement impact of the similarities and differences between IASC Standards and U.S. GAAP.[14] Later, in 1999 this study was updated to incorporate additional standards not covered in the original publication.[15] Each IASC standard was analyzed in an attempt to:

1. Identify similarities and differences of the IAS standard to U.S. GAAP
2. Assess the impact of these similarities and differences and their relative significance
3. Include examples wherever possible

These issues are discussed in more detail in the chapters of the text that address the topics covered by individual IASC standards.

Summary

Financial accounting is influenced by the environment in which it operates. A country's financial accounting policies are determined by the interaction of many variables relating to its history, values, and political and economic systems. U.S. companies increasingly must be able to compete in a global economy. This factor is complicated by the differences in accounting standards between countries. The International Accounting Standards Committee (IASC) was formed in 1973 to develop worldwide accounting standards. It is an independent private-sector body whose objective is to achieve uniformity in the accounting principles used for worldwide financial reporting. To this end, the IASC recently announced a plan to restructure the organization. The IASC has also developed a Framework for Financial Reporting to assist in the development of accounting standards. The FASB has become increasingly interested in the development of international accounting standards and has published a report outlining its views on the issue. The FASB also issues a response to the IASC's restructuring plan. In the readings contained on the text's webpage for Chapter 6, some additional international accounting issues are examined.

---

[14] Financial Accounting Standards Board, *The IASC-U.S. Comparison Project: A Report on the Similarities and Differences between IASC Standards and U.S. GAAP,* Carrie Bloom, ed., (Norwalk, CT: FASB, 1996).

[15] FASB, *The IASC-U.S. Comparison Project, op.cit.*

Cases

• Case 6-1 The Advantages and Disadvantages of Harmonization

The advantages and disadvantages of harmonizing accounting standards were summarized in this chapter.

Required:
Expand on these advantages and disadvantages. (*Hint:* You may wish to consult John N. Turner, "International Harmonization: A Professional Goal," *Journal of Accountancy* (January 1983), pp. 58–59; and Richard K. Goeltz, "International Accounting Harmonization: The Impossible [and Unnecessary?] Dream," *Accounting Horizons* (March 1991), pp. 85–88.)

• Case 6-2 The Approaches to Transnational Financial Reporting

Five approaches to transnational financial reporting were identified in the chapter.

Required:
a.   List some of the advantages and disadvantages of each approach.
b.   Which approach do you favor? Why?

• Case 6-3 The Purpose and Objectives of the IASC

The International Accounting Standards Committee (IASC) was formed in 1973.

Required:
a.   What is the purpose of the IASC?
b.   How does the IASC attempt to achieve its objectives?

• Case 6-4 Qualitative Characteristics Identified by the IASC

The International Accounting Standards Committee's Framework for the Preparation of Financial Statements identifies four primary qualitative characteristics.

Required:
a.   Discuss the four qualitative characteristics identified by the IASC.
b.   Contrast and compare these qualitative characteristics with the qualitative characteristics identified by the FASB in SFAC No. 2.

• Case 6-5 International vs. U.S. Standards

Under U.S. GAAP, property, plant, and equipment are reported at historical cost net of accumulated depreciation. These assets are written down to fair value when it is determined that they have been impaired.

A number of other countries, including Australia, Brazil, England, Mexico, and Singapore, permit the revaluation of property, plant, and equipment to their current cost as of the balance sheet date. The primary argument favoring revaluation is that the historical cost of assets purchased 10, 20, or 30 years ago is not meaningful. A primary argument against revaluation is the lack of objectivity in arriving at current cost estimates, particularly for old assets that either will or cannot be replaced with similar assets or for which there are no comparable or similar assets currently available for purchase.

Required:
a. Discuss the qualitative concept of comparability. In your opinion, would the financial statements of companies operating in one of the foreign countries listed above be comparable to a U.S. company's financial statements? Explain.
b. Discuss the concept of reliability. In your opinion, would the amounts reported by U.S. companies for property, plant, and equipment be more or less reliable than the current cost amounts reported by companies in England, Mexico, etc.?
c. Discuss the concept of relevance. In your opinion, would the amounts reported by U.S. companies for property, plant, and equipment be more or less relevant than the current cost amounts reported by companies in England, Mexico, etc.?

• Case 6-6 Accounting Standards

General Motors and Ford use LIFO to value their inventories. Honda (of Japan) and Daimler-Benz use FIFO. Under LIFO, recent costs are expensed as cost of goods sold; under FIFO, older costs are expensed as cost of goods sold.

Required:
a. Given the income statement effects of LIFO versus FIFO, how will the balance sheet inventory amounts differ between General Motors, Ford and Honda, and Daimler-Benz? In other words, will inventory be reported amounts representing recent costs or older historical costs? In your opinion, which balance sheet amounts would be more useful to financial statement users in making decisions to buy or sell shares of a company's stock?
b. Discuss the concept of conservatism. In your opinion, which is more conservative, General Motors, and Ford or Honda and Daimler-Benz? Explain.

Room for Debate

• Issue 1

The IASC framework for preparing and presenting financial statements defines assets as resources controlled by an enterprise as a result of past events from which future economic benefits are expected to flow to the enterprise. This definition is similar to that found in the FASB's conceptual framework.

As discussed in Chapter 15, the IASC requires consolidation of a subsidiary when the parent has the ability to control the subsidiary. In these cases, the subsidiary's assets are added to those of the parent company, and the total is reported in the balance sheet of the parent company. Under *SFAS No. 94*, consolidation is required only for those subsidiaries when the parent company has a majority ownership. The FASB has proposed that U.S. GAAP be changed to require consolidation for subsidiaries when the parent company controls the use of subsidiary assets. One goal of this proposal is harmonization of accounting standards among countries.

Team Debate:

Team 1.   Assume that you do not believe that control of subsidiary assets implies that those assets are, in substance, parent company assets. Argue for the FASB proposal based on the premise that harmonization of accounting standards among countries should be the paramount consideration. Cite relevant aspects of the U.S. and IASC conceptual frameworks in your argument.

Team 2.   Assume that you do not believe that control of subsidiary assets implies that those assets are, in substance, parent company assets. Argue against the FASB proposal based on the premise that harmonization of accounting standards among countries should not be the paramount consideration. Cite relevant aspects of the U.S. and IASC conceptual frameworks.

Recommended Additional Readings

American Accounting Association Financial Accounting Standards Committee. "Response to the IASC Discussion Paper: Shaping the IASC for the Future." *Accounting Horizons* (December 1999), pp. 443–452.

Barth, Mary E. "International Accounting Harmonization and Global Equity Markets." *Journal of Accounting and Economics* (January 1999), pp. 201–236.

Bloom, Robert. "Two Vision Statements on International Accounting Standard Setting." *Ohio CPA Journal* (January–March 2000), pp. 24–27.

Canfield, Christopher. "FASB v. IASC: Are the Structure and Standard Setting Process at the IASC Adequate for the Securities and Exchange Commission to Accept International Accounting Standards for Cross Border Offerings?" *Northwestern Journal of International Law and Business* (Fall 1999), pp. 125–144.

Daley, L. A., and G. G. Mueller. "Accounting in the Arena of World Politics." *Journal of Accountancy* (February 1982), pp. 40–46, 48, 50.

Financial Accounting Standards Board. *The IASC-U.S. Comparison Project: A Report on the Similarities and Differences between IASC Standards and U.S. GAAP.* 2nd ed. Carrie Bloom, ed. (Norwalk, CT: Financial Accounting Standards Board, 1999).

Goeltz, R. K. "International Accounting Harmonization: The Impossible (and Unnecessary?) Dream." *Accounting Horizons* (March 1991), pp. 85–88.

Gould, John D. "A Second Opinion on International Accounting Standards." *The CPA Journal* (January 1995), pp. 50–53.

Grove, Hugh D., and John D. Basley. "Disclosure Strategies for Harmonization of International Accounting Standards." *International Journal of Accounting Education and Research,*" Vol. 28, No. 2 (1993), pp. 116–128.

Harris, Mary. "The Market Valuation of IAS versus US-GAAP Accounting Measures Using Form 20-F Reconciliations." *Journal of Accounting and Economics* (January 1999), pp. 285–312.

Hofstede, G., "The Cultural Relativity of Organizational Practices and Theories." *Journal of International Business Studies* (Fall 1983), pp. 25–89.

Hofstede, G., "The Cultural Context of Accounting." In B. E. Cushing, (ed), *Accounting and Culture*. Sarasota, FL: American Accounting Association, 1987.

Most, Kenneth S. "Toward the International Harmonization of Accounting." *Advances in International Accounting*, Vol. 6 (1994), pp. 3–14.

Nobes, Christopher. "Toward a General Model of the Reasons for International Differences in Financial Reporting." *Abacus* (September 1998), pp. 162–188.

Pownall, Grace. "Implications of Accounting Research for the SEC's Consideration of International Accounting Standards for U.S. Securities Offerings." *Accounting Horizons* (September 1999), pp. 259–280.

Pratt, J., and G. Behr. "Environmental Factors, Transaction Costs and External Reporting: A Cross National Comparison." *International Journal of Accounting, Education and Research* (Spring 1987), pp. 159–175.

Schwartz, Donald. "The Future of Financial Accounting: Universal Standards." *Journal of Accountancy* (May 1996), pp. 20–21.

Turner, Lynn E. "Auditing, Earnings Management, and International Accounting Issues at the Securities and Exchange Commission." *Accounting Horizons* (September 1999), pp. 281–298.

Van Hulle, K. "The EC Experience of Harmonization: Part I." *Accountancy* (September 1989), pp. 76–77.

Van Hulle, K. "The EC Experience of Harmonization: Part II." *Accountancy* (October 1989), pp. 96–99.

Wyatt, Arthur R., and Joseph F. Yospe. "Wake-up Call to U.S. Business; International Accounting Standards Are on the Way." *Journal of Accountancy* (July 1993), pp. 80–85.

Bibliography

Al-Hashim, Dhia D., and Jeffrey S. Arpan. *International Dimensions of Accounting*. Boston, MA: PWS-Kent Publishing Company, 1993.

Benson, Sir Henry. "International Accounting—The Challenges of the Future." *Journal of Accountancy* (November 1977), pp. 93–96.

Berton, Lee. "Arthur Young Professors' Roundtable: The International World of Accounting." *Journal of Accountancy* (August 1980), pp. 74–79.

Brown, Jan G. "The Development of International Accounting Standards." *Woman CPA* (October 1977), pp. 9–11.

Cairns, David. "A New Thrust for International Standards." *The Accountant's Magazine* (July 1987), pp. 24–25.

Choi, F.D.S., and V. B. Bavishi. "International Accounting Standards: Issues Needing Attention." *Journal of Accountancy* (March 1983), pp. 62–68.

Choi, Frederick D. S., and Gerhard G. Mueller. *International Accounting*. Englewood Cliffs, NJ: Prentice-Hall, 1984.

Dewhurst, Charles S. "Accounting for International Operations." *The CPA Journal* (January 1988), pp. 78–81.

Evans, T. G., and M. E. Taylor. "Bottom Line Compliance with the IASC: A Comparative Analysis." *International Journal of Accounting* (Fall 1982), pp. 115–128.

Gould, J., D.J.P. McAllister, and L. L. Orsini. "Raising Capital Overseas." *Journal of Accountancy* (February 1997), pp. 33–37.

Hamid, Shaari, Russsell Craig, and Frank Clark. "Religion A Confounding Cultural Element in the International Harmonization of Accounting." *Abacus* (September 1993), pp. 131–148.

Hayes, Donald. "The International Accounting Standards Committee—Recent Developments and Current Problems." *International Journal of Accounting* (Fall 1980), pp. 1–10.

Kanaga, William S. "International Accounting: The Challenge and the Changes." *Journal of Accountancy* (November 1980), pp. 55–60.

Kirkpatrick, John L. "The Gaps in International GAAP." *Corporate Accounting* (Fall 1985), pp. 3–10.

Mueller, Gerhard G., Helen Gernon, and Gary Meek. *Accounting, An International Perspective.* 3rd ed. Homewood, IL: Richard D. Irwin, 1994.

Nobes, Christopher. "Is the IASC Successful?" *The Accountant* (August 21–28, 1985), pp. 20–21.

Nobes, Christopher, and Robert Parker, (eds). *Comparative International Accounting.* Homewood, IL: Richard D. Irwin, 1981.

Taylor, Stephen L. "International Accounting Standards: An Alternative Rationale." *Abacus* (September 1987), pp. 157–171.

Turner, J. N. "International Harmonization: A Professional Goal." *Journal of Accountancy* (January 1983), pp. 58–64, 66.

Violet, William J. "A Philosophical Perspective on the Development of International Accounting Standards." *International Journal of Accounting Education and Research* (Fall 1983), pp. 1–13.

Watt, George C., Richard M. Hammer, and Marianne Burge. *Accounting for the Multinational Corporation.* New York: Financial Executives Research Foundation, 1978.

Wesberry, James P., Jr. "The United States Constitution and International Accounting Standards." *The Government Accountants Journal* (Winter 1987), pp. 32–37.

Working
Capital

A company's *working capital* is the net short-term investment needed to carry on day-to-day activities. The measurement and disclosure of working capital on financial statements has been considered an appropriate accounting function for decades, and so the usefulness of this concept for financial analysis is accepted almost without question. This is not to say that the concept does not present some serious problems, namely: (1) inconsistencies in the measurements of the various components of working capital, (2) differences of opinion over what should be included as the elements of working capital, and (3) a lack of precision in the meaning of certain key terms involved in defining the elements of working capital, such as *liquidity* and *current*. This chapter examines the foundation of the working capital concept; reviews the concept and its components as currently understood; illustrates how the adequacy of a company's working capital position can be evaluated; and discusses how the concept might be modified to add to its usefulness.

Development of the Working Capital Concept

The concept of working capital originated with the distinction between fixed and circulating capital at the beginning of the 20th century. As noted in Chapter 1, at that time accounting was in its adolescent stage, and such concepts as asset, liability, income, and expense were not clearly understood.[1] The impetus for the fixed and circulating capital definitions came from court

---

[1] For a complete documentation of the history of the working capital concept, see William Huizingh, *Working Capital Classification* (Ann Arbor: Bureau of Business Research, Graduate School of Business Administration, University of Michigan, 1967).

decisions on the legality of dividends in Great Britain. As first defined, fixed capital was money expended that was sunk once and for all, while circulating capital was defined as items of stock in trade, which are parted with and replaced by similar items in the ordinary course of business.

These definitions were not readily accepted by members of the accounting profession, some of whom feared that the general public would misinterpret the distinction. Soon thereafter, British and American accountants began to examine the valuation bases of various assets and gave increased attention to a method of accounting termed the *double-account system*. This system divided the balance sheet horizontally into two sections. The upper portion contained all the long-lived assets, the capital, the debt, and a balancing figure that represented the difference between capital and long-term liabilities, and long-lived assets. The lower section contained all other assets, current liabilities, and the balancing figure from the top section.

During this same period, the notion of *liquidity* was becoming established as a basis for the classification of assets on the financial statements. Liquidity classification schemes were intended to report on the short-run solvency of the enterprise; however, criticisms arose which suggested that such schemes were in conflict with the going-concern concept. Nevertheless, the liquidity concept continued to gain acceptance among accountants and financial statement users and was included by Paton in his distinction between fixed and current assets.[2] Paton noted that length of life, rate of use, and method of consumption were important factors in distinguishing between fixed and current assets. He elaborated on these factors as follows: A fixed asset will remain in the enterprise two or more periods, whereas current assets will be used more rapidly; fixed assets may be charged to expense over many periods, whereas current assets are used more quickly; and fixed assets are used entirely to furnish a series of similar services, whereas current assets are consumed.[3]

During the first three decades of the 20th century, most users in the United States viewed the balance sheet as the principal financial statement. During this period, financial statements were prepared on the basis of their usefulness to creditors, and investors were left to make their decisions on whatever basis they felt applicable. In 1936 the American Institute of Certified Public Accountants attempted to modify this viewpoint when it acknowledged the different points of view of the creditor and investor, as follows.

> As a rule a creditor is more particularly interested in the liquidity of a business enterprise and the nature and adequacy of its working capital; hence the details of the current assets and current liabilities are to him of relatively more importance than details of long-term assets and liabilities. He also has a real interest in the earnings, because the ability to repay a loan may be dependent upon the profits of the enterprise. From an investor's point of view, it is generally recognized

[2] William A. Paton, *Accounting Theory* (New York: Ronald Press, 1922).
[3] Ibid., pp. 215–216.

that earning capacity is of vital importance and that the income account is at least as important as the balance sheet.[4]

By the 1940s, the concept of working capital as a basis for determining liquidity had become well established, even though there was some disagreement as to its exact meaning. The confusion centered on how to identify current assets and whether the classification should be based on those items that *will be* converted into cash in the short run or those that *could be* converted into cash. At this time, the one-year rule as the basis for classifying assets as current or noncurrent was fairly well established. But Anson Herrick, who was an active member of the American Institute of Certified Public Accountants, began to point out some of the fallacies of the one-year rule.

Herrick focused on the differences in preparing statements for credit and investment purposes and noted some inconsistencies in current practice, such as including inventories under the current classification when their turnover might take more than a year while excluding trade receivables due more than a year after the balance sheet date.[5] His thoughts are summarized in the following statement.

It is not logical to adopt a practice which may result in substantial difference between the reported amount of net current assets ... and the amount which would be shown if the statement were to be prepared a few days earlier or later.[6]

In lieu of the one-year rule, Herrick proposed the *operating cycle* as the basis for classifying assets as current. This distinction was based on the contrast of the assets' economic substance as either *fixed* or *circulating* capital.[7]

In 1947, while Herrick was a committee member, the Committee on Accounting Procedure issued *ARB No. 30*. This release defined current assets as "cash or other resources commonly identified as those which are reasonably expected to be realized in cash or sold or consumed during the normal operating cycle of the business." Current liabilities were defined as "debts or obligations, the liquidation or payment of which is reasonably expected to require the use of existing resources properly classifiable as current assets or the creation of other current liabilities."[8] The operating cycle was then defined as "the average time intervening between the acquisition of materials or services ... and the final cash realization." The committee also established one year as the basis for classification when the operating cycle was shorter than one year.[9] Although this distinction was slightly modified by

---

[4] *Examination of Financial Statements by Independent Public Accountants* (New York: AICPA, 1936), p. 4.

[5] Anson Herrick, "Current Assets and Current Liabilities," *Journal of Accountancy* (January 1944), pp. 48–55.

[6] Ibid., p. 49.

[7] Ibid., p. 50.

[8] *Accounting Research Bulletin No. 30*, pp. 248–249.

[9] Ibid., pp. 247, 249.

ARB NO. 43, it has stood essentially intact since that time and was recently reaffirmed in *SFAS No. 115* as discussed later in the chapter.

Current Usage

The working capital concept provides useful information by giving an indication of an entity's liquidity and the degree of protection given to short-term creditors. Specifically, the presentation of working capital can be said to add to the flow of information to financial statement users by (1) indicating the amount of margin or buffer available to meet current obligations, (2) presenting the flow of current assets and current liabilities from past periods, and (3) presenting information on which to base predictions of future inflows and outflows. In the following sections, we examine the measurement of the items included under working capital.

Components of Working Capital

The *ARB No. 43* definitions of current assets and current liabilities include examples of each classification as follows:

Current Assets

a.   *Cash available for current operations and items which are the equivalent of cash*
b.   *Inventories of merchandise, raw materials, goods in process, finished goods, operating supplies, and ordinary maintenance materials and parts*
c.   *Trade accounts, notes, and acceptances receivable*
d.   *Receivables from officers, employees, affiliates, and others if collectible in the ordinary course of business within a year*
e.   *Installment or deferred accounts and notes receivable if they conform generally to normal trade practices and terms within the business*
f.   *Marketable securities representing the investment of cash available for current operations*
g.   *Prepaid expenses, such as insurance, interest, rents, taxes, unused royalties, current paid advertising service not yet received, and operating supplies[10]*

Current Liabilities

a.   *obligations for items which have entered into the operating cycle, such as payables incurred in the acquisition of materials and supplies to be used in the production of goods or in providing services to be offered for sale*
b.   *collections received in advance of the delivery of goods or performance of services*
c.   *debts which arise from operations directly related to the operating cycle, such as accruals for wages, salaries and commission, rentals, royalties, and income and other taxes*
d.   *other liabilities whose regular and ordinary liquidation is expected to occur within a relatively short period of time, usually twelve months, are also intended for inclusion, such as short-term debts arising from the acquisition*

---

[10] *Accounting Research Bulletin No. 43*, "Restatement and Revision of Accounting Research Bulletins" (New York: AICPA, 1953), pars. 6010–11.

> *of capital assets, serial maturities of long-term obligations, amounts required to be expended within one year under sinking fund provisions and agency obligations arising from the collection or acceptance of cash or other assets for the account of third persons*[11]

These items will now be examined in more detail.

Current Assets

Cash

The accurate measurement of cash is important not only because cash represents the amount of resources available to meet emergency situations, but also because most accounting measurements are based on actual or expected cash inflows and outflows. The prediction of future cash flows is essential to investors, creditors, and management to enable these groups to determine (1) the availability of cash to meet maturing obligations, (2) the availability of cash to pay dividends, and (3) the amount of idle cash that can safely be invested for future use. Measuring cash normally includes counting not only the cash on hand and in banks but also formal negotiable paper, such as personal checks, cashier's checks, and bank drafts.

The amount of cash disclosed as a current asset must be available for current use and is not subject to any restrictions. For example, sinking fund cash should not be reported as a current asset because it is intended to be used to purchase long-term investments or to repay long-term debt.

It has also become commonplace for banks to require a portion of amounts borrowed to remain on deposit during the period of the loan. These deposits are called *compensating balances*. This type of agreement has two main effects: (1) It reduces the amount of cash available for current use, and (2) it increases the effective interest rate on the loan. In 1973, the SEC issued *Accounting Series Release No. 148*, which recommended that compensating balances against short-term loans be shown separately in the current assets section of the balance sheet. Compensating balances on long-term loans may be classified as either investments or other assets.[12]

Cash Equivalents

Firms frequently invest cash in excess of immediate needs in short-term, highly liquid investments. Whether cash is on hand, on deposit, or invested in a short-term investment that is readily convertible to cash is irrelevant to financial statement users' assessments of liquidity and future cash flows. The investment of idle funds in cash equivalents to earn interest is a part of the firm's cash management policy. This policy is in contrast to investing capital in the hope of benefiting from favorable price changes that may result from

---

[11] Ibid., par. 6011.

[12] "Amendments to Regulation S-X and Related Interpretations and Guidelines Regarding the Disclosure of Compensating Balances and Short-Term Borrowing Agreements," *Accounting Series Release No. 148* (Washington, DC: SEC, November 13, 1973).

changes in interest rates or other factors. In order to distinguish between cash management and investment policies, SFAS No. 95 defines cash equivalents as short-term investments that satisfy the following two criteria:

1. Readily convertible into a known amount of cash.
2. Sufficiently close to its maturity date so that its market value is relatively insensitive to interest rate changes.

Generally, only investments purchased within three months of their maturity value will satisfy these criteria. Examples of cash equivalents are short-term investments in U.S. Treasury Bills, commercial paper, and money market funds. The purchase and sale of these investments are viewed as part of the firm's cash management activities rather than part of its operating, financing, and investing activities. In addition, the FASB noted that different types of firms in different industries might pursue different cash management and investing strategies. Consequently, each firm must disclose its policy for treating items as cash equivalents, and any change in that policy must be treated as a change in accounting principle that requires the restatement of prior years' financial statements.

Temporary Investments
In the event that the cash and cash equivalent balances are larger than necessary to provide for current operations, it is advisable to invest idle funds until their use becomes necessary. Investments classified as current assets must be readily marketable and intended to be converted into cash within the operating cycle or a year, whichever is longer. Short-term investments are generally distinguished from cash equivalents by relatively longer investment perspectives, at relatively higher rates of return.

In theory, the procedures used to report the value of temporary investments on the balance sheet should provide investors with an indication of the resources that will be available for future use—that is, the amount of cash that could be generated from the disposal of these securities. Most temporary investments are unlike other assets in that an objectively determined measurement of their value is available in the securities market on a day-to-day basis. Therefore, accountants have been divided over the proper methods to use to value temporary investments. Three alternative methods for reporting temporary investments have been debated: *historical cost, market value,* and the *lower of cost or market.*

The *historical cost* method reports temporary investments at their acquisition cost until disposal. The advocates of historical cost believe that an objectively verified purchase price provides the most relevant information about investments to decision makers. They also argue that current market prices do not provide any better information on future prices than does original cost and that only realized gains and losses should be reported on the income statement.

Investments reported at *market value* are adjusted to reflect both upward and downward changes in value, and these changes are reported as either gains or losses on the income statement. Advocates of the market value method state that current amounts represent the current resources that would be needed to acquire the same securities now as well as the amount that would be received from sale of the securities. In addition, they note that fair value is as objectively determined as historical cost for most investments, and it also presents more timely information on the effect of holding investments.

The *lower of cost or market* method, as originally defined, reports only downward adjustments in the value of temporary investments. The proponents of this method believe that it provides users with more conservative balance sheet and income statement valuations. They argue that conservative valuations are necessary in order not to mislead investors.

In response to stock market conditions in 1973 and 1974, the FASB studied accounting for temporary investments when their value falls below cost. In 1973 and 1974 the stock market declined substantially from previous levels and then made a partial recovery. The general movement in stock prices during this period had two main effects on financial reporting for investments:

1.   Some companies used the historical cost method and did not write their investments down to reflect market prices and were therefore carrying their portfolios of investments at amounts above current market prices.

2.   Some companies used the lower of cost or market method, valued their investments at market values, and wrote their investments down to current prices when the stock market reached its lowest level. The partial recovery experienced by the stock market then could not be reflected on these companies' financial statements, which resulted in the companies carrying their investments at an amount below both cost and current market.

Subsequently, the FASB issued *SFAS No. 12*, "Accounting for Certain Marketable Securities," which attempted to alleviate this problem.[13]

According to the provisions of *SFAS No. 12*, marketable equity securities classified as current assets were to be valued at their aggregate cost or market value, whichever was lower on each balance sheet date. This determination was to be made by comparing the total cost of the entire portfolio of temporary investments in equity securities against its total market value. Losses in market value were to be accounted for as charges against income and reported on the balance sheet by way of a valuation account offset against the temporary investment account.

These requirements were not substantially different from previous practice. However, the FASB did provide for one major difference. If losses had previously been recorded, a subsequent recovery of market value was to be reported as income to the extent of previously recorded losses.

If all or any part of the portfolio was sold, a gain or loss was recognized on the sale by comparing the original cost of the securities sold with the pro-

[13] Financial Accounting Standards Board, *Statement of Financial Accounting Standards No. 12*, "Accounting for Certain Marketable Securities" (Stamford, CT: FASB, 1975).

ceeds from the sale. The valuation account was not affected by the sale of securities. Changes in the valuation account were recorded on the balance sheet date by comparing the cost of the remaining securities with their market value to determine the required balance in the valuation account. If no securities remained, the entire valuation account was eliminated.

It was anticipated that the provisions of *SFAS No. 12* would allow investors to evaluate the management of the temporary investment portfolio. For example, it might be possible to compare the yearly change in the market value of the portfolio to the overall trend in the stock market to assess the effect of management's temporary investment strategy.

SFAS No. 12 referred only to marketable equity securities and did not alter the accounting treatment required for other types of temporary investments. Under traditional GAAP, other temporary investments would have been reported by using either the cost or the lower of cost or market methods. However, if the lower of cost or market method was used, losses were recorded only when there had been a permanent impairment in value. Subsequent recoveries in market value were not recorded.

Later, concerns began to be expressed about the different accounting treatments allowed for investments in equity versus debt securities. Specifically, questions were raised about using the lower of cost or market method where diminished values were reported, whereas value appreciations were not reported. In addition, the issue of gains trading was raised. *Gains trading* is the practice of selling securities that appreciate in value in order to recognize a gain, while holding securities with unrealized losses.

As a result, the FASB undertook a project to address accounting for both equity and debt securities. This project was limited in scope because not all financial assets were included (e.g., receivables), and current accounting requirements for financial liabilities were not changed. The result of this project was the release of *Statement of Financial Accounting Standards No. 115,* "Accounting for Certain Investments in Debt and Equity Securities." The provisions of this statement became effective for fiscal periods beginning after December 15, 1993.

SFAS No. 115 requires companies to classify equity and debt securities into one of the following three categories:

Trading securities: Securities held for resale.

Securities available for sale: Securities not classified as trading securities or held-to-maturity securities.

Securities held to maturity: Securities for which the reporting enterprise has both the positive intent and ability to hold those securities to maturity.

Trading securities are reported at fair value, and all unrealized holding gains and losses are recognized in earnings. Available-for-sale securities are reported at fair value. However, unrealized holding gains and losses for these securities are not included in periodic net income; rather, they are reported as a component of other comprehensive income. Held-to-maturity securities are accounted for by the historical cost method, and any premium or discount, reflected as a difference between the acquisition price and the security's maturity value, is amortized over the remaining life of the security.

Trading securities are reported as current assets on the balance sheet. Individual held-to-maturity and available-for-sale securities are reported as either current assets or investments as appropriate. The appropriate classification is to be based on the definitions provided in *ARB No. 43*, discussed earlier.

The transfer of a security between investment categories is accounted for at fair value. At the date of the transfer, the security's unrealized holding gain or loss shall be accounted for as follows:

1. For a security transferred from the trading category, the unrealized holding gain or loss will already have been recognized in earnings, so no additional recognition is required.

2. For a security transferred into the trading category, the unrealized holding gain or loss at the date of the transfer shall be recognized immediately.

3. For a debt security transferred into the available-for-sale category from the held-to-maturity category, the unrealized holding gain or loss shall be recognized in a separate component of stockholders' equity.

4. For a debt security transferred into the held-to-maturity category from the available-for-sale category, the unrealized holding gain or loss shall continue to be reported in a separate component of stockholders' equity, but shall be amortized over the remaining life of the security as an adjustment to interest in a manner similar to the amortization of a premium or discount.

These requirements were adopted to further deter gains trading. If all transfers could be made at fair value and all holding gains and losses could be recognized immediately in earnings, the possibility of discretionary transfers to recognize earnings would be left open. The approach adopted is similar to recognizing holding gains and losses in a manner consistent with the category into which the security is being transferred.

Receivables
The term *receivables* encompasses a wide variety of claims held against others. Receivables are classified into two categories for financial statement presentation: (1) trade receivables and (2) nontrade receivables.

The outstanding receivables balance constitutes a major source of cash inflows to meet maturing obligations; therefore, the composition of this balance must be carefully evaluated so that financial statement users are not misled. In order for an item to be classified as a receivable, both the amount to be received and the expected due date must be subject to reasonable estimation.

Ideally, each enterprise would make only cash sales; however, given the nature of our economic society, most firms must extend various types of credit. Businesses sell on credit to increase sales, but when credit is extended, losses from nonpayments invariably occur. Once a business decides to sell on credit, it may record bad debts by one of the following procedures:

1. Bad debts aie recorded as the loss is discovered (the direct write-off method).

2. Bad debts are estimated in the year of the sale (the estimation, or allowance method).

Under the *direct write-off* method, a loss is recorded when a specific customer account is determined to be uncollectible. Frequently, this determination may not be made until a subsequent accounting period and, therefore, results in an improper matching of revenues and expenses. In addition, *SFAS No. 5* requires estimated losses to be accrued when it is probable that an asset has been impaired or a liability has been incurred, and the amount of the loss can be estimated. Since these conditions are usually satisfied for uncollectible accounts, most companies estimate bad debts.

Two methods may be used to estimate expected losses from nonpayment of outstanding accounts receivable: (1) the estimated loss is based on annual sales and (2) the estimated loss is based on the outstanding accounts receivable balance. When the estimated loss is based on annual sales, the matching process is enhanced because expenses are directly related to the revenues that caused the expenses. On the other hand, a more precise measure of anticipated losses can usually be made by reviewing the age and characteristics of the various accounts receivable. When the amount of loss is based on the outstanding accounts receivable, the net balance of the asset account closely resembles the expected amount to be collected in the future *(net realizable value)*. With the increased emphasis on the income statement as the primary financial statement, most accountants now recommend estimating losses on the basis of sales. However, where sales and credit policies are relatively stable, it is unlikely that use of either method of estimation will materially affect reported expenses.

Some accountants have also suggested that receivables should be carried at their present value by applying a discount factor. But others have argued that this treatment is not usually considered necessary due to the relatively short collection (or discount) period involved for most accounts receivable. The FASB's recent embrace of the asset and liability approach has also had implications for these issues. Under the provisions of *SFAS No. 114*, "Accounting by Creditors for the Impairment of a Loan," creditors must now evaluate the probability that receivables will be collected. If it is determined that amounts will probably not be collected, the present value of the expected future cash payments must be calculated. When this present value is less than the recorded value of the loan, a loss is recognized and charged to bad debt expense, and the receivable is reduced through a valuation allowance. Alternatively, loss impairment may be measured based on the fair market value of the receivable, or if collateralized, the fair market value of the collateral. The definition of a probable loss is that a future event is likely to occur, which is consistent with the definition provided in *SFAS No. 5*, "Accounting for Contingencies." (See Chapter 10 for a discussion of accounting for contingencies.)

Inventories

The term *inventory*

> *designate[s] the aggregate of those items of tangible personal property which: (1) are held for sale in the ordinary course of business, (2) are in process of produc-*

tion for such sale, or (3) are to be currently consumed in the production of goods or services to be available for sale.[14]

The valuation of inventories is of major importance for two reasons. First, inventories generally constitute a major portion of current assets; consequently, they have a significant impact on determining working capital and current position. Second, inventory valuation has a major and immediate impact on the reported amount of net profit.

Inventory valuation procedures differ from the valuation procedures associated with cash, cash equivalents, temporary investments, and receivables. The amounts disclosed for cash, cash equivalents, temporary investments, and receivables approximate the amount of funds expected to be received from these assets. The amount of inventory disclosed on the financial statements does not represent the future cash receipts expected to be generated. Rather, it represents the acquisition value of a cost expected to generate future revenues.

The proper valuation of inventories rests on answers to the following questions.

1. What amount of goods are on hand?
2. What cost flow assumption is most reasonable for the enterprise?
3. Has the market value of the inventory declined since its acquisition?

Inventory Quantity The inventory quantity question posed above involves determining the amount of goods on hand by (1) an actual count, (2) perpetual records, or (3) estimating procedures.

Business enterprises that issue audited financial statements are usually required to *actually count* all items of inventory at least once a year unless other methods provide reasonable assurance that the inventory figure is correct. When the inventory count is used to determine ending inventory, as in a *periodic inventory system,* the expectation is that all goods not on hand were sold. However, other factors, such as spoilage and pilferage, must be taken into consideration.

When inventory quantity is determined by the *perpetual records method,* all items of an inventory are tabulated as purchases and sales occur, and the amount of inventory on hand and the amount contained in the accounting records should be equal. However, it is usually necessary to verify the perpetual record by an actual count of inventory at least once a year. Accounting control over inventories is increased by the use of a perpetual system. But a perpetual system should be used only when the benefits derived from maintaining the records are greater than the cost of keeping the records.

Estimation methods are used when it is impossible or impractical to count or keep perpetual records for the inventory. Two methods may be used to estimate inventories: (1) the gross profit method and (2) the retail method.

[14] "Restatement and Revision of Accounting Research Bulletins," *Accounting Research and Terminology Bulletins, No. 43* (New York: AICPA, 1953).

The *gross profit* method computes the ending inventory on a dollar basis by subtracting the estimated cost of sales from the cost of goods available. This method is especially useful in estimating inventories for interim financial statements or in computing losses from casualties, such as fire or theft.

The *retail method* is used most frequently where merchandise is available for sale directly to customers, such as in department or discount stores. When using this method, the retail value of inventory is computed by subtracting the retail price of goods sold from the retail price of goods available. Inventory at cost is then computed by applying the average markup percentage to the ending inventory at retail.

Both the gross profit and retail methods, although approximating balance sheet values, fail to provide management with all available information concerning the quantity and unit prices of specific items of inventory. For this reason an actual count of goods on hand should be made annually.

Flow Assumptions Historically, the matching of costs with associated revenues has been the primary objective in inventory valuation. That is, balance sheet valuation was viewed as secondary to income determination. Each of the flow assumptions discussed below necessarily requires a trade-off between asset valuation and income determination. Four methods are available to account for the flow of goods from purchase to sale: (1) specific identification, (2) first in, first out, (3) last in, first out, and (4) averaging.

If an exact matching of expenses and revenues is the primary objective of inventory valuation, then *specific identification* of each item of merchandise sold may be the most appropriate method. However, even this method has low informational content to balance sheet readers because the valuation of inventories at original cost generally has little relation to future expectations. When using the specific identification method, the inventory cost is determined by keeping a separate record for each item acquired and totaling the cost of the inventory items on hand at the end of each accounting period. Most companies find that the cost of the required recordkeeping associated with the procedure outweighs any expected benefits, and so they turn to other methods. Specific identification is most feasible when the volume of sales is low and the cost of individual items is high, for example, jewelry, automobiles, and yachts.

The *first in, first out (FIFO) method* is based on assumptions about the actual flow of merchandise throughout the enterprise; in effect, it is an approximation of specific identification. In most cases, this assumption conforms to reality because the oldest items in the inventory are the items management wishes to sell first, and where perishables are involved, the oldest items must be sold quickly or they will spoil.

The FIFO flow assumption satisfies the historical cost and matching principles since the recorded amount for cost of goods sold is similar to the amount that would have been recorded under specific identification if the actual flow of goods were on a FIFO basis. Moreover, the valuation of inventory more closely resembles the replacement cost of the items on hand and thereby allows financial statement users to evaluate future working capital flows more accurately. During the last decade, rising inflation rates have caused accountants to question the desirability of using FIFO. Using older and lower unit costs during a period of inflation causes an inflated net profit figure that may mislead financial statement users. This inflated profit figure could also result in the payment of additional income taxes.

The *last in, first out (LIFO) method* of inventory valuation is based on the assumption that current costs should be matched against current revenues. Most advocates of LIFO cite the matching principle as the basis for their stand and argue that the past five decades of almost uninterrupted inflation require that LIFO be used to more closely approximate actual net income. These arguments are also based on the belief that price level changes should be eliminated from the statements, and LIFO is in effect a partial price level adjustment. (See Chapter 15 for a further discussion of price level adjustments.)

Use of LIFO can result in distortions of earnings when normal inventory levels are depleted. That is, if inventory levels fall below the normal number of units in any year, the older, usually much lower, cost of these items is charged to cost of goods sold and matched against current sales revenue dollars, resulting in an inflated net income amount that is not sustainable. When a material LIFO liquidation occurs, the SEC requires it to be disclosed in the company's 10-K report. This information is also usually included in the company's annual report to stockholders. For example, in 1998 Oxford Industries reported that inventory quantities were reduced, resulting in a LIFO liquidation that decreased cost of goods sold by $591,000 and increased after-tax earning by $361,000.

An added impetus to the use of LIFO in external financial reports is the Internal Revenue Service's requirement that this method must be used for reporting purposes when it is used for income tax purposes. LIFO can result in substantial tax savings, to the extent that cost of goods sold under LIFO and FIFO differ. This tax benefit is calculated as the difference in cost of goods sold times the company's marginal tax rate. As a consequence, many companies that might not otherwise use LIFO for reporting purposes do so because of income tax considerations. In 1999 *Accounting Trends and Techniques* reported that 319 of the 600 companies surveyed used LIFO for some portion of their inventory valuation.[15]

Averaging techniques are, in effect, a compromise position between FIFO and LIFO. When averaging is used, each purchase affects both inventory valuation and cost of goods sold. Therefore, averaging does not result in either a good match of costs with revenues or a proper valuation of inventories in fluctuating market conditions. Proponents of averaging base their arguments on the necessity of periodic presentation. That is, all the transactions during a particular period are viewed as reflective of the period as a whole rather than as individual transactions. The advocates of averaging maintain that

---

[15] AICPA, *Accounting Trends and Techniques,* George N. Dieta, Richard Rikert, and Andy Mrakovic, eds., 53rd ed. (New York, 1999), p. 359.

financial statements should reflect the operations of the entire period as a whole rather than a series of transactions

When the averaging method used is a weighted or moving weighted average, a claim can be made that the cost of goods sold is reflective of the total period's operations; however, the resulting inventory valuation is not representative of expected future cash flows. If the simple average method is used, the resulting valuations can result in completely distorted unit prices when lot sizes and prices are changing.

Market Fluctuations Many accountants have advocated valuing inventories at market because they believe that current assets should reflect current values. This might add to the information content of the working capital computation, but to date the doctrine of conservatism has been seen as overriding the advantages claimed by current valuation advocates. Nevertheless, when inventories have declined in value, traditional accounting holds that the future selling price will move in the same direction and that anticipated future losses should be recorded in the same period as the inventory decline.

The AICPA has provided the following definitions to use in applying the lower of cost or market rule to inventories.

> *As used in the phrase lower of cost or market the term market means current replacement cost (by purchase or reproduction, as the case may be) except that:*
>
> 1. *market should not exceed the net realizable value (i.e., estimated selling price in the ordinary course of business less reasonably predictable costs of completion and disposal), and*
>
> 2. *market should not be less than net realizable value reduced by an allowance for an approximately normal profit margin.*[16]

The application of the lower of cost or market rule results in inventory being recorded at an *expected utility* value and in the recording of a "normal profit" when the inventory is sold. Therefore, expenses are understated in the period of sale which may give rise to misinterpretations by external users.

Use of the lower of cost or market rule for inventories is consistent with the qualitative characteristics of accounting information contained in *SFAC No. 2* and the definitions of assets and losses contained in *SFAC No. 6*. That is, when the cost of inventory exceeds its expected benefit, a reduction of the inventory to its market value is a better measure of its expected future benefit.

The major criticism of the lower of cost or market rule is that it is applied only for downward adjustments. Therefore, holding losses are recognized, while holding gains are ignored. As noted earlier, this criticism has not been viewed as important as maintaining conservative financial statements, and the importance of the concept of conservatism was reaffirmed by the FASB in *SFAC No. 5*.

Prepaids

Prepaid items result from recording expected future benefits from services to be rendered. They do not represent current assets in the sense that they will

---

[16] Ibid., Chap. 4, par. 7.

be converted into cash, but rather in the sense that they will require the use of current assets during the operating cycle if they were not in existence.

The measurement of prepaids is generally the residual result of the attempt to charge their expiration to expense, and little attention is given to balance sheet valuations. Two main cost expiration methods are used in the measurement of prepaids: (1) specific identification and (2) time. Specific identification is used where the items are consumed, as with office supplies, and time is used where no tangible asset exists and rights are in evidence over a certain period, such as with unexpired insurance or prepaid rent.

In most cases, the amortization method is of little consequence because of the relative unimportance of these items. However, where substantial prepayments occur, care should be exercised to ensure that the allocation method is reasonable under the circumstances.

Current Liabilities

Payables
The measurement of payables presents no particular difficulty because the amount of the obligation is usually fixed by a transaction and involves a promise to pay at a subsequent date. As with receivables, recording discounts from face value is not considered necessary because the period of debt is generally short. However, where interest is not specifically stated on notes payable, *APB Opinion No. 21,* "Interest on Receivables and Payables," requires that interest be calculated for certain types of notes.[17] (See Chapter 10.) In addition to notes and accounts payable, dividends and taxes represent payables that require the use of current funds.

Liability recognition frequently results from the necessity to recognize an asset or an expense where the focus of attention is not on the liability. However, the recognition of short-term liabilities may have significant impact on the working position of the enterprise.

Deferrals
Generally, deferrals are a special type of liability whose settlement requires the performance of services rather than the payment of money. Examples of deferrals include such items as subscriptions collected in advance or unearned rent. They are similar to prepaid expenses in that they are generally the residual result of the attempt to measure another amount. In this case, the amount attempted to be measured is revenue, whereas it was an expense in the case of prepaids.

The placement of deferrals in the current liability section of the balance sheet has been criticized because since there is no claimant they are not really liabilities in the general sense of the term. However, unless they are unusually large, it is unlikely that recording deferrals as liabilities will have much

---

[17] *Accounting Principles Board Opinion No. 21,* "Interest on Receivables and Payables" (New York: AICPA, 1971).

impact on financial statement presentation. Care should be taken to ensure that the company is not being overly cautious in reporting income as a deferral and to determine that the deferral accounts are not being used as an additional allowance for uncollectible accounts.

Current Maturities

Unlike most assets, liabilities may be transferred from the long-term to the current classification with passage of time. Where the payment of long-term debt in the current period requires the use of current funds, proper accounting dictates that this amount be classified as current. Not all current maturities are classified as current liabilities. When the long-term liability is to be retired out of a special fund or by issuing additional long-term debt, the obligation should not be classified as current.

The proper classification of current maturities is of great importance because of the effect it can have on the working capital presentation. When adequate provision has not previously been made to retire current maturities, a company may find itself in a weak working capital position and future capital sources may evaporate.

Financial Analysis of a Company's Working Capital Position

The evaluation of a company's current operating cycle can highlight possible liquidity problems. Consider a large retailer such as the Nordstrom Department Store chain. The company purchases merchandise on credit from various manufacturers such as Bally shoes, Tommy Hilfiger clothes, and Giorgio cosmetics. The merchandise Nordstrom purchases is first shipped to the chain's warehouses and later to various stores throughout the country where it is displayed and sold to customers. Many of Nordstrom's sales are made on credit. Liquidity problems can arise when customer payments on account are not received in a timely manner. Several ratios in addition to working capital are available to assist in evaluating a company's liquidity, including the current ratio, the acid test (quick) ratio, cash flow from operations to current liabilities ratio, the accounts receivable turnover ratio, the inventory turnover ratio, and the accounts payable turnover ratio. The calculation and analysis of each of these ratios are illustrated here by using the information contained in Kroll-O'Gara Company's balance sheet, income statement, and statement of cash flows that are contained in Chapter 4 and 5. Each of the ratios is computed for both 1997 and 1998 for comparative purposes.

Kroll-O'Gara Company's working capital (current assets – current liabilities) for the two years is:

1998	**1997**
$148,805,822 – 65,435,424 =	$93,606,585 – 58,328,230 =
$83,370,398	$35,278,355

Management of a company's working capital is important for any business. This analysis indicates that Kroll-O'Gara Company's working capital increased by $48,092,043 during 1998. Nevertheless, calculating the amount of working capital provides limited information because it does not allow for easy comparisons with benchmarks, industry standards, or other companies. That is, it is an absolute amount that does not take into consideration the size of a company, and an amount that is adequate for one company may be considered inadequate for another larger company.

To overcome this deficiency, financial analysts compute the current ratio and the acid test (quick) ratio. The current ratio is calculated as follows.

$$\frac{\text{Current assets}}{\text{Current liabilities}}$$

Kroll-O'Gara Company's current ratios for 1998 and 1997 are calculated as:

1998	**1997**
$\dfrac{\$148,805,822}{\$ 65,435,424} = 2.27{:}1$	$\dfrac{\$93,606,585}{\$58,328,230} = 1.60{:}1$

Financial analysts generally consider a current ratio of 2:1 to indicate adequate short-term liquidity. These calculations indicate that the company's liquidity position improved during 1998 and is sufficient using the general benchmark. As indicated in Chapter 5, this ratio and other liquidity ratios might also be compared to industry standards and other companies in the same industry in order to assess their adequacy.

An additional concern is the composition of a company's current assets. That is, current liabilities must be satisfied through the payment of cash so an analysis of a company's liquidity should consider how a company's current assets might be used to repay its current debt. The acid test (quick) ratio provided a more rigid analysis of a company's ability to pay its current obligations as they become due because it only includes those current assets that can easily be converted into cash in the numerator. The acid test (quick) ratio is computed as:

$$\frac{\text{Cash} + \text{Marketable securities} + \text{Receivables}}{\text{Current liabilities}}$$

Kroll-O'Gara Company's acid test (quick) ratios for 1998 and 1997 are calculated as:

1998

$$\frac{\$12,862,928 + 13,285,322 + 55,570,815}{\$65,435,424} = 1.25{:}1$$

1997

$$\frac{\$9,765,422 + 22,969 + 40,796,471}{\$58,328,230} = 0.87{:}1$$

Financial analysts usually consider an acid test ratio of 1:1 as adequate for meeting short term liquidity needs. Kroll-O'Gara Company's acid test (quick) ratio improved during 1998 and meets the general benchmark

One final measure that can be used to evaluate a company's liquidity is the cash flow from operations to current liabilities ratio. This ratio indicates a company's ability to repay current liabilities from current operations. The cash flow from operations to current liabilities ratio is calculated as:

$$\frac{\text{Net cash provided from operating activities}}{\text{Average current liabilities}}$$

Notice that this ratio is calculated by using average current liabilities in the denominator. This results in the use of a consistent numerator and denominator since the net cash provided from operating activities represents the flow of cash over the year. Kroll-O'Gara Company's cash flow from operations to current liabilities ratios for 1998 and 1997 are calculated as:

1998	**1997**
$\dfrac{\$(12,435,025)}{(\$65,435,424 + 58,328,230)/2} = (0.20){:}1$	$\dfrac{\$6,194,818}{(\$58,328,230 + 49,289,202)/2^{18}} = 0.12{:}1$

These ratios indicate that the company is not currently generating enough cash flow from operations to be able to repay its current obligations.

The preceding ratios evaluated a company's liquidity. Other ratios are available that assist in evaluating how efficient a company is in utilizing its current assets and managing its current liabilities. The accounts receivable turnover ratio measures a company's ability to collect its receivables on a timely basis. The accounts receivable turnover ratio is computed as:

$$\frac{\text{Net credit sales}[19]}{\text{Average accounts receivable}}$$

Note that this ratio also uses an average amount in the denominator to provide consistency with the numerator. Kroll-O'Gara Company's accounts receivable turnover ratios for 1998 and 1997 are calculated as:

1998	**1997**
$\dfrac{\$264,844,847}{(\$55,570,815 + 40,796,471)/2} = 5.50$	$\dfrac{\$206,102,605}{(\$40,796,471 + 22,941,065)/2} = 6.47$

[18] 1996 amounts in this and succeeding calculations are taken from Kroll-O'Gara Company's 1997 annual report that is not illustrated in the text.

[19] The sales figure contained on most companies' income statement is the combined amount of cash and credit sales. Most companies make the greatest majority of their sales on credit, so the sales figure on the income statement can be used to approximate credit sales. However, if a company makes a large amount of cash sales, the result may be misleading.

These ratios indicate that the company's accounts receivable were paid off by customers an average of 6.47 times in 1997 and 5.50 times in 1998. To add perspective to the company's efficiency in collecting accounts receivable, financial analysts calculate the number of days in receivables as follows:

$$\frac{365}{\text{Asset turnover ratio}}$$

Kroll-O'Gara Company's days in receivables ratios for 1998 and 1997 are calculated as:

1998	**1997**
$\dfrac{365}{5.50} = 66.4 \text{ days}$	$\dfrac{365}{6.47} = 56.4 \text{ days}$

The calculation of average days in receivables allows a company to evaluate its ability to collect its accounts receivable within its normal credit period. For Kroll-O'Gara Company, this calculation indicates that the company may be experiencing difficulty in collecting its receivables when considering that normal trade credit policies generally require payment within 30 days. The comparative analysis also indicates that the company's average collection period increased about 10 days over the two-year period.

A company's efficiency in managing its inventory can be similarly analyzed by computing the inventory turnover ratio. This ratio is calculated as:

$$\frac{\text{Cost of goods sold}}{\text{Average inventory}}$$

Kroll-O'Gara Company's inventory turnover ratios for 1998 and 1997 are calculated as:

1998	**1997**
$\dfrac{\$173,317,466}{(\$22,397,939 + 19,562,899)/2} = 8.26$	$\dfrac{\$139,765,613}{(\$19,562,899 + 8,733,640)/2} = 9.88$

This ratio can be further analyzed by calculating the average days in inventory as follows:

$$\frac{365}{\text{Inventory turnover ratio}}$$

Kroll-O'Gara Company's average days in inventory for 1998 and 1997 are calculated as:

1998	**1997**
$\dfrac{365}{8.26} = 44.2 \text{ days}$	$\dfrac{365}{9.88} = 36.9 \text{ days}$

These ratios indicate that the company's ability to manage its inventory declined during 1998. However, care must be exercised in evaluating these ratios because they are highly industry dependent. For example, a grocery chain such as Safeway sells many perishables and would be expected to have a high inventory turnover ratio, whereas, for defense contractors such as Boeing, this ratio would probably be relatively lower.

The analysis of a company's working capital, current ratio, and inventory turnover ratios can be misleading for companies using LIFO inventory costing. In such cases, the amount of working capital and the current ratio will be understated because the average inventory amounts used in calculating these ratios will usually be much lower than if they had been computed using FIFO. This difference is termed the *LIFO reserve*. On the other hand, the inventory turnover ratio will generally be overstated because the average inventory amounts used in the denominator will be lower than if FIFO had been used. The company's inventory costing method is disclosed in its summary of significant accounting policies. Financial statement users should exercise care in interpreting the amount of working capital, the current ratio, and the inventory turnover ratio for companies using LIFO. For comparative purposes, the reported amount of LIFO inventory should be adjusted by the amount of the LIFO reserve.[20] This issue is not relevant to the interpretation of Kroll'O'Gara Company's ratios because it uses FIFO inventory costing as disclosed in its summary of significant accounting policies.

One final ratio helps evaluate a company's pattern of payments to suppliers by analyzing its accounts payable. A company's accounts payable turnover ratio is calculated as:

$$\frac{\text{Inventory purchases}^{21}}{\text{Average accounts payable}}$$

Kroll-O'Gara Company's accounts payable turnover ratios for 1998 and 1997 are calculated as:

1998	**1997**
$\dfrac{\$173,317,466 + 2,835,040}{(\$35,553,818 + 32,328,154)/2} = 5.19$	$\dfrac{\$139,765,613 + 10,829,259}{(\$32,328,154 + 15,997,708)/2} = 6.23$

This ratio can also be used to calculate the average days payables are outstanding, as follows:

$$\frac{365}{\text{Accounts payable turnover ratio}}$$

[20] This amount, or the replacement cost of the inventory, is a recommended disclosure by an AICPA Task Force and is reported by most companies that use LIFO. For example, in 1998 Oxford Industries reported the excess of replacement cost over the value of its LIFO inventory to be $39,205,000.

[21] This amount is not usually disclosed on corporate financial statements, but it can be estimated by cost of goods sold + increases or − decreases in inventory during the year.

For Kroll-O'Gara Company these amounts for 1998 and 1997 are:

1998	1997
$\dfrac{365}{5.19} = 70.3 \text{ days}$	$\dfrac{365}{6.23} = 46.4 \text{ days}$

These ratios indicate that the company's payable balances are not being satisfied in a timely manner in that normal trade policy is for payables to be satisfied within 30 days. The comparative analysis also indicates that the average days outstanding for the company's payables increased about 24 days over the two-year period.

A comprehensive analysis of Kroll-O'Gara Company's working capital position would combine the results of the above calculations. This analysis for 1998 indicates that:

> Accounts receivable are paid in approximately 66 days.
> Inventory remains on hand for approximately 44 days.
> Current operations are not generating sufficient cash to repay current liabilities.
> Accounts payable are being satisfied in approximately 70 days.

This analysis indicates a weakness of evaluating a company's liquidity by focusing solely on its working capital position. An initial analysis of Kroll-O'Gara Company's working capital position indicated that it had an adequate amount of current assets to satisfy its current obligations. Further analysis, however, revealed that the company is having difficulty collecting its receivables and is not generating enough cash from operating activities to pay current obligations. In fact, in 1998 its cash flow from operating activities was negative. As a consequence, the company is apparently unable to satisfy its current obligations in a timely manner.

Modification of the Working Capital Concept

Earlier it was suggested that the working capital concept was useful to investors, creditors, and management to indicate the amount of buffer available to meet current obligations, present information about cash flows, and predict future cash flows. However, current usage in the United States, and the inability of the IASC to agree on a workable definition of the concept, suggest that much of the foundation for the working capital concept is based on an evolution of long-established customs and conventions. That is, the historical examination of the development and the current status of the working capital concept suggests that it is more closely associated with the notion of circulating capital than with the fulfillment of various user needs concerning liquidity and cash flows.

Current U.S. and international practice is based on the assumption that the items classified as current assets will be used to retire existing current liabilities and that the measurement procedures used in valuing these items provide a valid indicator of the amount of cash expected to be realized or paid. Closer examination of these assumptions discloses two fallacies: (1) not all the items are measured in terms of their expected cash equivalent, and (2) some of the items will never be received or paid in cash.

On the current asset side only cash, which is actual, receivables, which are measured at expected net realizable value, and securities measured at fair market value show a high degree of correlation with the cash that will become available. Inventories are measured at cost, but the expectation is that they will be exchanged for amounts substantially above cost. Prepaid expenses have been included as current assets because if they had not been acquired, they would require the use of current assets in the normal operations of the business. However, prepaids will be used rather than exchanged for cash and, therefore, do not aid in predicting future cash flows. An enumeration of the valuation procedure associated with current liabilities exposes similar problems. Payables and the current portion of long-term debt represent the amounts to be paid in cash to retire these obligations during the coming period, but deferred credits will be retired by the performance of services rather than the payment of monies.

If the working capital concept is to become truly operational, it would seem necessary to modify it in such a manner as to show the amount of actual buffer between maturing obligations and the resources expected to be used in retiring these obligations. Such presentation should include only the current cash equivalent of the assets to be used to pay the existing debts. It would therefore seem more reasonable to base the working capital presentation on the monetary-nonmonetary dichotomy used in price level accounting. (See Chapter 15.) To review this concept briefly, monetary items are claims to or against specific amounts of money; all other assets and liabilities are nonmonetary.

The monetary working capital presentation would list as assets cash, cash equivalents, temporary investments, and receivables and would list as liabilities current payables. It is also suggested that more meaningful information could be provided if all temporary investments were measured by their current market price, including securities held to maturity. This presentation would have the following advantages: (1) it would be a more representative measure of liquidity and buffer because it would be more closely associated with future cash flows, (2) it would provide more information about actual flows because only items expected to be realized or retired by cash transactions would be included, and (3) it would allow greater predictive ability because actual cash flows could be traced.

The concept of working capital is a valid and useful device for presenting information to financial statement users. Yet its usefulness is impaired because much of the concept's foundation is based on tradition rather than on user needs. The implementation of new ideas into accounting theory is always a slow and tedious process, but the adoption of this new concept of working capital should more completely satisfy users' needs.

International Accounting Standards

The International Accounting Standards Committee has issued pronouncements on the following issues affecting working capital:

1. The presentation of current assets and current liabilities in *IAS No. 1*, "Presentation of Financial Statements."

2. The accounting for and disclosure of investment securities in *IAS No. 25*, "Accounting for Investments."

3. Accounting for inventories in *IAS No. 2*, "Inventories."

In its discussion of the presentation of current assets and current liabilities, the IASC does not attempt to deal with the valuation issues discussed earlier in the chapter. However, the committee noted that some financial statement users see the classification of assets and liabilities into current and noncurrent as a measure of the enterprise's liquidity, whereas others regard this classification as the identification of the circulating resources and obligations of the enterprise. The IASC then went on to note that since these two concepts are somewhat contradictory, it has led to the classification of items as current or noncurrent based on convention rather than on any one concept. *IAS No. 1* allows companies to determine whether or not to separately present current assets and current liabilities. This decision was apparently based on the committee's inability to agree on the usefulness of the concept because of the limitations noted earlier in this chapter. The statement suggests that each enterprise should choose, depending on the nature of its operations, whether to classify assets and liabilities as current or noncurrent. *IAS No. 1* notes that such classifications provide useful information for an enterprise that operates using a clearly defined operating cycle. If a classified balance sheet is used, classification of current items is based on the operating cycle or one year, whichever is most appropriate. In its review of *IAS No. 1*, the FASB staff noted that there are distinct similarities between the requirements for disclosing current assets and current liabilities in this release and U.S. GAAP.[22]

IAS No. 25 allows investments carried as current assets to be accounted for by either the market value or the lower of cost or market value methods. The carrying values of current investments are allowed to be determined on either an aggregate portfolio basis, in total or by investment category, or on an individual investment basis, but *IAS No. 25* stated a general preference for the aggregate portfolio or investment category bases. For enterprises that do not separately disclose current assets in their balance sheets, a distinction must be made for measurement purposes to determine the proper carrying values. The FASB has not undertaken a review of *IAS No. 25* because at the time the comprehensive review was undertaken, the topic of investments was under reconsideration by both the FASB and the IASC.

In *IAS No. 2*, the IASC noted that the objective of inventory reporting is to determine the proper amount of cost to recognize as an asset and carry forward until the related revenues are recognized. The committee

---

[22] Financial Accounting Standards Board, *The IASC-U.S. Comparison Project: A Report on the Similarities and Differences between IASC Standards and U.S. GAAP*, Carrie Bloomer, ed., 2nd Ed. (Norwalk, CT: Financial Accounting Standards Board: 1999), pp. 63–87.

stated a preference for the specific identification method of inventory valuation when the items are interchangeable or are produced and segregated for specific projects. This method was viewed as inappropriate when large numbers of interchangeable items are present. In these cases, the IASC stated a preference for either FIFO or weighted average methods; however, LIFO is an allowed alternative. In the event LIFO is used, the enterprise must also disclose the lower of LIFO cost and net realizable value, or the lower of current cost and net realizable value. The FASB staff's review of IAS No. 2 indicated that this standard is very similar to existing U.S. GAAP. However, it was noted that the wide range of accounting alternatives available within both U.S. GAAP and IASC standards makes intercompany comparison moot. It was also suggested that the lack of disclosure requirements makes such comparisons almost impossible, despite the significance of inventories and cost of goods sold to most manufacturing and merchandising companies.[23]

Summary

A review of the concept and components of working capital from a historical point of view shows that the concept has its foundation in an earlier period, when the focus was on the balance sheet and the ability to repay debts. Because of these factors, the presentation of working capital has not evolved fast enough to accommodate user needs.

An examination of the various measurement bases of current assets and current liabilities indicates that the measurement bases and methods of reporting the various accounts are dissimilar. We believe that user needs would be better satisfied if the working capital concept were modified to include only monetary items.

In the readings contained on the text's webpage for Chapter 7, the working capital concept is further analyzed.

Cases

• Case 7-1 Credit and Investment Policies

The Rivera Company, a small retail store, has been in business for a few years. The company's current policy is that all sales are made for cash, and all cash sales are deposited in the company's bank account. The bank account does not pay interest, and the company does not have any temporary investments. Rivera's sales average $90,000 a month, its gross profit is 40 percent, and the average checking account balance is $50,000.

Juan Rivera, the owner, recently hired a consultant to review the company's short-term liquid asset policy. The consultant recommended that

---

[23] FASB, *The IASC-U.S. Comparison Project,* pp. 89–98.

Rivera invest its idle cash in temporary investments and accept credit sales. Juan Rivera is investigating the following alternatives.

Temporary Investments

1. Invest in three-month certificates yielding 8.5 percent interest. Early withdrawals from this account will result in the loss of all interest earned.

2. Open an investment account earning 7.5 percent. The minimum amount that can be invested in this account is $25,000, and the bank must be notified seven days in advance for all withdrawals.

3. Open a NOW checking account paying 5.5 percent interest. No notification is required for withdrawals.

Credit Sales

1. Accept credit sales from customers holding a national credit card. One credit card company has offered Rivera a 5 percent service charge rate and will sustain all bad debt losses. If this offer is accepted, it is expected that monthly sales will increase by 15 percent, but 50 percent of the current cash customers will become credit customers.

2. Establish its own credit department. This alternative will require hiring an additional employee at an annual salary of $24,000. Monthly sales are expected to increase by 40 percent, and it is expected that 20 percent of the existing cash customers will become credit customers. It is estimated that bad debts will be 5 percent of credit sales.

Required:
a. Which short-term investment policy should Rivera adopt? Why?
b. Which credit policy should Rivera adopt? Why?

• Case 7-2 *SFAS No. 115*

SFAS No. 115 requires companies to assign their portfolio of investment securities into (1) trading securities, (2) securities available for sale, and (3) held-to-maturity securities.

Required:
a. Define each of these categories of securities and discuss the accounting treatment for each category.
b. Discuss how companies are required to assign each category of securities into its current and noncurrent portions.
c. Some individuals maintain that the only proper accounting treatment for all marketable securities is current value. Others maintain that this treatment might allow companies to "manage earnings." Discuss the arguments for each position.

• Case 7-3 Cost Flow Assumptions

Cost for inventory purposes should be determined by the inventory cost flow method most clearly reflecting periodic income.

Required:
a. Describe the fundamental cost flow assumptions of the average cost, FIFO, and LIFO inventory cost flow methods.
b. Discuss the reasons for using LIFO in an inflationary economy.
c. Where there is evidence that the utility of goods, in their disposal in the ordinary course of business, will be less than cost, what is the proper accounting treatment, and under what concept is that treatment justified?

• Case 7-4 Inventory Cost and Income

Steel Company, a wholesaler that has been in business for two years, purchases its inventories from various suppliers. During the two years, each purchase has been at a lower price than the previous purchase.

Steel uses the lower of FIFO cost or market method to value inventories. The original cost of the inventories is above replacement cost and below the net realizable value. The net realizable value less the normal profit margin is below the replacement cost.

Required:
a. In general, what criteria should be used to determine which costs should be included in inventory?
b. In general, why is the lower of cost or market rule used to report inventory?
c. At what amount should Steel's inventories be reported on the balance sheet? Explain the application of the lower of cost or market rule in this situation.
d. What would have been the effect on ending inventories and net income for the second year had Steel used the lower of average cost or market inventory method instead of the lower of FIFO cost or market inventory method? Why?

• Case 7-5 Uncollectible Accounts

Anth Company has significant amounts of trade accounts receivable. Anth uses the allowance method to estimate bad debts instead of the specific write-off method. During the year, some specific accounts were written off as uncollectible, and some that were previously written off as uncollectible were collected.

Anth also has some interest-bearing notes receivable for which the face amount plus interest at the prevailing rate of interest is due at maturity. The notes were received on July 1, 2000, and are due on June 30, 2002.

Required:
a. What are the deficiencies of the specific write-off method?
b. What are the two basic allowance methods used to estimate bad debts, and what is the theoretical justification for each?
c. How should Anth account for the collection of the specific accounts previously written off as uncollectible?
d. How should Anth report the effects of the interest-bearing notes receivable on its December 31, 2001, balance sheet and its income statement for the year ended December 31, 2001? Why?

- ## Case 7-6 Lower-of-Cost or Market Valuation of Inventories

Accountants generally follow the lower-of-cost or market basis of inventory valuations.

Required:
a. Define *cost* as applied to the valuation of inventories.
b. Define *market* as applied to the valuation of inventories.
c. Why are inventories valued at the lower-of-cost or market? Discuss.
d. List the arguments against the use of the lower-of-cost or market method of valuing inventories.

- ## Case 7-7 Accounting for Bad Debt Expense under the Allowance Method

On December 31, 2001, Carme Company had significant amounts of accounts receivables as a result of credit sales to its customers. Carme Company uses the allowance method based on credit sales to estimate bad debts. Based on past experience, 1 percent of credit sales normally will not be collected. This pattern is expected to continue.

Required:
a. Discuss the rationale for using the allowance method based on credit sales to estimate bad debts. Contrast this method with the allowance method based on the balance in the trade receivables accounts.
b. How should Carme Company report the allowance for bad debts account on its balance sheet at December 31, 2001? Also, describe the alternatives, if any, for presentation of bad debt expense in Carme Company's 2001 income statement.

- ## Case 7-8 Accounting for Trading and Available-for-Sales Securities

At the end of the first year of operations, Key Company had a current equity securities portfolio classified as available for sale securities with a cost of $500,000 and a fair value of $550,000. At the end of its second year of operations, Key Company had a current equity securities portfolio classified as available for sale securities with a cost of $525,000 and a fair value of $475,000. No securities were sold during the first year. One security with a cost of $80,000 and a fair value of $70,000 at the end of the first year was sold for $100,000 during the second year.

Required:
a. How should Key Company report the preceding facts in its balance sheets and income statements for both years? Discuss the rationale for your answer.
b. How would your answer have differed if the security had been classified as trading securities?

- ## Case 7-9 Alternate Inventory Valuations

Specific identification is sometimes said to be the ideal method for assigning cost to inventory and to cost of goods sold.

Required:
a. List the arguments for and against the foregoing statement.
b. First in, first-out; weighted average; and last-in, first-out methods are often used instead of specific identification. Compare each of these methods with the specific identification method. Include in your discussion analysis of the theoretical propriety of each method in the determination of income and asset valuation. (Do not define the methods or describe their technical accounting procedures.)

- ## Case 7-10 Net Realizable Value of Accounts Receivable

The theoretical valuation of receivables would be the present value of expected future cash flows. However, trade receivables are not discounted due to materiality considerations; hence, their net realizable value is the closest practical approximation to the theoretical valuation.

Required:
a. Define net realizable value.
b. The allowance method of accounting for bad debts may utilize an income statement or a balance sheet approach.
   i. Which approach provides the best estimate of net realizable value? Explain.
   ii. Working capital is intended to provide a measure of liquidity. Which approach provides a better measure of liquidity? Explain.
   iii. Which approach is consistent with the matching concept? Explain.
   iv. Which approach is consistent with the definition of comprehensive income? Explain.
   v. Which approach is more consistent with the concept of financial capital maintenance? Explain.
   vi. Which approach is more consistent with the concept of physical capital maintenance? Explain.

- ## Case 7-11 Accounting for Prepaids and Deferrals

Short-term deferrals (prepaids and unearned revenues) are classified as current assets and current liabilities. As such they are included in working capital.

Required:
a. Some argue that prepaids will not generate cash, and hence, are not liquid assets.
   i. Why do accountants include short-term prepaids as current assets? Do they meet the definition of assets found in the conceptual framework? Do they provide working capital? Explain.

    ii. Present arguments for excluding prepaids from current assets. Do they provide liquidity? Explain.
b. Some argue that deferred liabilities will not be "paid."
    i. Why do accountants include short-term unearned revenues as current liabilities? Do they meet the definition of liabilities found in the conceptual framework? Do they affect working capital? Explain.
c. Present arguments for excluding unearned revenues from current liabilities. Do they affect liquidity? Explain.

Room for Debate

• Issue 1

MVP Corp uses LIFO to value its inventory. The 19×8 inventory records disclose the following:

Beginning Inventory:	Units	Unit Costs
First layer	10,000	$ 15
Second Layer	22,000	18
Purchases	250,000	20

At 12/26/00, the company has a special, nonrecurring opportunity to purchase 40,000 units at $17 per unit. The purchase can be made and the units delivered on 12/30/00, or it can be delayed until the first week of January 19 01. The company plans to make the purchase, due to the obvious cost savings involved. Sales for 2000 totaled 245,000 units.

Team Debate:
Team 1. Describe the financial statement effects of making the purchase in 2000 as opposed to 2001. Argue for making the purchase during 19×8. Defend the use of LIFO. Use the matching concept in your defense.

Team 2. Given the financial statement effects of the decision to purchase in 2000, argue against the use of LIFO and in favor of FIFO. Base your arguments on the conceptual framework, for example, representational faithfulness and neutrality. Use the matching concept in your argument.

Recommended Additional Readings

Bohan, Michael P., and Steven Rubin. "LIFO: What Should Be Disclosed?" *Journal of Accountancy* (February 1985), pp. 72–77.

Gosman, Martin L., and Philip E. Meyer. "SFAS 94's Effect on Liquidity Disclosure." *Accounting Horizons* (March 1992), pp. 88–100.

Guenther, David A. "The LIFO Reserve and the Value of the Firm: Theory and Empirical Evidence." *Contemporary Accounting Research* (Spring 1994), pp. 433–452.

Reeve, James, and Keith Stanga. "Balance Sheet Impact of Using LIFO: An Empirical Study." *Accounting Horizons* (September 1987), pp. 9–16.

Schuetze, Walter P. "What Is an Asset?" *Accounting Horizons* (September 1993), pp. 66–70.

Long-Term Assets I: Property, Plant, and Equipment

The evolution of the circulating and noncirculating capital distinction of assets and liabilities into the working capital concept has been accompanied by the separate classification and disclosure of long-term assets. In this chapter we examine one of the categories of long-term assets—property, plant, and equipment. Long-term investments and intangibles are discussed in Chapter 9.

Property, Plant, and Equipment

The items of property, plant, and equipment generally represent a major source of future service potential to the enterprise. These assets represent a significant commitment of economic resources for companies in capital-intensive industries such as USX in the steel industry, Boeing in the airplane manufacturing industry and Exxon in the oil exploration and refining industry. Such companies may have as much as 75 percent of their total assets invested in property, plant, and equipment. The valuation of property, plant, and equipment assets is of interest to financial statement users because it indicates the physical resources available to the firm and may also give some indication of future liquidity and cash flows. These valuations are particularly important in capital-intensive industries such as automobile manufacturing because property, plant, and equipment constitutes a major component of the company's total assets. The objectives of plant and equipment accounting are

1. Accounting and reporting to investors on stewardship.
2. Accounting for the use and deterioration of plant and equipment.
3. Planning for new acquisitions, through budgeting.

4. Supplying information for taxing authorities.

5. Supplying rate-making information for regulated industries.

Accounting for Cost

Many business enterprises commit substantial corporate resources to acquire property, plant, and equipment. Investors, creditors, and other users rely on accountants to report the extent of corporate investment in these assets. The initial investment, or cost to the enterprise, represents the sacrifice of resources given up now to accomplish future objectives. Traditionally, accountants have placed a great deal of emphasis on the principle of objective evidence to determine the initial valuation of long-term assets. Cost, or the economic sacrifice incurred, is the preferred valuation method used to account for the acquisition of property, plant, and equipment because, as discussed in Chapter 3, cost is more reliable and verifiable than other valuation methods such as discounted present value, replacement cost, or net realizable value. There is also a presumption that the agreed-on purchase price represents the future service potential of the asset to the buyer in an arm's-length transaction.

Despite the reliability and verifiability of the purchase price as the basis for initially recording property, plant, and equipment, the assignment of cost to individual assets is not always as uncomplicated as might be expected. When assets are acquired in groups, when they are self-constructed, when they are acquired in nonmonetary exchanges, or when property contains assets that are to be removed, certain accounting problems arise. These issues are discussed in the following sections.

Group Purchases

When a group of assets is acquired for a lump-sum purchase price, such as the purchase of land, buildings, and equipment for a single purchase price, the total acquisition cost must be allocated to the individual assets so that this cost can be charged to expense as the service potential of the individual assets expires. The most frequent, though arbitrary, solution to this allocation problem has been to assign the acquisition cost to the various assets on the basis of the weighted average of their respective appraisal values. Where appraisal values are not available, the cost assignment may be based on the relative carrying values on the seller's books. Since no evidence exists that either of these values is the relative value to the purchaser, assignment by either of these procedures would seem to be a violation of the objectivity principle, but the use of these methods is usually justified on the basis of expediency and the lack of acceptable alternative methods.

Self-Constructed Assets

Self-constructed assets give rise to questions about the proper components of cost. Although it is generally agreed that all expenses directly associated with the construction process should be included in the recorded cost of the asset (material, direct labor, etc.), there are controversial issues regarding the assignment of fixed overhead and the capitalization of interest. The fixed-overhead issue has two aspects: (1) Should any fixed overhead be allocated?

and (2) If so, how much fixed overhead should be allocated? This problem has further ramifications. If a plant is operating at less than full capacity and fixed overhead is assigned to a self-constructed asset project, charging the project with a portion of the fixed overhead will cause the profit margin on all other products to increase during the period of construction. Three approaches are available to resolve this issue:

1. Allocate no fixed overhead to the self-construction project.
2. Allocate only incremental fixed overhead to the project.
3. Allocate fixed overhead to the project on the same basis as it is allocated to other products.

Some accountants favor the first approach. They argue that the allocation of fixed overhead is arbitrary and therefore only direct costs should be considered. Nevertheless, the prevailing opinion is that the construction of the asset required the use of some amount of fixed overhead, and fixed overhead is a proper component of cost. Consequently, no allocation is seen as a violation of the historical cost principle.

When the production of other products has been discontinued to produce a self-constructed asset, allocation of the entire amount of fixed overhead to the remaining products will cause reported profits on these products to decrease. (The same amount of overhead is allocated to fewer products.) Under these circumstances, the third approach seems most appropriate. On the other hand, it seems unlikely that an enterprise would discontinue operations of a profitable product to construct productive facilities except in unusual circumstances.

When operations are at less than full capacity, the second approach is the most logical. The decision to build the asset was probably connected with the availability of idle facilities. Increasing the profit margin on existing products by allocating a portion of the fixed overhead to the self-construction project will distort reported profits.

A corollary to the fixed overhead allocation question is the issue of the capitalization of interest charges during the period of the construction of the asset. During the construction period, extra financing for materials and supplies will undoubtedly be required, and these funds will frequently be obtained from external sources. The central question is the advisability of capitalizing the cost associated with the use of these funds. Some accountants have argued that interest is a financing rather than an operating charge and should not be charged against the asset. Others have noted that if the asset was acquired from outsiders, interest charges would undoubtedly be part of the cost basis to the seller and would be included in the sales price. In addition, public utilities normally capitalize both actual and implicit interest (when their own funds are used) on construction projects because future rates are based on the costs of services. Charging existing products for the expenses associated with a separate decision results in an improper matching of costs and revenues. Therefore, a more logical approach is to capitalize incremental interest charges during the construction period. Once the new asset is placed in service, interest is charged against operations.

The misapplication of this theory resulted in abuses during the first part of the 1970s when many companies adopted the policy of capitalizing all interest costs. However, in 1974 the SEC established a rule preventing this practice.[1] Later, in 1979, the FASB issued *SFAS No. 34*, "Capitalization of Interest Costs."[2] In this release, the FASB maintained that interest should be capitalized only when an asset requires a period of time to be prepared for its intended use.

The primary objective of *SFAS No. 34* is to recognize interest cost as a significant part of the historical cost of acquiring an asset. The criteria for determining whether an asset qualifies for interest capitalization are that the asset must not yet be ready for its intended purpose and must be undergoing activities necessary to get it ready. Qualified assets are defined as (1) assets that are constructed or otherwise produced for an enterprise's own use and (2) assets intended for sale or lease that are constructed or otherwise produced as discrete projects. *SFAS No. 34* also excludes interest capitalization for inventories that are routinely manufactured or otherwise produced in large quantities on a repetitive basis. Assets that are currently in use or are not undergoing the activities necessary to get them ready for use are also excluded.

An additional issue addressed by *SFAS No. 34* is the determination of the proper amount of interest to capitalize. The FASB decided that the amount of interest to be capitalized is the amount that could have been avoided if the asset had not been constructed. The interest rate to be used is either the weighted average rate of interest charges during the period or the interest charge on a specific debt instrument issued to finance the project. The amount of avoidable interest is determined by applying the appropriate interest rate to the average amount of accumulated expenditures for the asset during the construction period. The capitalized amount is the lesser of the calculated "avoidable" interest and the actual interest incurred. In addition, only actual interest costs on present obligations may be capitalized, not imputed interest on equity funds.

Removal of Existing Assets

When a firm acquires property containing existing structures that are to be removed, a question arises concerning the proper treatment of the cost of removing these structures. Current practice is to assign removal costs less any proceeds received from the sale of the assets to the land, since these costs are necessary to put the site in a state of readiness for construction.

Assets Acquired in Noncash Transactions

Assets may also be acquired by trading equity securities, or one asset may be exchanged in partial payment for another (trade-in). When equity securities are exchanged for assets, the cost principle dictates that the recorded value of the asset is the amount of consideration given. This amount is usually the market value of the securities exchanged. If the market value of the securi-

---

[1] "Capitalization of Interest by Companies Other Than Public Utilities," *SEC Accounting Series Release No. 163* (Washington, DC: SEC, 1974).

[2] Financial Accounting Standards Board, *Statement of Financial Accounting Standards No. 34*, "Capitalization of Interest Costs" (Stamford, CT: FASB, 1979), par. 9.

ties is not determinable, it is necessary to assign cost to the property on the basis of its fair market value. This procedure is a departure from the cost principle and can be viewed as an example of the use of replacement cost in current practice.

When assets are exchanged, for example, in trade-ins, additional complications arise. Accountants have long argued the relative merits of using the fair market value versus the book value of the exchanged asset. In 1973 the Accounting Principles Board released its *Opinion No. 29,* "Accounting for Nonmonetary Transactions," which concluded that fair value should *(generally)* be used as the basis of accountability.[3] Therefore, the cost of an asset acquired in a straight exchange for another asset is the fair market value of the surrendered asset.

This general rule is subject to one exception. In *Opinion No. 29* the APB stated that exchanges should be recorded at the book value of the asset given up when the exchange is not the culmination of the earning process. Two examples of exchanges that do not result in the culmination of the earning process are

1. Exchange of a *product or property held for sale* in the ordinary course of business (inventory) for a product or property to be sold in the same line of business to facilitate sales to customers other than parties to the exchange.

2. Exchange of a *productive asset* not held for sale in the ordinary course of business for a *similar* productive asset or an equivalent interest in the same or similar productive asset.[4]

If the exchanged assets are dissimilar, the presumption is that the earning process is complete, and the acquired asset is recorded at the fair value of the asset exchanged including any gain or loss. This requirement exists for straight exchanges and for exchanges accompanied by cash payments *(boot).* For example, if Company G exchanges cash of $2,000, and an asset with a book value of $10,000 and a fair market value of $13,000, for a dissimilar asset, a gain of $3,000 should be recognized [$13,000 − $10,000], and the new asset is recorded at $15,000.

On the other hand, accounting for the exchange of *similar productive assets* takes a somewhat different form. According to the provisions of *APB Opinion No. 29,* losses on the exchange of similar productive assets are always recognized in their entirety whether or not boot (cash) is involved. However, gains are never recognized unless boot is received. The recipient of boot recognizes a gain in the ratio of the boot to the total consideration received. In effect, the receiver of boot is recognizing a proportionate sale and proportionate trade-in. For example, assume Company S acquires an asset with a fair market value of $10,000 and $5,000 cash in exchange for an asset with a book

---

[3] *Accounting Principles Board Opinion No. 29,* "Accounting for Nonmonetary Transactions" (New York: AICPA, 1973).

[4] Ibid., par. 21.

value of $12,000 and a fair market value of $15,000. A gain of $1,000 is recognized. The recognized gain is calculated as follows.

$$\text{recorded gain} = \frac{\text{boot}}{\text{boot} + \text{fair market value of asset acquired}} \times \text{total gain*}$$

$$\frac{\$5,000}{\$5,000 + \$10,000} \times \$3,000^* = \$1,000$$

*($15,000 − 12,000) The new asset is recorded at $8,000 ($10,000 − 2,000 gain not recognized).

Donated and Discovery Values

Corporations sometimes acquire assets as gifts from municipalities, local citizens groups, or stockholders as inducements to locate facilities in certain areas. The FASB has defined such contributions as transfers "of cash or other assets to an entity or settlement or cancellation of its liability from a voluntary nonreciprocal transfer by another entity acting other than as an owner."[5] The cost principle holds that the recorded values of assets should be the consideration given in return, but since donations are nonreciprocal transfers, strict adherence to this principle will result in a failure to record donated assets at all. On the other hand, failure to report values for these assets on the balance sheet is inconsistent with the full disclosure principle.

Previous practice required donated assets to be recorded at their fair market values. A similar amount was recorded in an equity account termed *donated capital.* Thereafter, as the service potential of the donated assets declines, depreciation is charged to operations, as discussed later in the chapter. Recording donated assets at fair market values is defended on the grounds that if the donation had been in cash, the amount received would have been recorded as donated capital, and the cash could have been used to purchase the asset at its fair market value.

SFAS No. 116 requires that the inflow of assets from a donation be considered revenue.[6] If so, the fair market value of the assets received represents the appropriate measurement. However, this argument may be flawed. According to *SFAC No. 6,* revenues arise from the delivery or production of goods and the rendering of services. If the contribution is a nonreciprocal transfer, then it is difficult to see how a revenue has been earned. Alternatively, it may be argued that the inflow represents a gain. This latter argument is consistent with the Conceptual Framework's definition of a gain, as resulting from peripheral or incidental transactions and with the definition of comprehensive income as the change in net assets resulting from nonowner transactions. Under this approach,

---

[5] Financial Accounting Standards Board, *Statement of Financial Accounting Standards No. 116,* "Accounting for Contributions Received and Contributions Made" (Stamford, CT: FASB, 1993), par. 5.

[6] Ibid., par. 8.

the asset and gain would be recorded at the fair market value of the asset received, thereby allowing full disclosure of the asset in the balance sheet.

Similarly, valuable natural resources may be discovered on property subsequent to its acquisition, and the original cost may not provide all relevant information about the nature of the property. In such cases, the cost principle is modified to account for the appraisal increase in the property. A corresponding increase is reported as an unrealized gain in accumulated other comprehensive income. An alternative practice consistent with the Conceptual Framework's definition of comprehensive income would be to recognize the appraisal increase as a gain.

Financial Analysis of Property, Plant, and Equipment

In Chapter 5 we discussed analyzing a company's profitability by computing the return on assets ratio. The sustainability of earnings is a major consideration in this process. For capital-intensive companies, a large portion of their assets base will be investments in property, plant, and equipment, and a major question for investors analyzing such companies is their asset replacement policy. A company with a large investment in property, plant, and equipment that fails to systematically replace those assets will generally report an increasing return on assets over the useful life of its asset base. That is, the return on assets denominator will decrease by the amount of annual depreciation expense (discussed in the next section), resulting in an increasing return percentage for stable amounts of earnings. In addition, the general pattern of rising prices will tend to increase the selling price of the company's product, resulting in a further upward bias for the return on assets percentage.

An examination of a company's investing activity helps in analyzing the earnings sustainability of the return on assets percentage. For example, Kroll-O'Gara Company's statement of cash flows contained in Chapter 5 reveals that the company acquired $5,521,131 and $6,947,155 of property, plant, and equipment assets in 1997 and 1998, respectively. These amounts are 16.0 percent and 15.9 percent, respectively of the purchase price of its property, plant, and equipment assets, and provide evidence that the company's return on assets percentage is not being distorted by a failure to systematically replace its long-term assets.

Cost Allocation

Capitalizing the cost of an asset implies that the asset has future service potential. Future service potential indicates that the asset is expected to generate or be associated with future resource flows. As those flows materialize, the matching concept (discussed in Chapter 3) dictates that certain costs no longer have future service potential and should be charged to expense during the period the associated revenues are earned. Because the cost of property, plant, and equipment is incurred to benefit future periods, it must be spread, or allocated, to the periods benefited. The process of recognizing, or spreading, cost over multiple periods is termed *cost allocation*. For items of property, plant, and equipment, cost allocation is referred to as *depreciation.* As the asset is depreciated, the cost is said to expire—that is, it is expensed. (See Chapter 3 for a discussion of the process of cost expiration.)

As discussed earlier, balance sheet measurements should theoretically reflect the future service potential of assets at any moment in time. Accountants generally agree that cost reflects future service potential at acquisition. However, in subsequent periods, expectations about future resource flows may change. Also, the discount rate used to measure the present value of the future service potential may change. As a result, the asset may still be useful, but because of technological changes, its future service potential at the end of any given period may differ from what was originally anticipated. Systematic cost allocation methods do not attempt to measure changes in expectations or discount rates. Consequently, no systematic cost allocation method can provide balance sheet measures that consistently reflect future service potential.

The historical cost accounting model presently dominant in accounting practice requires that the costs incurred be allocated in a systematic and rational manner. Thomas, following extensive study of cost allocation, concluded that all allocation is based on arbitrary assumptions and that no one method of cost allocation is superior to another.[7] At the same time, it cannot be concluded that the present accounting model provides information that is not useful for investor decision making. A number of studies document an association between accounting income numbers and stock returns. This evidence implies that historical-cost-based accounting income, which employs cost allocation methods, has information content. (See Chapter 4 for further discussion of this issue.)

Depreciation

Once the appropriate cost of an asset has been determined, certain decisions must be made as to the expiration of that cost. At the extremes, the entire cost of the asset can be expensed when the asset is acquired; or, alternatively, cost can be retained in the accounting records until disposal of the asset when the entire cost is expensed. However, neither of these approaches provides for a satisfactory measure of periodic income. Thus, the concept of depreciation was devised in an effort to allocate the cost of property, plant, and equipment over the periods that receive benefit from use of long-term assets.

The desire of financial statement users for periodic presentation of information on the result of operations necessitated allocating asset cost to the periods receiving benefit from use of the asset. Because depreciation is a form of cost allocation, all depreciation concepts are related to some view of income measurement. A strict interpretation of the FASB's comprehensive income concept would require that changes in service potential be recorded in income. Economic depreciation has been defined as the change in the discounted present value of the items of property, plant, and equipment during

---

[7] Arthur L. Thomas, "The Allocation Program in Financial. Accounting Theory," *Studies in Accounting Research No. 3* (American Accounting Association, 1969), Evanston, IL.

a period. If the discounted present value measures the service potential of the asset at a point in time, the change in service potential interpretation is consistent with the economic concept of income.

As discussed in Chapter 3, recording cost expirations by the change in service potential is a difficult concept to operationalize. Consequently, accountants have adopted a transactions view of income determination, in which they see income as the end result of revenue recognition according to certain criteria, coupled with the appropriate matching of expenses with those revenues. Thus, most depreciation methods emphasize the matching concept, and little attention is directed to balance sheet valuation. Depreciation is typically described as a process of systematic and rational cost allocation that is not intended to result in the presentation of asset fair value on the balance sheet. This point was first emphasized by the Committee on Terminology of the American Institute of Certified Public Accountants as follows:

> *Depreciation accounting is a system of accounting which aims to distribute the cost or other basic value of tangible capital assets, less salvage value (if any), over the estimated useful life of the unit (which may be a group of assets) in a systematic and rational manner. It is a process of allocation, not valuation.*[8]

The AICPA's view of depreciation is particularly important to an understanding of the difference between accounting and economic concepts of income, and it also provides insight into many misunderstandings about accounting depreciation. Economists see depreciation as the decline in the real value of assets. Other individuals believe that depreciation charges and the resulting accumulated depreciation provide the source of funds for future replacement of assets. Still others have suggested that business investment decisions are influenced by the portion of the original asset cost that has been previously allocated. That is, new investments cannot be made because the old asset has not been fully depreciated. These views are not consistent with the stated objective of depreciation for accounting purposes. In the following section, we examine the accounting concept of depreciation more closely.

The Depreciation Process

The depreciation process for long-term assets comprises three separate factors:

1. Establishing the proper depreciation base.
2. Estimating the useful service life.
3. Choosing a cost apportionment method.

Depreciation Base
The depreciation base is that portion of the cost of the asset that should be charged to expense over its expected useful life. Because cost represents the future service potential of the asset embodied in future resource flows, the

---

[8] *Accounting Terminology Bulletin No. 1,* "Review and Resume" (New York: AICPA, 1953), p. 9513.

theoretical depreciation base is the present value of all resource flows over the life of the asset, until disposition of the asset. Hence, it should be cost minus the present value of the salvage value. In practice, salvage value is not discounted, and as a practical matter, it is typically ignored. Proper accounting treatment requires that salvage value be taken into consideration. For example, rental car agencies normally use automobiles for only a short period; the expected value of these automobiles at the time they are retired from service would be material and should be considered in establishing the depreciation base.

Useful Service Life

The useful service life of an asset is the period of time the asset is expected to function efficiently. Consequently, an asset's useful service life may be less than its physical life, and factors other than wear and tear should be examined to establish the useful service life.

Various authors have suggested possible obsolescence, inadequacy, supersession, and changes in the social environment as factors to be considered in establishing the expected service life. For example, jet airplanes have replaced most of the propeller-driven planes on the airlines, and ecological factors have caused changes in manufacturing processes in the steel industry. Estimating such factors requires a certain amount of clairvoyance—a quality difficult to acquire.

Depreciation Methods

Most of the controversy in depreciation accounting revolves around the question of the proper method to use in allocating the depreciation base over its estimated service life. Theoretically, the expired cost of the asset should be related to the value received from the asset in each period; however, it is extremely difficult to measure these amounts. Accountants have, therefore, attempted to estimate expired costs by other methods, namely:

1. Straight line
2. Accelerated
3. Units of activity
4. Group and composite
5. Retirement and replacement
6. Compound interest

Straight Line The straight-line method allocates an equal portion of the depreciable cost of an asset to each period the asset is used. Straight-line depreciation is often justified on the basis of the lack of evidence to support other methods. Since it is difficult to establish evidence that links the value received from an asset to any particular period, the advocates of straight-line depreciation accounting argue that other methods are arbitrary and therefore inappropriate. Use of the straight-line method implies that the asset is declining in service potential in equal amounts over its estimated service life.

Accelerated The-sum-of-the-year's-digits and fixed-percentage-of-declining-base are the most frequently encountered methods of accelerated depreciation.[9] These methods result in larger charges to expense in the earlier years of asset use, although little evidence supports the notion that assets actually decline in service potential in the manner suggested by these methods. Advocates contend that accelerated depreciation is preferred to straight-line because as the asset ages, the smaller depreciation charges are associated with higher maintenance charges. The resulting combined expense pattern provides a better matching against the associated revenue stream. Accelerated depreciation methods probably give balance sheet valuations that are closer to the actual value of the assets in question than straight-line, since most assets depreciate in value more rapidly in their earlier years of use. But since depreciation accounting is not intended to be a method of asset valuation, this factor should not be viewed as an advantage of using accelerated depreciation methods.

Units of Activity Where assets, such as machinery, are used in the actual production process, it is sometimes possible to determine the total expected output to be obtained from these assets. Depreciation may then be based on the number of units of output during an accounting period. The activity measures of depreciation assume that each product produced during the asset's existence receives the same amount of benefit from the asset. This assumption may or may not be realistic. In addition, care must be exercised in establishing a direct relationship between the measurement unit and the asset. For example, when direct labor hours are used as a measure of the units of output, a decline in productive efficiency in the later years of the asset's use may cause the addition of more direct labor hours per product, which would result in charging more cost per unit.

Group and Composite Group and composite depreciation are similar methods that apply depreciation to more than one asset during each accounting period. The advantage claimed for both methods is that they simplify recordkeeping; however, they may also obscure gains and losses on the disposal of individual assets. Group depreciation is used for homogeneous assets that are expected to have similar service lives and residual values. Composite depreciation is used for dissimilar assets with varying service lives and residual values.

In either case, the total cost of the assets is capitalized in a single account and treated as if it were a single asset for depreciation purposes. The depreciation rate is based on the average life of the assets, and periodic depreciation is calculated by multiplying the balance in the asset account by this rate. In the event an individual asset is taken out of service, no gain or loss is recognized because the entire asset has not been retired. In an individual retirement, accumulated depreciation is charged for the difference between the

---

[9] Since 1981, the Internal Revenue Code has specified various accelerated depreciation methods to be used to determine taxable income. The method to use depends on the year of acquisition of the asset and the type of asset.

original cost and the proceeds received. Any gain or loss is recorded when the entire group of assets has been taken out of service.

Retirement and Replacement Some accountants have advocated retirement and replacement methods as expedient alternatives to the other methods of depreciation. Although retirement and replacement methods have not gained wide acceptance, they are used by public utilities. These methods recognize depreciation only at the time an asset reaches the end of its service life. Under the retirement method, depreciation is charged only when the asset is taken out of service, whereas the replacement method charges to depreciation the cost of new assets while retaining the original cost of plant and equipment acquired as an asset. Where the number of assets in use is large and a similar number of replacements occurs each year, these methods might be justified, but in general they completely distort the matching process. Another disadvantage inherent in the use of the retirement and replacement methods is that they allow for the possibility of earnings management. That is, the computation of net income may be significantly influenced and manipulated by management through advancing or postponing the replacement period.

Compound Interest Compound interest methods of depreciation have received attention because they focus on cost recovery and rate of return on investments. As discussed previously, assets may be viewed as future services to be received over their service lives, and the cost of the asset may then be viewed as the present value of the periodic services discounted at a rate of interest that takes into consideration the risk of the investment. The two compound interest depreciation methods most often encountered are the annuity method and the sinking fund method.

Under the *annuity method,* depreciation is based on the theory that production should be charged not only with the depreciable cost of the property, but also with the unrecovered income that might have been earned if the funds had been invested in some other manner.

The major criticism voiced against use of the annuity method is including interest in the periodic depreciation charge. Including interest as an element of the cost of the asset may be theoretically correct, but it is not a generally accepted accounting procedure.

The *sinking fund method* is based on the assumption that an asset replacement fund is being established to replace the assets retired. The sinking fund method takes into consideration the time value of money, and it results in a constant rate of return on book value. This method has been criticized, however, because it yields an increasing charge to depreciation in each year of asset life, while accountants generally agree that the service potential of the asset actually decreases each year.

An important point to note about all the depreciation methods is that no matter how simple or complex the calculations involved, the end result is an arbitrary cost allocation. The asset value disclosed on the balance sheet may not even approximate the current value of the asset. Therefore, since the avowed purpose of depreciation methods is to allocate cost, not determine value, the depreciation method selected should provide the most appropriate allocation of cost to the periods of benefit.

Disclosure of Depreciation Methods

The largest majority of U.S. companies use straight-line depreciation as evidenced by the 1999 edition of *Accounting Trends and Techniques*, which reported that 577 of the 600 firms surveyed used straight-line depreciation for at least some of their assets.[10] Kroll-O'Gara Company uses straight-line depreciation. The following is excerpted from the company's summary of significant accounting policies:

> *Property, Plant, and Equipment—Property, plant and equipment are stated at cost. Depreciation is computed on the straight-line method over the estimated useful lives of the related assets as follows:*

Buildings and improvements	*5–40 years*
Furniture and fixtures	*5–10 years*
Machinery and equipment	*5–12 years*
Leasehold improvements	*Life of lease*
Vehicles	*5 years*

Accounting for Oil and Gas Properties

The assignment of cost to oil and gas properties has been a controversial subject for a number of years. These assets are unlike other long-term assets in that relatively large expenditures are required to find them, and for every successful discovery there are many "dry holes."

For a number of years, two major methods of accounting have been advocated for recording and expensing the costs incurred in the development and production of oil and gas properties. These methods are termed the successful-efforts and the full-cost methods.

Under the *successful-efforts* method, costs that are directly identifiable with successful projects are capitalized and the costs of nonproducing efforts are expensed. The *full-cost* method capitalizes all the costs (whether they result in successful or unsuccessful projects) incurred for exploration and drilling within a large geographic area or cost center. Under both methods, the capitalized costs are subsequently allocated to expense as depletion by the units of activity method, as discussed earlier in the chapter. These alternatives can yield significantly different periodic asset valuations and net income figures.

The proponents of full costing maintain that oil companies undertake exploration and drilling activities knowing that only a small proportion of that activity will be fruitful. Therefore, unsuccessful activities must be viewed in the overall context of the entire exploration effort, and all costs related to the overall effort must be matched with the production from the few successful wells. Opponents to full costing argue that exploration efforts in one geographical area often bear little resemblance or relationship to exploration efforts in another dissimilar geographical area. Therefore, it is theoretically incorrect to match the costs of unsuccessful wells with the revenue of successful wells discovered in other locations.

---

[10] AICPA, *Accounting Trends and Techniques*, George N. Dieta, Richard Rikert, and Andy Mrakovic, eds., 53rd ed. New York: 1999, p. 359.

A second area of controversy concerns the relative financial effects of the full-cost and successful-efforts methods. One argument centers on the relative valuation of assets and measurement of net income under each method. Proponents of the full-cost method contend that the capitalization of all drilling costs results in a measurement of assets that is closer to the present value of proved reserves and further results in a higher net income. The larger assets and higher income enable small producers to attract the capital necessary to continue operations.

The proponents of the successful-efforts method counter by saying that there will not be a significant restriction on the inflow of capital to smaller producers solely due to the accounting method utilized. The evidence in the accounting literature from the efficient market research (discussed in Chapter 2) indicates that the stock market does not respond to changes in income that are caused by using alternative accounting principles.[11]

The FASB undertook a study of these arguments, and, in December 1977, issued *SFAS No. 19*, "Financial Accounting and Reporting by Oil and Gas Companies." In this release, the board accepted the viewpoints advanced by the proponents of the successful-efforts method. The following is a summary of the rationale given for this decision.

1. Costs should be capitalized if they are expected to provide identifiable future benefits; otherwise they are considered to be an expense. The successful-efforts method is consistent with this concept while full cost is not.

2. Financial statements should report on the results of economic influences as they occur. If a firm's operations yield widely fluctuating earnings or only minor fluctuations, the financial statements should report them. If the statements do not show these differences that are perceived by investors and lenders as representing differences in risk, or if differences are shown that really do not exist, then capital may not be allocated equitably in the market. Full cost tends to obscure failure and risk by capitalizing both successful and unsuccessful activities; the successful-efforts method clearly depicts the risk involved by expensing unsuccessful operations.

3. Small companies argue that their ability to raise capital will be impaired if successful efforts are required because their income statements will more likely report net losses, and their balance sheets could report cumulative deficits in stockholders' equity. Studies on the effect of accounting methods on securities prices are not conclusive. The claim that successful efforts would inhibit a company's ability to obtain capital has not been demonstrated or refuted conclusively. In addition, accounting standards should not be designed to foster national economic goals but instead should objectively report the results of operations.

These issues contain elements of both agency theory and economic consequences arguments in addition to their efficient markets implications. If

---

[11] For a further discussion of these issues, see Steven M. Flory and Steven D. Grossman, "New Oil and Gas Accounting Requirements," *The CPA Journal* (May 1978), pp. 39–43.

small firms are more susceptible to earnings fluctuations, it will be expected that the managers of these firms will react by reducing or eliminating more risky drilling activities to protect their earnings. As a consequence, the total proven oil and gas reserves for U.S. companies will decline because some risky projects are successful.

Soon after the release of *SFAS No. 19*, many small oil and gas producers voiced objections and asked the U.S. Congress for relief from its provisions. This pressure ultimately resulted in three SEC Accounting Series Releases on oil and gas accounting. The result of these pronouncements was a posture of support for the FASB's overall efforts but a rejection of the provisions of *SFAS No. 19*.

In reaction to *SFAS No. 19*, the SEC asserted that both the full-cost and successful-efforts methods were so inadequate that it did not matter which was employed. As a substitute, the SEC recommended a method termed *reserve recognition accounting* (RRA). This method is a current-value approach that is based on the net present values of a company's oil and gas reserves. However, this recommendation has not been implemented because its use requires too many assumptions.

Later, the FASB issued *SFAS Nos. 33* and *39*. These releases required large publicly held oil and gas companies to report the effects of changing prices on certain types of assets. At this time, the board recognized that the accumulation of all the required information was placing a significant burden on oil- and gas-producing companies. The usefulness of the required data was also questioned, as was the failure to disclose other, seemingly more relevant information.

Thereafter, a task force comprised of individuals from the oil and gas industry and the financial and accounting community was formed to aid in the development of reporting standards for the oil and gas industry. The result of this review was the publication of *SFAS No. 69*, "Disclosures about Oil and Gas Producing Activities."

According to this release, publicly traded companies with significant oil and gas activities are required to disclose the following as supplementary information to their published financial statements.

1. Proven oil and gas reserve quantities.
2. Capitalized costs relating to oil- and gas-producing activities.
3. Costs incurred in oil and gas property acquisition, exploration, and development activities.
4. Results of operations for oil- and gas-producing activities.
5. A standardized measure of discounted future net cash flows relating to proven oil and gas reserve quantities.

Capital and Revenue Expenditures

The purchase and installation of plant and equipment does not eliminate expenditures associated with these assets. Almost all productive facilities require periodic maintenance that should be charged to current expense. The cost of the asset to the enterprise includes the initial cost plus all costs associated with keeping the asset in working order. However, if additional expenditures give rise to an increase in future service potential, these expenditures should not be charged to current operations. Expenditures that increase future service potential should be added to the remaining unexpired cost of the asset and be charged to expense over the estimated remaining period of benefit.

In most cases, the decision to expense or capitalize expenditures subject to acquisition is fairly simple and is based on whether the cost incurred is "ordinary and necessary" or "prolongs future life." But frequently this decision becomes more complicated, and additional rules have been formulated that assist in determining whether an expenditure should be recorded as a capital improvement. If the asset's life is increased, the efficiency provided is increased, or if output is increased, the cost of an expenditure should be capitalized and written off over the expected period of benefit. All other expenditures made subsequent to acquisition should be expensed as incurred.

Recognition and Measurement Issues

Accounting depreciation methods are objective because they use historical cost. Moreover, once selected, the resulting depreciation charges are generally reliable. Nevertheless, all accounting depreciation methods have similar recognition and measurement problems. Given that fixed assets are intended to provide service potential over multiple future years, each cost allocation method requires estimates of salvage value and useful life, and given the rapidly changing competitive environment, revisions of these estimates may be required each accounting period.

It can also be argued that accounting depreciation methods do not provide relevant information for users. Users desire information that is useful in predicting future cash flows. Users are also aware that management makes a decision each period either to reinvest in available long-term assets or to replace existing long-term assets with new ones. Consequently, a current-value approach to depreciation may be more consistent with investor needs.

Recording depreciation using a current-value balance sheet approach would require knowledge of the reinvestment value of each long-term asset at the end of each accounting period. Such a determination may be impracticable or even impossible. The assets in question may be old, or they may be so specialized that there is no readily determinable market value. Alternative discounted present-value techniques require estimates of future cash flows that may be unreliable. And appraisal values may not be realistic. Therefore, there is no simple answer to the determination of the most appropriate approach to depreciation. This determination depends, to a large extent, on an individual's perception of the necessary trade-off between relevance and reliability.

Impairment of Value

The *SFAC No. 6* definition of assets (see Chapter 5) implies that assets have future service potential and consequently value to the reporting entity. Future service potential implies that the asset is expected to generate future cash flows. When the present value of future cash flows decreases, the value of the asset to the firm declines. If the decline in value over the life of the asset is greater than the accumulated depreciation charges, the book value of the asset is overstated and the value of the asset is said to be impaired. Yet accountants have been reluctant to apply the lower of cost or market rule to account for fixed assets.

The FASB, noting divergent practices in the recognition of impairment of long-lived assets, issued *SFAS No. 121*,[12] which addresses the matter of when to recognize the impairment of long-lived assets and how to measure the loss. This release ignores current value as a determinant of impairment. Rather, the pronouncement states that impairment occurs when the carrying amount of the asset is not recoverable. The recoverable amount is defined as the sum of the future cash flows expected to result from use of the asset and its eventual disposal. Companies are required to review long-lived assets (including intangibles) for impairment whenever events or changes in circumstances indicate that book value may not be recoverable. Examples are:

1. A significant decrease in the market value of an asset.

2. A significant change in the extent or manner in which an asset is used.

3. A significant adverse change in legal factors or in business climate that affects the value of assets.

4. An accumulation of significant costs in excess of the amount originally expended to acquire or construct an asset.

5. A projection or forecast that demonstrates a history of continuing losses associated with the asset.

Although fair value is not used to determine impairment, *SFAS No. 121* requires that when impairment has occurred, a loss is to be recognized for the difference between the carrying value of an asset and its current value less estimated cost to dispose of the asset. The resulting reduced carrying value of the asset becomes its new cost basis and is depreciated over the remaining useful life of the asset.

International Accounting Standards

The International Accounting Standards Committee has issued pronouncements on the following issues affecting items of property, plant, and equipment:

1. The overall issues associated with accounting for property, plant, and equipment assets in *IAS No. 16*, "Property, Plant and Equipment."

---

[12] *Statement of Financial Accounting Standards No. 121*, "Accounting for the Impairment of Long-Lived Assets to Be Disposed Of" (Stamford, CT: Financial Accounting Standards Board, 1995).

2. The capitalization of interest costs on acquired assets in *IAS No. 23,* "Borrowing Costs."

3. The accounting treatment for impairment of assets in *IAS No. 36,* "Impairment of Assets."

4. Accounting for investment properties in *IAS No. 40,* "Investment Property."

IAS No. 16 allows for differences from U.S. GAAP in that items of property, plant, and equipment are allowed (but not required) to be periodically revalued to current market values. The standard also requires depreciation to be calculated in a manner that more closely resembles the actual decline in service potential of the assets.

IAS No. 16 indicates that items of property, plant, and equipment should be recognized as assets when it is probable that the future economic benefit associated with these assets will flow to the enterprise and that their cost can be reliably measured. Under these circumstances, the initial measurement of the value of the asset is defined as its cost. Subsequently, the stated preferred treatment is to depreciate the asset's historical cost; however, an allowed alternative treatment is to periodically revalue the asset at its fair market value. When such revaluations occur, increases in value are to be recorded in stockholders' equity, unless a previously existing reevaluation surplus exists, whereas decreases are recorded as current-period expenses. In the event a revaluation is undertaken, the statement requires that the entire group of assets to which the revalued asset belongs also be revalued. Examples of groups of property, plant, and equipment assets are land, buildings, and machinery. Finally, the required disclosures for items of property, plant, and equipment include the measurement bases used for the assets, as well as a reconciliation of the beginning and ending balances to include disposals and acquisitions and any revaluation adjustments.

IAS No. 16 also requires companies to periodically review the carrying amounts of items of property, plant, and equipment to determine whether the recoverable amount of the asset has declined below its carrying amount. When such a decline has occurred, the carrying amount of the asset must be reduced to the recoverable amount, and this reduction is recognized as an expense in the current period. *IAS No. 16* also requires write-ups when the circumstances or events that led to write-downs cease to exist. This treatment contrasts to the requirements of *SFAS No. 121,* which prohibits recognition of subsequent recoveries.

With respect to depreciation, *IAS No. 16* indicated that the periodic charge should be allocated in a systematic basis over the asset's useful life and that the depreciation method selected should reflect the pattern in which the asset's economic benefits are consumed. Finally, the standard requires periodic review of the pattern of economic benefits consumed, and when a change in the pattern of benefits is in evidence, the method of depreciation must be changed to reflect this new pattern of benefits. Such changes in depreciation methods are to be accounted for as changes in accounting principles. This treatment differs substantially from U.S. GAAP where the depreciation method selected is only required to be systematic and rational, and changes in depreciation methods are allowed only in unusual circumstances.

The FASB staff review of *IAS No. 16* indicated concern over several areas of difference between this standard and existing U.S. GAAP. Of particular concern was the allowed alternative treatment of periodically revaluing items of property, plant, and equipment on the basis of their fair values. The use of this alternative treatment, which is not allowed under U.S. GAAP, was seen as distorting intercompany comparability and decreasing the use of similar accounting procedures in similar circumstances. The staff also expressed concern that the guidelines for determining fair value were unclear and inconsistent in that both current value and value in use definitions were used in suggesting how to calculate fair value. Other expressed areas of concern were the concept of depreciation by pattern of use, the failure to specifically address accounting for assets in the extractive industries, and the failure to specify clear rules for capitalization of subsequent expenditures related to assets.[13]

IAS No. 23 allows companies to choose between two methods of accounting for borrowing costs. Under the benchmark treatment, companies are required to recognize interest costs in the period in which they are incurred. Under the allowed alternative treatment, interest costs that are directly attributable to the acquisition, construction, or production of a qualifying asset are capitalized as part of that asset. The interest costs that are to be capitalized are the costs that could be avoided if the expenditure for the qualifying asset had not been made. As a result, the IASC alternative accounting treatment for capitalized interest costs is similar to U.S. GAAP. In its review of *IAS No. 23*, the FASB staff expressed concern over companies' ability to choose one of two possible treatments for the same transaction. Of additional concern was the fact that this recognition flexibility (immediate recognition versus capitalization) might have a profound effect on reported net income.[14]

IAS No. 36 requires an impairment loss to be recognized whenever the recoverable amount of an asset is less than its carrying amount (its book value). The recoverable amount of an asset is the higher of its net selling price and its value in use. Both are based on present-value calculations as follows:

Net selling price is the amount obtainable from the sale of an asset in an arm's length transaction between knowledgeable willing parties, less the costs of disposal.

[13] Financial Accounting Standards Board, *The IASC-U.S. Comparison Project: A Report on the Similarities and Differences between IASC Standards and U.S. GAAP,* 2nd ed., Carrie Bloomer, ed. (Norwalk, CT. Financial Accounting Standards Board, 1999), pp. 173–186.

[14] Ibid., pp. 321–328.

Value in use is the amount obtainable from use of an asset until the end of its useful life and from its subsequent disposal. Value in use is calculated as the present value of estimated future cash flows. The discount rate should be a pretax rate that reflects current market assessments of the time value of money and the risks specific to the asset.

An impairment loss should be recognized as an expense in the income statement for assets carried at cost and should be treated as a revaluation decrease for assets carried at a revalued amount. An impairment loss should be reversed (and income recognized) when there has been a change in the estimates used to determine an asset's recoverable amount since the last impairment loss was recognized.

In determining value in use, an enterprise should use:

a. Cash flow projections based on reasonable and supportable assumptions that reflect the asset in its current condition and represent management's best estimate of the set of economic conditions that will exist over the remaining useful life of the asset. Estimates of future cash flows should include all estimated future cash inflows and cash outflows except for cash flows from financing activities and income tax receipts and payments.

b. A pretax discount rate that reflects current market assessments of the time value of money and the risks specific to the asset. The discount rate should not reflect risks for which the future cash flows have been adjusted.

If an asset does not generate cash inflows that are largely independent of the cash inflows from other assets, an enterprise should determine the recoverable amount of the cash-generating unit to which the asset belongs. A cash-generating unit is the smallest identifiable group of assets that generates cash inflows that are largely independent of the cash inflows from other assets or group of assets.

Impairment losses recognized in prior years should be reversed if, and only if, there has been a change in the estimates used to determine recoverable amount since the last impairment loss was recognized. However, an impairment loss should only be reversed to the extent the reversal does not increase the carrying amount of the asset above the carrying amount that would have been determined for the asset (net of amortization or depreciation) had no impairment loss been recognized. An impairment loss for goodwill should be reversed only if the specific external event that caused the recognition of the impairment loss reverses. A reversal of an impairment loss should be recognized as income in the income statement for assets carried at cost and treated as a revaluation increase for assets carried at revalued amount.

The FASB staff review of *IAS No. 36* indicated that it takes a similar approach to identifying impaired assets as that contained in *SFAS No. 121*. However, it was noted that the two statements are significantly different in their approaches to recognizing, measuring, and reversing impairment losses. *IAS No. 36* requires that its impairment provisions be applied to all assets, whereas *SFAS No. 121* requires that different recognition and measurement provisions be applied to assets to be held and used than to assets to be disposed of. Although both statements require an impairment trigger to record a loss, *IAS No. 36* uses the higher of an asset's net selling price or value in use and incorporates discounting, whereas *SFAS No. 121* uses the sum of an asset's undiscounted future cash flows. As a result, companies using *IAS No. 36* will normally recognize impairment losses sooner than if they had used *SFAS No. 121*. *IAS No. 36* requires that an impairment loss be measured as the amount by which an asset's carrying value exceeds its impairment recognition trigger, whereas *SFAS No. 121* measures the loss as the difference between the assets carrying value and its fair value. These differences can cause the recognition of substantially different amount of loss. Finally, *IAS No. 36* requires the reversal of previously recorded impairment losses for both assets held and used and assets disposed of, while *SFAS No. 121* does not permit the reversal of impairment losses for assets held and used. This difference is likely to increase the volatility of the amounts reported under *IAS No. 36*.[15]

IAS No. 40 was released in March 2000 and became effective for accounting periods beginning on or after January 1, 2001. It covers investment property held by all enterprises. Investment property is defined as property (land or buildings) held to earn rentals or for capital appreciation, or both. In accounting for these properties under *IAS No. 40*, an enterprise must choose either

A fair value model whereby investment property is measured at fair value and changes in fair value are recognized in the income statement; or

A cost model (the same as the benchmark treatment in *IAS No. 16*, "Property, Plant and Equipment," whereby investment property is measured at depreciated cost (less any accumulated impairment losses). An enterprise that chooses the cost model should disclose the fair value of its investment property. *IAS No. 40* indicates that the model chosen must be used to account for all of its investment properties, and a change from one model to the other model should be made only if the change will result in a more appropriate presentation. The standard states that this is highly unlikely to be the case for a change from the fair value model to the cost model. The FASB staff had not reviewed *IAS No. 40* at the time this text was published. A summary of its review will be added to the text's website when it becomes available.

Summary

Property, plant, and equipment are usually the major long-term assets of a company. The overall objectives in accounting for these assets are to

---

[15] Ibid., pp. 413–430.

give management, investors, and government authorities useful information about these assets and to plan for a new acquisition through realistic budgeting. A number of problems arise in choosing methods for assigning costs for these assets. Generally accepted accounting principles have been developed to handle most of these troublesome areas. Assigning asset cost to the period of benefit remains the major problem in accounting for property, plant, and equipment. There are a number of views on depreciation as well as a number of alternative methods of calculating and assigning these costs.

In the readings contained on the text's webpage for Chapter 8, some additional issues associated with accounting for property, plant and equipment are examined.

Cases

• Case 8-1 Donated Assets

The City of Martinsville donated land to Essex Company. The fair value of the land was $100,000. The land had cost the city $45,000.

Required:
a. Describe the current accounting treatment for the land. Include in your answer the amount at which the land would be valued by Essex Company and any other income statement or balance sheet effect.
b. Under the recommendations outlined in *SFAS No. 116,* the FASB required that donated assets be recorded at fair value and that revenue be recognized equivalent to the amount recorded for a donation.
  i.   Defend the FASB's position. In your answer refer to the Conceptual Framework.
  ii. Criticize the FASB's position. In your answer refer to the Conceptual Framework.
c. Assume that immediately before the donation, Essex had assets totaling $800,000 and liabilities totaling $350,000. Compare the financial statement effects of the FASB requirement with previous practice. For example, how would EPS or ratios such as debt-to-equity be affected?

• Case 8-2 Purchase of Assets

On October 10, 2000, Mason Engineering Company completed negotiations on a contract for the purchase of new equipment. Under the terms of the agreement, the equipment may be purchased now or Mason may wait until January 10, 2001, to make the purchase. The cost of the equipment is $400,000. It will be financed by a note-bearing interest at the market rate of interest. Straight-line depreciation over a 10-year life will be used for book purposes. A double-declining balance over seven years will be used for tax purposes. (One-half year's depreciation will be taken in the year of purchase regardless of the date of purchase.)

Required:
a. Discuss the financial statement impacts of postponing the purchase of the equipment. Would the market price of the firm's common stock be affected by any or all of these impacts? Do not assume in your discussion that the postponement will have impact on revenues or any operating costs, other than depreciation.
b. Discuss any cash flow impacts related to postponing the purchase of the equipment.
c. Efficient markets assume that stockholder wealth is affected by the amount and timing of cash flows. Which alternative is more favorable to them: purchasing before year-end or waiting until January? Explain your answer.

• Case 8-3 Accounting for Natural Resources

During 2000 (its first year of operations), the Jerry Oil and Gas Rigging Company drilled 9 oil wells. One is producing, and it cost $700,000 to drill. Seven are dry holes, costing $500,000 each. Jerry is still drilling the other well. So far, Jerry has sunk $220,000 into this well.

The producing well is expected to provide 5 million barrels of oil.

Required:
a. Assume production and sale of 2,000 barrels in 2000. What will be the cost of sales under the successful-efforts method and the full-cost method? What other expense(s), if any, related to drilling will be recognized under each case?
b. Which alternative will allow Jerry to present more favorable-looking financial statements? Explain.
c. Which method is more representationally faithful? Explain.
d. Discuss whether drilling the dry holes qualifies as an asset under the Conceptual Framework's definition of assets. Give pros and cons.

• Case 8-4 Depreciation Accounting

Depreciation continues to be one of the most controversial, difficult, and important problem areas in accounting.

Required:
a. Explain the conventional accounting concept of depreciation accounting.
b. Discuss its conceptual merit with respect to
   i. The value of the asset.
   ii. The charge(s) to expense.
   iii. The discretion of management in selecting the method.
c. Explain the factors that should be considered when applying the conventional concept of depreciation to the determination of how the value of a newly acquired computer system should be assigned to expense for financial reporting purposes (income tax considerations should be ignored).

d.   What depreciation methods might be used for the computer system? Describe the advantages and disadvantages of each.

• Case 8-5 Self-Constructed Assets

Jay Manufacturing, Inc. began operations five years ago producing probos, a new type of instrument it hoped to sell to doctors, dentists, and hospitals. The demand for probos far exceeded initial expectations, and the company was unable to produce enough probos to meet that demand.

The company was manufacturing probos on equipment it built at the start of its operations, but to meet demand more efficient equipment was needed. Company management decided to design and build the equipment since equipment that was currently available on the market was unsuitable for producing probos.

In 2001 a section of the plant was devoted to development of the new equipment, and a special staff of personnel was hired. Within six months a machine was developed at a cost of $170,000 that successfully increased production and reduced labor cost substantially. Sparked by the success of the new machine, the company built three more machines of the same type at a cost of $80,000 each.

Required:
a.   In addition to satisfying a need that outsiders cannot meet within the desired time, what other reasons might cause a firm to construct fixed assets for its own use?
b.   In general, what costs should be capitalized for a self-constructed asset?
c.   Discuss the proprietary (give pros and cons) of including in the capitalized cost of self-constructed assets:
    i.   The increase in overhead caused by the self-construction of fixed assets.
    ii. A proportionate share of overhead on the same basis as that applied to goods manufactured for sale. Take into consideration whether or not the company is at full capacity.
d.   Discuss the proper accounting treatment of the $90,000 ($170,000 – $80,000) by which the cost of the first machine exceeded the cost of the subsequent machines.

• Case 8-6 Accounting for Land

Your client found three suitable sites, each having certain unique advantages, for a new plant facility. In order to thoroughly investigate the advantages and disadvantages of each site, one-year options were purchased for an amount equal to 5 percent of the contract price of each site. The costs of the options cannot be applied against the contracts. Before the options expire, one of the sites was purchased at the contract price of $60,000. The option on this site had cost $3,000. The two options not exercised had cost $3,500 each.

Required:
Present arguments in support of recording the cost of the land at each of the following amounts:
a. $60,000
b. $63,000
c. $70,000

• Case 8-7 Depreciation Accounting

Property, plant, and equipment (plant assets) generally represent a material portion of the total assets of most companies. Accounting for the acquisition and usage of such assets is, therefore, an important part of the financial reporting process.

Required:
a. Distinguish between revenue and capital expenditures and explain why this distinction is important.
b. Briefly define depreciation as used in accounting.
c. Identify the factors that are relevant in determining the annual depreciation and explain whether these factors are determined objectively or whether they are based on judgment.
d. Explain why depreciation is shown as an adjustment to cash in the operations section on the statement of cash flows.

• Case 8-8 Accounting for Land and Plant Assets

A company may acquire plant assets (among other ways) for cash, on a deferred payment plan, by exchanging other assets or by a combination of these ways.

Required:
a. Identify six costs that should be capitalized as the cost of the land. For your answer, assume that land with an existing building is acquired for cash and that the existing building is to be removed in the immediate future so that a new building can be constructed on the site.
b. At what amount should a company record a plant asset acquired on a deferred payment plan?
c. In general, at what amount should plant assets received in exchange for other nonmonetary assets be recorded? Specifically, at what amount should a company record a new machine acquired by exchanging an older similar machine and paying cash? Would your answer be the same if cash were received?

• Case 8-9 Acquisition and Sale of Plant Assets

George Company purchased land for use as its corporate headquarters. A small factory that was on the land when it was purchased was torn down before construction of the office building began. Furthermore, a substantial amount of rock blasting and removal had to be done to the site before construction of the building foundation began. Because the office building was set back on the land far from the public road, George Company had the contractor construct a paved road that led from the public road to the parking lot of the office building.

Three years after the office building was occupied, George Company added four stories to the office building. The four stories had an estimated useful life of five years more than the remaining estimated life of the original building.

Ten years later the land and buildings were sold at an amount more than their net book value, and George Company had a new office building constructed in another state for use as its new corporate headquarters.

Required:
a. Which of the preceding expenditures should be capitalized? How should each be depreciated or amortized? Discuss the rationale for your answers.
b. How would the sale of the land and building be accounted for? Include in your answer how to determine the net book value at the date of sale. Discuss the rationale for your answer.

• Case 8-10 Accounting for Property, Plant, and Equipment

Among the principal topics related to the accounting for the property, plant, and equipment of a company are acquisitions and retirements.

Required:
a. What expenditures should be capitalized when equipment is acquired for cash?
b. Assume the market value of equipment is not determinable by reference to a similar purchase for cash. Describe how the acquiring company should determine the capitalized cost of equipment purchased by exchanging it for each of the following:
   i.   Bonds having an established market price.
   ii. Common stock not having an established market price.
   iii. Similar equipment not having a determinable market price.
c. Describe the factors that determine whether expenditures relating to property, plant, and equipment already in use should be capitalized.
d. Describe how to account for the gain or loss on the sale of property, plant, or equipment.

• Case 8-11 Individual vs. Composite Depreciation

Management frequently calls on a certified public accountant for advice regarding methods of computing depreciation. Although the question arises less frequently, of comparable importance is whether the depreciation method should be based on the consideration of assets as units, or as a group, or as having a composite life.

Required.
a. Briefly describe the depreciation methods based on treating assets as
   i. Units.
   ii. A group or having a composite life.
b. Present arguments for and against the use of each of the two methods.
c. Describe how retirements are recorded under each of the two methods. Give the rationale for each case.

• Case 8-12 Environmental Costs

Joe Mason acquired land on which he will construct a new restaurant. A chemical plant had once occupied the site. Government regulations require Joe to clean up the chemical residue before building. The cost of the clean-up is material.

Required:
a. Under current GAAP, an asset is charged with historical cost, which includes the purchase price and all costs incident to getting the asset ready for its intended use. Defend the historical cost principle. Use the conceptual framework concepts and definitions in your defense.
b. How should Joe treat the cost of the clean-up? Is it a land cost, a building cost, or an expense? Explain.

• Case 8-13 Cost Allocation

Keeping an asset implies reinvestment in the asset. Finance theory is consistent with the notion that reinvestment is at current value, or replacement cost. Such a decision is presumably based on comparing expected future cash flows that will be generated by the asset and the cost of replacing it with a new one that may generate the same or different cash flows.

According to the conceptual framework, the purpose of financial statements is to provide information regarding performance. Investment or reinvestment decisions are a part of that performance. Yet, the historical cost of fixed assets is retained and allocated over subsequent accounting periods.

Required:
a. Present arguments in favor of cost allocation.
b. Does cost allocation provide relevant information?
c. Would a current-value approach to measurement of fixed assets be preferable? Why?
d. Would a current-value approach be consistent with the physical capital maintenance concept? Explain.
e. What problems and limitations are associated with using replacement cost for fixed assets?

Room for Debate

• Issue 1

According to *SFAS No. 34*, interest on self-constructed assets should be capitalized.

Team Debate:

Team 1. Present arguments in favor of capitalizing interest. Tie your arguments to the concepts and definitions found in the conceptual framework.

Team 2. Criticize the provisions of *SFAS No. 34*. Present arguments against capitalizing interest. Tie your arguments to the concepts and definitions found in the conceptual framework. (Finance theory would say that interest is a return to the capital provider, the lender. Finance theory may assist you in your argument.)

Recommended Additional Readings

Barefield, Russell M., and Eugene Comiskey. "Depreciation Policy and the Behavior of Corporate Profits." *Journal of Accounting Research* (Autumn 1971), pp. 351–358.

Bennett, Anthony H. "Depreciation and Business Decision Making." *Accounting and Business Research* (Winter 1972), pp. 3–28.

Brown, Lawrence D., Ronald J. Huefner, and Ralph W. Sanders, Jr. "A Test of the Reliability of Current Cost Disclosures." *Abacus* (March 1994), pp. 2–18.

Burt, Oscar R. "Unified Theory of Depreciation." *Journal of Accounting Research* (Spring 1970), pp. 28–57.

Cooper, Jean C., and Frank H. Selto. "An Experimental Examination of the Effects of SFAS No. 2 on R & D Decisions." *Accounting, Organizations and Society* Vol. 3, No. 1 (1991), pp. 227–243.

Grinyer, J. R. "A New Approach to Depreciation." *Abacus* (March 1987), pp. 43–54.

Johnson, Orace. "Two General Concepts of Depreciation." *Journal of Accounting Research* (Spring 1968), pp. 29–37.

Kim, M., and G. Moore. "Economic vs. Accounting Depreciation." *Journal of Accounting and Economics* (April 1988), pp. 111–126.

Lowe, Howard. "The Essential of a General Theory of Depreciation." *The Accounting Review* (April 1963), pp. 293–301.

McKeown, James C. "Comparative Application of Market and Cost Based Accounting Models." *Journal of Accounting Research* (Spring 1973), pp. 65–78.

Smith, Kenneth J. "Asset Impairment Disclosures," *Journal of Accountancy* (December 1994), pp. 57–64.

Snavely, Howard J. "Current Cost for Long-Lived Assets: A Critical View." *The Accounting Review* (April 1969), pp. 344–353.

Wright, F. K. "Toward A General Theory of Depreciation." *Journal of Accounting Research* (Spring 1964), pp. 80–90.

Bibliography

Alciatore, Mimi L. "The Reliability and Relevance of Reserve Value Accounting Data: A Review of the Empirical Research." *Journal of Accounting Literature* (1990), pp. 1–38.

Anthony, Robert N. *Accounting for the Cost of Interest.* Lexington, MA: Lexington Books, 1975.

Arcady, Alex T., and Charles E. Baker. "Capitalization of Interest Cost—Implementing FASB Statement No. 34." *The Ohio CPA* (Autumn 1980), pp. 137–141.

Arnett, Harold E. "APB Opinion No. 29: Accounting for Nonmonetary Transactions—Some New Perspectives." *Management Accounting* (October 1978), pp. 41–48.

Barnea, Amir. "Note on the Cash-flow Approach to Valuation and Depreciation of Productive Assets." *Journal of Financial and Quantitative Analysis* (June 1972), pp. 1841–1846.

Baxter, W. T. "Depreciating Assets: The Forward Looking Approach to Value." *Abacus* (December 1970), pp. 120–131.

Beidelman, Carl R. "Valuation of Used Capital Assets." *Studies in Accounting Research* No. 7. American Accounting Association, 1973.

Bierman, Harold, Jr., and Thomas R. Dyckman. "Accounting for Interest During Construction." *Accounting and Business Research* (Autumn 1979), pp. 267–272.

Cappettini, Robert, and Thomas E. King. "Exchanges of Nonmonetary Assets: Some Changes." *The Accounting Review* (January 1976), pp. 142–147.

Castellano, Joseph F., Clarence E. Campbell, and Harper A. Roehm. "An Application of APB Opinion 29." *The Ohio CPA* (Winter 1976), pp. 17–19.

Chambers, Raymond J. "Asset Measurement and Valuation." *Cost and Management* (March–April 1971), pp. 30–35.

Cotteleer, Thomas F. "Depreciation, an Accounting Enigma." *Management Accounting* (February 1971), pp. 23–24, 27.

Coughlan, Joseph D., and William K. Strand. *Depreciation: Accounting, Taxes, and Business Decisions.* New York: Ronald Press, 1969.

Dixon, Robert L. "Decreasing Charge Depreciation—A Search for Logic." *The Accounting Review* (October 1960), pp. 590–597.

Flory, Steven M., and Steven D. Grossman. "New Oil and Gas Accounting." *The CPA Journal* (May 1978), pp. 39–43.

Goldberg, L. "Concepts of Depreciation." In W. T. Baxter and Sidney Davidson (eds.). *Studies in Accounting Theory.* Homewood, IL: Richard D. Irwin, 1962, pp. 236–258.

Gray, O. Ronald. "Implementation of FASB Statement No. 34: Capitalization of Interest Cost." *The National Public Accountant* (April 1980), pp. 23–25.

Greipel, Rudolph C. "Accounting for Nonmonetary Transactions—A Review of APB Opinion No. 29." *The CPA Journal* (January 1974), pp. 34–39.

Grossman, Steven D., Alan G. Mayper, and Robert B. Welker. "Oil and Gas Disclosures—The FASB Reacts." *The CPA Journal* (May 1983), pp. 24–29.

Harris, Trevor S., and James A. Ohlson. "Accounting Disclosures and the Market's Valuation of Oil and Gas Properties: Evaluation of Market Efficiency and Functional Fixation." *The Accounting Review* (October 1990), pp. 764–780.

Imhoff, Eugene A., and Paul A. Janell. "Opinion No. 29: A New Valuation Method." *Management Accounting* (March 1979), pp. 50–53.

Lambert, S. J., and Joyce C. Lambert. "Concepts and Applications in APB Opinion No. 29." *Journal of Accountancy* (March 1977), pp. 60–68.

Lamden, Charles W., Dale L. Gerboth, and Thomas W. McRae. *Accounting for Depreciable Assets.* New York: American Institute of Certified Public Accountants, 1975.

Lev, Baruch, and Henri Theil. "A Maximum Entropy Approach to the Choice of Asset Depreciation." *Journal of Accounting Research* (Autumn 1978), pp. 286–293.

McIntyre, Edward V. "Present Value Depreciation and the Disaggregation Problem." *The Accounting Review* (January 1977), pp. 261–271.

Most, Kenneth S. "Depreciation in Economic and Accounting Theories." *Accountant* (February 25, 1971), pp. 237–240.

Mullen, Louis E. "Spotlight on Estimated Economic Life of Depreciable Assets." *The CPA Journal* (August 1973), pp. 662–666.

NAA Management Accounting Practices Committee. "Fixed Asset Accounting: The Allocation of Costs." *Management Accounting* (January 1974), pp. 43–49.

NAA Management Accounting Practices Committee. "Fixed Asset Accounting: The Capitalization of Costs." *The CPA Journal* (March 1973), pp. 193–207.

Nikolai, Loren A. "Simplifying Nonmonetary Exchanges." *The CPA Journal* (January 1977), pp. 69–71.

Paton, William A. "Depreciation—Concept and Measurement." *Journal of Accountancy* (October 1959), pp. 38–43.

Peasnell, K. V. "The CCA Depreciation Problem—An Analysis and Proposal." *Abacus* (December 1977), pp. 123–140.

Pidock, Wayne L. "Accounting for Net Salvage." *Management Accounting* (December 1970), pp. 49–52.

Thomas, Arthur L. *Studies in Accounting Research No. 9.* "The Allocation Problem: Part Two." Sarasota, FL: American Accounting Association, 1974.

Warrell, C. J. "The Enterprise Value Concept of Asset Valuation." *Accounting and Business Research* (Summer 1974), pp. 220–226.

Young, T. N., and C. G. Peirson. "Depreciation—Future Services Basis." *The Accounting Review* (April 1967), pp. 338–341.

Long-Term
Assets II:
Investments
and Intangibles

Investments in the securities of other corporations are made for a variety of reasons such as obtaining additional income, creating desirable relationships with suppliers, obtaining partial or full control over related companies, or adding new products. The decision to classify these investments as long-term rather than as current assets is based on the concept of *managerial intent*. When management intends to use the securities for long-term purposes, they are separately classified on the balance sheet as long-term investments rather than as temporary investments.

As discussed in Chapter 5, the balance sheet category, investments, includes investments in equity and debt securities of other enterprises, assets not currently in use, and special funds. This chapter discusses investments in equity and debt securities. Detailed discussion of equity investments will be limited to those that do not result in consolidated financial statements. In addition, the topic of intangible assets will be addressed.

Investments in Equity Securities

The term *equity securities* is defined in *SFAS No. 115* as:

> *Any security representing an ownership interest in an enterprise (for example, common, preferred, or other capital stock) or the right to acquire (for example, warrants, rights, and call options) or dispose of (for example, put options) an ownership interest in an enterprise at fixed or determinable prices.*[1]

[1] Financial Accounting Standards Board, *Statement of Financial Accounting Standards No. 115*, "Accounting for Certain Investments in Debt and Equity Securities" (Stamford, CT: FASB, 1993), par. 137.

Equity securities do not include redeemable preferred stock or convertible bonds.

Equity securities may be acquired on an organized stock exchange, over the counter, or by direct sale. In addition, warrants, rights, and options may be attached to other securities (bonds or preferred stock), or they may be received from the issuer, cost free, to enable the enterprise to maintain its present proportionate share of ownership.[2] The recorded cost of investments in equity securities includes the purchase price of the securities plus any brokerage fees, transfer costs, or taxes on transfer. When equity securities are obtained in a nonmonetary transaction, the recorded cost is based on fair market value of the consideration given, or, if fair market value is unavailable, the fair market value of the marketable equity security received.

Subsequent to acquisition, five methods of accounting and financial statement presentation are utilized under current GAAP for the various types of equity securities: (1) consolidation, (2) the equity method, (3) the cost method, (4) the lower of cost or market method, (5) the fair value method, and (6) the market value method. These methods are not alternatives for recording investments in equity securities. They are applied on the basis of the investee's percentage of ownership or surrounding circumstances. Each method and the circumstances under which it is applicable are described in the following paragraphs.

Consolidation

Consolidated financial statements are required when an investor owns enough common stock to obtain control over the investee. *Control* is defined in *SFAS No. 94* as ownership of a majority voting interest (over 50 percent) unless the parent company is precluded from exercising control or unless control is temporary.[3] *Consolidation* requires that at the balance sheet date the investment account (accounted for during the year under the equity method described below) be replaced by the assets and liabilities of the investee company. In the consolidation process, the investee assets and liabilities are consolidated with (added to) those of the controlling parent company. Consolidated financial statements are discussed in detail in Chapter 15.

The Equity Method

The *equity method* is used when an investor has the ability to significantly influence the financing and operating decisions of an investee, even though it holds less than 50 percent of the voting stock. Ability to exercise significant influence can be determined in a number of ways, including

---

[2] Allowing investors to maintain their proportionate share of ownership is one of the basic rights of common stock ownership. This right is referred to as the preemptive right.

[3] Financial Accounting Standards Board, *Statement of Financial Accounting Standards No. 94,* "Consolidation of all Majority-Owned Subsidiaries" (Stamford, CT: FASB, 1988), par. 13.

Strobel, Caroline D., and Ollie S. Powers. "Accounting for Inventories: Where We Stand." *The CPA Journal* (May 1981), pp. 41–46.
Wyatt, Arthur. "The SEC Says: Mark to Market." *Accounting Horizons* (March 1991), pp. 80–84.

Bibliography

Barden, Horace G. *The Accounting Basis of Inventories*. New York: American Institute of Certified Public Accountants, 1973.

Bastable, C. W., and Jacob D. Merriwether. "FIFO in an Inflationary Environment." *Journal of Accountancy* (March 1976), pp. 49–55.

Beresford, Dennis R., and Michael H. Sietta. "Short-Term Debt Agreements—Classification Issues." *The CPA Journal* (August 1983), pp. 32–37.

Bohan, Michael P., and Steven Rubin. "LIFO: What Should Be Disclosed." *Journal of Accountancy* (February 1985), pp. 72–77.

Buckley, John W., and James R. Goode. "Inventory Valuation and Income Measurement: An Improved System." *Abacus* (June 1976), pp. 34–48.

Copeland, Ronald M., Joseph F. Wojdak, and John K. Shank. "Use Lifo to Offset Inflation." *Harvard Business Review* (May–June 1971), pp. 91–100.

Cramer, Joe J. "Incompatibility of Bad Debt 'Expense' with Contemporary Accounting Theory." *The Accounting Review* (July 1972), pp. 596–598.

Dun, L. C. "Working Capital A Logical Concept." *Australian Accountant* (October 1969), pp. 461–464.

Fox, Harold F. "Exploring the Facts of Lifo." *National Public Accountant* (October 1971), pp. 22–25.

Gambling, Trevor E. "Lifo vs. Fifo under Conditions of 'Certainty.'" *The Accounting Review* (April 1968), pp. 387–389.

Haried, Andrew A., and Ralph E. Smith. "Accounting for Marketable Equity Securities." *Journal of Accountancy* (February 1977), pp. 54–62.

Hirschman, Robert W. "A Look at 'Current' Classifications." *Journal of Accountancy* (November 1967), pp. 54–58.

Hoffman, Raymond A., and Henry Gunders. *Inventories: Control, Costing and Effect upon Income and Taxes*, 2d ed. New York: Ronald Press, 1970.

Holmes, William. "Market Value of Inventories—Perils and Pitfalls." *Journal of Commercial Bank Lending* (April 1973), pp. 30–35.

Huizingh, William. *Working Capital Classification*. Ann Arbor: Bureau of Business Research, Graduate School of Business Administration, University of Michigan, 1967.

Hunter, Robert D. "Concept of Working Capital." *Journal of Commercial Bank Lending* (March 1972), pp. 24–30.

Johnson, Charles E. "Inventory Valuation—The Accountant's Achilles Heel." *The Accounting Review* (April 1954), pp. 15–26.

Lemke, Kenneth W. "The Evaluation of Liquidity: An Analytical Study." *Journal of Accounting Research* (Spring 1970), pp. 47–77.

McAnly, Herbert T. "How LIFO Began." *Management Accounting* (May 1975), pp. 24–26.

Moonitz, Maurice. "The Case against Lifo as an Inventory-Pricing Formula." *Journal of Accountancy* (June 1953), pp. 682–690.

Moonitz, Maurice. "Accounting for Investments in Debt Securities." In Stephen A. Zeff, Joel Demski, and Nicholas Dopuch, (eds.), *Essays in Honor of William A. Paton*. Ann Arbor: University of Michigan Graduate School of Business Administration Division of Research, 1979, pp. 57–72.

Morse, Dale, and Gordon Richardson. "The LIFO/FIFO Decision." *Journal of Accounting Research* (Spring 1983), pp. 106–127.

Munter, Paul, and Tommy Moores. "Transfers of Receivables with Recourse." *The CPA Journal* (July 1984), pp. 52–60.

O'Connor, Stephen J. "LIFO: Still a Valid Management Tool?" *Financial Executive* (September 1978), pp. 26–30.

Pantiack, Wayne G. "Last-In First-Out Accounting for Inventories." *The CPA Journal* (July 1985), pp. 42–48.

Skinner, R. C. "Combining LIFO and FIFO." *International Journal of Accounting, Education and Research* (Spring 1975), pp. 127–134.

Staubus, George J. "Testing Inventory Accounting." *The Accounting Review* (July 1968), pp. 413–424.

Storey, Reed K., and Maurice Moonitz. *Market Value Methods for Intercorporate Investments in Stock*. New York: American Institute of Certified Public Accountants, 1976.

Sunder, Shyam. "Optional Choice between FIFO and LIFO." *Journal of Accounting Research* (Autumn 1976), pp. 277–300.

1. Representation on the board of directors.
2. Participation in policy-making processes.
3. Material intercompany transactions.
4. Interchange of managerial personnel.
5. Technological dependency.
6. The percent of ownership the investor has in relation to other holdings.[4]

When using the *equity method,* adjustments are made to the recorded cost of the investment to account for the profits and losses of the investee and the distributions of earnings. These adjustments are based on the investor's percentage of ownership of the investee. For example, if the investee reports a profit, the investor will report as income its pro-rata ownership share of the investee profit and increase the carrying value of the investment account by the same amount. On the other hand, dividends received are recorded as a decrease in the carrying value of the investment account for the amount of the dividend received. Dividends are not recorded as income since the investee's income is recorded by the investor as it is earned by the investee. In other words, under the equity method, dividends are viewed as distributions of accumulated earnings. Because the accumulation of earnings increases the investment account, the distribution of earnings decreases the investment account. Consequently, the investment account represents the investee's equity in the investment.

In *ARB No. 51,* the Committee on Accounting Procedure described the equity method[5] and stated that it is the preferred method of accounting for unconsolidated subsidiaries.[6] In 1971, the Accounting Principles Board (APB) reported its conclusions on a study of the accounting for long-term investments in stocks by issuing *APB Opinion No. 18,* "The Equity Method of Accounting for Investments in Common Stock."[7] *APB Opinion No. 18,* clarified the applicability of the equity method to investments of common stock in subsidiaries; however, it was noted that the equity method was not a valid substitute for consolidation.[8]

The Board also noted that determining the ability to influence is not always clear and "in order to achieve a reasonable degree of uniformity in application"[9] an investment of 20 percent or more of the voting stock of the

---

[4] Ibid., par. 17.

[5] *ARB No. 51* did not refer to the equity method by name.

[6] Committee on Accounting Procedure, *Accounting Research Bulletin No. 51,* "Consolidated Financial Statements" (New York: AICPA, 1959), par. 19. The APB reiterated this position in *APB Opinion No. 10,* "Omnibus Opinion of 1966" (par. 3), and referred to the procedure described in *ARB No. 51* as the equity method.

[7] Accounting Principles Board, *Opinion No. 18,* "The Equity Method of Accounting for Investments in Common Stock" (New York: AICPA, 1971).

[8] Ibid., par. 14.

[9] Ibid.

investee is deemed to constitute evidence of a presumption of the ability to exercise significant influence. Conversely, ownership of less than 20 percent of the voting stock leads to the presumption that the investor does not have significant influence unless an ability to exercise significant influence can be demonstrated.[10] Consequently, it was concluded that significant influence is normally attained when an investor holds 20 percent or more of the voting stock of an investee unless the surrounding circumstances indicate a lack of ability to influence.

FASB, *Interpretation No. 35*, suggests that the following facts and circumstances might preclude an investor from using the equity method even if an investment of 20 percent or more is held:

1. *Opposition by the investee, such as litigation or complaints to governmental regulatory authorities, challenges the investor's ability to exercise significant influence.*

2. *The investor and investee sign an agreement under which the investor surrenders significant rights as a shareholder.*

3. *Majority ownership of the investee is concentrated among a small group of shareholders who operate the investee without regard to the views of the investor.*

4. *The investor needs or wants more financial information to apply the equity method than is available to the investee's other shareholders (e.g., the investor wants quarterly financial information from an investee that publicly reports only annually), tries to obtain that information, and fails.*

5. *The investor tries and fails to obtain representation on the investee's board of directors.[11]*

The APB's decision to endorse the equity method was based on the objectives of accrual accounting—that is, the reporting of transactions when they occur rather than as cash is collected. When the investor can exercise significant influence over the investee, the results of operating decisions better reflect the periodic outcomes resulting from making the investment, rather than distributions of the investor's share of accumulated profits, which in and of themselves may be unrelated to performance. The Board apparently believed that the cash flow needs of investors can be satisfied by the significant influence test and that reporting needs are of primary importance.

The Cost Method

When there is a lack of significant influence or control, investments in common stocks are accounted for under either the cost method or the fair value

[10] Ibid.

[11] Financial Accounting Standards Board, *Interpretation No. 35*, "Criteria for Applying the Equity Method of Accounting for Investments in Common Stock" (Stamford, CT: FASB, 1981), par. 4.

method. These methods also apply to all other equity securities. When there is no readily determinable market price for equity securities, the cost method must be used. Use of a fair value approach is currently required under *SFAS No. 115* for all equity securities for which fair value is readily determinable and for which neither consolidation nor the equity method is required.

Under the cost method, an investment in equity securities is carried at its historical cost. Revenue is recorded and reported as dividends are received. The cost method can be criticized because it does not measure current fair value. Historical cost provides information relevant for determining recovery when the securities are acquired. Current fair market value would provide a similar measure for the current accounting period. If the purpose of financial statements is to provide investors, creditors, and other users with information useful in assessing future cash flows, the current assessment of recoverable amounts, current market values, would be relevant. Even for those equity securities that are not actively traded, an estimate of current fair value may be more relevant than cost.

Despite some speculation at the time *APB Opinion No. 18* was issued that the APB might espouse fair market value, *APB Opinion No. 18* did little to add to its acceptability. The use of fair value is a departure from the historical cost principle. The APB apparently was not prepared to take the radical step of endorsing a departure from historical cost, despite the fact that the information needed to determine the fair values for most investments is readily available. However, the FASB reversed this position in *SFAS No. 115*. Fair value accounting is now required in several circumstances, as discussed later in the chapter.

The Lower of Cost or Market Method

As discussed earlier in Chapter 7, in 1975 the FASB issued *SFAS No. 12*. This release required that equity securities having readily determinable market values that were not accounted for under the equity method or consolidation be accounted for by applying lower of cost or market (LCM). Under the LCM method as prescribed by *SFAS No. 12*, marketable equity securities were separated into current and long-term portfolios. Each portfolio was carried on the balance sheet at the lower of that portfolio's aggregate cost or market value. This process was accomplished by the use of a valuation allowance for each portfolio, which measured the amount by which the aggregate cost of the investment portfolio exceeded aggregate market value at the balance sheet date. For temporary investments in marketable equity securities, the unrealized losses and subsequent recoveries were recognized in the income statement. In contrast, for long-term investments in marketable equity securities, the cumulative effect of unrealized losses and recoveries was reported as negative stockholders' equity.

The FASB's advocacy of the LCM method in *SFAS No. 12* was not a strict departure from historical cost. Rather, it was simply further evidence of the overriding concern for conservatism discussed earlier in Chapter 4. LCM for marketable securities can be defended on the grounds that the recording of cost implies recovery of that cost. It is reasonable to assume that management would not invest in assets that are not recoverable. By the same token, when recovery has declined temporarily through decline in market value, it is reasonable to reduce the book value of assets to the lower market value.

The LCM method was criticized because it did not result in consistent treatment of all marketable equity securities. Gains were treated differently from losses, and temporary investments were treated differently from long-term investments without a rational explanation. Furthermore, it is inconsistent to recognize market value increases up to cost but not to market. Opponents of *SFAS No. 12* argued that the consequent recognition of unrealized gains was so arbitrary that no recognition of these gains would be preferable.

Finally, the determination of LCM on an aggregate basis may be deceptive. Unrealized losses are offset against unrealized gains. In a subsequent period when a security was sold, prior cumulative unrecognized gains and losses were recognized, causing a mismatching of gain and loss recognition within the period in which it occurred.

The Fair Value Method

SFAS No. 115, "Accounting for Certain Investments in Debt and Equity Securities,"[12] describes the current GAAP for equity securities that have readily determinable fair values and that are not subject to the equity method under *APB Opinion No. 18* or to consolidation. According to *SFAS No. 115,* the fair value of an equity security is readily determinable if

1. *The sales prices or bid-and-ask quotations are currently available on a securities exchange registered with the Securities and Exchange Commission (SEC) or in the over-the-counter market when they are publicly reported by the National Association of Securities Dealers Automated Quotations systems or by the National Quotation Bureau.*

2. *The security is traded only in foreign markets and if the foreign market is of a breadth and scope comparable to one of the U.S. markets referred to above.*

3. *The investment is in a mutual fund that has a fair value per share (unit) that is published and is the basis for current transactions.*[13]

Under the fair value method, at acquisition, equity securities are to be classified as either **trading** or **available-for-sale.** As discussed earlier in Chapter 6, *trading securities* are defined as "securities that are bought and held principally for the purpose of selling them in the near term (thus held for only a short period of time)."[14] Trading securities are actively and frequently bought and sold, generally with the objective of generating profits from short-term price movements. *Available-for-sale securities* are those equity secu-

---

[12] Financial Accounting Standards Board, *Statement of Financial Accounting Standards No. 115,* "Accounting for Certain Investments in Debt and Equity Securities" (Stamford, CT: FASB, 1993).

[13] Ibid., par. 3.

[14] Ibid., par. 12.

rities having readily determinable market prices that are not considered trading securities.[15] All trading securities are to be classified as current assets. Available-for-sale securities are to be classified as current or long-term depending on whether they meet the *ARB No. 43* definition of current assets, described in Chapters 5 and 6. Accordingly, these securities will be classified as current if they are reasonably expected to be realized in cash or sold or consumed during the normal operating cycle of the business or one year, whichever is longer. All other available-for-sale securities will be classified as long-term investments.

At each balance sheet date, long-term equity securities subject to the *SFAS No. 115* provisions are to be reported at fair value. Unrealized holding gains and losses for available-for-sale securities (current and long-term) will be excluded from earnings. The cumulative unrealized holding gains and losses for these securities will be reported as a net amount as a component of accumulated other comprehensive income. Dividend income for available-for-sale securities will continue to be included in earnings.

When an equity security is transferred from the trading category to the available-for-sale category or vice versa, the transfer is to be accounted for at fair value at the date of transfer. The treatment of unrealized holding gains shall be as follows:

1. *For a transfer from the trading category to the available-for-sale category, the unrealized holding gain or loss is recognized in income up to the date of transfer. It is not reversed.*

2. *For a transfer from the available-for-sale category to the trading category, the unrecognized holding gain or loss at the date of transfer is recognized immediately in earnings.*[16]

The FASB's primary impetus for requiring fair value accounting for investments in equity securities is relevance. The advocates of fair value accounting for investments in securities believe that fair value is useful in assisting investors, creditors, and other users in evaluating the performance of enterprise investing strategies. According to *SFAC No. 1,* users of financial information are interested in assessing the amount, timing, and risk associated with expected net cash inflows to the enterprise. These assessments aid in evaluating the potential outcome of their own personal investing strategies because the expected cash flows to the enterprise are the main source of expected cash flows from the enterprise to them. Fair value is market determined. It reflects the market consensus regarding the expected resource flows of a security discounted by the current interest rate adjusted for the risk associated with that security.

In addition, the fair value method partially eliminates the uneven-handed treatment that *SFAS No. 12* afforded to gains and losses. All unrealized gains and unrealized losses will be treated the same for asset valuation purposes. For

[15] Ibid.

[16] Ibid., par. 15.

trading securities, the gains and losses will be recognized in those periods in which they occur. Thus, for these assets the method is consistent with other accrual accounting requirements. It is also consistent with the *SFAC No. 6* definition of comprehensive income because comprehensive income is based on changes in net assets and would include changes in the market values of assets. For trading securities, there will be no further masking of gains against losses that occurred under the aggregate valuation approach of *SFAS No. 12.*

However, inconsistent income statement treatment for equity securities will continue. Unrealized gains and losses for available-for-sale securities will not be recognized until they are reclassified as trading securities and sold. Thus, for these securities there will be no accrual accounting based matching of market gains and losses in the period in which they are incurred. The result will be a distortion of reported earnings.

Finally, the readily determinable criteria preclude fair value accounting for those securities that are not actively traded. Some advocates of fair value would argue that other estimates of fair value would be more meaningful than historical cost. Nevertheless, the FASB decided to limit the scope of fair value accounting for investments in equity securities to those that are readily determinable in the market. These measures are reliable and do not depend on imprecise measures that subjective judgments regarding market values would entail.

The Market Value Method

Under the market value method, investment income is recorded for dividends received, and unrealized gains and losses are recognized in earnings, rather than as a component of other comprehensive income. All upward and downward changes in the market value of the investment shares are recorded as income or losses. Changes in the market value of the investment require adjustment to the carrying value of the investment account. Thus, the market value method is analogous to the fair value method for trading securities described above. It has become accepted industry practice for certain industries, such as mutual funds, where it has attained the status of GAAP.

Figure 9.1 summarizes the approaches that are considered current GAAP for investments in equity securities. Table 9.1 on page 276 summarizes the effects of various events on the investment account and the reported income of the investor under each of these methods. Consolidation is omitted from Table 9.1 because it is a reporting method and not a method for recording transactions and events.

Investments in Debt Securities

Investments in debt securities, such as bonds or government securities, are initially recorded at cost, and it is not unusual for the purchase price of a debt instrument to differ from its face value. This difference reflects the fluctuations in market interest rates that have occurred since the time the debt instrument was initially offered for sale to the present. Thus, debt instru-

FIGURE 9.1 *Accounting for Investments in Equity Securities*

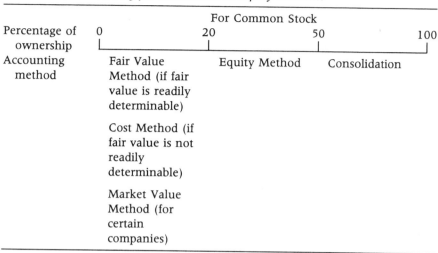

	For Common Stock			
Percentage of ownership	0	20	50	100
Accounting method	Fair Value Method (if fair value is readily determinable)	Equity Method	Consolidation	
	Cost Method (if fair value is not readily determinable)			
	Market Value Method (for certain companies)			

ments are often sold at a premium or discount. For a detailed discussion of how the amount of a bond premium or discount is determined and their effects on interest, see Chapter 10.

The provisions of *SFAS No. 115* also apply to all investments in debt securities. Prior to the issuance of *SFAS No. 115,* all debt securities that were classified as long-term were accounted for by amortizing the premium or discount over the term of the bond, regardless of the intent or ability of the investing entity to hold the investment to maturity or whether the investment had a readily determinable fair value. Regulators and others expressed concerns that the recognition and measurement of investments in debt securities, particularly those held by financial institutions, should better reflect the investor's intent to hold, make available to sell, or trade these securities. Moreover, the provisions of *SFAS No. 12* did not apply to investments in debt securities. Some enterprises applied LCM to these securities; others accounted for them under the cost method. The result was that the accounting treatment for these securities was inconsistent from one entity to the next; therefore, it was difficult to compare the performance of these investments across companies.

SFAS No. 115 requires that at acquisition individual investments in debt securities be classified as trading, available-for-sale, or held-to-maturity. Those debt securities that are classified as trading or available-for-sale are to be treated in the same manner as equity securities that are similarly classified. That is, the fair value method described above will apply to these securities. Thus, the discussion that follows will be limited to those debt securities that are classified as held-to-maturity.

TABLE 9.1 *Effects of the Cost, Fair Value, Equity, and Market Value Methods on Investment and Income*

Event	Cost	Fair Value		Equity	Market Value
		Trading Securities	Available-for-Sale Securities		
Acquire 25% of common stock of S Company for $100,000	Investment increased $100,000	Investment increased $100,000	Investment increased $100,000	Investment increased $100,000	Investment increased $100,000
Investee reports net income of $10,000	No effect on investment or income	No effect on investment or income	No effect on investment or income	Investment increased $2,500; income increased $2,500	No effect on investment or income
Investee pays dividends of $5,000 (25% investor)	No effect on investment; income increased $1,250	No effect on investment; income increased $1,250	No effect on investment; income increased $1,250	Investment decreased $1,250; no effect on income	No effect on investment; income increased $1,250
Investor's shares increased in value by 5% of original cost	No effect on investment or income	Investment increased $5,000; income increased $5,000	Investment increased $5,000; no effect on income	No effect on investment or income	Investment increased $5,000; income increased $5,000
Investor's shares decreased in value by 10% of original cost	No effect on investment or income	Investment decreased $10,000; income decreased $10,000	Investment decreased $10,000; no effect on income	No effect on investment or income	Investment decreased $10,000; income decreased $10,000

Debt instruments are to be classified as *held-to-maturity* "only if the reporting enterprise has the positive intent and ability to hold those securities to maturity."[17] A debt security may continue to be classified as held-to-maturity even if sold or called prior to maturity if (a) the sale date (or call date if exercise of the call is probable) occurs so near to the maturity date that interest rate risk has no substantial effect on fair value or (b) the sale occurs after the enterprise has already collected a substantial portion (85 percent or more) of the principal outstanding at acquisition.[18]

Debt securities that are classified as held-to-maturity are to be measured at *amortized cost*. When these debt securities are sold at a premium or discount, the total interest income to the investing enterprise over the life of the debt instrument from acquisition to maturity is affected by the amount of the premium or discount. Measurement at amortized cost means that the premium or discount is amortized each period to calculate interest income. (Chapter 10 illustrates how a premium or discount affects interest over the life of a bond.) Amortization of the premium or discount is treated as an adjustment to interest income and to the investment account.

Two methods of debt premium or discount amortization are available: straight-line and effective interest. Under the *straight-line* method, the premium or discount is divided by the number of periods remaining in the life of the debt issue. In each subsequent period, an equal amount of premium or discount is written off as an interest income adjustment. The rationale underlying the use of the straight-line method is its ease of computation and the belief its use results in premium or discount amortization results that are not materially different from other measurement methods.

When the effective interest method is used, the actual rate of return on the debt instrument must be computed at the time the investment is acquired. This interest rate is then applied to the carrying value of the investment in each interest period to determine the interest income. Using the effective interest method results in a uniform rate of return over the life of the investment. Use of this method is based on the belief that the investment was acquired at a certain yield and that the financial statements issued in subsequent periods should reflect the effects of that decision.

When it is evident that the investor has changed intent to hold a debt security to maturity, the security is transferred to either the trading or the available-for-sale category. The transfer is accounted for at fair value. If the security is transferred to the trading category, the unrealized gain or loss at the date of transfer is recognized in income. If the security is transferred to the available-for-sale category, the unrealized gain or loss at the date of transfer is recognized as a component of other comprehensive income. When a change from the available-for-sale category to the held-to-maturity category occurs, the amount of accumulated unrealized holding gains and losses that exists at the date of transfer will continue to be included as a component of

---

[17] Ibid., par. 7.

[18] Ibid., par. 11.

other comprehensive income that is reported in the stockholders' equity section of the balance sheet, and will be amortized over the remaining life of the debt security as an adjustment to interest income. The effect of this treatment is that interest income each period will be what it would have been under the amortized cost method, but the carrying value of the debt security on the balance sheet in subsequent periods will reflect the amortized market value at the date of transfer, rather than the amortized cost.

A change in circumstances may result in the change of intent to hold a debt security to maturity, but may not call into question the classification of other debt as held-to-maturity if the change in circumstances is due to one or more of the following:

1. Evidence of significant deterioration in the issuer's credit worthiness.

2. A tax law change that eliminates or reduces the tax-exempt status of interest on the debt security.

3. A major business combination or disposition (such as sale of a segment of the business) that necessitates the sale or transfer of the debt security in order to maintain the enterprise's existing interest rate risk position or credit risk policy.

4. A change in statutory or regulatory requirements that significantly modifies either what constitutes a permissible investment or the maximum level of investment that the enterprise can hold in certain kinds of securities.

5. A change in regulatory requirements that significantly increases the enterprise's industry capital requirements that causes the enterprise to downsize.

6. A significant increase in the risk weights of debt securities used for regulatory risk-based capital purposes.

A debt security will not be classified as held-to-maturity if the enterprise intends to hold the security for an indefinite period. An indefinite holding period is presumed if, for example, the debt security would be available to be sold in response to:

1. Changes in market interest rates and related changes in the security's prepayment risk.

2. Need for liquidity. Examples indicating a need for liquidity include: for financial institutions, the withdrawal of deposits or the increased demand for loans and for insurance companies, the surrender of insurance policies, or the payment of insurance claims.

3. Changes in the availability and yield on alternative investments.

4. Changes in funding sources and terms.

5. Changes in foreign currency risk.[19]

---

[19] Ibid., par. 9.

SFAS No. 115 addresses issues concerning the relevance of fair value to investors, creditors, and other users. However, in allowing the continued use of amortized cost for debt securities that are intended to be held to maturity, it does not address concerns that use of the amortized cost method permits the recognition of holding gains through the selective sale of appreciated debt instruments recorded at amortized cost at the date of sale. This affords management the opportunity to engage in gains trading and to selectively manage reported earnings. Moreover, it does not address the criticism that accounting for debt securities is based on management's plan for holding or disposing of the investment rather than on the characteristics of the asset itself. In allowing three distinct categories, the same company could give three different accounting treatments to three otherwise identical debt securities. Critics argue that these issues can be resolved only by reporting all debt and equity securities that have determinable fair values at fair value and by including all unrealized gains and losses in earnings as they occur.

The FASB countered that the procedures outlined in *SFAS No. 115* reflect the economic consequences of events and transactions. The reporting requirements better reflect the manner in which enterprises manage their investments and the impact of economic events on the overall enterprise. Moreover, the following disclosure requirements should provide fair value information that should prove useful to investor decision making in addition to the reporting requirements outlined above. For securities classified as available-for-sale and separately for securities classified as held-to-maturity, the enterprise is to report

1. Aggregate fair value.
2. Gross unrealized holding gains.
3. Gross unrealized holding losses.
4. The amortized cost basis by major security type.

Permanent Decline in Fair Value

When a decline in the fair value of a long-term investment that is classified as available-for-sale is determined to be other than temporary, an *other-than-temporary impairment* will be considered to have occurred. In this case, the investment account balance for this security is written down to fair value, a loss is included in earnings, and a new cost basis is established. The new cost basis for recognition of gain or loss on reclassification or sale will not be adjusted for subsequent recoveries of the recognized loss. All subsequent increases in fair value will be recorded as components of other comprehensive income, in the same manner as subsequent unrealized losses.[20] Similar treatment will be given for other-than-permanent declines in investments in debt securities that are classified as held-to-maturity.

---

[20] Ibid., par. 16.

Impairment of Investments in Unsecuritized Debt

Investments in unsecuritized debt, principally accounts and notes receivable, are subject to the provisions of *SFAS No. 114*, "Accounting by Creditors for Impairment of Loans."[21] Recall from Chapter 7 that these loans are "impaired when, based on current information and events, it is probable that a creditor will be unable to collect all amounts due according to the contractual terms of the loan agreement,"[22] including interest. To reiterate, in these cases, impairment is measured based on the present value of expected future cash flows discounted at the loan's effective interest rate as determined at the origin or acquisition of the loan. Alternatively, impairment may be measured using the market price for the loan or, if the loan is collateralized, the fair value of the collateral. If the resulting measurement of impairment is less than the carrying value of the loan (including interest and unamortized loan fees, premium, or discount), the impairment is recognized by creating a valuation allowance and making a corresponding charge to bad debt expense.[23]

In subsequent accounting periods, for those impairments that were calculated by discounting cash flows, impairment is remeasured to reflect any significant changes (positive or negative) in the cash flow expectations used to calculate the original loan impairment. For those impairments that were measured using fair values, similar remeasurements are made to reflect subsequent significant changes in fair value. However, the loan-carrying value may not be written up to a value that exceeds the recorded investment in the loan. For balance sheet purposes, the changes are reflected in the valuation allowance account.[24]

For income statement purposes, changes in the present value of the expected future cash flows of an impaired loan may be treated in one of two ways:

1. Increases that are attributable to the passage of time are reported as interest income; the balance of the change in present value is an adjustment to bad debt expense.

2. The entire change in present value is reported as an adjustment to bad debt expense.[25]

All changes in the measurement of impairment that are based on changes in fair value are reflected in earnings as adjustments to bad debt expense.[26]

---

[21] Financial Accounting Standards Board, *Statement of Financial Accounting Standards No. 114*, "Accounting by Creditors for Impairment of a Loan" (Stamford, CT: FASB, 1993).

[22] Ibid., par. 8.

[23] Ibid., pars. 13 and 14.

[24] Ibid., par. 16.

[25] Ibid., par. 17.

[26] Ibid., par. 18.

At each balance sheet date, the following disclosures are required:

1. The recorded investment in the impaired loans.
2. The beginning and ending balance in the allowance account and the activity occurring during the period in that account.
3. The income recognition policy, including the amount of interest income recognized due to changes in the present value of the impaired loan.[27]

SFAS No. 114 is intended to address whether present-value measures should be used to measure loan impairment. The pronouncement clarifies present GAAP for loan impairments by specifying that both principal and interest receivable should be considered when calculating loan impairment. The prescribed measurement methods should reflect the amount that is expected to be recovered by the creditor so that investors, creditors, and other users can better assess the amount and timing of future cash flows. The initial present value recorded for the loan reflected the expectations at that time regarding expected future cash flows. Because the loan was originally recorded at a discounted amount, ongoing assessment for impairment should be treated in a similar manner. The added uncertainty associated with expectations regarding the future cash flows from impaired loans should not preclude the use of discounted cash flows. The impairment represents a deterioration in quality as reflected in the change in cash flow expectations. Thus, the impairment itself does not indicate that a new loan has replaced the old one. Rather, the old loan is continuing, but expectations about future cash flows have changed. Consequently, the contractual interest rate is the appropriate rate to discount those cash flows.

Critics argue that the effect of impairment is a change in the character of the loan that should be measured directly. If so, the contractual interest rate is no longer relevant. The most desirable direct measure of an impaired loan is fair value. If no market value exists, the creditor should discount the expected future cash flows utilizing an interest rate that is commensurate with the risk involved. Moreover, allowing the use of a fair value alternative is inconsistent with requiring the original loan interest rate to be used when the discounting alternative is selected. To be consistent in approach, the discounting should require an interest rate commensurate with the risk associated with the current status of the loan. Such a rate is implicit in the fair value of the loan. In addition, the pronouncement allows three alternative measures of loan impairment, with no guidance on when to use one method over the other. Allowing alternatives in this manner enables enterprises to utilize the provisions of this pronouncement to manage their financial statements.

---

[27] Ibid., par. 20.

Transfers of Financial Assets

Financial assets include investments in debt and equity securities. Accounting for financial assets was first outlined in *SFAS No. 125*[28] which was recently replaced by *SFAS No. 140.*[29] This statement adopts a financial consequences approach which requires an entity to recognize the financial assets it controls and the liabilities it has incurred, and to derecognize financial assets when control has been surrendered and to derecognize financial liabilities when they are extinguished.

According to SFAS No. 140, the transferor surrenders control over transferred assets if and only if all of the following conditions are met:

1. The transferred assets have been isolated from the transferor—put beyond the transferor's reach as well as the reach of its creditors.

2. Each transferee (or, if the transferee is a qualifying special purpose entity, each holder of its beneficial interests) has the right to pledge or exchange the assets (or beneficial interests) it received, and no condition both constrains the transferee (or holder) from taking advantage of its right to pledge or exchange and provides more than a trivial benefit to the transferor.

3. The transferor does not maintain effective control over the transferred asset by having an agreement that obligates it to repurchase or redeem the asset before maturity or by having an agreement that allows it to repurchase or redeem assets that are not readily obtainable.

A transfer of financial assets is accounted for as a sale to the extent that consideration other than beneficial interests in the transferred asset are received in exchange. Liabilities and derivatives incurred in a transfer of financial asset are initially measured at their fair market values. Servicing assets and liabilities are measured by amortization over the period of servicing income or loss, and assessment for asset impairment or increased obligation based on their fair market values. Liabilities are derecognized only when repaid or when the debtor is legally relieved of the obligation. That is, in-substance defeasance is not permitted.

Intangibles

It is difficult to define the term *intangibles* adequately. Kohler defined it as capital assets that have no physical existence and whose value depends on the rights and benefits that possession confers on the owner.[30] However,

---

[28] *Statement of Financial Accounting Standards No. 125,* "Accounting for Transfers and Servicing of Financial Assets and Extinguishments of Liabilities" (Stamford, CT: FASB, 1996).

[29] *Statement of Financial Accounting Standards No. 140,* "Accounting for Transfers and Servicing of Financial Assets and Extinguishments of Liabilities"—a replacement of FASB Statement No. 125" (Stamford, CT: FASB, 2000).

[30] Eric L. Kohler, *A Dictionary for Accountants,* 3rd ed. (Englewood Cliffs, NJ: Prentice-Hall, 1963), p. 269.

Paton had previously noted that the lack of physical existence test was not particularly helpful and suggested that intangibles are assets more closely related to the enterprise as a whole than to any components.[31] It should also be noted that many intangibles convey a sort of monopolistic right to their owners. Examples of intangibles are patents, copyrights, franchises, leaseholds, and goodwill.

Intangible assets derive their value from the special rights and privileges they convey, and accounting for these assets involves the same problems as accounting for other long-term assets. Specifically, an initial carrying amount must be determined; this initial carrying value must be systematically and rationally allocated to the periods that receive benefit; under the provisions of *SFAS No. 121*, if the asset's carrying value is not recoverable, the carrying value must be written down to fair value. These problems are magnified in the case of intangibles because their very nature makes evidence elusive. Both the value and the useful lives of intangibles are difficult to determine.

In reviewing the topic of intangibles, the Accounting Principles Board noted that these assets might be classified on several different bases.

Identifiability—separately identifiable or lacking specific identification.

Manner of acquisition—acquired singularly, in groups, or in business combinations, or developed internally.

Expected period of benefit—limited by law or contract, related to human or economic factors, or having indefinite or indeterminate duration.

Separability from an entire enterprise—rights transferable without title, salable, or inseparable from the enterprise or a substantial part of it.[32]

Today, the cost of internally developed intangibles, such as patents, are considered costs of research and development and are expensed as incurred under *SFAS No. 2*, as discussed later in the chapter.

The foregoing definitions suggest that intangibles may be classified according to whether they are *externally acquired* (purchased from outsiders) or *internally developed*. In addition, they may be classified as *identifiable* or *unidentifiable*. These last two classifications relate to the Type (a) and Type (b) classifications contained in *ARB No. 43* and discussed later in the chapter.

Accounting for Cost

The initial valuation process for intangible assets generally follows the same standards employed for other long-lived assets. Cost includes all expenditures necessary to acquire an individual asset and make it ready for use. When intangibles are purchased from outsiders, assigning cost is fairly easy, and the methods used in allocating cost to groups of assets and by exchanges of other assets are similar to those discussed for tangible fixed assets

[31] William A. Paton and William A. Paton, Jr., *Asset Accounting* (New York: Macmillan Co., 1952), pp. 485–490.

[32] *Accounting Principles Board Opinion No. 17*, "Intangible Assets" (New York: AICPA, 1970).

Companies frequently develop intangible assets internally. The Accounting Principles Board addressed the problems inherent in accounting for internally developed intangibles in *Opinion No. 17*. The Board's conclusions are based on the identifiability characteristic defined earlier.

> *A company should record as assets the costs of intangible assets acquired from other enterprises or individuals. Costs of developing, maintaining, or restoring intangible assets which are not specifically identifiable, have indeterminate lives, or are inherent in a continuing business and related to the enterprise as a whole— such as goodwill—should be deducted from income when incurred.*[33]

The identifiability criterion alleviated much of the problem in accounting for the cost of intangible assets and is yet another example of the APB's attempts to narrow alternatives. Where a specific cost can be assigned to a specific asset, intangibles are carried forward at recorded values. Where either a specific asset or specific amount is indeterminable, no attempt should be made to carry values forward.

Amortization

The matching principle dictates that the cost of intangible assets be apportioned to the expected periods of benefit. *ARB No. 43* noted that this process involved two separate types of intangibles.

> a.   *those having a term of existence limited by law, regulation, or agreement, or by their nature (such as patents, copyrights, leases, licenses, franchises for a fixed term and goodwill as to which there is evidence of limited duration).*
>
> b.   *those having no such term of existence and as to which there is, at the time of acquisition, no indication of limited life (such as goodwill generally, going value, trade names, secret processes, subscription lists, perpetual franchises, and organization costs).*[34]

This release resulted in the adoption of a classification scheme that identified intangibles as either Type (a) or Type (b). These terms became widely used in discussing the issues associated with recording and amortizing intangible assets. In *APB Opinion No. 17*, the terms *Type (a)* and *Type (b)* were not specifically used, and the terms *identifiable* and *unidentifiable* were substituted. In this release, the APB noted that then-current practices allowed for the following variations in treatment of unidentifiable intangibles: (1) retention of cost until a reduction of value was apparent, (2) amortization over an arbitrary period, (3) amortization over estimated useful life with specified minimum and maximum periods, and (4) deduction from equity as acquired.[35]

---

[33] Ibid., par. 24.

[34] *Accounting Research Bulletin No. 43*, "Restatement and Revision of Accounting Research Bulletins" (New York: AICPA, 1953), p. 6019.

[35] *APB Opinion No. 17*, op. cit.

In *Opinion No. 17* the APB concluded that intangible assets should be amortized by systematic charges to income over the estimated period to be benefited. The Board also suggested that the following factors should be considered in estimating the useful lives of intangibles:

1. Legal, regulatory, or contractual provisions may limit the maximum useful life.
2. Provisions for renewal or extension may alter a specific limit on useful life.
3. Effects of obsolescence, demand, competition, and other economic factors may reduce a useful life.
4. A useful life may parallel the service life expectancies of individuals or groups of employees.
5. Expected actions of competitors and others may restrict present competitive advantages.
6. An apparently unlimited useful life may in fact be indefinite, and benefits cannot be reasonably projected.
7. An intangible asset may be a composite of many individual factors with varying effective lives.[36]

The period of amortization should be determined from a review of the foregoing factors but should not exceed 40 years. Use of the straight-line method of amortization was required unless another method could be demonstrated to be more appropriate.

As observed earlier, the release of *APB Opinion No. 17* narrowed the accounting treatment available for similar transactions; however, whether or not it created the desired result is subject to question. *APB Opinion No. 17* has been criticized because it places values on the balance sheet that relate to future expectations (for example, purchased goodwill). Others disagree with the Board's conclusions because it assigns costs to arbitrary periods where there is no evidence that costs have expired (for example, perpetual franchises). Further evidence of this pronouncement's lack of acceptability lies in the fact that originally it was part of *APB Opinion No. 16*, "Business Combinations." However, since enough members of the APB objected to various provisions of both Opinions, it was necessary to separate them to obtain the required majority for passage.

Goodwill

The topic of goodwill has been of interest for many years. As initially conceived, it was viewed as good relations with customers. Such factors as a convenient location and habits of customers were viewed as adding to the value of the business. Yang described it as everything that might contribute to the advantage an established business possesses over a business to be started anew.[37] Since that time, the concept of goodwill has evolved into

[36] Ibid., par. 27.

[37] J. M. Yang, *Goodwill and Other Intangibles* (New York: Ronald Press, 1927), p. 29.

an earning power concept in which the value of goodwill is determined by subtracting the book value of a firm's net assets from the total value of the enterprise.

Catlett and Olson summarized the characteristics of goodwill that distinguish it from other elements of value as follows:

1. *The value of goodwill has no reliable or predictable relationship to costs that may have been incurred in its creation.*

2. *Individual intangible factors that may contribute to goodwill cannot be valued.*

3. *Goodwill attaches only to a business as a whole.*

4. *The value of goodwill may, and does, fluctuate suddenly and widely because of the innumerable factors that influence that value.*

5. *Goodwill is not utilized or consumed in the production of earnings.*

6. *Goodwill appears to be an element of value that runs directly to the investor or owner in a business enterprise.*[38]

In theory, the value of goodwill is equal to the discounted present value of expected superior earnings (expected future earnings less normal earnings for the industry). Thus the process of estimating the value of goodwill involves forecasting future earnings and choosing an appropriate discount rate.

The forecasting of future earnings is a risky proposition. Since the past is the best indicator of the future, prior and current revenue and expense figures should be used. However, the following points are relevant to this process:

1. The use of too few or too many years may distort projections.

2. Trends in earnings should be considered.

3. Industry trends are important.

4. Overall economic conditions can be significant.

In choosing the discount rate to be used in making goodwill calculations, the objective is to approximate the existing cost of capital for the company. This approximation must take into consideration existing and expected risk conditions as well as earnings potential.

Although goodwill may exist at any point in time, in practice, it is recognized for accounting purposes only when it is acquired through purchase of an existing business.[39] Only then is the value of goodwill readily determinable because the purchase embodies an arm's length transaction wherein assets, often cash or marketable securities, are exchanged. The

---

[38] George R. Catlett and Norman O. Olson, *Accounting for Goodwill* (New York: AICPA, 1968), pp. 20–21.

[39] In certain cases, goodwill is recognized when a new partner is admitted to a partnership or when a partner leaves a partnership.

value of the assets exchanged indicates a total fair value for the business entity acquired. The excess of total fair value over the fair value of identifiable net assets is considered goodwill. This practice fulfills the stewardship function of accounting and facilitates the managers' accountability to stockholders. However, it can be argued that when a company acquires stock so that it can exercise significant influence or control, part of the purchase price represents an influence or control premium and is not a payment for goodwill. In this case, two intangible assets are purchased and should be given separate accounting treatment.

When goodwill is recorded, it is considered an intangible asset. As such, it has been subject to the *APB Opinion No. 17* requirements for amortization of cost over useful life, or 40 years, whichever comes first.[40] The case for amortization was based on accrual accounting. The company has paid for the goodwill. The goodwill will presumably generate future earnings, and thus its cost should be matched against those future earnings as they arise. However, in the case of goodwill, it is difficult, if not impossible, to estimate what that useful life will be. If goodwill measures excess earning power, how long can it be expected to last? An economist would say that it would not last very long because competition would drive it away. If so, it should be written off over a relatively short period of time. On the other hand, if the goodwill is attributable to some ability associated with the enterprise, its employees, or management that would be difficult for others to duplicate, then it may have an indefinite useful life, in which case it may be inappropriate to amortize goodwill at all.

Some accountants argue that goodwill should be written off when it is acquired because it would then receive the same treatment as inherent goodwill (goodwill that exists but is not paid for). There are costs associated with developing inherent goodwill. These costs are written off as they are incurred. Moreover, when goodwill is acquired, further cost will be incurred to continue excess earnings ability. Hence, to amortize the cost of goodwill acquired over future periods represents a double counting of cost. The immediate write-off of purchased goodwill could be treated as an extraordinary item because it represents a transaction outside the normal trading activity of the acquiring or investee enterprise.

Opponents of immediate write-off of goodwill contend that the purchase of goodwill implies future profitability; thus, it is inconsistent and perhaps misleading to investors to write off the cost of goodwill because it represents an asset having future service potential. This is particularly true for investments in people-intensive companies, for example, in service industries. For these investments, the amount of goodwill acquired relative to other assets is high. Thus, the immediate write-off would be material and would have a major and misleading impact on financial ratios, partic-

---

[40] The Revenue Reconciliation Act of 1993 allows goodwill to be written off over a 15-year period for income tax purposes. Consequently, a new income tax timing difference has been created by this legislation, and the previous permanent difference has been eliminated.

ularly debt to equity and return on investment. Moreover, future profits would be inflated because they would not be matched against the cost of the investment.

The FASB recently revisited this issue and tentatively decided to adopt an impairment approach whereby goodwill will only be expensed when its recorded value exceeds its fair value.

Brand Recognition Accounting

Brand recognition, embodied, for example, in tradenames and trademarks or as the result of advertising efforts, is similar to goodwill. It, too, may result in future profits that otherwise would not accrue; thus, brand recognition has future service potential and may be considered an asset. If so, investors interested in evaluating a company may take this asset into consideration even though it may not appear on the corporate balance sheet.

In current practice, trademarks and tradenames are recognized only if purchased. Research and development costs and the cost of advertising that eventually result in brand recognition are expensed as incurred. Hence, brand recognition rarely appears in published financial statements. When it is recorded, the asset is considered an intangible asset and is amortized in accordance with *APB Opinion No. 17*. Like goodwill, determination of useful life is questionable, and useful life could even be indefinite. Unlike goodwill, brand recognition is not likely to be driven away by competition. Thus, the write-off under the rules for intangible assets may be questionable.

When an enterprise invests in a business that has brand recognition, that part of the purchase price that is normally considered goodwill may actually be due, at least in part, to brand recognition. Some accountants argue that the excess of cost over the fair value of identifiable net assets should be allocated between goodwill and brand recognition, and that due to differences in anticipated useful lives should be subjected to different amortization periods or rules. Perhaps the purchase price attributable to goodwill should be amortized, and the cost attributable to brand recognition should not.

There are obvious measurement problems associated with such an allocation. Because the current value of goodwill and brand recognition is a function of the future profits that each will generate, the separation of cost into goodwill and brand recognition components would require the separate measurement and discounting of cash flow expected to be derived from each component. At a minimum, it would be necessary to derive a fair value for one component and presume that the rest of the cost paid applied to the other component. But how would the acquiring firm identify which cash flows would result from which asset? Excess earnings would be provided by both assets, but it would be difficult to determine how much of the excess earnings would be derived from each asset. Such a measurement is further complicated when it is felt that some of the purchase price of the investment has been paid for an influence or control premium. In this case, an allocation should be made to three separate intangible assets.

Research and Development Costs

Large corporations are continually attempting to improve their product lines, bring out new products, improve manufacturing methods, and develop improved manufacturing facilities. Accounting for the cost of the research department's activities is a complicated process because some costs may never result in future benefits. For those costs that will provide future benefit, an asset exists. However, due to the uncertainty surrounding the present determination of which costs will result in future benefits, and over what periods those future benefits will be realized, many accountants view such determinations as too subjective and unreliable. In the past, many corporations recognized the importance of developing accounting procedures to allow such costs to be capitalized and amortized on a reasonable basis. For example, one study suggested that such costs might be classified as follows:

1. *Basic research:* Experimentation with no specific commercial objective.
2. *New product development:* Experimental effort toward previously untried products.
3. *Product improvement:* Effort toward improving the quality or functional performance of current product lines.
4. *Cost and/or capacity improvement:* Development of new and improved processes, manufacturing equipment, and the like, to reduce operations costs or expand capacity.
5. *Safety, health, and convenience:* Improvement of working conditions generally for purposes of employee welfare, community relations, and so on.[41]

This classification scheme would make it easier to identify the costs that should be deferred and those that should be expensed. The authors of this study suggested that categories (1), (2), and (3) should generally be deferred and amortized, whereas (4) and (5) should be charged to expense because of the difficulty in determining the future periods expected to receive benefit.

APB Opinion No. 17 requires the immediate expensing of intangible assets that are not specifically identifiable because these costs do not specifically generate revenue and have dubious future service potential. This provision was adopted to discourage the manipulation of research and development expenses. (Many companies were capitalizing research and development costs in low-profit years and writing them off in a lump sum in high-profit years.)

Later, the FASB restudied the issue of research and development costs and issued *SFAS No. 2.* This release requires all research and development costs to be charged to expense as incurred. To distinguish research and development costs from other costs, the FASB provided the following definitions.

---

[41] Donald L. Madden, Levis D. McCullers, and Relmond P. Van Daniker, "Classification of Research and Development Expenditures: A Guide to Better Accounting." *The CPA Journal* (February 1972), pp. 139–142.

Research is planned search or critical investigation aimed at the discovery of new knowledge with the hope that such knowledge will be useful in developing a new product or service or a new process or technique or in bringing about a significant improvement to an existing product or process.

Development is the translation of research findings or other knowledge into a plan or design for a new product or process or for a significant improvement to an existing product or process whether intended for sale or use. It includes the conceptual formulation, design, and testing of product alternatives, construction of prototypes, and operation of pilot plants. It does not include routine or periodic alterations to existing products, production lines, manufacturing processes, and other ongoing operations, even though these alterations may represent improvements and it does not include market research or market testing activities.[42]

Research and Development Activities	*Activities Not Considered Research and Development*
Laboratory research aimed at discovery of a new knowledge	Engineering follow-through in an early phase of commercial production
Searching for applications of new research findings	Quality control during commercial production including routine testing
Conceptual formulation and design of possible product or process alternatives	Troubleshooting breakdowns during production
Testing in search for or evaluation of product or process alternatives	Routine, ongoing efforts to refine, enrich, or improve the qualities of an existing product
Modification of the design of a product or process	Adaptation of an existing capability to a particular requirement or customer's need
Design, construction, and testing of preproduction prototypes and models	Periodic design changes to existing products
Design of tools, jigs, molds, and dies involving new technology	Routine design of tools, jigs, molds, and dies
Design, construction, and operation of a pilot plant not useful for commercial production	Activity, including design and construction engineering, related to the construction, relocation, rearrangement, or start-up of facilities or equipment.
Engineering activity required to advance the design of a product to the manufacturing stage	Legal work on patent applications, sale, licensing, or litigation

---

[42] Financial Accounting Standards Board, *Statement of Financial Accounting Standards No. 2,* "Accounting for Research and Development Costs" (Stamford, CT: FASB, October 1974), par. 8.

Since many costs may have characteristics similar to research and development costs, the FASB also listed activities that would and would not be included in the category of research and development costs as shown on page 290.

The disclosure of research and development costs in annual reports was the subject of a recent research study (contained on the webpage by Gary Entwistle). Entwistle found that only approximately 1 percent of the firms he surveyed made R&D disclosures in the financial statements and that such disclosures were located throughout the annual report. An examination of Kroll-O'Gara Company's 1998 financial statements revealed the following from part (n) of the summary of significant accounting policies:

> *Research and Development—Research and development costs are expensed as incurred. The Company incurred approximately $130,000, $136,000 and $537,000 for the years ended December 31, 1996, 1997 and 1998, respectively, for research and development. These costs are included in general and administrative expenses in the accompanying consolidated statements of operations.*

International Accounting Standards

The International Accounting Standards Committee has issued pronouncements on the following issues:

1. Accounting for investments in associates in *IAS No. 28*, "Accounting for Investments in Associates."
2. Accounting for goodwill in *IAS No. 22*, "Business Combinations."
3. Accounting for intangibles in *IAS No. 38*, "Intangible Assets."
4. Accounting for financial assets in *IAS No. 32*, "Financial Instruments: Disclosure and Presentation."
5. The recognition and measurement of financial assets in *IAS No. 39*, "Financial Instruments: Recognition and Measurement."

In *IAS No. 28*, the IASC addressed accounting for investments where the investor does not own a majority interest but has the ability to significantly influence the investee. The reporting requirements contained in this statement are quite similar to U.S. GAAP discussed in *APB Opinion No. 18*. In its review of *IAS No. 28*, the FASB staff indicated that the requirements for use of the equity method are essentially the same as those contained in U.S. GAAP. However, concern was voiced over the lack of disclosure requirements in *IAS No. 28*. *ABP Opinion No. 18* requires the disclosure of summary information about assets, liabilities, and the results of operations when an investee is material to an investor. *IAS No. 28* does not require similar disclosures. These disclosures were seen as crucial to the analysis of companies using the equity method.[43]

---

[43] Financial Accounting Standards Board, *The IAS-U. S. Comparison Project: A Report on the Similarities and Differences between IAS Standards and U.S. GAAP,* Carrie Bloomer ed., 2nd ed. (Norwalk, CT: Financial Accounting Standards Board, 1999), pp. 289–320.

With respect to goodwill, the IAS, in an amendment to *IAS No. 22,* indicated that it should be recognized as an asset and amortized over a period not to exceed 20 years unless evidence exists that a longer period is justified. This treatment contrasts to current U.S. GAAP which allows amortization periods of up to 40 years. *IAS No. 22* also proscribes the accounting treatment for "negative goodwill." (Cost is less than the fair market value of the assets acquired.) The preferred practice is to attempt to proportionally reduce the values of the acquired assets; however, if it is not possible to completely eliminate the amount, this excess is recognized as deferred income and amortized on a systematic basis over a five-year period unless a longer period of up to 20 years can be justified. Alternatively, a company may choose to disregard the attempt to proportionally reduce the excess, record it all as deferred income, and amortize it over the appropriate periods. The FASB staff analysis of the impact of using a relatively shorter amortization period for goodwill under the reporting requirements of *IAS No. 22* was seen as negligible in that it would usually be possible for users to assess the impact of different amortization periods for comparative analysis based on the disclosure requirements contained in *IAS No. 22.*[42]

IAS No. 38, "Intangible Assets," applies to all intangible assets that are not specifically dealt with in other international accounting standards. It specifically applies to expenditures for advertising, training, start-up, and R&D activities. Specifically, *IAS No. 38* indicates that an intangible asset should be recognized initially, at cost, in the financial statements if

a.   The asset meets the definition of an intangible asset. In particular, there should be an identifiable asset that is controlled and clearly distinguishable from an enterprise's goodwill.
b.   It is probable that the future economic benefits that are attributable to the asset will flow to the enterprise.
c.   The cost of the asset can be measured reliably.

These requirements apply whether an intangible asset is acquired externally or generated internally. If an intangible item does not meet both the definition and the criteria for the recognition of an intangible asset, it is expensed when incurred. All expenditures on research are to be immediately recognized as expenses, and internally generated intangibles such as goodwill cannot be recognized as assets.

After initial recognition in the financial statements, *IAS No. 38* indicates that intangible assets should be measured under one of the following two treatments:

a.   Benchmark treatment: historical cost less any amortization and impairment losses; or
b.   Allowed alternative treatment: revalued amount (based on fair value) less any subsequent amortization and impairment losses. The main difference from the treatment for revaluations of property, plant, and equipment under *IAS No. 16* is that revaluations for intangible assets are permitted only if fair value can be determined by reference to an active market. Active markets are expected to be rare for intangible assets.

The statement requires intangible assets to be amortized over the best estimate of their useful life, and it includes the presumption that the useful life of an intangible asset will not exceed 20 years from the date when the asset is available for use. In rare cases, where persuasive evidence suggests that the useful life of an intangible asset will exceed 20 years, an enterprise should amortize the intangible asset over the best estimate of its useful life and

a. Test the intangible asset for impairment at least annually in accordance with *IAS No. 36*, Impairment of Assets; and

b. Disclose the reasons why the presumption that the useful life of an intangible asset will not exceed 20 years is rebutted and also the factor(s) that played a significant role in determining the useful life of the asset.

In its review of *IAS No. 38*, the FASB staff indicated that it is similar to *APB Opinion No. 17* in that both address accounting for acquired and internally generated intangible assets. However, it was noted that analyzing *IAS No. 38* is difficult because some of the issues it contains are scattered throughout U.S. GAAP. The primary differences include the following: *IAS No. 38* addresses research and development costs as separate components of internally generated intangible assets and similar to *SFAS No. 2*, requires research costs to be charged to expenses, but unlike *SFAS No. 2* allows for the capitalization of development costs under certain circumstances. The staff review noted that the alternate treatment allowed by *IAS No. 38* is not allowed under U.S. GAAP. Finally, the two standards differ in the maximum amortization period, with *IAS No. 38* allowing up to 20 years and *APB Opinion No. 17* up to 40 years.

In *IAS No. 32*, financial assets were defined as cash, a right to receive cash or other financial assets from another enterprise, and a contractual right to exchange financial assets with another enterprise under potential favorable conditions or equity instruments of other enterprises. The information to be disclosed concerning financial assets includes how they might affect the amount, timing, and certainty of future cash flows, and the associated accounting policies and basis of measurement applied. For each class of financial assets, a company must disclose information about its exposure to credit risk (the risk that the other party will fail to discharge its obligation and cause the enterprise to incur a loss), including the amount that best represents its maximum risk and significant concentrations of credit risk. Finally, information about the financial assets fair value is to be disclosed.

Under *IAS No. 39*, which became effective for all companies for annual periods beginning on or after January 1, 2001, all financial assets are recognized on the balance sheet, including all derivatives. They are initially measured at cost, which is the fair value of whatever was paid or received to acquire the financial asset. An enterprise should recognize normal purchases of securities in the marketplace either at trade date or settlement date, with recognition of certain value changes between trade and settlement dates if settlement date accounting is used. Transaction costs should be included in the initial measurement of all financial instruments.

Subsequent to initial recognition, all financial assets are remeasured to fair value, except for the following, which should be carried at amortized cost:

a. Loans and receivables originated by the enterprise and not held for trading.
b. Other fixed maturity investments, such as debt securities and mandatorily redeemable preferred shares, that the enterprise intends and is able to hold to maturity.
c. Financial assets whose fair value cannot be reliably measured (generally limited to some equity securities with no quoted market price and forwards and options on unquoted equity securities).

An intended or actual sale of a held-to-maturity security due to a non-recurring and not reasonably anticipated circumstance beyond the enterprise's control should not call into question the enterprise's ability to hold its remaining portfolio to maturity. If an enterprise is prohibited from classifying financial assets as held-to-maturity because it has sold more than an insignificant amount of assets that it had previously said it intended to hold to maturity, that prohibition should expire at the end of the second financial year following the premature sales. For those financial assets that are remeasured to fair value, an enterprise will have a single, enterprisewide option either to:

a. Recognize the entire adjustment in net profit or loss for the period; or
b. Recognize in net profit or loss for the period only those changes in fair value relating to financial assets held for trading, with the nontrading value changes reported in equity until the financial asset is sold, at which time the realized gain or loss is reported in net profit or loss. For this purpose, derivatives are always deemed held for trading unless they are designated as hedging instruments.

IAS No. 39 requires that an impairment loss be recognized for a financial asset whose recoverable amount is less than the carrying amount and establishes conditions for determining when control over a financial asset has been transferred to another party. For financial assets, a transfer normally will be recognized if (a) the transferee has the right to sell or pledge the asset and (b) the transferor does not have the right to reacquire the transferred assets unless either the asset is readily obtainable in the market or the reacquisition price is fair value at the time of reacquisition. If part of a financial asset is sold or extinguished, the carrying amount is split based on relative fair values. If fair values are not determinable, a cost recovery approach to profit recognition is taken. The FASB staff had not reviewed *IAS No. 39* at the time this text was published. A summary of the staff review will be available on the text's webpage when it is released.

Summary

A number of measurement problems arise in accounting for investments in equity and debt securities and for intangibles. Less than majority investments in common stock are accounted for by the cost method, the fair value method, the equity method, or the market value method, according to the percentage of ownership in the investee held by the investor or the surrounding circumstances. The equity method satisfies the requirements of accrual accounting for those investments wherein the investor has the ability to exercise significant influence over the investee. The fair value method provides information relevant to investor decision making for investments in debt and equity securities that have readily determinable fair values. Dividend and interest income for these securities are recognized as received or receivable.

Investments in debt securities that management intends to hold to maturity are carried at amortized cost. Income from debt is recognized as interest is paid and is adjusted at year-end for amounts that have accrued since the last interest payment date. The interest income is adjusted for the amortization of discounts and premiums to reflect the total interest earned over the life of the debt instrument from the purchase date to the maturity date. The straight-line or effective interest methods can be used to amortize discounts or premiums.

Intangible assets are identified as either identifiable or unidentifiable. Identifiable intangible assets are written off over their period of benefit. Unidentifiable intangible assets, purchased from outsiders, are written off over their period of benefit, not to exceed 40 years.

In the articles contained on the webpage for Chapter 9, accounting for investments and intangibles is further examined.

Cases

• Case 9-1 Value of Intangible Assets

On June 30, 2001, your client, the Vandiver Corporation, was granted patents covering plastic cartons that it has been producing and marketing profitably for the past three years. One patent covers the manufacturing process, and the other covers the related products.

Vandiver executives tell you that these patents represent the most significant breakthrough in the industry in the past 30 years. The products have been marketed under the registered trademarks Safetainer, Duratainer, and Sealrite. Licenses under the patents have already been granted by your client to other manufacturers in the United States and abroad and are producing substantial royalties.

On July 1, 2001, Vandiver commenced patent infringement actions against several companies whose names you recognize as those of substantial and prominent competitors. Vandiver's management is optimistic that these suits will result in a permanent injunction against the manufacture and sale of the infringing products and collection of damages for loss of profits caused by the alleged infringements.

The financial executive has suggested that the patents be recorded at the discounted value of expected net royalty receipts.

Required:

a. What is an intangible asset? Explain.

b. Discuss whether the patents, in this case, fit the *SFAC No. 6* definition of assets. Would your answer be the same if Vandiver was expected to lose the lawsuit? Explain.

c. i. What is the meaning of "discounted value of expected net royalty receipts"? Explain.

    ii. How would such a value be calculated for net royalty receipts?

d. What basis of valuation for Vandiver's patents would be generally accepted in accounting? Give supporting reasons for this basis.

e. i. Assuming no practical problems of implementation and ignoring generally accepted accounting principles, what is the preferable basis of valuation for patents? Explain.

    ii. What would be the preferable theoretical basis of amortization? Explain.

f. What recognition, if any, should be made of the infringement litigation in the financial statements and in the notes to the financial statements for the year ended September 30, 2001? Discuss.

Case 9-2 Accounting for Investments

Xavier Co. purchased $1,000,000 face amount of Yodel Corp., 16 percent bonds on December 31, 2000, for $881,000. Two years later Zandale Co. purchased $1,000,000 face amount of Yodel Corp. bonds for $1,164,000. Each purchasing company plans to hold the bonds until maturity, 12/31/08.

Under current GAAP, Xavier and Zandale will recognize the following amounts in their financial statements.

	Xavier		Zandale	
12/31	Asset	Income	Asset	Income
2000	$881,000	$ 0		
2001	889,000	168,000		
2002	898,000	169,000	$1,164,000	$ 0
2003	908,000	170,000	1,144,000	140,000
2004	921,000	173,000	1,122,000	138,000
2005	936,000	175,000	1,096,000	132,000
2006	954,000	178,000	1,068,000	132,000
2007	975,000	181,000	1,036,000	128,000
2008	0	185,000	0	124,000
		$1,399,000		$796,000

During this time period, the market price of the Yodel bonds varied widely. At the end of each year, the closing price and related market interest rates were as follows:

12/31	Closing Price	Yield
2001	88.1	19%
2002	104.2	15
2003	116.4	12
2004	122.8	10
2005	115.5	11
2006	97.8	17
2007	98.4	17
2008	97.4	19

Required:

a. Even though Xavier and Zandale have purchased the same par value bonds, their financial statements reflect different amounts each year. How are they accounting for the bonds, and why do their financial statements differ?

b. Assume that Xavier had classified their investment in Yodel bonds as available-for-sale but long-term. How would their assets and income differ, if any, over the above time period? Discuss this accounting treatment. In your answer, construct a table similar to the one above and show the amounts that would appear in assets and income. Show a separate column for interest income and unrealized gains, if any, that would be reflected in earnings.

c. Would your answer to (b) be different if Xavier had classified the investment as available-for-sale but short-term? Explain.

d. Assume that Zandale had classified their investment in Yodel bonds as trading. How would their assets and income differ, if any, over the above time period? Discuss this accounting treatment. In your answer, construct a table similar to the one above and show the amounts that would appear in assets and income. Show a separate column for interest income and unrealized gains, if any, that would be reflected in earnings?

e. Discuss the FASB's rationale for the three different classifications.

f. Which approach to classification do you think is more relevant to investors? Why?

• Case 9-3 Investment Classification and Managerial Intent

Qtip Corp. owns stock in Maxey Corp. The investment represents a 10 percent interest, and Qtip is unable to exercise significant influence over Maxey.

The Maxey stock was purchased by Qtip on January 1, 1997, for $23,000. The stock consistently pays an annual dividend to Qtip of $2,000. Qtip classifies the stock as available-for-sale. Its fair value at 12/31/00 was $21,600. This amount was properly reported as an asset in the balance sheet. Due to the development of a new Maxey product line, the market value of Qtip's investment rose to $27,000 at 12/31/01.

The Qtip management team is aware of the provisions of *SFAS No. 115*. The possibility of changing the classification from available-for-sale to trading is discussed. This change is justified, management says, because they intend to sell the security at some point in 2002 so that they can realize the gain.

Required:

a. Discuss the role that managerial intention plays in the accounting treatment of equity securities that have a readily determinable fair value.
b. What income statement effect, if any, would the change in classification have for Qtip?
c. Discuss the ethical considerations of this case.
d. Opponents of *SFAS No. 115* contend that allowing a change in classification masks the effects of unrealized losses and results in improper matching of market value changes with accounting periods. Describe how the accounting treatment and the proposed change in classification would result in this sort of mismatching.

• Case 9-4 Income Effects of Investments

Victoria Company has both current and noncurrent equity securities portfolios. All of the equity securities have readily determinable fair values. Those equity securities in the current portfolio are considered trading securities. At the beginning of the year, the market value of each security exceeded cost.

During the year, some of the securities increased in value. These securities (some in the current portfolio and some in the long-term portfolio) were sold. At the end of the year, the market value of each of the remaining securities was less than the original cost.

Victoria also has investments in long-term bonds, which the company intends to hold to maturity. All of the bonds were purchased at face value. During the year some of these bonds were called by the issuer prior to maturity. In each case, the call price was in excess of par value. Three months before the end of the year, additional similar bonds were purchased for face value plus two months' accrued interest.

Required:

a. How should Victoria account for the sale of the securities from each portfolio? Why?
b. How should Victoria account for the marketable equity securities portfolios at year-end? Why?
c. How should Victoria account for the disposition prior to their maturity of the long-term bonds called by their issuer? Why?
d. How should Victoria report the purchase of the additional similar bonds at the date of acquisition? Why?

• Case 9-5 Financial Statement Disclosures of the Use of the Equity Method

On July 1, 2001, Dynamic Company purchased for cash 40 percent of the outstanding capital stock of Cart Company. Both Dynamic Company and Cart Company have a December 31 year-end. Cart Company, whose common stock is actively traded in the over-the-counter market, reported its total net income for the year to Dynamic Company, and also paid cash dividends on November 15, 2001, to Dynamic and its other stockholders.

Required:
How should Dynamic Company report the foregoing facts in its December 31, 2001, balance sheet and its income statement for the year then ended? Discuss the rationale for your answer.

• Case 9-6 Accounting for Research and Development Activities

The Thomas Company is in the process of developing a revolutionary new product. A new division of the company was formed to develop, manufacture, and market this new product. As of year-end (December 31, 2001), the new product has not been manufactured for resale; however, a prototype unit was built and is in operation.

Throughout 2001 the new division incurred certain costs. These costs include design and engineering studies, prototype manufacturing costs, administrative expenses (including salaries of administrative personnel), and market research costs. In addition, approximately $500,000 in equipment (estimated useful life, 10 years) was purchased for use in developing and manufacturing the preproduction prototype and will be used to manufacture the new product. Approximately $200,000 of this equipment was built specifically for the design and development of the new product; the remaining $300,000 of equipment was used to manufacture the new product once it is in commercial production.

Required:
a. What is the definition of *research and development* as defined in *Statement of Financial Accounting Standards No. 2?*
b. Briefly indicate the practical and conceptual reasons for the conclusion reached by the FASB on accounting and reporting practices for research and development costs.
c. In accordance with *Statement of Financial Accounting Standards No. 2,* how should the various costs Thomas just described be recorded in the financial statements for the year ended December 31, 2001?

• Case 9-7 Trading vs. Available-for-Sale Securities

The Financial Accounting Standards Board issued *Statement of Financial Standards No. 115* to describe the accounting treatment that should be afforded to equity securities that have readily determinable market values which are not accounted for under the equity method or consolidation. An important part of the statement concerns the distinction between trading securities and available-for-sale securities.

Required:
a. Compare and contrast trading securities and available-for-sale securities.
b. How are the trading securities and available-for-sale securities classified in the balance sheet? In your answer, discuss the factors that should be

considered in determining whether a security is classified as trading or available-for-sale and as current or noncurrent.

c. How do the above classifications affect the accounting treatment for unrealized losses?

d. Why does a company maintain an investment portfolio containing current and noncurrent securities?

• Case 9-8 Accounting for Investments in Equity Securities

Presented below are four unrelated situations involving equity securities that have readily determinable fair values.

Situation 1
A noncurrent portfolio with an aggregate market value in excess of cost includes one particular security whose market value has declined to less than one-half of the original cost. The decline in value is considered to be other than temporary.

Situation 2
The balance sheet of a company does not classify assets and liabilities as current and noncurrent. The portfolio of marketable equity securities includes securities normally considered to be trading securities that have a net cost in excess of market value of $2,000. The remainder of the portfolio is considered noncurrent and has a net market value in excess of cost of $5,000.

Situation 3
A marketable equity security, whose market value is currently less than cost, is classified as a noncurrent security that is available-for-sale but is to be reclassified as a trading security.

Situation 4
A company's noncurrent portfolio of marketable equity securities consists of the common stock of one company. At the end of the prior year, the market value of the security was 50 percent of original cost, and the effect was properly reflected in the balance sheet. However, at the end of the current year, the market value of the security had appreciated to twice the original cost. The security is still considered noncurrent at year-end.

Required:
Determine the effect on classification, carrying value, and earnings for each of the preceding situations. Complete your response to each situation before proceeding to the next situation.

• Case 9-9 Equity Securities: GAAP Versus International Accounting Standards

SFAS No. 115 prescribes the accounting treatment for investments in equity securities having readily determined fair values for which the equity method and consolidation do not apply. *IAS No. 25* prescribes international accounting practice for similar securities.

Required:
a. Compare and contrast U.S. GAAP for investments in equity securities under *SFAS No. 115* with the provisions of *IAS No. 25*.
b. Discuss whether U.S. GAAP under *SFAS No. 115* or the requirements of *IAS No. 25* are more consistent with the following concepts:
  i. Conservatism
  ii. Comparability
  iii. Relevance
  iv. Neutrality
  v. Representational faithfulness
  vi. Physical capital maintenance

• Case 9-10 Accounting for Goodwill

Kallus Corp. is an industry leader in the manufacture of toys. Each year, its design staff comes up with new ideas that are a great success. As a result, Kallus sales and profits consistently exceed those of other toy manufacturers. Over the past 10 years, Kallus has earned average net profits of $189 million compared to $122 million for the typical company in the toy industry.

Required:
Answer the following questions:
a. Does Kallus have goodwill? Explain.
b. Is goodwill an asset? Explain. (Does it meet the definition of an asset found in *SFAS No. 6?*)
c. If you believe Kallus has goodwill, how would you go about measuring it? Explain.
d. Should Kallus Corp. report goodwill in the balance sheet? Why or why not?

Room for Debate

• Issue 1

SFAS No. 115 was issued in response to concerns by regulators and others regarding the recognition and measurement of investments in debt securities.

Team Debate:
Team 1. Present arguments supporting the provisions of *SFAS No. 115*. You may consider tying your arguments to theories of capital maintenance and/or the conceptual framework.
Team 2. Present arguments describing the deficiencies of *SFAS No. 115*. You may consider tying your arguments to theories of capital maintenance and/or the conceptual framework.

• Issue 2

Under current GAAP, goodwill is recorded when purchased.

Team Debate:

Team 1. Present arguments in favor of the capitalization of "purchased" goodwill. You may consider tying your arguments to theories of capital maintenance and/or the conceptual framework.

Team 2. Present arguments against the capitalization of "purchased" goodwill. You may consider tying your arguments to theories of capital maintenance and/or the conceptual framework.

Recommended Additional Readings

Bierman, Harold, Jr., and Roland E. Dukes. "Accounting for Research and Development Costs." *Journal of Accountancy* (April 1975), pp. 44–55.

Clark, Stanley J., and Charles E. Jordan. "Accounting for Asset Impairment under SFAS No. 121." *The Ohio CPA Journal* (February 1996), pp. 15–18.

Davis, Michael. "Goodwill Accounting: Time for an Overhaul." *Journal of Accountancy* (June 1992), pp. 75–78, 80, 82, 83.

Duval, Linda, Ross Jennings, John Robinson, and Robert B. Thompson II. "Can Investors Unravel the Effects of Goodwill Accounting?" *Accounting Horizons* (June 1992), pp. 1–14.

Munter, Paul. "SFAS No. 121 and Impairment of Assets." *The CPA Journal* (October 1995), pp. 54–55.

Nix, Paul E., and David E. Nix. "A Historical Review of the Accounting Treatment of Research and Development Costs." *The Accounting Historians' Journal* (June 1992), pp. 51–78.

Pactor, Paul A. "Applying APB Opinion No. 18—Equity Method." *Journal of Accountancy* (September 1971), pp. 54–62.

Parks, James T. "The Portfolio Accounting Controversy." *Journal of Accountancy* (November 1989), pp. 81–84, 86.

Pizzy, Alan. "Accounting for Goodwill and Brands." *Management Accounting* (September 1991), pp. 22, 23, 26.

Smith, Kimberly J. "Asset Impairment Disclosures: Will Accounting for Asset Impairment Lead to Performance Impairment?" *Journal of Accountancy* (December 1994), pp. 57–61.

Swieringa, Robert J. "Recognition and Measurement Issues in Accounting for Secured Assets." *Journal of Accounting Auditing and Finance* (Spring 1989), pp. 169–186.

Wines, Grueme, and Colin Ferguson. "An Empirical Investigation of Accounting Methods for Goodwill and Intangible Assets." *Abacus* (March 1993), pp. 90–105.

Bibliography

Abdel-khalik, A. Rashad. "Advertising Effectiveness and Accounting Policy." *The Accounting Review* (October 1975), pp. 657–670.

Barrett, M. Edgar. "Accounting for Intercorporate Investments: A Behavioral Field Experiment." *Journal of Accounting Research. Empirical Research in Accounting* (1971), pp. 50–65.

Barrett, M. Edgar. "APB Opinion No. 18: A Move Toward Preferences of Users." *Financial Analysts Journal* (July–August 1972), pp. 47–50, 52–55.

Catlett, George R., and Norman O. Olson. "Accounting for Goodwill." *Accounting Research Study No. 10.* New York: AICPA, 1968.

Clinch, Greg, and Joseph Magliolo. "Market Perceptions of Reserve Disclosures under SFAS No. 69." *The Accounting Review* (October 1992), pp. 843–861.

Copeland, Ronald M., Robert Strawser, and John G. Binns. "Accounting for Investments in Common Stock." *Financial Executive* (February 1972), pp. 36–38ff.

Dukes, Roland E. "An Investigation of the Effects of Expensing Research and Development Costs on Security Prices." In Michael Schiff and George Sorter (eds.), *Proceedings in the Conference on Tropical Research in Accounting.* New York: New York University, 1976, pp. 147–193.

Elliot, John, Gordon Richardson, Thomas Dyckman, and Roland Dukes. "The Impact of SFAS No. 2 on Firm Expenditures on Research and Development: Replications and Extensions." *Journal of Accounting Research* (Spring 1984), pp. 85–102.

Falk, Haim, and Joseph C. Miller. "Amortization of Advertising Expenditures." *Journal of Accounting Research* (Spring 1977), pp. 12–22.

Gellein, Oscar S., and Maurice S. Newman. "Accounting for Research and Development Expenditures." *Accounting Research Study No. 14.* New York: AICPA, 1973.

Gridley, F. W. "Accounting for R&D Costs." *Financial Executive* (April 1974), pp. 18–22.

Gynther, Reg S. "Some Conceptualizing on Goodwill." *The Accounting Review* (April 1969), pp. 247–255.

Johnson, Orace. "A Consequential Approach to Accounting for R&D." *Journal of Accounting Research* (Autumn 1967), pp. 164–172.

Lall, R. M. "Conceptual Veracity of Goodwill." *Accountancy* (October 1968), pp. 728–732.

Lee, T. A. "Goodwill: An Example of Will-o'-the-Wisp Accounting." *Accounting and Business Research* (Autumn 1971), pp. 318–328.

Lynch, Thomas Edward. "Accounting for Investments in Equity Securities by the Equity and Market Value Methods." *Financial Analysts' Journal* (January–February 1975), pp. 62–69.

MacIntosh, J.C.C. "Problem of Accounting for Goodwill." *Accountancy* (November 1974), pp. 30–32.

Miller, Malcolm C. "Goodwill—An Aggregation Issue." *The Accounting Review* (April 1973), pp. 280–291.

Munter, Paul, and Thomas A. Ratcliff. "Accounting for Research and Development Activities." *The CPA Journal* (April 1983), pp. 54–65.

Newman, Maurice S. "Accounting for Research and Development Expenditures." *The CPA Journal* (April 1974), pp. 55–58.

O'Connor, Melvin C., and James C. Hamre. "Alternative Methods of Accounting for Long-Term Nonsubsidiary Intercorporate Investments in Common Stock." *The Accounting Review* (April 1972), pp. 308–319.

Picconi, Mario J. "A Reconsideration of the Recognition of Advertising Assets on Financial Statements." *Journal of Accounting Research* (Autumn 1977), pp. 317–326.

Sands, John E. *Wealth, Income and Intangibles.* Toronto: Toronto University Press, 1963.

Tearney, Michael G. "Accounting for Goodwill: A Realistic Approach." *Journal of Accountancy* (July 1973), pp. 41–45.

Tearney, Michael G. "Compliance with the AICPA Pronouncements on Accounting for Goodwill." *The CPA Journal* (February 1973), pp. 121–125.

Weinwurm, Ernest H. "Modernizing the Goodwill Concept." *Management Accounting* (December 1971), pp. 31–34.

Wesley, Charles E., and Thomas J. Linsmeier. "A Further Examination of the Economic Consequences of SFAS No. 2." *Journal of Accounting Research* (Spring 1992), pp. 156–164.

Zucca, Linda J., and David R. Campbell. "A Closer Look at Discretionary Writedowns of Impaired Assets." *Accounting Horizons* (September 1992), pp. 30–41.

Long-Term

Liabilities

The importance of short-term liabilities as an element of working capital was discussed in Chapter 6. In this chapter we examine the nature of long-term liabilities. The emphasis is on recognition and measurement of transactions and events as liabilities, with specific attention to some of the more troublesome aspects, and analysis of the risk associated with a company's use of long-term debt.

Investors, creditors, and other users view the separation of liabilities into their current and noncurrent elements as important because their decision models utilize the working capital concept, current ratios, and projections of expected future cash flows to analyze and compare the performance of firms. The amount of long-term debt relative to equity is also relevant because the debt-to-equity ratio is directly related to the risk associated with investing in the firm's stock.[1] As the debt-to-equity ratio of a firm increases, the market's perception of the riskiness of investing in the firm's stock also rises. Thus, it is important that accountants have criteria to appropriately classify liabilities as short-term or long-term so that decision makers can reliably evaluate the firm's ability to meet current needs and to determine the level of riskiness inherent in projections of future cash flows over time.

---

[1] See Robert S. Hamada, "The Effect of the Firm's Capital Structure on the Systematic Risk of Common Stocks," *The Journal of Finance* (March 1969), pp. 13–31, and Mark E. Rubinstein, "A Mean-Variance Synthesis of Corporate Financial Theory," *The Journal of Finance* (May 1973), pp. 167–181.

The Definition of Liabilities

Statement of Financial Accounting Concepts (SFAC) No. 6 describes the elements comprising the balance sheet as assets, liabilities, and equity. Assets have future economic benefit. Liabilities and equity provide resources (capital) for the acquisition of assets. The amount of liabilities a firm has relative to equity is termed the firm's capital structure.

In current accounting practice, liabilities and equity are treated as two separate and distinct elements of the firm's capital structure. This distinction is apparent in the fundamental accounting equation.

$$\text{assets} = \text{liabilities} + \text{equity}$$

Accordingly, liabilities and equity are both claimants to enterprise assets; but equity represents an ownership interest, whereas liabilities are creditor claims. These interests are different, and their separate disclosure is relevant to decision makers who rely on published financial information.[2]

Theories of equity postulate how the balance sheet elements are related and have implications for the definitions of both liabilities and equity. The two prominent theories of equity—entity theory and proprietary theory—imply unique relationships between assets, liabilities, and equity.

The *entity theory* depicts the accounting equation as

$$\text{assets} = \text{equities}$$

According to the entity theory, there is no fundamental difference between liabilities and owners' equity.[3] Both provide capital to the business entity and receive income in return in the form of interest and dividends. Under entity theory, liabilities and equity would require separate line disclosure in the balance sheet, but there would be no subtotals for total liabilities or total equity, and no need for separate or distinct definitions for each.

The *proprietary theory* views the net assets of the firm as belonging to the owners.[4] Under this theory, equity is equal to the net worth of the owners. The proprietary theory relationship is articulated as

$$\text{assets} - \text{liabilities} = \text{equity}$$

Although the AICPA, APB, and FASB have not formally described this relationship as the theory underlying the elements of financial statements, the APB defined liabilities and owners' equity in *Statement No. 4* and stated that

---

[2] See Myrtle W. Clark, "Entity Theory, Modern Capital Structure Theory, and the Distinction between Debt and Equity," *Accounting Horizons* (September 1993). pp. 14–31.

[3] William A. Paton, *Accounting Theory* (New York: Ronald Press Co., 1922), p. 73.

[4] Henry Rand Hatfield, *Accounting, Its Principles and Problems* (New York: D. Appleton & Co., 1927), pp. 171, 221.

the approach implicit in their definitions is that assets minus liabilities equals owners' equity.[5]

In addition, *SFAC No. 6* has defined liabilities and equities in a manner that is also consistent with proprietary theory as follows.

> *Liabilities—probable future sacrifices of economic benefits arising from present obligations of a particular entity to transfer assets or provide services to other entities in the future as a result of past transactions or events.*

> *Equities—the residual interest in the assets of an entity that remains after deducting its liabilities. In a business enterprise the equity is the ownership.[6]*

Recognition and Measurement of Liabilities

According to *SFAC No. 5*, for an item to be recognized as a liability in financial statements, it must meet the definition of liabilities found in *SFAC No. 6*, and it must be measurable. Accountants take a transactions approach to measuring liabilities.[7] Liabilities are measured at the amount established in an exchange. Theoretically, liabilities should be measured at the present value of the future cash flows, discounted at the market rate of interest. The discounted present value measures the fair market value of the liability at issuance. For example, as described in detail in a later section, the issue price of a bond represents the present value of the interest payments and the maturity value, discounted at the market rate of interest. Discounting is generally ignored for current liabilities because the undiscounted value is not materially different from the discounted present value.

The classification and measurement of items as liabilities is not always straightforward. For example, the FASB has issued a pronouncement requiring that the present value of postretirement benefits, such as health care for retired employees be recognized as liabilities, even though the benefits may not be paid for many years in the future and there is a great deal of uncertainty surrounding projections of future cash flows. The FASB supports this kind of recognition by referring to the *SFAC No. 6* definition of liabilities. Postretirement benefits represent sacrifices of future resources resulting from employees having earned those future benefits during present and prior accounting periods.

Unfortunately, the definitions in *SFAC No. 6*, like those in *APB Statement No. 4*, leave many unresolved questions. In the following section we examine some of these questions and attempt to develop more specific criteria for the proper classification of items as liabilities.

---

[5] *Accounting Principles Board, Statement No. 4*, "Basic Concepts and Accounting Principles Underlying Financial Statements of Business Enterprises" (New York: AICPA, 1970), par. 132.

[6] Financial Accounting Standards Board, *Statement of Financial Accounting Concepts No. 6*, "Elements of Financial Statements" (Stamford, CT: FASB, 1985), pars. 35 and 49.

[7] Ibid., par. 67, and APB, op. cit., par. 181.

Debt Versus Equity

The preceding definitions require the classification of all items on the right-hand side of the balance sheet into their liability or equity components. This requirement presumes that all financial interests in the enterprise are liability or equity interests, and it further presumes that these distinctions are readily apparent to whoever is preparing financial statements. There are at least two fallacies in these assumptions: (1) the wide variety of securities issued by the modern complex corporation does not readily lend itself to classification schemes, and (2) to date there are no authoritative guidelines to use in applying the classification schemes. What one individual may view as debt another may view as equity.

An example of a security presenting this type of dilemma is redeemable preferred stock. Under current GAAP, redeemable preferred stock is considered equity, even though it must be repaid. Nevertheless, the SEC has ruled that future cash obligations attached to preferred stock subject to mandatory redemption or whose redemption is outside the issuer's control should be highlighted so as to distinguish it from permanent capital.[8] These securities must not be included under the heading of stockholders' equity. Moreover, they may not be included in total liabilities. The SEC has in effect created a separate "temporary" equity balance sheet category. *SFAC No. 6* does not recognize such a category as an element of financial statements.

As long as accountants feel that the present sharp distinction between debt and equity should be continued, such examples point to the need for accountants to develop additional criteria to aid in classifying items on the right-hand side of the accounting equation as either debt or equity. The following section discusses some of the decision factors that may be used.

Consolidated Set of Decision Factors

The following set of 13 factors is presented as a guide to assist in determining the classification of items on the right-hand side of the accounting equation as either debt or equity. The sequence in which the factors are presented is not intended to reflect any judgment about their relative importance.

Maturity Date

Debt instruments typically have a fixed maturity date, whereas equity instruments do not mature. Because they do mature, debt instruments set forth the redemption requirements. One of the requirements may be the establishment of a sinking fund in order to ensure that funds will be available for the redemption.

Claim on Assets

In the event the business is liquidated, creditors' claims take precedence over those of the owners. There are two possible interpretations of this factor. The

---

[8] U.S. Securities and Exchange Commission, Accounting Series Release No. 268, Presentation in Financial Statements of "Redeemable Preferred Stocks," in *SEC Accounting Rules* (Chicago: Commerce Clearing House, 1983).

first is that all claims other than the first priority are equity claims. The second is that all claims other than the last are creditor claims. The problem area involves all claims between these two interpretations: those claims that are subordinated to the first claim but take precedence over the last claim.

Claim on Income

A fixed dividend or interest rate has a preference over other dividend or interest payments. That it is cumulative in the event it is not paid for a particular period is said to indicate a debt security. On the other hand, a security that does not provide for a fixed rate, one that gives the holder the right to participate with common stockholders in any income distribution, or one whose claim is subordinate to other claims, may indicate an ownership interest.

Market Valuations

Market valuations of liabilities are not affected by company performance as long as the company is solvent. Conversely, the market price of equity securities is affected by the earnings of the company and investor expectations regarding future dividend payments.

Voice in Management

A voting right is the most frequent evidence of a voice in the management of a corporation. This right is normally limited to common stockholders, but it may be extended to other investors if the company defaults on some predetermined conditions. For example, if interest is not paid when due or profits fall below a certain level, voting rights may be granted to other security holders, thus suggesting that the security in question has ownership characteristics.

Maturity Value

A liability has a fixed maturity value that does not change throughout the life of the liability. An ownership interest does not mature, except in the event of liquidation; consequently, there is no maturity value.

Intent of Parties

The courts have determined that the intent of the parties is one factor to be evaluated in ruling on the debt or equity nature of a particular security. Investor attitude and investment character are two subfactors that help in making this determination. Investors may be divided into those who want safety and those who want capital growth, and the investments may be divided into those that provide either safety or an opportunity for capital gains or losses. If the investor was motivated to make a particular investment on the basis of safety and if the corporation included in the issue those features normally equated with safety, then the security may be debt rather than equity. However, if the investor was motivated to acquire the security by the possibility of capital growth and if the security offered the opportunity of capital growth, the security would be viewed as equity rather than debt.

Preemptive Right

A security that is included in the preemptive right of common stockholders (the right to purchase common shares in a new stock offering by the corporation) may be considered to have an equity characteristic. Securities not carrying this right may be considered debt.

Conversion Features

A security that may be converted into common stock has at least the potential to become equity if it is not currently considered equity. A historical study of eventual conversion or liquidation may be useful in evaluating this particular factor.

Potential Dilution of Earnings per Share

This factor might be considered as a subfactor of *conversion* because the conversion feature of a security is the most likely cause of dilution of earnings per share, other than a new issue of common stock. In any event, a security that has the potential to dilute earnings per share is assumed to have equity characteristics.

Right to Enforce Payments

From a legal point of view, creditors have the right to receive periodic interest at the agreed-upon date and to have the maturity value paid at the maturity date. The enforcement of this right may result in the corporation being placed in receivership. Owners have no such legal right; therefore, the existence of the right to enforce payment is an indication of a debt instrument.

Good Business Reasons for Issuing

Determining what constitutes good business reasons for issuing a security with certain features rather than one with different features presents a difficult problem. Two relevant subfactors are the alternatives available and the amount of capitalization. Securities issued by a company in financial difficulty or with a low level of capitalization may be considered equity on the grounds that only those with an ownership interest would be willing to accept the risk, whereas securities issued by a company with a high level of capitalization may be viewed as debt.

Identity of Interest Between Creditors and Owners

When the individuals who invest in debt securities are the same individuals, or family members, who hold the common stock, an ownership interest is indicated.

The FASB, recognizing that these problems exist, resurrected a discussion memorandum titled "Distinguishing between Liability and Equity Instruments and Accounting for Instruments with Characteristics of Both."[9] The impetus for the discussion memorandum is the increasing use of *complex financial instruments,* which have both debt and equity characteristics. In late 2000 the FASB issued an exposure draft of a proposed statement, "Accounting for Financial Instruments with Characteristics of Liabilities, Equity or Both,"[10] and a proposed amendment to SFAC No. 6 that would revise the definition of liabilities.

---

[9] FASB Discussion Memorandum, "Distinguishing between Liability and Equity Instruments and Accounting for Instruments with Characteristics of Both" (Stamford, CT: FASB, August 20, 1990).

[10] FASB Exposure Draft, "Accounting for Financial Instruments with Characteristics of Liabilities, Equity or Both" (Stamford, CT: FASB, October 27, 2000).

The Board's tentative conclusions have led to the development of an approach based on the characteristics of liabilities and equity. The first step in this approach is to determine whether the component includes an obligation. An obligation is a contractual provision that requires the issuer to perform by transferring to the holder either cash, other assets, or the issuer's stock. Those financial instrument components that embody obligations that require settlement by a transfer of cash or other assets are classified as liabilities because they do not give rise to the possibility of establishing an ownership interest by the holder. Obligations permitting or requiring settlement by the issuance of stock give rise to liability-equity classification questions. These components should be classified as equity if they convey the risks and rewards of ownership to the holder. If the relationship is that of a debtor and creditor, the component should be classified as a liability. The proceeds of issuance of a compound financial instrument that includes both liability and equity components should be allocated to its liability and equity components using the relative fair-value method unless that is impracticable. Interest, dividends, gains and losses relating to financial instrument components classified as liabilities are reported in income. Similar amounts related to equity components are to be reported in equity.

Long-Term Debt Classification

Once a particular security has been classified as a liability, it may be reported as either a current or a long-term liability. The classification of an item as a long-term liability is based on the one-year or current-operating-cycle rule. If the settlement of an existing obligation is not expected to use an asset properly classified as current or be replaced by another current liability, it is classified as a long-term liability. The most frequently encountered long-term liabilities are bonds payable, long-term notes payable, lease obligations, pension obligations, deferred taxes, other long-term deferrals, and, occasionally, contingent liabilities. Leases, pensions, and taxes are discussed separately in the following chapters. In this section we examine the recording and reporting requirements for bonds, notes, deferrals, and contingencies.

Bonds Payable

When additional funds are needed to expand the business or for current operations, a corporation has the choice of issuing debt or equity securities. There are four basic reasons why a corporation may wish to issue debt rather than equity securities.

1. *Bonds may be the only available source of funds.* Many small and medium-size companies may appear too risky for investors to make a permanent investment.
2. *Debt financing has a lower cost.* Since bonds have a lower investment risk than stock, they traditionally have paid relatively low rates of interest. Investors acquiring equity securities generally expect a greater return.

3. ***Debt financing offers a tax advantage*** Payments to debtholders in the form of interest are deductible for income tax purposes, whereas dividends on equity securities are not.

4. ***The voting privilege is not shared.*** If a stockholder wishes to maintain his or her present percentage ownership in a corporation, he or she must purchase the current ownership portion of each new common stock issue. Debt issues do not carry ownership or voting rights; consequently, they do not dilute voting power. Where the portion of ownership is small and holdings are widespread, this consideration is probably not very important.

The use of borrowed funds is known as *financial leverage*. The customary reason for using borrowed funds is the expectation of investing them in a capital project that will provide a return in excess of the cost of the acquired funds. The stockholders' investment serves as protection for the bondholders' principal and income, and the strength of current earnings and the debt-equity relationship both influence the rate of interest required by the debtholder. When using debt financing, it should be recognized that financial leverage increases the rate of return to common stockholders only when the return on the project is greater than the cost of the borrowed funds. Earnings (less their related tax effect) in excess of interest payments will increase earnings per share. However, if the return on the investment project falls below the stipulated bond interest rate, earnings per share will decline. The assessment of a company's use of financial leverage is discussed later in the chapter.

Bond Classifications

Bonds frequently are classified by the nature of the protection offered by the company. Bonds that are secured by a lien against specific assets of the corporation are known as *mortgage bonds.* In the event the corporation becomes bankrupt and is liquidated, the holders of mortgage bonds have first claim against the proceeds from the sale of the assets that secured their debt. If the proceeds from the sale of secured assets are not sufficient to repay the debt, mortgage bondholders become general creditors for the remainder of the unpaid debt.

   Debenture bonds are not secured by any property or assets, and their marketability is based on the corporation's general credit. A long period of earnings and continued favorable predictions are necessary for a company to sell debenture bonds. Debenture bondholders become general creditors of the corporation in the event of liquidation.

Bond Selling Prices

Bonds are generally sold in $1,000 denominations and carry a stated amount of interest. *The stated interest rate* is printed on the *bond indenture* (contract). It determines the amount of interest that will be paid to the investor at the end of each interest period. The stated rate will approximate the rate that management believes necessary to sell the bonds given the current state of the economy and the perceived risk associated with the bonds. A bond issued with a relatively low amount of perceived risk will offer a lower interest rate than a bond issue with a relatively higher amount of risk.

The decision to issue bonds and their subsequent sale may take place over a relatively long period of time. From the time the bonds are authorized until they are issued, economic conditions affecting interest rates may change. As a result, at issuance the stated interest rate may differ from the *market rate* for bonds of similar perceived risk. The investor will be unwilling to invest in a bond yielding interest at a rate less than the market rate. Similarly, the issuing company will be unwilling to issue a bond yielding an interest rate that is higher than the market rate. Because the stated rate is predetermined and cannot be changed, the market price of the bonds is adjusted so that *effective rate* of interest is equal to the market rate.

The rate of interest necessary to sell a bond issue is known as the *yield rate* on the bonds. The amount investors are willing to invest is the amount that will yield the market rate of interest, given the amount and timing of the stated interest payments and the *maturity value* of the bonds. Thus, the issue price of the bond is equal to the sum of the present values of the principal and interest payments, discounted at the yield rate. If investors are willing to accept the interest rate stated on the bonds, they will be sold at their *face value*, or *par*, and the yield rate will equal the stated interest rate. When the market rate of interest exceeds the stated interest rate, the bonds will sell below face value (at a *discount*), thereby increasing the effective interest rate. Alternatively, when the market rate of interest is less than the stated interest rate, the bonds will sell above face value (at a *premium*), thereby lowering the effective interest rate.

To illustrate, assume that the XYZ Corporation issued $100,000 of 10 percent, 10-year bonds on January 1, 2001. Interest on these bonds is to be paid annually each December 31. If these bonds are actually sold to yield 9 percent, the bond selling price will be calculated as follows.

Present value of maturity value	
$100,000 × 0.422411[a]	$42,241.10
Present value of interest payments	
$10,000 × 6.417658[b]	64,176.58
Bond issue price	$106,417.68

[a] Present value of $1: $i = 0.09$, $n = 10$.
[b] Present value of an ordinary annuity of $1: $i = 0.09$, $n = 10$.

Since investors must accept an interest rate lower than the rate stated on the bonds, the bond selling price will be higher than the face value of the bonds. The increased selling price has the effect of lowering the yield rate. That is, the amount of interest stipulated on the bonds will be the amount paid to investors each interest payment date, but the actual cash amount invested has increased. The result is that total interest expense over the life of the bonds will be less than the stated amount of interest by the amount of the premium.

Total interest paid		
$10,000 × 10	$100,000.00	$100,000.00
Principal payment at maturity	100,000.00	
Total paid by the borrower	$200,000.00	
Issue price	106,417.68	
Total interest expense	$93,582.32	
		93,582.32
Premium on the bonds		$ 6,417.68

On the other hand, assume that the rate of interest required by investors is 12 percent. The bond selling price will be reduced to achieve a higher yield rate as follows.

Present value of maturity value	
$100,000 × 0.321973[a]	$32,197.30
Present value of interest payments	
$10,000 × 5.650223[b]	56,502.23
Bond issue price	$88,699.53

[a]Present value of $1: i = 12, n = 10.

[b]Present value of an ordinary annuity of $1: i = 12, n = 10.

In this case, the yield rate is higher than the stated rate because the cash payment to investors remains the same while the amount borrowed has decreased. The total interest expense over the life of the bonds will exceed the total interest payments by the amount of the discount, $11,300.47 ($100,000 − 88,699.53).

When bonds are issued between interest payment dates, because interest payments are fixed by the bond indenture, investors will receive the full amount of the interest payment on the interest payment date, even though the bonds have not been held for the entire interest period. To compensate the issuer, the investor pays interest accrued from the contract date to the date of issuance. The *accrued interest* will be repaid to the investor on the next interest payment date and therefore is a current liability to the issuing corporation. The issue price is determined by discounting the maturity value and interest payments from the contract date to maturity plus the return on the bond from the contract date to the date of issuance minus the amount of accrued interest paid.

Bond Issue Costs

The costs to issue bonds may be substantial. The issuing corporation incurs attorney's fees, costs to print the bonds, the cost of preparing the bond prospectus, and sales brokerage commissions. Under *APB Opinion No. 21, bond issue costs* are treated as a deferred charge and shown on the balance sheet as an asset. The asset is amortized from the date of issue to the maturity date of the bonds. The rationale for this treatment is that the costs were incurred to derive benefit from the issuance of the bonds because the debt proceeds contribute to the earnings process. Consequently, they represent future service potential and are assets.

In contrast, debt issue costs were cited by *SFAC No. 6* as an expenditure that does not meet the definition of an asset.[11] The FASB argued that these costs reduce the proceeds of borrowing, resulting in a higher effective interest rate. Consequently, they have no future benefit. This argument provides a basis for subtracting unamortized bond issue costs from the initial carrying value of the debt and allowing it to affect the calculation of periodic interest expense. Alternatively, the FASB stated that because they provide no future benefit, debt issue costs may be treated as an expense of the period of borrowing.[12]

Bond Interest Expense

Interest is the cost of borrowing, and because debt is borrowed over a period of time, it should be allocated over the period benefited. As shown above, the total interest over the life of the bond issue is affected by the presence of a premium or discount. In these cases, the calculation of *interest expense* involves amortization of the premium or discount. There are two methods of allocating interest expense and the associated premium or discount over the life of the bond issue: (1) the straight-line method and (2) the effective interest method. Under the *straight-line method,* the total discount or premium is divided by the total number of interest periods to arrive at the amount to be amortized each period. This method gives an equal allocation per period and results in a stable interest cost per period.

The assumption of a stable interest cost per interest period is not realistic, however, when a premium or discount is involved. The original selling price of the bonds was set to yield the market rate of interest. Therefore, the more valid assumption is that the yield rate should be reflected over the life of the bond issue. The *effective interest method* satisfies this objective by applying the yield rate to the varying value of the bonds in each successive period to determine the amount of interest expense to record. When using the effective interest method, the premium or discount amortization is determined by finding the difference between the stated interest payment and the amount of interest expense recorded for the period.

The effective interest method is theoretically preferable because it results in a stable interest rate per period and discloses a liability balance on the balance sheet equivalent to the present value of the future cash flows discounted at the original market rate of interest. In addition, *APB Opinion No. 21* requires use of the effective interest method unless the results obtained from use of the straight-line method are not materially different. Some companies use the straight-line method because it is easy to calculate and because the difference between income statement and balance sheet values reported under the two methods from period to period are relatively minor.

[11] *SFAC No. 6*, op. cit., par. 237.

[12] Ibid.

Zero Coupon Bonds

A *zero coupon* or *deep discount bond* is a bond sold at considerably less than its face value that does not provide periodic interest payments or carry a stated rate of interest. The interest cost to the issuer is determined by the effective interest method and the total discount is amortized over the life of the bond issue. For example, if $100,000 of zero coupon bonds with a life of 10 years are issued to yield 12 percent, the issue price will be $32,197 and the unamortized discount will be $67,803.

Many accountants have questioned the logic of purchasing zero coupon bonds because of the Internal Revenue Code regulation that requires investors to include the yearly discount amortization as income prior to the time the cash interest is actually received. However, zero coupon bonds became popular with pension funds because (1) they usually do not contain a call provision, and therefore the stated return is guaranteed until maturity and (2) they offer *reinvestment return,* which means that all the interest is reinvested at the same rate of return over the life of the issue. In addition, the income from pension investments is tax deferred. No tax is paid until distributions are made during retirement.

Call Provisions

Long-term debt is issued under the prevailing market conditions at the time it is issued. When market conditions are unfavorable, it may be necessary to pay unusually high interest rates or to include promises in the *bond indenture* (the agreement between the issuing corporation and the bondholders) that inhibit the financial operation of the company. For example, the indenture may include restrictions on dividends, a promise to maintain a certain working capital position, or the maintenance of a certain debt-equity relationship.

Most companies protect themselves from the inability to take advantage of future favorable changes in market conditions by including a call provision in the bond indenture. This provision allows the company to recall debt at a prestated percentage of the issue price.

The recall, or *early extinguishment,* of debt may take two forms: (1) the borrowed funds may no longer be needed and the debt is therefore canceled, which is termed *debt retirement;* or (2) the existing debt may be replaced with another debt issue, termed *debt refunding.*

The cancellation of existing debt poses no particular accounting problem. Any gain or loss resulting from the difference between the carrying value and the call price is treated as a gain or loss in the year the cancellation takes place. The theory behind this treatment is that the recall of the debt was a current decision and should therefore be reflected in current income.

The argument is not quite so convincing in the case of refunding transactions. In *ARB No. 43,* three methods of accounting for the gain or loss from a refunding transaction were discussed.

1. Make a direct write-off of the gain or loss in the year of the transaction.
2. Amortize the gain or loss over the remaining life of the original issue.

3. Amortize the gain or loss over the life of the new issue.[13]

Some accountants favor recognizing the gain or loss over the remaining life of the old issue because they view this as the period of benefit—that is, a higher interest cost would have been incurred during this period if the old issue had not been refunded. Those who favor recognizing the gain or loss over the life of the new issue base their argument on the matching concept— that is, the lower interest rates obtained by the refunding should be adjusted to reflect any refunding gain or loss. Finally, those accountants favoring immediate write-off argue that this method is the most logical because the value of the debt has changed over time, and paying the call price is the most favorable method of eliminating the debt.

ARB No. 43 stated a preference for the first method and allowed the second. Later, *APB Opinion No 6* allowed the use of the third method under certain circumstances.[14] In effect, these two releases frequently permitted a company to use any one of three available methods.

After a subsequent reexamination of the topic, the APB issued *Opinion No. 26*, "Early Extinguishment of Debt."[15] In this release, the Board maintained that all early extinguishments were fundamentally alike (whether retirements or refundings) and that they should be accounted for in the same manner. Since the accounting treatment of retirements was to reflect any gain or loss in the period of recall, it was concluded that any gains or losses from refunding should also be reflected currently in income. Thus, options two and three are no longer considered acceptable under generally accepted accounting principles.

A short time later, the FASB undertook a study of the reporting requirements for gains and losses arising from early extinguishment of debt. This review was undertaken because of pressure from the SEC. Prevailing market conditions in 1973 and 1974 allowed several companies to reacquire long-term debt at prices well below face value. For example, in 1973 United Brands was able to realize a $37.5 million gain by exchanging $12.5 million in cash and $75 million in $9^{1}/_{8}$ percent debentures for $125 million of $5^{1}/_{2}$ percent convertible subordinated debentures. This entire gain was reported as ordinary income.

Upon completion of its study, *SFAS No. 4*, "Reporting Gains and Losses from Extinguishment of Debt,"[16] was issued. This release requires that gains and losses on all extinguishments, whether early or at scheduled maturity, be

[13] *Accounting Research Bulletin No. 43*, "Restatement and Revision of Accounting Research Bulletins" (New York: AICPA, 1953).

[14] *Accounting Principles Board Opinion No. 6*, "Status of Accounting Research Bulletins" (New York: AICPA, 1965).

[15] *Accounting Principles Board Opinion No. 26*, "Early Extinguishment of Debt" (New York: AICPA, 1972).

[16] Financial Accounting Standards Board, *Statement of Financial Accounting Standards No. 4*, "Reporting Gains and Losses from Extinguishment of Debt" (Stamford, CT: FASB, 1975).

classified as extraordinary items without regard to the criteria of "unusual nature" or "infrequency of occurrence." In addition, the following disclosures are required.

1. *A description of the extinguishment transactions, including the sources of any funds used to extinguish debt if it is practicable to identify the sources.*

2. *The income tax effect in the period of extinguishment.*

3. *The per-share amount of the aggregate gain or loss net of related tax effect.*[17]

Subsequently, *APB Opinion No. 26* was amended by *SFAS No. 76*, "Extinguishment of Debt." This release made the provisions of *APB Opinion No. 26* applicable to all debt extinguishments, whether early or not, except those specifically exempted by other pronouncements (e.g., debt restructurings). Debt was considered to be extinguished in the following circumstances.

1. The debtor has paid the creditor and is relieved of all obligations regardless of whether the securities are canceled or held as treasury bonds by the debtor.

2. The debtor is legally released from being the primary obligor by the creditor, and it is probable that no future payment will be required *(legal defeasance)*.

3. The debtor places cash or other essentially risk-free securities (such as government securities) in a trust used solely for satisfying both the scheduled interest payments and principal of a specific obligation, with the possibility of future payments being remote *(in-substance defeasance)*.

Under the third situation, known as in substance defeasance, the debt was considered extinguished even though the debtor is not legally released from being the primary obligor of the debt. *SFAS No. 76* allowed the debt and the assets placed into the irrevocable trust to be derecognized. This practice was criticized as being inconsistent with economic reality. It was argued that the transaction does not have sufficient economic substance to justify derecognition or gain recognition. Moreover, it allowed management to manipulate income by recording a gain even though the debtor had not been legally released from the obligation

The FASB reviewed in-substance defeasance as part of their project on financial instruments and off-balance sheet financing (discussed later in this chapter). The Board subsequently issued *SFAS No. 125*,[18] which eliminated the reporting of these transactions as early extinguishments of debt. This release indicated that a debt should be extinguished if and only if the following two conditions are met:

---

[17] Ibid., par. 9.

[18] *Statement of Financial Accounting Standards No. 125*, "Accounting for Transfers and Servicing of Financial Assets and Extinguishments of Liabilities" (Stamford, CT: FASB 1996).

1. The debtor pays the creditor and is relieved of its obligation. Payment may be in the form of cash, other financial assets, goods, or services or reacquisition of debt securities.

2. The debtor is legally released from being the primary obligor.

It was argued that an in-substance defeasance transaction does not meet the conditions necessary for derecognition of a liability or an asset because it lacks the following essential characteristics:

1. Placing the assets in a trust does not release the debtor from the debt. If the assets should prove insufficient, the debtor must make up the difference.

2. The lender is not limited to the cash flows generated by the trust.

3. The lender does not have the ability to dispose of the assets or to terminate the trust.

4. If the assets in the trust exceed the amounts necessary to meet scheduled interest and principal payments, the debtor can remove the assets.

5. The lender is not a contractual party to establishing the trust.

6. The debtor does not surrender control of the benefits of the assets. The debtor continues to derive benefit because the assets are being used to extinguish the debt.

The FASB recently amended *SFAS No. 125* by issuing *SFAS No. 140*. This release eliminated liability extinguishment by in-substance defeasance. (See Chapter 9 for a discussion of *SFAS No. 140*.)

Convertible Debt

Senior securities (bonds or preferred stock) that are convertible into common stock at the election of the bondholder play a frequent role in corporate financing. There is rather widespread agreement that firms sell convertible securities for one of two primary reasons. Either the firm wants to increase equity capital and decides that convertible securities are the most advantageous way, or the firm wants to increase its debt or preferred stock and discovers that the conversion feature is necessary to make the security sufficiently marketable at a reasonable interest or dividend rate. In addition, there are several other factors that, at one time or another, may motivate corporate management to decide to issue convertible debt. Among these are to

1. Avoid the downward price pressures on the firm's stock that placing a large new issue of common stock on the market would cause.

2. Avoid dilution of earnings and increased dividend requirements while an expansion program is getting under way.

3. Avoid the direct sale of common stock when the corporation believes that its stock is currently undervalued in the market.

4. Penetrate that segment of the capital market that is unwilling or unable to participate in a direct common stock issue.

5. Minimize the flotation cost (cost associated with selling securities).

The remainder of this section will concentrate on convertible debt. Convertible preferred stock is discussed in Chapter 13.

Accounting for *convertible debt* has been the subject of controversy for a number of years. Convertible debt is a *complex financial instrument.* Complex financial instruments combine two or more fundamental financial instruments. Convertible debt combines debt with the option to convert. This combination raises questions regarding the nature of convertible debt and as a result raises questions regarding the appropriate accounting treatment.

There is no question regarding the nature of straight-debt issues. These bonds are liabilities and nothing more. Convertible debt, however, can be viewed in a number of ways. One possibility is to ignore the conversion feature and treat convertible debt like a straight-debt issue. This is the currently required treatment under *APB Opinion No. 14.* This approach is defended on the basis that the bond and conversion option are not separable. Thus, the conversion feature itself, regardless of its nature, has no marketable valuation. Opponents of the current requirement argue that it results in an understatement of interest expense and an overstatement of bond indebtedness.[19]

A second view holds that the conversion feature is equity, and as such, its value should be separated from the bond and included in stockholders' equity as additional paid-in capital. Proponents of this view argue that the conversion feature has value that is a function of the price of the stock, not the bond. Investors are willing to pay for the option to convert. Moreover, due to the flexibility to convert or hold the bond, they may also accept a lower interest rate on the debt than would otherwise be obtainable. Therefore, the valuation of the equity component would be the difference between the price at which the bonds might have been sold and the price at which they were sold. This position was initially embraced by the APB in *Opinion No. 10,*[20] but shortly after, due to widespread opposition by corporate management, it was superseded by *APB Opinion No. 12.*[21]

A third view is that convertible debt should be classified according to its governing characteristic.[22] The governing characteristic is based on whether

---

[19] It should be noted that *APB Opinion No. 14* was issued prior to the availability of the Black-Scholes options pricing model (discussed in Chapter 14). Use of the Black-Scholes model allows for separating the debt and equity portions of convertible bonds.

[20] *Accounting Principles Board Opinion No. 10,* "Omnibus Opinion—1966" (New York: AICPA, 1966).

[21] *Accounting Principles Board Opinion No. 12,* "Omnibus Opinion—1967" (New York: AICPA, 1967).

[22] Financial Accounting Standards Board, Discussion Memorandum, "Distinguishing between Liability and Equity Instruments and Accounting for Instruments with Characteristics of Both" (Stamford, CT: 1990), par. 287.

the instrument satisfies the definition of a liability or equity at the date of issuance. The FASB has described four alternative approaches by which the governing characteristic might be determined. The first three would classify convertible debt as a liability. The approaches are:

1. Classify based on the contractual terms in effect at issuance. Without conversion, interest and maturity payments must be made; therefore convertible debt should be classified as a liability.

2. Classify as a liability if the instrument embodies an obligation to transfer financial instruments to the holder if the option were exercised.

3. Classify in accordance with the fundamental financial instrument having the highest value.

4. Classify based on the most probable outcome. A convertible bond would be classified as an equity security if conversion were deemed to be the more probable outcome.[23]

A fifth view is based on alternative 2 above. This view considers the bond and the option to be two distinct liabilities that warrant separate disclosure.[24] Because the option obligates the corporation to transfer stock to the bondholder upon conversion, the option itself may be considered a liability. The corporation may satisfy the obligation at any time before exercise by buying the bonds in the open market or by exercising a call. At exercise, because the corporation could have sold the stock at market value, the securities exchanged represent compensation. That is, common stock is used in lieu of cash. An exercise would typically occur when the market price of the stock is high enough to motivate conversion. Thus, at exercise the corporation would receive less than it would have received had the stock transaction occurred at market price. Consequently, the decision to allow the bonds to be exercised causes the corporation to suffer a loss. Since equity transactions are between the corporation and stockholders acting as owners, such a loss is inconsistent with the definition of equity. Finally, if the options are never exercised, the initial value received for the conversion feature cannot be equity because the bondholders never acted in an ownership capacity.

Long-Term Notes Payable

Long-term notes payable are similar to debenture bonds in that they represent future obligations to repay debt. The promise to pay is generally accompanied by a provision for interest on the borrowed funds. The amount of interest charged will depend on such factors as the credit standing of the borrower, the amount of current debt, and usual business customs.

During the early 1970s, the Accounting Principles Board studied the notes receivable and payable phenomenon. This study disclosed a rather unusual occurrence in that some note transactions were being conducted

---

[23] Ibid., par. 289, 290.

[24] Clark, op. cit.

without an accompanying interest charge. These transactions were apparently being carried out for such purposes as maintaining favorable customer relations, maintaining current suppliers, or ensuring future services. After this study, the APB issued *Opinion No. 21*, "Interest on Receivables and Payables,"[25] which provided guidelines for cases in which no rate of interest was stipulated on notes or the rate stipulated was clearly inappropriate.

The provisions of *APB Opinion No. 21*, in summary form, are as follows.

1. Notes exchanged solely for cash are assumed to have a present value equal to the cash exchanged.

2. Notes exchanged for property, goods, and services are presumed to have a proper rate of interest.

3. If no interest is stated or the amount of interest is clearly inappropriate on notes exchanged for property, goods, and services, the present value of the note should be determined by (whichever is more clearly determinable):
    a. Determining the fair market value of the property, goods, and services exchanged.
    b. Determining the market value of the note at the time of the transaction.

4. If neither 3a nor 3b is determinable, the present value of the note should be determined by discounting all future payments to the present at an imputed rate of interest. This imputed rate should approximate the rate of similar independent borrowers and lenders in arm's-length transactions.[26]

When the face value of the note differs from its present value, the difference is shown as a premium or discount on the face value of the note and is amortized over the life of the note by the *effective interest method* in such a manner as to reflect a constant rate of interest. This amortization will be deducted from the premium or discount each year, as discussed earlier for bond discount and premiums, in such a manner that at the time of repayment the face value and carrying value are equal.

Although *APB Opinion No. 21* was designed to require the recording of interest on most notes receivable and payable, it specifically *exempted* the following types of transactions.

1. Normal trade transactions not exceeding a year.

2. Amounts that will be applied to the purchase of property, goods, and services.

3. Security deposits.

4. Customary activities of financial institutions.

---

[25] *Accounting Principles Board Opinion No. 21*, "Interest on Receivables and Payables" (New York: AICPA, 1971).

[26] Ibid., pars. 11–13.

5. Transactions where the rate is affected by the regulations of government agencies.

6. Transactions between parent and subsidiaries and between subsidiaries of a common parent.

Short-Term Debt Expected to Be Refinanced

Some corporations have attempted to improve their liquidity position by excluding that portion of short-term debt from current liabilities that was expected to be refinanced on a long-term basis. This treatment resulted in disclosure variations between companies and led to the issuance of *SFAS No. 6*, "Classification of Short Term Obligations Expected to Be Refinanced." In this release, the FASB took the position that short-term obligations cannot be disclosed as long-term liabilities unless the following conditions exist: (1) there is an intention to refinance current liabilities on a long-term basis and (2) the corporation demonstrates the ability to refinance such liabilities. The intent of the company to refinance current obligations means that working capital will not be reduced by satisfaction of the obligation. The ability to refinance means that the company has an agreement to refinance the obligations on a long-term basis with a qualified creditor.

A company may refinance short-term debt on a long-term basis by replacing a current liability with long-term debt or ownership securities. In addition, refinancing may be demonstrated if the current liability is extended, renewed, or replaced by other short-term debt.

A short-term obligation that is excluded from the current liability section of the balance sheet requires disclosure in the financial statement footnotes. This disclosure must include a general description of the financing agreement and the terms of any new obligation incurred or expected to be incurred or equity securities issued or expected to be issued as a result of the refinancing.

Deferred Credits

Deferred credits are not liabilities in the usual sense of the word, in that they will not normally be satisfied by the payment of funds but rather by the performance of services. They result from the double-entry accounting system, which requires a credit for every debit. The most frequently encountered deferred credits are (1) income received in advance; and (2) unrealized gross profit on installment sales (usually no longer appropriate). These items represent anticipated future revenues (unearned income). But there is no assurance that all deferrals will ultimately be included in income determination.

Although unearned revenues fit the definition of liabilities found in *SFAC No. 6*, deferred gross profit on installment sales does not.[27] Unearned revenues reflect liabilities to perform future services resulting from transactions for which the company was compensated in advance. Deferred gross profits arise from prior performance of services, the compensation for which has not

---

[27] *SFAC No. 6*, op. cit., par. 233.

yet been received and the future receipt of which is in doubt. The corporation has no further obligation to the customer or client; rather, it is the customer or client who is obligated to the corporation. Because the deferred gross profit resulted from recognition of a receivable that continues to reflect unrecovered cost, the deferred gross profit is conceptually an asset valuation and should be shown as a contra to the receivable on the balance sheet.[28]

The deferral section of the balance sheet is grounded in the principle of conservatism. As discussed in Chapter 3, this principle requires that revenue recognition be postponed until there is assurance that it is earned, but expenses are to be recorded as incurred.

Contingencies

A contingency is a possible future event that will have some impact on the firm. Although *Accounting Principles Board Statement No. 4* required the disclosure of contingencies,[29] it made no effort to define or give examples of them. Among the most frequently encountered contingencies are

1. Pending lawsuits.
2. Income tax disputes.
3. Notes receivable discounted.
4. Accommodation endorsements.

The decision to record contingencies should be based on the principle of disclosure. That is, when the disclosure of an event adds to the information content of financial statements, it should be reported. Some authors have argued for basing this decision on expected value criteria. That is, if a potential obligation has a high probability of occurrence, it should be recorded as a liability, whereas potential obligations with low probabilities are reported in footnotes.

On the other hand, the reporting of some types of contingencies may result in a self-fulfilling prophecy. For example, a frequently encountered contingency problem is the question of including the possible loss from a lawsuit in the liability section of the balance sheet. The dollar value of the loss can generally be determined by applying expected value criteria, but placing the item on the balance sheet may supply the plaintiff with additional evidence of the company's guilt. Here the corporation is faced with the dilemma of conflicting responsibilities to its financial statement users to disclose all pertinent information while at the same time minimizing losses.

The FASB reviewed the nature of contingencies in *SFAS No. 5*, "Accounting for Contingencies."[30] This release defines two types of contingencies—

---

[28] Ibid., par. 234.

[29] *APB Statement No. 4*, op. cit.

[30] Financial Accounting Standards Board, *Statement of Financial Accounting Standards No. 5*, "Accounting for Contingencies" (Stamford, CT: FASB, 1975).

gain contingencies (expected future gains) and loss contingencies (expected future losses).

With respect to gain contingencies, the board held that these events should not usually be reflected currently in the financial statement because to do so might result in revenue recognition before realization. However, adequate disclosure should be made of all gain contingencies while exercising due care to avoid misleading implications as to the likelihood of realization.[31]

The criteria established for recording loss contingencies require that the likelihood of loss be determined as follows.

Probable.   The future event is likely to occur.
Reasonably possible.   The chance of occurrence is more than remote but less than likely.
Remote.   The chance of occurrence is slight.

Once the likelihood of a loss is determined, contingencies are charged against income and a liability is recorded if both of the following conditions are met.

1. Information available prior to the issuance of the financial statements indicates that it is probable that an asset had been impaired or a liability had been incurred at the date of the financial statements.

2. The amount of the loss can be reasonably estimated.[32]

If a loss is not accrued because one or both of these conditions has not been met, footnote disclosure of the contingency should be made when there is at least a reasonable possibility that a loss may have been incurred.

SFAS No. 5 is evidence of the FASB's preference for the conservatism convention. However, this statement resulted in the application of separate standards for the reporting of revenues and expenses. The provisions of *SFAS No. 5* might cause one company to record a liability without a corresponding asset being recorded by the claimant company. These procedures are not conducive to the development of a general theory of accounting and are further evidence of the need to establish a broad framework within which to establish consistent accounting principles.

An examination of the Kroll-O'Gara Company balance sheet presented in Chapter 5 revealed a line item termed contingencies and commitments. No dollar amounts accompanied this line item; however, the company included it in order to highlight the existence of contingencies to financial statement users. These contingencies relate to letters of credit, purchase commitments, employment contracts, and legal matters, and are disclosed in Footnote (12) to the company's financial statements and contained on the text's webpage.

[31] Ibid.
[32] Ibid., par. 8.

Other Liability Measurement Issues

During the past several years, some additional measurement issues relating to liabilities have arisen. Among the most important of these are the disclosure of "off-balance sheet" financing arrangements and derivatives.

Off-Balance Sheet Financing

The proportion of debt in a firm's capital structure is perceived as an indicator of the level of risk associated with investing in that company. Recently, some innovative financing arrangements have been structured by corporations in such a manner that they do not satisfy liability recognition criteria. These arrangements are termed *off-balance sheet* financing. The principal goal of these arrangements is to keep debt off the balance sheet. For example, several oil companies may form a joint venture to drill for offshore oil and may agree to make payments to support the venture over time, or a company may engage in a lease agreement that does not require it to capitalize the cost of acquiring a productive asset.[33] In such cases, neither their share of the assets nor the future liability will appear on the balance sheet. In essence, the companies have acquired the use of economic resources (assets), without recording the corresponding economic obligation (liabilities).

The FASB has an off-balance sheet financing project on its agenda. The objective of this project is to develop broad standards of financial accounting and reporting about financial instruments and related transactions. Due to the complexity of these issues, the FASB has decided to give the widest possible exposure to proposed statements prior to their release. As an interim step, the Board determined that improved disclosure of certain information is necessary. Subsequently, the FASB completed two disclosure phases, which resulted in the issuance of *SFAS No. 105*, "Disclosure of Information about Financial Instruments with Off-Balance Sheet Risk and Financial Instruments with Concentrations of Credit Risk" in 1990, and the issuance of *SFAS No. 107*, "Disclosures about Fair Value of Financial Instruments," in 1991.

SFAS No. 105 defined a financial instrument as cash, evidence of an ownership interest in an entity, or a contract that both

1. Imposes on one entity a contractual obligation to (a) deliver cash or another financial instrument to a second entity, or (b) exchange financial instruments on potentially unfavorable terms with the second entity.

2. Conveys to the second entity a contractual right to (a) receive cash or another financial instrument from the first entity, or (b) exchange other financial instruments on potentially favorable terms with the first entity.

Examples of financial instruments with off-balance sheet risk are outstanding loan commitments, outstanding commercial letters of credit, financial guarantees, recourse obligations on receivables sold, obligations to repurchase securities sold, outstanding commitments to purchase or sell financial instruments at predetermined prices, and future contracts. The risk

---

[33] This is termed an operating lease. Accounting for leases is discussed in Chapter 12.

of loss from financial instruments includes the possibility that a loss may occur due to the failure of another party to perform according to the terms of the contract *(credit risk)* and the possibility that future changes in market price may make a financial instrument less valuable *(market risk)*.

In addition, entities are required to disclose all significant concentrations of credit risk arising from all financial instruments, whether from individual counterparties or groups of counterparties. Group concentractions of credit risk exist if a number of counterparties are engaged in similar activities having similar economic characteristics that would cause their ability to meet contractual obligations to be similarly affected by changes in economic or other conditions. The following is to be disclosed for each significant concentration:

1. Information about the activity, region, or economic characteristic that identifies the concentration.
2. The amount of loss due to credit risk that the entity would incur if the parties to the concentration failed to perform the contract.
3. The entity's policy of requiring collateral to support financial instruments subject to credit risk, information about the entity's access to that collateral, and the nature and description of the collateral supporting the financial instruments.

This statement, though still applicable at the time this text was published, will be superseded by *SFAS No. 133* (discussed later in the chapter) when it becomes effective.

SFAS No. 107 requires the disclosure of fair value of financial instruments for which an estimate of fair value is practicable. The methods and assumptions used to estimate fair value also must be disclosed. The fair value of a financial instrument is defined as "the amount at which the instrument could be exchanged in a current transaction between willing parties, other than in a forced or liquidation sale."[34] A quoted market price is cited as the best evidence of fair value.

These disclosure requirements apply to financial instruments regardless of whether they are assets or liabilities or whether or not they are reported in the balance sheet. The following are exempt from the *SFAS No. 107* requirements. Many of them already have extensive disclosure requirements.

1. Deferred compensation arrangements such as pensions, postretirement benefits, and employee stock option and purchase plans.
2. Debt extinguished and the related assets removed from the balance sheet in cases of in-substance defeasance. (No longer applicable.)
3. Insurance contracts, other than financial guarantees and investment contracts.

[34] Financial Accounting Standards Board, *Statement of Financial Accounting Standards No. 107*, "Disclosures about Fair Value of Financial Instruments" (Stamford, CT: FASB, 1991), par. 5.

4. Leases.

5. Warranty obligations and rights.

6. Unconditional purchase obligations.

7. Investments accounted for under the equity method.

8. Minority interest.

9. Equity investments in consolidated subsidiaries.

10. Equity instruments classified in stockholders' equity.[35]

In addition, fair value disclosure is not required for trade receivables whose carrying amount approximates fair value.[36] *SFAS No. 133* (discussed in the next section) amends *SFAS No. 107* to include the footnote disclosure provisions relating to credit risk contained in *SFAS No. 105*.

Derivatives
A derivative is a transaction, or contract, whose value depends on the value of an underlying asset or index. (That is, its value is derived from an underlying asset or index.) In such a transaction, a party with exposure to unwanted risk can pass some or all of that risk on to a second party.[37] When derivatives are employed, the first party can (1) assume a different risk from the second party, (2) pay the second party to assume the risk, or (3) use some combination of (1) and (2).

The rise in the use of derivatives can be traced to the abandonment of currencies fixed against the value of gold, whereby most currencies have been allowed to float to exchange levels determined by market forces. In addition, most governments now allow interest rates to fluctuate more freely than they did in the past, and exposure to exchange risk has increased due to the growth of international commerce.

All derivative transactions stem from two types of transactions—forwards and options. A *forward* transaction obligates one party to buy and another to sell a specified item, such as 10,000 German marks, at a specified price on a specified future date. On the other hand, an *option* gives its holder the right, but not the obligation, to buy or sell the specific item, such as the 10,000 German marks, at a specified price on a specified date in the future. The major difference between the two types of transactions is that a forward requires performance, whereas an option will be exercised only if it is financially advantageous to do so. But in either case the future price is locked in advance.

The participants in derivative transactions can be categorized as dealers and end-users. There are only a small number of dealers (less than 200) worldwide. Dealers are generally banks, although some are independent brokers. The number of end-users is constantly increasing as business and government organizations become involved in international financial transactions.

---

[35] Ibid., par. 8.

[36] Ibid., par. 13.

[37] Risk is defined in this case as the possibility that the actual return from holding a security will deviate from the original expected return when the security was acquired.

End-users include businesses, banks, securities firms, mutual and pension funds, governmental units, and even the World Bank.

The goals of end-users vary. Some use derivatives so that the risk of financial operations can be controlled, whereas others attempt to manage foreign exchange rate fluctuation exposure. Speculators may seek profits from simultaneous price differentials in different foreign markets. Or others may attempt to hedge exposure to currency rate changes.

Five types of derivatives that transfer elements of risk can be identified: forward contracts, futures, options, asset swaps, and hybrids. Each of these types carries an associated risk; however, although the associated risk is not unique to derivatives, they are difficult to manage because derivative products are complex. Moreover, there is difficulty in measuring the actual risk associated with the various types of derivatives. These five types of derivatives are summarized in Table 10.1.

Each of these derivatives carries risk that can be identified as market, credit, operational, legal, and systems. *Market risk* is the exposure to the possibility of financial loss resulting from an unfavorable movement in interest rates, exchange rates, stock prices, or commodity prices. Estimating the market value of a derivative at any point in time is difficult because it is influenced by a variety of factors such as exchange rates, interest rates, and time until settlement. *Credit risk* is the exposure to the possibility of financial loss resulting from the other party's failure to meet its financial obligations. *Operational risk* is the exposure to the possibility of financial loss resulting from inadequate internal controls, fraud, or human error. *Legal risk* is the exposure to the possibility of financial losses resulting from an action by a court, regulatory agency, or legislative body that invalidates all or part of an existing derivative contract. *Systems risk* is the exposure to the possibility of financial losses resulting from the disruption at a firm, in a market segment, or to a settlement system, that in turn could cause difficulties at other firms, in other market systems, or in the financial system as a whole.

The FASB first addressed the question of derivatives in *SFAS No. 105* and defined these securities under the broad category of financial instruments. This category includes not only traditional assets and liabilities such as notes receivable and bonds payable, but also innovative financial instruments such as forward contracts, futures, options, and asset swaps discussed above. Disclosure of the fair value of these financial instruments (whether or not recognized) was subsequently required by *SFAS No. 107* when it was practicable to estimate fair value. Finally, in Statement No. 119, *Disclosure about Derivative Financial Instruments and Fair Values of Financial Instruments*, companies were required to disclose information about derivative financial instruments and changed the methods of disclosure of such information.

In 1998, the FASB issued *SFAS No. 133, Accounting for Derivative Instruments and Hedging Activities.*[38] This statement establishes accounting and

---

[38] Financial Accounting Standards Board, *Statement of Financial Accounting Standards No. 133*, "Accounting for Derivative Instruments and Hedging Activities" (Stamford, CT: FASB, 1998).

Modification of Terms

A restructuring agreement involving a modification of terms is accounted for on a prospective basis and results in one of the two following situations.

1. The amount of principal and interest to be repaid is greater than the current carrying value of the liability; therefore, the debtor recognizes no gain.

2. The amount of principal and interest to be repaid is less than the current carrying value of the liability; therefore, the debtor recognizes a gain.

In the event it is determined that the total amount to be repaid exceeds the carrying value of the debt on the date of the restructuring agreement, no adjustment is made to the original carrying value of the liability. However, it is necessary to determine the effective interest rate that equates the total future payments with the current carrying value. This rate is then applied to the carrying value of the obligation each year to determine the amount of interest expense. The difference between the recorded amount of interest expense and any cash payment reduces the carrying value of the liability.

If the total future cash payments are determined to be less than the carrying value of the obligation, the amount of the liability is reduced to the total amount of the cash to be repaid. The debtor then recognizes an extraordinary gain for the amount of this adjustment, and all future payments are recorded as reductions in the amount of the liability. That is, the debt is treated as though there were no interest rate.

Under *SFAS No. 15,* a creditor treated a troubled debt restructuring resulting in a modification of terms in a manner similar to the debtor. No loss was recognized when the total amount receivable from the debtor under the modified arrangement was greater than the current carrying value of the receivable. Similarly, when the total future cash flows under the modified terms were less than the current carrying value, a loss was recognized for the difference.

This practice was criticized because the creditor would recognize a loss only when the total future cash flows were less than the current carrying value of the loan. The loss recognized would result in a carrying value of the impaired loan equal to the total future cash flows. Consequently, no interest income could be recorded over the term of the new agreement. In the case where no loss is recognized, the current loan amount was presumed to be the amount borrowed, forcing the interest rate on the modified loan arrangement to be unrealistically low. These results were inconsistent with other reporting requirements for similar financial instruments. Initially, the restructured financial instruments were not recorded at fair value, nor is interest calculated using the market rate implied in the loan agreement.

As a part of its financial instruments project, the FASB addressed the issue of whether a creditor should measure an impaired loan based on the present value of the future cash flows related to the loan. The Board concluded that it would be inappropriate to continue to ignore the time value of money and issued *SFAS No. 114,* "Accounting by Creditors for Impairment of a Loan."[42]

SFAS No. 114 requires creditors to measure receivables that result from a troubled debt restructure involving a modification of terms at the present value of expected future cash flows discounted at the loan's effective interest rate.[43] A bad debt loss is recognized, and a valuation allowance is credited for the difference between the restructured measurement and the current carrying value of the loan. The effective interest rate used to discount the expected future cash flows is to be the rate on the original contractual agreement rather than the rate specified in the restructuring agreement.[44] The rationale for use of the original loan rate is that the restructure represents continuing efforts to recover the original loan.

As a practical expedient, the creditor may alternatively value the receivable based on the loan's observable market price. If the receivable is collateralized, it may be valued at the fair value of the collateral.[45]

Income over the life of the restructured loan may be recognized in one of two ways.

1. Changes in the present value of expected future cash flows that are due to the passage of time are reported as interest income, whereas those changes attributable to changes in expectations regarding future cash flows are reported as bad debt expense.

2. All changes in the present value of expected future cash flows are treated as adjustments to bad debt expense.[46]

SFAS No. 114 may be criticized because its requirements are inconsistent with the intent of the pronouncement. The resulting restructured loan measurements will not provide the fair value of the restructured loan because the interest rate used was based on prior conditions and probably does not reflect current conditions or the risk inherent in the restructured cash flows.

SFAS No. 114 does not mention the debtor. Therefore, the debtor will continue to record the restructure in accordance with *SFAS No. 15*. This results in a lack of symmetry between debtor and creditor treatment of the same financial instrument.

Satisfaction of the Debt Through an Asset or Equity Swap

When a debtor exchanges an asset or an equity interest in satisfaction of a liability, the transfer is recorded on the basis of the fair market value of the asset or equity interest transferred. Market value is determined at the time of the exchange by the fair market value of the asset or equity exchanged unless the

---

[42] Financial Accounting Standards Board, *Statement of Financial Accounting Standards No. 114,* "Accounting by Creditors for Impairment of a Loan" (Stamford, CT: FASB, 1993).

[43] Ibid., par. 13.

[44] Ibid., par. 14.

[45] Ibid., par. 13.

[46] Ibid., par. 17.

This adjustment indicates how all available information can be used to help evaluate a company's financial position.

The interest coverage (or times interest earned) ratio provides information about a company's ability to generate sufficient sustainable income to pay its interest obligation. This ratio is calculated as:

$$\frac{\text{Operating income before interest and taxes}}{\text{Interest expense}}$$

Kroll-O'Gara Company's 1997 and 1998 interest coverage ratios are calculated as:

1997

$$\frac{\$5,905,511 + 5,092,372}{\$5,092,372} = 2.16$$

1998

$$\frac{\$20,555,370 + 4,881,822}{\$4,881,823} = 5.59$$

These ratios indicate that Kroll-O'Gara Company has made a significant improvement in its ability to generate enough income to cover its debt service payments during 1998. This analysis can also be expanded to include debt repayment amounts for a company expecting to retire a portion of its long-term debt during the next annual period. An examination of Kroll-O'Gara Company's Footnote 8 indicates that much of its long-term debt is payable in installments. As a consequence, its interest coverage ratio should be interpreted in light of the additional debt retirement payments.

A criticism of the interest coverage ratio is that it does not consider the cash flow effects of net income. That is, interest payments require a cash outflow, and the ratio does not consider the cash effects of the company's income generating ability. The debt service coverage ratio attempts to overcome this criticism by using cash flow from operating activities in the numerator and is calculated as:

$$\frac{\text{Cash flow from operating activities before interest and taxes}}{\text{Interest expense}}$$

Kroll-O'Gara Company's debt service coverage ratios for 1997 and 1998 are calculated as:

1997

$$\frac{\$6,194,818 + 3,304,993 + 5,092,372^{50}}{5,092,372} = 2.87$$

1998

$$\frac{\$(12,435,025) + 7,466,464 + 4,481,882}{4,481,822} = (0.11)$$

---

[50] Approximated as cash flows from operating activities + income tax expense + interest expense. Most companies disclose actual cash income tax and interest expense.

An examination of the results of these calculations indicates that the company's ability to generate sufficient cash to service its debt deteriorated significantly during 1998. This analysis in conjunction with the previous analysis that indicated the company has installment debt repayment amounts due over the next several years highlights a potential solvency for the company.

A final method of solvency analysis involves assessing a company's financial flexibility, that is, its ability to react to changing economic conditions. This assessment is made by attempting to prepare pro-forma financial statements that are subsequently evaluated in light of a company's ability to react to various scenarios such as economic downturns or rising interest rates.

International Accounting Standards

The IASC addressed the following issues relating to long-term liabilities:

1. Debt and equity classification in *IAS No. 32*, "Financial Instruments: Disclosure and Presentation."

2. Contingencies in *IAS No. 37*, "Provisions, Contingent Liabilities and Contingent Assets."

3. Financial Instruments in *IAS No. 39*, "Financial Instruments Recognition and Measurement."

In *IAS No. 32*, financial liabilities are defined as contractual obligations to deliver cash or another financial asset to another enterprise, or to exchange financial instruments with another enterprise under conditions that are potentially unfavorable. Equity instruments are defined as contracts that evidence a residual interest in the assets of an enterprise after deducting all of its liabilities. The statement requires companies to disclose certain information about its financial liabilities, including how they might affect the amount, timing, and certainty of future cash flows, and the associated accounting policies and basis of measurement applied. The exposure of an enterprise's liabilities to interest rate risk (the risk that the value of a financial instrument may fluctuate due to changes in market rates of interest) must be disclosed, including repricing or maturity dates and effective interest rates. Finally, information about the fair value of an enterprise's financial liabilities must be disclosed.

The FASB staff review of the accounting requirements for financial liabilities contained in *IAS No. 32*[51] indicated that, despite the guidance for initial recognition of liabilities, some financial instruments that would be classified as liabilities under IASC standards would be classified as equity under U.S. GAAP. In addition, IASC standards currently require the issuer of a compound financial instrument containing both liability and equity components to separably measure these components. Current U.S. GAAP does not now require a similar treatment, but the issue is under study by the FASB.

---

[51] Financial Accounting Standards Board, *The IASC-U.S. Comparison Project: A Report on the Similarities and Differences between IASC Standards and U.S. GAAP.* Carrie Bloomer, ed., 2nd ed. (Norwalk, CT: Financial Accounting Standards Board, 1999), pp. 463–495.

IAS No. 37 indicated that provisions should be recognized in the balance sheet when an enterprise has a present obligation (legal or constructive) as a result of a past event. It is probable (i.e., more likely than not) that an outflow of resources embodying economic benefits will be required to settle the obligation, and a reliable estimate can be made of the amount of the obligation. Provisions should be measured on the balance sheet at the best estimate of the expenditure required to settle the present obligation at the balance sheet date—in other words, the amount that an enterprise would rationally pay to settle the obligation or to transfer it to a third party at that date. The amount of a provision should not be reduced by gains from the expected disposal of assets (even if the expected disposal is closely linked to the event giving rise to the provision) or by expected reimbursements (for example, through insurance contracts, indemnity clauses, or suppliers' warranties). When it is virtually certain that reimbursement will be received if the enterprise settles the obligation, the reimbursement should be recognized as a separate asset. A provision should be used only for expenditures for which the provision was originally recognized and should be reversed if an outflow of resources is no longer probable. The FASB staff review of the accounting requirements for financial liabilities contained in *IAS No. 32*[52] indicated that comparison among companies using U.S. GAAP has been difficult because of various interpretations of the applicability of the term *probable* and that such comparisons are likely to be more difficult with companies using IAS standards. That is, *IAS No. 37* uses the term *probable* to describe a situation that is more likely than not to occur, whereas *SFAS No. 5* uses it to define an outcome that is likely to occur. In addition, the likelihood of occupance criteria has a different threshold for recognition in that the term *probable* under U.S. GAAP is generally understood to be an approximate 80 percent chance of occupance, whereas the more likely than not criteria in *IAS No. 37* are understood to mean a greater than 50 percent chance of occupance.

Under *IAS No. 39*, financial liabilities are recognized on the balance sheet, including all derivatives. They are initially measured at cost, which is the fair value of whatever was paid or received to acquire the financial asset or liability. After acquisition, most financial liabilities are measured at original recorded amount less principal repayments and amortization. Only derivatives and liabilities held for trading (such as securities borrowed by a short seller) are remeasured to fair value. For those financial liabilities that are remeasured to fair value, an enterprise will have a single, enterprisewide option to

a. Recognize the entire adjustment in net profit or loss for the period; or

b. Recognize in net profit or loss for the period only those changes in fair value relating to financial liabilities held for trading. For this purpose, derivatives are always deemed held for trading unless they are designated as hedging instruments.

For accounting purposes, hedging means designating a derivative or (only for hedges of foreign currency risks) a nonderivative financial instru-

---

[52] Ibid., pp. 431–450.

ment as an offset in net profit or loss, in whole or in part, to the change in fair value or cash flows of a hedged item. Under certain circumstances, hedge accounting is permitted under *IAS No. 39*, provided that the hedging relationship is clearly defined, measurable, and actually effective. Hedge accounting is permitted only if an enterprise designates a specific hedging instrument as a hedge of a change in value or cash flow of a specific hedged item rather than as a hedge of an overall net balance sheet position. However, in some cases the approximate income statement effect of hedge accounting for an overall net position can be achieved by designating part of one of the underlying items as the hedged position. The FASB staff's review of this standard was very limited because neither it nor *SFAS No. 133* was effective at the time of its review.[53]

Summary

A review of the recording and reporting criteria for the components of long-term debt indicates that balance sheets items are classified as either debt or equity according to the basic concept of accounting being employed. Debt can be viewed as a separate component of the balance sheet or as part of the overall equity invested in the enterprise. The separate classification of items as debt is the generally accepted method, and a number of criteria may be used as a frame of reference in classifying specific items as debt or equity.

There are various components of long-term debt: bonds, convertible debt, long-term notes payable, deferred credits, contingencies, derivatives and so forth. The review of the accounting treatment for each of these items focused on troublesome areas and the accepted accounting treatment where definitive answers are available.

In the readings contained on the text's webpage for Chapter 10, some additional issues impacting on accounting for long-term liabilities are examined.

Cases

• Case 10-1 Reporting Bond Liabilities

On January 1, 2001, Plywood Homes, Inc., issued 20-year, 4 percent bonds having a face value of $1 million. The interest on the bonds is payable semiannually on June 30 and December 31. The proceeds to the company were $975,000 (i.e., on the day they were issued the bonds had a market value of $975,000). On June 30, 2001, the company's fiscal closing date, when the bonds were being traded at $98^1/_2$, each of the following amounts was suggested as a possible valuation basis for reporting the bond liability on the balance sheet.

1. $975,625 (proceeds, plus six months' straight-line amortization)

2. $1 million (face value)

---

[53] Ibid., pp. 463–495.

3. $1,780,000 (face value plus interest payments)
4. $985,000 (fair value)

Required:
a. Distinguish between nominal and effective interest rates.
b. Explain the nature of the $25,000 difference between the face value and market value of the bonds on January 1, 2001.
c. Between January 1 and June 30, the market value of the company's bonds increased from $975,000 to $985,000. Explain. Discuss the significance of the increase to the company.
d. Evaluate each of the four suggested alternatives for reporting the bond liability on the balance sheet, giving arguments for and against each alternative. Your answer should take the investor and the reporting company into consideration.

• Case 10-2 Debt Restructuring

Whiley Company issued a $100,000, five-year, 10 percent note to Security Co. on January 2, 2000. Interest was to be paid annually each December 31. The stated rate of interest reflected the market rate of interest on similar notes.

Whiley made the first interest payment on December 31, 2000, but due to financial difficulties was unable to pay any interest on December 31, 2001. Security agreed to the following terms:

1. The $100,000 principal would be payable in five equal installments, beginning December 31, 2002.
2. The accrued interest at December 31, 2001, would be forgiven.
3. Whiley Company would be required to make no other payments.

Because of the risk associated with the note, it has no determinable fair value. The note is secured by equipment having a fair value of $80,000 at December 31, 2001. The present value of the five equal installments discounted at 10 percent is $75,815.

Required:
a. Under current GAAP, at which amount would Whiley report the restructured liability at December 31, 2001? Explain. How much gain would Whiley recognize in its income statement for 2001? Explain. How much interest expense would Whiley recognize in 2002? Explain.
b. Under current GAAP, what alternatives does Security have for reporting the restructured receivable? Explain. How would each alternative affect the 2001 income statement and future interest revenue? Explain.
c. Discuss the pros and cons of the alternatives in (b) and compare them to the prior GAAP treatment (treatment that was reciprocal to the debtor).
d. If the provisions of *SFAS No. 114* were to be extended to debtors, what would be the incremental effect (difference between what would be reported under *SFAS No. 114* and current GAAP for debtors) on Whiley's financial statements, debt-to-equity ratio, and EPS for 2001 and 2002? Explain.

- ## Case 10-3 Alternative Financing Decision

Baker Company needs $1 million to expand its existing plant. Baker management is considering the following two alternative forms of financing.

1. At the beginning of 2001, issue $1 million of convertible, 10-year, 10 percent bonds. Each $1,000 bond can be converted into 20 shares of Baker $10.00 par value common stock. The conversion may take place any time after three years.

2. At the beginning of 2001, issue 10,000 shares of $100 par value, $10, redeemable preferred stock. The preferred is redeemable at $102, 10 years from the date of issue.

Baker's management is concerned about the effects of the two alternatives on cash flows, their financial statements, and future financing for other planned expansion activities. Also, there are existing debt covenants that restrict the debt-to-equity ratio to 2:1; $1 million in new debt would cause the debt-to-equity ratio to be close to 2:1. Baker believes that either the bonds or the preferred stock could be sold at par value. Their income tax rate is 34 percent.

The Baker Company common stock is currently selling for $45.00 per share.

Required:
a. Discuss the theoretical and currently generally accepted accounting treatments for convertible bonds.
b. Discuss the SEC and currently generally accepted accounting treatments for redeemable preferred stock.
c. Compare the effects of the two financing alternatives on Baker Company's balance sheet, income statement, and cash flows under current GAAP. Your comparison should consider 2001 and future years, the potential conversion of the bonds, and the debt covenant restrictions.
d. If the FASB were to decide to recognize the value for conversion (conversion feature) as equity, would this have an impact on Baker Company's decision, and how would Baker Company's financial statements be affected if it chose the convertible bond alternative? Would the decision to select convertible bonds versus redeemable preferred stock be affected, especially in light of the concern regarding the debt covenant restrictions?

- ## Case 10-4 Effective Interest Amortization of Premiums and Discounts

The appropriate method of amortizing a premium or discount on issuance of bonds is the effective interest method.

Required:
a. What is the effective interest method of amortization, and how is it different from or similar to the straight-line method of amortization?
b. How are interest and the amount of discount or premium amortization computed using the effective interest method, and why and how do

amounts obtained using the effective interest method differ from amounts computed under the straight-line method?

c. Generally, the effective interest method is defended on the grounds that it provides the appropriate amount of interest expense. Does it also provide an appropriate balance sheet amount for the liability balance? Why, or why not?

• Case 10-5 Early Extinguishment of Debt

Gains or losses from the early extinguishment of debt that is refunded can theoretically be accounted for in three ways.

1. Amortized over the life of old debt.
2. Amortized over the life of the new debt issue.
3. Recognized in the period of extinguishment.

Required:

a. Discuss the supporting arguments for each of the three theoretical methods of accounting for gains and losses from the early extinguishment of debt.
b. Which of the three methods would provide a balance sheet measure that reflects the present value of the future cash flows discounted at the interest rate that is commensurate with the risk associated with the new debt issue? Why?
c. Which of the three methods is generally accepted, and how should the appropriate amount of gain or loss be shown in a company's financial statements?

• Case 10-6 Contingencies

Angela Company is a manufacturer of toys. During the year, the following situations arose.

- A safety hazard related to one of its toy products was discovered. It is considered probable that liabilities have been incurred. Based on past experience, a reasonable estimate of the amount of loss can be made.

- One of its small warehouses is located on the bank of a river and can no longer be insured against flood losses. No flood losses occurred after the date the insurance became unavailable.

- This year, Angela began promoting a new toy by including a coupon, redeemable for a movie ticket, in each toy's carton. The movie ticket, which cost Angela $2, is purchased in advance and then mailed to the customer when Angela receives the coupon. Based on past experience, Angela estimated that 60 percent of the coupons would be redeemed. Forty percent of the coupons would be actually redeemed this year, and the remaining 20 percent of the coupons were expected to be redeemed next year.

Required:

a. How should Angela report the safety hazard? Why? Do not discuss deferred tax implications.

b. How should Angela report the uninsured flood risk? Why?

c. How should Angela account for the toy promotion campaign in this year?

• Case 10-7 Accounting for Notes Payable

Business transactions often involve the exchange of property, goods, or services for notes on similar instruments that may stipulate no interest rate or an interest rate that varies from prevailing rates.

Required:

a. When a note is exchanged for property, goods, or services, what value should be placed on the note
   i. if it bears interest at a reasonable rate and is issued in a bargained transaction entered into at arm's length? Explain.
   ii. if it bears no interest and/or is not issued in a bargained transaction entered into at arm's length? Explain.

b. if the recorded value of a note differs from the face value,
   i. How should the difference be accounted for? Explain.
   ii. How should this difference be presented in the financial statements? Explain.

• Case 10-8 Accounting for Bonds Payable

On April 1, 2001, Janine Corporation sold some of its five-year, $1,000 face value 12 percent term bonds dated March 1, 2001, at an effective annual interest rate (yield) of 10 percent. Interest is payable semiannually, and the first interest payment date is September 1, 2001. Janine uses the interest method of amortization. Bond issue costs were incurred in preparing and selling the bond issue.

On November 1, 2001, Janine sold directly to underwriters, at lump-sum price, $1,000 face value, 9 percent serial bonds dated November 1, 2001, at an effective interest rate (yield) of 11 percent. A total of 25 percent of these serial bonds are due on November 1, 2002; a total of 30 percent on November 1, 2003; and the rest on November 1, 2004. Interest is payable semiannually, and the first interest payment date is May 1, 2002. Janine uses the interest method of amortization. Bond issue costs were incurred in preparing and selling the bond issue.

Required:

a. How would the market price of the term bonds and the serial bonds be determined?

b. i. How would all items related to the term bonds, except for bond issue costs, be presented in a balance sheet prepared immediately after the term bond issue was sold?
   ii. How would all items related to the serial bonds, except for bond issue costs, be presented in a balance sheet prepared immediately after the serial bond issue was sold?

c. What alternative methods could be used to account for the bond issue costs for the term bonds in 2001? Which method(s) is (are) considered current GAAP? Which method(s), if any, would affect the calculation of interest expense? Why?

d. How would the amount of interest expense for the term bonds and the serial bonds be determined for 2001?

• Case 10-9 Accounting Concepts and Contingencies

The two basic requirements for the accrual of a loss contingency are supported by several basic concepts of accounting. Four of these concepts are periodicity (time periods), measurement, objectivity, and relevance.

Required:
Discuss how the two basic requirements for accrual of a loss contingency relate to the four concepts listed above.

• Case 10-10 Reporting Contingencies

The following three independent sets of facts relate to (1) the possible accrual or (2) the possible disclosure by other means of a loss contingency.

Situation 1
A company offers a one-way warranty for the product that it manufactures. A history of warranty claims has been compiled, and the probable amount of claims related to sales for a given period can be determined.

Situation 2
Subsequent to the date of a set of financial statements, but prior to the issuance of the financial statements, a company enters into a contract that will probably result in a significant loss to the company. The amount of the loss can be reasonably estimated.

Situation 3
A company has adopted a policy of recording self-insurance for any possible losses resulting from injury to others by the company's vehicles. The premium for an insurance policy for the same risk from an independent insurance company would have an annual cost of $2,000. During the period covered by the financial statements, there were no accidents involving the company's vehicles that resulted in injury to others.

Required:
Discuss the accrual of a loss contingency and/or type of disclosure necessary (if any) and the reason(s) why such a disclosure is appropriate for each of the three independent sets of facts above. Complete your response to each situation before proceeding to the next situation.

• Case 10-11 Debtor and Creditor Accounting for Troubled Debt Restructings

Debtors currently report the consequences of troubled debt restructures under *SFAS No. 15*. Creditors are required to report the same consequences under *SFAS No. 114*.

Required:
a. Describe the accounting treatment for debtors when there is a modification of terms under a troubled debt restructure.
b. Describe the accounting treatment for creditors when there is a modification of terms under a troubled debt restructure.
c. Are the measurements reported in financial statements by debtors and creditors for troubled debt restructures when there is a modification of terms symmetrical? Explain. If so, in your opinion, are the two different treatments justifiable? In your opinion, does either approach, or both, report the economic substance of the transaction? Explain.
d. If both parties to the same transaction, in this case a troubled debt restructure, report the transaction differently, in your opinion, which representation is more representationally faithful? Explain.

• Case 10-12 Accounting for Debt

Under *SFAS No. 115,* investors are required to report investments in debt securities that are not to be held-to-maturity at fair value rather than at amortized cost. Debtors are not covered by the provisions of *SFAS No. 115.* Debtors report their obligations for the same securities as liabilities, measured at amortized cost.

At 12/31/x1, IOU Corp. reported a $100,000, 8 percent bond payable due in 16 years as a long-term liability net of unamortized premium of $1,450. Interest rates have risen since the bond was issued, and the current market price for the bond is $98,000.

Required:
a. Under *SFAS No. 115,* the investor reported the IOU bond at $98,000. Because the bond was classified as available-for-sale, the holding loss was reported as a component of comprehensive income. Explain the rationale for this reporting procedure.
b. In your opinion, why, under GAAP, would IOU report the same debt instrument in a different way? Are the circumstances for the debtor different from those for the creditor? Can one party to the instrument have a loss and the other not have a gain? Explain. (In your answer, assume that IOU does not plan to pay the debt off until maturity.)
c. Would your answer to (b) be different if IOU planned to pay off the debt in the near future? Explain.
d. Ignoring transaction costs, such as bond issue costs, if IOU can pay off the debt at $98,000 but chooses not to, is there an economic gain or loss to the company? What should IOU take into consideration in making a decision to pay the debt?

e. Assume that IOU has the opportunity to refund the bonds by issuing similar debt having a fair value of $98,000. What would be the effects of the refunding on the IOU financial statements? Since no cash changed hands, is the economic substance of the refunding transaction really different from simply leaving the same debt outstanding? If not, do you believe that IOU should report the existing debt at $98,000 or should it leave it at amortized cost? Explain.

Room for Debate

• Issue 1

In a recent discussion memorandum, "Distinguishing between Liability and Equity Instruments and Accounting for Instruments with Characteristics of Both," the FASB addressed the issue of whether redeemable preferred stock is debt or equity.

Team Debate:

Team 1. Present arguments in favor of presenting redeemable preferred stock as debt. Your arguments should take into consideration definitions of the elements of financial statements in *SFAS No. 6* and any other relevant aspects of the conceptual framework, as well as implications regarding the usefulness of financial statement information to investors.

Team 2. Present arguments in favor of presenting redeemable preferred stock as equity. Your arguments should take into consideration definitions of the elements of financial statements in *SFAS No. 6* and any other relevant aspects of the conceptual framework, as well as implications regarding the usefulness of financial statement information to investors.

Recommended Additional Readings

Arutt, Diane, Kenneth Bosin, Susan Fresbour, J. Robert Hitchings, John McEnerny, and Jaruloch Whitehead. "Implementation of SFAS No. 114, Accounting by Creditors for Impairment of a Loan." *The CPA Journal* (January 1995), pp. 36–41.

Beatty, Anne. "Assessing the Use of Derivatives as Part of a Risk-Management Strategy." *Journal of Accounting and Economics* (January 1999), pp. 353–358.

Bloom, Robert. "An Overview of FASB Statement 133—Accounting for Derivative Instruments and Hedging Activities." *Ohio CPA Journal* (January–March 1999), pp. 23–29.

Byington, J. Ralph, and Paul Munter. "Disclosures about Financial Instruments." *The CPA Journal* (September 1990), pp. 42–44, 46–48.

Guay, Wayne R. "The Impact of Derivatives on Firm Risk: An Empirical Examination of New Derivative Users." *Journal of Accounting and Economics* (January 1999), pp. 319–352.

Jones, Jefferson P. "The Effect of Accounting for Derivatives on Other comprehensive Income." *The CPA Journal* (March 2000), pp. 54–56.

King, Thomas E., Alan K. Ortegren, and Robin M. King. "A Reassessment of the Allocation of Convertible Debt Proceeds and the Implications for Other Hybrid Financial Instruments." *Accounting Horizons* (September 1990), pp. 10–19.

Kulkarni, Deepak. "The Valuation of Liabilities." *Accounting and Business Research* (Summer 1980), pp. 291–297.

Nair, R. D., Larry E. Rittenberg, and Jerry J. Weygandt. "Accounting for Interest Rate Swaps—A Critical Evaluation." *Accounting Horizons* (September 1990), pp. 20–30.

Pariser, David B. "Financial Reporting Implications of Troubled Debt." *The CPA Journal* (February 1989), pp. 33–39.

Rasch, Ronald H. "New Accounting for Derivatives Illustrated." *The CPA Journal* (November 1998), pp. 56–59.

Roulstone, Darren T. "Effect of SEC Financial Reporting Release No. 48 on Derivative and Market Risk Disclosures." *Accounting Horizons* (December 1999), pp. 343–363.

Stephens, Matthew J. "Inseparability and the Valuation of Convertible Bonds." *Journal of Accountancy* (August 1971), pp. 54–62.

Wald, John K. "How Firm Characteristics Affect Capital Structure." *The Journal of Financial Management* (Summer 1999), pp. 161–188.

Bibliography

Amble, Joan Lordi. "The FASB's New ED on Disclosures." *Journal of Accountancy* (November 1989), pp. 63, 64, 66–69.

Anton, Hector R. "Accounting for Bond Liabilities." *Journal of Accountancy* (September 1956), pp. 53–56.

Bevis, Herman. "Contingencies and Probabilities in Financial Statements." *Journal of Accountancy* (October 1968), pp. 37–41.

Carpenter, Charles G., and Joseph F. Wojdak. "Capitalizing Executory Contracts: A Perspective. *New York CPA* (January 1971), pp. 40–47.

Castellano, Joseph F., and Gerald E. Keyes. "An Application of APB Opinion No. 21." *The Ohio CPA Journal* (Summer 1972), pp. 86–91.

Clancy, Donald K. "What Is a Convertible Debenture? A Review of the Literature in the U.S.A." *Abacus* (December 1978), pp. 171–179.

Cloud, Douglas, Jack E. Smith, and Edwin Waters. "When Is a Liability Not a Liability?" *National Public Accountant* (December 1986), pp. 42–47.

Collier, Boyd, and Curtis Carnes. "Convertible Bonds and Financial Reality." *Management Accounting* (February 1979), pp. 47, 48, 52.

Cramer, Joe J., Jr. "The Nature and Importance of Discounted Present Value in Financial Accounting and Reporting." *The Arthur Andersen Chronicle* (September 1977), pp. 27–39.

Davis, Larry R., Linda M. Lovata, and Kirk L. Philipich. "The Effect of Debt Defeasance on the Decisions of Loan Officers." *Accounting Horizons* (June 1991), pp. 64–70.

Dudley, L. W., and F. P. Schadler. "Reporting the Relative Equity Portion of Convertible Debt Issues," *Journal of Accounting, Auditing and Finance"* (Summer 1994), pp. 561–578.

Falk, Haim, and Stephen L. Buzby. "What's Missing in Accounting for Convertible Bonds?" *CA Magazine* (July 1978), pp. 40–45.

Ford, Allen. "Should Cost Be Assigned to Conversion Value?" *The Accounting Review* (October 1969), pp. 818–822.

Gamble, George O., and Joe J. Cramer, Jr. "The Role of Present Value in the Measurement and Recording of Nonmonetary Financial Assets and Liabilities: An Examination." *Accounting Horizons* (December 1992), pp. 32–41.

Henderson, M. S. "Nature of Liabilities." *Australian Accountant* (July 1974), pp. 328–330, 333–334.

Hughes, John S. "Toward a Contract Basis of Valuation in Accounting." *The Accounting Review* (October 1978), pp. 882–894.

Imdieke, Leroy F., and Jerry J. Weygandt. "Accounting for That Imputed Discount Factor." *Journal of Accountancy* (June 1970), pp. 54–58.

Jacobsen, Lyle E. "Liabilities and Quasi Liabilities." In Morton Backer (ed.), *Modern Accounting Theory,* Englewood Cliffs, NJ: Prentice-Hall, 1966, pp. 232–249.

King, Raymond D. "The Effect of Convertible Bond Equity Values on Dilution and Leverage." *The Accounting Review* (July 1984), pp. 419–431.

Linsmeier, Thomas J., and Neil D. Pearson. 1997. "Quantitative Disclosures of Market Risk in the SEC Release." *Accounting Horizons* (March), pp. 110–111.

Ma, Ronald, and Malcolm C. Miller. "Conceptualizing the Liability." *Accounting and Business Research* (Autumn 1978), pp. 258–265.

McCullers, Levis D. "An Alternative to APB Opinion No. 14." *Journal of Accounting Research* (Spring 1971), pp. 160–164.

Melcher, Beatrice. *Stockholders' Equity.* New York: American Institute of Certified Public Accountants, 1973.

Meyers, Stephen L. "Accounting for Long Term Notes." *Management Accounting* (July 1973), pp. 49–51.

Mielke, David E., and James Seifert. "A Survey on the Effects of Defeasing Debt." *Journal of Accounting, Auditing and Finance* (1987), pp. 65–78.

Miller, Jerry D. "Accounting for Warrants and Convertible Bonds." *Management Accounting* (January 1973), pp. 26–28.

Moonitz, Maurice. "The Changing Concept of Liabilities." *Journal of Accountancy* (May 1960), pp. 41–46.

Munter, Paul. "The Financial Instruments Project Marches On." *The CPA Journal* (July 1992), pp. 30–32, 34–36.

Pacter, Paul. "A Synopsis of APB Opinion No. 21: An Explanation of the Provisions of the APB Opinion on Interest on Receivables and Payables." *Journal of Accountancy* (March 1972), pp. 57–67.

Roden, Peyton F. "The Financial Implications of In-Substance Defeasance." *Journal of Accounting Auditing and Finance* (1987), pp. 79–89.

Rogers, Richard L., and Krishnagopal Menon. "Accounting for Deferred-Payment Notes." *The Accounting Review* (July 1985), pp. 547–557.

Savage, Charles L. "Review of APB Opinion No. 28—Early Extinguishment of Debt." *The CPA Journal* (April 1973), pp. 283–285.

Shoenthal, Edward R. "Contingent Legal Liabilities." *The CPA Journal* (March 1976), pp. 30–34.

Sprouse, Robert, T. "Accounting for What-You-May-Call-Its." *Journal of Accountancy* (October 1966), pp. 45–53.

Swieringa, Robert J., and Dale Morse. "Accounting for Hybrid Convertible Debentures." *The Accounting Review* (January 1985), pp. 127–133.

Waxman, Robert N. "Review of APB Opinion No. 21—Interest on Receivables and Payables." *The CPA Journal* (August 1972), pp. 627–633.

Weil, Roman L. "Role of Time Value of Money in Financial Reporting." *Accounting Horizons* (December 1990), pp. 47–67.

CHAPTER 11

Accounting for

Income Taxes

Most accountants agree that corporate income tax is an expense. Treating income tax as an expense is required under current generally accepted accounting principles (GAAP). This treatment is consistent with proprietary theory because the earnings that accrue to owners are reduced by corporate obligations to the government. Also, because the income tax does not result from transactions with owners, expensing corporate income tax is consistent with the *SFAC No. 6* definition of comprehensive income. Thus, on the surface accounting for income taxes would appear to be a nonissue.

Yet accounting for income taxes has been a most controversial financial accounting topic for many years. The controversy centers around a number of reporting and measurement issues. This chapter traces the historical development of GAAP for income taxes. We will examine the theoretical accounting issues as well as the reporting requirements of *APB Opinion No. 11, SFAS No. 96*, and the current authoritative pronouncement, *SFAS No. 109*.

Historical Perspective

Accounting for income taxes became a significant issue in the 1940s when the Internal Revenue Code (IRC) permitted companies to depreciate the cost of emergency facilities considered essential to the war effort over a period of 60 months.[1] For a five-year period, businesses were able to reduce taxable income below what it would have been under the accounting method of depreciation. The total depreciation charge over the life of the asset was the same for finan-

[1] Frank R. Rayburn, "A Chronological Review of the Authoritative Literature on Interperiod Tax Allocation: 1940–1985," *The Accounting Historians Journal* (Fall 1986), p. 91.

cial accounting income and for taxable income, but the allocation of cost to financial accounting income in each accounting period differed significantly from the allocation to taxable income. Prior to this Internal Revenue Service regulation, accounting practitioners expensed income tax as it was incurred per the corporate tax return. Some accountants argued that when accelerated tax depreciation is allowed, expensing the amount of the tax liability incurred in each period results in material distortions of periodic earnings. For example, when pretax financial accounting income is the same in each accounting period, tax expense fluctuates and reported earnings is not normalized.

The Committee on Accounting Procedure responded in 1944 by issuing *ARB No. 23*, "Accounting for Income Taxes."[2] *ARB No. 23* subsequently became Chapter 10, Section B of the AICPA's consolidated set of accounting procedures, *ARB No. 43*.[3] This release stated,

> *Income taxes are an expense that should be allocated, when necessary and practicable, to income and other accounts, as other expenses are allocated. What the income statement should reflect ... is the expense properly allocable to the income included in the income statement for the year.[4]*

It follows that items reported in the income statement have tax consequences. These tax consequences are expenses and should be treated in a manner similar to other expenses reported in the income statement. Accrual accounting requires the recognition of revenues and expenses in the period incurred, without regard to the timing of cash receipts and payments. Consequently, the tax effects of business transactions should be recorded in a similar manner. That is, income tax should be allocated to periods so that the items reported on the income statement are matched with their respective tax consequences. The allocation of income taxes to accounting periods is termed *interperiod tax allocation*.

ARB No. 23 did not apply to those cases where "differences between the tax return and the income statement will recur regularly over a comparatively long period of time."[5] A debate ensued as to whether the tax consequences of all items resulting in tax treatment that differs from accounting treatment should be allocated. In addition, *ARB No. 23* did not provide clear guidance on how to measure specific tax consequences. The nature of income taxes was subsequently studied by the Accounting Principles Board, which issued *APB Opinion No. 11*, "Accounting for Income Taxes."[6] *APB Opin-*

---

[2] American Institute of Accountants, Committee on Accounting Procedure, "Accounting for Income Taxes," *Accounting Research Bulletin No. 23* (New York: AIA, 1944).

[3] American Institute of Accountants, Committee on Accounting Procedure, "Restatement and Revision of Accounting Research Bulletins," *Accounting Research Bulletin No. 43* (New York: AIA, 1953).

[4] Ibid., Section B, par. 4.

[5] Ibid., Section B, par. 1.

[6] Accounting Principles Board, *Opinion No. 11*, "Accounting for Income Taxes" (New York: AICPA, 1967).

ion No. 11 extended interperiod tax allocation to all items, resulting in differences in the timing of revenue and expense recognition in the income statement and the tax return. The measurement and reporting procedures required under *APB Opinion No. 11* were consistent with the income statement approach outlined in *ARB No. 43*. Nevertheless, this *Opinion* was widely criticized. Opponents argued that the resulting balance sheet amounts did not reflect the future tax consequences of economic events and transactions. In response, the FASB issued *SFAS No. 96*, "Accounting for Income Taxes,"[7] which proscribed a balance sheet approach to allocating income taxes among accounting periods. But *SFAS No. 96* did not silence the critics of accounting for income taxes, and some of the provisions of *SFAS No. 96* were so controversial that the FASB was compelled to delay the effective date of the pronouncement twice. Subsequently, *SFAS No. 96* was superseded by *SFAS No. 109*, "Accounting for Income Taxes."[8]

The Income Tax Allocation Issue

According to *Statement of Financial Accounting Concepts (SFAC) No. 1*, the objective of financial reporting is to provide information that is useful in predicting the amounts and timing of future cash flows.[9] GAAP guide the reporting and measurement of economic events and transactions to meet this goal.

Most economic events and transactions have tax cash flow consequences. These consequences are reported on tax returns in accordance with the IRC. The IRC is enacted by Congress, and its goal is to provide revenue, in an equitable manner, to operate the federal government. On occasion, the IRC may also be used to regulate the economy. The same economic events that give rise to taxable income are also reported in published financial statements by following GAAP. In general, revenue becomes taxable when taxpayers receive cash or expenses are deductible when cash is paid (the ability to pay criterion). Consequently, income tax accounting is more closely associated with cash basis accounting than is financial accounting. Because the IRC is based on an ability to pay criterion, the IRC's reporting requirements differ from the reporting requirements for financial accounting as defined by GAAP. As a result, the taxes paid in a given year may not reflect the tax consequences of events and transactions that are reported in the income statement for that same year.

When the IRC requires that revenues and expenses be recognized in different accounting periods from GAAP, taxable income is temporarily different from pretax financial accounting income. This temporary difference is

---

[7] Financial Accounting Standards Board, *Statement of Financial Accounting Standards No. 96*, "Accounting for Income Taxes" (Stamford, CT: FASB, 1987).

[8] Financial Accounting Standards Board, *Statement of Financial Accounting Standards No. 109*, "Accounting for Income Taxes" (Stamford, CT: FASB, 1992).

[9] Financial Accounting Standards Board, *Statement of Financial Accounting Concepts No. 1*, "Objectives of Financial Reporting by Business Enterprises" (Stamford, CT: FASB, 1978), par. 37.

termed an *originating difference*. In a subsequent period the event that caused the originating difference will reverse itself. The reversal is termed a *reversing difference*. Originating and reversing temporary differences cause an accounting problem that is termed the *Income tax allocation issue*.

The objectives of accounting for income taxes are to recognize the amount of taxes payable or refundable for the current year and to recognize the future tax consequences of temporary differences as well as net operating losses (NOLs) and unused tax credits.[10] To facilitate discussion of the issues raised by the concept of interperiod tax allocation, we first examine the nature of differences among pretax financial income, taxable income, and NOLs.

Permanent and Temporary Differences

Differences between pretax financial accounting income and taxable income are either permanent or temporary. Temporary differences between pretax financial accounting income and taxable income affect two or more accounting periods and thus are the focus of the income tax allocation issue. Permanent differences do not have income tax allocation consequences.

Permanent Differences

Most *permanent differences* between pretax financial accounting income and taxable income occur when specific provisions of the IRC exempt certain types of revenue from taxation or prohibit the deduction of certain types of expenses. Others occur when the IRC allows tax deductions that are not expenses under GAAP. Permanent differences arise because of federal economic policy or because Congress may wish to alleviate a provision of the IRC that falls too heavily on one segment of the economy. There are three types of permanent differences:

1. ***Revenue recognized for financial accounting reporting purposes that is never taxable.*** Examples include interest on municipal bonds and life insurance proceeds payable to a corporation for an insured employee.

2. ***Expenses recognized for financial accounting reporting purposes that are never deductible for income tax purposes.*** An example is life insurance premiums on employees.

3. ***Income tax deductions that do not qualify as expenses under GAAP.*** Examples include percentage depletion in excess of cost depletion and the special dividend exclusion.[11]

Permanent differences affect pretax financial accounting income or taxable income but not both. A corporation that has nontaxable revenue or additional

---

[10] *SFAC No. 109*, op. cit., pars. 3 and 6.

[11] Corporations are allowed to deduct between 80 and 100 percent of the dividends received from other corporations, depending on their percentage of ownership, in computing their taxable income.

deductions for income tax reporting purposes will report a relatively lower taxable income as compared to pretax financial accounting income than it would have if these items were not present, whereas a corporation with expenses that are not tax deductible will report a relatively higher taxable income.

Temporary Differences

Temporary differences between pretax financial accounting income and taxable income arise because the timing of revenues, gains, expenses, or losses in financial accounting income occurs in a different period from taxable income. These timing differences result in assets and liabilities having different bases for financial accounting purposes than for income tax purposes at the end of a given accounting period. Additional temporary differences occur because specific provisions of the IRC create different bases for depreciation or for gain or loss recognition for income taxes purposes than are used for financial accounting purposes. Since many of these additional temporary differences relate to more complex provisions of the tax laws, only timing differences are discussed in detail.

Reversals of originating differences that cause current taxable income to be less than current financial accounting income cause future taxable income to exceed future financial accounting income. The difference is taxable in future accounting periods. In this case, the amount of the reversal is termed a *taxable amount*. The opposite occurs for originating differences that cause current taxable income to exceed current financial accounting income. These temporary differences result in future *deductible amounts*. The existence of future taxable or deductible amounts implies that temporary differences have future tax consequences. The future tax consequences argument rests on the inherent GAAP assumption that reported amounts of assets and liabilities will be recovered or settled, respectively. For example, GAAP requires lower-of-cost-or-market for assets when full recovery of cost is not expected. This assumption implies that reversals of temporary differences occur when reported amounts of assets are recovered or reported amounts of liabilities are settled.[12]

APB Opinion No. 11 limited the scope of temporary differences to timing differences. *Timing differences* occur when taxable revenues or gains, or tax deductible expenses or losses, are recognized in one accounting period for financial accounting reporting purposes and in a different accounting period for income tax purposes. The resulting tax consequences affect current and future accounting periods.

Timing differences may be classified into two broad categories:

Current Financial Accounting Income Exceeds Current Taxable Income[13]

1. *Revenues or gains are included in financial accounting income prior to the time they are included in taxable income.* For example, gross profit on

[12] *SFAC No. 109*, op. cit., pars. 3 and 6.

[13] *SFAS No. 109* describes these temporary differences in par. 11.

installment sales is included in financial accounting income at the point of sale but is generally reported for tax purposes as the cash is collected.

2. *Expenses or losses are deducted to compute taxable income prior to the time they are deducted to compute financial accounting income.* For example, a fixed asset may be depreciated by MACRS depreciation for income tax purposes and by the straight-line method for financial accounting purposes.[14]

**Current Financial Accounting Income Is Less
Than Current Taxable Income**

1. *Revenues or gains are included in taxable income prior to the time they are included in financial accounting income.* For example, rent received in advance is taxable when it is received, but it is recorded for financial accounting purposes under the accrual method as it is earned.

2. *Expenses or losses are deducted to compute financial accounting income prior to the time they are deducted to determine taxable income.* For example, product warranty costs are estimated and recorded as expenses at the time of sale of the product for financial accounting purposes, but deducted as actually incurred in later years to determine taxable income.

SFASs No. 96 and *No. 109* broadened the scope of temporary differences by including all "events that create differences between the tax bases of assets and liabilities and their amounts for financial reporting."[15] For example, an asset donated to a business has a zero basis for tax purposes but is recorded at its fair market value for financial accounting purposes. This creates a temporary difference that will reverse either through depreciation or sale of the asset. Thus, these additional temporary differences also result in tax consequences that affect two or more accounting periods.

Additional Temporary Differences[16]

1. *A reduction in the tax basis of depreciable assets because of tax credits.* The amounts received on future recovery of the amount of the asset for financial accounting purposes will be taxable when the asset is recovered. For example, the IRC allows taxpayers to reduce the depreciation basis of assets by half of the amount of the investment tax credit (ITC) taken for the asset. As a result, future taxable incomes will exceed future pretax financial accounting income by the amount of the tax basis reduction. Hence, the basis reduction is a temporary difference that creates a future taxable amount. The future taxable amount is equivalent to the amount needed to recover the additional financial accounting asset cost basis.

---

[14] MACRS is the only allowable accelerated depreciation method allowed under the IRC. It frequently results in relatively higher depreciation amounts than straight-line depreciation in the early years of an asset's life.

[15] Ibid, par. 3.

[16] These temporary differences are also described in *SFAS No. 109*, op. cit., par. 11.

2. ***The ITC accounted for by the deferred method.*** Recall that the preferred treatment of accounting for the ITC is to reduce the cost of the related asset by the amount of the ITC. If this method is used, the amounts received on future recovery of the reduced cost of the asset for financial accounting purposes will be less than the tax basis of the asset. The difference will be tax deductible when the asset is recovered.

3. ***Foreign operations for which the reporting currency is the functional currency.*** The provisions of *SFAS No. 52,* "Foreign Currency Translation,"[17] require certain assets to be remeasured from the foreign currency to U.S. dollars using historical exchange rates when the reporting currency is the functional currency.[18] If exchange rates subsequently change, there will be a difference between the foreign tax basis and the U.S. dollar historical cost of assets and liabilities. That difference will be taxable or deductible for foreign tax purposes when the reported amounts of the assets and liabilities are recovered and settled, respectively.

4. ***An increase in the tax basis of assets because of indexing for inflation.*** The tax law may require adjustment of the tax basis of a depreciable asset for the effects of inflation. The inflation-adjusted basis of the asset will then be used to compute future tax deductions for depreciation, or the gain or loss on the sale of the asset. Amounts received on future recovery of the remaining cost of the asset recorded for financial accounting purposes will then be less than the remaining tax basis of the asset, and the difference will be tax deductible when the asset is recovered.

5. ***Business combinations accounted for by the purchase method.*** There may be differences between the assigned value and the tax basis of the assets and liabilities recognized in a business combination accounted for as a purchase.[19] These differences will result in taxable or deductible amounts when the recorded amounts of the assets are recovered or the recorded amounts of the liabilities are settled.

Under current GAAP, published financial statements should reflect the tax consequences of economic events and transactions reported in those financial statements. Because temporary differences affect current and future tax payments, the current period income tax expense comprises the *current provision for taxes* (taxes payable in the tax return) and the results of interperiod tax allocation *(deferred income taxes).* The deferred tax component of tax expense reflects the tax consequences of current period originating and

---

[17] Financial Accounting Standards Board, *Statement of Financial Accounting Standards No. 52,* "Foreign Currency Translation" (Stamford, CT: FASB, 1981).

[18] *SFAS No. 52* defines the functional currency as the currency of the primary economic environment in which an entity operates. See Chapter 15 for a discussion of foreign currency translation.

[19] Under the purchase method of accounting for business combinations, the assets and liabilities acquired are recorded at their fair market values, not their previous book values. See Chapter 15 for a discussion of business combinations.

reversing differences. The expected cash flows of future tax consequences resulting from temporary differences between pretax financial accounting income and taxable income reflect anticipated future tax benefits *(deferred tax assets)* or payables *(deferred tax liabilities)*.

Net Operating Losses

A NOL occurs when the amount of total tax deductions and losses is greater than the amount of total taxable revenues and gains during an accounting period. The IRC allows corporations reporting NOLs to carry these losses back and forward to offset other reported taxable income (currently back three years and forward 15 years).

A NOL carryback is applied to the taxable income of the three preceding years in reverse order beginning with the earliest year and moving forward to the most recent year. If unused NOLs are still available, they are carried forward for up to 15 years to offset any future taxable income.[20] NOL carrybacks result in the refund of prior taxes paid. Thus, the tax benefits of NOL carrybacks are currently realizable and are recorded for financial accounting purposes as reductions in the current period loss. A receivable is recognized on the balance sheet, and the associated benefit is shown on the current year's income statement.

Whether to recognize the potential benefit of an NOL carryforward has added controversy to the income tax accounting debate. The APB argued that the benefit of an NOL carryforward is generally not assured in the loss period.[21] Nevertheless, *APB Opinion No. 11* allowed the recognition of anticipated benefit to be realized from an NOL carryforward in the unusual circumstances when realization is assured beyond any reasonable doubt.[22] *SFAS No. 96* did not allow the potential tax benefits of NOL carryforwards to be treated as assets. This position was based on the following argument:

> *Incurring losses or generating profits in future years are future events that are not recognized in financial statements for the current year and are not inherently assumed in financial statements for the current year. Those future events shall not be anticipated, regardless of probability, for purposes of recognizing or measuring … [income taxes] … in the current year.[23]*

SFAS No. 109 liberalizes the policies for recognizing tax assets (as discussed later) and, thus, for the financial accounting treatment of NOL carryforwards.

Conceptual Issues

The questions raised by the income tax allocation issue involve whether and how to account for the tax effects of the differences between taxable income,

---

[20] A company may choose not to use the carryback provisions and only carryforward net operating losses. Such an election might occur if Congress were expected to increase tax rates in the near future.

[21] APB *Opinion No. 11*, op. cit., par. 43.

[22] Ibid.

[23] Ibid., par. 15.

as determined by the IRC, and pretax financial accounting income, as determined under GAAP. Some accountants believe that it is inappropriate to give any accounting recognition to the tax effects of these differences. Others believe that recognition is appropriate but disagree on the method to use. There is also disagreement on the appropriate tax rate to use and whether reported future tax effects should be discounted to their present values. Finally, there is a lack of consensus over whether interperiod tax allocation should be applied comprehensively to all differences or only to those expected to reverse in the future. Each of these conceptual issues is examined in more detail in the following paragraphs.

Allocation Versus Nonallocation
Although authoritative pronouncements have consistently required interperiod tax allocation, some individuals maintain that the amount of income tax expense reported on a company's income statement should be the same as the income taxes payable for the accounting period as determined by the income tax return. Under this approach, no interperiod allocation of income taxes is necessary.

Advocates of nonallocation argue as follows:

1. Income taxes result only from taxable income. Whether or not the company has accounting income is irrelevant. Hence, attempts to match income taxes with accounting income provide no relevant information for users of published financial statements.

2. Income taxes are different from other expenses; therefore, allocation in a manner similar to other expenses is not relevant. Expense is a measure of the cost of generating revenue; income taxes generate no revenues. They are not incurred in anticipation of future benefits, nor are they expirations of cost to provide facilities to generate revenues.

3. Income taxes are levied on total taxable income, not on individual items of revenue and expense. Therefore, there can be no temporary differences related to these items.

4. Interperiod tax allocation hides an economic difference between a company that employs tax strategies that reduce current tax payments (and is therefore economically better off) and one that does not.

5. Reporting a company's income tax expense at the amount paid or currently payable is a better predictor of the company's future cash outflows because many of the deferred taxes will never be paid, or will be paid only in the distant future.

6. Income tax allocation entails an implicit forecasting of future profits. To incorporate such forecasting into the preparation of financial information is inconsistent with the longstanding principle of conservatism.

7. There is no present obligation for the potential or future tax consequences of present or prior transactions because there is no legal liability to pay taxes until an actual future tax return is prepared.

8. The accounting recordkeeping and procedures involving interperiod tax allocation are too costly for the purported benefits.

On the other hand, the advocates of interperiod tax allocation cite the following reasons to counter the preceding arguments or to criticize nonallocation:

1. Income taxes result from the incurrence of transactions and events. As a result, income tax expense should be based on the results of the transactions or events that are included in financial accounting income.

2. Income taxes are an expense of doing business and should involve the same accrual, deferral, and estimation concepts that are applied to other expenses.

3. Differences between the timing of revenues and expenses do result in temporary differences that will reverse in the future. Expanding, growing businesses experience increasing asset and liability balances. Old assets are collected, old liabilities are paid, and new ones take their place. Deferred tax balances grow in a similar manner.

4. Interperiod tax allocation makes a company's net income a more useful measure of its long-term earning power and avoids periodic income distortions resulting from income tax regulations.

5. Nonallocation of a company's income tax expense hinders the prediction of its future cash flows. For instance, a company's future cash inflows from installment sales collection would usually be offset by related cash outflows for taxes.

6. A company is a going concern, and income taxes that are currently deferred will eventually be paid. The validity of other assets and liabilities reported in the balance sheet depends on the presumption of a viable company and hence the incurrence of future net income.

7. Temporary differences are associated with future tax consequences. For example, reversals of originating differences that provide present tax savings are associated with higher future taxable incomes and therefore higher future tax payments. In this sense, deferred tax liabilities are similar to other contingent liabilities that are currently reported under GAAP.

Comprehensive Versus Partial Allocation
If the arguments in favor of the interperiod allocation of income taxes are accepted, the next issue to address is whether allocation should be applied on a comprehensive or partial basis. Under *comprehensive allocation,* the income tax expense reported in an accounting period is affected by all transactions and events entering into the determination of pretax financial accounting income for that period. Comprehensive allocation results in including the tax consequences of all temporary differences as deferred tax assets and liabilities, regardless of how significant or recurrent. Proponents of comprehensive allocation view all transactions and events that create temporary differences as affecting cash flows in the accounting periods when the originating differences reverse. Under this view, an originating temporary difference is analogous to an unpaid accounts receivable or accounts payable invoice; when a temporary difference reverses, it is collected or paid.

In contrast, under *partial allocation,* the income tax expense reported in an accounting period will not be affected by those temporary differences that are not expected to reverse in the future. That is, proponents of partial allocation argue that, in certain cases, groups of similar transactions or events may continually create originating differences in the future that will offset any reversing differences, resulting in an indefinite postponement of deferred tax consequences. In effect, these types of temporary differences are more like permanent differences. Examples of these types of differences include depreciation for manufacturing companies with large amounts of depreciable assets and installment sales for merchandising companies.

Advocates of comprehensive allocation raise the following arguments:

1. Individual temporary differences do reverse. By definition, a temporary difference cannot be permanent; the offsetting effect of future events should not be assumed. It is inappropriate to look at the effect of a group of temporary differences on income taxes; the focus should be on the individual items comprising the group. Temporary differences should be viewed in the same manner as accounts payable. That is, although the total balance of accounts payable may not change, many individual credit and payment transactions affect the total.

2. Accounting is primarily historical. It is inappropriate to offset the income tax effects of possible future transactions against the tax effects of transactions that have already occurred.

3. The income tax effects of temporary differences should be reported in the same period as the related transactions and events in pretax financial accounting income.

4. Accounting results should not be subject to manipulation by management. That is, a company's management should not be able to alter the company's results of operations and ending financial position by arbitrarily deciding what temporary differences will and will not reverse in the future.

In contrast, advocates of partial income tax allocation argue that

1. All groups of income tax temporary differences are not similar to certain other groups of accounting items, such as accounts payable. Accounts payable "roll over" as a result of actual individual credit and payment transactions. Income taxes, however, are based on total taxable income and not on the individual items constituting that income. Therefore, consideration of the impact of the *group* of temporary differences on income taxes is the appropriate viewpoint.

2. Comprehensive income tax allocation distorts economic reality. The income tax regulations that cause the temporary differences will continue to exist in the future. For instance, Congress is not likely to reduce investment incentives with respect to depreciation. Consequently, future investments are virtually certain to result in originating depreciation differences of an amount to at least offset reversing differences. Thus, consideration should be given to the impact of future, as well as historical, transactions.

3. Assessment of a company's future cash flows is enhanced by using the partial allocation approach. That is, the deferred income taxes (if any) reported on a company's balance sheet under partial allocation will be more reflective of the future cash flows.

4. Accounting results should not be distorted by the use of a rigid, mechanical approach, such as comprehensive tax allocation. Furthermore, an objective of the audit function is to identify and deter any management manipulation.

Discounting Deferred Taxes

Current GAAP requires comprehensive interperiod income tax allocation. Reported deferred tax assets and liabilities reflect anticipated future tax consequences resulting from temporary differences between pretax financial accounting income and taxable income. Specific measurement issues, such as the appropriate method and tax rate to use to calculate deferred tax balances, are discussed in the following sections. This section addresses the issue of whether deferred taxes, regardless of the measurement method used, should be discounted.

Proponents of reporting deferred taxes at their discounted amounts argue that the company that reduces tax payments is economically better off. It is their belief that by discounting deferred taxes, a company best reflects the operational advantages in its financial statements. Furthermore, proponents feel that discounting deferred taxes is consistent with the accounting principles established for such items as notes receivable and notes payable, pension costs, and leases. They argue that discounted amounts are considered to be the most appropriate indicators of future cash flows.

Critics of discounting counter that discounting deferred taxes mismatches taxable transactions and the related tax effects. That is, the taxable transaction would be reported in one period and the related tax effects over several periods. They also argue that discounting would conceal a company's actual tax burden by reporting as interest expense the discount factor that would otherwise be reported as part of income tax expense. Furthermore, deferred taxes may be considered as interest-free loans from the government that do not require discounting because the effective interest rate is zero.

Alternative Interperiod Tax Allocation Methods

Three methods of income tax allocation may be used in conjunction with either the comprehensive or partial allocation approach. These are (1) the deferred method, (2) the asset/liability method, and (3) the net-of-tax method.

The Deferred Method

The *deferred method* of income tax allocation is an income statement approach. It is based on the concept that income tax expense is related to the period in which income is recognized. The deferred method measures income tax expense as though the current period pretax financial accounting income is reported on the current year's income tax return. The tax effect of a temporary difference is the difference between income taxes computed with and without inclusion of the temporary difference. The resulting difference between income tax expense and income taxes currently payable is a debit or credit to the deferred income tax account.

The deferred tax account balance is reported in the balance sheet as a deferred tax credit or deferred tax charge. *Under the deferred method, the deferred tax amount reported on the balance sheets is the effect of temporary differences that will reverse in the future and that are measured using the income tax rates and laws in effect when the differences originated.* No adjustments are made to deferred taxes for changes in the income tax rates or tax laws that occur after the period of origination. When the deferrals reverse, the tax effects are recorded at the rates in existence *when the temporary differences originated.*

APB Opinion No. 11 required comprehensive interperiod income tax allocation using the deferred method.[24] Like its predecessor, *ARB No. 43, APB Opinion No. 11* concluded that "income tax expense should include the tax effects of revenue and expense transactions included in the determination of pretax accounting income."[25] Use of the deferred method caused considerable controversy. The primary criticism was that neither deferred tax charges nor deferred tax credits have the essential characteristics of assets or liabilities. Because the deferred method does not use tax rates that will be in effect when temporary differences reverse, they do not measure probable future benefits or sacrifices; hence, the resulting deferred taxes do not meet the definition of assets or liabilities in *SFAC No. 6.* The deferred tax balances simply represent the cumulative effects of temporary differences waiting to be adjusted in the matching process of some future accounting period.

Arguments in favor of the deferred method of interperiod tax allocation include the following:

1. The income statement is the most important financial statement, and matching is a critical aspect of the accounting process. Thus, it is of little consequence that deferred taxes are not true assets or liabilities in the conceptual sense.

2. Deferred taxes are the result of historical transactions or events that created the temporary differences. Since accounting reports most economic events on an historical cost basis, deferred taxes should be reported in a similar manner.

3. Historical income tax rates are verifiable. Reporting deferred taxes based on historical rates increases the reliability of accounting information.

The Asset/Liability Method

The *asset/liability method* of income tax allocation is balance sheet oriented. The intent is to accrue and report the total tax benefit or taxes payable that will

---

[24] *APB Opinion No. 11*, op. cit., pars. 34 and 35.

[25] Ibid., par. 34.

actually be realized or assessed on temporary differences when they reverse. A temporary difference is viewed as giving rise to either a tax benefit that will result in a decrease in future tax payments or a tax liability that will be paid in the future at the then-current tax rates. Theoretically, the future tax rates used should be estimated, based on expectations regarding future tax law changes. However, current GAAP requires that the future tax rates used to determine current period deferred tax asset and liability balances be based on currently enacted tax law.[26] *Under the asset/liability method, as defined by current GAAP, the deferred tax amount reported on the balance sheet is the effect of temporary differences that will reverse in the future and that are measured using the currently enacted tax rates and laws that will be in effect when the temporary differences reverse.* Adjustments, however, are made to deferred tax asset and liability accounts for any changes in the income tax rates or laws when these changes are enacted.

When using the asset/liability method, income tax expense is the sum of (or difference between) the changes in deferred tax asset and liability balances[27] and the current provision for income taxes per the tax return. According to the FASB, deferred taxes under the asset/liability method meet the conceptual definitions of assets and liabilities established in *SFAC No. 6.*[28] For instance, the resulting deferred tax credit balances of an entity can be viewed as probable future sacrifices (i.e., tax payments based on future tax rates) arising from present obligations (taxes owed) as a result of past transactions (originating differences). That is, deferred taxes measure future resource flows that result from transactions or events already recognized for financial accounting purposes.

Arguments in favor of the asset/liability method of interperiod tax allocation include the following:

1. The balance sheet is becoming a more important financial statement. Reporting deferred taxes based on the expected tax rates when the temporary differences reverse increases the predictive value of future cash flows, liquidity, and financial flexibility.

2. As discussed earlier, reporting deferred taxes based on the expected tax rates is conceptually more sound because the reported amount represents either the likely future economic sacrifice (future tax payments) or economic benefit (future reduction in taxes).

3. Deferred taxes may be the result of historical transactions, but, by definition, they are taxes that are postponed and will be paid (or will reduce taxes) in the future at the future tax rates.

4. Estimates are used extensively in accounting. The use of estimated future tax rates for deferred taxes poses no more of a problem regarding verifiability and reliability than using, say, estimated lives for depreciation.

---

[26] *FASB Statement No. 109,* op. cit., par. 8.

[27] Under *SFAS No. 109,* there may also be a valuation allowance for deferred tax assets. Changes in the valuation allowance would also affect income tax expense. The valuation allowance is discussed later in the chapter.

[28] *FASB Statement No. 109,* op. cit., par. 63.

5. Because the tax expense results from changes in balance sheet values, its measurement is consistent with the *SFAC No. 6* and *SFAS No. 130* definitions of comprehensive income.

The Net-of-Tax Method

The *net-of-tax method* is more a method of disclosure than a different method of calculating deferred taxes. Under this method, the income tax effects of temporary differences are computed by applying either the deferred method or the asset/liability method. The resulting deferred taxes, however, are not separately disclosed on the balance sheet. Instead, *under the net-of-tax method the deferred charges (tax assets) or deferred credits (tax liabilities) are treated as adjustments of the accounts to which the temporary differences relate.* Generally, the accounts are adjusted through the use of a valuation allowance rather than directly. For instance, if a temporary difference results from additional tax depreciation, the related tax effect will be subtracted (by means of a valuation account) from the cost of the asset (along with accumulated depreciation) to determine the carrying value of the depreciable asset. Similarly, the carrying value of installment accounts receivable would be reduced for the expected increase in income taxes that will occur when the receivable is collected (and taxed). Reversals of temporary differences would reduce the valuation allowance accounts.

Two alternatives exist for disclosing the periodic income tax expense on the income statement under the net-of-tax method. Under the first alternative, the tax effects of temporary differences are included in the total income tax expense. Thus, the income tax expense is reported in a manner similar to the deferred method or the asset/liability method. Under the second alternative, income tax expense is reported at the same amount as current income taxes payable, and the tax effects of temporary differences are combined with the revenue or expense items to which they relate. For instance, the tax effect of additional tax depreciation would be reported as an adjustment to depreciation expense.

The basic argument in favor of the net-of-tax method of interperiod tax allocation centers on the notion that all revenue and expense transactions involve changes in specific asset and liability accounts and are recorded accordingly. Therefore, accounting for the tax effects of temporary differences should be no different. Because temporary differences are the result of events that affect the future taxability and tax deductibility of specific assets and liabilities, they have future economic consequences that should be reflected in the value of the related assets and liabilities. For instance, when tax depreciation exceeds financial accounting depreciation, income tax expense is higher than current income taxes payable because an excess amount of the cost of the depreciable asset has been charged against taxable income. Thus, the excess (temporary difference) has reduced the future tax deductibility of the depreciable asset cost, and the carrying value of the asset should be reduced accordingly.

There are several arguments against the net-of-tax method. The primary argument is that many factors affect the value of assets and liabilities but are not recorded in the accounts. To single out one factor (impact on future taxes) as affecting value is inappropriate. Besides, it is not always possible to determine the related asset or liability account.[29] Furthermore, it is argued that the net-of-tax method is too complex to use and distorts traditional concepts for measuring assets and liabilities.

FASB Dissatisfaction with the Deferred Method

The deferred method was prescribed by *APB Opinion No. 11*. In 1982, the FASB, prompted by criticisms and concerns voiced in the literature and letters to the Board regarding the deferred method, began to reconsider accounting for income taxes. In *SFAC No. 6*, the FASB indicated that deferred income tax amounts reported on the balance sheet did not meet the newly established definitions for assets and liabilities.[30] The application of the deferred method by business enterprises most frequently resulted in reporting a deferred tax credit balance. Under the deferred method, deferred tax credits result when the payment of income tax is deferred to a later period. However, the tax rate used to measure the deferral may not be in effect when the deferred taxes are actually paid. If deferred income tax credit balances are liabilities, then the amounts reported in balance sheets should reflect the future resource outflows that will be required to settle them. Thus, any changes in tax rates and tax law that would change the future impact of temporary differences on income tax payments should be recognized for financial reporting purposes in the period when tax rate and tax law changes are enacted.

Subsequently, the Tax Reform Act of 1986 significantly reduced income tax rates and created additional pressure to consider a change in the method of accounting for temporary differences. After weighing the various arguments in favor of nonallocation and interperiod income tax allocation, the comprehensive and partial income allocation approaches, and the deferred, asset/liability, and net-of-tax methods of applying income tax allocation, in 1987 the FASB released *SFAS No. 96*, which concluded that

1. Interperiod income tax allocation of temporary differences is appropriate.
2. The comprehensive allocation approach should be applied.
3. The asset/liability method of income tax allocation should be used.

In addition to accepting the arguments presented earlier in favor of the asset/liability method, the FASB expanded on these arguments and provided the following rationale for its conclusions:

1. The income tax consequences of an event should be recognized in the same accounting period as that event is recognized in the financial state-

[29] Net operating losses (NOLs) create deferred tax asset balances under current GAAP. NOLs do not result from temporary differences deriving from any single transaction or event. There are no assets or liabilities on the balance sheet for NOLs.

[30] Financial Accounting Standards Board, *Statement of Financial Accounting Concepts No. 6*, "Elements of Financial Statements" (Stamford, CT: FASB, 1985), par. 241.

ments. Although most events affect taxable income and pretax financial accounting income in the same accounting period, the income tax consequences of some events are deferred. Temporary differences result from events that have deferred tax consequences.

2. Recognition of deferred income taxes is consistent with accrual accounting. Under accrual accounting, there is an assumption that there will be future recovery and settlement of reported amounts of assets and liabilities, respectively. That assumption necessitates the recognition of deferred tax consequences of those temporary differences that will become refundable or payable when the reported amounts of assets and liabilities are recovered and settled, respectively. On the other hand, earning future income and incurring future losses are events that are *not* assumed in the current accounting period under accrual accounting; thus, they should not be assumed for income tax accounting.

3. Under the asset/liability method, the deferred tax consequences of temporary differences generally are recognizable liabilities and assets. That is, a deferred tax liability represents the amount of income taxes that will be payable in future years when temporary differences result in taxable income at that time. Similarly, a deferred tax asset represents that amount of income taxes that will be refundable when temporary differences result in tax deductible amounts in future years.

Note that the FASB emphasized that temporary differences result in future tax consequences, rather than the allocation of tax among accounting periods. Nonallocation, partial allocation, and the deferred and net-of-tax methods were rejected and are *not* GAAP. Furthermore, reporting deferred taxes using a present-value approach was not considered by the FASB and is also *not* acceptable accounting for income taxes. The asset/liability approach presumably measures the future tax consequences for prior events or transactions. The following sections describe the *SFAS No. 96* arguments and conclusions regarding the nature of deferred tax liabilities and deferred tax assets, and how they should be measured and reported.

Deferred Tax Liability
The three essential characteristics of a liability established by *SFAC No. 6* are that (1) it must embody a present responsibility to another entity that involves settlement by probable future transfer or use of assets at a specified or determinable date, on occurrence of a specified event, or on demand; (2) the responsibility obligates the entity, leaving it little or no discretion to avoid the future sacrifice; and (3) the transaction or event obligating the entity has already happened. The deferred tax consequences of temporary differences that will result in net taxable amounts in future years meet these characteristics.[31] The first characteristic is met by a deferred tax liability because (1) the deferred tax consequences stem from the requirements of tax law and hence are a responsibility to the government, (2) settlement will involve a probable

---

[31] Financial Accounting Standards Board, *Statement of Financial Accounting Standards No. 96*, "Accounting for Income Taxes" (Stamford, CT: FASB, 1997), pars. 83–89.

future transfer or use of assets when the taxes are paid, and (3) settlement will result from events specified by the tax law. The second characteristic is met because, based on the government's tax rules and regulations, income taxes definitely will be payable when temporary differences result in net taxable amounts in future years. The third characteristic is met because the past events that created the temporary differences are the same past events that result in the deferred tax obligation.

Deferred Tax Asset

The three essential characteristics of an asset are that (1) it must embody a probable future benefit that involves a capacity to contribute to future net cash inflows, (2) the entity must be able to obtain the benefit and control other entities' access to it, and (3) the transaction or other event resulting in the entity's right to or control of the benefit must already have occurred. The deferred tax consequences of temporary differences that will result in net deductible amounts in future years that may be *carried back* as permitted by tax law meet these characteristics.[32] The first characteristic is met because a tax benefit is guaranteed. When the future year actually occurs, one of two events will occur. Either the deductible amount will be used to reduce actual income taxes for that year, or the deductible amount will result in a refund of taxes paid in the current or preceding years. The second characteristic is met because the entity will have an exclusive right to the tax benefit resulting from the carryback. Finally, the third characteristic is met because the entity must have earned taxable income in the current or past years for a carryback to be considered realizable.

On the other hand, a net deductible amount that cannot be carried back to the present or prior periods or an unused NOL carryforward does not have a refund guarantee. These deductions must be carried to future years in order to obtain a tax benefit. Consequently, the entity must have future taxable income for a future tax benefit to occur. Since earning income in future years has not yet occurred and is not inherently assumed in preparing financial statements, the third characteristic is *not* met for net deductible amounts that cannot be carried back to obtain a refund of taxes already paid. Nor is it met for NOL carryforwards. In other words, these items represent gain contingencies that may not be realized.

In summary, the deferred tax consequences of temporary differences that result in net deductible amounts in future years that may be carried back to present and prior years are an asset. But *SFAS No. 96* limited the recognition of benefit of all other net deductible amounts to reductions of deferred tax liabilities. Under this pronouncement, they were not recorded as assets— a treatment consistent with the treatment of other gain contingencies.

Business Dissatisfaction with *SFAS No. 96*

After *SFAS No. 96* was issued, and prior to its mandatory implementation date, many businesses expressed concern regarding the effect the standard

---

[32] Ibid., pars. 97–102.

would have on their financial statements and the cost that would be incurred in implementing the standard. These objections became so widespread that the implementation date was first postponed from 1988 to 1989[33] and later from 1989 to 1991.[34]

The major objections to *SFAS No. 96* centered on the cost of scheduling that would be necessary to determine whether a deferred tax asset could be recognized and the loss of some deferred tax assets because of the zero future income assumption. Prior to the effective date of *SFAS No. 96*, the FASB received (1) requests for about 20 different limited-scope amendments to its provisions; (2) many requests to change the criteria for recognition and measurement of deferred tax assets to anticipate, in certain circumstances, the tax consequences of future income; and (3) requests to reduce the complexity of scheduling the future reversals of temporary differences and considering hypothetical tax planning strategies. On June 5, 1991, the Board issued an Exposure Draft proposing a new standard to supersede *SFAS No. 96*. Later, on June 17, 1991, the Board issued another Exposure Draft to delay the effective date for the implementation of *SFAS No. 96* for a third time to December 15, 1992 (effective for 1993 statements) to allow time for interested parties to respond to the June 5, 1991, Exposure Draft. Finally, in early 1992 *SFAS No. 109* was issued.

SFAS No. 109

The FASB was convinced by the critics of *SFAS No. 96* that deferred tax assets should be treated similarly to deferred tax liabilities and that the scheduling requirements of *SFAS No. 96* were often too complex and costly. However, the Board did not want to return to the deferred method and remained committed to the asset/liability method. *SFAS No. 109* responded to these concerns by allowing the separate recognition and measurement of deferred tax assets and liabilities without regard to future income considerations,[35] using the average enacted tax rates[36] for future years. The deferred tax asset is to be reduced by a *tax valuation allowance* if available evidence indicates that it is *more likely than not (a likelihood of more than 50 percent)* that some portion or all of the deferred tax asset will not be realized.[37]

---

[33] Financial Accounting Standards Board, *Statement of Financial Accounting Standards No. 100*, "Accounting for Income Taxes—Deferral of the Effective Date of FASB Statement No. 96" (Stamford, CT: FASB, 1988).

[34] Financial Accounting Standards Board, *Statement of Financial Accounting Standards No. 103*, "Accounting for Income Taxes—Deferral of the Effective Date of FASB Statement No. 96" (Stamford, CT: 1989).

[35] *SFAS No. 109*, par. 17.

[36] For most companies, the marginal tax rate and the average tax rate are the same. Those companies for which a graduated tax rate is a significant factor are to use the average graduated tax rate applicable to the amount of estimated taxable income for the years when the deferred tax assets or liabilities are expected to be settled. Ibid., par. 18.

[37] Ibid., par. 17.

These requirements result in the following more simplified series of steps for determining deferred tax liability and asset balances:[38]

1. Identify temporary differences, NOL carryforwards, and unused tax credits.
2. Measure the total deferred tax liability by applying the expected tax rate to future taxable amounts.
3. Measure the total deferred tax asset by applying the expected future tax rate to future deductible amounts and NOL carryforwards.
4. Measure deferred tax assets for each type of unused tax credit.
5. Measure the valuation allowance based on the above more likely than not criterion.

The Valuation Allowance

The deferred tax asset measures potential benefits to be received in future years from NOL carryovers, deductible amounts arising from temporary differences, or unused tax credits. Because there may be insufficient future taxable income to actually derive a benefit from a recorded deferred tax asset, *SFAS No. 109* requires a *valuation allowance* sufficient to reduce the deferred tax asset to the amount that is more likely than not to be realized. The *more likely than not* criterion is a new measurement yardstick for the FASB. Previously, in establishing standards for contingent liabilities, the FASB introduced the terms *probable, reasonably probable,* and *remote.* The use of these terms for deferred tax assets would imply *an affirmative judgment approach* wherein recognition would require probable realization; however, no recognition would be given to deferred tax assets when the likelihood of realization was less than probable. The Board decided against the use of this approach to solve the income tax issue because it felt that probable was too stringent a benchmark for the recognition of deferred tax assets.[39]

The FASB also considered an *impairment approach* that would require deferred tax asset recognition unless it is probable that the asset will not be realized. The impairment approach was also deemed problematic because it would result in recognition of a deferred tax asset that is not expected to be realized when the likelihood of its not being realized is less than probable.[40]

The more likely than not criterion was selected because it would eliminate any distinction between the affirmative judgment and impairment approaches. As a practical matter, use of this criterion would provide both of the following results:

a. Recognition of a deferred tax asset if the likelihood of realizing the future tax benefit is more than 50 percent (the affirmative judgment approach).

[38] Ibid., par. 17.
[39] Ibid., par. 95.
[40] Ibid.

b.   Recognition of a deferred tax asset unless the likelihood of not realizing the future tax benefit is more than 50 percent (the impairment approach).[41]

In other words, the FASB chose a middle ground, which in effect embraced both approaches, *rather than selecting one over the other.* Use of the more likely than not criterion allows practitioners to ignore the zero future income assumption. That is, accountants may assume that there will be sufficient future taxable income to realize deferred tax assets unless evidence indicates that it is more likely than not that it will not be realized.

The Board considered various criteria to determine when impairment might apply but did not come to any definitive conclusions. The realization of future benefit from a deductible temporary difference or carryover ultimately depends on the incurrence of taxable income that is of an appropriate character to utilize the carryover of a NOL or credit, or against which a deductible amount may be applied. *SFAS No. 109* cited the following as possible sources of taxable income (affirmative evidence) that may enable the realization of deferred tax assets:

1.   Future reversals of existing taxable temporary differences.

2.   Future taxable income exclusive of taxable temporary differences and carryovers.

3.   Taxable income in the current or prior years to which deductible amounts resulting from temporary differences could be carried back.

4.   In order to prevent a NOL or tax credit carryover from expiring, prudent and feasible tax planning strategies that an enterprise ordinarily might not take may be employed to
     a.   Accelerate taxable amounts against which to apply carryforwards.
     b.   Change the character of taxable or deductible amounts from ordinary income or loss to capital gain or loss.
     c.   Switch from tax-exempt to taxable investments.[42]

SFAS No. 109 stressed that the exercise of judgment is necessary to determine whether a valuation allowance should be reported and, if so, the level of impairment of the deferred tax asset that is more likely than not to occur. On the downside, negative evidence (potential impairment) might include the following:

1.   A history of NOL or tax credit carryforwards expiring unused.

2.   Anticipated losses (by a presently profitable enterprise).

3.   Unsettled circumstances that may adversely affect future operations and profits.

4.   A carryover period that is so brief that it would limit realization of deferred tax benefits if (a) a significant deductible temporary difference

---

[41] Ibid.

[42] Ibid., pars. 21 and 22.

is expected to reverse in a single year or (b) the business operating cycle is traditionally cyclical.[43]

This type of negative evidence should be weighed against positive evidence such as

1. Existing contracts or sales backlog.
2. Significant appreciation of an asset's value over its tax basis.
3. A strong earnings history (exclusive of the NOL or deductible temporary differences) coupled with evidence that the loss is an aberration rather than a continuing condition.[44]

By relaxing the future income assumption, the necessity of scheduling that was required under *SFAS No. 96* is greatly reduced. If it is assumed that there will be sufficient taxable income in future years to realize the tax benefit of existing deductible amounts, the carryback and carryforward provisions of *SFAS No. 96* will not be needed. If, on the other hand, it is not possible to assume sufficient future taxable income, then scheduling may be needed to determine the balance in the valuation allowance account. However, scheduling is no longer required to determine the proper classification of the deferred amount between current and noncurrent. The deferred tax balance is to be classified as current or noncurrent in the same manner as the assets and liabilities to which the deferred taxes relate.

The adoption of the *more likely than not* approach led the FASB to conclude that a similar approach should be used for NOLs, unused credits, and deductible amounts resulting from temporary differences. Under *SFAS No. 109*, NOLs will now result in deferred tax assets unless it is more likely than not that they will not be able to be applied against future taxable income. This is a significant change in that millions of dollars of potential benefit that have heretofore been unreported will be included in the assets of companies.

Shift in Interpretation of Future Tax Consequences

In requiring the separate measurement of deferred tax liabilities and deferred tax assets and the reduction of deferred tax assets by the valuation allowance, the resulting balance sheet amounts would not reflect the effects of netting deductible amounts against taxable amounts or the certain guarantee of realization for deferred tax assets that would have occurred under *SFAS No. 96*. In short, the *SFAS No. 109* provisions introduced different levels of certainty regarding expected future cash flows. As a result, the FASB reexamined whether the resulting deferred tax liabilities and deferred tax assets fit the definitions of liabilities and assets found in *SFAC No. 6*. The Board concluded that they do and that the information provided is useful, understandable, and no more complex than any other approach to accounting for

---

[43] Ibid., par. 23.
[44] Ibid., par. 24.

income taxes.[45] These conclusions are based on the following arguments regarding the *SFAS No. 109* deferred tax liability and deferred tax asset.

Deferred Tax Liability

In requiring the separate measurement of deferred tax assets and deferred tax liabilities, deferred tax liabilities will not measure the effects of net taxable amounts. Nevertheless, according to *SFAS No. 109*, the resulting deferred tax liabilities meet all three essential characteristics of liabilities outlined in *SFAC No. 6* (described previously).[46] Again, the first characteristic of a liability is that it embodies a present obligation to the enterprise to settle by probable future transfer or use of assets upon the occurrence of a specified event, or on demand. This characteristic is met because the deferred tax liability measures an obligation to the government resulting from the deferred tax consequences of taxable temporary differences that stem from the requirements of the tax law.

The second characteristic, that the enterprise is obligated and has little or no discretion to avoid future sacrifice, is also met. It may be possible to delay future reversals of temporary differences by postponing events such as recovery or settlement of assets or liabilities; but, eventually, these temporary differences will become taxable. Hence, the only relevant question is when, not whether, the tax consequences will occur. Finally, the future payment of tax is the result of past transactions or events that created the originating temporary differences. This satisfies the third characteristic of a liability—that the transaction or event that obligates the enterprise has already happened.

Deferred Tax Asset

The FASB also concluded that *SFAS No. 109* deferred tax assets, reduced by the valuation allowance, meet the *SFAC No. 6* characteristics of assets.[47] The first characteristic of an asset is that it embodies a capacity to contribute directly or indirectly to enterprise future net cash inflows. There is no question that deductible amounts that may be carried back to offset taxable income that has already been incurred embody a probable future benefit because they contribute directly to future net cash inflows. Other deductible amounts and carryovers under the more likely than not criterion, because they may be used to reduce future taxable amounts, will contribute indirectly to future cash flows.

The second characteristic of an asset is that the enterprise can obtain the benefit and can control others' access to it. To the extent that these benefits will occur, the enterprise has an exclusive right to those benefits as they are realized and therefore can control access to them.

---

[45] Ibid., par. 63.

[46] Ibid., pars. 75–79.

[47] Ibid., pars. 80–86.

The third characteristic of an asset is that the transaction or event that resulted in the enterprise obtaining the right to control the benefit has already occurred. Because deferred tax asset realization under *SFAS No. 96* was guaranteed, the critical event giving rise to the asset was prior taxable income. However, *SFAS No. 109* allows recognition if the weight of the evidence implies that it is more likely than not that realization will occur. Thus, the existence or absence of future taxable income is critical to deferred tax asset recognition under current GAAP for those deductible amounts and carryforwards that will not result in a refund of prior taxes paid. "The Board concluded that earning taxable income in future years (a) is the event that confirms the existence of recognizable tax benefit at the end of the current year and (b) is not the prerequisite event that must occur before a tax benefit may be recognized as was the case under the requirements of [SFAS No.] 96."[48]

Financial Statement Disclosure

Several disclosure issues arise in connection with the reporting of income taxes on financial statements.

Income Statement Presentation and Related Disclosures

The portrayal of the effects of taxation on major segments of the income statement and on items carried directly to retained earnings is enhanced by allocating the income tax expense for a period among these items. The allocation of income tax within an accounting period is termed *intraperiod tax allocation*. Intraperiod tax allocation is required under current GAAP.[49] Income tax expense (or benefit) is disclosed for net income from continuing operations, gains or losses resulting from the disposal of a segment of a business, extraordinary items, and the cumulative effect of changes in accounting principles. In addition, the tax effect of any prior period adjustments to Retained Earnings must be disclosed.

SFAS No. 109 also requires disclosure of the significant components of income tax attributable to income from continuing operations. These components include

1. The current provision (or benefit) for income taxes.
2. Deferred tax expense or benefit (exclusive of items 3–8 listed below).
3. Investment tax credits.
4. Government grants (to the extent that they reduce income tax expense).
5. The benefits of operating loss carryforwards.
6. Tax expense that results from allocations of tax benefits to balance sheets in a business combination.
7. Adjustments to the deferred tax liability or asset for enacted changes in tax laws or a change in the tax status of the reporting entity.

[48] Ibid., par. 86.
[49] Ibid., par. 43.

8. Adjustments of the beginning balance of the valuation allowance because of a change in circumstances that causes a change in judgment about the realizability of the related deferred tax asset.

Balance Sheet Presentation and Related Disclosures

The current provision (or benefit) is reported in the balance sheet as a current liability or asset. Deferred tax balances are reported as assets and liabilities. They are classified as (1) the net current amount and (2) the net noncurrent amount. This classification is based on the classification of the related asset or liability that caused the deferred item.[50] That is, a deferred tax asset or liability is related to an asset or liability if a reduction of the asset or liability will cause the temporary difference to reverse. A deferred tax asset or liability that is not related to an asset or liability, including deferred tax assets created by NOL or tax credit carryforwards, is classified as current or noncurrent according to the expected reversal date of the temporary difference. A net noncurrent deferred tax asset is classified as an Other Asset. A noncurrent net deferred tax liability is classified as a Long-term Liability. The valuation allowance (and the net change in it) associated with deferred tax assets that do not meet the *more likely than not to be realized* criterion must be disclosed. Also, companies must disclose the approximate tax effect of each item that gives rise to a significant portion of deferred tax liabilities and assets (exclusive of the valuation allowance).[51]

SEC Disclosure Requirements

The Securities and Exchange Commission (SEC) has also adopted disclosure requirements for corporations issuing publicly traded securities. The disclosures required include

1. A reconciliation of the difference between income tax expense and the amount of tax expense that would have been reported by applying the normal rate to reported income for the company. This requirement highlights the special provisions of the tax code that benefited the company.

2. The amount of any temporary difference that is due to the deferral of investment tax credits (when and if the ITC is applicable).

These requirements are intended to provide information to investors and others on the effective tax rates of corporations.

Financial Analysis of Income Taxes

Taken together, the SEC and *SFAS No. 109* financial statement disclosure requirements allow investors, creditors, and other users of financial information to make better decisions. Specifically,

1. The quality of earnings can be assessed because special situations that give rise to one-time earnings are highlighted.

[50] Ibid., par. 41.

[51] Ibid., par. 43.

2. Future cash flows can be more easily assessed because reversals of deferred tax assets and liabilities are highlighted.

3. Government regulation of the economy is enhanced because it is easier to calculate actual tax rates.

One area of interest to accounting researchers has been the establishment of deferred assets and liabilities and the related valuation account necessary if a company determines that some of its deferred assets may not be realized in the future. The FASB indicated that the determination of the valuation account according to the more likely than not criterion reflects a trade-off between relevance and objectivity. Consequently, an examination of the components of the deferred accounts may help to illuminate how companies are assessing this trade-off. In addition, research has found that deferred taxes help predict future earnings, which, in turn, affects the value of the firm and security prices,[52] and that the data required to be provided is value relevant.[53] The magnitude of the valuation allowance has also been found to vary widely consistent with the level of managerial discretion allowed by *SFAS No. 109*. However, preliminary evidence suggests that this variation is not the result of earnings management activities.[54]

The footnotes to a company's financial statements provide information that can be used to analyze its income tax amounts. Specifically, most companies will disclose

a. Information on the amount of taxes that would be paid at the federal statutory rate and the amount actually paid.

b. Changes in the deferred tax asset and liability accounts.

c. Information concerning income tax carrybacks and carryforwards.

Footnote 5 to Kroll-O'Gara Company's financial statements (contained on the text's webpage) discloses information regarding the company's income tax. From this information we can see that the company's 1998 provision for income taxes (taxes payable) was 36.3 percent, while the federal statutory rate was 34.4 percent. This difference was even more pronounced in 1997 when the amounts were 56.0 and 34.0, respectively. This analysis indicates that these differences were being affected by nondeductible expenses, changes in the deferred tax valuation account, and the effects of foreign income.

In reviewing changes in the deferred accounts, it can be seen that both the deferred tax asset and deferred tax liability increased during 1998. The

---

[52] David A Guenther and Richard C. Sansing, "Valuation of the Firm in the Presence of Temporary Book-Tax Differences: The Role of Deferred Tax Assets and Liabilities," *The Accounting Review* (January 2000), pp. 1–12.

[53] Benjamin C. Ayers, "Deferred Tax Accounting under *SFAS No. 109:* An Empirical Investigation of Its Incremental Value-Relevance to *APB No. 11*," *The Accounting Review* (April 1998), pp. 195–212.

[54] Gregory S. Miller and Douglas J. Skinner, "Determinants of the Valuation Allowance for Deferred Tax Assets under *SFAS No. 109*," *The Accounting Review* (April 1998), pp. 213–233.

increase in the deferred tax asset was attributable mainly to an increase in payroll and benefit items, and acquisition costs, whereas the increase in deferred liabilities was largely caused by an increase in deferred revenues. These changes are all consistent with the company's increased level of operations during 1998. Finally, the company discloses that it has foreign and domestic net operating loss carryforwards but that the realization of the foreign carryforwards is uncertain.

International Accounting Standards

The IASC's discussion of accounting for income taxes is contained in *IAS No. 12,* "Accounting for Taxes on Income." In 1996, this statement was revised to reduce the number of options companies have when accounting for deferred taxes. Previously, companies were allowed to account for income tax timing differences by either the deferred or the liability method. Under the revised standard, only the liability method is allowed. The revised standard is quite similar to U.S. GAAP as outlined in *SFAS No. 109.* The IASC is currently considering some additional issues such as whether the tax consequences of recovering the carrying amount of certain assets and liabilities may depend on the manner of recovery or settlement (e.g., different tax rates on capital gains). If so, deferred tax assets and liabilities will be measured on the basis of the tax consequences that would follow from the expected manner of recovery or settlement. A requirement to disclose a reconciliation between tax expense and accounting profit is also being considered. The FASB staff did not undertake a comprehensive review of the revised *IAS No. 12* because the IASC was still in the process of developing the new standard when the FASB study was published.

Summary

Interperiod income tax allocation has been a controversial issue for many years. The CAP, the APB, and the FASB have all examined the topic and issued pronouncements. In *SFAS No. 109,* the FASB recommended the use of an asset/liability approach that allows for the recognition of both assets and liabilities that arise from interperiod tax allocation. In addition, the potential tax benefit of net operating loss carrybacks and carryforwards can be recognized if it is more likely than not that they will be realized.

In the reading located on the webpage for this chapter accounting for income taxes is examined further.

Cases

• Case 11-1 Income Tax Implications of Capital Investment Decisions

The Whitley Corporation's year-end is December 31. It is now October 1, 2001. The Whitley management team is taking a look at the prior nine months and attempting to make some short-term strategy decisions.

Whitley has experienced steady growth over the five preceding years. The result has been a steadily increasing EPS. Last year Whitley reported an EPS of 1.95.

This year, due to a mild recession, Whitley's sales have fallen off. Management is looking for strategies that may improve the appearance of their financial statements. At the same time, there is a need for new equipment in the plant. Despite the recession, Whitley has enough cash to make the purchase.

Based on the year's performance to date and extrapolation of the results to year-end, management feels that the pretax financial accounting income for the year will be $200,000. Transactions from prior years have resulted in a deferred tax asset of $15,000 and a deferred tax liability of $70,000 at the beginning of 2001. The temporary difference of $37,500 that resulted in the deferred tax asset is expected to completely reverse by the end of 2001. The deferred tax liability resulted totally from temporary depreciation differences. There will be a pretax reversal of $42,500 in this temporary difference during 2001.

Based on presently enacted tax law, the purchase of the equipment will result in a future taxable amount of $50,000. Whitley management feels that it can wait four to six months to purchase the machine. Whitley's tax rate is 40 percent.

Required:

a. Determine the projected amount of income tax expense that would be reported if Whitley waits until next year to purchase the equipment.
b. Determine the projected amount of income tax expense that would be reported if Whitley purchases the equipment in 2001.
c. Should Whitley wait to purchase the equipment? Your answer should take into consideration the expected financial statement effects, as well as the effect on EPS. Support your conclusions with pro-forma data. The number of shares that Whitley will use to calculate EPS is 55,500.
d. What are the ethical considerations of this case?

• Case 11-2 Discounting Deferred Taxes

The FASB has carefully avoided the issue of discounting deferred taxes. *Statement of Financial Accounting Standards No. 109,* "Accounting for Income Taxes," states that

> *"a deferred tax liability or asset should be recognized for the deferred tax consequences of temporary differences and operating loss or tax credit carryforwards. ... Under the requirements of this Statement: ... Deferred tax liabilities and assets are not discounted."*

Required:

a. Assuming that the firm's deferred tax liabilities exceed its deferred tax assets, select that approach to measurement—discounting or nondiscounting—that is best supported by the qualitative characteristics of *SFAC No. 2* by placing an X in the following evaluation matrix under the measurement approach selected. For example, if you feel that discounting has higher representational faithfulness, put an X under column 2 beside

representational faithfulness. Column 3 is provided for those cases for which a given concept is not applicable.
b. Discuss the reasons for your evaluations.
c. Present arguments supporting the discounting of deferred taxes.
d. Present arguments opposing the discounting of deferred taxes.

SFAC No. 2 Qualitative Characteristic	Nondiscounting (1)	Discounting (2)	Neither (3)
1. Relevance			
a. Timeliness			
b. Predictive and feedback value			
2. Reliability			
a. Representational faithfulness			
b. Verifiability and neutrality			
3. Understandability			
4. Comparability			

• Case 11-3 Accounting for Deferred Tax Assets

One of the main criticisms of *SFAS No. 96* was that most deferred tax assets could not be recognized. *SFAS No. 109* liberalized the recognition of deferred tax assets. Deferred tax assets are now recognized for all deductible amounts and carryovers. However, the amount reported may be reduced or eliminated by a valuation allowance if it is more likely than not that the deferred tax asset will not be realized.

Required:
a. Describe how the more likely than not criterion satisfied both the affirmative judgment approach and the impairment approach to asset recognition. How does this differ from typical asset recognition?
b. Cite examples that indicate affirmative evidence supporting the recognition of deferred tax assets.
c. Cite examples of potential impairment of deferred tax assets.
d. Given that some of each type of evidence may exist, how might the more likely than not criterion present management with an ethical dilemma? Explain.

• Case 11-4 Intraperiod vs. Interperiod Income Tax Allocation

Income tax allocation is an integral part of generally accepted accounting principles. The applications of intraperiod income tax allocation (within a period) and interperiod tax allocation (among periods) are both required.

Required:
a. Explain the need for intraperiod income tax allocation.
b. Accountants who favor interperiod income tax allocation argue that income taxes are an expense rather than a distribution of earnings. Explain

the significance of this argument. Do not explain the definitions of expense or distribution of earnings.

c. Discuss the nature of the deferred income tax accounts and possible classifications in a company's balance sheet.

d. Indicate and explain whether each of the following independent situations should be treated as a temporary difference or a permanent difference.

    i. Estimated warranty costs (covering a three-year period) are expensed for accounting purposes when incurred.

    ii. Depreciation for accounting and income tax purposes differs because of different bases of carrying the related property. The different bases are a result of a business combination treated as a purchase for accounting purposes and as a tax-free exchange for income tax purposes.

    iii. A company properly uses the equity method to account for its 30 percent investment in another company. The investee pays dividends that are about 10 percent of its annual earnings.

e. For each of the above independent situations, determine whether those situations that are treated as temporary differences will result in future taxable amounts or future deductible amounts and whether they will result in deferred tax assets or deferred tax liabilities. Explain.

• Case 11-5 Temporary Differences

Statement of Financial Accounting Standards No. 109, "Accounting for Income Taxes," requires interperiod income tax allocation for temporary differences.

Required:
a. Define the term *temporary difference.*
b. List the examples of temporary differences contained in *SFAS No. 109.*
c. Defend comprehensive interperiod income tax allocation.

• Case 11-6 Asset/Liability Method

Statement of Financial Accounting Standards No. 109, "Accounting for Income Taxes," requires companies to use the asset/liability method of interperiod income tax allocation.

Required:
a. Discuss the criteria for recognizing deferred tax assets and deferred tax liabilities under the provisions of *SFAS No. 109.*
b. Compare and contrast the asset/liability method and the deferred method.

• Case 11-7 Methods of Interperiod Income Tax Allocation

There are three general views regarding interperiod income tax allocation: no allocation, partial allocation, and comprehensive allocation.

Required:
a. Defend the position of no allocation or income taxes.
b. Defend the position of partial allocation of income taxes.
c. Defend the position of comprehensive allocation of income taxes.

- ## Case 11-8 Accounting for Income Taxes: Different Approaches

Mark or Make is a bourbon distillery. Sales have been steady for the past three years, and operating costs have remained unchanged. On 1/1/×1 Mark or Make took advantage of a special deal to prepay its rent for three years at a substantial savings. The amount of the prepayment was $60,000. The following income statement items (excluding the rent) are shown below.

	20×1	20×2	20×3
Gross profit on sales	350,000	349,000	351,000
Operating expense	210,000	210,000	210,000

Assume that the rental is deducted on the corporate tax purposes in 20×1 and that there are no other temporary differences between taxable income and pretax accounting income. In addition, there are no permanent differences between taxable income and pretax accounting income. The corporate tax rate for all three years is 30 percent.

Required:
a. Construct income statements for 20×1, 20×2, and 20×3 under the following approaches to interperiod income tax allocation:
    i.   No allocation.
    ii. Comprehensive allocation.
b. Do you believe that no allocation distorts Mark or Make's net income? Explain.
c. For years 20×1 and 20×2, Mark or Make reported net income applying the concept of comprehensive interperiod income tax allocation. During 20×2 Congress passed a new tax law that will increase the corporate tax rate from 30 to 33 percent.
    Reconstruct the income statements for 20×2 and 20×3 under the following assumptions:
    i.   Mark or Make uses the deferred method to account for interperiod income tax allocation.
    ii. Mark or Make uses the asset/liability approach to account for interperiod income tax allocation.
d. Which of the two approaches used in (d) provides measures of income and liabilities that are useful to decision makers? Explain.

Room for Debate

- ## Issue 1

The APB required comprehensive interperiod income tax allocation under the deferred method. The FASB requires comprehensive interperiod income tax allocation under the asset/liability approach.

Team Debate:

Team 1. Defend the deferred method of accounting for interperiod income tax allocation. You may take into consideration the definitions of the elements of financial statements found in *SFAC No. 6* and other theoretical concepts such as relevance, reliability, and matching.

Team 2. Defend the asset/liability approach of accounting for interperiod income tax allocation. You may take into consideration the definitions of elements of financial statements found in *SFAC No. 6* and other theoretical concepts such as relevance, reliability, and matching.

Recommended Additional Readings

Amir, Eli. "The Valuation of Deferred Taxes." *Contemporary Accounting Research* (Winter 1997), pp. 597–623.

Ayers, Benjamin C. "Deferred Tax Accounting under *SFAS No. 109:* An Empirical Investigation of Its Incremental Value-Relevance to *APB No. 11*," *The Accounting Review* (April 1998), pp. 195–212.

Guenther, David A., and Richard C. Sansing. "Valuation of the Firm in the Presence of Temporary Book-Tax Differences: The Role of Deferred Tax Assets and Liabilities." *The Accounting Review* (January 2000), pp. 1–12.

Heiman-Hoffman, Vicky, and James M. Patton. "An Experimental Investigation of Deferred Tax Asset Judgments under *SFAS No. 109*." *Accounting Horizons* (March 1994), pp. 1–7.

Miller, Gregory S., and Douglas J. Skinner. "Determinants of the Valuation Allowance for Deferred Tax Assets under *SFAS No. 109*." *The Accounting Review* (April 1998), pp. 213–233.

Petree, Thomas R., George J. Gregory, and Randall J. Vitray. "Evaluating Deferred Tax Assets." *Journal of Accountancy* (March 1995), pp. 71–76.

Smith, Darlene A., and Gary Freeman. "*SFAS 109*, Accounting for Income Taxes," *The CPA Journal* (April 1992), pp. 16–25.

Spece, Thomas C. "Case Study: Implementation of SFAS No. 109." *The Ohio CPA Journal* (April 1995), pp. 32–37.

Bibliography

Arthur Andersen & Co. *Accounting for Income Taxes.* Chicago: Arthur Andersen & Co., 1961.

Barton, A. U. "Company Income Tax and Interperiod Allocation." *Abacus* (September 1970), pp. 3–24.

Baylis, A. W. "Income Tax Allocation—A Defense." *Abacus* (December 1971), pp. 161–172. See also A. D. Barton. "Reply to Mr. Baylis." *Abacus* (December 1971), pp. 173–175.

Beaver, William, and Roland E. Dukes. "Interperiod Tax Allocation and Delta-Depreciation Methods: Some Empirical Results." *The Accounting Review* (July 1973), pp. 549–595.

Bevis, Donald J., and Raymond E. Perry. *Accounting for Income Taxes.* New York: AICPA, 1969.

Bierman, Harold, Jr. "One More Reason to Revise Statement 96." *Accounting Horizons* (June 1990), pp. 42–46.

Bierman, Harold, and Thomas R. Dyckman. "New Look at Deferred Taxes." *Financial Executive* (January 1974), pp. 40ff.

Black, Homer A. "Interperiod Allocation of Corporate Income Taxes." *Accounting Research Study No. 9.* New York: AICPA, 1966.

Chambers, R. J. "Tax Allocation and Financial Reporting." *Abacus* (December 1968), pp. 99–123.

Chaney, Paul K., and Debra C. Jeter. "Accounting for Deferred Income Taxes: Simplicity? Usefulness?" *Accounting Horizons* (June 1989), pp. 6–13.

Cramer, Joe, J., Jr., and William J. Schrader. "Investment Tax Credit." *Business Horizons* (February 1970), pp. 85–89.

Givoly, Dan, and Carla Hayn. "The Valuation of the Deferred Tax Liability: Evidence from the Stock Market." *The Accounting Review* (April 1992), pp. 394–410.

Godlick, Neil B., and Richard P. Miller. "Applying APB Opinions Nos. 23 and 24." *Journal of Accountancy* (November 1973), pp. 55–63.

Hill, Thomas, "Some Arguments Against the Interperiod Allocation of Income Taxes." *The Accounting Review* (July 1957), pp. 528–537.

Kissinger, John N. "In Defense of Interperiod Income Tax Allocation." *Journal of Accounting Auditing and Finance* (Spring 1986), pp. 90–101.

Laibstain, Samuel. "New Look at Accounting for Operating Loss Carry-Forwards." *The Accounting Review* (April 1971), pp. 342–351.

Meonske, Norman R., and Hans Sprohge. "How to Apply the New Accounting Rules for Deferred Taxes." *The Practical Accountant* (June 1988), pp. 15–50.

Moonitz, Maurice. "Some Reflections on the Investment Credit Experience." *Journal of Accounting Research* (Spring 1966), pp. 47–61.

Moore, Carl L. "Deferred Income Tax—Is It a Liability?" *New York CPA* (February 1970), pp. 130–138.

Norgaard, Corine T. "Financial Implications of Comprehensive Income Tax Allocation." *Financial Analysts Journal* (January–February 1969), pp. 81–85.

Nurnberg, Hugo. "Critique of the Deferred Method of Interperiod Tax Allocation." *New York CPA* (December 1969), pp. 958–961.

Nurnberg, Hugo. "Deferred Tax Assets under FASB *Statement No. 96*." *Accounting Horizons* (December 1989), pp. 49–56.

Pointer, Larry Gene. "Disclosing Corporate Tax Policy." *Journal of Accountancy* (July 1973), pp. 56–61.

Price Waterhouse & Co. *Is Generally Accepted Accounting for Income Taxes Possibly Misleading Investors?* New York: Price Waterhouse & Co., 1967.

Raiburn, Michael H., Michael R. Lane, and D. D. Raiburn. "Purchased Loss Carryforwards: An Unresolved Issue." *Journal of Accountancy* (November 1983), pp. 98–108.

Rayburn, Frank R. "A Chronological Review of the Authoritative Literature on Interperiod Tax Allocation: 1945–1985." *The Accounting Historians Journal* (Fall 1986), pp. 89–108.

Read, William J., and Robert A. J. Bartsch. "The FASB's Proposed Rules for Deferred Taxes." *Journal of Accountancy* (August 1991), pp. 44–46, 48, 50–53.

Revsine, Lawrence. "Some Controversy Concerning Controversial Accounting Changes." *The Accounting Review* (April 1969), pp. 354–358.

Rosenfield, Paul, and William C. Dent. "No More Deferred Taxes." *Journal of Accountancy* (February 1983), pp. 44–55.

Smith, Willis A. "Tax Allocation Revisited—Another Viewpoint." *The CPA Journal* (September 1984), pp. 52–56.

Stamp, Edward. "Some Further Reflections on the Investment Credit." *Journal of Accounting Research* (Spring 1967), pp. 124–128.

Throckmorton, Jerry J. "Theoretical Concepts for Interpreting the Investment Credit." *Journal of Accountancy* (April 1970), pp. 45–52.

Voss, William M. "Accelerated Depreciation and Deferred Tax Allocation." *Journal of Accounting Research* (Autumn 1968), pp. 262–269.

Watson, Peter L. "Accounting for Deferred Tax on Depreciable Assets." *Accounting and Business Research* (Autumn 1979), pp. 338–347.

Weber, Richard P. "Misleading Tax Figures: A Problem for Accountants." *The Accounting Review* (January 1977), pp. 172–185.

Wheeler, James E., and Willard H. Galliart. *An Appraisal of Interperiod Income Tax Allocation.* New York: Financial Executives Research Foundation, 1974.

Williams, Edward E., and M. Chapman Findly. "Discounting Deferred Tax Liabilities: Some Clarifying Comments." *Journal of Business Finance and Accounting* (Spring 1975), pp. 121–133.

Wolk, Harry I., Dale R. Martin, and Virginia A. Nichols. "Statement of Financial Accounting Standards No. 96: Some Theoretical Problems." *Accounting Horizons* (June 1989), pp. 1–5.

Wolk, Harry I., and Michael G. Tearney. "Income Tax Allocation and Loss Carry-Forwards: Exploring Uncharted Ground." *The Accounting Review* (April 1973), pp. 292–299.

Wyatt, Arthur R., Richard Dieter, and John E. Stewart. "Tax Allocation Revisited." *The CPA Journal* (1984), pp. 10, 12, 14–16, 18.

Leases

Business firms generally acquire *property rights* in long-term assets through purchases that are funded by internal sources or by externally borrowed funds. The accounting issues associated with the purchase of long-term assets were discussed in Chapter 7. Leasing is an alternative means of acquiring long-term assets to be used by business firms. Leases that are not in-substance purchases provide for the *right-to use* property by lessees in contrast to purchases that transfer property rights to the user of the long-term asset. Lease terms generally obligate lessees to make a series of payments over a future period of time. As such, they are similar to long-term debt. However, if a lease is correctly structured, it enables the lessee to engage in *off-balance sheet financing* (discussed in Chapter 10) because certain leases are not recorded as long-term debt on the balance sheet. Business managers frequently wish to use off-balance sheet financing in order to improve the financial position of their companies. However, as noted earlier in the text, efficient market research indicates that off-balance sheet financing techniques are incorporated into user decision models in determining the value of a company.

Leasing has become a popular method of acquiring property because it has the following advantages:

1. It offers 100 percent financing.
2. It offers protection against obsolescence.
3. It is frequently less costly than other forms of financing the cost of the acquisition of fixed assets.
4. If the lease qualifies as an operating lease, it does not add debt to the balance sheet.

Many long-term leases possess most of the attributes of long-term debt. That is, they create an obligation for payment under an agreement that is noncancelable. The adverse effects of debt are also present in leases in that an inability to pay may result in insolvency. Consequently, even though there are statutory limitations on lease obligations in bankruptcy proceedings, these limits do not have an impact on the probability of the adverse effects of non-payment on asset values and credit standing in the event of nonpayment of lease obligations. The statutory limitations involve only the evaluation of the amount owed after insolvency proceedings have commenced.

Management's choice between purchasing and leasing is a function of strategic investment and capital structure objectives, the comparative costs of purchases of assets versus leasing assets, the availability of tax benefits, and perceived financial reporting advantages. The tax benefit advantage is a major factor in leasing decisions. From a macroeconomic standpoint, the tax benefits of owning assets may be maximized by transferring them to the party in the higher marginal tax bracket. Firms with lower effective tax rates may engage in more leasing transactions than firms in higher tax brackets since the tax benefits are passed on to the lessor. El-Gazzar et al.[1] found evidence to support this theory; firms with lower effective tax rates were found to have a higher proportion of leased debt to total assets than did firms with higher effective tax rates.

Some lease agreements are in-substance long-term installment purchases of assets that have been structured to gain tax or other benefits to the parties. Since leases may take different forms, it is necessary to examine the underlying nature of the original transaction to determine the appropriate method of accounting for these agreements. That is, they should be reported in a manner that describes the intent of the lessor and lessee rather than the form of the agreement.

Over the years, two methods for allocating lease revenues and expenses to the periods covered by the lease agreement have emerged in accounting practice. One method, termed a *capital lease,* is based on the view that the lease constitutes an agreement through which the lessor finances the acquisition of assets by the lessee. Consequently, capital leases are in-substance installment purchases of assets. The other method is termed an *operating lease* and is based on the view that the lease constitutes a rental agreement between the lessor and lessee.

Two basic accounting questions are associated with leases: (1) What characteristics of the lease agreement require a lease to be reported as an in-substance long-term purchase of an asset? (2) Which characteristics allow the lease to be recorded as a long-term rental agreement?

The accounting profession first recognized the problems associated with leases in *Accounting Research Bulletin (ARB) No. 38.* This release recommended that if a lease agreement was in substance an installment purchase of prop-

---

[1] Shamir M, El-Gazzar, Steven Lilien, and Victor Pastena, "Accounting for Leases by Lessees," *Journal of Accounting and Economics* (October 1986), pp. 217–237.

erty, the lessee should record it as an asset and a liability. As with many of the ARBs, the recommendations of this pronouncement were largely ignored in practice, and the lease disclosure problem remained an important accounting issue.

Later, in 1964, the Accounting Principles Board issued *Opinion No. 5*, "Reporting of Leases in Financial Statements of Lessees." The provisions of *APB Opinion No. 5* (discussed later in the chapter) required leases that were in-substance purchases to be capitalized on the financial statements of lessees. This conclusion was no match for the countervailing forces against the capitalization of leases that were motivated by the ability to present a more favorable financial structure and patterns of income determination. As a result, relatively few leases were capitalized under the provisions of *APB Opinion No. 5*.

The APB also issued three other statements dealing with accounting for leases by lessors and lessees: *APB Opinion No. 7*, "Accounting for Leases in Financial Statement of Lessors"; *APB Opinion No. 27*, "Accounting for Lease Transactions by Manufacturers or Dealer Lessors"; and *APB Opinion No. 31*, "Disclosure of Lease Transactions by Lessees." Nevertheless, the overall result of these statements was that few leases were being capitalized and that lessor and lessee accounting for leases lacked symmetry. That is, these four *Opinions* allowed differences in recording and reporting the same lease by lessors and lessees.

In November 1976, the FASB issued *SFAS No. 13*, "Accounting for Leases," which superseded *APB Opinion Nos. 5, 7, 27*, and *31*. A major purpose of *SFAS No. 13* was to achieve a greater degree of symmetry of accounting between lessees and lessors. In an effort to accomplish this goal, the statement established standards of financial accounting and reporting for both lessees and lessors. As noted above, one of the problems associated with the four *Opinions* issued by the APB was that they allowed differences in recording and reporting the same lease by lessors and lessees. Adherence to *SFAS No. 13* substantially reduces (though does not completely eliminate) this possibility.

The conceptual foundation underlying *SFAS No. 13* is based on the view that "a lease that transfers substantially all of the benefits and risks inherent in the ownership of property should be accounted for as the acquisition of an asset and the incurrence of an obligation by the lessee and as a sale or financing lease by the lessor."[2] This viewpoint leads immediately to three basic conclusions: (1) The characteristics that indicate that substantially all the benefits and risks of ownership have been transferred to the lessee must be identified. These leases should be recorded as if they involved the purchase and sale of assets *(capital leases)*. (2) The same characteristics should apply to both the lessee and lessor; therefore, the inconsistency in accounting treatment that previously existed should be eliminated. (3) Those leases that do not meet the characteristics identified in (1) should be accounted for as rental agreements *(operating leases)*.

---

[2] Financial Accounting Standards Board, *Statement of Financial Accounting Standards No. 13*, "Accounting for Leases" (Stamford, CT: FASB, 1976), par. 60. This statement was later amended in 1980 to incorporate several FASB pronouncements that expanded on the principles outlined in the original pronouncement.

It has been suggested that the choice of structuring a lease as either an operating or a capital lease is not independent of the original nature of leasing as opposed to buying the asset. As indicated earlier, companies engaging in lease transactions may attempt to transfer the benefits of owning assets to the lease party in the higher tax bracket. In addition, Smith and Wakeman[3] identified eight nontax factors that make leasing more attractive than purchase:

1. The period of use is short relative to the overall life of the asset.
2. The lessor has a comparative advantage over the lessee in reselling the asset.
3. Corporate bond covenants of the lessee contain restrictions relating to financial policies the firm must follow (maximum debt to equity ratios).
4. Management compensation contracts contain provisions expressing compensation as a function of return on invested capital.
5. Lessee ownership is closely held so that risk reduction is important.
6. The lessor (manufacturer) has market power and can thus generate higher profits by leasing the asset (and controlling the terms of the lease) than by selling the asset.
7. The asset is not specialized to the firm.
8. The asset's value is not sensitive to use or abuse (the owner takes better care of the asset than does the lessee).

Obviously, some of these reasons are not subject to lessee choice but are motivated by the lessor and/or the type of asset involved. However, short periods of use and the resale factor favor the accounting treatment of a lease as operating, whereas the bond covenant and management compensation incentives favor a structuring of the lease as a capital lease. In addition, lessors may be more inclined to seek to structure leases as capital leases to allow earlier recognition of revenue and net income. That is, a lease that is reported as an in-substance sale by the lessor frequently allows for revenue recognition at the time of the original transaction in addition to interest revenue over the life of the lease.

Criteria for Classifying Leases

In *SFAS No. 13*, the FASB outlined specific criteria to help classify leases as either capital or operating leases. In the case of the lessee, if at its inception the lease meets any one of the following four criteria, the lease is classified as a capital lease; otherwise, it is classified as an operating lease:

1. The lease transfers ownership of the property to the lessee by the end of the lease term. This includes the fixed noncancelable term of the lease plus various specified renewal options and periods.

---

[3] Clifford Smith, Jr., and L. Macdonald Wakeman, "Determinants of Corporate Leasing Policy," *Journal of Finance* (July 1985), pp. 895–908.

2. The lease contains a bargain purchase option. This means that the stated purchase price is sufficiently lower than the expected fair market value of the property at the date the option becomes exercisable and that exercise of the option appears, at the inception of the lease, to be reasonably assured.

3. The lease term is equal to 75 percent or more of the estimated remaining economic life of the leased property, unless the beginning of the lease term falls within the last 25 percent of the total estimated economic life of the leased property.

4. At the beginning of the lease term, the present value of the minimum lease payments (the amounts of the payments the lessee is required to make excluding that portion of the payments representing executory costs such as insurance, maintenance, and taxes to be paid by the lessee) equals or exceeds 90 percent of the fair value of the leased property less any related investment tax credit retained by the lessor. (This criterion is also ignored when the lease term falls within the last 25 percent of the total estimated economic life of the leased property).[4]

The criteria for capitalization of leases are based on the assumption that a lease that transfers to the lessee the risks and benefits of using an asset should be recorded as an acquisition of a long-term asset. However, the criteria are seen as arbitrary because the FASB provided no explanation for choosing a lease term of 75 percent, or a fair value of 90 percent as the cutoff points. In addition, the criteria have been viewed as redundant and essentially based on the fourth criterion (see the article by Coughlan on the webpage for Chapter 12).

In the case of the lessor (except for leveraged leases, discussed later), if a lease meets any one of the preceding four criteria plus *both* of the following additional criteria, it is classified as a sales type or direct financing lease (a capital lease):

1. Collectibility of the minimum lease payments is reasonably predictable.

2. No important uncertainties surround the amount of unreimbursable costs yet to be incurred by the lessor under the lease.[5]

Accounting and Reporting by Lessees under *SFAS No. 13*

Historically, the primary concern in accounting for lease transactions by lessees has been the appropriate recognition of assets and liabilities on the lessee's balance sheet. This concern has overridden the corollary question of revenue recognition on the part of lessors. Therefore, the usual position of accountants has been that if the lease agreement was in substance an installment purchase, the "leased" property should be accounted for as an asset by the lessee, together with its corresponding liability. Failure to do so results in

[4] Ibid., par. 7.

[5] Ibid., par. 8.

an understatement of assets and liabilities on the balance sheet. Lease arrangements that are not considered installment purchases constitute *off-balance sheet financing* arrangements and should be properly disclosed in the footnotes to financial statements.

As early as 1962, the accounting research division of the AICPA recognized that there was little consistency in the disclosure of leases by lessees and that most companies were not capitalizing leases. It therefore authorized a research study on the reporting of leases by lessees. Among the recommendations of this study were the following:

> To the extent, then, that leases give rise to property rights, those rights and related liabilities should be measured and incorporated in the balance sheet.
>
> To the extent, then, that the rental payments represent a means of financing the acquisition of property rights which the lessee has in his possession and under his control, the transaction constitutes the acquisition of an asset with a related obligation to pay for it.
>
> To the extent, however, that the rental payments are for services such as maintenance, insurance, property taxes, heat, light, and elevator service, no asset has been acquired, and none should be recorded....
>
> The measurement of the asset value and the related liability involves two steps: (1) the determination of the part of the rentals which constitutes payment for property rights, and (2) the discounting of these rentals at an appropriate rate of interest.[6]

The crucial difference in the conclusion of this study and the existing practice was the emphasis on *property rights* (the right to use property), as opposed to the *rights in property*—ownership of equity interest in the property.

The APB considered the recommendations of this study and agreed that certain lease agreements should result in the lessee recording an asset and liability. The board concluded that the important criterion to be applied was whether the lease was in substance a purchase, that is, rights in property, rather than the existence of property rights. This conclusion indicated that the APB agreed that assets and liabilities should be recorded when the lease transaction was in substance an installment purchase in the same manner as other purchase arrangements. The APB, however, did not agree that the right to use property in exchange for future rental payments gives rise to the recording of assets and liabilities, since no equity in property is created.

In *Opinion No. 5*, the APB asserted that a noncancelable lease, or a lease cancelable only on the occurrence of some remote contingency, was probably in substance a purchase if either of the two following conditions exists:

1. The initial term is materially less than the useful life of the property, and the lessee has the option to renew the lease for the remaining useful life of the property at substantially less than the fair rental value.

2. The lessee has the right, during or at the expiration of the lease, to acquire the property at a price that at the inception of the lease appears

---

[6] John H. Myers, *Accounting Research Study No. 4*, "Reporting of Leases in Financial Statements" (New York: AICPA, 1962), pp. 4–5.

to be substantially less than the probable fair value of the property at the time or times of permitted acquisition by the lessee.[7]

The presence of either of these two conditions was seen as convincing evidence that the lessee was building equity in the property.

The APB went on to say that one or more of the following circumstances tend to indicate that a lease arrangement is in substance a purchase:

1. The property was acquired by the lessor to meet the special needs of the lessee and will probably be usable only for that purpose and only by the lessee.

2. The term of the lease corresponds substantially to the estimated useful life of the property, and the lessee is obligated to pay costs such as taxes, insurance, and maintenance, which are usually considered incidental to ownership.

3. The lessee has guaranteed the obligations of the lessor with respect to the leased property.

4. The lessee has treated the lease as a purchase for tax purposes.[8]

In addition, the lease might be considered a purchase if the lessor and lessee were related even in the absence of the preceding conditions and circumstances. In that case,

> *A lease should be recorded as a purchase if a primary purpose of ownership of the property by the lessor is to lease it to the lessee and (1) the lease payments are pledged to secure the debts of the lessor or (2) the lessee is able, directly or indirectly, to control or influence significantly the actions of the lessor with respect to the lease.[9]*

These conclusions caused controversy in the financial community because some individuals believed that they resulted in disincentives to leasing. Those holding this view maintained that noncapitalized leases provide the following benefits:

1. Improved accounting rate of return and debt ratios, thereby improving the financial picture of the company.

2. Better debt ratings.

3. Increased availability of capital.

On the other hand, the advocates of lease capitalization hold that these arguments are, in essence, attempts to deceive financial statement users. That is, a company should fully disclose the impact of all its financing and investing activities and not attempt to hide the economic substance of external transactions. (This issue is discussed in more detail later in the chapter.)

---

[7] *Accounting Principles Board Opinion No. 5,* "Reporting of Leases in Financial Statements of Lessees" (New York: AICPA, 1964), par. 10.

[8] Ibid., par. 11.

[9] Ibid., par. 12.

Capital Leases

The views expressed in *APB Opinion No. 5* concerning the capitalization of those leases that are "in-substance installment purchases" are significant from a historical point of view for two reasons. First, in *SFAS No. 13*, the FASB based its conclusion on the concept that a lease that "Transfers substantially all of the benefits and risks of the ownership of property should be accounted for as the acquisition of an asset and the incurrence of an obligation by the lessee, and as a sale or financing by the lessor." Second, to a great extent, the accounting provisions of *SFAS No. 13* applicable to lessees generally follow *APB Opinion No. 5*.

The provisions of *SFAS No. 13* require a lessee entering into a capital lease agreement to record both an asset and a liability at the lower of the following:

1. The sum of the present value of the *minimum lease payments* at the inception of the lease (see the following discussion).
2. The fair value of the leased property at the inception of the lease.

The rules for determining minimum lease payments were specifically set forth by the Board. In summary, those payments that the lessee is obligated to make or can be required to make with the exception of executory costs should be included. Consequently, the following items are subject to inclusion in the determination of the minimum lease payments:

1. Minimum rental payments over the life of the lease.
2. Payment called for by a bargain purchase option.
3. Any guarantee by the lessee of the residual value at the expiration of the lease term.
4. Any penalties that the lessee can be required to pay for failure to renew the lease.[10]

Once the minimum lease payments or fair market value is determined, the next step is to compute the present value of the lease payments. The interest rate to be used in this computation is generally the lessee's incremental borrowing rate. This is the rate the lessee would have been charged had he or she borrowed funds to buy the asset with repayments over the same term. If the lessee can readily determine the implicit interest rate used by the lessor and if that rate is lower than his or her incremental borrowing rate, then the lessee is to use the lessor's implicit interest rate for calculating the present value of the minimum lease payments. If the lessee does not know the lessor's interest rate (a likely situation), or if the lessor's implicit interest rate is higher than the lessee's incremental borrowing rate, the lessee and lessor will have different amortization schedules to recognize interest expense and interest revenue, respectively.

Capital lease assets and liabilities are to be separately identified in the lessee's balance sheet or in the accompanying footnotes. The liability should

---

[10] *SFAS No. 13*, op. cit., par. 5.

be classified as current and noncurrent on the same basis as all other liabilities, that is, according to when the obligation must be paid.

Unless the lease involves land, the asset recorded under a capital lease is to be amortized by one of two methods. Leases that meet either criterion 1 or 2 on pages 387–388 are to be amortized in a manner consistent with the lessee's normal depreciation policy for owned assets. That is, the asset's economic life to the lessee is used as the amortization period. Leases that do not meet criterion 1 or 2 but meet either criterion 3 or 4 are to be amortized in a manner consistent with the lessee's normal depreciation policy, using the lease term as the period of amortization. In conformity with *APB Opinion No. 21,* "Interest on Receivables and Payables," *SFAS No. 13* requires that each minimum payment under a capital lease be allocated between a reduction of the liability and interest expense. This allocation is to be made in such a manner that the interest expense reflects a constant interest rate on the outstanding balance of the obligation (i.e., the effective interest method). Thus, as with any loan payment schedule, each successive payment allocates a greater amount to the reduction of the principal and a lesser amount to interest expense. This procedure results in the loan being reflected on the balance sheet at the present value of the future cash flows discounted at the effective interest rate.

Disclosure Requirements for Capital Leases

SFAS No. 13 also requires the disclosure of additional information for capital leases. The following information must be disclosed in the lessee's financial statements or in the accompanying footnotes:

1. The gross amount of assets recorded under capital leases as of the date of each balance sheet presented by major classes according to nature or function.
2. Future minimum lease payments as of the date of the latest balance sheet presented, in the aggregate and for each of the five succeeding fiscal years.
3. The total minimum sublease rentals to be received in the future under noncancelable subleases as of the date of the latest balance sheet presented.
4. Total contingent rentals (rentals on which the amounts are dependent on some factor other than the passage of time) actually incurred for each period for which an income statement is presented.[11]

Operating Leases

All leases that do not meet any of the four criteria for capitalization are to be classified as operating leases by the lessee. Failure to meet any of the criteria means that the lease is simply a rental arrangement and, in essence, should be accounted for in the same manner as any other rental agreement, with certain exceptions. The rent payments made on an operating lease are normally charged to expense as they become payable over the life of the lease.

---

[11] Ibid., par. 16.

An exception is made if the rental schedule does not result in a straight-line basis of payment. In such cases, the rent expense is to be recognized on a straight line basis, unless the lessee can demonstrate that some other method gives a more systematic and rational periodic charge.

In *Opinion No. 31,* "Disclosure of Lease Commitments by Lessees," the APB observed that many different users of financial statements were dissatisfied with the information being provided about leases. Although many criticisms were being voiced over accounting for leases, the focus of this opinion was on the information that should be disclosed about noncapitalized leases.

The following disclosures are required for operating leases by lessees:

1. *For operating leases having initial or remaining noncancelable lease terms in excess of one year:*
   a. *Future minimum rental payments required as of the date of the latest balance sheet presented in the aggregate and for each of the five succeeding fiscal years.*
   b. *The total of minimum rentals to be received in the future under noncancelable subleases as of the date of the latest balance sheet presented.*

2. *For all operating leases, rental expense for each period for which an income statement is presented, with separate amounts for minimum rentals, contingent rentals and sublease rentals.*

3. *A general description of the lessee's leasing arrangements including, but not limited to the following:*
   a. *The basis on which contingent rental payments are determined.*
   b. *The existence and terms of renewals or purchase options and escalation clauses.*
   c. *Restrictions imposed by lease agreements, such as those concerning dividends, additional debt, and further leasing.*[12]

The FASB contends that the preceding accounting and disclosure requirements for capital and operating leases by lessees give users information useful in assessing a company's financial position and results of operations. The requirements also provide many specific and detailed rules, which should lead to greater consistency in the presentation of lease information.

Accounting and Reporting by Lessors

The major concern in accounting for leases in the financial statements of lessors is the appropriate allocation of revenues and expenses to the period covered by the lease. This concern contrasts with the lessee's focus on the balance sheet presentation of leases. As a general rule, lease agreements include a specific schedule of the date and amounts of payments the lessee is to make to the lessor. The fact that the lessor knows the date and amount of payment does not necessarily indicate that revenue should be recorded in the same period the cash is received. Accrual accounting frequently gives rise to

[12] Ibid., par. 16.

situations in which revenue is recognized in a period other than when payment is received, in order to measure the results of operations more fairly.

The nature of the lease and the rent schedule may make it necessary for the lessor to recognize revenue that is more or less than the payments received in a given period. Furthermore, the lessor must allocate the acquisition and operating costs of the leased property, together with any costs of negotiating and closing the lease, to the accounting periods receiving benefits in a systematic and rational manner consistent with the timing of revenue recognition. The latter point is consistent with the application of the matching principle in accounting, that is, determining the amount of revenue to be recognized in a period and then ascertaining which costs should be matched with that revenue.

The criterion for choosing between accounting for lease revenue by either the capital or operating methods historically was based on the accounting objective of fairly stating the lessor's periodic net income. Whichever method would best accomplish this objective should be followed. *SFAS No. 13* set forth specific criteria for determining the type of lease as well as the reporting and disclosure requirements for each type.

According to *SFAS No. 13*, if at its inception a lease agreement meets the lessor criteria for classification as a capital lease and if the two additional criteria for lessors contained on page 388 are met, the lessor is to classify the lease either as a *sales-type lease* or a *direct financing lease*, whichever is appropriate. All other leases, except leveraged leases (discussed in a separate section), are to be classified as operating leases.

Sales-Type Leases

A capital lease should be recorded as a *sales-type lease* by the lessor when there is a manufacturer's or dealer's profit (or loss). This implies that the leased asset is an item of inventory and the seller is earning a gross profit on the sale. Sales-type leases arise when manufacturers or dealers use leasing as a means of marketing their products.

Table 12.1 depicts the major steps involved in accounting for a sales-type lease by a lessor. The amount to be recorded as gross investment (a) is the total amount of the minimum lease payments over the life of the lease, plus any unguaranteed residual value accruing to the benefit of the lessor. Once the gross investment has been determined, it is to be discounted to its present value (b) using an interest rate that causes the aggregate present value at the beginning of the lease term to be equal to the fair value of the leased property. The rate thus determined is referred to as the interest rate implicit in the lease.

The difference between the gross investment (a) and the present value of the gross investment (b) is to be recorded as unearned interest income (c). The unearned interest income is to be amortized as interest income over the life of the lease using the interest method described in *APB Opinion No. 21*. Applying the interest method results in a constant rate of return on the net investment in the lease. The difference between the gross investment (a) and the unearned interest income (c) is the amount of net investment (d), which is equal to the present value of the gross investment (b). This amount is classified as a current or noncurrent asset on the lessor's balance sheet in the same manner as all other assets. Revenue from sales-type leases is thus reflected by two differ-

TABLE 12.1 *Accounting Steps for Sales-Type Leases*

Gross investment (a) *minus*	XX
Present value of gross investment (b) *equals*	XX
Unearned income (c)	XX
Gross investment (a) *minus*	XX
Unearned income (c) *equals*	XX
Net investment (d)	XX
Sales (e) *minus*	XX
Cost of goods sold (f) *equals*	XX
Profit or loss (g)	XX

two amounts: (1) the gross profit (or loss) on the sale in the year of the lease agreement and (2) interest on the remaining net investment over the life of the lease agreement.

For sales-type leases, because the critical event is the sale, the initial direct costs associated with obtaining the lease agreement are written off when the sale is recorded at the inception of the lease. These costs are disclosed as selling expenses on the income statement.

Direct Financing Leases
When no manufacturer's or dealer's profit (or loss) is recorded, a capital lease should be accounted for as a direct financing lease by the lessor. Under the direct financing method, the lessor is essentially viewed as a lending institution for revenue recognition purposes. If a lessor records a capital lease under the direct financing method, each payment must be allocated between interest revenue and investment recovery. In the early periods of the agreement, a significant portion of the payment will be recorded as interest, but each succeeding payment will result in a decreasing amount of interest revenue and an increasing amount of investment recovery due to the fact that the amount of the net investment is decreasing.

For direct financing leases, the FASB adopted the approach of requiring the recording of the total minimum lease payments as a receivable on the date of the transaction and treating the difference between that amount and the asset cost as unearned income. Subsequently, as each rental payment is received, the receivable is reduced by the full amount of the payment, and a portion of the unearned income is transferred to earned income.

Table 12.2 illustrates the accounting steps for direct financing leases. Gross investment (a) is determined in the same way as in sales-type leases, but unearned income (c) is computed as the difference between gross invest-

TABLE 12.2 *Accounting Steps for Direct Financing Leases*

Gross investment (a) *minus*	XX
Cost (b) *equals*	XX
Unearned income (c)	XX
Gross investment (a) *minus*	XX
Unearned income (c) *equals*	XX
Net investment (d)	XX
Unearned income (c) *minus*	XX
Initial direct costs (e) *equals*	XX
Unearned income to be amortized (f)	XX

ment and the cost (b) of the leased property. The difference between gross investment (a) and unearned income (c) is net investment (d), which is the same as (b) in the sales-type lease.

Initial direct costs (e) in financing leases are treated as an adjustment to the investment in the leased asset. Because financing the lease is the revenue-generating activity, *SFAS No. 91* requires that this cost be matched in proportion to the recognition of interest revenue. In each accounting period over the life of the lease, the unearned interest income (c) minus the indirect cost (e) is amortized by the effective interest method. Because the net investment is increased by an amount equal to the initial direct costs, a new effective interest rate must be determined in order to apply the interest method to the declining net investment balance. Under direct financing leases, the only revenue recorded by the lessor is disclosed as interest revenue over the lease term. Since initial direct costs increase the amount disclosed as the net investment, the interest income reported represents interest net of the write-off of the initial direct cost.

Disclosure Requirements for Sales-Type and Direct Financing Leases

In addition to the specific procedures required to account for sales-type and direct financing leases, the FASB established certain disclosure requirements. The following information is to be disclosed when leasing constitutes a significant part of the lessor's business activities in terms of revenue, net income, or assets:

1. *The components of the net investment in leases as of the date of each balance sheet presented:*
   a. *Future minimum lease payments to be received with deduction for any executory costs included in payments and allowance for uncollectibles.*
   b. *The unguaranteed residual value.*
   c. *Unearned income.*

2. *Future minimum lease payments to be received for each of the five succeeding fiscal years as of the date of the latest balance sheet presented.*

3. *The amount of unearned income included in income to offset initial direct costs charged against income for each period for which an income statement is presented. (For direct financing leases only.)*

4. *Total contingent rentals included in income for each period for which an income statement is presented.*

5. *A general description of the lessor's leasing arrangements.*[13]

The Board indicated that these disclosures by the lessor, as with the disclosures by lessees, would aid the users of financial statements in their assessment of the financial condition and results of operations of lessors. Note also that these requirements make the information disclosed by lessors and lessees more consistent.

Operating Leases

Those leases that do not meet the criteria for classification as sales-type or direct financing leases are accounted for as operating leases by the lessor. As a result, the leased property is reported with or near other property, plant, and equipment on the lessor's balance sheet and is depreciated following the lessor's normal depreciation policy.

Rental payments are recognized as revenue when they become receivables unless the payments are not made on a straight-line basis. In that case, as with the lessee, the recognition of revenue is to be on a straight-line basis. Initial direct costs associated with the lease are to be deferred and allocated over the lease term in the same manner as rental revenue (usually on a straight-line basis). However, if these costs are not material, they may be charged to expense as incurred.

If leasing is a significant part of the lessor's business activities, the following information is to be disclosed for operating leases:

1. *The cost and carrying amount, if different, of property on lease or held for leasing by major classes of property according to nature or function, and the amount of accumulated depreciation in total as of the date of the latest balance sheet presented.*

2. *Minimum future rentals on noncancelable leases as of the date of the latest balance sheet presented, in the aggregate and for each of the five succeeding fiscal years.*

3. *Total contingent rentals included in income for each period for which an income statement is presented.*

4. *A general description of the lessor's leasing arrangements.*[14]

[13] Ibid., par. 23.
[14] Ibid., par. 23.

Sales and Leasebacks

In a sale and leaseback transaction, the owner of property sells the property and then immediately leases it back from the buyer. These transactions frequently occur when companies have limited cash resources or when they result in tax advantages. Tax advantages occur because the sales price of the asset is usually its current market value and this amount generally exceeds the carrying value of the asset on the seller's books. Therefore, the tax deductible periodic rental payments are higher than the previously recorded amount of depreciation expense.

Most sales and leaseback transactions are treated as a single economic event according to the lease classification criteria previously discussed on pages 387–388. That is, the lessee-seller applies the *SFAS No. 13* criteria to the lease agreement and records the lease as either capital or operating, and the gain or on the sale is amortized over the lease term, whereas, if a loss occurs, it is recognized immediately. However, in certain circumstances where the lessee retains significantly smaller rights to use the property, a gain may be immediately recognized. In this case, it is argued that two distinctly different transactions have occurred because the rights to use have changed.

Leveraged Leases

A leveraged lease is defined as a special leasing arrangement involving three different parties: (1) the equity holder—the lessor; (2) the asset user—the lessee; and (3) the debtholder—a long-term financer.[15] A leveraged lease may be illustrated as follows:

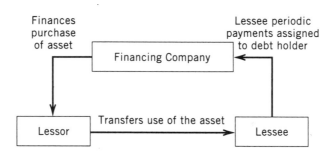

The major issue in accounting for leveraged leases is whether the transaction should be recorded as a single economic event or as separate transactions. All leveraged leases meet the criteria for direct financing leases. However, a leveraged lease might be accounted for as a lease with an additional debt transaction or as a single transaction. The FASB determined that a leveraged lease should be accounted for as a single transaction, and it provided the following guidelines.

---

[15] A fourth party may also be involved when the owner-lessor initially purchases the property from a manufacturer.

The lessee records the lease as a capital lease. The lessor records the lease as a direct financing lease, and the investment in capital leases is the net result of several factors:

1. *Rentals receivable, net of that portion of the rental applicable to principal and interest on the nonrecourse debt.*

2. *A receivable for the amount of the investment tax credit to be realized on the transaction.*

3. *The estimated residual value of the leased asset.*

4. *Unearned and deferred income consisting of the estimated pretax lease income (or loss), after deducting initial direct costs remaining to be allocated to income over the lease term and the investment tax credit remaining to be allocated to income over the lease term.[16]*

Once the original investment has been determined, the next step is to project cash receipts and disbursements over the term of the lease, and then compute a rate of return on the net investment in those years in which it is positive. Annual cash flow is the sum of gross lease rental and residual value (in the final year), less loan interest payments plus or minus income tax credits or charges, less loan principal payments, plus investment tax credit realized. The rate to be used in the computation is that "which when applied to the net investment in the years in which the net investment is positive will distribute the net income to those years."[17]

In a footnote to an illustration of the allocation of annual cash flow to investment and income, *SFAS No. 13* includes the following comment:

[The rate used for the allocation] is calculated by a trial and error process. The allocation is calculated based upon an initial estimate of the rate as a starting point. If the total thus allocated to income differs under the estimated rate from the net cash flow the estimated rate is increased or decreased, as appropriate, to devise a revised allocation. This process is repeated until a rate is selected which develops a total amount allocated to income that is precisely equal to the net cash flow. As a practical matter, a computer program is used to calculate [the allocation] under successive iterations until the correct rate is determined.[18]

This method of accounting for leveraged leases was considered to associate the income with the unrecovered balance of the earning asset in a manner consistent with the investor's view of the transaction. Income is recognized at a level rate on net investment in years in which the net investment is positive and is thus identified as "primary" earnings from the lease.

In recent years companies have tried to circumvent *SFAS No. 13.* These efforts are used mainly by lessees who do not wish to report increased liabilities or adversely affect their debt-equity ratios. However, unlike lessees,

---

[16] *FASB Statement No. 13*, op. cit., par. 43.

[17] Ibid., par. 44.

[18] Ibid., par. 123.

lessors do not wish to avoid recording lease transactions as capital leases. Consequently, the trick is to allow the lessee to record a lease as an operating lease while the lessor records it as either a sales-type or direct financing.

Accounting for Loan Origination Fees and Costs

In 1986, the FASB issued *SFAS No. 91*, "Accounting for Nonrefundable Fees and Costs Associated with Originating or Acquiring Loans and Initial Direct Costs of Leases." This release was issued in response to the controversy surrounding loan fee accounting and has a significant impact on lenders and investors in debt obligations, particularly banks, finance companies, mortgage companies, leasing companies, and insurance companies. The issue involves accounting for front-end, loan-origination fees that are charged for loans or lines of credit. These fees are not generally refundable even if the loan is repaid prior to maturity or if the borrower decides not to exercise the line of credit.

Previously, these origination fees were accounted for by one of the following methods.

Income Lenders generally view loan origination fees as compensation for the cost of evaluating the creditworthiness of borrowers. Consequently, many recognized these fees as income when the loan was made or the line of credit expired. In addition, loan origination costs are expensed as incurred. As a result, origination fees and the related expenses were regarded as separate activities from lending.

Discount on the loan Under this method, origination fees are considered a discount on the loan, and the amount of funds received by the borrower is equal to the principal amount less the origination fee. This method views origination fees and costs as an integral part of the lending process; consequently, these fees and costs are deferred and amortized over the life of the loan as a yield adjustment.

SFAS No. 91 requires the second method. That is, all loan fees and costs must be amortized as a yield adjustment using the interest method. In addition, the unamortized balance of the deferred loan fee/cost must be included as a part of the related loan balance.

SFAS No. 91 improves the comparability of the financial statements of lending and leasing companies; however, this improvement creates additional costs. Among these are the cost of changing accounting methods as well as reduced earning over the short term because of the deferral of origination fees. *SFAS No. 91* recommends restating prior years' earnings when preparing comparative statements to minimize the second cost.

Financial Analysis of Leases

In Chapter 10 we illustrated some procedures that a financial analyst might use to evaluate a company's long-term debt position and indicated that the use of operating leases can have an impact on this type of analysis. The use of leases can also have an impact on a company's liquidity and profitability ratios. That is, a company employing operating leases to acquire its assets will have a relatively better working capital position and relatively higher current ratio and return on assets ratio than it would have if it had recorded the transaction as a capital lease. To illustrate, Samson Company has the following summarized balance sheet on 12/31/01 prior to entering into a lease transaction:

Current assets	$ 50,000
Long-term assets	250,000
Total assets	$300,000
Current liabilities	$ 20,000
Long-term debt	130,000
Stockholders' equity	150,000
Total liabilities and stockholders' equity	$300,000

Assume that the company enters into a lease agreement on December 31, 2001, whereby it promises to pay a lessor $10,000 annually for the next five years for the use of an asset. If the lease is accounted for as an operating lease, neither the asset nor the liability is recorded on Samson's balance sheet, and its working capital, current ratio, and return on assets ratios for December 31, 2001 will appear as follows. (Assume the company earned net income of $25,000 during 2001.)

$$\text{Working capital} = \$50,000 - 20,000 = \$30,000$$
$$\text{Current ratio} = \$50,000/\$20,000 = 2.5{:}1$$
$$\text{Return on asset ratio} = \$25,000/\$300,000^{19} = 8.3\%$$

Alternatively, if the lease agreement is recorded as a capital lease, the discounted present value of both the asset and liability is recorded on the company's balance sheet. In addition, the lease liability is separated into its current and long-term components, and the company's December 31, 2001 balance sheet will now appear as follows (assuming a discount rate of 10 percent):

Current assets	$ 50,000
Long-term assets	250,000
Capital leases	37,908
Total assets	$337,908
Current liabilities	$ 20,000
Current lease obligation	9,091
Long-term debt	130,000
Long-term lease obligation	28,817
Stockholders' equity	150,000
Total liabilities and stockholders' equity	$337,908

---

[19] Assume the company's total assets remained constant throughout the year.

The company's working capital, current ratio, and return on assets ratios will now be computed:

$$\text{Working capital} = \$50,000 - 29,091 = \$20,909$$
$$\text{Current ratio} = \$50,000/\$29,091 = 1.7:1$$
$$\text{Return on asset ratio} = \$25,000/\$318,945[20] = 7.8\%$$

Using a similar analysis for the Kroll-O'Gara Company, footnote 9 extracted from its financial statements indicates that the company has entered into several operating lease agreements:

OPERATING LEASES

The Company leases office space and certain equipment and supplies under agreements with terms from one to ten years. The following is a schedule, by year, of approximate future minimum rental or usage payments required under operating leases that have initial or noncancelable lease terms in excess of one year as of December 31, 1998:

	TOTAL
1999	*$ 6,442,482*
2000	*5,503,777*
2001	*3,708,492*
2002	*2,843,961*
2003	*2,438,388*
Thereafter	*8,766,311*
	$29,703,411

Rental expense charged against current operations amounted to approximately $4,595,000, $4,115,000 and $6,430,000, for the years ended December 31, 1996, 1997 and 1998, respectively.

As a result, the company's working capital and current ratio illustrated in Chapter 7 and its return on assets ratios illustrated in Chapter 9 are all overstated when the company's lease financing policy is incorporated into the analysis. The extent of these overstatements can be estimated by discounting the 1999 obligation of $6,442,482 for one year to arrive at the current portion of its lease obligation and the remaining $23,260,929 to arrive at the long-term obligation. The present value of the sum of these two amounts is equal to the amount capitalized as a leased asset.[21]

---

[20] ($300,000 + 337,908)/2.

[21] In order to make this calculation, a discount factor must be assumed, and the annual amounts of the total of $8,766,311 payments due after 2003 must be estimated. If a discount rate of 12 percent and equal annual payments for 5 years after 2003 of $1,753,262 are assumed, the present value of the current obligation is $5,752,234, the present value of the long-term obligation is $13,445,073, and the property under leased assets is $19,197,307.

International Accounting Standards

IAS No. 17, "Accounting for Leases" deals with lease accounting issues. This standard is quite similar to U.S. GAAP as outlined in *SFAS No. 13.* One difference in terminology, however, is that in-substance purchases of assets are termed *financing leases* in *IAS No. 17* rather than capital leases. In addition, the terminology sales-type and direct financing are not used in conjunction with the reporting requirements specified for lessors. Nevertheless, the required accounting treatment for lessors is similar to that outlined in *SFAS No. 13.*

The comparative analysis of *IAS No. 17* and *SFAS No. 13* by the FASB staff indicated that companies following the international standard would tend to follow U.S. GAAP. However, concern was voiced that the guidance provided by *IAS No. 17* is broader and less specific than that provided in *SFAS No. 13.* For example, it was noted that *SFAS No. 13* requires that certain criteria be assessed in determining whether a lease qualifies as a capital lease, whereas *IAS No. 17* requires a judgmental determination based on the substance of the leasing transaction. The staff study also revealed that much of the reporting and disclosure guidance of *IAS No. 17* was presented as a suggestion or was optional, which makes it difficult to determine if these provisions must be followed, and if not, how accounting and reporting under *IAS No. 17* would differ from accounting and reporting under *SFAS No. 13.*[22]

Summary

SFAS No. 13 sets forth clear criteria for identifying leases that are to be capitalized by lessees and treated as sales-type or direct financing leases by lessors. The criteria were designed to achieve symmetry in accounting between lessees and lessors. The achievement of symmetry, however, will depend on such things as whether the lessee and lessor use comparable interest rates in calculating the present value of the minimum lease rentals, whether the two certainty criteria applied by the lessor are met, and whether current leasing techniques are continued or new off-balance sheet techniques are found. Thus, the statement may achieve its stated objective, or it may simply cause the demise of current leasing activities and the creation of some different approaches for securing and providing the use of the assets.

SFAS No. 13 significantly curtailed one of the most widely used methods of off-balance sheet financing. However, some corporate managers may still attempt to circumvent the requirements of *SFAS No. 13* and to generally understate long-term debt in an effort to improve the financial picture of their companies. A careful reading of the footnotes to the financial statements and management's comments may shed light on the possible existence of unrecorded liabilities.

---

[22] Financial Accounting Standards Board, *The IASC-U.S. Comparison Project: A Report on the Similarities and Differences between IASC Standards and U.S. GAAP,* Carrie Bloomer ed., 2nd ed. (Norwalk, CT: Financial Accounting Standards Board, 1999), pp. 187–205.

In the articles contained on the webpage for Chapter 12, several problems associated with *SFAS No. 13* are addressed.

Cases

• Case 12-1 Capital vs. Operating Leases

On January 2, 2001, two identical companies, Daggar Corp. and Bayshore Company, lease similar assets with the following characteristics:

1. The economic life is eight years.
2. The term of the lease is five years.
3. Lease payment of $20,000 per year is due at the beginning of each year beginning January 2, 2001.
4. The fair market value of the leased property is $96,000.
5. Each firm has an incremental borrowing rate of 8 percent and a tax rate of 40 percent.

Daggar capitalizes the lease, whereas Bayshore records the lease as an operating lease. Both firms depreciate assets by the straight-line method, and both treat the lease as an operating lease for federal income tax purposes.

Required:
a. Determine earnings (i) before interest and taxes and (ii) before taxes for both firms. Identify the source of any differences between the companies.
b. Compute any deferred taxes resulting from the lease for each firm in the first year of the lease.
c. Compute the effect of the lease on the 2001 reported cash from operations for both firms. Explain any differences.
d. Compute the effect of the lease on 2001 reported cash flows from investing activities for both firms. Explain any differences.
e. Compute the effect of the lease on 2001 reported cash flow from financing activities for both firms. Explain any differences.
f. Compute the effect of the lease on total 2001 cash flows for both companies. Explain any differences.
g. Give reasons why Daggar and Bayshore may have wanted to use different methods to report similar transactions.

• Case 12-2 Lessee and Lessor Accounting for Leases

On January 2, 2001, Grant Corporation leases an asset to Pippin Corporation under the following conditions:

1. Annual lease payments of $10,000 for 20 years.

2. At the end of the lease term, the asset is expected to have a value of $2,750.

3. The fair market value of the asset at the inception of the lease is $92,625.

4. The estimated economic life of the lease is 30 years.

5. Grant's implicit interest rate is 12 percent; Pippin's incremental borrowing rate is 10 percent.

6. The asset is recorded in Grant's inventory at $75,000 just prior to the lease transaction.

Required:

a. What type of lease is this for Pippin? Why?

b. Assume Grant capitalizes the lease. What financial statement accounts are affected by this lease, and what is the amount of each effect?

c. Assume Grant uses straight-line depreciation. What are the income statement, balance sheet, and statement of cash flow effects for 2001?

d. How should Grant record this lease? Why? Would any additional information be helpful in making this decision?

e. Assume that Grant treats the lease as a sales-type lease and the residual value is not guaranteed by Pippin. What financial statement accounts are affected on January 2, 2001?

f. Assume instead that Grant records the lease as an operating lease and uses straight-line depreciation. What are the income statement, balance sheet, and statement of cash flow effects on December 31, 2001?

• Case 12-3 Lessee Accounting for Leases

To meet the need for its expanding operations, Johnson Corporation obtained a charter for a separate corporation whose purpose was to buy a land site, build and equip a new building, and lease the entire facility to Johnson Corporation for a period of 20 years. Rental to be paid by Johnson was set at an amount sufficient to cover expenses of operation and debt service on the corporation's 20-year serial mortgage bonds. During the term of the lease, the lessee has the option of purchasing the facilities at a price that will retire the bonds and cover the costs of liquidation of the corporation. Alternatively, at the termination of the lease, the properties will be transferred to Johnson for a small consideration. At the exercise of the option or at the termination of the lease, the lessor corporation will be dissolved.

Required:

a. Under certain conditions, generally accepted accounting principles provide that leased property be included in the balance sheet of a lessee even though legal title remains with the lessor.

    i. Discuss the conditions that would require financial statement recognition of the asset and the related liability by a lessee.

    ii. Describe the accounting treatment that should be employed by a lessee under the conditions you described in your answer to part (i).

b. Unless the conditions referred to in (a) are present, generally accepted accounting principles do not embrace asset recognition of leases in the financial statements of lessees. However, some accountants do advocate recognition by lessees that have acquired *property rights*. Explain what is meant by property rights and discuss the conditions under which these rights might be considered to have been acquired by a lessee.

c. Under the circumstances described in the case, how should the Johnson Corporation account for the lease transactions in its financial statements? Explain your answer.

• Case 12-4 Application of SFAS No. 13

On January 1, 2001, Lani Company entered into a noncancelable lease for a machine to be used in its manufacturing operations. The lease transfers ownership of the machine to Lani by the end of the lease term. The term of the lease is eight years. The minimum lease payment made by Lani on January 1, 2001, was one of eight equal annual payments. At the inception of the lease, the criteria established for classification as a capital lease by the lessee were met.

Required:
a. What is the theoretical basis for the accounting standard that requires certain long-term leases to be capitalized by the lessee? Do not discuss the specific criteria for classifying a specific lease as a capital lease.
b. How should Lani account for this lease at its inception and determine the amount to be recorded?
c. What expenses related to this lease will Lani incur during the first year of the lease, and how will they be determined?
d. How should Lani report the lease transaction on its December 31, 2001, balance sheet?

• Case 12-5 Lease Classifications

Doherty Company leased equipment from Lambert Company. The classification of the lease makes a difference in the amounts reflected on the balance sheet and income statement of both Doherty Company and Lambert Company.

Required:
a. What criteria must be met by the lease in order that Doherty Company classify it as a capital lease?
b. What criteria must the lease meet in order that Lambert Company classify it as a sales-type or direct financing lease?
c. Contrast a sales-type lease with a direct financing lease.

• Case 12-6 Lease Accounting: Various Issues

On January 1, Borman Company, a lessee, entered into three noncancelable leases for brand-new equipment, Lease J, Lease K, and Lease L. None of the three leases transfers ownership of the equipment to Borman at the end of the lease term. For each of the three leases, the present value at the beginning of the lease term of the minimum lease payments, excluding that portion of the payments representing executory costs such as insurance, maintenance, and taxes to be paid by the lessor, including any profit thereon, is 75 percent of the excess of the fair value of the equipment to the lessor at the inception of the lease over any related investment tax credit retained by the lessor and expected to be realized by the lessor.

The following information is peculiar to each lease:

Lease J does not contain a bargain purchase option; the lease term is equal to 80 percent of the estimated economic life of the equipment.

Lease K contains a bargain purchase option; the lease term is equal to 50 percent of the estimated economic life of the equipment.

Lease L does not contain a bargain purchase option; the lease term is equal to 50 percent of the estimated economic life of the equipment.

Required:
a. How should Borman Company classify each of the three leases and why? Discuss the rationale for your answer.
b. What amount, if any, should Borman record as a liability at the inception of the lease for each of the three leases?
c. Assuming that the minimum lease payments are made on a straight-line basis, how should Borman record each minimum lease payment for each of the three leases?

• Case 12-7 Sales Type vs. Direct Financing Leases

1. Capital leases and operating leases are the two classifications of leases described in FASB pronouncements from the standpoint of the lessee.

Required:
a. Describe how a capital lease would be accounted for by the lessee both at the inception of the lease and during the first year of the lease, assuming the lease transfers ownership of the property to the lessee by the end of the lease.
b. Describe how an operating lease would be accounted for by the lessee both at the inception of the lease and during the first year of the lease, assuming the lessee makes equal monthly payments at the beginning of each month of the lease. Describe the change in accounting, if any, when rental payments are not made on a straightline basis. Do not discuss the criteria for distinguishing between capital leases and operating leases.

2. Sales-type leases and direct financing leases are two of the classifications of leases described in FASB pronouncements, from the standpoint of the lessor.

Required.
Compare and contrast a sales-type lease with a direct financing lease as follows:
a. Gross investment in the lease.

b.   Amortization of unearned interest income.
c.   Manufacturer's or dealer's profit.

Do not discuss the criteria for distinguishing between the leases described above and operating leases.

• Case 12-8 Lease Issues

Milton Corporation entered into a lease arrangement with James Leasing Corporation for a certain machine. James's primary business is leasing, and it is not a manufacturer or dealer. Milton will lease the machine for a period of three years, which is 50 percent of the machine's economic life. James will take possession of the machine at the end of the initial three-year lease and lease it to another, smaller company that does not need the most current version of the machine. Milton does not guarantee any residual value for the machine and will not purchase the machine at the end of the lease term.

Milton's incremental borrowing rate is 10 percent, and the implicit rate in the lease is $8\frac{1}{2}$ percent. Milton has no way of knowing the implicit rate used by James. Using either rate, the present value of the minimum lease payment is between 90 percent and 100 percent of the fair value of the machine at the date of the lease agreement.

James is reasonably certain that Milton will pay all lease payments, and because Milton has agreed to pay all executory costs, there are no important uncertainties regarding costs to be incurred by James.

Required:
a.   With respect to Milton (the lessee), answer the following.
    i.   What type of lease has been entered into? Explain the reason for your answer.
    ii.   How should Milton compute the appropriate amount to be recorded for the lease or asset acquired?
    iii.   What accounts will be created or affected by this transaction, and how will the lease or asset and other costs related to the transaction be matched with earnings?
    iv.   What disclosures must Milton make regarding this lease or asset?
b.   With respect to James (the lessor), answer the following.
    i.   What type of leasing arrangement has been entered into? Explain the reason for your answer.
    ii.   How should this lease be recorded by James, and how are the appropriate amounts determined?
    iii.   How should James determine the appropriate amount of earnings to be recognized from each lease payment?
    iv.   What disclosures must James make regarding this lease?

• Case 12-9 Lease Capitalization Criteria

On January 1, 2001, Von Company entered into two noncancelable leases for new machines to be used in its manufacturing operations. The first lease does not contain a bargain purchase option; the lease term is equal to 80 percent of the estimated economic life of the machine. The second lease contains a bargain purchase option; the lease term is equal to 50 percent of the estimated economic life of the machine.

Required:

a. What is the theoretical basis for requiring lessees to capitalize certain long-term leases? *Do not discuss the specific criteria for classifying a lease as a capital lease.*
b. How should a lessee account for a capital lease at its inception?
c. How should a lessee record each minimum lease payment for a capital lease?
d. How should Von classify each of the two leases? Why?

• Case 12-10 Leasing and Off-Balance Sheet Financing

SFAS No. 94 requires consolidation of majority-owned subsidiaries. The pronouncement was issued in response to criticisms of "off-balance sheet financing." For example, prior to *SFAS No. 94* companies with leasing subsidiaries did not have to consolidate them. Below are the unconsolidated balance sheets of Pesky Company and its wholly owned subsidiary, Smart Leasing Corp.

Pesky Company		Smart Leasing Corp	
Current Assets	$ 450,000	Current Assets	$ 5,000
Investment in Smart	8,500		
Plant Assets	980,000	Leased Assets	375,000
Total Assets	$1,438,500	Total Assets	$380,000
Current Liabilities	$ 290,000	Current Liabilities	$ 1,500
Long-Term Debt	300,000	Long-Term Debt	20,000
		Lease Obligations	350,000
Common Stock	520,000	Common Stock	40,000
Retained Earnings	328,500	Retained Earnings	(31,500)
Total Liabilities & SE	$1,438,500	Total Liabilities & SE	$380,000

Following is the consolidated balance sheet for Pesky Company and its subsidiary:

Current Assets	$ 455,000
Plant Assets	980,000
Leased Assets	375,000
Total Assets	$1,810,000
Current Liabilities	$ 291,500
Long-Term Debt	320,000
Lease Obligations	350,000
Common Stock	520,000
Retained Earnings	328,500
Total Liabilities & SE	$1,810,000

Required:
a. Describe the balance sheet effects of eliminating off-balance sheet financing by consolidating Smart Leasing.
b. What are the effects on important ratios, such as debt-to-equity, liquidity ratios, return on assets, and so on.
c. Do you believe Pesky should be allowed to report the leases "off-balance sheet?" What are the ethical considerations?

Room for Debate

• Issue 1

Under *SFAS No. 13*, leases that do not meet one of the four criteria for a capital lease are treated as operating leases.

Team Debate:
Team 1. Argue for the capitalization of leases that do not meet any of the *SFAS No. 13* criteria for a capital lease. Your argument should take into consideration the conceptual framework definitions of assets and liabilities.
Team 2. Argue against the capitalization of leases that do not meet any of the *SFAS No. 13* criteria for a capital lease. Your arguments should take into consideration the matching principle and full disclosure.

Recommended Additional Readings

El-Gazzar, Shamir M., Steven Lilien, and Victor Pastena. "Accounting for Leases by Lessees." *Journal of Accounting and Economics* (October 1986), pp. 217–237.

El-Gazzar, Shamir M., Steven Lilien, and Victor Pastena. "Use of Off-Balance Sheet Financing to Circumvent Financial Covenant Restrictions." *Journal of Accounting Auditing and Finance* (Spring 1989), pp. 217–231.

Hartman, Bart P., and Heibatollah Sami. "Impact of Accounting Treatment of Leasing Contracts on User Decision Making: A Field Experiment." *Advances in Accounting* (1989), pp. 23–35.

Imhoff, Eugene A., Robert C. Lipe, and David W. Wright. "Operating Leases: Impact of Constructive Capitalization." *Accounting Horizons* (March 1991), pp. 51–63.

Imhoff, Eugene A., and Jacob K. Thomas. "Economic Consequences of Accounting Standards: The Lease Disclosure Rule Change." *Journal of Accounting and Economics* (December 1988), pp. 277–310.

Lewis, Craig M., and James Schallheim. "Are Debt and Leases Substitutes?" *Journal of Financial and Quantitative Analysis* (December 1992), pp. 497–511.

Schiffman, Alan T. "Accounting for Leases: How to Work with the Complex Rules of FASB 13." *Practical Accountant* (July 1980), pp. 57–69.

Smith, Clifford, Jr., and L. MacDonald Wakeman. "Determinants of Corporate Leasing Policy." *Journal of Finance* (July 1985), pp. 895–908.

Bibliography

Abdel-Khalik, A. Rashad, Robert B. Thompson, and Robert E. Taylor. "The Impact of Reporting Leases Off the Balance Sheet on Bond Risk Premiums: Two Exploratory Studies." *Economic Consequences of Financial Accounting Standards.* FASB, 1978, pp. 103–155.

Anton, Hector R. "Leveraged Leases—A Marriage of Economics, Taxation and Accounting." In Alfred R. Roberts (ed.). *DR Scott Memorial Lectures in Accountancy,* Vol. 6. Columbia: University of Missouri Press, 1974, pp. 81–113.

Berger, Peter, and Kenneth Blomster. "Lease Accounting Issues." *The CPA Journal* (December 1988), pp. 76–78.

Bowman, Robert G. "The Debt Equivalence of Leases: An Empirical Investigation." *The Accounting Review* (April 1980), pp. 237–253.

Clay, Raymond J., and William W. Holder. "A Practitioner's Guide to Accounting for Leases." *Journal of Accountancy* (August 1977), pp. 61–68.

Collins, William A. "Accounting for Leases-Flowcharts." *Journal of Accountancy* (September 1978), pp. 60–63.

DeFliese, Philip L. "Accounting for Leases: A Broader Perspective." *Financial Executive* (July 1974), pp. 14–23.

Deming, John R. "An Analysis of FASB No. 13." *Financial Executive* (March 1978), pp. 46–51.

Dieter, Richard. "Is Lessee Accounting Working?" *The CPA Journal* (August 1979), pp. 13–19.

Elam, Rick. "Effect of Leases Data on the Predictive Ability of Financial Ratios." *The Accounting Review* (January 1975), pp. 25–43.

FASB Discussion Memorandum. *Accounting for Leases.* Stamford, CT: Financial Accounting Standards Board, 1974.

Finnerty, Joseph F., Rich N. Fitzsimmons, and Thomas W. Oliver. "Lease Capitalization and Systematic Risk." *The Accounting Review* (October 1980), pp. 731–739.

Grinnel, D. Jacque, and Richard F. Kochanek. "The New Accounting Standards for Leases." *The CPA Journal* (October 1977), pp. 15–21.

Hawkins, David. "Objectives, Not Rules for Lease Accounting." *Financial Executive* (November 1970), p. 34.

Hawkins, David F., and Mary M. Wehle. *Accounting for Leases.* New York: Financial Executives Research Foundation, 1973.

Hazard, Albert W., and Raymond E. Perry. "What FASB Statement No. 91 Means for Accountants and Auditors." *Journal of Accountancy* (February 1988), pp. 28, 30, 32–34, 36.

Ingberman, Monroe, Joshua Ronen, and George H. Sorter. "How Lease Capitalization under FASB Statement No. 13 Will Affect Financial Ratios." *Financial Analysts Journal* (January–February 1979), pp. 28–31.

Kuo, Horng-Ching. "Evaluation of Alternative Approaches to Lessee Accounting in the Context of Risk Assessment." *Review of Business and Economic Research* (Fall 1988), pp. 31–44.

Lander, Gerald, and Alan Reinstein. "Coping with SFAS No. 91." *The CPA Journal* (April 1988), pp. 73–75.

Ma, Ronald. "Accounting for Long-Term Leases." *Abacus* (June 1972), pp. 12–34.

Myers, John H. *Reporting of Leases in Financial Statements.* New York: American Institute of Certified Public Accounts, 1962.

Shachner, Leopold. "The New Accounting for Leases." *Financial Executive* (February 1978), pp. 40–47.

Swieringa, Robert J. "When Current Is Noncurrent and Vice Versa." *The Accounting Review* (January 1984), pp. 123–130.

Wyatt, Arthur R. "Leases Should Be Capitalized." *The CPA Journal* (September 1974), pp. 35–58.

Zises, Alvin. "The Pseudo-Lease—Trap and Time Bomb." *Financial Executive* (August 1973), pp. 20–25.

CHAPTER

13

Pensions and

Other

Postretirement

Benefits

For many years, employers have been concerned with providing for the retirement needs of their work force. This concern resulted in the adoption of pension plans on a massive scale after World War II. Generally, companies provide for pension benefits by making periodic payments to an outside third party, termed a funding agency. This agency then assumes responsibility for investing the pension funds and making periodic payments to the recipients of benefits.

The two most frequently encountered types of pension plans are defined contribution plans and defined benefit plans. In a *defined contribution plan,* the employer promises to contribute a certain amount into the plan each period. For example, the employer may promise to contribute 8 percent of the employee's salary each year. However, no promise is made concerning the ultimate benefits to be paid. Retirement benefits are determined by the return earned on the invested pension funds during the investment period.

In a *defined benefit plan,* the amount of pension benefits to be received in the future is defined by the terms of the plan. For example, the retirement plan of a company may promise that an employee retiring at age 65 will receive 2 percent of the average of the highest five years' salary for every year of service. An employee working for this company for 30 years will receive a pension for life equal to 60 percent of the average of his or her highest five salary years. When a company establishes a defined benefit pension plan, it is necessary to determine the annual contribution needed to meet the benefit requirements in the future.

Accounting for defined contribution plans is relatively straightforward. Since the risk for future benefits is borne by the employee, the employer's only expense is the annual promised contribution to the pension plan. This amount of contribution is the periodic pension expense. When a company adopts a defined contribution pension plan, the employer's financial statements should disclose the existence of the plan, the employee groups covered, the basis for determining contributions, and any significant matters affecting comparability from period to period (such as amendments increasing the annual contribution percentage).

On the other hand, accounting for defined benefit plans is much more complex. In these plans, the pension benefits to be received in the future are affected by uncertain variables such as turnover, mortality, length of employee service, compensation levels, and the earnings of the pension fund assets. In defined benefit plans, the risks are borne by employers because they must make large enough contributions to meet the pension benefits promised. As a result, the amount of periodic pension expense incurred may not be equal to the cash contributed to the plan.

Since the future pension benefits are affected by uncertain variables, employers hire actuaries to help determine the amount of periodic contributions necessary to satisfy future requirements. The actuary takes into consideration the future benefits promised and the characteristics of the employee group (such as age and sex). He or she then makes assumptions about such factors as employee turnover, future salary levels, and the earnings rate on the funds invested, and arrives at the present value of the expected benefits to be received in the future. The employer then determines the funding pattern necessary to satisfy the future obligation.

The employer's actuarial funding method may be either a cost approach or a benefit approach. A *cost approach* estimates the total retirement benefits to be paid in the future and then determines the equal annual payment that will be necessary to fund those benefits. The annual payment necessary is adjusted for the amount of interest assumed to be earned by funds contributed to the plan.

A *benefit approach* determines the amount of pension benefits earned by employee service to date and then estimates the present value of those benefits. Two benefit approaches may be used: (1) the accumulated benefits approach and (2) the benefits/years of service approach. The major difference between these two methods is that under the *accumulated benefits approach,* the annual pension cost and liability are based on existing salary levels, whereas under the *benefits/years of service approach* (also called the *projected unit credit method*) the annual pension cost and liability are based on the estimated final pay at retirement. The liability for pension benefits under the accumulated benefits approach is termed the *accumulated benefits obligation,* whereas the liability computed under the benefits/years of service approach is termed the *projected benefit obligation.*

Even though the actuarial funding approaches have been defined, accounting for the cost of pension plans has caused a great deal of controversy over the years, and several authoritative pronouncements have been issued. In the following sections we trace the evolution of pension accounting standards.

Historical Perspective

The rapidly increasing number of pension plans adopted by companies immediately following World War II caused accountants to question the then current treatment of accounting for pension costs. A major concern was the fact that many new pension plans gave employees credit for their years of service before adoption of the plan. The point at issue was the most appropriate treatment of costs associated with this past service. In *Accounting Research Bulletin No. 47*, "Accounting for Costs of Pension Plans," the Committee on Accounting Procedure of the AICPA stated its preference that costs based on current and future service be systematically accrued during the expected period of active service of the covered employees and that costs based on past services be charged off over some reasonable period. The allocation of past service cost was to be made on a systematic and rational basis and was not to cause distortion of the operating results in any one year.

Later, the APB observed that despite *ARB No. 47*, accounting for the cost of pension plans was inconsistent from year to year, both among companies and within a single company. Sometimes the cost charged to operations was equal to the amount paid into the fund during a given year; at other times no actual funding occurred. Moreover, the amortization of past service cost ranged up to 40 years.

Accounting inconsistencies and the growing importance of pension plan costs prompted the APB to authorize *Accounting Research Study No. 8*, "Accounting for the Cost of Pension Plans." This study was published in 1965, and, after careful examination of its recommendations, the APB issued *Opinion No. 8*, "Accounting for the Cost of Pension Plans" in 1966. Since the conclusions of the APB were generally similar to those of the research study, we shall review only the *Opinion* here.

APB Opinion No. 8

APB Opinion No. 8 identified the basic problems associated with accounting for the cost of pension plans as (1) measuring the total amount of costs associated with a pension plan, (2) allocating the total pension costs to the proper accounting periods, (3) providing the cash to fund the pension plan, and (4) disclosing the significant aspects of the pension plan on the financial statements.

The APB's conclusions concerning these questions were based to a large extent on two basic beliefs or assumptions. First, the Board believed that most companies will continue the benefits called for in a pension plan even if the plan is not fully funded on a year-to-year basis. Therefore, the cost should be recognized annually whether or not funded. Second, the Board adopted the view that the cost of all past service should be charged against income after the adoption or amendment of a plan and that no portion of such cost should be charged directly to retained earnings. In *APB Opinion No. 8*, several issues were addressed, and various terms were introduced. In the following paragraphs we examine these issues and terms as originally defined by the APB. However, it should be noted that subsequent pronouncements have modified these definitions and/or changed the terminology.

Normal Cost

The current expense provision of pension cost was termed normal cost in *APB Opinion No. 8*. This was the amount that was required to be expensed each year based on the current number of employees and the actuarial cost method being used. As noted earlier, the actuarial cost method must take into consideration such factors as employee turnover, mortality, and the treatment of actuarial gains and losses.

Past Service Cost

When a pension plan is adopted, the employees are usually given credit for previous years of service. These benefits were referred to as *past service cost* and should be charged as expense in current and future periods. Past service cost is calculated by determining the present value of the amount of future benefits accruing to the current employee group. Prior to the issuance of *APB Opinion No. 8*, many companies charged past service costs against retained earnings as prior period adjustments. This policy was based on the theory that the benefits of employee service had been obtained in prior periods; therefore, the cost associated with those benefits should be charged to previous periods. *APB Opinion No. 8* eliminated this treatment of past service costs, and later pronouncements concurred.

Prior Service Cost

Prior service costs were pension costs assigned to years prior to the date of a particular actuarial valuation. Prior service cost arose as a result of an amendment to the original pension agreement or changes in the actuarial assumptions of the pension plan. When the pension agreement is amended or the underlying assumptions change, it becomes necessary to recalculate the expected future benefits accruing to the current employee group. This calculation is similar to the determination of past service cost.

Actuarial Gains and Losses

The pension cost for any period is based on several assumptions. These assumptions frequently do not coincide with actual results. It is therefore necessary to make periodic adjustments so that actual experience is recognized in the recorded amount of pension expense. Under *APB Opinion No. 8*, periodic pension expense included normal cost and amortization of past and prior service costs. These costs were estimated based on actuarial assumptions. If in a subsequent period, the actuary would revise his or her assumptions based on new information, a periodic adjustment would be required. *APB Opinion No. 8* termed the deviations between the actuarial assumptions and subsequent changes in assumptions due to actual experience *actuarial gains and losses.*

The amount of any actuarial gain or loss was to be recognized over current and future periods by one of two acceptable methods:

1. *Spreading.* The net actuarial gains and losses were applied to current and future costs through an adjustment to either normal cost or past service cost each year.

2. ***Averaging.*** An average of the sum of previously expensed annual actuarial gains and losses and expected future actuarial gains and losses was applied to normal cost.

Basic Accounting Method

Before *APB Opinion No. 8* was issued, the Board could not completely agree on the most appropriate measure of cost to be included in each period. Consequently, it was decided that annual cost should be measured by an acceptable actuarial cost method, consistently applied, that produces an amount between a specified minimum and maximum. (In this context, an acceptable actuarial cost method should be rational and systematic and should be consistently applied so that the cost is reasonably stable from year to year.)

The minimum annual provision for pension cost could not be less than the total of

1. Normal cost (cost associated with the years after the date of adoption or amendment of the plan).
2. An amount equivalent to interest on any unfunded past or prior service cost.
3. If indicated, a provision for vested benefits (benefits that are not contingent on the employee continuing in the service of the company).

The maximum annual provision for pension cost could not be more than the total of

1. Normal cost.
2. Ten percent of the past service cost (until fully amortized).
3. Ten percent of the amounts of any increase or decrease in prior service cost arising from amendments of the plan (until fully amortized).
4. Interest equivalents on the difference between pension costs and amounts funded.

The Board's disagreement revolved around two differing viewpoints regarding the nature of pension cost. One view held that pensions are a means of promoting efficiency by (1) providing for the systematic retirement of older people and (2) fulfilling a social obligation expected of a business enterprise. Accordingly, pension costs are associated with the plan itself rather than specific employees, and the amount of pension expense is the amount that must be contributed annually in order to keep the plan in existence indefinitely. The alternative view was that pensions are a form of supplement benefit to the current employee group, so that the amount of pension expense in any period is related to specific employees. This view is rooted in labor economics and is based on the theory that employees contract for wages based on their marginal revenue product. Thus, a pension represents payments during retirement of deferred wages that were earned during each year of employment, and the amount of pension expense is established by determining the benefits expected to become payable to specific employees in the future. Under either view, annual pension expense would include normal costs. However, only the second view would include past and prior service costs in the determination of annual pension cost.

By requiring the specified minimum and maximum provisions, *APB Opinion No. 8* did narrow the range of practices previously employed in determining the annual provision of pension cost. However, it should be noted that these minimum and maximum provisions were arbitrarily determined. Thus, the only theoretical justification for their use was a higher degree of uniformity. In addition, the Board decided that only the difference between the amount charged against income and the amount funded should be shown in the balance sheet as accrued or prepaid pension cost. The unamortized and unfunded past and prior service cost was not considered to be a liability by the Board and was not required to be disclosed on the balance sheet. This decision caused a great deal of controversy and resulted in many debates among accountants over the proper amount of future pension costs to be disclosed on financial statements.

The Pension Liability Issue

In 1981, the FASB proposed a significant change in the method to account for pension cost. The board enumerated several reasons for this proposed change. First, the number of pension plans had grown enormously since the issuance of *APB Opinion No. 8* in 1966. A research study performed by Coopers & Lybrand indicated there were approximately 500,000 private pension plans in the United States in 1979, with total plan assets in excess of $320 billion. There had also been significant changes in laws, regulations, and economic factors affecting pension plans, not the least of which was double-digit inflation.

Second, the Board contended that pension information was inadequate, despite the increased disclosures mandated by *SFAS No. 36*. Finally, the flexibility of permitted actuarial methods resulted in a lack of comparability among reporting companies, according to some financial statement users.

The basic issues involved in the FASB's proposal entitled "Preliminary Views" were

1. What is the period over which the cost of pensions should be recognized? In 1981, pension costs could be recognized over a 30- to 40-year period, which is generally longer than the current work force is expected to continue working.

2. How should pension costs be spread among or allocated to the individual periods? The basic question here was whether the practice of choosing among a variety of acceptable costs and funding methods met the needs of financial statement users.

3. Should information about the status of pensions be included in the statement of changes in financial position? This was undoubtedly the most controversial of the issues considered.

The positions taken in the FASB's "Preliminary Views" would have required an employer sponsoring a defined benefit pension plan to recognize a net pension liability (or asset) on its balance sheet. This disclosure would have been composed of the following three components: *the pension benefit obligation* less *the plan's net assets available for benefits* plus or minus a *measurement valuation allowance.* This calculation of pension cost coincides with the view that pension expense should be recognized in the period in which the employees render their services. This view is consistent with the matching principle.

One organization that opposed the position of the "Preliminary View" was the AICPA task force on pension plans and pension costs. This group's opposition was expressed in several general areas:

1. The amounts involved did not meet the definition of assets or liabilities under *SFAC No. 3* (now *SFAC No. 6*).

2. A pension arrangement is essentially an executory contract that under existing generally accepted accounting principles is accounted for only as the covered services are performed.

3. Too much subjectivity is involved in determining the amount of the net pension liability—that is, the number is too "soft" to be reported in basic financial statements.

4. Finally, the FASB had not demonstrated the need to amend *APB Opinion No. 8* extensively.

Despite this opposition, the FASB remained steadfast in its determination to change previous pension accounting methods. Under the method originally advocated in "Preliminary Views," the pension benefit obligation would have comprised an accrual for benefits earned by the employees but not yet paid, including prior service credits granted when a plan is initiated or amended. The obligation would include both vested and nonvested benefits and would be measured based on estimates of future compensation levels.

The measure of the pension benefit obligation proposed was called the *actuarial present value of accumulated benefits with salary progression.* As a result, the proposed method would have required a forecast of salary growth for pension plans that define benefits in terms of an employee's future salary. Since most sponsors utilize financial pay plans, the salary growth assumption would result in pension benefit obligations larger than those previously being reported.

On the other hand, if plan assets exceeded the benefit obligation, a company would report a net pension asset on its balance sheet. The plan's investment assets available for benefits would be measured at fair value, consistent with *SFAS No. 35*, "Accounting and Reporting for Defined Benefit Pension Plans" (discussed later in this chapter).

The third component of the net pension liability was to be the measurement valuation allowance. This component was intended to reduce the volatility of the net pension liability inherent in the prediction of future events, such as changes in the pension benefit obligation and the plan assets, due to experience gains and losses or changes in actuarial assumptions.

Under "Preliminary Views," the amount of annual pension expense that an employer would recognize would have been the sum of

1. The increase in the pension benefit obligation attributable to employee service during the period (conceptually similar to "normal cost").

2. The increase in the pension benefit obligation attributable to the accrual of interest on the obligation (resulting from the fact that the obligation is the discounted present value of estimated future payments).

3. The increase in plan assets resulting from earnings on the assets at the assumed rate (reducing the periodic pension expense).

4. The amortization of the measurement valuation allowance, which may either increase or decrease the pension expense. Actuarial gains or losses would be included in the measurement of the valuation allowance.

SFAS No. 87

After deliberating the issues addressed in "Preliminary Views" for several years, the FASB reached a consensus in 1985 and issued *SFAS No. 87*, "Employers' Accounting for Pensions." This release was the product of compromises and resulted in several differences from the FASB's original position expressed in "Preliminary Views." *SFAS No. 87* maintained that pension information should be prepared on the accrual basis and retained three fundamental aspects of past pension accounting: (1) delaying recognition of certain events, (2) reporting net cost, and (3) offsetting assets and liabilities.

The delayed-recognition feature results in systematic recognition of changes in the pension obligation (such as plan amendments). It also results in changes in the values of assets set aside to meet those obligations.

The net cost feature results in reporting as a single amount the recognized consequences of the events that affected the pension plan. Three items are aggregated to arrive at this amount: (1) the annual cost of the benefits promised, (2) the interest cost resulting from the deferred payment of those benefits, and (3) the result of investing the pension assets.

Offsetting means that the value of the assets contributed to a pension plan and the liabilities recognized as pension cost in previous periods are disclosed as a single net amount in the employer's financial statements.

The members of the FASB expressed the view that understandability, comparability, and the usefulness of pension information would be improved by narrowing the range of methods available for allocating the cost of an employee's pension to individual periods of service. The Board also stated that the pension plan's benefit formula provides the most relevant and reliable indicator of how pension costs and pension benefits are incurred. Therefore, *SFAS No. 87* required three changes in previous pension accounting:

1. A standardized method of measuring net pension cost. The Board indicated that requiring all companies with defined benefit plans to measure net period pension cost, taking into consideration the plan formula and the service period, would improve comparability and understandability.

2. Immediate recognition of a pension liability when the accumulated benefit obligation exceeds the fair value of the pension assets. The accumulated benefit obligation is calculated using present salary levels. Because salary levels generally rise, the amount of the unfunded accumulated benefit obligation represents a conservative floor for the present obligation for future benefits already earned by the employees.

3. Expanded disclosures intended to provide more complete and current information than can be practically incorporated into the financial statements at this time.

Pension Cost

Under the provisions of *SFAS No. 87,* the several components of net pension cost reflect different aspects of the benefits earned by employees and the method of financing those benefits by the employer. The net pension cost recognized by an employer sponsoring a defined benefit pension plan must include the following components:

1. Service cost
2. Interest cost
3. Return on plan assets
4. Amortization of unrecognized prior service cost
5. Amortization of gains and losses
6. Amortization of the unrecognized net obligation or unrecognized net asset at the date of the initial application of *SFAS No. 87* (the transition amount)

The *service cost* component is determined as the actuarial present value of the benefits attributed by the pension formula to employee service for that period. This requirement means that one of the benefit approaches discussed earlier must be used as the basis for assigning pension cost to an accounting period. It also means that the benefits/years of service approach should be used to calculate pension cost for all plans that use this benefit approach in calculating earned pension benefits. The FASB's position is that the terms of the agreement should form the basis for recording the expense and obligation, and the plan's benefit formula is the best measure of the amount of cost incurred each period. The discount rate to be used in calculating service cost is the rate at which the pension benefits could be settled, such as by purchasing annuity contracts from an insurance company. This rate is termed the *settlement-basis discount rate.*

The *interest cost* component is determined as the increase in the projected benefit obligation due to the passage of time. Recall that the pension liability is calculated on a discounted basis and accrues interest each year. The interest cost component is determined by accruing interest on the previous year's pension liability at the settlement-basis discount rate.

The *return on plan assets* component is the difference between the fair value of these assets from the beginning to the end of the period, adjusted for contributions, benefits, and payments. That is, the interest and dividends earned on the funds actually contributed to the pension fund combined with changes in the market value of invested assets will reduce the amount of net pension cost for the period. *SFAS No. 87* allows the use of either the actual return or the expected return on plan assets when calculating this component of pension expense.

Prior service cost is the total cost of retroactive benefits at the date the pension plan is initiated or amended. Prior service cost is assigned to the expected remaining service period of each employee expected to receive benefits. (As a practical matter, the FASB allows for a simplified method of assigning this cost to future periods; the company may assign this cost on a straight-line basis over the average remaining service life of its active employees.)

Gains and losses include *actuarial* gains and losses or *experience* gains and losses. Actuarial gains and losses occur when the actuary changes assumptions, resulting in a change in the projected benefit obligation. For example, if the actuary increases the discount rate, the beginning projected benefit obligation is reduced. This means that prior expense recognition for interest, service cost, and prior service cost was overstated. Thus, the amount of the change in the beginning projected benefit obligation is an actuarial gain. Experience gains and losses occur when net pension cost includes the expected, rather than the actual, return on plan assets. The expected return presumes that plan assets will grow to a particular amount by the end of the period. If, for example, the actual return is greater than expected, future pension costs will be defrayed further and an experience gain takes place. *SFAS No. 87* contains a minimum requirement for the recognition of these gains and losses. At a minimum, the amount of gain or loss to be amortized in a given period is the amount by which the cumulative unamortized gains and losses exceed what the pronouncement termed the *corridor.* The corridor is defined as 10 percent of the greater of the projected benefit obligation or market value of the plan assets. The excess, if any, is divided by the average remaining service period of employees expected to receive benefits. The rationale for using the corridor approach is that typically these gains and losses are random errors and should have an expected value of zero. That is, over time, actuarial gains and losses should offset each other. Only extreme values should be recognized. The corridor procedure is similar to statistical procedures that are designed to identify outliers.

SFAS No. 87 requires significant changes in pension accounting from what was previously required in *APB Opinion No. 8.* As a result, the Board decided to allow for a relatively long transition period. Most companies were not required to follow the provisions of *SFAS No. 87* until the 1987 calendar year. In addition, the minimum liability provision (discussed in the next section) was not required to be reported until calendar year 1989. Since these changes were so significant, an *unrecognized net obligation* or *unrecognized net asset* frequently resulted when changing to the new reporting requirements. Therefore, the provisions of *SFAS No. 87* required companies to determine, on the date the provisions of this statement were first applied, the amount of (1) the projected benefit obligation and (2) the fair value of the plan assets. This resulted in either an unrecognized net obligation or an unrecognized net asset. This amount, termed the *transition amount,* was to be amortized on a straight-line basis over the average remaining service period of employees expecting to receive benefits.

Minimum Liability Recognition

Unlike other expenses that are recognized in the income statement, periodic pension cost is not tied to changes in balance sheet accounts. *SFAS No. 87* requires amortization of prior service cost, gains and losses, and the transition amount, but the unamortized amounts for these items are not recorded. Hence, the *funded status* of the plan (the difference between the projected benefit obligation and the fair value of plan assets) is not recognized in the accounting records. Recall that the FASB's original position on this issue, expressed in "Preliminary Views," was that a liability exists when the projected benefit obligation exceeds the plan assets (i.e., the plan is underfunded) or that an asset exists when the reverse is true. Since agreement on this issue could not be reached, the Board developed a compromise position that requires recognition of a liability, termed *the minimum liability,* when the accumulated benefit obligation exceeds the fair value of the plan assets. Thus, even though future salary levels are used to calculate pension expense, the liability reported on the balance sheet need only take into consideration present salary levels. The result is that the balance sheet and income statements are not articulated, a condition that is contrary to the Conceptual Framework.

The portion of the underfunded pension obligation that is not already recognized in the accounting records occurs because the company has unamortized prior service cost or unamortized gains and losses. Because the minimum liability is based on current salary levels and is therefore likely to be less than the underfunded projected benefit obligation, total unamortized prior service cost and unamortized gains and losses are likely to exceed the amount needed to increase the pension liability to the minimum required. *SFAS No. 87* requires that when an additional liability is recognized to meet the minimum liability requirement, the offsetting debit is to be allocated first to an intangible asset for the unamortized prior service cost. The remainder, if any, is due to unamortized net losses and is reported as an element of other comprehensive income. The minimum liability is reassessed at the end of each accounting period, and necessary adjustments are made directly to the intangible asset or stockholders' equity.

Disclosures

SFAS No. 87 requires employers to disclose information beyond that previously required. Perhaps the most significant of these added disclosures are the components of net pension cost and the funding status of the plan. Specifically, employers sponsoring defined benefit plans must disclose the following information:

1. A description of the plan, including employee groups covered, type of benefit formula, funding policy, types of assets held, significant nonbenefit liabilities if any, and the nature and effect of significant matters affecting comparability of information for all periods presented.

2. The amount of net periodic pension cost for the period showing separately the service cost component, the interest cost component, the actual return on assets for the period, and the net total of other components.

3. A schedule reconciling the funded status of the plan with amounts reported in the employer's statement of financial position, showing separately
   a. The fair value of plan assets.
   b. The projected benefit obligation identifying the accumulated benefit obligation and the vested benefit obligation.
   c. The amount of unrecognized prior service cost.
   d. The amount of unrecognized prior net gain or loss.
   e. The amount of any remaining unrecognized net obligation or net asset existing at the date of initial application of *SFAS No. 87*.
   f. The amount of any additional liability recognized.
   g. The amount of net pension asset or liability recognized in the statement of financial positions (this is the net result of combining the preceding six items).
   h. The weighted average assumed discount rate and the weighted average expected long-term rate of return on plan assets.

The annual pension cost reported by corporations under *SFAS No. 87* will usually be different from the cost previously disclosed under the provisions of *APB Opinion No. 8*. The magnitude of these differences depends on such factors as the pension plan's benefit formula, employees' remaining service periods, investment returns, and prior accounting and funding policies. Companies that have underfunded pension plans with a relatively short future employee service period may be required to report significantly higher pension expense.

In releasing *SFAS No. 87*, the Board stated that this pronouncement was a continuation of its evolutionary search for more meaningful and more useful pension accounting information. The Board also stated that while it believes that the conclusions it reached are a worthwhile and significant step in that direction, these conclusions are not likely to be the final step in the evolution. Table 13.1 compares the evolution of these standards from *APB Opinion No. 8* through "Preliminary Views" to *SFAS No. 87*.

SFAS No. 87—Theoretical Issues

The issuance of *SFAS No. 87* may have created as many issues as it resolved. Criticism of the pronouncement has been directed at the projected benefits approach, use of the settlement rate to discount projected benefits, allowing alternative measures of return, and the minimum liability requirement.

TABLE 13.1 *Comparison of Previous Accounting Practice With FASB's "Preliminary Views" and* Statement of Financial *Accounting Standards No. 87*

Issue	Previous Accounting	Preliminary Views	SFAS No. 87
Recognition of a liability.	A liability recognized equal to accumulated expense based on an acceptable actuarial method less amounts funded.	Recognizes a net pension liability (or asset) based on services rendered by the employees, using an actuarial method the FASB concludes is most appropriate for accounting purposes.	Recognition of a liability if periodic cost exceeds contributions to the plan. Additional "minimum liability" recognized when the accumulated benefit obligation exceeds the fair value of the plan assets.
Recognition of plan assets as employer's assets.	Not recognized as employer's assets.	Recognizes plan assets as an offset against the pension obligation. Could result in a net asset.	Not recognized as employer's assets.
Measurement of pension liability and expense.	Based on a number of actuarial cost methods that achieve systematic and rational allocation of pension cost.	Proposes one method as most appropriate for accounting purposes; the projected-unit-credit method for final pay and career-average pay plans, and the accumulated benefits method for flat benefit plans.	Based on the terms of the pension agreement. Uses the accumulated benefits approach for plans based on existing salary levels and the benefits per years of service approach for plans based on future salary levels.
Accounting for changes in the plan, including a new one that gives credit for past service.	No immediate recognition of an accounting liability.	Recognizes the increased pension benefit obligation (liability) and records an intangible asset representing expected future economic benefits.	No immediate recognition of the liability.

(continues)

425

TABLE 13.1. (*Continued*)

Issue	Previous Accounting	Preliminary Views	*SFAS No. 87*
	Pension expense and the related actuarial liabilities are recognized over a number of future periods.	Pension expense would include amortization of prior service cost over the average remaining service period of active plan participants.	Recognizes increased pension expense over the expected remaining service period of employees expected to receive benefit.
Accounting for actuarial gains or losses (measurement changes).	Included in pension expense in a systematic and rational manner (i.e., spread or averaged over a period of 10 to 20 years).	Establishes a measurement valuation allowance consisting of realized and unrealized experience gains and losses and effects of changes in actuarial assumptions, which would be a component of the net pension liability.	No immediate recognition of the liability.
		Recognizes measurement changes prospectively through amortization of the measurement valuation allowance based on the average remaining service period of active plan participants.	Corridor approach adopted. Ten percent of the excess of any annual gain or loss in excess of the greater of the projected benefit obligation or the market value of the plan assets is recognized over the average service period of employees expected to receive benefits.

Source: Adapted from Coopers & Lybrand, *Executive Alert Newsletter*, Dec.–Jan. 1985, p. 14.

Projected Benefits Approach

When the benefit formula utilizes future salary levels, *SFAS No. 87* requires that service cost and the employer's present obligation for future benefits earned to date be measured utilizing projected future salary levels. This measurement can be defended on the basis that employees contract for retirement benefits. These benefits are earned while the employee works; thus, matching would dictate that they be an accrued expense. Also, the projected benefit obligation represents a present obligation to pay the future benefits. Thus, the projected benefit obligation qualifies as a liability under *SFAS No. 6*.

Critics contend that the projected obligation implies that the benefits earned to date will be paid. This is true only for those employees who have vested benefits or who will remain employees until the benefits do vest. Some feel that only vested benefits should be considered a present liability because vested benefits are the only portion that the company has a present legal obligation to pay if the plan were terminated. Others feel that the accumulated benefits approach provides the more appropriate measure because it is a conservative estimate of the present obligation for future benefits and would be the amount that the employer would set aside if the plan were terminated and the employer wanted to provide for all employees who were vested and might vest in the future. Moreover, the accumulated benefits approach does not require subjective projections of future salary levels. At the other extreme, some believe that the projected benefits approach understates the present liability because it does not take into consideration projected years of service.

The Settlement Rate

SFAS No. 87 requires that the actuarially determined projected benefit obligation be calculated utilizing a discount rate at which the plan could be effectively settled. For example, the rate at which the company could currently obtain an annuity contract to provide the projected future benefits would be an appropriate settlement rate. The FASB felt that the actuary's rate should not be affected by the return expected on funded assets. The projected benefit obligation is a liability. The discount rate selected is chosen to measure the liability and has nothing to do with how the assets that are set aside to satisfy that liability are invested.

Opponents argue that the settlement rate is a short-term current rate and that the pension obligation is not going to be settled currently; rather, it is a long-term phenomenon. The settlement rates fluctuate from period to period, resulting in volatile measures of the projected benefit obligation, service cost, and interest. Some agree with the FASB that the discount rate used need not be the expected return on plan assets but argue that it should be based on a more long-run measure of typical pension fund asset returns over time. Others contend that the fund provides the means by which the company will settle the pension obligation, and thus the return on the plan assets is the relevant rate at which to discount projected benefits.

Return on Plan Assets

SFAS No. 87 requires that net pension cost include the actual return or that the actual return be adjusted to the expected return. Allowing these two alternatives represents a compromise. The FASB favors including the actual return. For the most part, the actual return is a realized return. Furthermore, recognition of the actual return is consistent with the comprehensive income concept. Nevertheless, the Board's preference for measuring the return component was criticized because it would produce volatile measures of pension expense from period to period. The FASB conceded by allowing the expected return to be included, instead utilizing the expected rate of return on plan assets applied to the market-related asset value of the plan assets. The market-related asset value is a long-term measure of asset value. Hence, the expected return should allow the smoothing of net periodic pension cost. At the same time, allowing the minimum amortization of actuarial and experience gains and losses should provide further assurance of a smoother, less volatile periodic pension expense.

Reporting the Minimum Liability

One aim of *SFAS No. 87* was to report the net pension obligation on the balance sheet. However, for many companies, reporting the net obligation measured using projected benefits would have a dramatic effect on total liabilities and debt-to-equity ratios. Moreover, some contended that the projected benefit obligation overstates the pension liability because it does not represent the legal liability or the most likely settlement amount. The Board acquiesced to these concerns and opted for a minimum liability measurement based on the more conservative accumulated benefit obligation.

If the projected benefit obligation provides the more appropriate measure, then reporting the minimum liability understates liabilities. Furthermore, it is inconsistent with the measurement of periodic pension expense, which is measured utilizing projected benefits. Such an inconsistency perpetuates the criticism regarding pension reporting under *APB Opinion No. 8* that pension accounting is contrary to the fundamental notion that the financial statements should be articulated. Empirical research has demonstrated that pension obligations are considered liabilities,[1] but to date there is no conclusive evidence that the market perceives one method of measuring the obligation or pension expense to be better than another.

Accounting for the Pension Fund

Until 1980, accounting practice often relied on the actuary's funding and cash flow considerations for measuring pension costs and accumulated pension benefits. At that time, *APB Board Opinion No. 8* stated that accounting for pension expense and related liabilities was separate and distinct from actuarial costing for funding purposes. However, according to *SFAS No. 35,* "Accounting and Reporting by Defined Benefit Pension Plans," the status of plans for financial reporting purposes is to be determined by actuarial

---

[1] See, for example, W. Landsman, "An Empirical Investigation of Pension Fund Property Rights," *The Accounting Review* (October 1986), pp. 662–691, and D. S. Dhaliwal, "Measurement of Financial Leverage in the Presence of Unfunded Pension Obligations," *The Accounting Review* (October 1986), pp. 651–661.

methodology designed not for funding purposes but for financial reporting purposes.

Neither the FASB nor its predecessors had issued authoritative accounting standards specifically applicable to pension plans. Therefore, the financial reporting by those plans varied widely. *SFAS No. 35* establishes accounting and reporting standards designed to correct this shortcoming.

The primary objective of *SFAS No. 35* is to provide financial information that is useful in assessing a pension plan's current and future ability to pay benefits when due. In attempting to accomplish this objective, *SFAS No. 35* requires that pension plan financial statements include four basic categories of information:

1. Net assets available for benefits.
2. Changes in net assets during the reporting period.
3. The actuarial present value of accumulated plan benefits.
4. The significant effects of factors such as plan amendments and changes in actuarial assumptions on the year-to-year change in the actuarial present value of accumulated plan benefits.

Information about net assets must be available for plan benefits at the end of the plan year and must be prepared using the accrual basis of accounting.

The statement also sets standards for information regarding participants' accumulated plan benefits. Accumulated plan benefits are defined as those future benefit payments attributable under the plan's provisions to employees' service rendered to date. Information about accumulated benefits may be presented at either the beginning or the end of the plan year. Accumulated plan benefits are to be measured at their actuarial present value, based primarily on history of pay and service and other appropriate factors.

The Employee Retirement Income Security Act

In 1974, Congress passed the Employee Retirement Income Security Act (ERISA), also known as the Pension Reform Act of 1974. The basic goals of this legislation were to create standards for the operation of pension funds and to correct abuses in the handling of pension funds.

ERISA establishes guidelines for employee participation in pension plans, vesting provisions, minimum funding requirements, financial statement disclosure of pension plans, and the administration of the pension plan. Shortly thereafter, the FASB undertook a study of the impact of ERISA on *APB Opinion No. 8*. The conclusions of this study are contained in *FASB Interpretation No. 3*. In essence, *FASB Interpretation No. 3* states that ERISA is concerned with pension funding requirements and that the provisions of *APB Opinion No. 8* were not affected by ERISA. The provisions of *SFAS No. 87* are also not affected by ERISA. The APB's and FASB's pronouncements are concerned with periodic expense and liability recognition, whereas the provisions of ERISA are concerned mainly with the funding policies of pension plans.

Other Postretirement Benefits

In December 1990, the FASB issued *SFAS No. 106*, "Employers' Accounting for Postretirement Benefits Other Than Pensions."[2] This pronouncement deals with the accounting for all benefits, other than pension benefits, offered to retired employees, commonly referred to as other postretirement benefits (OPEB). Although its provisions apply to a wide variety of postretirement benefits, such as tuition assistance, day care, legal services, and housing subsidies, the most significant OPEBs are retiree health care benefits and life insurance. Based on the notion that management promises OPEBs in exchange for current services, the Board felt that OPEBs are similar to defined benefit pension plans and as such deserve similar treatment. Consequently, *SFAS No. 106* requires that the cost of OPEBs be accrued over the working lives of the employees expected to receive them. However, due to the controversial nature surrounding measurement and reporting issues related to the employer's obligation for OPEBs, the Board decided not to require minimum liability balance sheet disclosure.

Although on the surface OPEBs are similar to defined benefit pension plans, they have characteristics that necessitate different accounting considerations and that have been the source of considerable controversy:

1. Defined benefit pension payments are determined by formula, whereas the future cash outlays for OPEBs depend on the amount of services, such as medical care, that the employees will eventually receive. Unlike pension plan payments, there is no "cap" on the amount of benefits to be paid to participants. Hence, the future cash flows associated with OPEBs are much more difficult to predict.

2. Unlike defined pension benefits, employees do not accumulate additional OPEB benefits with each year of service.

3. OPEBs do not vest. That is, employees who leave have no further claim to future benefits. Employees have no statutory right to vested health care benefits. Defined benefits are covered by stringent minimum vesting, participation, and funding standards, and are insured by the Pension Benefit Guaranty Corporation under ERISA. Health and other OPEBs are explicitly excluded from ERISA.

SFAS No. 106

SFAS No. 106 requires that the periodic postretirement benefit expenses comprise the same six components as pension expense. Nevertheless, there are measurement differences owing to the foregoing differences between the characteristics of OPEBs and those of defined benefit pension plans. The determination of the return on assets and the amortization of gains and losses for OPEBs and defined benefit pension plans are the same. We will concentrate on those components that are treated differently.

---

[2] Financial Accounting Standards Board, *Statement of Financial Accounting Standards No. 106*, "Employers' Accounting for Postretirement Benefits Other Than Pensions" (Stamford, CT: FASB, 1990).

Service Cost

The service cost component of net periodic pension cost is that portion of the ending projected benefit obligation attributable to employee service during the current period. The basis for computing OPEB service cost is the expected postretirement benefit obligation (EPBO), which is defined as the actuarial present value of the total benefits expected to be paid assuming full eligibility is achieved.[3] Measurements included in the calculation of the EPBO include estimated effects of medical cost, inflation, and the impact of technological advancements and future delivery patterns. The service cost component for OPEBs is the ratable portion of the EPBO attributable to employee service in the current period.

Interest

Interest is calculated by applying the discount rate by the *accumulated postretirement benefit obligation* (APBO). The APBO is that portion of the EPBO attributable to employee service rendered to the measurement date. Once the employee is fully eligible to receive OPEB benefits, the APBO and the EPBO are equivalent.[4]

Amortization of Prior Service Costs

For OPEBs *prior service cost* is the increase in the APBO attributed to an increase in benefits to employee service rendered in prior periods. *SFAS No. 106* requires that prior service cost be recognized over the life expectancy of the employees when most participants are fully eligible to receive benefits. If employees are not fully eligible, prior service cost is amortized to the date of full eligibility. OPEB gains on decreases in benefits are required to be offset against both unrecognized prior service cost and unrecognized transition obligations.

Amortization of the Transition Obligation

The transition obligation under *SFAS No. 106* is the difference between the APBO and the fair value of funded OPEB assets. The transition amount may be recognized immediately, or it may be amortized over the average remaining service lives of active participants. The employer may elect a minimum amortization period of 20 years. The amount of amortization allowed is constrained. The cumulative expense recognized as a result of electing to defer recognition of the transition amount may not exceed the cumulative expense that would occur on a pay-as-you-go basis.

Disclosure

Like *SFAS No. 87, SFAS No. 106* requires the disclosure of plan details, including the funding policy and amounts and types of funded assets, the components of net periodic cost, and a reconciliation of the funded status of the plan with amounts reported in the statement of financial position. Recognizing the sensitivity of the assumptions used to measure OPEB costs, *SFAS No. 106* also requires disclosure of

1. The assumed health care cost trend rates used to measure the EPBO.
2. The effects of a one-percentage-point increase in the assumed health care cost trend rates.

[3] Ibid., par. 20.

[4] Ibid., pars. 20 and 21.

Postemployment Benefits

In addition to postretirement benefits, employers often provide benefits to employees who are inactive due to, for example, a layoff or disability, but not retired. In *SFAS No. 112*, "Employers' Accounting for Postemployment Benefits,"[5] the FASB determined that these benefits are compensation for services rendered, and as such the provisions of *SFAS No. 5*, "Accounting for Contingencies," and *SFAS No. 43*, "Accounting for Compensated Absences," provide the appropriate accounting treatment. Hence, a loss contingency should be accrued when the payment of postemployment benefits is probable, the amount of the loss contingency can be reasonably estimated, the employer's obligation is attributable to employee services already rendered, and the employee's rights to postemployment benefits vest or accumulate.

SFAS No. 132

SFAS No. 132 standardizes the disclosure requirements for pensions and other postretirement benefits, requires the disclosure of additional information on changes in the benefit obligation and fair value of plan assets in order to facilitate financial analysis, and eliminates certain other disclosure requirements contained in *SFAS Nos. 87, 88*, and *106*. The benefits to financial statement users include the disclosure of disaggregated information on the six components of periodic pension cost and other postretirement benefits and information on changes in the projected benefit obligation and plan assets. The statement suggests a combined format for the presentation of both pensions and other postretirement benefits. *SFAS No. 132* is analyzed in more detail in an article by Kenneth Shaw contained on the text's webpage for Chapter 13.

Financial Analysis of Retirement Benefits

The combined effect of *SFAS Nos. 87, 106*, and *132* is to provide investors with additional information about the future cash flows associated with retirement benefits. The individual components of periodic pension cost have been found to convey different amounts of information to financial statement users. Service cost, interest cost, and the expected return on plan assets have been found to provide information on a company's sustainable income; whereas the other components of pension cost were not found to provide significant additional information.[6] Similarly, the disclosure of the accumulated postretirement benefit obligation for other postretirement benefits was found to be negatively correlated with the price of a company's stock.[7] However,

---

[5] Financial Accounting Standards Board, *Statement of Financial Accounting Standards No. 112*, "Employers' Accounting for Postemployment Benefits" (Stamford, CT: FASB, 1992).

[6] M. E. Barth, W. H. Braver, and W. R. Landsman, "The Market Value Implications of Net Periodic Pension Cost Components," *Journal of Accounting and Economics* (March 1992), pp. 27–62.

[7] B. Choi, D. W. Collins and W. B. Johnson, "Valuation Implications of Reliability Differences: The Case of Non-Pension Postretirement Obligations," *The Accounting Review* (July 1997), pp. 351–383.

the release of *SFAS No. 106* also has had economic consequences. Prior to the issuance of *SFAS No. 106*, employers accounted for OPEBs on a pay-as-you-go basis, postponing any recognition of expense until the postretirement period. Due to the magnitude of these expenditures, particularly in light of rising health care costs, requiring firms to change from a cash basis to an accrual basis would have had a major impact on financial reporting. A *Wall Street Journal* article described *SFAS No. 106* as "one of the most significant changes in accounting ever … that could cut corporate profits by hundreds of billions of dollars."[8] Because of the pronouncement's expected impact some have argued that its provisions may cause management to curtail or even eliminate OPEBs. As a result, *SFAS No. 106* may eventually have adverse economic consequences for employees. The reduction or elimination of OPEBs could significantly affect an individual's ability to finance future health and life insurance costs. Ultimately, it could also result in additional costs to the federal government, and therefore to the taxpayer, through increased Medicare payments. Later, these implications were partially confirmed by a survey reported in the *Wall Street Journal* which indicated that up to 80 percent of the firms in a survey might reduce or terminate their health care benefits in an effort to reduce the reported amount of the accumulated postretirement benefit obligation.[9]

Kroll-O'Gara Company does not have a defined benefit pension plan for its employees and did not disclose any information on other postretirement benefits. The following footnote relates to a defined contribution pension plan offered by the company.

> *(a) Defined Contribution Plans—The Company and its subsidiaries have established various non-contributory profit sharing/401(k) plans covering substantially all of the Company's employees. Contributions to the plans are discretionary and are determined annually by the Company's Board of Directors. Certain plans also offer a matching contribution whereby the Company will contribute a percentage of the amount a participant contributes, limited to certain maximum amounts. Plan contribution expense charged against current operations for all such plans amounted to approximately $1,243,000, $1,211,140 and $797,003, for the years ended December 31, 1996, 1997 and 1998, respectively.*

Disclosure of the information for pension and other postretirement benefits under the provisions of *SFAS Nos. 87, 106,* and *132* is illustrated for Coca-Cola. The following footnote was extracted from the company's 1999 financial statements:

> *Our Company sponsors and/or contributes to pension and postretirement health care and life insurance benefit plans covering substantially all U.S. employees and certain employees in international locations. We also sponsor nonqualified, unfunded defined benefit pension plans for certain officers and other employees. In*

[8] "FASB Issues Rule Change on Benefits," *The Wall Street Journal*, December 29, 1990, p. A3.

[9] "UNYSIS Corp Says It Will Stop Paying Medical Benefits in Three Years," *Wall Street Journal* (November 4, 1992), B1.

addition, our Company and its subsidiaries have various pension plans and other forms of postretirement arrangements outside the United States.

Total expense for all benefit plans, including defined benefit pension plans and postretirement health care and life insurance benefit plans, amounted to approximately $108 million in 1999, $119 million in 1998 and $109 million in 1997. Net periodic cost for our pension and other benefit plans consists of the following (in millions):

	Pension Benefits		
Year Ended December 31	1999	1998	1997
Service Cost	$ 67	$ 56	$ 49
Interest Cost	111	105	93
Expected return on plan assets	(119)	(105)	(95)
Amortization of prior service cost	6	3	7
Recognized net actuarial loss	7	9	14
Net periodic pension cost	$ 72	$ 68	$ 68

	Pension Benefits		
Year Ended December 31	1999	1998	1997
Service Cost	$ 14	$ 14	$ 11
Interest Cost	22	25	23
Expected return on plan assets	(1)	(1)	(1)
Recognized net actuarial gain	—	—	(1)
Net periodic cost	$ 35	$ 38	$32

The following table sets forth the change in benefit obligation for our benefit plans (in millions):

	Pension Benefits		Other Benefits	
Year Ended December 31	1999	1998	1999	1998
Benefit obligation at beginning of year	$ 1,717	$ 1,488	$ 381	$ 327
Service cost	67	56	14	14
Interest cost	111	105	22	25
Foreign currency exchange rate changes	(13)	25	—	—
Amendments	4	8	—	—
Actuarial (gain) loss	(137)	124	(101)	31
Benefits paid	(84)	(86)	(14)	(16)
Other	5	(3)	1	—
Benefit obligation at end of year	$ 1,670	$ 1,717	$ 303	$ 381

The following table sets forth the change in plan assets for our benefit plans (in millions):

Year Ended December 31	Pension Benefits		Other Benefits	
	1999	1998	1999	1998
Fair value of plan assets at beginning of year	$ 1,516	$ 1,408	$ 36	$ 40
Actual return on plan assets	259	129	1	2
Employer contribution	34	25	5	10
Foreign currency exchange rate changes	(20)	18	—	—
benefits paid	(69)	(68)	(14)	(16)
Other	2	4	1	—
Fair value of plan assets at end of year	$ 1,722	$ 1,516	$ 29	$ 36

The projected benefit obligation, accumulated benefit obligation, and fair value of plan assets for the pension plans with accumulated benefit obligations in excess of plan assets were $556 million, $434 million, and $161 million, respectively, as of December 31, 1999, and $536 million, $418 million, and $149 million, respectively, as of December 31, 1998.

International Accounting Standards

The IASC has issued two standards for retirement benefits:

1. *IAS No. 19*, "Retirement Benefit Costs."
2. *IAS No. 26*, "Accounting and Reporting by Retirement Benefit Plans."

In *IAS No. 19*, as amended in 1998, the IASC delineated the procedures to account for both defined contribution and defined benefit pension plans. With respect to defined contribution plans, the amount contributed is to be recognized as a current period expense. This treatment is consistent with current U.S. GAAP. For defined benefit plans, current service cost is required to be recognized as a current period expense. Past service costs, experience adjustments, the effects of changes in actuarial assumptions, and plan adjustments are generally to be recognized as expenses (or income) in a systematic manner over the remaining working lives of the current employees. The preferred method of determining costs under defined benefit plans is the *accrued benefit valuation method;* however, the *projected benefit valuation method* is an acceptable alternative. This treatment allows for more variation in measuring pension cost than is available under U.S. GAAP, and *IAS No. 19* does not address the minimum liability issue contained in *SFAS No. 87*.

In its review of the original *IAS No. 19*, the FASB staff noted that the social contract between the employer and the employee in many foreign countries is different from that in the United States. Both the government and the employer may provide pension benefits; thereby lowering the firm's pension liability.[10] In its review of the revised *IAS No. 19*, the FASB staff noted that since it eliminated many of the differences between it and U.S. GAAP, the new statement represents a significant improvement. On the other hand, it was noted that it still allows similar plans to be accounted for in a different manner under IAS and U.S. GAAP. Specifically, *IAS No. 19* does not provide a definition for a defined contribution plan. That is, if a plan is not a defined benefit plan, it is by default a defined contribution plan. As a result, it is possible that a plan that would be accounted for as a defined benefit plan under U.S. GAAP could be accounted for as a defined contribution plan under *IAS No. 19*. In addition, the calculation of the minimum liability amounts may differ under the provisions of the two plans.[11]

IAS No. 26 establishes separate standards for reporting by defined contribution plans and by defined benefit plans. For defined contribution plans, the statement indicates that the objective of reporting is to provide information about the plan and the performance of its investments. As a result, the information should be provided concerning significant activities affecting the plan, changes relating to the plan, investment performance, and a description of the plan's investment policies. For defined benefit plans, *IAS No. 26* indicates that the objective is to provide information about the financial resources and activities that will be useful in assessing the relationship between plan resources and future benefits. Accordingly, information should be provided concerning significant activities affecting the plan, changes relating to the plan, investment performance actuarial information, and a description of the plan's investment policies These requirements are similar to U.S. GAAP for reporting on pension plan assets as outlined in *SFAS No. 35*. The FASB Staff did not review *IAS No. 26* because it was not part of the core standards accounting project.

Summary

Accounting for the cost of pension plans continues to be a controversial issue. Although both the APB and the FASB have addressed this issue, complete consensus has not been achieved. There still are differing views on what constitutes a company's liability and periodic expense for a pension plan. There are also a variety of views on how to measure and disclose pension assets and liabilities on financial statements. Finally, the SFAS on accounting for other postretirement benefits has created a great deal of controversy.

In the articles for Chapter 13 contained on the text's webpage, some additional issues associated with accounting for pensions and other postretirement benefits are addressed.

[10] Financial Accounting Standards Board, *The IASC-U.S. Comparison Project: A Report on the Similarities and Differences between IASC Standards and U.S. GAAP,* Carrie Bloomer (ed.) (Norwalk, CT: Financial Accounting Standards Board, 1996), pp. 281–296.

[11] Financial Accounting Standards Board, *The IASC-U.S. Comparison Project: A Report on the Similarities and Differences between IASC Standards and U.S. GAAP,* Carrie Bloomer (ed.), 2nd ed. (Norwalk, CT: Financial Accounting Standards Board, 1999), pp. 229–271.

Cases

• Case 13-1 Adoption of SFAS No. 87 Issues

Michaels Corporation has a defined benefit pension plan. In 1987, Michaels adopted the provisions of *SFAS No. 87*. At January 1, 1987, the projected benefit obligation (PBO) was $400,000. Cumulative funding and cumulative pension expense under *APB Opinion No. 8* were equal. Plan assets were heavily invested in the stock market, and due to a bear market, the market value of plan assets at January 1, 1987, was $590,000. Michaels Corporation elected to write off the transition amount over a 15-year period.

For the year 1987, net periodic pension cost was negative.

Required:
a. Is the transition amount considered an asset or a liability? Explain.
b. Discuss how the transition amount in this case would affect net periodic pension expense.
c. Discuss why net periodic pension expense would be negative. In your answer list and describe any and all factors that may cause net periodic pension expense to be negative.
d. Would the pension expense for Michaels have been negative prior to the adoption of *SFAS No. 87?* Why the difference, if any?

• Case 13-2 Pension Benefits

Pension accounting has become more closely associated with the method of determining pension benefits.

Required:
a. Discuss the following methods of determining pension benefits.
   i. Defined contribution plan
   ii. Defined benefit plan
b. Discuss the following actuarial funding methods.
   i. Cost approach
   ii. Benefit approach

• Case 13-3 Pension Accounting Termonology

Statement of Financial Accounting Standards No. 87, "Employers Accounting for Pensions," requires an understanding of certain terms.

Required:
a. Discuss the following components of annual pension cost.
   i. Service cost
   ii. Interest cost
   iii. Actual return on plan assets
   iv. Amortization of unrecognized prior service cost
   v. Amortization of the transition amount
b. Discuss the composition and treatment of the minimum liability provision.

• Case 13-4 Application of SFAS No. 87.

Carson Company sponsors a single-employer defined benefit pension plan. The plan provides that pension benefits are determined by age, years of service, and compensation. Among the components that should be included in the net pension cost recognized for a period are service cost, interest cost, and actual return on plan assets.

Required:
a. What two accounting problems result from the nature of the defined benefit pension plan? Why do these problems arise?
b. How should Carson determine the service cost component of the net pension cost?
c. How should Carson determine the interest cost component of the net pension cost?
d. How should Carson determine the actual return on plan assets component of the net pension cost?

• Case 13-5 Accounting for Other Postretirement Benefits

Postretirement benefits other than pensions (OPEBs) are similar to defined benefit pension plans in some respects and different in others.

Required:
a. Discuss the characteristics of OPEBs that make them different from defined benefit pension plans.
b. Discuss how the accounting for OPEBs differs from the accounting for defined benefit pension plans.
c. In what respects are OPEBs similar to defined benefit pension plans? Explain.
d. In what respects is the accounting for OPEBs similar to, or the same as, the accounting for defined benefit pension plans? Explain.

• Case 13-6 Pension Funding Status

Under *SFAS No. 87,* pension expense for defined benefit pension plans is measured using projected benefits. At a minimum, companies must report the excess of the accumulated benefit obligation over the fair value of funded assets as a liability.

Penny Pincher Company has a defined benefit pension plan for its employees. The following pension data are available at year-end (in millions):

Accumulated benefit obligation	142
Projected benefit obligation	205
Fair value of plan assets	175

There is no balance in prepaid/accrued pension costs.

Required:

a. Calculate the funded status of the plan (i.e., the excess of the projected benefit obligation over the fair value of plan assets). Is the plan over funded or underfunded?

b. If the projected benefit obligation provides the appropriate measure of the company's obligation for pension benefits and the assets in the fund are viewed as satisfying all or part of that obligation, what is Penny Pincher's liability, if any, for the pension plan at year-end? Explain, citing the conceptual framework's definition of liabilities in your explanation.

c. What amount will Penny Pincher have to report in its balance sheet?

d. Assume that the accumulated benefit obligation is 190 and that Penny Pincher reports the minimum liability in the balance sheet. What amount will be reported? Will the Penny Pincher financial statements be "articulated?" Explain.

• Case 13-7 Effect of the Settlement Rate on Periodic Pension Cost

Critics of *SFAS No. 87* argue that its requirements result in reporting pension expense that is volatile. One of the factors causing volatility is changing the discount rate used to calculate service cost and the projected benefit obligation. The FASB requires use of the "settlement rate" to discount projected benefits.

Required:

a. What is the settlement rate?

b. Explain why the FASB chose the settlement rate to discount projected benefits.

c. What alternative rate, or rates, might be preferred by opponents of the settlement rate? Why?

d. Why might companies object to increased volatility of pension expense? Discuss.

Room for Debate

• Issue 1

SFAS No. 87 requires that projected benefits be utilized to measure pension expense and that a minimum liability measurement utilize accumulated benefits. Some feel that projected benefits are appropriate to measure pension expense and liability. Others feel that accumulated benefits are appropriate to measure expense and liability.

Team Debate:

Team 1. Argue for the use of projected benefits for pension expense and liability purposes. Relate your arguments to appropriate accounting theory, including the conceptual framework and capital maintenance concepts. You may find the article, "Alternative Accounting Treatments for Pensions," *The Accounting Review* (October 1982), pp. 806–823, helpful in lending support for your arguments.

Team 2. Argue for the use of accumulated benefits for pension expense and liability purposes. Relate your arguments to appropriate accounting theory, including the conceptual framework and capital maintenance concepts. You may find the article, "Alternative Accounting Treatments for Pensions," *The Accounting Review* (October 1982), pp. 806–823, helpful in bolstering your arguments.

Recommended Additional Readings

Barth, Mary E., William H. Braver, and Wayne. R. Landsman. "The Market Value Implications of Net Periodic Pension Cost Components." *Journal of Accounting and Economics* (March 1992), pp. 27–62.

Choi, Byeonghee, Daniel. W. Collins, and W. Bruce. Johnson. "Valuation Implications of Reliability Differences: The Case of Non-Pension Postretirement Obligations." *The Accounting Review* (July 1997), pp. 351–383.

Harper, Robert M., Jr., William G. Mister, and Jerry R. Strawser. "The Effect of Recognition versus Disclosure of Unfunded Postretirement Benefits on Lenders' Perceptions of Debt." *Accounting Horizons* (September 1991), pp. 50–56.

Langer, Russell, and Baruch Lev. "The FASB's Policy of Extended Adoption for New Standards: An Examination of FAS No. 87." *The Accounting Review* (July 1993), pp. 515–533.

Lillian, Steven, and Martin Mellman. "Time for Realism in Accounting for Employers' Pension Plans." *The CPA Journal* (June 1994), pp. 54–57.

Lucas, Timothy S., and Betsy Ann Hollowell. "Pension Accounting: The Liability Question." *Journal of Accountancy* (October 1981), pp. 57–67.

Mills, Robert H. "SFAS 87: An Improvement in Pension Reporting?" *The CPA Journal* (July 1989), pp. 37, 38, 40–42.

Revsine, Lawrence. "Understanding Financial Accounting Standard 87." *Financial Analysts Journal* (January–February 1989), pp. 61–68.

Thomas, Paula B., and Larry E. Farmer. "OPEB: Improved Reporting or the Last Straw?" *Journal of Accountancy* (November 1990), pp. 102–104, 107, 109, 110, 112.

Wilbert, James R., and Kenneth E. Dakduk. "The New FASB 106: How to Account for Postretirement Benefits." *Journal of Accountancy* (August 1991), pp. 36–41.

Wyatt, Arthur. "OPEB Costs: The FASB Establishes Accountability." *Accounting Horizons* (March 1990), pp. 108–110.

Bibliography

Abrams, Reuben W. "Accounting for the Cost of Pension Plans and Deferred Compensation Contracts." *New York CPA* (April 1970), pp. 300–307.

Brownler, E. Richard, and S. David Young. "Pension Accounting: A New Proposal." *The CPA Journal* (July 1985), pp. 28–34.

Cassell, Jules M., and Diana W. Kahn. "FASB Statement No. 35: Not Enough about the Future?" *Financial Executive* (December 1980), pp. 44–51.

Deaton, William C., and Jerry J. Weygandt. "Disclosures Related to Pension Plans." *Journal of Accountancy* (January 1975), pp. 44–51.

Deitrick, James W., and C. Wayne Alderman. "Pension Plans: What Companies Do—and Do Not—Disclose." *Management Accounting* (April 1980), pp. 24–29.

Dewhirst, John F. "A Conceptual Approach to Pension Accounting." *The Accounting Review* (April 1971), pp. 365–373.

Doley, Lane Alan. "The Valuations of Reported Pension Measures for Firms Sponsoring Defined Benefit Plans." *The Accounting Review* (April 1984), pp. 177–198.

Goldberg, Seymour. "Pension Planning and the CPA." *Journal of Accountancy* (May 1984), pp. 68–72.

Goldstein, Leo. "Unfunded Pension Liabilities May Be Dangerous to Corporate Health." *Management Accounting* (April 1980), pp. 20–22.

Grant, Edward B., and Thomas R. Weirich. "Current Developments in Pension Accounting." *The National Public Accountant* (July 1980), pp. 11–15.

Hicks, Ernest L. "Accounting for the Cost of Pension Plans." *Accounting Research Study No. 8*. New York: AICPA, 1965.

Kirk, Donald J. "Pension Accounting: Where the FASB Now Stands." *Journal of Accountancy* (June 1980), pp. 82–88.

Kwon, S. "Economic Determinants of the Assumed Interest Rate in Pension Accounting." *Advances in Accounting,* Vol. 12 (1994), pp. 67–86.

Langenderfer, Harold Q. "Accrued Past-Service Pension Costs Should Be Capitalized." *New York CPA* (February 1971), pp. 137–143.

Lorensen, Leonard, and Paul Rosenfield. "Vested Benefits—A Company's Only Pension Liability." *Journal of Accountancy* (October 1983), pp. 64–76.

Ostuw, Richard. "How to Deal with Retiree Needs under OPEP." *Financial Executive* (January/February 1989), pp. 37–40.

Philips, G. Edward. "Pension Liabilities and Assets." *The Accounting Review* (January 1968), pp. 10–17.

Schuchart, J. A., and W. L. Sanders, Jr. "Pension Fund Considerations." *Management Accounting* (March 1972), pp. 49–52.

Smith, Jack L. "Actuarial Cost Methods—Basics for CPA." *Journal of Accountancy* (February 1977), pp. 62–66.

Smith, Jack L. "Needed: Improved Pension Accounting and Reporting." *Management Accounting* (May 1978), pp. 43–46.

Stone, Mary C. "The Changing Picture for Pension Accounting." *The CPA Journal* (April 1983), pp. 32–42.

Stone, Mary, and Robert Ingram. "The Effect of Statement No. 87 on the Financial Reports of Early Adopters." *Accounting Horizons* (September 1988), pp. 48–61.

Walken, David M. "Accounting for Reversions from Pension Plans." *Journal of Accountancy* (February 1985), pp. 64–70.

Equity

Equity is the basic risk capital of an enterprise. Equity capital has no guaranteed return and no timetable for the repayment of the capital investment. From the standpoint of enterprise stability and exposure to risk of insolvency, a basic characteristic of equity capital is that it is permanent and can be counted on to remain invested in good times as well as bad. Consequently, equity funds can be most confidently invested in long-term assets and be exposed to the greatest risks.

The investor in the common stock of an enterprise must balance the existence of debt, which represents a risk of loss of investment, against the potential of high profits from financial leverage. The mix of debt and equity investments in a company is termed its *capital structure*. There has been considerable debate over the years over whether the cost of capital for an enterprise varies with different capital structures, that is, with different mixtures of debt and equity. Modigliani and Miller[1] found that an enterprise's cost of capital is, except for the tax deductibility of interest, not affected by the mix of debt and equity. This is true, they asserted, because each individual stockholder can inject his or her own blend of risk into the total investment position.

In this chapter we maintain that the degree of risk of an enterprise as perceived by a potential investor is a given. In the following paragraphs we review some theories of equity and discuss the theoretical issues associated with recording the various components of equity.

---

[1] F. Modigliani and M. Miller, "Cost of Capital, Corporation Finance and the Theory of Investment," *American Economic Review* (June 1958), pp. 261–297.

Theories of Equity

Chapter 10 introduced two theories of equity, the proprietary theory and the entity theory. These and several other theories may provide a frame of reference for the presentation of financial statements. When viewing the applicability of the various theories of equity, it is important to remember that the purpose of a theory is to provide a rationale or explanation for some action. The proprietary theory gained prominence because the interests of the owner(s) were seen as the guiding force in the preparation of financial statements. However, as the interests of other users became more significant, accountants made changes in financial report formats without adopting a particular equity theory.

In the following discussion, the student should keep in mind that the adoption of a particular theory could influence a number of accounting and reporting procedures. The student should also note that the theories represent a point of view toward the firm for accounting purposes that is not necessarily the same as the legal view of the firm.

Proprietary Theory

According to the proprietary theory, the firm is owned by some specified person or group. The ownership interest may be represented by a sole proprietor, a partnership, or a number of stockholders. The assets of the firm belong to these owners, and any liabilities of the firm are also the owners' liabilities. Revenues received by the firm immediately increase the owner's net interest in the firm, and, likewise, all expenses incurred by the firm immediately decrease the net proprietary interest in the firm. This theory holds that all profits or losses immediately become the property of the owners, and not the firm, whether or not they are distributed. Therefore, the firm exists simply to provide the means to carry on transactions for the owners, and the net worth or equity section of the balance sheet should be viewed as

$$\text{assets} - \text{liabilities} = \text{proprietorship}$$

Under the proprietary theory, financial reporting is based on the premise that the owner is the primary focus of the financial statements. The proprietary theory is particularly applicable to sole proprietorships where the owner is the decision maker. When the form of the enterprise grows more complex, and the ownership and management separate, this theory becomes less acceptable. An attempt has been made to retain the concepts of the proprietary theory in the corporate situation; however, many accountants have asserted that it cannot meet the requirements of the corporate form of organization.[2] Nevertheless, we still find significant accounting policies that can be justified only through acceptance of the proprietary theory. For example, the

---

[2] See, for example, William J. Vatter, "Corporate Stock Equities," Part 1, in Morton Backer (ed.), *Modern Accounting Theory* (Englewood Cliffs, NJ: Prentice-Hall, 1966), p. 251.

calculation and presentation of earnings per share figures are relevant only if we assume that those earnings belong to the shareholders prior to the declaration of dividends.

Entity Theory

The rise of the corporate form of organization, which (1) was accompanied by the separation of ownership and management, (2) limited the liability of owners, and (3) resulted in the legal definition of a corporation as a person, encouraged the evolution of new theories of ownership. Among the first of these theories was the entity theory, which is expressed as

$$\text{assets} = \text{equities}$$

The entity theory, like the proprietary theory, is a point of view toward the firm and the people concerned with its operation. This viewpoint places the firm, and not the owners, at the center of interest for accounting and financial reporting purposes. The essence of the entity theory is that creditors as well as stockholders contribute resources to the firm, and the firm exists as a separate and distinct entity apart from these groups. The assets and liabilities belong to the firm and not the owners. As revenue is received, it becomes the property of the entity, and expenses incurred are obligations of the entity. Any profits are the property of the entity and accrue to the stockholders only when a dividend is declared. Under this theory, all the items on the right-hand side of the balance sheet, except retained earnings that belong to the firm, are viewed as claims against the assets of the firm, and individual items are distinguished by the nature of their claims. Some items are identified as creditor claims and others as owner claims; nevertheless, they are claims against the firm as a separate entity.

Goldberg has illustrated the difference between the proprietary and entity theories through an example involving a small child in possession of his or her first unit of monetary exchange.

> *Suppose that a small child is given, say £1, with which he can do whatever he likes. If (as is most likely) he is not familiar with the idea of ownership, he will think (I) "Here is £1"; and (ii) "This £1 is mine." These thoughts comprise the essence of the proprietary viewpoint and of double entry, for if the child were a born accountant, he would express the same thoughts as (I) "There exists an asset," and (ii) "I have a proprietary interest in that asset." That is to say, the £1 is regarded from two aspects: (1) as something that exists—an asset; and (ii) as belonging to somebody—my asset. Suppose further that, until the child can decide what he will do with the £1 he puts it in a money box. The entity theory can be introduced here by personalizing the money box—it involves adopting the point of view that the money box now has the £1 and owes £1 to the child.[3]*

---

[3] Louis Goldberg, *An Inquiry into the Nature of Accounting* (American Accounting Association, Monograph No. 7, 1963), p. 126.

Embedded in this illustration is the fundamental distinction between the proprietary and entity theories—perceptions of the right-hand side of the balance sheet. Individuals who view net income as accruing only to owners will favor the proprietary approach, whereas those taking a broader view of the nature of the beneficiaries of income will favor the entity approach.

Entity theory makes no distinction between debt and equity. Both are considered sources of capital, and the operations of the firm are not affected by the amount of debt relative to equity.[4] Thus, under entity theory debt-to-equity ratios would not provide relevant information for investor decision making.[5] Yet present accounting practice makes a sharp distinction between debt and equity. Moreover, the amount of debt relative to equity is generally considered an important indicator of risk.[6] Such a distinction implies that accountants must separately identify and classify liabilities from equities. Nevertheless, complex financial instruments such as convertible bonds may comprise debt and equity components. Due to the problems associated with identifying and measuring the fundamental components of these financial instruments, the FASB was prompted to issue a discussion memorandum (DM), "Distinguishing between Liability and Equity Instruments and Accounting for Instruments with the Characteristics of Both."[7] The DM asks whether the sharp distinction should be continued. In other words, should accounting follow entity theory, or should accounting attempt to identify and separately report the elements of debt and equity? If the distinction is to continue, decisions must be made regarding the nature of fundamental financial instruments and how to appropriately measure and report them.

Other Theoretical Approaches

Several authors have noted inadequacies in the entity and proprietary approaches and have developed additional viewpoints or perspectives from which to rationalize the recording and reporting of accounting information. The most notable of these new viewpoints are the fund theory, the commander theory, the enterprise theory, and the residual equity theory. Each of these theories is considered separately.

Fund Theory
Vatter attacked the proprietary theory as too simplistic for modern corporate reporting.[8] He saw no logical basis for viewing the corporation as a person in the legal sense, and he argued that the corporation is the people it represents.

[4] W. A. Paton, *Accounting Theory* (New York: Roland Press, 1922).

[5] M. W. Clark, "Entity Theory, Modern Capital Structure Theory, and the Distinction Between Debt and Equity," *Accounting Horizons* (September 1993), pp. 14–31.

[6] Ibid.

[7] Financial Accounting Standards Board, *Discussion Memorandum: Distinguishing between Liability and Equity Instruments and Accounting for Instruments with Characteristics of Both* (Stamford, CT: FASB, 1990).

[8] William J. Vatter, *The Fund Theory of Accounting and Its Implications for Financial Reports* (Chicago, IL: University of Chicago Press, 1947).

The fund theory attempts to abandon the personal relationship advocated by the proprietary theory and the personalization of the firm advocated by the entity theory. Under the fund approach, the measurement of net income plays a role secondary to satisfying the special interests of management, social control agencies (e.g., government agencies), and the overall process of credit extension and investment. The fund theory is expressed by the following equation:

$$\text{assets} = \text{restrictions on assets}$$

This theory explains the financial recording of an organization in terms of three features:

1. *Fund* An area of attention defined by the activities and operations surrounding any one set of accounting records and for which a self-balancing set of accounts is created.

2. *Assets* Economic services and potentials.

3. *Restrictions* Limitations on the use of assets.

These features are applied to each homogeneous set of activities and functions within the organization, thus providing a separate accounting for each area of economic concern.

   The fund theory has not gained general acceptance in financial accounting; it is more suitable to governmental accounting. This theory is a somewhat radical change from current practices, and the added volume of bookkeeping it would require has inhibited its adoption. Use of the fund approach in government accounting is attributed principally to the legal restrictions typically imposed on each fund, thus requiring a separate accounting for each.

Commander Theory
The entity theory adopts the point of view of the business entity, whereas the proprietary theory takes the viewpoint of the proprietor. But, asks Goldberg, "What of the point of view of the managers, that is, of the activity force in a ... company?"[9] Goldberg argues that this question is of major importance because of the divergent self-interested viewpoints of owners and managers in large-scale corporations. In fact, so relevant is this divergence "that in recent years a whole new field of study, going under the name of 'management accounting' and an ancillary literature have grown up, in which the emphasis is laid upon accountants for information to enable them (the managers) to carry out their function of control of property with a view to its increase."[10]

   The commander approach is offered as a replacement for the proprietary and entity theories because it is argued that the goals of the manager (commander) are at least equally important to those of the proprietor or entity. The proprietary, entity, and fund approaches emphasize persons, personal-

[9] Goldberg, op. cit., p. 152.
[10] Ibid.

ization, and funds, respectively, but the commander theory emphasizes control. Everyone who has resources to deploy is viewed as a commander.

The commander theory, unlike the proprietary, entity, and fund approaches, has applicability to all organizational forms (i.e., sole proprietorship, partnership, and corporation). The form of organization does not negate the applicability of the commander view because the commander can take on more than one identity in any organization. In sole proprietorships or partnerships, the proprietors or partners are both owners and commanders. Under the corporate form, both the managers and stockholders are commanders in that each maintains some control over resources (i.e., managers control the enterprise resources, and stockholders control returns on investment emerging from the enterprise).

The commander theory argues that the notion of control is broad enough to encompass all relevant parties to the exclusion of none. The function of accounting, then, takes on an element of stewardship, and the question of where resource increments flow is not relevant. Rather, the relevant factor is how the commander allocates resources to the benefit of all parties. Responsibility accounting is consistent with the commander theory. Responsibility accounting identifies the revenues and costs that are under the control of various "commanders" within the organization, and financial statements are organized to highlight the contributions of each level of control to enterprise profits. The commander theory is not on the surface a radical move from current accounting practices, and it has generated little reaction in accounting circles.

Enterprise Theory

Under the enterprise theory, business units, most notably those listed on national or regional stock exchanges, are viewed as social institutions, composed of capital contributors having "a common purpose or purposes and, to a certain extent, roles of common action."[11] Management within this framework essentially maintains an arm's-length relationship with owners and has as its primary responsibilities the distribution of adequate dividends and the maintenance of friendly terms with employees, consumers, and government units. Because this theory applies only to large nationally or regionally traded issues, it is generally considered to have only minor impact on accounting theory or the development of accounting principles and practices.

Residual Equity Theory

Staubus defines residual equity as "the equitable interest in organization assets which will absorb the effect upon those assets of any economic event that no interested party has specifically agreed to."[12] Here, the common shareholders hold the residual equity in the enterprise by virtue of having the final claim on income, yet they are the first to be charged for losses. The residual equity holders are vital to the firm's existence in that they are the

[11] Waino Soujanen, "Enterprise Theory and Corporate Balance Sheets," *The Accounting Review* (January 1958), p. 56.

[12] George J. Staubus, "The Residual Equity Point of View in Accounting," *The Accounting Review* (January 1959), p. 3.

highest risk takers and provide a substantial volume of capital during the firm's developmental stage.

The residual equity theory is formulated as

$$\text{assets} - \text{specific equities} = \text{residual equities}$$

Under this approach, the residual of assets, net of the claim of specific equity holders (creditors and preferred stockholders), accrue to residual owners. In this framework, the role of financial reporting is to provide prospective and current residual owners with information regarding enterprise resource flows so that they can assess the value of their residual claim. Management is in effect a trustee responsible for maximizing the wealth of residual equity holders. Income accrues to the residual owners after the claims of specific equity holders are met. Thus, the income to specific equity holders, including interest on debt and dividends to preferred stockholders, would be deducted in arriving at residual net income. This theory is consistent with models that are formulated in the finance literature[13] with current financial statement presentation of earnings per share and with the conceptual framework's emphasis on the relevance of projecting cash flows. Again, as with the fund, commander, and enterprise theories, the residual equity approach has gained little attention in financial accounting.

Definition of Equity

SFAC No. 6 defines equity as a residual interest. However, the residual interest described therein is not equivalent to residual equity defined above. Rather, it is the difference between assets and liabilities.[14] Consequently, under *SFAC No. 6*, the definition and characteristics of equity hinge on the definitions and characteristics of assets and liabilities. *SFAC No. 6* defines equity in total but does not define the attributes of the elements of equity. It does note that enterprises may have more than one class of equity, such as common stock and preferred stock. Equity is defined as the difference between assets and liabilities, and liabilities are described as embodying an obligation to transfer assets or provide services to another entity in the future as the result of some prior transaction or event. Consequently, the distinguishing feature between liabilities and equities is that equities do not obligate the entity to transfer future resources or provide services. There is no obligation to distribute resources to equity holders until declared by the board of directors or unless the entity is liquidated.

Under the *SFAC No. 6* definition, if a financial instrument issued by the enterprise does not fit the definition of a liability, then it must be an equity instrument. The DM questions whether the definition of equity should continue to be governed by the definition of liabilities or whether it should be separately defined. If equity were independently defined, then the liabilities

---

[13] Clark, op. cit.

[14] Financial Accounting Standards Board, *Statement of Financial Accounting Concepts No. 6*, "Elements of Financial Statements" (Stamford, CT: FASB, 1985), par. 60.

might be the residual outcome of identifying assets and equity. In this case, the equation describing the relationship between financial statement elements could be stated as

$$assets - equity = liabilities$$

Alternatively, equity might be defined as an absolute residual, as under the residual equity theory, and a third category added to the balance sheet—"quasi-equity." The quasi-equity category might include items such as preferred stock or minority interest. This category would allow accountants to retain the definition of liabilities and treat the quasi-equity category as a residual. If this form of financial statement presentation should emerge, then other issues would have to be addressed, such as the definition of earnings. For example, as stated before, a residual equity definition of equity would imply that preferred dividends would be subtracted in the determination of net income.

Recording Equity

The American economy is characterized by three forms of business organization: sole proprietorships, partnerships, and corporations. Although the number of sole proprietorships greatly exceeds the number of partnerships and corporations in the United States, the greatest amount of economic activity is carried out by corporations. This is due to the efficiency of corporate production and distribution systems. Several advantages accrue to the corporate form and help to explain its emergence. Among these are

1. *Limited liability* Stockholders are liable only for the amount of their original investment (unless that investment is less than the par value of the shares). Creditors may not look to the assets of individual owners for debt repayments in the event of a liquidation as is possible in the case of sole proprietorships and partnerships.

2. *Continuity* The corporation's life is not affected by the death or resignation of owners.

3. *Investment liquidity* Corporate shares may be freely exchanged on the open market. Many shares are listed on national security exchanges, which improves their marketability.

4. *Variety of ownership interest* Shares of corporate stock usually contain four basic rights: the right to vote for members of the board of directors of the corporation and thereby participate in management, the right to receive dividends, the right to receive assets on the liquidation of the corporation, and the preemptive right to purchase additional shares in the same proportion to current ownership interest if new issues of stock are marketed. Shareholders may sacrifice any or all of these rights in return for special privileges. This results in an additional class of stock termed *preferred stock*, which may have either or both of the following features:
   a. Preference as to dividends.
   b. Preference as to assets in liquidation.

Traditionally, utilities were the largest issuers of preferred stock because selling preferred shares does not impact on a company's debt cost. Recently, banks and other financial institutions have also become more active in preferred stock offerings because of new federal requirements. Preferred stock is most often acquired by corporate investors because of the dividend exclusion allowance rule allowed under the Internal Revenue Code.

The corporate form of business organization allows management specialists to be employed. The owners thereby gain an expertise not normally available in sole proprietorships or partnerships. Evidence of the extent of this advantage can be found in the growth of business schools in the major universities. A large percentage of the students in these programs are in training to obtain employment in large corporations.

As noted earlier, two major types of stock may be found in any corporation, preferred stock and common stock. Preferred stockholders give up one or more of the rights usually accruing to stockholders for preference as to dividends or to assets in liquidation. Common stockholders retain these rights and have a residual claim on both the earnings and assets in liquidation. A corporation's capital section usually is subdivided into several components. In addition to disclosing the legal claims ownership groups have against the assets of the corporation, the separation of the components of capital gives information on the sources of capital, dividend requirements, and priorities in liquidation.

The components of the capital section are classified by source in the following manner:

I. Paid-in capital (contributed capital)
   A. Legal capital-par, stated value, or entire proceeds if no par or stated value accompanies the stock issue
   B. Additional paid-in capital—amounts received in excess of par or stated value
II. Earned capital
   A. Appropriated
   B. Unappropriated
III. Other comprehensive income

Each of these components is discussed in further detail in the following sections.

Paid-in Capital

The limited liability advantage of the corporate form of business organization provides that creditors may look only to the assets of the corporation to satisfy their claims. This factor has caused various states to enact laws that attempt to protect creditors and inform them of the true nature of the assets and liabilities of individual corporations. State laws generally protect creditors by establishing the concept of *legal capital*—the amount of net assets that cannot be distributed to stockholders. These laws vary from state to state, but the par or stated value of the outstanding shares generally constitutes a corporation's legal capital. State laws generally require legal capital to be reported separately from the total amount invested. As a result, ownership interests are classified as capital stock or additional paid-in capital in excess of par value. The classification, *additional paid-in capital,* includes all amounts originally received for shares of stock in excess of par or stated value. In unusual cases, stock may be sold for less than par value. In the event the corporation is liquidated, the holders of securities acquired for less than their par value could be required to pay the corporation the amount of the difference between the original investment and par value in order to protect creditors.

Stock Subscriptions

Large corporations frequently sell entire issues of stock to a group of investment advisors, or *underwriters,* who then attempt to resell the shares to the public. When a corporation sells shares of stock directly to individuals, it is common practice for individuals to contract to purchase shares on an installment basis. These individuals, termed *subscribers,* usually receive the rights of ownership when they contract to purchase the shares on subscription but do not actually receive any shares until the company has received payment for all subscribed shares. That is, each installment received is viewed as a percentage payment on each contracted share, and no shares are issued until all are paid in full. In some states, capital stock subscribed is viewed as part of legal capital, even though the shares are not outstanding. In other states, the subscribed shares are included in legal capital only after they have been fully paid and issued.

When a stock subscription takes place, the corporation has a legally enforceable claim against the subscribers for the balance due on the subscriptions. Therefore, receivables resulting from stock subscriptions embody probable future economic benefits and fit the definition of assets. However, present practice typically follows SEC Regulation S-X, which requires stock subscriptions receivable to be disclosed in stockholders' equity. Proponents of this treatment argue that the enterprise's recourse if the receivable is not collected is not to issue the stock. Moreover, the enterprise may not pursue collection, and therefore these receivables are sufficiently uncertain to qualify them as recognizable assets. It is also argued that stock subscriptions receivable are different from other receivables because they do not result from transferring assets or providing services.

Special Features

Securities other than common stock may contain features that allow (1) the holders of these securities to become common stockholders, (2) the corporation to reacquire these securities, or (3) the rate of return on the securities to fluctuate. Among these features are convertible provisions, call provisions, cumulative provisions, participating provisions, and redemption provisions. These provisions are found most frequently on preferred stock, but some of them may also be found on long-term debt, as discussed in Chapter 10.

Conversion

A convertible feature is included on a preferred stock issue to make it more attractive to potential investors. Usually, a conversion feature is attached to allow the corporation to sell its preferred shares at a relatively lower dividend rate than is found on other securities with the same degree of risk. The conversion rate is normally set above the current relationship of the market value of the common share to the market value of the preferred convertible shares. For example, if the corporation's common stock is selling at $10 per share and the preferred stock has a selling price of $100 per share, the conversion rate might be set at eight shares of common for one preferred. All other things being equal, it would appear to be profitable for the preferred shareholders to convert to common when the value of the common shares rises above $12.50 per share. However, it is normal for the market price of the preferred shares to fluctuate in proportion to the market price of the common; therefore, an individual would not be able to make a profit by simply converting one type of security to another. Convertible stock is attractive to investors because the exchange ratio tends to tie the market price of the preferred stock to the market price of the common stock.

When preferred stock is converted to common stock, the proper accounting treatment is to transfer the par value of the preferred, plus a proportionate share of any additional paid-in capital on the preferred stock, to common stock. If this amount differs from the par or stated value of common stock, it is apportioned between par or stated value and additional paid-in capital on common stock.

If a residual equity approach were adopted to define the components of equity, then a determination would need to be made regarding the conversion feature. The recognition and measurement problems associated with separate recognition of the conversion feature of preferred stock would be similar to those associated with convertible bonds (see Chapter 10 for a discussion of these recognition and measurement issues). However, even if current practice is retained and preferred stock continues to be disclosed as an element of stockholders' equity, separate disclosure of the conversion feature may have information content.[15]

Call Provisions

Call provisions allow the corporation to reacquire preferred stock at some predetermined amount. Corporations include call provisions on securities because of uncertain future conditions. Current conditions dictate the return on investment that will be attractive to potential investors, but conditions may change so that the corporation may offer a lower return on investment in the future. In addition, market conditions may make it necessary to promise a certain debt-equity relationship at the time of issue. Call provisions allow the corporation to take advantage of future favorable conditions and indicate how the securities may be retired. The existence of a call price tends to set an upward limit on the market price of nonconvertible securities, since investors will not normally be inclined to purchase shares that could be recalled momentarily at a lower price.

[15] Clark, op. cit.

Cumulative Provisions

Preferred shareholders normally have a preference as to dividends. That is, no common dividends may be paid in any one year until all required preferred dividends for that year are paid. Usually, corporations also include added protection for preferred shareholders in the form of a cumulative provision. This provision states that if all or any part of the stated preferred dividend is not paid in any one year, the unpaid portion accumulates and must be paid in subsequent years before any dividend can be paid on common stock. Any unpaid dividend on cumulative preferred stock constitutes a dividend in arrears and should be disclosed in the notes to the financial statements, even though it is not a liability until the board of directors of the corporation actually declares it so. Dividends in arrears are important in predicting future cash flows and as an indicator of financial flexibility and liquidity.

Participating Provisions

Participating provisions allow preferred stockholders to share dividends in excess of normal returns with common shareholders. For example, a participating provision might indicate that preferred shares are to participate in dividends on a 1:1 basis with common stock on all dividends in excess of $5 per share. This provision requires that any payments of more than $5 per share to the common stockholder also be made on a dollar-for-dollar basis to each share of preferred.

Redemption Provision

A redemption provision indicates that the shareholder may exchange preferred stock for cash in the future. The redemption provision may include a mandatory maturity date or may specify a redemption price. Redeemable preferred stock has several of the debt characteristics discussed earlier in Chapter 10. In fact, the SEC requires separate disclosure of such shares in its reports because of their special nature. At present, the FASB does not require similar treatment, although footnote disclosure is required.

Stock Options and Warrants

Many corporations have agreements with employees and security holders termed *stock options* and *stock warrants* that may result in the issuance of additional shares of common stock. Stock option and stock warrant agreements can significantly affect the amount of common stock outstanding, and the method of accounting for them should be carefully evaluated.

Stock Option Plans

Executive stock option plans have become an important element of the compensation package for corporate officers. These plans allow corporate officials to purchase a stated number of shares of stock at an established price for some predetermined period. In the past, stock option plans were especially advantageous because of income tax regulations that taxed proceeds at the capital gains rate when the securities purchased under stock option plans were sold. Current tax laws have substantially reduced the tax advantage of stock options. Nevertheless, many corporations still use them as part of the total compensation package.

Stock option plans are most valuable when the option price is lower than the market price. For this reason, stock option plans are viewed as an incentive that influences the holders of options to try to increase corporate profits and thereby increase the value of the company's common shares on the stock market. These plans have a potentially dilutive effect on other shareholders, since exercising options results in additional stockholder claims against the same amount of income. The relative effects of this potential dilution versus the effect of management's incentive to increase profits should be examined by current and potential shareholders. Such measurements are, of course, quite difficult.

In 1972 the Accounting Principles Board reviewed the issue of accounting for stock options and issued *APB Opinion No. 25*, "Accounting for Stock Issued to Employees."[16] Two types of plans were defined, noncompensatory and compensatory.

A *noncompensatory stock option plan* was defined as one not primarily designed as a method of compensation, but rather as a source of additional capital or of more widespread ownership among employees. Four essential characteristics of noncompensatory plans were defined: (1) the participation of all full-time employees, (2) the offering of stock on an equal basis or as a uniform percentage of salary to all employees, (3) a limited time for exercise of the option, and (4) a discount from market price that would not differ from a reasonable offer to stockholders. When these conditions are met, the plan does not discriminate in favor of company employees; thus, the corporation is not required to record any compensation expense.

Compensatory stock option plans, on the other hand, give employees an option that is not offered to all employees or to stockholders. These plans involve the recording of an expense, and the timing of the measurement of this expense can greatly affect its impact on financial reports. The six possible measurement dates to determine the amount of compensation expense associated with a stock option plan originally discussed in *ARB No. 43* were reviewed in Appendix B to *APB Opinion No. 25*. These dates are

1. The date of the adoption of an option plan.
2. The date on which an option is granted to a specific individual.
3. The date on which the grantee has performed any conditions precedent to exercise of the option.
4. The date on which the grantee may first exercise the option.
5. The date on which the option is exercised by the grantee.
6. The date on which the grantee disposes of the stock acquired.[17]

The APB concluded that compensation expense should be measured on the first date on which both the number of shares to be received by a particular

---

[16] *Accounting Principles Board Opinion No. 25*, "Accounting for Stock Issued to Employees" (New York: AICPA, 1972).

[17] Ibid., par. 6.

individual and the option price are known. In most cases, this will be the date on which the option is granted to a specific individual. The compensation expense is equal to the difference between the market price of the stock on the measurement date and the price the employee is required to pay.

The determination of the measurement date is of primary importance for compensatory stock option plans. In some plans, the date of the grant is the measurement date, and, therefore, the amount of compensation is known. In other plans the measurement date is later than the date of the grant and the annual compensation expense must be estimated.

If the date of the grant and the measurement date are the same, deferred compensation and common stock options are established for the total amount of compensation cost. The deferred compensation cost is offset against the common stock options in the stockholders' equity section and amortized to expense over the period of benefit. In the event the measurement date is later than the date of the grant, total compensation cost cannot be precisely measured on the date of the grant. Therefore, annual compensation expense is estimated, and common stock options are recorded during each period until the measurement date is reached.

Occasionally, available stock options may not be exercised. In the event an option is not exercised prior to the expiration date, previously recognized compensation expense is not affected; however, on the expiration date, the value of any previously recorded common stock options is transferred to additional paid-in capital.

The rationale for use of the *APB Opinion No. 25* measurement date is that it coincides with the date that the corporation commits to a specified number of shares. Because the shares could have been sold in the market rather than set aside for the employees, the difference between the market value of those shares and the option price on the date committed represents the opportunity cost associated with the options and thus the total compensation. An alternative argument, in favor of the *APB Opinion No. 25* measurement date, relies on labor economic theory. From the employee's perspective, the employees contract for services based on the amount of marginal revenue product they provide. Accordingly, the employee accepts the options in lieu of current wages. Consequently, the difference between the current market price and the option of the shares represents employee compensation.

The ultimate value of this investment lies somewhere between zero— when the market price never exceeds the option price—and a very large return—when the market price rises substantially above the option price. Some accountants have advocated recording the value of the option at the expected value that lies between these two extremes. However, this procedure would result in a more subjective valuation. The recording and measurement of common stock option plans will undoubtedly continue to be a controversial issue in the near future. In addition, recent innovations utilizing leverage and preferred stock have added to the complexity of employee stock option plans.

SFAS No. 123 Many accountants believe that the procedures for recognizing common stock options under the provisions of *APB Opinion No. 25* result in understated income statement and balance sheet valuations. They maintain that employees accepting stock options are accepting an investment in the firm in lieu of additional cash compensation. For example, in 1984, Walt Disney Company granted stock options to its chairman of the board, Michael Eisner. These options allowed him to purchase shares at approximately $57.44 per share. By 1992, when he exercised most of his options, the split-adjusted value of the shares had risen to approximately $646.00 As a result, Eisner realized a profit of over $126,900,000. However, the accounting rules in place at the time did not require Disney to record any expense at the time the options were granted.[18] As the result of many similar situations, several organizations interested in the development of accounting standards asked the FASB to reconsider the reporting requirements contained in *APB Opinion No. 25*. The FASB subsequently undertook a study of accounting for the value of stock options and initially concluded in an exposure draft (ED) that they should be recognized as expenses based on the fair value method. The release of this ED resulted in widespread opposition to its provisions. Senator Joseph Lieberman (D, Connecticut) sponsored a Sense of the Senate resolution that called on the FASB not to change its treatment of stock options. He also proposed establishing government controls on accounting rule-making by requiring SEC approval for accounting rule changes. The concerns voiced were based on economic consequences arguments about the effect on reported income and a perceived inability to measure the amount of compensation accurately enough to include it in the income statement as an expense.

After further deliberations, the FASB issued *SFAS No. 123*, "Accounting for Stock Based Compensation." This statement adopts the fair value approach to accounting for employee stock option plans contained in the previously released ED and encourages companies to adopt this method. It also allows companies to continue to use the *intrinsic value method* proscribed in *APB Opinion No. 25*. Companies that choose to continue reporting for stock option plans under the provisions of *APB No. 25* must now disclose the pro-forma effects on net income and earnings per share based on the fair value method.

Under the provisions of *SFAS No. 123*, compensation cost may be measured at its fair value on the date of the grant based on the value of the award and recognized over the service period (generally the vesting period). Fair value is to be measured using an option pricing model that takes into account as of the grant date: exercise price, expected volatility (if public), expected dividends on the stock, and a risk-free interest rate for the term of the option. Several alternative option pricing models are available with which to measure fair value; however, the most popular of these is the Black-Scholes model. This model assumes that stock prices follow a skewed lognormal distribution that results in a normal bell curve distribution for changes in stock prices. For example, under this approach, the value assigned to Michalel Eisner's stock options would have been somewhere between $3 million and $8

[18] Thomas Barton, William Shenkir, and Frederick Cole, "Other Voices," *Barron's*, November 14, 1994, pp. 65–68.

million.[19] Use of the Black-Scholes model to determine the fair value of stock options is discussed in greater detail in the article by James Mountain on the text's webpage for Chapter 14. Most stock options do not have an intrinsic value on the date of the grant. Consequently, compensation expense was seldom recorded under the requirements contained in *APB Opinion No. 25. SFAS No. 123* now requires compensation cost to be measured and, at least, disclosed.

Stock Warrants

Stock warrants are certificates that allow holders to acquire shares of stock at certain prices within stated periods. These certificates are generally issued under one of two conditions:

1. As evidence of the *preemptive right* of current shareholders to purchase additional shares of common stock from new stock issues in proportion to their current ownership percentage.
2. As an inducement originally attached to debt or preferred shares to increase the marketability of these securities.

Under current practice, the accounting for the preemptive right of existing shareholders creates no particular problem. These warrants are not recorded except as memoranda in the formal accounting records. In the event warrants of this type are exercised, the value of the shares of stock issued is measured at the amount of cash exchanged.

Detachable warrants attached to other securities require a separate valuation because they may be traded on the open market. The amount to be attributed to these types of warrants depends on their value in the securities market. Their value is measured by determining the percentage relationship of the price of the warrant to the total market price of the security and warrant, and applying this percentage to the proceeds of the security issue. This procedure should be followed whether the warrants are associated with bonds or with preferred stock.

In *APB Opinion No. 14,* the Accounting Principles Board supported this approach when it stated,

> *The Board is of the opinion that the portion of the proceeds of debt securities issued with detachable stock purchase warrants which is applicable to the warrants should be accounted for as paid-in capital. The allocation should be based on the relative fair value of the two securities at the time of issuance.*[20]

If the warrants are exercised, their value will be added to the cash received to arrive at the carrying value of the common stock. In the event the warrants are not exercised within the designated period, the portion of the cost of the security allocated to the warrants will remain on the books as paid-in capital.

---

[19] Ibid.

[20] *Accounting Principles Board Opinion No. 14,* "Accounting for Convertible Debt and Debt Issued with Stock Purchase Warrants" (New York: AICPA, 1969), par. 16.

The Equity/Liability Question

The DM on distinguishing between debt and equity questions whether financial option contracts that obligate the enterprise to issue its own stock are liabilities or equity. In present practice, these contracts are treated as equity. This practice implies that exercise of an option involves a nonreciprocal transfer wherein the issuing enterprise receives something of value (e.g., employee services) but gives up nothing of value in return. Therefore, financial option contracts that do not result in the eventual payment of assets or the performance of services do not qualify as liabilities. Moreover, unlike debt securities, the value of options written on an enterprise's own stock is a function of the market price of the underlying common stock.

Alternatively, financial option contracts can be viewed as obligations to issue stock conditional upon exercise by the holder. They give the holder the right to exchange financial instruments on specified terms. The shares issued represent compensation for the cash received. Because the shares could have been sold at market value, they are issued to the option holder in lieu of cash. The obligation to make the exchange may be satisfied at any time by buying the option at the current market price. Financial option contracts entail a contractual obligation of the issuing corporation to deliver financial instruments upon exercise on potentially unfavorable terms to preexisting common stockholders. At exercise, the corporation receives less cash than it would if the stock issues were sold at the current market price. Consequently, the issuer's decision to allow exercise to occur results in a loss. The loss is an opportunity cost, which "is financed by diluting the preexisting stockholders' wealth."[21] That is, the option holders profit at the expense of preexisting stockholders. Therefore, they are not acting in the role of owners.

Retained Earnings

Legal restrictions in most states allow corporations to pay dividends only when there are accumulated, undistributed earnings. These restrictions have resulted in the reporting of earned capital as a component of owners' equity separate from paid-in capital. Although some states allow dividends from paid-in capital in the event of deficits, corporate managements generally do not wish to deplete capital, and distributions of this type are rare.

Retained earnings represent the accumulated net profits of a corporation that have not been distributed as dividends. It also should be noted that accumulated retained earnings do not necessarily mean that a corporation has the cash available with which to pay dividends. Accumulated earnings allow corporations to distribute dividends; the actual cash funds to pay these dividends must be available or acquired from other sources.

In many cases, the retained earnings balance disclosed on the financial statements is divided into appropriated and unappropriated sections. Appropriated retained earnings comprise that portion of retained earnings that are not available to distribute as dividends. Appropriations may arise from legal

---

[21] FASB, op. cit., par. 134.

restrictions, contractual restrictions, or internal decisions. However, an appropriation does not provide the funds with which to accomplish stated objectives, and it can be argued that these disclosures might be just as effective as footnotes.

Stock Dividends

As noted previously, corporations may have accumulated earnings but not have the funds available to distribute these earnings as cash dividends to stockholders. In such cases, the company may elect to distribute some of its own shares of stock as dividends to current stockholders. Distributions of this type are termed *stock dividends*. When stock dividends are minor, relative to the total number of shares outstanding, retained earnings is reduced by the market value of the shares distributed. Capital stock and additional paid-in capital are increased by the par value of the shares and any excess, respectively. In theory, a relatively small stock dividend will not adversely affect the previously established market value of the stock. The rationale behind stock dividend distributions is that the stockholders will receive additional shares with the same value per share as those previously held. Nevertheless, stock dividends are not income to the recipients. They represent no distribution of corporate assets to the owners and are simply a reclassification of ownership interests.

Stock Splits

A procedure somewhat similar to stock dividends, but with a different purpose, is a *stock split*. The most economical method of purchasing and selling stock in the stock market is in blocks of 100 shares, and this practice affects the marketability of the stock. The higher the price of an individual share of stock, the fewer are the number of people able to purchase the stock in blocks of 100. For this reason, many corporations seek to maintain the price of their stock within certain ranges. When the price climbs above that range, the firm may decide to issue additional shares to all existing stockholders (or split the stock). In a stock split, each stockholder receives a stated multiple of the number of shares currently held (usually 2 or 3 for 1), which lowers the market price per share. In theory, this lower price should be calculated by dividing the current price by the multiple of shares in the split, but intervening variables in the marketplace frequently affect prices simultaneously. A stock split does not cause any change in the stockholder's equity section except to increase the number of actual shares outstanding and reduce the par or stated value per share. No additional values are assigned to the shares of stock issued in a stock split because no distribution of assets or reclassification of ownership interests occurs.

A question sometimes arises as to whether a stock dividend is in actuality a stock split and should be treated accordingly. In a stock dividend, no material change in the market price of the shares is anticipated, whereas stock splits are undertaken specifically to change the market price of the shares. A large stock dividend can cause market prices to decline regardless of the terminology attached to the distribution. A rule of thumb is that if a stock dividend is at least 20 to 25 percent of the outstanding shares, the distribution should be recorded in a manner similar to a stock split. Stock distributions of this magnitude are termed *large stock dividends*. When large stock dividends are declared, standard practice is to capitalize an amount of retained earnings equal to the par value of the shares issued.

Treasury Stock

Capital may be reduced by formally repurchasing and canceling outstanding shares of stock; however, the corporation may informally reduce capital by acquiring shares on the open market without canceling them. These reacquired shares are termed *treasury stock*. Reacquisition of a company's own stock reduces both assets and stockholder equity and results in a legal restriction on retained earnings. The amount of shares repurchased is usually limited by the amount of a company's retained earnings.

In general, finance theory interprets stock repurchase announcements as an indication that management views them as underpriced in the marketplace.[22] In addition, a company may reacquire its own shares in order to offer employee stock options.

Two methods of accounting for treasury stock are found in current practice: the cost method and the par value method. Under the *cost method,* the presumption is that the shares acquired will be resold, and two events are assumed: (1) the purchase of the shares by the corporation and (2) the reissuance to a new stockholder. The reacquired shares are recorded at cost, and this amount is disclosed as negative stockholders' equity by deducting it from total capital until the shares are resold. Because treasury stock transactions are transactions with owners, any difference between the acquisition price and the sales price is generally treated as an adjustment to paid-in capital (unless sufficient additional paid-in capital is not available to offset any "loss"; in such cases retained earnings is charged).

Under the *par value method,* it is assumed that the corporation's relationship with the original stockholder is ended. The transaction is in substance a retirement; hence, the shares are considered constructively retired. Therefore, legal capital and additional paid-in capital are reduced for the original issue price of the reacquired shares. Any difference between the original issue price and the reacquisition price is treated as an adjustment to additional paid-in capital (unless a sufficient balance is not available to offset a "loss" and retained earnings is charged). The par value of the reacquired shares is disclosed as a deduction from capital stock until the treasury shares are reissued.

The disclosure requirements for treasury stock in financial statements are not clearly defined by generally accepted accounting principles. For example, *APB Opinion No. 6* states:

> *When a corporation's stock is acquired for purposes other than retirement (formal or constructive), or when ultimate disposition has not yet been decided, the cost of acquired stock may be shown separately, as a deduction from the total capital*

[22] William Pugh and John S. Jahera, Jr., "Stock Repurchases and Execs Returns: An Empirical Examination," *The Financial Review* (February 1990), pp. 127–143.

stock, capital surplus, and retained earnings, or may be accorded the accounting treatment appropriate for retired stock, or in some circumstances may be shown as an asset.[23]

This *Opinion,* in effect, allows for virtually any presentation of treasury stock desired by a corporation and disregards the reasons for the acquisition of the shares. Treasury stock is clearly not an asset because a company cannot own itself, and dividends are not paid on treasury shares. Similarly, "gains" and "losses" on treasury stock transactions are not to be reported on the income statement because of the possibility of income manipulation and because gains and losses cannot result from investments by owners or distributions to owners. The presentation of treasury shares on the financial statements should be reviewed by the FASB, and a presentation that more closely resembles the purpose of the acquisition of treasury shares should be required.

Other Comprehensive Income

Items recorded as other comprehensive income arise from events not connected with the issuance of stock or the normal profit-directed operations of the company. They result from the need to recognize assets or changes in value of other balance sheet items that have been excluded from the components of income by an authoritative body. The recognition issues for these items are discussed elsewhere in the text. The major examples of other comprehensive income are (1) unrealized gains and losses on investments in debt and equity securities classified as available for sale securities (discussed in Chapter 8) and (2) unrealized gains and losses resulting from the translation of certain investments in foreign subsidiaries (discussed in Chapter 15). Although these items are not included in earnings under current GAAP, they are defined in *SFAS No. 133* as components of comprehensive income.

Quasi-Reorganizations

A corporation that suffers losses over an extended period of time may find it difficult to attract new capital. That is, debtholders and stockholders wish to receive a return on their investments, but a period of unprofitable operations may restrict the corporation's ability to offer interest and dividend payments. This is particularly true for stockholders who cannot receive dividends unless there is a positive retained earnings balance.

In some cases a corporate reorganization allowed under the provisions of state law may be attempted as an alternative to bankruptcy. These situations are termed *quasi-reorganizations,* and the company is given a fresh start by eliminating the deficit balance in retained earnings and writing down any overvalued assets. If a quasi-reorganization is undertaken, the corporation

---

[23] *Accounting Principles Board Opinion No. 6,* "Status of Accounting Research Bulletins" (New York: AICPA, 1965), par. 12.

must clearly disclose its plan to the stockholders and receive their formal approval.

Modigliani and Miller[24] found that the actual payment of dividends did not affect the market value of an enterprise, whereas the ability to pay dividends did affect a firm's market value. A quasi-reorganization gives a firm the ability to pay dividends sooner than it would have been able to without a quasi-reorganization, and a quasi-reorganization can positively affect the market value of a reorganized enterprise. Therefore, a firm that is unable to pay dividends because of negative retained earnings will be able to raise new capital more economically if it first engages in a quasi-reorganization.

The steps involved in a quasi-reorganization are

1. Assets are written down to their fair market value against retained earnings or additional paid-in capital.
2. The retained earnings deficit is eliminated against additional paid-in capital or legal capital.
3. The zero retained earnings balance is dated, and this date is retained until it loses its significance (typically 5 to 10 years).

Financial Analysis of Stockholders' Equity

The financial analysis of investment returns was introduced in Chapter 5. The return on assets ratio measures the average return on investment to all investors regardless of their relationship to the company. This ratio is based on the entity theory in that it does not distinguish among investors and reports on overall firm performance. A ratio that reports on a company's performance from the point of view of its common stockholders is the return on common shareholders' equity (ROCSE). This ratio is based on the proprietary theory in that borrowing costs are considered expenses rather than a return on investment and is based on sustainable income. It is calculated as:

$$\text{ROCSE} = \frac{\text{Net income available to common shareholders}}{\text{Average common stockholders' equity}}$$

Kroll-O'Gara Company's 1998 and 1997 ROCSE are calculated as follows:

	1998	**1997**
ROCSE =	$\dfrac{\$13,088,906}{[(\$206,856 + 149,993,769) + (\$147,952 + 58,912,209)]/2}$	$\dfrac{\$2,406,643 + 193,875 + 360,000}{[(\$147,952 + 58,912,209) + (\$135,905 + 50,589,966)^{25}]/2}$
=	12.5%	5.4%

---

[24] Modigliani and Miller, op. cit., pp. 261–297.

[25] From the company's 1997 10-K report.

The ROCSE is impacted by both profitability and the extent to which a company employs financial leverage. As discussed in Chapter 10, financial leverage increases the rate of return to common stockholders when the return on investment projects is greater than the cost of the borrowed funds. Kroll-O'Gara Company's ROCSE increased from 5.4 percent in 1997 to 12.5 percent in 1998. These returns are somewhat different than the return on asset measures of 1.88 percent and 6.6 percent for 1997 and 1998, respectively, that were illustrated in Chapter 5. A company's use of financial leverage can also be evaluated by calculating the common stock earnings ratio and the financial structure ratio.

The common stock earnings leverage ratio (CSELR) indicates the proportion of net operating profit after taxes that belongs to the common stockholders and is calculated as:

$$CSELR = \frac{\text{Net income available to common stockholders}}{\text{Net operating profit after taxes}^{26}}$$

The financial structure ratio (FSR) indicates the proportion of the company's assets that are being financed by the stockholders and is calculated as:

$$FSR = \frac{\text{Average assets}}{\text{Average common stockholders' equity}}$$

Kroll-O'Gara Company's CSELR and FSR for 1998 are:

$$CSELR = \frac{13,088,906}{\$13,088,906 + 2,868,376^{27}}$$
$$= 82.0\%$$

$$FSR = \frac{(\$248,956,059 + 150,484,480)/2}{[(\$206,856 + 149,993,769)}$$
$$+ (\$147,952 + 58,912,209)]/2$$
$$= 1.91$$

These ratios indicate that the company's use of financial leverage is resulting in a rate of return to the common stockholders that is in excess of what the company earns on all of its assets.

International Accounting Standards

In "Framework for the Preparation and Presentation of Financial Statements," the IASC indicated a preference for the proprietary theory when it

[26] Amounts obtained from the company's income statement contained in Chapter 4. The calculation of NOPAT is illustrated in Chapter 5.

[27] See Chapter 5 for a discussion of the calculation of net operating profit after taxes.

stated, "*Equity* is the residual interest in the assets of the enterprise after deducting all its liabilities."[28] The IASC then indicated that equity may be subclassified to disclose amounts contributed by stockholders, retained earnings, reserves, and capital maintenance adjustments. These subclassifications are viewed as relevant to the decision-making needs of the users of financial statements because they indicate any current legal restrictions and may reflect the fact that different ownership interests have different rights. The IASC has not yet addressed any specific equity reporting issues.

Summary

There are a number of theoretical approaches to the recording and reporting of ownership equity. The proprietary and entity theories are the two major approaches, but accounting theorists have developed other viewpoints, including the fund, commander, enterprise, and residual equity theories.

In addition to an understanding of the theoretical bases of equity reporting, it is important to understand the generally accepted accounting principles associated with the recording and reporting of equity. Preferred stock, common stock, additional paid-in capital, subscriptions, options, and warrants all require somewhat different accounting treatments.

Another aspect of equity reporting is the valuation of retained earnings. Although retained earnings exist in an accounting sense and allow the distribution of cash dividends, the actual funds for such distribution may not be available. In addition, stock dividends, stock splits, treasury stock, and quasi-reorganization all affect the reporting of equity securities, and each of these has its own reporting requirements.

In the readings, contained on the text's webpage for Chapter 14, accounting for stockholders' equity is further addressed.

Cases

• Case 14-1 Preparation of the Stockholders' Equity Section of the Balance Sheet

Raun Company had the following account titles on its December 31, 2001, trial balance:

> Six percent cumulative convertible preferred stock, $100 par value
> Premium on preferred stock
> Common stock, $1 stated value
> Premium on common stock
> Retained earnings

---

[28] International Accounting Standards Committee, "Framework for the Preparation and Presentation of Financial Statements," (1989), par. 49(c).

The following additional information about the Raun Company was available for the year ended December 31, 2001.

1. There were 2 million shares of preferred stock authorized, of which 1 million were outstanding. All 1 million shares outstanding were issued on January 2, 1985, for $120 a share. The preferred stock is convertible into common stock on a one-for-one basis until December 31, 2002; thereafter, the preferred stock ceases to be convertible and is callable at par value by the company. No preferred stock has been converted into common stock, and there were no dividends in arrears at December 31, 2001.

2. The common stock has been issued at amounts above stated value per share since incorporation in 1955. Of the million shares authorized, there were 3.5 million shares outstanding at January 1, 2001. The market price of the outstanding common stock has increased slowly, but consistently, for the last five years.

3. The company has an employee stock option plan in which certain key employees and officers may purchase shares of common stock at 100 percent of the market price at the date of the option grant. All options are exercisable in installments of one-third each year, commencing one year after the date of the grant, and they expire if not exercised within four years of the grant date. On January 1, 2001, options for 70,000 shares were outstanding at prices ranging from $47 to $83 a share. Options for 20,000 shares were exercised at $47 to $79 a share during 2001. No options expired during 2001, and additional options for 15,000 shares were granted at $86 a share. Of these, 30,000 were exercisable at that date at prices ranging from $54 to $79 a share.

4. The company also has an employee stock purchase plan through which the company pays one-half and the employee pays one-half of the market price of the stock at the date of the subscription. During 2001 employees subscribed to 60,000 shares at an average price of $87 a share. All 60,000 shares were paid for and issued late in September 2001.

5. On December 31, 2001, a total of 355,000 shares of common stock were set aside for the granting of future stock options and for future purchases under the employee stock purchase plan. The only changes in the stockholders' equity for 2001 were those described previously, 2001 net income, and cash dividends paid.

Required:

a. Prepare a stockholders' equity section of the balance sheet of Raun Company at December 31, 2001; substitute, where appropriate, Xs for unknown dollar amounts. Use good form and provide full disclosure. Write appropriate footnotes as they should appear in the published financial statements.

b. Provide theoretical justification for your treatment of the employee stock option plan. In your discussion, explain why your treatment fits the definition of equity or liabilities, whichever is appropriate.

- ## Case 14-2 Accounting for Employee Stock Option: Theoretical Arguments

Arts Corp. offers a generous employee compensation package that includes employee stock options. The exercise price has always been equal to the market price of the stock at the date of grant. The corporate controller, John Jones, believes that employee stock options, like all obligations to issue the corporation's own stock, are equity. The new staff accountant, Marcy Means, disagrees. Marcy argues that when a company issues stock for less than current value, the value of preexisting stockholders' shares is diluted.

Required:
a. Under existing generally accepted accounting principles, describe how Arts Corp. should account for its employee stock option plan.
b. Pretend you are hired to debate the issue of the proper treatment of options written on a company's own stock. Formulate your argument, citing concepts and definitions to buttress your case assuming
    i. You are siding with John.
    ii. You are siding with Marcy.

- ## Case 14-3 Preparation of Financial Statements Under Various Theories of Equity

Drake Company reported the following for 2001:

Current Assets	$ 87,000
Current Liabilities	19,000
Revenues	450,000
Cost of Goods Sold	220,000
Noncurrent Assets	186,000
Bonds Payable (10%, issued at par)	100,000
Preferred Stock, $5, $100 Par	20,000
Common Stock, $10 Par	50,000
Paid-in-Capital in Excess of Par	48,000
Operating Expenses	64,000
Retained Earnings	36,000

Common stockholders received a $2 dividend during the year. The preferred stock is noncumulative and nonparticipating.

Required:
a. Ignoring income taxes, prepare an income statement and balance sheet for Drake Company at December 31, 2001, that is consistent with each of the following theories of equity:
    i. Entity theory
    ii. Proprietary theory
    iii. Residual equity theory
b. For each theory cited above, compute the December 31, 2001, debt-to-equity ratio. If none would be computed, discuss why.

• Case 14-4 Accounting for Treasury Stock

For numerous reasons, a corporation may reacquire shares of its own capital stock. When a company purchases treasury stock, it has two options as to how to account for the shares: the cost method and the par value method.

Required:
Compare and contrast the cost method and the par value method for each of the following.
a. Purchase of shares at a price less than par value.
b. Purchase of shares at a price greater than par value.
c. Subsequent resale of treasury shares at a price less than purchase price but more than par value.
d. Subsequent resale of treasury shares at a price greater than both purchase price and par value.
e. Effect on net income.

• Case 14-5 Accounting for a Quasi-Reorganization

Carrol, Inc., accomplished a quasi-reorganization effective December 31, 2001. Immediately prior to the quasi-reorganization, the stockholders' equity was as follows:

Common stock, par value $10 per share authorized issued and outstanding 400,000 shares	$4,000,000
Additional paid-in capital	600,000
Retained earnings (deficit)	(900,000)

Under the terms of the quasi-reorganization, the par value of the common stock was reduced from $10 per share to $5 per share and equipment was written down by $1.2 million.

Required:
Discuss the accounting treatment necessary to accomplish this quasi-reorganization.

• Case 14-6 Stock Options: Various Methods

Stock options are widely used as a form of compensation for corporate executives.

Required:
a. Identify five methods that have been proposed for determining the value of executive stock options.
b. Discuss the conceptual merits of each of these proposed methods.

• Case 14-7 Effects of Stock Options

On January 1, 2001, as an incentive to improved performance of duties, Recycling Corporation adopted a qualified stock option plan to grant corporate executives nontransferable stock options to 500,000 shares of its unissued $1 par value common stock. The options were granted on May 1, 2001, at $25 per share, the market price on that date. All the options were exercisable one year later and for four years thereafter, providing that the grantee was employed by the corporation at the date of exercise.

The market price of this stock was $40 per share on May 1, 2002. All options were exercised before December 31, 2002, at times when the market price varied between $40 and $50 per share.

Required:
a. What information on this option plan should be presented in the financial statements of Recycling Corporation at (1) December 31, 2001, and (2) December 31, 2002? Explain.
b. It has been said that the exercise of such a stock option would dilute the equity of existing stockholders in the corporation.
    i.   How could this happen? Discuss.
    ii. What conditions could prevent a dilution of existing equities from taking place in this transaction? Discuss.

• Case 14-8 Theoretical Implications of Various Theories of Equity

The proprietary theory, the entity theory, and the funds theory are three approaches to accounting for equities.

Required:
a. Describe briefly each of these theories.
b. State your reasons for emphasizing the application of one of these theories to each of the following.
    i.   Single proprietorship
    ii. Partnership
    iii. Financial institutions (banks)
    iv. Consolidated statements
    v.   Estate accounting

• Case 14-9 Classification of Stockholders' Equity

The total owners' equity (excess of assets over liabilities) is usually shown under a number of subcaptions on the corporation's balance sheet.

Required:
a. List the major subdivisions of the stockholders' equity section of a corporate balance sheet and describe briefly the nature of the amounts that will appear in each section.
b. Explain fully the reasons for subdividing the amount of stockholders' equity, including legal, accounting, and other considerations.
c. Describe four different kinds of transactions that will result in paid-in or permanent capital in excess of legal or stated capital.

d. Various accounting authorities have recommended that the terms *paid-in surplus* and *earned surplus* not be used in published financial statements. Explain briefly the reason for this suggestion and indicate acceptable substitutes for the terms.

• Case 14-10 Stock Dividends

The directors of Lenox Corporation are considering issuing a stock dividend.

Required:
The directors have asked you to discuss the proposed action by answering the following questions.
a. What is a stock dividend? How is a stock dividend distinguished from a stock split from a legal standpoint? from an accounting standpoint?
b. For what reasons does a corporation usually declare a stock dividend? a stock split?
c. Discuss the amount, if any, of retained earnings to be capitalized in connection with a stock dividend.

• Case 14-11 Stocks Splits and Stock Dividends

A corporation may use stock splits and stock dividends to change the number of shares of its stock outstanding.

Required:
a. What is meant by a stock split effected in the form of a dividend?
b. From an accounting viewpoint, explain how the stock split effected in the form of a dividend differs from an ordinary stock dividend.
c. How should a stock dividend that has been declared but not yet issued be classified in a statement of financial position? Why?

• Case 14-12 Accounting for ESOPs

Growth Corp. offered the following stock option plan to its employees:
    Each employee will receive 1,000 options to purchase shares of stock at an option price equal to the market price of the company's common shares on the grant date, 1/1/x1. On that date:

The market price per share was	$ 22
The fair value of an option was	$ 3

Required:
a. Describe how the ESOPs will be reported under *APB Opinion No. 25*.
b. Analyze and explain the consequences of the *APB Opinion No. 25* accounting treatment. Your analysis should consider the following:
    i.   The conceptual framework
    ii. Any ethical implications
    iii. The impact on financial statements
    iv. The impact on financial ratios

c. The FASB encourages companies to adopt the fair value method of accounting for ESOPs as described in *SFAS No. 123*. Describe how the ESOPs will be reported under this method.

d. Analyze and explain the consequences of using fair value to measure and report the ESOPs. Your analysis should consider the following:
   i. The conceptual framework
   ii. Any ethical implications
   iii. The impact on financial statements
   iv. The impact on financial ratios

• Case 14-13 Debt vs. Equity

The entity theory of equity implies that there should be no need for financial statements to distinguish between debt and equity. Alternatively, proprietary theory implies that such a distinction is necessary and yields information vital to owners and potential stockholders.

Required:

a. Discuss the entity theory rationale for making no distinction between debt and equity.

b. Is entity theory or proprietary theory consistent with modern theories of finance—that is, does the firm's capital structure make a difference? Explain.

Room for Debate

• Issue 1

In the 1990 discussion memorandum, "Distinguishing between Liability and Equity Instruments and Accounting for Instruments with Characteristics of Both," the FASB presented arguments relating to the presentation and measurement of a company's stock options and warrants. Under current GAAP, stock options and warrants are measured at the historical fair value of consideration received at issuance. The amount received is reported as an element of stockholders' equity.

Some theorists argue that stock options and warrants represent obligations of the issuing entity and should be reported as liabilities. Moreover, a more appropriate measure would be fair value of the options or warrants at the balance sheet date.

Team Debate:

Team 1. Argue for the current GAAP treatment for the issuance and subsequent reporting stock options and warrants.

Team 2. Argue for reporting stock options and warrants as liabilities measured at current fair value.

Recommended Additional Readings

Cheatham, Carole, Leo R. Cheatham, and Michelle McEacharn. "ESOPs Fable: The Goose that Laid the Golden Egg." *The National Public Accountant* (April 1995), pp. 33–37.

Ciccotello, Conrad S., and C. Terry Grant. "Employee Stock Option Accounting Changes." *Journal of Accountancy* (January 1995), pp. 72–76.

Davis, Michael L., and James A. Largay III. "Quasi reorganization: Fresh or False Start." *Journal of Accountancy* (July 1995), pp. 79–84.

Haley, Brian W., and Thomas A. Ratcliff. "Accounting for Incentive Stock Options." *The CPA Journal* (1982), pp. 32–39.

Kimmel, Paul, and Terry D. Warfield. "Variation in Attributes of Redeemable Preferred Stock: Implications for Accounting Standards." *Accounting Horizons* (June 1993), pp. 30–40.

Mountain, James R. "FASB 123: Putting Together the Pieces." *Journal of Accountancy* (January 1996), pp. 73–78.

Nair, R. D., Larry E. Rittenberg, and Jerry J. Weygandt. "Accounting for Redeemable Preferred Stock: Unresolved Issues." *Accounting Horizons* (June 1990), pp. 33–41.

Roberts, Michael L., William D. Samson, and Michael T. Dugan. "The Stockholders' Equity Section: Form Without Substance." *Accounting Horizons* (December 1990), pp. 35–46.

Bibliography

Alvin, Gerald. "Accounting for Investment and Stock Rights: The Market Value Method." *The CPA Journal* (February 1973), pp. 126–131.

Bird, Francis, A., Lewis F. Davidson, and Charles H. Smith. "Perceptions of External Accounting Transfers under Entity and Proprietary Theory." *The Accounting Review* (April 1975), pp. 233–244.

Birnberg, Jacob G. "An Information Oriented Approach to the Presentation of Common Stockholders' Equity." *The Accounting Review* (October 1964), pp. 963–971.

Boudreaux, Kenneth J., and Stephen A. Zeff. "A Note on the Measure of Compensation Implicit in Employee Stock Options." *Journal of Accounting Research* (Spring 1976), pp. 158–162.

Chang, Emily C. "Accounting for Stock Splits." *Financial Executive* (March 1969), pp. 79–80, 82–84.

Committee on Tax and Financial Entity Theory. "Report of the Committee on Tax and Financial Entity Theory." *The Accounting Review,* supplement to Vol. 48 (1973), pp. 187–192.

Foster, Taylor W., III, and Don Vickrey. "The Information Content of Stock Dividend Announcements." *The Accounting Review* (April 1976), pp. 360–370.

Goldberg, Louis. *An Inquiry into the Nature of Accounting.* American Accounting Association, Monograph No. 7, 1963.

Gynther, Reginald S. "Accounting Concepts and Behavioral Hypotheses." *The Accounting Review* (April 1967), pp. 274–290.

Hawkins, David F., and Walter J. Campbell. *Equity Valuation: Models, Analysis and Implications.* New York: Financial Executives Research Foundation, 1978.

Husband, George. "The Corporate-Entity Fiction and Accounting Theory." *The Accounting Review* (September 1938), pp. 241–253.

Li, David H. "The Nature of Corporate Residual Equity under the Entity Concept." *The Accounting Review* (April 1960), pp. 197–201.

Lowe, Howard D. "The Classification of Corporate Stock Equities." *The Accounting Review* (July 1961), pp. 425–433.

Melcher, Beatrice. *Accounting Research Study No. 15.* "Stockholders' Equity." New York: AICPA, 1973.

Millar, James A. "Split or Dividend: Do the Words Really Matter?" *The Accounting Review* (January 1977), pp. 52–55.

Modigliani, F., and M. Miller. "Cost of Capital, Corporation Finance and the Theory of Investment." *American Economic Review* (June 1958), pp. 261–297.

1964 Concepts and Standards Research Committee—The Business Entity. "The Entity Concept." *The Accounting Review* (April 1965), pp. 358–367.

Pusker, Henri C. "Accounting for Capital Stock Distributions (Stock Split-Ups and Dividends)." *New York CPA* (May 1971), pp. 347–352.

Rogers, Donald R., and R. W. Schattke. "Buy-Outs of Stock Options: Compensation or Capital?" *Journal of Accountancy* (August 1972), pp. 55–59.

Scott, Richard A. "Owners' Equity, the Anachronistic Element." *The Accounting Review* (October 1979), pp. 750–763.

Simons, Donald R., and Jerry J. Weygandt. "Stock Options Revisited: Accounting for Option Buy-Outs." *The CPA Journal* (September 1973), pp. 779–783.

Smith, Clifford W., Jr., and Jerold L. Zimmerman. "Valuing Employer Stock Option Plans Using Option Pricing Methods." *Journal of Accounting Research* (Autumn 1976), pp. 357–364.

Smith, Ralph E., and Leroy F. Imdieke. "Accounting for Stock Issued to Employees." *Journal of Accountancy* (November 1974), pp. 68–75.

Soujanen, Waino. "Enterprise Theory and Corporate Balance Sheets." *The Accounting Review* (January 1958), pp. 56–65.

Sprouse, Robert T. "The Significance of the Concept of the Corporation in Accounting Analyses." *The Accounting Review* (July 1957), pp. 369–378.

Staubus, George J. "The Residual Equity Point of View in Accounting." *The Accounting Review* (January 1959), pp. 3–13.

Thomas, Paula Bevels, and Larry E. Farmer. "Accounting for Stock Options and SARs: The Equality Question." *Journal of Accountancy* (June 1984), pp. 92–98.

Vatter, William J. "Corporate Stock Equities." In Morton Backer (ed.), *Modern Accounting Theory.* Englewood Cliffs, NJ: Prentice-Hall, 1966.

Vatter, William J. *The Fund Theory of Accounting and Its Implications for Financial Reports.* Chicago, IL: University of Chicago Press, 1947.

Weygandt, Jerry J. "Valuation of Stock Option Contracts." *The Accounting Review* (January 1977), pp. 40–51.

Accounting for
Multiple Entities

Since the inception of the corporate form of organization, business enter-prises have found it beneficial to combine operations to achieve economies of scale. These combined operations may vary from corporate joint ventures in which two or more corporations join together as a partnership for a par-ticular project, such as drilling an offshore oil well, to the sale of one com-pany to another. Accounting for the acquisition of one company by another is complicated by the fact that various terms may be used to describe these acquisitions. Such terms as *consolidation, combination, merger, pooling of interest,* and *purchase* have all been used interchangeably despite the fact that they are not all the same and some are subclassifications of others. In this chapter we focus on five aspects of accounting for multiple entities: (1) the acquisition of one company by another—*combinations,* (2) the reporting of parent and sub-sidiary relationships—*consolidations* and *segment reporting,* (3) accounting for the acquisition of a company by acquiring stock directly from the stockhold-ers—*tender offers,* (4) accounting for acquired subsidiaries—*push-down account-ing,* and (5) foreign currency translation for international subsidiaries.

Business Combinations

Combining two or more previously separate business organizations into a single entity has been an observable phenomenon since the late 1800s. Wyatt categorized this phenomenon as follows:

The classical era   The period from 1890 to 1904, following the passage of the Sherman Act. These combinations were generally accomplished through a holding company whose purpose was vertical integration of all operations from the acquisition of raw materials to the sale of the product.

Second wave   The period from the end of World War I to the end of the 1920s. These combinations were generally piecemeal acquisitions whose purpose was to expand the operations of the acquiring company.

Third wave   The period from the end of the World War II through the 1960s. Again these were piecemeal acquisitions designed to strengthen competitive position, diversify into new areas, or keep up with technological changes.[1]

In addition to the foregoing reasons, several other factors may cause a business organization to consider combining with another organization.

Tax consequences   The purchasing corporation may accrue the benefits of operating loss carryforwards from acquired corporations.

Growth and diversification   The purchasing corporation may wish to acquire a new product or enter a new market.

Financial considerations   A larger asset base may make it easier for the corporation to acquire additional funds from capital markets.

Competitive pressure   Economies of scale may alleviate a highly competitive market situation.

Profit and retirement   The seller may be motivated by a high profit or the desire to retire.[2]

Accounting for Business Combinations

After the Securities and Exchange Commission was established during the 1930s, two methods of accounting for business combinations evolved: *purchase* and *pooling of interests*. These methods are described in more detail in the following comments.

In accounting for business combinations, it is essential to recall that fair reporting of the results of economic events for a particular enterprise is the essence of the accounting process. These reports should not be biased in favor of any group and must be based on the underlying substance of the economic events. There are two methods of achieving majority ownership in another corporation: (1) the acquiring corporation purchases the voting stock of the acquired corporation for cash or (2) the acquiring corporation exchanges its voting stock for the voting stock of the acquired corporation. The essential question then becomes: Is the economic substance of these events different enough to warrant different methods of accounting?

As noted earlier, under current GAAP two methods of accounting for business combinations are permitted: (1) purchase and (2) pooling of interests. Under the *purchase* method, the assets of the acquired company are recorded at their market value in the same manner as was discussed in Chapter 7 for group purchases of assets. That is, the individual *fair market value* of each asset is recorded. Any liabilities assumed by the acquiring company are

---

[1] Arthur R. Wyatt, *A Critical Study of Accounting for Business Combinations* (New York: AICPA, 1963), pp. 1–5.

[2] Ibid., pp. 6–8.

then deducted from this amount, and any excess between the net assets received and the cash paid is recorded as *goodwill.*

As discussed in Chapter 9, under current GAAP, goodwill is amortized over a period not to exceed 40 years. However, in late 2000 the FASB tentatively decided that goodwill should no longer be amortized. Rather, goodwill would be accounted for by using an impairment approach and expensed only when its recorded value exceeds its fair value. This treatment would require companies to periodically review the amount of goodwill recorded on their balance sheets to determine if it is overvalued, and could have troublesome effects for companies whose stock prices have significantly declined such as Aenna or Blockbuster during 2000. That is, companies reporting goodwill values in excess of their market values might be required to record large charges against earnings. (This issue is evolving and will be updated on the text's webpage).

Under current GAAP, if the difference between the net assets received and the cash paid is negative, noncurrent assets (other than investments) are reduced. If the balance of the noncurrent assets is reduced to zero, a deferred credit is created and amortized. In addition, reported income for the new combined company will include the acquiring company's income for the entire year and the acquired company's income since the date of acquisition. In a previous exposure draft, the Board, proposed that "negative" goodwill be allocated first to intangible assets for which there is no observable market, and that any excess then be allocated to acquired depreciable and intangible assets. Finally, any remaining excess would be recognized as an extraordinary item.[3]

The *pooling of interests* method accounts for the combination as the uniting of ownership interests. That is, it is not accounted for as an acquisition but rather as a fusion of two or more previously separate entities. The recorded amounts of assets and liabilities of the merging companies are added together on the balance sheet of the combined corporation, and goodwill is *not* recorded. The par value of the stock of the acquiring company, which was issued to obtain the acquired entity, replaces the stock of the acquired entity. The remaining stockholders' equity amounts for the two entities are then combined. Moreover, income for the new reporting unit includes the income since the last reporting date for each of the previously separate companies. For example, if P Corporation acquired S Corporation on December 15, 2000, and both companies' fiscal year ended on December 31, the combined corporation reports S's net income for the entire year of 2000.

In addressing the question posed earlier on the propriety of using different recording and reporting techniques, it should be noted that two distinctly different economic events may occur in a business combination. When cash is exchanged, only one ownership group remains, even though there may be two separate legal entities; because one controls the other, only one entity in essence survives. When voting stock is exchanged, all the previous owners are still present, and the companies have simply united to carry on their pre-

[3] Exposure Draft, "Business Combinations and Intangible Assets," September 7, 1999.

viously separate operations. Logically, the purchase method is appropriate for business combinations resulting from cash transactions. However, the pooling of interests method may be appropriate when the ownership of two or more entities is combined.

The Accounting Principles Board reviewed this question and in 1970 issued *Opinion No. 16*, "Business Combinations."[4] The Board found merit in the use of both methods and did not propose that one method be used to the exclusion of the other. The APB noted that the two methods were not alternatives for accounting for the same transaction and established specific criteria for determining whether a combination should be accounted for as a purchase or as a pooling of interests. All transactions that involve the exchange of cash are to be recorded as purchases, whereas exchanges of voting stock are to be reported as pooling of interests subject to certain specific criteria. If any of the criteria is violated, the combination must be recorded as a purchase. These criteria are classified as (1) attributes of the combining companies, (2) manner of combining interests, and (3) absence of planned transactions. In essence, the criteria were established to ensure that a combination could not be recorded as a pooling of interests where one group of stockholders achieved an advantage over another, or where the combined corporation did not plan to carry on the activities of the previously separate companies. These requirements are summarized as follows.

Attributes of the Combining Companies

1. Each of the combining companies is autonomous and has not been a subsidiary or division of another corporation within two years before the plan of combination is initiated.

2. Each of the combining companies is independent of the other combining companies. (*Independent* means no more than 10 percent investment in the outstanding voting stock of any combining company at the date of acquisition.)

These attributes are intended to ensure a true fusion of two previously separate, distinct stockholder interests and assets. Consequently, criterion 1 prohibits fragments of prior entities from being pooled, whereas criterion 2 prohibits prior relationships between the two entities. Prior relationships between the combining entities would mean that the present combination combines only the previously uncombined segment. In addition, prior relationships between the combined entity and other entities would indicate that only a portion of another entity is combined with the acquiring entity.

Manner of Combining Interests

1. The combination is effected in a single transaction or is completed in accordance with a specific plan within one year after the plan is initiated.

---

[4] *Accounting Principles Board Opinion No. 16*, "Business Combinations" (New York: APB, 1970).

2. A corporation offers and issues only common stock with rights identical to those of the majority of its outstanding voting common stock in exchange for substantially all the voting common stock interest of another company at the date the plan of combination is consummated. (*Substantially all* means 90 percent or more of the outstanding voting common stock at the date the plan is consummated.)

3. None of the combining companies changes the equity interest of the voting common stock in contemplation of effecting the combination within two years before the plan is initiated or between the date the plan is initiated and the date it is consummated. (Such changes might include distribution to stockholders, exchanges, retirements, or additional issuances.)

4. Each of the combining companies reacquires shares of voting common stock only for purposes other than business combinations, and no company reacquires more than a normal number of shares between the date the combination is initiated and consummated (normal reacquisition determined by pattern prior to initiation of the plan).

5. The ratio of the interest of an individual common stockholder to those of other common stockholders in a combining company remains the same as a result of the exchange of stock to effect the combination. (The proportion of shares received is equal to each individual stockholder's relative proportion of previous ownership.)

6. The voting rights to which the common stock ownership interests in the resulting combined corporation are entitled are exercisable by the stockholders; the stockholders are neither deprived of nor restricted in exercising those rights for a period.

7. The combination is resolved at the date the plan is consummated, and no provisions of the plan relating to the issue of securities or other considerations are pending.

The intent of the manner of combining interests attributes is to ensure that the continuation of prior ownership interests of the combining companies occurs in a manner that leaves their interests in the combined assets virtually unchanged. Under these conditions, all stockholders of the acquired entity are treated in an even-handed manner. There are no transactions designed to manipulate and bring about the combination or to favor one group of stockholders over another.

Absence of Planned Transactions

1. The combined corporation does not agree directly or indirectly to retire or reacquire all or part of the common stock issued to effect the combination.

2. The combined corporation does not enter into other financial arrangements for the benefit of former stockholders of a combining company, such as a guaranty of loans secured by stock issued in the combination, which in effect negates the exchange of equity securities.

3. The combined corporation does not intend or plan to dispose of a significant part of the assets of the combining companies within two years after the combination other than disposals in the ordinary course of business of the formerly separate companies and to eliminate duplicate facilities or excess capacity.[5]

Such planned transactions would have counteracted the conditions for a continuation of prior ownership interests. In effect, they would allow a purchase to be disguised as a pooling of interests. The parties to a business combination may prefer that it be recorded as a pooling of interests. Poolings do not change the recorded values of assets combined with the acquiring entity regardless of the value of the stock exchanged. The revenues and expenses (and subsequent cash flows) of the acquired entity would presumably be unaffected by the form of business combination, but, under the purchase method, recorded asset costs tend to be higher than under a pooling of interests. Those additional costs are written off against profits, resulting in lower earnings. Consequently, management may be prompted to structure the terms of a business combination to comply with the pooling criteria.

It should be emphasized that pooling of interests is appropriate only when there is an exchange of voting stock and each of the foregoing conditions has been met. Where a combination has been effected by a cash transaction or any *one* of the foregoing conditions has been violated, the purchase method must be used. In addition, when the purchase method is appropriate for combinations involving the exchange of voting common stock, the fair market value of the securities exchanged is the measure of the acquisition price.

Criticism of the Pooling of Interests Method

Critics of the pooling method argue that business combinations reported under this method are similar to those reported under the purchase method, yet pooled financial statements are substantially different from those produced by the purchase method. Unlike the purchase method, pooling ignores the values exchanged in a business combination. As a result, under the pooling method, information regarding how much was invested is not disclosed, and assets that were not previously recorded by the combining companies are ignored. The consequent understatement of assets and overstatement of income in subsequent years hampers the investor's ability to assess return on investment. Moreover, because the acquired assets are not measured in a manner similar to other acquisitions, it is difficult to compare the performance of pooled entities and other companies. The end result may be the disruption of the efficient allocation of resources in the capital markets.

Another consideration is that the pooling of interests method is generally not allowed under international accounting standards. This condition further exacerbates intercompany comparisons of financial condition and perform-

[5] Ibid., pars. 46–48.

ance. In early 2000, the FASB voted to eliminate the pooling of interests method for all business combinations occurring after January 1, 2001. This decision resulted in economic consequences arguments about its effect on mergers. Critics of the decision to eliminate the pooling method contend that it will have a negative effect on the ability of companies to engage in mergers in the future and that many of the mergers that took place during the 1990s would not have been consummated if the rule had been in place at that time. As a result, on October 3, 2000 two members of Congress, Representatives Christopher Cox (R-CA) and Calvin Dooley (D-CA) introduced a bill in the House of Representatives that would delay the completion of the project on business combinations. This action was immediately criticized by the Chairman of the FASB, Edmund L. Jenkins, as legislative interference with the FASB's ability to do its job. Subsequently, five members of Congress (four of whom were CPAs) issued dear colleague letters opposing the bill. These events caused the FASB to revisit the issue but in early 2001 the FASB reaffirmed its decision to eliminate pooling of interests accounting. (This issue is evolving and will be updated on the text's webpage.)

The Fresh-Start Method

A stumbling block to the FASB's efforts to eliminate the pooling of interests method is the notion that some business combinations are essentially mergers of equals. In these cases, none of the combining entities continues. Instead, a new combined entity emerges that is substantially different from its predecessor companies. In a 1998 position paper, the FASB determined that neither the purchase nor the pooling of interests methods may be appropriate for these types of business combinations, and it proposed a new method, termed the *fresh-start method*. Under the fresh-start method, all assets of the combined, surviving entity would be revalued. The resulting financial statements would depict net assets and performance as though the enterprise were a newly formed business entity. Such a revaluation would be similar to that under the purchase method; all the net assets of all combined parties would be revalued rather than just those of the acquired entity.[6]

Consolidations

When a business organization acquires control over one or more others through the acquisition of a majority of the outstanding voting stock, stockholders of the acquiring company (the *parent* company) have an interest in the assets of combined parent/*subsidiary* entity. It is logical to presume that financial statements that combine the results of both parent company and subsidiary operations and financial position would be more meaningful, at least to parent company stockholders, than presenting the separate financial statements of the parent company and each individual subsidiary company.[7]

---

[6] Invitation to Comment, "Methods of Accounting for Business Combinations: Recommendations of the G4 + 1 for Achieving Convergence," FASB, December 15, 1998.

For accounting purposes, the entire group is considered a unified whole, and *SFAS No. 94* requires majority-owned subsidiaries to be *consolidated* unless the parent is precluded from exercising control or control is temporary.[8]

The criteria for preparing consolidated financial statements were originally described in *Accounting Research Bulletin No. 51* as follows:

1. A parent-subsidiary relationship must exist. (The parent must own at least 51 percent of the subsidiary.)

2. The parent exercises control over the subsidiary. (Where the courts are exercising control as in a bankruptcy, consolidation is not appropriate.)

3. The parent plans to maintain control over the subsidiary during the near future. (Subsidiaries that are to be sold in the near future should not be consolidated.)

4. The parent and subsidiary should operate as an integrated unit, and non-homogeneous operations should be excluded.

5. The fiscal years of the units should approximate each other. (Generally, they should fall within 93 days of each other, or appropriate adjustments should be made to reflect similar closing dates.[9]

The underlying philosophy of both *ARB No. 51* and *SFAS No. 94* is the presentation of a single, though fictional, entity with economic but not legal substance. In the preparation of consolidated financial statements, two overriding principles prevail. The first is balance sheet oriented, and the second is income statement oriented.

1. The entity cannot own or owe itself.

2. The entity cannot make a profit by selling to itself.

The result of the first principle is to eliminate all assets on one company's books that are offset by liabilities on the other, for example, an account receivable on the parent's books relating to a corresponding account payable on the subsidiary's books. In the preparation of consolidated statements, the parent's account receivable is eliminated against the subsidiary's account payable. In applying the second principle, all intercompany sales and profits are eliminated. For example, a sale by one company is offset against a purchase by an affiliated company. (A detailed discussion of the preparation of consolidated financial statements is beyond the scope of this text.)

The Concept of Control

The impetus for consolidations is the control of the parent company over the subsidiary. Control is defined as "the power of one entity to direct or cause the direction of the management and operating and financing policies of

---

[7] Committee on Accounting Procedure, *Accounting Research Bulletin No. 51*, "Consolidated Financial Statements" (New York: AICPA, 1959), par. 1.

[8] Financial Accounting Standards Board, *Statement of Financial Accounting Standards No. 94*, "Consolidation of All Majority-Owned Subsidiaries" (Stamford, CT: FASB, 1987).

[9] *Accounting Research Bulletin No. 51*, op. cit.

another entity."[10] Control is normally presumed when the parent owns, either directly or indirectly, a majority of the voting stock of the subsidiary. The following exceptions indicating an inability to control a majority owned subsidiary are cited by *SFAS No. 94:*

1. The subsidiary is in a legal reorganization or bankruptcy.
2. There are severe governmentally imposed uncertainties.

The issuance of *SFAS No. 94* was prompted by concerns over off-balance sheet financing. *ARB No. 51* allowed majority-owned subsidiaries to be excluded from consolidation (1) when the subsidiary is a foreign subsidiary, (2) when the minority interest in the subsidiary (subsidiary shares not owned by the parent company) is large relative to the equity interest of parent company stockholders in the consolidated net assets, and (3) when the subsidiary has nonhomogeneous operations.[11] The last exception, the *nonhomogeneity exception,* allowed parent companies to create financing subsidiaries or leasing companies and to keep debt or capital lease obligations off the parent company balance sheets. *SFAS No. 94* eliminated these three exceptions.

In a 1991 discussion memorandum on consolidation policy and procedures, the FASB addressed the issue of whether control and the level of ownership are synonymous.[12] In other words, the Board posed the question: Should consolidation be extended to situations where the parent company has control but less than majority ownership? Subsequently, the FASB issued an exposure draft, "Consolidated Financial Statements: Policy and Procedures," in which control over an entity was defined as "power over its assets."[13] As such, control implies that one entity has the power to use or direct the use of the assets of another entity by:

- Establishing the controlled entity's policies and its capital and operating budgets.
- Selecting, determining the compensation of, and terminating personnel responsible for implementing the controlled entity's policies and decisions.

Hence, a controlling entity can use or direct the use of the controlled entity's assets to receive future benefit. It follows that the assets of the controlled entity have future service potential to the controlling entity and should be consolidated.

According to the exposure draft, in the absence of evidence to the contrary, effective control is evident when the controlling entity has one or more of the following:

---

[10] Financial Accounting Standards Board, *Discussion Memorandum: An Analysis of Issues Related to Consolidation Policy and Procedures* (Stamford, CT: FASB, 1991), par. 122.

[11] Ibid.

[12] Ibid.

[13] Financial Accounting Standards Board, *Exposure Draft: Consolidated Financial Statements: Policy and Procedures* (Stamford, CT: FASB, October 16, 1995), par. 9.

- Ownership of a large minority voting interest (approximately 40 percent) when no other party or group has a significant interest.

- An ability to dominate the process of nominating candidates to another entity's governing board and to cast a majority of the votes cast in electing board members.

- A unilateral ability to obtain a majority voting interest through ownership of convertible securities or other rights that may be converted or exercised to obtain voting shares.

- A relationship with an entity that has no voting stock or member voting rights but has legally enforceable provisions that (a) can only be changed by the creator and (b) limit the entity to activities that provide substantially all of the entity's future economic benefits to the creator.

- A unilateral ability to dissolve an entity and assume control of its assets, subject to claims against those assets, without assuming economic costs in excess of benefits expected from the dissolution.

- A sole general partnership interest in a limited partnership.

Opponents of consolidation of entities where legal control (majority ownership) does not exist contend that the determination of other than legal control is too subjective for practical implementation. Nevertheless, there is widespread use of the control rather than the majority ownership criterion in other countries, for example, Canada, Australia, and the United Kingdom.

The FASB is currently reviewing the definition of control. In late 2000 the FASB reviewed its embracement of the control-based consolidation approach and decided to proceed with the modified approach. The Board intends to issue an exposure draft on this issue by the second quarter of 2001. Under the modified approach, a party that has a financial relationship with an entity would assess whether consolidation is required by applying the four following steps:

1. The party having the financial relationship will assess whether the entity is a qualifying special-purpose entity and if the party is the transferor or its affiliate. If so, the standard does not apply and SFAS No. 140 applies. (Discussed in Chapter 9).

2. The party assesses whether the permitted activities and powers of the entity are significantly limited. If not, the modified approach does not apply and the presumption of control remains.

3. If the permitted activities and powers are significantly limited, the party assesses whether it has a current ability to change the entity's purpose or powers. If so, the party consolidates only if that ability can be exercised (a) without further significant cash outlay or investment or (b) with a significant cash outlaw or investment that is expected to result in benefits that exceed further investments.

4. If the party is not required to consolidate under Step 3, the party assesses whether its financial interests in the entity (a) are a significant

portion of all such variable interests and (b) are significantly greater than such variable interests held by any other party. If both of these conditions exist, the party is required to consolidate unless other circumstances prohibit it from having an ongoing ability to affect the nature, timing or volume of the entity's operating activities.

The Board has tentatively decided to establish an effective date of implementation of this treatment for financial statements of companies with fiscal years beginning after June 15, 2002.

Theories of Consolidation

There are two prominent theories of consolidation: *entity theory* and *parent company theory.* Each theory implies a unique philosophy regarding the nature and purpose of consolidated financial statements. Current practice conforms strictly to neither theory; rather, it retains elements of both theories. Beams describes this hybrid of concepts underlying current consolidation practices and theories as *contemporary theory.*[14]

Entity Theory

According to entity theory (discussed in Chapter 14), the consolidated group (parent company and subsidiaries) is an entity separate from its owners. Thus, the emphasis is on control of the group of legal entities operating as a single unit. Consolidated assets belong to the consolidated entity, and the income earned by investing in those assets is income to the consolidated entity rather than to the parent company stockholders. Consequently, the purpose of consolidated statements is to provide information to all shareholders—parent company stockholders and outside minority stockholders of the subsidiaries.

Parent Company Theory

Parent company theory evolved from the proprietary theory of equity described in Chapter 13. Under parent company theory, parent company stockholders are viewed as having a proprietary interest in the net assets of the consolidated group. The purpose of consolidated statements is to provide information primarily for parent company stockholders. The resulting financial statements reflect a parent company perspective. The assets and liabilities of the subsidiary are substituted for the parent company's investment in the subsidiary, the parent company stockholders' equity is equal to consolidated stockholders' equity, and the subsidiary revenues, expenses, gains, and losses are substituted for the parent company's investment income in the subsidiary.

---

[14] Floyd A. Beams, *Advanced Accounting,* 5th ed. (Englewood Cliffs, NJ: Prentice-Hall, 1991), pp. 437–439.

Minority Interest

When a portion of a subsidiary's stock is owned by investors outside the parent company, this ownership interest is referred to as a *minority interest*. The value of this investment results from holding shares in an affiliated company, and the determination of equity, the payment of dividends, and the basis for a claim, should a liquidation ensue, are all based on a claim against a particular subsidiary. Therefore, the minority interest must gauge its financial status from the subsidiary company, not the parent or the consolidated group. Under current practice, the minority interest is calculated as the percentage ownership in the subsidiary's net assets at the date of acquisition, plus the percentage of retained earnings since acquisition.

The classification of minority interest on consolidated balance sheets poses a problem. The prevailing pronouncements on consolidations, *ARB No. 51* and *SFAS No. 94*, neither define what minority interest is nor describe how it should be treated in published financial statements. Moreover, the prevailing consolidation theories imply different interpretations of the very nature of minority interest. In practice, minority interest has been variously (1) disclosed as a liability, (2) separately presented between liabilities and stockholders' equity, and (3) disclosed as a part of stockholders' equity.

The first two alternative treatments are consistent with parent company theory. Under parent company theory, only parent company stockholders play a proprietary role; hence, minority shares are an outside interest and should not be included in stockholders' equity. It is argued that the consolidation process has no impact on the reporting entity and is of no benefit to minority shareholders. Yet minority interest does not fit the definition of liabilities found in *SFAC No. 6*; therefore, there is no established theoretical basis for reporting minority interest as debt. At the same time, minority stockholders do not enjoy the ownership privileges of parent company stockholders. Their interest is in only part of the consolidated entity, over which they cannot exercise control, and, thus, they are unable to act as owners in the usual sense. Some proponents of parent company theory argue that the unique nature of minority interest is best portrayed by placing it between liabilities and stockholders' equity.

Entity theory implies that minority interest is an equity interest. The consolidated enterprise is considered one economic unit, and minority shareholders contribute resources in the same manner as parent company stockholders. Moreover, like parent company stockholders, their respective interest is enhanced or burdened by changes in net assets from nonowner sources—a prerequisite for equities as described in *SFAC No. 6*, paragraph 62. Although the FASB has not officially defined minority interest, *SFAC No. 6* identified minority interest as an example of an equity interest stating that minority stockholders have ownership or residual interests in the consolidated enterprise.[15]

Because the FASB has proposed that consolidation should be required for controlled entities in which the controlling entity has less than a major-

---

[15] Financial Accounting Standards Board, *Statement of Financial Accounting Concepts No. 6*, "Elements of Financial Statements" (Stamford, CT: FASB, 1985), par. 254.

ity ownership, the outside interest would no longer be comprised of a minority of common stockholders in the controlled entity. Hence, the term *minority interest* would no longer apply. The exposure draft on consolidation policy and procedures proposes that the outside interest should be labeled as *noncontrolling interest in subsidiaries*. Moreover, consistent with their position in *SFAS No. 6*, the noncontrolling interest would be reported in the consolidated balance sheet as a separate component of equity.

Proportionate Consolidation

Because of the controversy surrounding the inability to reach a consensus on the nature of minority interest, some accountants advocate an alternative, proportionate consolidation. Proportionate consolidation would ignore minority interest altogether. Under this approach, the parent company would report only its share of the assets and liabilities of the subsidiary entity, and no minority interest would need to be reported. Rosenfield and Rubin[16] contend that when the parent company acquires the voting stock of the subsidiary, it obtains a right to receive its pro-rata share of the subsidiary company's dividends, implying that only the corresponding pro-rata share of subsidiary net assets is relevant to parent company stockholders. This argument ignores the concept of control that is fundamental to the very nature of consolidations. If the parent company controls the net assets of the subsidiary entity, then it controls 100 percent of those net assets, and not just its proportionate share. It follows that if consolidated financial statements are intended to report the results of utilizing the assets controlled, consolidation of 100 percent of subsidiary net assets would be relevant.

A determination of the nature of minority interest is important because it affects the underlying premises of alternative accounting treatments for the recognition and measurement of consolidated assets and earnings. A complete discussion of the issues involved is beyond the scope of this text. In the next section we describe the implications of consolidation theories and minority interest recognition and measurement. Similar implications apply to other consolidated net assets.

Goodwill

Goodwill, described in Chapter 8 as an intangible asset, is recorded when a purchase business combination occurs. In current practice, the measurement of goodwill is consistent with parent company theory. Goodwill is recorded as the difference between the cost of the investment made to acquire the subsidiary shares and the fair value of the parent company's proportionate share of the identifiable net assets of the subsidiary. No goodwill is attributed to minority interest. The result is that the value of minority interest reported on the consolidated financial statements is not affected by the consolidation

[16] Paul Rosenfield and Steven Rubin, "Minority Interest: Opposing Views," *Journal of Accountancy* (March 1986), pp. 78–80, 82, 84, 86, 88–90.

process. Thus, it reflects the minority interest's share of the reported book value of the subsidiary entity.

Under entity theory, because the emphasis is on the entity and not the parent company, goodwill would be valued at its total market value implied by the purchase price paid for the parent company investment. In this case, the equity interest in goodwill would be allocated between the parent company and minority interest. The result would be that the minority interest, like the parent company interest, would be measured at fair value. The balance sheet would then reflect the total fair value of the goodwill under the control of the parent company.

The FASB supports the entity theory for the valuation of identifiable net assets and the parent company theory for the valuation of goodwill. The exposure draft on consolidation policy and procedures would require subsidiary assets, such as inventory, land, and buildings, to be valued at 100 percent of fair value at acquisition. Hence, a portion of the difference between fair value and book value acquired would be attributed to the noncontrolling interest. This requirement would be contrary to existing practice. Goodwill would continue to be reported as the difference between the cost of the acquisition and that portion of the fair value of net identifiable assets acquired.

Drawbacks of Consolidation

The growth of business combinations has created companies with diversified operations termed *conglomerates*. The result has been the aggregation of financial information from various lines of business into one set of financial reports. Moreover, if the FASB does extend the definition of control below 50 percent ownership, the result will be even higher levels of aggregation and even greater loss of information regarding the performance of the individual combined companies. Each new business combination results in the loss of some information to the investing public because previously reported data is now combined with existing data in consolidating financial reports.

The loss of information may be further exacerbated by the reporting requirements of *SFAS No. 94*. Assets and liabilities of heterogeneous companies are now required to be consolidated. Although empirical research indicates that the liabilities of previously unconsolidated subsidiaries may be perceived by market participants as parent company liabilities,[17] one would expect a loss of comparability among the financial information provided across companies comprising varying combinations of different types of business entities. In addition, proponents of proportionate consolidation argue that the consolidation process exaggerates reported amounts for assets and liabilities and hence affects the calculation of performance measures, such as debt-to-equity ratios.

Some accountants would prefer that in addition to consolidated financial statements, companies also report the separate financial statements of the individual companies that constitute the consolidated group. In this way,

[17] E. E. Comiskey, R. A. McEwen, and C. W. Mulford, "A Test of Pro Forma Consolidation of Finance Subsidiaries," *Financial Management* (Autumn 1987), pp. 45–50.

users would evaluate the individual as well as the combined performance and financial position of the group and might better be able to assess the incremental addition of each unit to the total combined reporting entity

Segment Reporting

Current generally accepted accounting principles (GAAP) do not require the reporting of separate financial statements of the companies composing a consolidated group. Nevertheless, *segment reporting*, the reporting of financial information on a less than total enterprise basis, is required under *SFAS No. 131*.

Previous GAAP required or recommended less than total enterprise reporting only in limited areas. For example, *ARB No. 43* recommended certain disclosures about foreign operations, *APB No. 18* required the disclosure of certain information about companies accounted for by the equity method of accounting, and *APB No. 30* mandated the disclosure of information about discontinued segments. However, segmental information became an increasing part of corporate reporting during the 1970s because of two factors:

1. In 1969, the SEC required line-of-business reporting in registration statements, and in 1970 these requirements were extended to the 10-K reports.

2. In 1973, the New York Stock Exchange urged that line-of-business reporting, similar to that provided on the 10-K reports, be included in the annual reports to stockholders.

The proponents of segmental reporting base their arguments on two points:

1. Various types of operations may have differing prospects for growth, rates of profitability, and degrees of risk.

2. Since management responsibility is frequently decentralized, the assessment of management ability requires less than total enterprise information.[18]

Subsequent study of the problem resulted in the issuance of *SFAS No. 14* in 1976.[19] This pronouncement required that a corporation issuing a complete set of financial statements disclose

1. The enterprise's operations in different industries.

2. Its foreign operations and export sales.

3. Its major customers.[20]

---

[18] *An Analysis of Issues Related to Financial Reporting for Segments of a Business Enterprise,* FASB Discussion Memorandum (Stamford, CT: FASB, 1974), pp. 6–7.

[19] *Statement of Financial Accounting Standards No. 14,* "Financial Reporting for Segments of a Business Enterprise" (Stamford, CT: FASB, 1976).

[20] Ibid.

In requiring these disclosures, *SFAS No. 14* provided the following definitions:

1. **Industry segment**   Component of an enterprise engaged in providing a product or service or group of related products and services primarily to unaffiliated customers for a profit.
2. **Reportable segment**   An industry segment for which information is required to be reported by this segment.
3. **Revenue**   Sales to unaffiliated customers and intersegment transactions similar to those with unaffiliated customers.
4. **Operating profit or loss**   Revenue minus all operating expenses, including the allocation of corporate overhead.
5. **Identifiable assets**   Tangible and intangible enterprise assets that are used by the industry.

In response to criticisms of the reporting requirements of *SFAS No. 14*, *SFAS No. 131* restructured segment reporting to include a greater number of segments for some enterprises and segmentation that corresponds more closely to internal decision making regarding business segments, and extended segment reporting to interim reports. The resulting segment reporting practices are intended to provide information to help users make better assessments of enterprise performance and thereby make more informed decisions about the enterprise as a whole.

Under the provisions of *SFAS No. 131,* companies are required to report separately income statement and balance sheet information about each operating segment. In addition to a measure of a segment's profit or loss and total assets, companies are to report specific information if it is included in the measure of segment profit or loss by the chief operating decision maker. The list of such segment disclosures is as follows:

a.   Revenues from external users.
b.   Revenues from transactions with other operating segments of the same enterprise.
c.   Interest revenue.
d.   Interest expense.
e.   Depreciation, depletion, and amortization expense.
f.   Unusual items.
g.   Equity in the net income of investees under the equity method.
h.   Income tax expense or benefit.
i.   Extraordinary item.
j.   Significant noncash items other than depreciation, depletion, and amortization expense.[21]

Additional disclosures include the amount of investment in equity method investees and total expenditures for long-lived assets, productive assets,

---

[21] *SFAS No. 131,* "Disclosures about Segments of an Enterprise and Related Information" (Stamford, CT: FASB, 1997), par. 27.

mortgage and other servicing rights, and deferred tax assets for those items that are included in total segment assets. Companies are also required to report certain geographic information and information regarding the extent of reliance on major (10 percent or more of total revenue) customers.

Operating Segments

A goal of *SFAS No. 131* is to utilize the enterprise's internal organization in such a way that reportable operating segments will be readily evident to the financial statement preparer. The resulting "management approach" to identifying operating segments is based on the manner in which management organizes the segments for making operating decisions and assessing performance.

SFAS No. 131 defines an operating segment as a component of the enterprise

a. That engages in business activities from which it may earn revenues and incur expenses.
b. Whose operating results are regularly reviewed by the chief operating decision maker of the enterprise in making decisions about allocating resources to the segment and in assessing segment performance.
c. For which discrete financial information is available.

Reportable segments include those operating segments that meet any of the following quantitative thresholds:

a. Reported revenue is at least 10 percent of combined revenue.
b. Reported profit (loss) is at least 10 percent of combined profit (loss).
c. Assets are 10 percent or more of combined assets.

In analyzing segmental information, the user should keep in mind that comparison of a segment from one enterprise with a similar segment from another enterprise has limited usefulness unless both companies use similar disaggregation and cost allocation procedures. Because segments are identified by analyzing a company's internal organization structure, comparisons between companies may be difficult for companies with different organizational structures.

The major problems associated with these disclosures are (1) the determination of reportable segments, (2) the allocation of joint costs, and (3) transfer pricing. In determining its reportable segments, an enterprise is required to identify the individual products and services from which it derives its revenue, group these products by industry lines and segments, and select those segments that are significant with respect to the industry as a whole. These procedures require a considerable amount of managerial judgment, and the following guidelines are presented:

1. ***Existing profit centers*** The smallest units of activity for which revenue and expense information is accumulated for internal planning and control purposes represent a logical starting point for determining industry segments.

2. **Management organization** The company's internal organizational structure generally corresponds to management's view of the major segments.

3. **Investor expectations** The information provided should coincide with the type of information needed by the public.

4. **Competitive factors** Although the disclosure of all industry segment information might injure a company's competitive position, the required disclosures are not more detailed than those typically provided by an enterprise operating within a single industry.[22]

The problems associated with the allocation of joint costs and transfer pricing also cause some difficulty in reporting segmental information. Joint costs should be allocated to the various segments in the most rational manner possible. However, since the allocation process is frequently quite arbitrary, this process may have a profound effect on reporting segmental income.

The transfer pricing problem arises when products are transferred from division to division, and one division's product becomes another's raw material. In many cases, these interdivisional transfers are recorded at cost plus an amount of profit. Most accountants advocate eliminating the profit from interdivisional transfers before they are reported as segmental information.

Tender Offers

It has been suggested that the period since 1970 constitutes a fourth major merger period. Since 1970, the tender offer has become an increasingly popular method of creating a merger. A *tender offer* is an attempt by outsiders to obtain control of a firm by offering to buy the outstanding common stock at a specified price during a specified period of time. A tender offer will occur when the outsiders believe that the target firm's assets can be used more efficiently. This new wave of mergers was aided by relaxing antitrust rules against vertical and horizontal mergers and deregulating certain industries. A tender offer differs from the more traditional merger proposal in that it is made directly to the target's stockholders. Consequently, tender offers require neither the approval nor even notification of the target's managers or board of directors. A traditional merger proposal usually must be approved by the target company's board of directors before it is submitted to a vote of shareholders.

Both tender offers and mergers are voluntary exchanges and will be agreed on only if both parties to the exchange expect to benefit. In mergers, not only must the acquiring firm and shareholders of the target firm benefit, but so, too, must the managers of the target firm. However, in tender offers, management is not a party to the exchange. In such cases, management may not be perceived to benefit from the tender offer and in fact may be harmed.

[22] Ibid., par. 13.

For this reason, tender offers are sometimes hostile (opposed by management) and sometimes friendly, whereas mergers are always friendly.

The noninvolvement of target management in a tender offer has been argued to be a desirable feature of this method of transferring ownership of a company since it may provide the benefit of displacing poorly performing management. Management's major responsibility is to the corporate shareholders. However, because of the difficulty in day-to-day oversight, firms have the incentive to devote part of their resources to enhancing management prerogatives rather than profit maximization. If this occurs, the firm will not be operating efficiently and its stock will be undervalued. It is argued that the market for corporate control can act as an external check on management. Undervalued shares invite takeover attempts as outsiders realize that gains can be made by expelling inefficient, entrenched management. That is, replacing entrenched managers with executives who are more willing to seek a profit maximization strategy should improve the valuation of the firm's shares in the market.

Tender offers are frequently financed by leveraged buy-outs. In a *leveraged buy-out*, a small group of investors acquires a company. The financing for this buy-out is obtained largely by issuing debt. This debt is frequently called *junk bonds* because of the associated high interest rate and perceived degree of risk. When a tender offer is financed by a leveraged buy-out, the debt is ultimately repaid either from sale of part of the acquired company's assets or from operations. Some authors claim that this process imposes a pool of costs on society and argue that a socioeconomic impact study should accompany each potential takeover.[23] Others contend that takeovers create compelling economic incentives, resulting in a greater devotion to efficiency and risk-taking by management. The tender offer phenomenon has produced a new jargon to describe the behavior of management, the raider, and stockholders in a takeover situation. Some of these terms are as follows:[24]

Crown Jewel   The most valued asset held by a target. Divestiture of this asset by the target is frequently a defense to resist a takeover.

Golden Parachute   The provisions of the employment contracts of top-level management that provide for severance pay or other compensation should they lose their jobs in a takeover.

Greenmail   The premium paid by a targeted company to a raider in exchange for his or her shares of the targeted company.

Lockup Defense   The right given to a friendly party to purchase assets of the targeted firm, in particular the crown jewel, thus dissuading a takeover attempt.

---

[23] See, for example, A. J. Briloff, "Cannibalizing the Transcendent Margin: Reflections on Conglomeration, LBOs, Recapitalizations and Other Manifestations of Corporate Mania," *Financial Analysts Journal* (May–June 1988), pp. 74–80.

[24] M. Ott and G. J. Santoni, "Mergers and Takeovers—The Value of Predators' Information," *Bulletin, Federal Reserve Bank of St. Louis* (December 1985), p. 17.

Poison Pill   The right given stockholders, other than those involved in a hostile takeover, to purchase securities at a very favorable price in the event of a takeover.

Raiders   The person(s) or corporation attempting a takeover.

Shark Repellents   Antitakeover corporate charter amendments such as staggered terms for directors, super-majority requirement for approving a merger, or mandate that bidders pay the same price for all shares in a buy-out.

Stripper   A successful raider who, once the target is acquired, sells off some of the assets of the target company.

Target   The company at which a takeover attempt is directed.

Two-Tier Offer   A takeover offer that provides a cash price for sufficient shares to obtain control of the corporation, then a lower (noncash securities) price for the remaining shares.

White Knight   A merger partner solicited by management of a target who offers an alternative merger plan to that offered by a raider, which protects the target company from the attempted takeover.

The increased number of tender offers have tested the loyalty of corporate managers to their shareholders. If managers do not resist a takeover, they often lose their jobs, while the defeat of a lucrative offer from a raider can be costly to shareholders. There is even evidence that managers frequently resist the sale of their firms when the bids substantially exceed current market values. This evidence is an example of agency theory (discussed in Chapter 2) and serves as evidence that managers may tend to serve in their own interests at stockholders' expense.

One of the most common examples of a managerial action that is in conflict with shareholders' interest is the payment of greenmail. This practice is also frequently accompanied by a standstill agreement, which prohibits the raiders from owning any of the target firm's shares for a specified period. Another antitakeover defense is the use of poison pills that make the target less attractive to the raider.

A management operating in the best interest of its shareholders will attempt to increase the takeover premium if it senses that a takeover is possible. One method of accomplishing this is to encourage a bidding contest in which uninformed potential acquirers are invited to bid and to provide them with the information necessary to realize a profit from taking over the target.

Push-Down Accounting

Under the purchase method of accounting for consolidations, the parent company values subsidiary assets to reflect market value, but the subsidiary accounting for these asset values is not changed. Push-down accounting is a controversial accounting technique that requires a subsidiary company issuing separate financial statements to restate the reported value of its assets to the carrying amounts reported by the parent on the consolidated financial statements. That is, the subsidiary revalues its assets and liabilities to fair market value and recognizes goodwill in its own statements. Push-down accounting is required for publicly held companies whenever substantially all the common stock is acquired and the company has no outstanding public debt or preferred stock.[25] In 1979, the AICPA's task force on consolidations examined the issues associated with push-down accounting.[26]

Later, the FASB issued a discussion memorandum that contained arguments for and against push-down accounting.[27] The proponents of push-down accounting base their arguments on the following considerations:

1. The price paid by the new owners, when there is a substantial change in ownership, is the most relevant basis for the measurement of assets, liabilities, and results of operations of the entity.

2. The substance of transactions resulting in changes in ownership is the same as if the new owners purchased the net assets of an existing business and established a new entity.

3. *APB Opinion No. 16* requires consolidated financial statements to reflect the parent's purchase price. The separate financial statements should also reflect that purchase price for purposes of symmetry.

4. The parent's purchase of the subsidiary is an exchange that justifies the establishment of a new cost basis.

Others argue that push-down accounting is not appropriate for the following reasons:

1. Transactions of the entity's shareholders are not transactions of the entity and, therefore, should not affect the method of accounting employed by the entity.

2. Consistency is impaired for those who depend on comparable financial statements.

3. Push-down accounting may create problems for the subsidiary in maintaining compliance with previous agreements with outsiders (e.g., debt covenants) because those agreements were based on financial data prepared on the old basis of accounting.

4. There is no logical method of determining which owners' transactions should qualify for push-down accounting.

[25] Securities and Exchange Commission Staff, Accounting Bulletin No. 54, *Staff Views on the Application of the "Push Down" Basis of Accounting in the Separate Financial Statements of Subsidiaries Acquired in Purchase Transactions* (Washington, DC: November 3, 1983).

[26] Accounting Standards Executive Committee, Issues Paper, *"Push Down" Accounting* (New York: AICPA, October 30, 1979).

[27] Financial Accounting Standards Board, Discussion Memorandum, *An Analysis of Issues Related to Accounting for Business Combinations and Purchased Intangibles* (Stamford, CT: FASB, 1976), pars. 399–405.

The impact of push-down accounting is illustrated in Table 15.1. Assume a group of investors acquires a company in a leveraged buy-out transaction. The investors use $2,500 of their own funds and borrow $8,000 to acquire 100 percent of an entity's outstanding common stock. The lender required the loan to be recorded on the books of the acquired company ·because it was secured by the acquired company's assets. The estimated value of the acquired company's property plant and equipment was $12,000. Table 15.1 illustrates the acquired company's balance sheet under historical and push-down accounting.

Under the historical cost treatment, the cost of the acquired shares will be disclosed as treasury shares at cost, and the company's financial position appears dismal. That is, the company's total equity has a deficit balance, and the book value of the property, plant, and equipment is less than the debt they are securing. The push-down treatment paints an entirely different picture. It reflects the equity contribution of the new owners and the debt in light of the more realistic value of the fair market value of the property, plant, and equipment.

Despite these advantages, push-down accounting has been viewed as causing two major complications arising from its implementation—a reduction in reported net income and a violation of consistency. Net income is reduced when push-down accounting is used because the book value of assets is usually increased. The increased carrying value of assets leads to higher depreciation charges, resulting in relatively lower reported net income. However, this criticism has been seen to conflict with the concept of neutrality articulated in *SFAC No. 2*.[28] That is, accounting standards should be based on the relevance and reliability of the information produced, not on the effect the rules may have on any interest group.

The consistency issue can be resolved if the users of financial statements are provided adequate disclosures that allow them to evaluate the impact of push-down accounting. For example, companies might prepare pro-forma financial statements indicating how the company's financial statements might have appeared if the company had not implemented push-down accounting.

An additional issue is raised when the parent acquires less than 100 percent of the subsidiary's common stock. That is, should 100 percent of the assets' book value be revalued for push-down accounting purposes? Or should the assets be revalued only to the extent of the common stock acquired by the parent? This question has not been completely resolved. The SEC requires push-down accounting only when substantially all the company's common stock is acquired. The SEC also allows recording the new basis of a subsidiary's assets only to the extent of the common stock acquired. That is, if 90 percent of the outstanding common stock is acquired, each asset

[28] P. B. Thomas and J. L. Hagler, "Push Down Accounting: A Descriptive Assessment," *Accounting Horizons* (September 1988), pp. 26–31.

TABLE 15.1 *Historical Cost v. Push-Down*

	Alternative 1		Alternative 2	
	(1)	(2)	(3)	(4)
		(in thousands)		
	Historical Cost		Push-Down Treatment	
	Before Purchase	After Purchase	Push-Down Entries	Purchase Bases
Cash	$ 1,300	$ 1,300	$ —	$ 1,300
Accounts receivable	3,500	3,500	—	3,500
Inventories	1,400	1,400	—	1,400
Prepaid expenses	200	200	—	200
Total current assets	6,400	6,400		6,400
Property and equipment, net	8,900	8,900	3,100[1]	12,000
Other assets	400	400	—	400
Excess of cost over book value of net assets acquired	—	—	1,400[1]	1,400
	$15,700	$15,700	$4,500	$20,200
Accounts payable	$ 2,900	$ 2,900	$ —	$ 2,900
Notes payable	1,200	1,200	—	1,200
Accrued expenses	800	800	—	800
Total current liabilities	4,900	4,900	—	4,900
Long-term debt	4,800	12,800	8,000[2]	12,800
Deferred income taxes	1,800	1,800	(1,800)[1]	—
			2,500[3]	
Common stock	1,000	3,500	(1,000)[4]	2,500
Retained earnings	3,200	3,200	(3,200)[4]	
	4,200	6,700	(1,700)	2,500
Treasury stock	—	(10,500)	—	—
Total stockholders' equity (deficit)	4,200	(3,800)	(1,700)	2,500
	$15,700	$15,700	$4,500	$20,200

Push-down entry components applied to column 1:

[1] Purchase accounting adjustments per *APB Opinion No. 16.*

[2] To record borrowed financing for acquisition.

[3] To record equity financing for acquisition.

[4] To record purchase of outstanding shares.

Source: Adapted from Michael E. Cunningham, "Push Down Accounting Pros and Cons," *Journal of Accountancy* (June 1984), p. 75.

will be recorded at 90 percent of the difference between its book value and market value.

Foreign Currency Translation

Foreign operations by U.S. corporations have increased substantially in recent years. At the same time, devaluation of the dollar, which allowed it to float on world currency markets, accentuated the impact of foreign currency fluctuation on the accounting information and reporting systems of multinational companies. As a result, foreign currency translation has become an important and widely debated accounting and reporting issue. More specifically, the issue is this: How does a U.S.-based corporation measure monetary unit differences and changes in those differences in its foreign branches and subsidiaries?[29]

The problem arises in the following manner: The foreign subsidiary handles its transactions in foreign currency, which may include anything from long-term borrowing agreements for assets acquired to credit sales carried as accounts receivable. When management or outside investors wish to evaluate the company's operations as a whole, it becomes necessary to express all activities, foreign and domestic, in common financial terms. Useful comparisons and calculations can be made only if measures of a company's profitability and financial position are expressed in a common unit of measurement (usually the domestic currency); foreign monetary measures must be converted to domestic units. This process is known as *translation.*

In translating foreign currency, the foreign exchange rate defines the relationship between two monetary scales. The foreign currency is stated as a ratio to the U.S. dollar, and this ratio becomes the multiplying factor to determine the equivalent amount of domestic currency. For example, if the British pound (£) is quoted as $1.20 and an American subsidiary acquires an asset valued at £10,000, the translation into dollars will be $12,000 (10,000 × $1.20). Foreign exchange rates change over time in response to the forces of supply and demand and to the relative degree of inflation between countries. These changes are classified into three types—fluctuation, devaluation, and revaluation. *Fluctuation* denotes a rate change within the narrow margin allowed by the International Monetary Fund (IMF) (a deviation of $2\frac{1}{4}$ percent above or below that country's official exchange rate). If the IMF allows an entirely new support level of the foreign currency and the dollar rate falls, it is called *devaluation. Revaluation* occurs when the dollar rate of the foreign currency rises to a new support level.

The translation process in no way changes the inherent characteristics of the assets or liabilities measured. That is, translation is a single process that

---

[29] It has been argued that in reality it is impossible to isolate the translation process from general price-level adjustments, since foreign exchange rates do, to some extent, reflect changes in the price level. But even though inflationary relationships between countries may be indirectly reflected in official exchange rates, translation is still considered to be an independent process.

merely restates an asset or liability initially valued in foreign currency in terms of a common currency measurement by applying the rate of exchange factor; It does not restate historical cost. Translation is a completely separate process, just as adjusting for general price level changes is a separate process. The translation process is analogous to price-level adjustments in that neither changes any accounting principles; they merely change the unit of measurement.

If the exchange rate remained constant between a particular foreign country and the United States, translation would be a relatively simple process involving a constant exchange rate. However, recent history indicates that this is unlikely, and a method of translation must be established that adequately discloses the effect of changes in exchange rates on financial statements. There has been considerable debate among accountants on how to achieve this objective. In the following sections we review the proposals advocated by several individuals and groups.

Historically, four methods of translation were proposed by various authors prior to the release of any official pronouncements by the APB or FASB: the current-noncurrent method, the monetary-nonmonetary method, the current rate method, and the temporal method.[30]

Current-Noncurrent Method

The current-noncurrent method is based on the distinction between current and noncurrent assets and liabilities. It was initially recommended by the American Institute of Certified Public Accountants (AICPA) in 1931 and updated in *Accounting Research Bulletin No. 43* in 1953.[31] This method requires all current items (cash, receivables, inventory, and short-term liabilities) to be translated at the foreign exchange rate existing at the balance sheet date. The noncurrent items (plant, equipment, property, and long-term liabilities) are translated using the rate in effect when the items were acquired or incurred (the historical rate). The rationale for the dichotomy between current and noncurrent items is that those items that will not be converted into cash in the upcoming period (noncurrent) are not affected by changes in current rates. Thus, in using this method, it is assumed that items translated at the historical exchange rate are not exposed to gains and losses caused by changes in the relative value of currencies. In 1965, *ARB No. 43* (Chapter 12) was modified by *APB Opinion No. 6* to allow long-term payables and receivables to be translated at the current rather than historical rate if this treatment resulted in a better representation of a company's position.[32] With respect to the income statement, *ARB No. 43* required revenues and expenses

[30] See Leonard Lorensen, "Reporting Foreign Operations of U.S. Companies in U.S. Dollars," *Accounting Research Study No. 12* (New York: AICPA, 1972).

[31] *Accounting Research Bulletin No. 43* (New York: AICPA, 1953), Chapter 12.

[32] *Accounting Principles Board Opinion No. 6*, "Status of Accounting Research Bulletins" (New York: AICPA, 1965), par. 18.

to be translated at the average exchange rate applicable to each month, except for depreciation, which was translated at the historical rate.

Monetary-Nonmonetary Method

The monetary-nonmonetary method was first advocated by Samuel Hepworth,[33] and the National Association of Accountants' support of Hepworth's method in 1960 resulted in more widespread acceptance of its provisions.[34] The monetary-nonmonetary method requires that a distinction be made between monetary items (accounts representing cash or claims on cash, such as receivables, notes payable, and bonds payable) and nonmonetary items (accounts not representing claims on a specific amount of cash such as land, inventory, plant, equipment, and capital stock). Monetary items are translated at the exchange rate in effect at the balance sheet date, whereas nonmonetary items retain the historical exchange rate.

The only difference between the two methods for the reporting of assets is in the translation of inventories. If the current-noncurrent method is used, inventories are considered to be current assets (sensitive to foreign exchange gains and losses) and are translated at the current rate, whereas the monetary-nonmonetary method classifies inventories as nonmonetary assets that are subsequently translated at the historical or preexisting rate. A difference also arises in translating long-term debt. The current-noncurrent approach uses the historical translation rate, whereas the monetary-nonmonetary method considers long-term debt to be monetary and uses the current rate. This difference between the two methods disappears, however, if the current-noncurrent approach is modified as was required by *APB Opinion No. 6*. Both approaches result in a foreign exchange gain or loss in order to balance the assets with the liabilities and equities, thereby creating a reporting problem. That is, how should a gain or loss on foreign currency translation be reported on the financial statements? (We will discuss this issue later in the chapter.)

Although these two translation methods dominated accounting practices for approximately 40 years, the late 1960s and the early 1970s produced a proliferation of new proposals for dealing with foreign exchange problems. After 1971, when the dollar was devalued and allowed to float on the world monetary market, dissatisfaction with the traditional methods came to the forefront. Most authors advocating new approaches contend that new problems surfaced in 1971 because foreign currencies were appreciating rather than depreciating in relation to the dollar, and these problems could not be resolved by the traditional approaches. Two other methods, the current rate method and the temporal method, have been advocated to alleviate this problem.

---

[33] Samuel Hepworth, "Reporting Foreign Operations," *Michigan Business Studies* (University of Michigan, 1956).

[34] National Association of Accountants, "Management Accounting Problems in Foreign Operations," *NAA Research Report No. 36* (New York, 1960).

Current Rate Method

The current rate method requires the translation of *all* assets and liabilities at the exchange rate in effect on the balance sheet date (current rate). It is, therefore, the only method that translates fixed assets at current rather than historical rates. Proponents of the current rate method claim that it most clearly represents the true economic facts because stating all items currently presents the true earnings of a foreign operation at that time—particularly since from the investor's point of view the only real earnings are those that can actually be distributed.

Although the current rate method has drawn some support, it is not without critics. Proponents argue that it presents true economic facts by stating all items at the current rate, thus retaining operating relationships intact. However, critics attack the use of the current rate for fixed assets, stating that the resulting figure on the translated consolidated balance sheet does not represent the historical cost. They maintain that until the entire reporting system is changed, the current rate method will not be acceptable.

Temporal Method

In 1972, Lorensen advocated another approach, termed the *temporal principle of translation*.[35] Under this method monetary measurements depend on the temporal characteristics of assets and liabilities. That is, the time of measurement of the elements depends on certain characteristics. Lorensen summarized this process as follows:

> Money and receivables and payables measured at the amounts promised should be translated at the foreign exchange rate in effect at the balance sheet date. Assets and liabilities measured at money prices should be translated at the foreign exchange rate in effect at the dates to which the money prices pertain.[36]

This principle is simply an application of the fair value principle in the area of foreign translation. By stating foreign money receivables and payables at the balance sheet rate, the foreign currency's command over U.S. dollars is measured. (Lorensen believes that this attribute, command over U.S. dollars, is of paramount importance.) Nevertheless, the results from use of this method are generally identical to those from the monetary-nonmonetary method except when the inventory valuation is based on the lower of cost or market rule.

Lorensen's main concern was that the generally accepted accounting principles being followed should not be changed by the translation process. Consequently, he strongly opposed any translation method that ultimately changed the attributes of a balance sheet account (e.g., historical cost being transformed into replacement cost or selling price). Unfortunately, the temporal method does not provide any solution to the problem of reporting

---

[35] Lorensen, op. cit.

[36] Ibid., p. 19.

exchange gains and losses that plague the traditional methods. Moreover, using the historical rate to translate fixed assets, while translating the long-term debt incurred to finance those assets at the current rate, may be inappropriate and may result in large gains and losses that will not be realized in the near future. Furthermore, it is argued that because subsidiary assets are acquired with foreign, not the parent's, currency, use of the historic exchange rate is simply not relevant.

It must be stressed that none of these methods of translation provides a perfect representation of value because of the nature of the world's monetary systems. A country's currency is basically a one-dimensional scale that measures and compares economic values within that one political entity. Thus, even the best translation method that attempts to restate a foreign asset or liability in terms of domestic currency will inevitably be limited in its representation of economic reality.

The FASB and Foreign Currency Translation

The Financial Accounting Standards Board took this issue under advisement and originally issued *SFAS No. 8,* "Accounting for the Translation of Foreign Currency Transactions and Foreign Currency Financial Statements.[37] The Board stated that the overall objective of foreign currency translation is to measure and express, in dollars and in conformity with U.S. GAAP, the assets, liabilities, revenue, and expenses initially measured in foreign currency. The following translation principles applied:

1. Each transaction was recorded at the historical exchange rate (the exchange rate in effect at the transaction date).

2. All cash, receivables, and payables denominated in foreign currencies were adjusted using the current rate at the balance sheet date.

3. All assets carried at market price were adjusted to equivalent dollar prices on the balance sheet date.

4. For all other assets, the particular measurement bases were used to determine the translation rate.

5. Revenues and expenses were translated in a manner that produced approximately the same dollar amount that would have resulted had the underlying transactions been translated into dollars on the dates they occurred. An average rate could be used in most cases.

6. All exchange gains and losses were included in the determination of net income.

7. Gains and losses on forward exchange contracts (agreements to exchange currencies at a predetermined rate) entered into to hedge a for-

---

[37] Financial Accounting Standards Board, *Statement of Financial Accounting Standards No. 8,* "Accounting for the Translation of Foreign Currency Transactions and Foreign Currency Financial Statements" (Stamford, CT: FASB, 1975).

eign currency exposed net asset or liability position or to speculate were included in net income, while gains and losses on forward exchange contracts intended to hedge an identifiable foreign currency commitment were typically deferred.

This statement did not specifically advocate any one of the translation methods previously discussed, and none was adopted intact. Nevertheless, the general objectives of translation originally advocated by the FASB are most closely satisfied by the temporal method.

SFAS No. 52

The requirements of *SFAS No. 8* produced some perceived distortions in financial reporting that resulted in questions by many accountants and financial statement users as to the relevance, reliability, and predictive value of the information presented. Among these perceived distortions were the following:

1. The results of the application of *SFAS No. 8* were economically incompatible with reality. Since nonmonetary items such as inventory were translated at the historical rate, a loss could be reported during a period in which a foreign currency actually strengthened in relation to the dollar.
2. Matching of costs and revenues was inappropriate. For example, sales were measured and translated at current prices, whereas inventory was measured and translated at historical rates.
3. The volatility of earnings. *SFAS No. 8* required all translation gains and losses to be included in income. However, exchange rate changes are urealized and frequently short-term. This produced a so-called yo-yo effect on earnings. Critics contended that this reporting requirement tended to obscure long-term trends.

The FASB took these criticisms under advisement and later replaced *SFAS No. 8* with *SFAS No. 52*, "Foreign Currency Translation."[38] The following translation objectives were adopted in this release:

1. To provide information that is generally compatible with the expected economic effects of a rate change on an enterprise's cash flow and equity.
2. To reflect in consolidated statements the financial results and relationships of the individual consolidated entities in conformity with U.S. generally accepted accounting principles.

SFAS No. 52 adopts the *functional currency* approach to translation. An entity's functional currency is defined as the currency of the *primary economic environment* in which it operates, which will normally be the environment in which it expends cash. Most frequently, the functional currency will be the

---

[38] Financial Accounting Standards Board, *Statement of Financial Accounting Standards No. 52*, "Foreign Currency Translation" (Stamford, CT: FASB, 1981).

local currency, and four general procedures are involved in the translation process when the local currency is defined as the functional currency:

1. The financial statements of each individual foreign entity are initially recorded in that entity's functional currency. For example, a Japanese subsidiary would initially prepare its financial statements in terms of yen, for that would be the currency it generally uses to carry out cash transactions.

2. The foreign entity's statements must be adjusted (if necessary) to comply with generally accepted accounting principles in the United States.

3. The financial statements of the foreign entity are translated into the reporting currency of the parent company (usually the U.S. dollar). Assets and liabilities are translated at the current exchange rate at the balance sheet date. Revenues, expenses, gains, and losses are translated at the rate in effect at the date they were first recognized, or alternatively, at the average rate for the period.

4. Translation gains and losses are accumulated and reported as a component of other comprehensive income.

SFAS No. 52 defined two situations in which the local currency would not be the functional currency:

1. The foreign country's economic environment is highly inflationary (over 100 percent cumulative inflation over the past three years such as experienced by Argentina and Brazil in the recent past).

2. The company's investment is not considered long-term.

In these cases the foreign company's functional currency is the U.S. dollar, and the financial statements are translated using the *SFAS No. 8* approach. Thus, the resulting exchange gains and losses are reported as a component of net income.

Proponents feel that the situational approach adopted by *SFAS No. 52* gives a true picture of economic reality. When the functional currency is the local currency, the translated accounting numbers parallel the local perspective of foreign operations. Moreover, the major criticism leveled against *SFAS No. 8* is eliminated. Because translation gains and losses are included in other comprehensive income, rather than in ordinary income, the bottom line is not adversely affected by the volatility of foreign exchange rates.

Nevertheless, critics maintain that the functional currency approach may afford management too much leeway in the selection of the functional currency. As a result, a given subsidiary's functional currency may be chosen to manipulate reported net income. Furthermore, when the current rate is applied to historical costs, the result is an accounting model that at best is a hybrid of historical cost. Moreover, when these numbers are aggregated with the parent company's historical costs, the resulting consolidated financial statements are a mixed bag and may not provide useful information.

Translation versus Remeasurement

Under the provisions of *SFAS No. 52, translation* is the process of expressing in the reporting currency of the enterprise those amounts that are denominated or measured in a different currency. The translation process is performed in order to prepare financial statements, and it assumes that the foreign subsidiary is free standing and that the foreign accounts *will not* be liquidated into U.S. dollars. Therefore, translation adjustments are disclosed as a part of other comprehensive income rather than as adjustments to net income.

Remeasurement is the process of measuring transactions originally denominated in a different unit of currency (e.g., purchases of a German subsidiary of a U.S. company payable in French francs). Remeasurement is required when

1. A foreign entity operates in a highly inflationary economy.
2. The accounts of an entity are maintained in a currency other than its functional currency.
3. A foreign entity is a party to a transaction that produces a monetary asset or liability denominated in a currency other than its functional currency.

Remeasurement is accomplished by the same procedures as described earlier under the temporal method. That is, the financial statement elements are restated according to their original measurement bases. Remeasurement assumes that the foreign accounts will be liquidated into U.S. dollars and that an exchange of currencies will occur at the exchange rate prevailing on the date of remeasurement. This produces a foreign exchange gain or loss if the exchange rate fluctuates between the date of the original transaction and the date of the assumed exchange. Therefore, any exchange gain or loss is included in net income in the period in which it occurs.

Foreign Currency Hedges

In issuing *SFAS No. 133*, the FASB intended to increase the consistency of hedge accounting guidance by broadening the scope of eligible foreign currency hedges from what was previously allowed in *SFAS No. 52*. Under the provisions of *SFAS No. 133*, an entity may designate the following types of foreign currency exposure.

a. A fair value hedge of an unrecognized firm commitment or an available-for-sale security.
b. A cash flow hedge of a forecasted foreign-currency-denominated transaction or a forecasted intercompany foreign-currency-denominated transaction.
c. A hedge of a net investment in a foreign operation

Foreign currency fair value hedge A derivative instrument that is designated as hedging changes in the fair value of an unrecognized firm commitment qualifies for the accounting treatment of a fair value hedge if all of the specified criteria for hedge accounting under *SFAS No. 133* are met. A derivative instrument that is designated as hedging the changes in the fair value of an available-for-sale security also qualifies for the accounting treatment of a fair value hedge if all of the same specified criteria are met.

Foreign currency cash flow hedge Nonderivative financial instruments are not allowed to be designated as foreign currency cash flow hedges. Derivative instruments designated as hedging the foreign currency exposure to the variability in the functional-currency-equivalent cash flows associated with either a forecasted foreign-currency-denominated transaction (a forecasted export sale to an unaffiliated entity with the price to be denominated in a foreign currency) or a forecasted intercompany foreign-currency-denominated transaction (a forecasted sale to a foreign subsidiary) qualify for hedge accounting under the following conditions:

a. The company with the foreign currency exposure is a party to the hedging instrument
b. The hedged transaction is denominated in a currency other than that unit's functional currency
c. All of the qualifying criteria for hedge accounting contained in *SFAS No. 133* are met.

Hedge of a net investment in a foreign operation Occurs when dealing with a foreign currency to offset the effects of changes in exchange rates on the company's total investment in a foreign operation. For example, borrowing *REAIS* to hedge against the possible devaluation of that currency on an investment in Brazil. Accounting for foreign currency gains or losses depends on whether the dollar or the foreign currency is the functional currency. Usually the dollar is the functional currency because devaluations usually take place in highly inflationary economies. In such cases, remeasurement is required and the gain or loss is reported on the income statement. In the event the functional currency is the foreign currency, the gain or loss is reported in other comprehensive income. Derivative instruments that have been designated as hedges of foreign currency exposure of a net investment in a foreign subsidiary shall be reported in the same manner as the translation adjustment required by *SFAS No. 52* is reported.

International Accounting Standards

The IASC has issued the following pronouncements dealing with multiple entities:

1. *IAS No. 22*, "Business Combinations."
2. *IAS No. 27*, "Consolidated Financial Statements and Accounting for Investments in Subsidiaries."
3. *IAS No. 14*, "Reporting Financial Information by Segment," and an exposure draft, E51, with the same title.
4. *IAS No. 21*, "The Effects of Changes in Foreign Exchange Rates."

In *IAS No. 22*, the IASC addressed the purchase versus pooling of interests issue by distinguishing between *acquisitions* and *uniting of interests*. Acquisitions are accounted for by the purchase method, and uniting of interests is accounted for by the pooling of interests method. Although the criteria for use of the pooling of interests method are not as extensive as those contained in *APB No. 16*, the requirements are similar. Acquisitions are defined as business combinations where one of the combining companies obtains control over the other. (This is consistent with the recent exposure draft issued by the FASB.) As a result, *IAS No. 22* is more restrictive than U.S. GAAP in allowing business combinations to be accounted for by the use of the pooling of interests method. Uniting of interests results when the shareholders of the combining enterprises join in a substantially equal arrangement to share control. The criteria for use of pooling are:

a. The substantial majority of the voting common shares of the combining enterprises are exchanged.
b. The fair value of one enterprise is not significantly different from that of the other.
c. The shareholders of each enterprise maintain substantially the same relative rights in the combined entity.

One major difference with U.S. GAAP is in the treatment of goodwill arising from an acquisition. As discussed in Chapter 9, current IASC standards require goodwill to be recognized as an asset and amortized by the straight-line method over 5 years unless another amortization method is more appropriate. Amortization periods not to exceed 20 years may be used if they can be justified as more appropriate. (A proposed standard would change the 5-year period to 20 years and require amortization by a method that reflects use of the pattern of benefits.) Finally, as discussed in Chapter 9, negative goodwill is recognized as deferred income and amortized on a systematic basis over a 5-year period unless a longer period of up to 20 years can be justified.

In its review of *IAS No. 22*, the FASB staff indicated that fewer business combinations would qualify to be treated as pooling of interests under *IAS No. 22* because an acquirer can be identified in most business combinations. Consequently, intercompany comparability problems might occur when some combinations are accounting for using U.S. GAAP, while others are accounted for by using the provisions of *IAS No. 22*. It was also noted that financial analysts might prefer the IASC's treatment of business combinations and the write-offs of goodwill and acquired research and development costs.[39]

In *IAS No. 27*, the IASC addressed the issue of business combinations. This statement indicated that parent companies should present consolidated financial statements when it has the ability to control its subsidiaries unless that control is temporary or the parent operates under restrictions that impair its ability to obtain subsidiary funds which is similar to U.S. GAAP. However, the concept of control is defined somewhat differently. *IAS No. 27* defines control as the

[39] Financial Accounting Standards Board, *The IASC-U.S. Comparison Project: A Report on the Similarities and Differences between IASC Standards and U.S. GAAP*, 2nd ed., Carrie Bloomer (ed.) Norwalk, CT: Financial Accounting Standards Board, 1999), pp. 337–347.

power to govern a subsidiary, whereas U.S. GAAP focuses on ownership of a majority voting interest.

The FASB staff's review of the provisions of *IAS No. 27* indicated that more entities would likely qualify for consolidation under its provisions than under U.S. GAAP because of the IASC's emphasis on control rather than ownership of a majority voting interest. This difference could cause some intercompany comparability problems. In addition, it was noted that *IAS No. 27* provides more guidance on consolidation procedures than is currently available under U.S. GAAP.[40]

In 1997 *IAS No. 14* was revised and now requires all public companies to report segmental information along (1) product and service lines and (2) geographical lines. Segments are defined as organizational units for which information is reported to the board of directors and the CEO unless those organizational units are not along product/service or geographical lines, in which case use is made of the next lower level of internal segmentation that reports product and geographical information. One basis of segmentation is to be defined as primary, while the other is secondary.

The segment accounting policies used should be the same as those used for consolidated reporting purposes. In addition, the following information is required to be disclosed for each primary segment revenue (external and intersegment shown separately); operating result (before interest and taxes); carrying amount of segment assets; carrying amount of segment liabilities; cost to acquire property, plant, equipment, and intangibles; depreciation and amortization; all noncash expenses other than depreciation; the company's share of profit or loss of equity and joint venture investments; and the basis of intersegment pricing.

The following information is required to be disclosed for each secondary segment: revenue (external and intersegment shown separately); carrying amount of segment assets; cost to acquire property, plant, equipment, and intangibles; and the basis of intersegment pricing.

The FASB staff review of the revised *IAS No. 14* noted that the most significant differences between it and *SFAS No. 131* were in three areas.

1. *The process the standards prescribe for identifying reportable segments*   Under *IAS No. 14*, companies must report both business segments and geographical segments and identify the one as primary and the other as secondary. The dominant source and nature of a company's risks and returns govern the designation as primary and secondary. In contrast, *SFAS No. 131* adopts a management approach that relies on the form and content of the information provided by the company's internal reporting system for identifying reportable segments. The reportable segments are those that are regularly reviewed by the company's chief decision maker. As a result of this difference, significant differences can result in the identification of reportable segments under the provisions of the two standards.

[40] Ibid., pp. 349–361.

2. *The treatment for vertically integrated segments* IAS No. 14 encourages the disclosure of vertically integrated segments as separate segments, whereas *SFAS No. 131* only requires that they be disclosed separately if that is how the company is managed. This can result in different information being presented under the two standards.

3. *The basis of accounting* IAS No. 14 requires that segment information be prepared in conformity with the same accounting methods used for preparing the consolidated financial statements of the company. *SFAS No. 131* does not prescribe the accounting methods to be used, thus permitting alternative methods to be used as long as it is on the same basis as those used for internal reporting purposes. As a result, the reported results could differ significantly under the provisions of the two standards.[41]

In *IAS No. 21*, the IASC outlined accounting for foreign currency translation. Foreign currency transactions are to be initially recorded at the historical exchange rate. Subsequently, monetary items are reported at the balance sheet date exchange rate, and nonmonetary items are carried at either the historical rate or the current rate depending on whether the foreign currency denomination was determined by using historical cost or fair value. Exchange differences resulting from investments in foreign entities are to be classified as stockholders' equity until they are disposed of, at which time they are recognized in income. These procedures are similar to U.S. GAAP contained in *SFAS No. 52*.

The FASB staff review of *IAS No. 21* concluded that the standard takes an approach that is similar to U.S. GAAP. However, concern was expressed over some specific requirements contained in *IAS No. 21* involving hedge accounting and the possible use of historical rather than current rates to translate goodwill arising from the acquisition of a foreign subsidiary. These possible differences were seen as having a significant impact on the comparability of financial statements prepared using IASC standards with those using U.S. GAAP.[42]

Summary

There are several aspects to consider in accounting for multiple entities: (1) recording the acquisition of one company by another—combinations, (2) recording and reporting parent and subsidiary relations—consolidations and segment accounting, and (3) reporting the separate statements of subsidiaries—push-down accounting.

In accounting for business combinations, two methods of acquisition may be used. A subsidiary may be acquired by a cash exchange or by an exchange of voting stock. In addition, two methods of accounting—the purchase and pooling of interests methods—may be used to record these acquisitions. These two methods are not alternatives for recording the same transaction.

[41] Ibid.

[42] Ibid., pp. 277–287.

Exchanges of voting stock that satisfy certain criteria are recorded as pooling of interests; all other combinations are recorded as purchases.

Accounting for consolidations involves four major problems: (1) the presentation of consolidated assets, liabilities, and equity; (2) the presentation of consolidated net income; (3) the presentation of minority interest; and (4) accounting for fluctuations in currencies for foreign subsidiaries. Guidelines have been established for handling each of these problems. In addition, *SFAS No. 13* established criteria for the disclosure of segmental information.

In the readings that appear on the webpage for Chapter 15, some additional issues associated with accounting for multiple entities are addressed.

Cases

• Case 15-1 Purchase vs. Pooling of Interests: Various Issues

The board of directors of Kessler Corporation, Bar Company, Cohen, Inc., and Mason Corporation are meeting jointly to discuss plans for a business combination. Each of the corporations has one class of common stock outstanding. Bar also has one class of preferred stock outstanding. Although terms have not yet been settled, Kessler will be the acquiring or issuing corporation. Because the directors want to conform to generally accepted accounting principles, they have asked you to attend the meeting as an advisor.

Consider the following questions independently of the others and answer each in accordance with generally accepted accounting principles. Explain your answers.

Required;

a. Assume that the combination will be consummated on August 31, 2001. Explain the philosophy underlying the accounting and how the balance sheet accounts of each of the four corporations will appear on Kessler's consolidated balance sheet on September 1, 2001, if the combination is accounted for as a
   i.   Pooling of interests
   ii. Purchase
b. Assume that the combination will be consummated on August 31, 2001. Explain how the income statement accounts of each of the four corporations will be accounted for in preparing Kessler's consolidated income statement for the year ended December 31, 2001, if the combination is accounted for as a
   i.   Pooling of interests
   ii. Purchase
c. Some of the directors believe that the terms of the combination should be agreed on immediately and that the method of accounting to be used (whether pooling of interests, purchase, or a mixture) may be chosen at some later date. Others believe that the terms of the combination and the method to be used are very closely related. Which position is correct?

d. Kessler and Mason are comparable in size; Cohen and Bar are much smaller. How do these facts affect the choice of accounting method?

e. Bar was formerly a subsidiary of Tucker Corporation, which has no other relationship to any of the four companies discussing combination. Eighteen months ago Tucker voluntarily spun off Bar. What effect, if any, do these facts have on the choice of accounting method?

f. Kessler holds 2,000 of Bar's 10,000 outstanding shares of preferred stock and 15,000 of Cohen's 100,000 outstanding shares of common stock. All of Kessler's holdings were acquired during the first three months of 2001. What effect, if any, do these facts have on the choice of accounting method?

g. It is almost certain that Mrs. Victor Mason, Sr., who holds 5 percent of Mason's common stock, will object to the combination. Assume that Kessler is able to acquire only 95 percent (rather than 100 percent) of Mason's stock, issuing Kessler common stock in exchange.

   i. Which accounting method is applicable?

   ii. If Kessler is able to acquire the remaining 5 percent at some future time—in five years, for instance—in exchange for its own common stock, which accounting method will be applicable to this second acquisition?

h. Since the directors feel that one of Mason's major divisions will not be compatible with the operations of the combined company, they anticipate that it will be sold as soon as possible after the combination is consummated. They expect to have no trouble in finding a buyer. What effect, if any, do these facts have on the choice of accounting method?

• Case 15-2 Consolidated Financial Statements: Various Issues

Because of irreconcilable differences of opinion, a dissenting group within the management and board of directors of the Algo Company resigned and formed the Bevo Corporation to purchase a manufacturing division of the Algo Company. After negotiation of the agreement, but just before closing and actual transfer of the property, a minority stockholder of Algo notified Bevo that a prior stockholder's agreement with Algo empowered him to prevent the sale. The minority stockholder's claim was acknowledged by Bevo's board of directors. Bevo's board then organized Casco, Inc., to acquire the minority stockholder's interest in Algo for $75,000, and Bevo advanced the cash to Casco. Bevo exercised control over Casco as a subsidiary corporation with common officers and directors. Casco paid the minority stockholder $75,000 (about twice the market value of the Algo stock) for his interest in Algo. Bevo then purchased the manufacturing division from Algo.

Required:

a. What expenditures are usually included in the cost of property, plant, and equipment acquired in a purchase?

b.   i. What are the criteria for determining whether to consolidate the financial statements of Bevo Corporation and Casco, Inc.?

    ii. Should the financial statements of Bevo Corporation and Casco, Inc., be consolidated? Discuss.

c. Assume that unconsolidated financial statements are prepared. Discuss the propriety of treating the $75,000 expenditure in the financial statements of the Bevo Corporation as

    i. An account receivable from Casco

    ii. An investment in Casco

    iii. Part of the cost of the property, plant, and equipment

    iv. A loss

• Case 15-3 Segmental Reporting

The most recently published statement of consolidated earnings of National Industries, Inc., appears as follows:

NATIONAL INDUSTRIES, INC.
Statement of Consolidated Earnings
for the Year Ended March 31, 1999

Net sales	$38,041,200
Other revenue	407,400
Total revenue	$38,448,600
Cost of products sold	$27,173,300
Selling and administrative expenses	8,687,500
Interest expense	296,900
Total cost and expense	$36,157,700
Earnings before income taxes	$2,290,900
Provision for income taxes	1,005,200
Net earnings	$1,285,700

    Charles Norton, a representative of a firm of security analysts, visited the central headquarters of National Industries for the purpose of obtaining more information about the company's operations.

    In the annual report, National's president stated that National was engaged in the pharmaceutical, food processing, toy manufacturing, and metal-working industries. Norton complained that the published statement of earnings was of limited utility in his analysis of the firm's operations. He said that National should have disclosed separately the profit earned in each of its component industries. Further, he maintained that several items appearing on the statement of consolidated retained earnings should have been included on the statement of earnings, namely, a gain of $633,400 on the sale of the furniture division in early March of the current year and an assessment for additional income taxes of $164,900 resulting from an examination of the returns covering the years ended March 31, 2001 and 2002.

Required:

a. Discuss the accounting problems involved in measuring net profit by industry segments within a company.

b. With reference to National Industries' statement of consolidated earnings, identify the specific items where difficulty might be encountered in measuring profit by each of its industry segments and explain the nature of the difficulty.

c. i. What criteria should be applied in determining whether a gain or loss should be excluded from the determination of net earnings?

ii. What criteria should be applied in determining whether a gain or loss that is properly included in the determination of net earnings should be included in the results of ordinary operations or shown separately as an extraordinary item after all other terms of revenue and expense?

iii. How should the gain on the sale of the furniture division and the assessment of additional taxes each be presented in National's financial statements?

• Case 15-4 Tender Offers

A tender offer is one method of creating a merger. Tender offers are frequently financed by leveraged buy-outs.

Required:

a. Discuss how a merger is created when a tender offer is financed by a leveraged buy-out.

b. Discuss the following terms that are associated with tender offers.
   i. Crown jewel
   ii. Golden parachute
   iii. Greenmail
   iv. Poison pill
   v. Raider
   vi. Shark repellent
   vii. Target
   viii. Two-tier offer
   ix. White knight

• Case 15-5 Push-down Accounting

Push-down accounting is now required for reporting the separate subsidiary financial statements for companies acquired and accounted for by the purchase method.

Required:

a. Discuss the accounting treatment required by push-down accounting for a subsidiary acquired and accounted for under the purchase method of accounting.

b. Discuss the arguments for and against push-down accounting.

• Case 15-6 Business Combinations

The Whit Company and the Berry Company, a manufacturer and retailer, respectively, entered into a business combination whereby the Whit Company acquired for cash all the outstanding voting common stock of the Berry Company.

Required:
a. The Whit Company is preparing consolidated financial statements immediately after the consummation of the newly formed business combination. How should the Whit Company determine in general the amounts to be reported for the assets and liabilities of Berry Company? Assuming that the business combination resulted in goodwill, indicate how the amount of goodwill is determined.
b. Why and under what circumstances should Berry Company be included in the entity's consolidated financial statements?

• Case 15-7 Segmental Reporting: Required Information

A central issue in reporting on industry segments of a business enterprise is the determination of which segments are reportable.

Required:
a. What is a reportable segment?
b. Explain how a preparer would determine which operating segments to report segment information for.
c. What types of segment information are required to be reported?

• Case 15-8 Foreign Currency Translation: Measure vs. Denominate

The FASB has discussed certain terminology essential to both the translation of foreign currency transactions and foreign currency financial statements. Included in the discussion is a definition of and distinction between the terms *measure* and *denominate*.

Required:
Define the terms *measure* and *denominate* as discussed by the FASB and give a brief example that demonstrates the distinction between accounts measured in a particular currency and accounts denominated in a particular currency.

• Case 15-9 Foreign Currency Translation: Various Methods

Several methods of translating foreign currency transactions or accounts are reflected in foreign currency financial statements. Among these methods are the current-noncurrent, monetary-nonmonetary, current rate, and temporal methods.

Required:
Define the temporal method of translating foreign currency financial statements. Specifically include in your answer the treatment of the following four accounts.
a. Long-term accounts receivable.
b. Deferred income.
c. Inventory valued at cost.
d. Long-term debt.

• Case 15-10 Forward Exchange Contracts

Reporting forward exchange contracts continues to be a significant issue in accounting for foreign currency translation adjustments.

Required:
a. Describe a fair value hedge and discuss how to account for forward exchange contracts that are entered into for fair value hedges.
b. Describe foreign currency fair value hedges and discuss the accounting for these types of hedges.
c. Describe foreign currency cash flow hedges and discuss the accounting for these types of hedges.

Case 15-11 Foreign Currency Translation: Functional Currency Approach

In *SFAS No. 52*, the FASB adopted standards for financial reporting of foreign currency exchanges. This release adopts the functional currency approach to foreign currency translation.

Required:
a. Discuss the functional currency approach to foreign currency translation.
b. Discuss the terms *translation* and *remeasurement* as they relate to foreign currency translation.

Room for Debate

• Issue 1

In their 1995 exposure draft, "Consolidated Financial Statements: Policy and Procedures," the FASB proposed that a company's outside interest ("noncontrolling interest") be reported as an element of stockholders' equity. This practice would differ from *IAS No. 27*, which requires that noncontrolling interest be presented above stockholders' equity as well as from the majority of current practice that conforms to the international requirement.

Team Debate:

Team 1. Argue in favor of presenting the noncontrolling interest as an element of stockholders' equity. Your arguments should consider the conceptual framework and be grounded on a theory of consolidation (entity theory or parent company theory).

Team 2. Argue in favor of presenting the noncontrolling interest outside of stockholders' equity. Your arguments should consider the conceptual framework and be grounded on a theory of consolidation (entity theory or parent company theory).

Recommended Additional Readings

Bierman, Harold, Jr. "Proportionate Consolidation and Financial Analysis." *Accounting Horizons* (December 1992), pp. 5–17.

Briloff, Abraham J. "Dirty Pooling." *The Accounting Review* (July 1967), pp. 489–496.

Brownlee, E. Richard, II, Norman S. Siegel, and Kurt D. Rasmuss. "Mergers and Acquisitions, New Considerations." *The CPA Journal* (March 1989), pp. 12–14, 16, 18–20.

Dove, Robert "A Two-Tier Slice for Segments." *Accountancy* (April 1996), pp. 65–66.

Hector, Gary. "Are Shareholders Cheated by LBOs?" *Fortune* (January 19, 1987), pp. 98–100.

Knoeber, Charles R. "Golden Parachutes, Shark Repellents, and Hostile Tender Offers." *The American Economic Review* (March 1986), pp. 155–167.

McConnell, Patricia, and Paul Pactor. "IASC and FASB Proposals Would Enhance Segment Reporting." *The CPA Journal* (August 1995), pp. 32–38.

Moore, James. "Push-Down Accounting: FAS 200?" *Management Accounting* (November 1988), pp. 53–58.

Mortensen, R. "Accounting for Business Combinations in the Global Economy: Purchase, Pooling, or ———?" *Journal of Accounting Education* (Winter 1994), p. 81.

Pactor, Paul. "Revising GAAP for Consolidations: Join the Debate." *The CPA Journal* (July 1992), pp. 38–40, 42, 44, 47.

Rosenfield, Paul, and Steven Rubin. "Minority Interest: Opposing Views." *Journal of Accountancy* (March 1986), pp. 78–80, 82, 84, 86, 88–90.

Bibliography

Backman, Jules. "Economist Looks at Accounting for Business Combinations." *Financial Analysts Journal* (July–August 1970), pp. 39–48.

Baldwin, Bruce A. "Segment Earnings Disclosure and the Ability of Security Analysts to Forecast Earnings per Share." *The Accounting Review* (July 1984), pp. 376–384.

Bartlett, Thomas M., Jr. "Problems in Accounting for a Business Purchase." *Financial Executive* (April 1973), pp. 52–71.

Baxter, George C., and James C. Spinney. "A Closer Look at Consolidated Financial Statement Theory." *CA Magazine* (January 1975), pp. 31–36.

Benjamin, James J., and Steven D. Grossman. "Foreign Currency Translation: An Update." *The CPA Journal* (February 1981), pp. 38–42.

Bergstein, Sol. "More on Pooling of Interest." *Journal of Accountancy* (March 1972), pp. 83–86.

Brenner, Vincent C. "Empirical Study of Support for APB Opinion No. 16." *Journal of Accounting Research* (Spring 1972), pp. 200–208.

Brown, Frank A., and Philip L. Kintzele. "The Effects of FASB Statement No. 14 on Annual Reports." *The Ohio CPA* (Summer 1979), pp. 98–103.

Burton, John C. *Accounting for Business Combinations: A Practical and Empirical Comment.* New York: Financial Executives Research Foundation, 1970.

Cohen, Stuart. "Segment Reporting by Diversified Corporations." *Massachusetts CPA Review* (March–April 1979), pp. 15–20.

Dewberry, J. Terry. "A New Approach to Business Combinations." *Management Accounting* (November 1979), pp. 44–49.

Eigen, Martin M. "Is Pooling Really Necessary?" *The Accounting Review* (July 1965), pp. 563–570.

Eiteman, Dean S. *Pooling and Purchase Accounting.* Ann Arbor: University of Michigan, 1967.

Evans, Thomas G. "Some Concerns about Exposure after the FASB's Statement No. 8." *Financial Executive* (November 1976), pp. 28–30.

Fantl, Irving L. "Problems with Currency Translation—A Report on FASB No. 8." *Financial Executive* (December 1979), pp. 33–37.

Foster, William C. "Does Pooling Present Fairly?" *The CPA Journal* (December 1974), pp. 36–41.

Foster, William C. "The Illogic of Pooling." *Financial Executive* (December 1974), pp. 16–21.

Fotenos, James F. "Accounting for Business Combinations: A Critique of APB Opinion Number 16." *Stanford Law Review* (January 1971), pp. 330–346.

Fritzemeyer, Joe R. "Accounting for Business Combinations: The Evolution of an APB Opinion." *Journal of Accountancy* (August 1969), pp. 35–49.

Gagnon, Jean-Marie. "Purchase-Pooling Choice: Some Empirical Evidence." *Journal of Accounting Research* (Spring 1971), pp. 52–72.

Gitres, David L. "Negative Goodwill Paradox." *The CPA Journal* (December 1978), pp. 45–48.

Gosman, Martin L., and Philip E. Meyer. "SFAS 94's Effect on Liquidity Disclosure." *Accounting Horizons* (March 1992), pp. 88–100.

Gunther, Samuel P. "Lingering Pooling Problems." *The CPA Journal* (June 1973), pp. 459–463.

Harmon, David Perry, Jr. "Pooling of Interests: A Case Study." *Financial Analysts Journal* (March–April 1968), pp. 82–88.

Heian, James B., and James B. Thies. "Consolidation of Finance Subsidiaries: $230 Billion in Off-Balance-Sheet Financing Comes Home to Roost." *Accounting Horizons* (March 1989), pp. 1–9.

Lauver, R. C. "The Case for Poolings." *The Accounting Review* (January 1966), pp. 65–74.

Lurie, Adolph. "Segment Reporting—Past, Present, and Future." *The CPA Journal* (August 1979), pp. 27–30.

Lurie, Adolph. "Selecting Segments of a Business." *Financial Executive* (April 1980), pp. 34–44.

Mednick, Robert. "Companies Slice and Serve Up their Financial Results under FASB 14." *Financial Executive* (March 1979), pp. 44–56.

Moonitz, Maurice. *The Entity Theory of Consolidated Statements.* Brooklyn, NY: Foundation Press, 1951.

Moville, Wig De, and A. George Petrie. "Accounting for a Bargain Purchase in a Business Combination." *Accounting Horizons* (September 1989), pp. 38–43.

Ott, Mack, and G. J. Santoni. "Mergers and Takeovers—The Value of Predators' Information." *Bulletin: Federal Reserve Bank of St. Louis* (December 1985), pp. 16–28.

Rappaport, Alfred, and Eugene M. Lerner. *A Framework for Financial Reporting by Diversified Companies.* New York: National Association of Accountants, 1969.

Rappaport, Alfred, and Eugene M. Lerner. *Segment Reporting for Managers and Investors.* New York: National Association of Accountants, 1972.

Sapienza, Samuel R. "Business Combinations." In Morton Backer (ed.), *Modern Accounting Theory.* Englewood Cliffs, NJ: Prentice-Hall, 1966, pp. 339–365.

Sapienza, Samuel R. "Distinguishing between Purchase and Pooling." *Journal of Accountancy* (June 1961), pp. 35–40.

Sapienza, Samuel R. "Divided House of Consolidations." *The Accounting Review* (July 1960), pp. 503–510.

Savage, Allan H., and B. J. Linder. "Meeting the Requirements of Line of Business Reporting." *Financial Executive* (November 1980), pp. 38–44.

Savage, Linda, and Joel Siegel. "Disposal of a Segment of a Business." *The CPA Journal* (September 1978), pp. 32–37.

Schrader, William J., Robert E. Malcom, and John J. Willingham. "In Support of Pooling." *Financial Executive* (December 1969), pp. 54–63.

Seidler, Lee J. "An Income Approach to the Translation of Foreign Currency Financial Statements." *The CPA Journal* (January 1972), pp. 26–35.

Shank, John K. "FASB Statement No. 8 Resolved Foreign Currency Accounting—or Did It?" *Financial Analysts Journal* (July–August 1976), pp. 55–61.

Shank, John K., Jesse F. Dillard, and Richard J. Murdock. *Assessing the Economic Impact of FASB No. 8.* New York: Financial Executives Research Foundation, 1979.

Shank, John K., Jesse F. Dillard, and Richard J. Murdock. "FASB No. 8 and the Decision Makers." *Financial Executive* (February 1980), pp. 18–23.

Shieifer, Andrei, and Robert Vishny. "Greenmail, White Knights and Shareholders' Interest." *Rand Journal of Economics* (Autumn 1986), pp. 293–309.

Shwayder, Keith R. "Accounting for Exchange Rate Fluctuations." *The Accounting Review* (October 1972), pp. 747–760.

Slesinger, Reuben E. "Conglomeration: Growth and Techniques." *Accounting and Business Research* (Spring 1971), pp. 145–154.

Snavely, Howard J. "'Pooling' Is Good Accounting." *Financial Analysts Journal* (November–December 1968), pp. 85–89.

Snavely, Howard J. "Pooling Should Be Mandatory." *The CPA Journal* (December 1975), pp. 23–26 and (April 1976), pp. 5–6.

Solomons, David. *Divisional Performance: Measurement and Control.* Homewood, IL: Richard D. Irwin, 1968.

Sprouse, Robert T. "Diversified Views about Diversified Companies." *Journal of Accounting Research* (Spring 1969), pp. 137–159.

Steedle, Lamont F. "Disclosure of Segment Information—SFAS 14." *The CPA Journal* (October 1983), pp. 34–47.

Thomas, Paula B., and J. Larry Hagler. "Push Down Accounting: A Descriptive Assessment." *Accounting Horizons* (September 1988), pp. 26–31.

Weidenbaum, Murry, and Stephen Vogt. "Takeovers and Stockholders: Winners and Losers." *California Management Review* (Summer 1987), pp. 157–168.

Wyatt, Arthur R. *A Critical Study of Accounting for Business Combinations.* New York: American Institute of Certified Public Accountants, 1963.

Wyatt, Arthur R. "Inequities in Accounting for Business Combinations." *Financial Executive* (December 1972), pp. 28–35.

Financial Reporting Disclosure Requirements and Ethical Responsibilities

In the preceding chapters of this text, we have attempted to give a concise yet comprehensive explanation of current generally accepted accounting principles. We have given primary attention to those principles promulgated by the Financial Accounting Standards Board and its predecessors in their roles as the bodies of the accounting profession authorized to issue financial accounting standards. The discussion, therefore, has frequently been directed toward identifying transactions to be treated as accounting information, the appropriate measurement of those transactions, criteria for classifying the data in the financial statements, and the reporting and disclosure requirements of the various Accounting Research Bulletins, APB Opinions, and Statements of Financial Accounting Standards. In this chapter we look more closely at the concept of disclosure and examine accountants' ethical responsibility to society.

Disclosure Requirements

As indicated in Chapter 1, current standards are impacted by the conceptual framework of accounting and involve the concept of disclosure. However, various disclosure techniques are available, and the selection of the best method of disclosure depends on the nature of the information and its relative importance. The most common types of disclosure are:

1. The financial statements.
2. Footnotes to the financial statements.
3. Supplementary statements and schedules.
4. The auditor's certificate.
5. Management's Discussion and Analysis.

The *financial statements* should contain the most relevant and significant information about the corporation expressed in quantitative terms. The form and arrangement of the financial statements should ensure that the most vital information is readily apparent and understandable to the financial statement users.

The *footnotes* should present information that cannot be easily incorporated into the financial statements themselves. However, footnotes should never be used to substitute for the proper valuation of a financial statement element, nor should they be used to contradict information contained in the financial statements. The most common examples of footnotes are

1. Schedules and exhibits such as long-term debt.
2. Explanations of financial statement items such as pensions.
3. General information about the company such as subsequent events or contingencies.

Supplementary statements and schedules are intended to improve the understandability of the financial statements. They may be used to highlight trends such as five-year summaries, or they may be required by FASB pronouncements such as information on current costs.

The *auditor's certificate* is a form of disclosure in that it informs users of the reliability of the financial statements. That is, an unqualified opinion should indicate more reliable financial statements than does a qualified or adverse opinion.

The Securities and Exchange Commission requires publicly held companies to provide *Management's Discussion and Analysis* (MD&A) of the reasons for a company's performance during the preceding annual period. These disclosures involve the presentation of information pertaining to liquidity, capital resources, and the results of operations. The SEC also requires management to highlight favorable or unfavorable trends and to identify significant events and uncertainties that affect these three factors. This discussion is also intended to allow financial statement users to assess the likelihood that past performance is indicative of future performance. That is, the company must disclose matters known presently that could affect financial statements in the future. These discussions involve a number of subjective estimations, but the SEC believes that the relevance of this information exceeds its potential unreliability. In order to encourage these presentations, the SEC has provided "safe-harbor against fraud charges as long as estimates are prepared in a reasonable manner and disclosed in good faith."[1] The evaluation of the MD&A section of corporate annual reports has become of added interest to financial analysts in recent years. Clarkson et al. (1999), for example, found that MD&As were a source of useful information, especially in the financial analysis of a company.[2] Earlier, however, Pava and Epstein (1993)

---

[1] Safe-harbor Rule for Protection, Release No. 5993 (Washington, DC: SEC, 1979).

[2] Peter M. Clarkson, Jennifer L. Koa, and Gordon D. Richardson, "Evidence That Management Discussion and Analysis (MD&A) is a part of a Firm's Overall Disclosure Package," *Contemporary Accounting Research* (Spring 1999), pp. 111–134.

found that very few companies were making predictions, and when prospective data were disclosed, there was a strong bias in favor of reporting positive trends while negative trends tended to be ignored or not fully reported.[3] The financial analysis of the MD&A section of the annual report is discussed in further detail in the article by Nicholas Schroeder and Charles Gibson on the text's webpage for Chapter 16.

Kroll-O'Gara Company's footnotes to the financial statements, supplementary statements and schedules, auditor's certificate, and Management's Discussion and Analysis are all contained in the company's annual 10-K report contained on the text's webpage.

In addition, the SEC now requires a discussion of the quantitative and qualitative aspects of its market risk associated with derivative transactions in this section. Kroll-O'Gara Company's disclosure of this information is contained in Item 7(a) of its 10-K report. This issue is discussed in more detail in Chapter 10 and in the articles on the text's webpage for Chapter 10.

The presentation of financial statement information also involves the preparer's decision on the level of sophistication shown by the financial statements users. That is, preparers should decide whether the information provided is to be understandable to the relatively uninformed investor or to individuals working with the information on a day-to-day basis such as security analysts. The FASB addressed this issue when it stated in *SFAC No. 1* that financial information should be comprehensible to those who have a reasonable understanding of business and economic activities and are willing to study the information with reasonable diligence.

This chapter seeks to draw additional attention to the special importance of disclosure in financial reporting. Specifically, we review the disclosure requirements issued by

1. Private-sector authoritative bodies in various publications.
2. The Securities and Exchange Commission.

Private-Sector Authoritative Bodies

A casual perusal of the Accounting Research Bulletins, Opinions of the APB, and Statements of the FASB provides unmistakable evidence of the increased attention given to disclosure by the groups authorized to issue accounting pronouncements over the years. The ARBs contain only three disclosure requirements. One of these pertains to income taxes, another to long-term leases, and the third to contingencies, and in each case the discussion is rather brief. Of course, the text of the ARBs contains several references to disclosure, but the primary attention is directed toward recording and reporting procedures.

The increased concern with disclosure becomes apparent in *APB Opinion No. 5*, "Reporting of Leases in Financial Statements of Lessees," issued in September 1964. This release contains three paragraphs under the disclosure

---

[3] Moses L. Pava and Marc Epstein, "How Good Is MD&A as an Investment Tool?" *Journal of Accountancy* (March 1993), pp. 51–54.

caption. From that point forward, approximately one-half of the APB Opinions contain such captions, frequently with several paragraphs devoted to the topic, and almost every one includes a reference to disclosure. Similarly, virtually every FASB Statement includes a section devoted to disclosure.

APB Opinion No. 22, "Disclosure of Accounting Policies," provides another example of the increased concern for disclosure by the APB. In *Opinion No. 22* the APB reviewed the issue of the impact of various alternative accounting policies on net income and noted that these policies could have a significant effect on the usefulness of financial statements in making economic decisions. The APB concluded that the disclosure of information on the accounting policies selected is essential for financial statement users.

Accordingly, the Board stated that the accounting policies followed by the reporting entity and the methods used in applying these policies should be disclosed as a "Summary of Significant Accounting Policies" preceding the footnotes or as the first footnote. In particular, it was stated that accounting methods and procedures that involved the following cases should be disclosed:

1. A selection from existing acceptable alternatives.
2. Principles and methods peculiar to the industry in which the reporting entity operates.
3. Unusual or innovative applications of generally accepted accounting principles.

The Board's principal objective in issuing *APB Opinion No. 22* was to provide information that allows investors to utilize existing data in comparing firms across and between industries. Nevertheless, *APB Opinion No. 22* has been criticized as not going far enough. That is, simply saying that one company uses a 10-year straight-line depreciation method whereas another uses an 8-year double-declining balance depreciation method adds little to the information content of financial statements. A more important question is the effect on income of using one accounting procedure instead of another. Those who criticize *APB Opinion No. 22* on this basis would prefer industry-by-industry standards or additional information that would allow more exact comparisons to be made.

Securities and Exchange Commission

The Securities and Exchange Commission (SEC) is a regulatory agency with responsibility for administering federal securities laws. The purpose of these laws is to protect investors and to ensure that all investors have relevant information about companies that issue publicly traded securities. The SEC enforces all of the laws passed by Congress that impact on the public trading of securities. Among these laws are the Securities Act of 1933, the Securities Exchange Act of 1934, and the Foreign Corrupt Practices Act of 1977. These acts stress the need to provide prospective investors with full and fair disclosure of the activities of a company offering and selling securities to the public.

The Securities Act of 1933 regulates the initial public distribution of a corporation's securities. The disclosure issue addressed by the 1933 Act is the protection of the public from fraud when a company is initially issuing securities to the general public *(going public)*. The disclosure system necessary under this legislation has developed over the years and emphasizes the disclosure of "relevant information." The disclosure requirements under the 1933 Act include the filing of a registration statement and a prospectus for review by the SEC. Once a registration statement is filed, it becomes effective on the twentieth day after filing unless the SEC requires amendments. This 20-day period is termed the *waiting period,* and it is unlawful for a company to offer to sell securities during this period. The registration of securities under the provisions of the 1933 Act is designed to provide adequate disclosures of material facts to allow investors to assess the degree of potential risk. It should be emphasized that the registration of securities with the SEC does not protect investors from loss, and it is unlawful for anyone to suggest that registration prevents possible losses.

The Securities Exchange Act of 1934 regulates the trading of securities of publicly held companies. The disclosure issues addressed by the 1934 Act are the personal duties of corporate officers and owners *(insiders)* and the corporate reporting requirements. Periodic reporting for publicly held companies is termed *being public.* The disclosure system developed under this Act deals primarily with the formal content of the information contained in the corporate annual reports and interim reports issued to shareholders. One of the major goals of this legislation is to ensure that any *corporate insider* (broadly defined as any corporate officer, director, or 10-percent-or-more shareholder) does not achieve an advantage in the purchase or sale of securities because of a relationship with the corporation. Thus, the 1934 Act established civil and criminal liabilities for insiders making false or misleading statements when trading corporate securities. The specific SEC reporting requirements for going public and being public are beyond the scope of this text. In the following paragraphs we focus on some of the major disclosure issues adopted by the SEC.

The SEC's Integrated Disclosure System
The dual reporting system generated by the 1933 and 1934 Acts frequently resulted in reporting much of the same information several times in slightly different forms. In addition, the audited financial statements included in the annual report to shareholders were not explicitly covered by either piece of legislation.

In 1980, the SEC adopted a new integrated disclosure system for virtually all the reports covered by the 1933 and 1934 Acts. The new system was accomplished by revamping the two basic regulations of the SEC. These are Regulation S-X, which establishes the requirement for audited financial statements, and Regulation S-K, which covers other types of disclosure. The major change in Regulation S-X was that the audited financial statements included in the annual reports must conform and be identical to those required in the prospectus and all other reports filed with the SEC.

The major changes in Regulation S-K were (1) a requirement to include five years of selected data to highlight trends and (2) a revision of the requirements for management's discussion and analysis of financial condition and results of operations. The main items now required to be analyzed and discussed by management are

1. Unusual or infrequent events that materially affect the reported amount of income.
2. Trends or uncertainties having or expected to have a significant impact on reported income.
3. Changes in volume or price and the introduction of new products that materially affect income.
4. Factors that might have an impact on the company's liquidity or ability to generate enough cash to maintain operations.
5. Commitments for capital projects and anticipated sources of funds to finance these projects.
6. The impact of inflation on the company's operations (narrative presentation for companies not covered by *SFAS No. 33*).
7. The fact that companies are encouraged but not required to provide financial forecasts.

The Securities Act of 1933 is implemented primarily through the requirement that a nonexempt firm that desires to offer securities for public sale must file a registration statement with the SEC and provide potential investors with a prospectus. The prospectus contains most of the information provided to the SEC in the registration statement; therefore, here we review only the registration statement. Furthermore, our review is limited to SEC Form S-1, the general form to be used by all security issuers that are not required to use any of the many other S series forms.

The disclosure requirements of Form S-1 are listed in two parts, as shown in Table 16.1. Part I information must be included in the prospectus, while Part II lists additional information that may be required.

The Securities Exchange Act of 1934 established extensive reporting requirements to provide continuous full and fair disclosure. Again, there are numerous forms, and the corporation must select those that are appropriate for presenting the desired disclosure. The most common forms are the following.

1. Form 10, for registration of a class of security for which no other form is specified.
2. Form 10-K, the annual report to be used when no other form is specified. This form is the annual report counterpart of Form 10, which is used for registration.
3. Form 10-Q, a quarterly report of operations used by all firms.
4. Proxy statement, which is used when the firm makes a proxy solicitation for stockholder meetings.

TABLE 16.1 *Requirements of SEC Form S-1*

Part I	Part II
1. Distribution spread	22. Marketing arrangements
2. Plan of distribution	23. Other expenses of issuance
3. Use of proceeds	24. Relationship with registrants of
4. Sales other than for cash	experts named in statements
5. Capital structure	25. Sales to special parties
6. Summary of earnings	26. Recent sales of unregistered secu-
7. Organization of registrant	rities
8. Parents of registrant	27. Subsidiaries of registrant
9. Description of business	28. Franchises and concessions
10. Description of property	29. Indemnification of directors and
11. Organization within five years	officers
12. Pending legal proceedings	30. Treatment of proceeds from stock
13. Capital stocks being registered	being registered
14. Long-term debt being registered	31. Financial statements
15. Other securities being registered	
16. Directors and executive officers	
17. Remuneration of directors and of-ficers	
18. Options to purchase securities	
19. Principal holders of securities	
20. Interest of management in cer-tain transactions	
21. Certified financial statements	

Form 10-K is usually considered to be the most important of these forms because it is the annual report; it must be filed within 90 days after the end of the firm's fiscal year. The new disclosure rules adopted by the SEC restructured Form 10-K. This restructuring was intended to encourage companies to combine Form 10-K with the annual shareholders' report, thereby satisfying the purposes of both reports. The major disclosure items of Form 10-K are shown in Table 16.2.

The chief executive officer, the chief financial officer, the chief accounting officer, and a majority of the board of directors must sign Form 10-K. This requirement is intended to encourage the directors to devote the needed attention to reviewing the form and to obtain professional help whenever it is necessary.

The fact that much of the information provided to the SEC must be certified by an independent certified public accountant has been a significant factor in the growth and importance of the public accounting profession. Accumulating information for the various reports, as well as assisting in their preparation, also requires a substantial internal accounting effort, which has contributed to the growth and prestige of that segment of accounting.

TABLE 16.2 *Requirements of SEC Form 10-K*

Part I	Part II	Part III	Part IV
1. Business 2. Properties 3. Pending legal proceedings 4. Security ownership of certain beneficial owners and management	5. Market for the registrant's common stock and related security holder matters 6. Selected financial data 7. Management's discussion and analysis of financial condition and results of operations 8. Financial statements and supplemental data	9. Directors and executive officers of the registrant 10. Management remuneration and transactions	11. Exhibits, financial statements, and reports

Both internal and independent accountants, however, probably consider the SEC a mixed blessing at best because of the detailed information required and the legal liability involved. The 1933 Act makes clear that anyone connected with the registration statement is liable to investors for the accuracy of the statements. The external accountant's liability under this Act has been summarized as follows:

1. *Any person acquiring securities described in the Registration Statement may sue the accountant, regardless of the fact that he is not the client of the accountant.*

2. *[The plaintiff's] claim may be based upon an alleged false statement or misleading omission in the financial statements, which constitutes his prima facie case. The plaintiff does not have the further burden of proving that the accountants were negligent or fraudulent in certifying to the financial statement involved.*

3. *The plaintiff does not have to prove that he relied upon the statement or that the loss which he suffered was the proximate result of the falsity or misleading character of the financial statement.*

4. *The accountant has thrust upon him the burden of establishing his freedom from negligence and fraud by proving that he had, after reasonable investigation, reasonable ground to believe and did believe that the financial statements to which he certified were true not only as of the date of the financial statements, but beyond that, as of the time when the Registration Statement became effective.*

5. *The accountant has the burden of establishing by way of defense or in reduc-tion of alleged damages, that the loss of the plaintiff resulted in whole or part from causes other than the false statements or the misleading omissions in the financial statements. Under the common law it would have been the plain-tiff's affirmative case to prove that the damages which he claims he sustained were proximately caused by the negligence or fraud of the accountant.*[4]

The magnitude of this liability has almost certainly been a factor in the continual increase in both voluntary and required financial statement disclo-sures. In addition, the SEC is constantly expanding and asserting its role in providing the investor with full and fair disclosure.

Organizational Structure of the SEC

The SEC is directed by four commissioners appointed by the president with the approval of the U.S. Senate. Each commissioner is appointed for a five-year term, and one member is designated by the president as the chairman of the SEC.

The SEC is administered from its Washington, DC, headquarters but has regional and branch offices in the major financial centers of the United States. The commission is assisted by a professional staff of accountants, engi-neers, lawyers, and securities analysts. These individuals are assigned to the various offices throughout the United States.

The SEC staff is organized into the divisions and offices with specific responsibility for various segments of the federal securities laws. The SEC has five divisions:

1. *Corporation Finance* Responsible for ensuring that disclosure require-ments are met by publicly held companies registered with the SEC. It reviews all registration statements, prospectuses, quarterly and annual reports, proxy statements, and sales literature for corporations offering securities for sale to the public.

2. *Market Regulation* Responsible for overseeing the securities markets and their self-regulatory organizations.

3. *Investment Management* Responsible for regulating investment compa-nies (companies engaged in trading corporate securities).

4. *Division of Enforcement* Charged with enforcing federal securities laws. Responsible for determining whether the available evidence supports allegations or complaints filed against publicly held companies.

5. *Office of Compliance Inspections and Examinations* Responsible for conducting and coordinating all compliance inspection programs of bro-kers, dealers, and self-regulatory organizations.

The SEC office that is of primary importance to accountants is the Office of the Chief Accountant. The Chief Accountant consults with representatives of the accounting profession and the FASB regarding the promulgation of new or revised standards. These duties pertain to a major SEC objective of

---

[4] Saul Levy, *C.P.A. Handbook* (New York: AICPA, 1952), p. 39.

improving accounting and auditing standards and maintaining high standards of professional conduct by independent accountants. The office also administers the statutes and rules which require that accountants examining financial statements filed with the SEC be independent of their clients (discussed further in the next section of this chapter).

Duties of Public Accountants

Public accountants engaged in practicing before the SEC must conform to both SEC requirements and the AICPA Code of Professional Ethics (discussed later in the chapter). A public accountant is considered to be practicing before the SEC if he or she prepares any portion of a registration statement, application, or report and allows his or her name to be associated with the filing. The SEC is particularly sensitive to the *independence* of public accountants, which is defined in the Code of Professional Ethics as complete separation from the financial and business interests of the client.

Regulation S-X contains the SEC's independence requirements. This rule states two conditions that will call the public accountant's independence into question:

1. Any direct financial interest or any material indirect financial interest in the issuer.

2. Any connection with the issuer of the securities as a promoter, underwriter, director, officer, or employee.

The 1933 Act establishes the liability of public accountants to third parties when the accountant makes an untrue statement of a material fact (or omits a material fact) in a registration statement. The accountant's main defense in such cases is *due diligence*. That is, after reasonable investigation, he or she had reasonable grounds to believe that the facts as presented by the client were true.

Under the 1934 Act, the accountant has the responsibility of acting in good faith. If an investor acted on false and misleading financial statements filed with the SEC, the accountant must prove that he or she had no knowledge that the financial statements were false or misleading. That is, the test is *gross negligence*, which means that the accountant acted with less care than would be exercised by a reasonable person under the circumstances.

Foreign Corrupt Practices Act of 1977

The Foreign Corrupt Practices Act (FCPA) enacted by Congress in 1977 has been viewed as the culmination of a trend toward upgrading the ethical behavior of American firms engaged in international trade. The FCPA has two main elements. The first makes it a criminal offense to offer bribes to political or governmental officials outside the United States and imposes fines on offending firms. It also provides for fines and imprisonment of officers, directors, or stockholders of offending firms.

The second element of the FCPA is the requirement that all public companies must (1) keep reasonably detailed records that accurately and fairly reflect company financial activity and (2) devise and maintain a system of internal control that provides reasonable assurance that transactions were properly authorized, recorded, and accounted for. This element is an amendment to the Securities and Exchange Act of 1934 and therefore applies to all corporations that are subject to the 1934 Act's provisions. The disclosure issues involved in this legislation are the prevention of bribery of foreign officials and the maintenance of adequate financial records.

Ethical Responsibilities

The study of ethics from a philosophical perspective explores and analyzes moral judgments, choices, and standards, and asks the question: How should I act? Consequently, society's moral value judgments and the bases for choices of moral beliefs and standards require more comprehensive analysis than is attainable from the data of other disciplines. For example, consider the distinction between science and philosophy. While acting in a professional capacity, the scientist does not find it necessary to pass value judgments on his or her work. In fact, the scientist may disclaim responsibility for the uses of his or her findings, as in the case of nuclear weapons. However, philosophers do evaluate and pass moral judgments on the work of scientists, since the goal of philosophy is to evaluate all aspects of human character, conduct, and experience. Similarly, the scientist (and also the accountant), as a thinking person, is required to make value judgments concerning his or her own work and its consequences.

The terms *ethics* and *morals* are not used interchangeably. In general, ethics (derived from the Greek *elhike*—the science of character) is the study of moral issues, whereas morals (derived from the Greek *mores*—customs and manners) are standards that individuals observe in their daily conduct. The professions, including accounting, provide an exception to this general rule. Professional Codes of Conduct delineate minimum standards for the practice of a profession. Violation of these standards makes a professional unethical. For a layperson, the violation of his or her personal code of ethics makes the individual immoral.

The ethical philosophy of Western civilization is based largely on the concept of *utilitarianism,* the greatest happiness of the greatest number, as refined by John Stuart Mill.[5] Professional ethics by accountants prescribe a duty that goes beyond that of an ordinary citizen. The special responsibility accountants have to society was summarized by Chief Justice Warren Burger as discussed in Chapter 1 (see pages 28 and 29). Meeting this responsibility requires accountants to maintain high ethical standards of professional conduct. Society has granted many of the professions autonomy, including self-regulation, as a privilege. In return, these professions must assume the obligation to promote ethical conduct among their members, or public policy makers may react by reducing or removing self-regulation and autonomy. Ethical conduct by accountants, based on the concept of utilitarianism, should include consideration of all possible consequences of professional

[5] See, for example, J. B. Schneewind, *Mill's Ethical Writings* (New York: Collier, 1965).

decisions for all individuals or groups affected by a decision. Among these individuals or groups are actual and potential stockholders, creditors, suppliers, customers, employees, and society as a whole.

The practice of professional accounting is characterized by uncertainties that can create ethical dilemmas. Loeb[6] has identified several major ethical issues or dilemmas that may confront individual accountants and accounting firms.

1. ***Independence***   The concept of independence requires the complete separation of the business and financial interests of the public accountant from the client corporation. Consequently, the auditor must serve the role of an impartial observer maintaining the public watchdog function. How do firms develop policies to ensure that this duty is maintained?

2. ***Scope of services***   What other services (e.g., consulting, tax return preparation, tax advice) are compatible with financial auditing? At what point does the auditor lose independence by providing nonaudit services to a client?

3. ***Confidentiality***   When does the auditor's public watchdog function conflict with his or her duty to keep client activities confidential?

4. ***Practice development***   The removal of the rule prohibiting advertising (discussed later in the chapter) allows a great deal of latitude; however, an advertisement cannot be misleading or untrue. How do firms develop policies to delineate the nature and extent of professional development activities?

5. ***Differences on accounting issues***   How do public accounting firms develop policies to deal with situations in which a company wishes to account for a transaction in a manner not believed to be acceptable to the firm? (In these situations, the company may threaten to fire the auditor and seek a public accounting firm that will agree with management's position on the accounting issue. This is termed *opinion shopping.*)

The resolution of ethical dilemmas can be assisted through a framework of analysis. The purpose of such frameworks is to help identify the ethical issues and to decide on an appropriate course of action. For example, the following six-step approach may be used:

1.   Obtain the relevant facts.

2.   Identify the ethical issues.

3.   Determine the individuals or groups affected by the dilemma.

4.   Identify the possible alternative solutions.

5.   Determine how the individuals or groups are affected by the alternative solutions.

6.   Decide on the appropriate action.

---

[6] Stephen S. Loeb, "Ethical Committees and Consultants in Public Accounting," *Accounting Horizons* (December 1989), pp. 1–10.

Another aspect of the ethics issue is the legal-ethical question. That is, if a particular action is legal, does that automatically make it ethical? The obvious answer to this question is no, given that slavery was once legal in the United States. In fact, there is a general presumption in our society that ethical behavior should be at a higher level than legal behavior. Consequently, acts that are consistent with current ethical standards but inconsistent with current legal standards may be necessary to change unethical legal standards. For example, consider the issues of sexual and racial discrimination. Not many years ago public accounting firms did not hire either women or racial minorities. Various actions throughout society, some illegal under the then-current legal statutes, helped to eliminate these practices to the point that today over 50 percent of new hires by large public accounting firms are women; and the profession and public accounting firms are currently engaging in a variety of activities to encourage racial minorities to choose accounting as a career.

The Professional Code of Conduct

Accountants, as professionals, are expected to maintain a level of ethical conduct that goes beyond society's laws. The reason for this high level of ethical conduct is the need for public confidence in the quality of services provided by the profession, regardless of the individual providing the service. Public confidence in the quality of professional service is enhanced when the profession encourages high standards of performance and ethical conduct by its members.

Over the years, the American Institute of Certified Public Accountants (AICPA) has represented itself as an ethical professional body engaged in practicing an art rather than a science. Accounting was to be viewed by society, in a manner similar to the medical and legal professions, as more influenced by a service motive than entirely by a profit motive. As an art, the judgmental nature of accounting precludes a uniform set of rules to cover all situations; consequently, the foundation of the profession rests not on standardization and regulation but on ethical conduct.

In attempting to solidify this view by society, the accounting profession in the United States has had some form of a Code of Professional Conduct since the early twentieth century. The original code, which was part of the bylaws of the American Association of Professional Accountants (AAPA), a predecessor of the AICPA, was first published in 1905 and contained only two rules. One prohibited members from allowing nonmembers to practice in the member's name, thereby requiring all members of the firm to join the AAPA, not just the managing partner. The second rule prohibited the payment of referral fees now commonly known as "kickbacks." This limited scope of the earliest version of the code was based on a belief that a written code could not and should not be taken as a complete representation of the moral obligations of accounting's responsibility to society.

Later, in 1917 and through subsequent adopted rules, the renamed organization, the American Institute of Accountants, amended the Code of

Professional Conduct to include rules prohibiting various actions such as contingency fees, competitive bidding, advertising, the formation of partnerships, forecasts, and a substantial financial interest in a public corporation client. In addition, in response to the Securities Acts of 1933 and 1934, a rule on independence was adopted in 1934. Later, in 1941, the rules were codified into a new code that included a section on technical standards.

As discussed in Chapter 1, during the period following the collapse of the stock market in 1929, accountants were viewed very favorably by society. Consequently, it was not necessary for the profession to undertake any drastic measures to attain the public's confidence. Up to 1941, the profession's main concerns were bound up with the concepts of confidentiality, competence, and independence. The main emphasis of the profession's disciplinary actions during this period, and even somewhat later, was directed toward restrictions on unprofessional competitive practices such as competitive bidding, advertising, encroachment on the practice of other CPAs, and the pirating of other firms' employees. The rules prohibiting such actions were based on the belief that they would erode independence and destroy harmony among practitioners.[7]

In 1962 the Code of Professional Conduct was again amended. Although this amended code contained essentially the same rules as did the 1941 code, they were classified into five separate articles. Article 1, "Relations with Clients and Public," contained a more explicit description of independence. Article 2 defined "Technical Standards." Article 3 covered advertising, promotional practices, and competitive bidding and was titled "Promotional Practices." Article 4 discussed the rules of membership and was termed "Operating Practices." Finally, Article 5, "Relations with Fellow Members," defined unacceptable client and employee acquisition practices.

The subsequent social upheaval of the 1960s, and the impact of the Watergate investigation of 1974, also affected the accounting profession. For example, it was found that many of the largest corporations had made illegal contributions to the Republican Party, and investigations discovered secret bank accounts that were used to hide illegal bribes and kickbacks. The profession argued that it was difficult, if not impossible, to discover such transactions in a normal audit. It was also maintained that, even if detected, such illegal transactions would not have a material effect on companies' financial statements and, therefore, did not require disclosure. Nevertheless, the failure to uncover these illegal activities by normal audits served to erode confidence in the ethical conduct of the accounting profession. As a result of these issues, and due to the fact that public accounting firms had failed to detect imminent bankruptcies for several large audit clients such as National Student Marketing, Penn Central, and Equity Funding, in 1977 the United States Congress published a study that asserted an alarming lack of independence and a lack of dedication to public protection by the largest public accounting firms.[8]

---

[7] W. E., Olson, *The Accounting Profession: Years of Trial: 1969–1980* (New York: AICPA, 1982).

[8] U.S. Congress, *The Accounting Establishment: 95th Congress*, 1st session (Washington, DC: GPO, 1977).

During this period, the House Subcommittee on Oversight and Investigations (the congressional body that oversees the SEC) was also engaging in an inquiry of accounting practices in the oil and gas industry that culminated in a much larger investigation. In a report issued in 1978,[9] the Committee's chair, John Moss, summarized Congress's concern over the incidents that had occurred. Especially troubling were events such as bankruptcies with no prior warnings from auditors to investors that anything was amiss, the demise of over 100 brokerage firms in the late 1960s because of inconsistent methods of determining capital ratios, lack of uniform accounting procedures in the energy industry, and the incidents discovered in relation to the Watergate incident.

Subsequently, in the mid-1980s congressional interest in the accounting profession emerged again in the form of more hearings before the House Subcommittee on Oversight and Investigations previously chaired by Representative John Dingell. The committee's primary concern was the role of auditors in the detection of fraud. Representative Dingell questioned whether the public's and the profession's perception of accountants' responsibility coincided. He also asked: Were the rules deficient? Were the qualifications to be a CPA sufficient? Was self-policing of the accounting profession adequate?[10] In other words, he was questioning the maintenance of ethical standards by the profession and suggesting that the profession did not have the ability to regulate itself.

Public policy makers were not the only ones voicing concerns. During the 1970s some accountants were joining the critics of the accounting profession. For example, Abraham Briloff, an accounting professor at Baruch College, City University of New York, in a series of books, articles, and testimony before Congress,[11] maintained that many published financial statements were not "prepared fairly" in accordance with generally accepted accounting principles; the FASB had not fulfilled its responsibility to develop accounting standards; and public accounting firms had not adequately resolved the differences in accounting issues dilemmas discussed above, resulting in several cases of successful "opinion shopping."

The events of the 1970s and 1980s served to question the ability of accountants to detect fraud, uncover illegal contributions, and predict bankruptcy; consequently, their competence as professionals was being questioned. As a result, the profession was facing legislation that threatened to regulate the practice of accounting.

[9] U.S. Congress, *Accounting and Auditing Practices and Procedures: 95th Congress,* 1st session (Washington, DC: GPO, 1978).

[10] J. Dingell, "Accountants Must Clean Up Their Act: Rep. John Dingell Speaks Out," *Management Accounting* (May 1985), pp. 52–55.

[11] See, for example, *Unaccountable Accounting* (New York: Harper & Row, 1972); *More Debits Than Credits* (New York: Harper & Row, 1976); *The Truth about Corporate Accounting* (New York: Harper & Row, 1981); "Standards Without Standards/Principles Without Principles/Fairness Without Fairness," *Advances in Accounting* (1986), pp. 25–50; and "Accounting and Society: A Covenant Desecrated," *Critical Perspectives on Accounting* (March 1990), pp. 5–30.

Partially in response to these issues, the AICPA engaged in several activities in an attempt to neutralize criticism of the accounting profession. In 1973 the Code of Professional Conduct was again amended. A major feature of this amended Code was the requirement to comply with auditing standards and the prohibition from expressing an opinion that financial statements are prepared in conformity with generally accepted accounting standards if such statements depart from an accounting principle. As discussed earlier in the text, the inclusion of this rule made ARBs, APB Opinions, and SFASs enforceable under the Code of Professional Conduct. The 1973 Code also included a discussion of the philosophical fashion by which the rules flow from the concepts and why these concepts were of importance to the profession.

Next, in 1974 the AICPA formed a commission on auditors' responsibilities. The final report of this commission, known as the Cohen Report, called upon the Auditing Standards Executive Committee to consider developing an improved auditor's report. The report also recommended the development of criteria for the evaluation of internal accounting controls and the establishment of independent audit committees. Later, the AICPA established a new division for CPA firms with two sections, one for firms with clients registered with the SEC and one for firms that had private practice clients. Membership in the SEC Practice Section requires self-regulation, including external peer review of its practice procedures. In addition, the activities of the SEC Practice Section are monitored by a Public Oversight Board.

As noted by Representative Dingell, some of the criticism of the professional practice of accounting can be attributed to an *expectations gap*. That is, there is a difference between what financial statement users and society as a whole perceive as the responsibility of public accountants versus what accountants and the profession perceive as their responsibility. As a result, the AICPA's Auditing Standards Board issued nine new Standards in 1988 in an attempt to narrow this expectations gap. Specifically, with respect to addressing some of the problem areas identified by critics, the effect of these new standards was to (1) broaden auditors' responsibility to consider the reliability of a company's internal control system when planning an audit, (2) delineate the responsibility of auditors for reporting errors, irregularities, and illegal acts by clients, and (3) require auditors to evaluate a company's ability to continue as a going concern.

At about this same time, the Code of Professional Conduct was undergoing a review. In 1983 the AICPA appointed a Special Committee to study the relevance and effectiveness of the Code in the then-current environment. The report of this committee, commonly known as the Anderson Report, indicated that effective performance should meet six criteria:

1. Safeguard the public's interest.
2. Recognize the CPA's paramount role in the financial reporting process.
3. Help assure quality performance and eliminate substandard performance.
4. Help assure objectivity and integrity in public service.

5. Enhance the CPA's prestige and credibility.
6. Provide guidance as to proper conduct.[12]

The members of the AICPA accepted the recommendations of the Anderson Report and amended the Code of Professional Conduct in 1988. The Code now consists of four sections as follows:

Principles   The standards of ethical conduct stated in philosophical terms.

Rules of conduct   Minimum standards of ethical conduct.

Interpretations   Interpretations of the rules by the AICPA Division of Professional Ethics.

Ethical rulings   Published explanations and answers to questions about the rules submitted to the AICPA by practicing accountants and others interested in ethical requirements.

The first two sections of the Code of Professional Conduct consist of general statements emphasizing positive activities that encourage a high level of performance (principles) and minimum levels of performance that must be maintained (rules). Consequently, implicit in the Code of Professional Conduct is the expectation that the CPAs will abide by the rules at the minimum and strive to achieve the principles at the maximum. The following six ethical principles, which are not enforceable, are contained in the Code of Professional Conduct:

1. *Responsibilities*   In carrying out their responsibilities as professionals, members should exercise sensitive professional and moral judgments in all their activities.
2. *The public interest*   Members should accept the obligation to act in a way that will serve the public interest, honor the public trust, and demonstrate commitment to professionalism.
3. *Integrity*   To maintain and broaden public confidence, members should perform all professional responsibilities with the highest level of integrity.
4. *Objectivity and independence*   A member should maintain objectivity and be free of conflict of interest in discharging professional responsibilities. A member in public practice should be independent in fact and appearance when providing auditing and other attestation services.
5. *Due care*   A member should observe the profession's technical and ethical standards, strive continually to improve competence and the quality of services, and discharge professional responsibility to the best of the member's ability.
6. *Scope and nature of services*   A member in public practice should observe the Principles of the Code of Professional Conduct in determining the scope and nature of services to be provided.

---

[12] AICPA, *Recruiting Professional Standards to Achieve Professional Excellence in a Changing Environment* (New York: AICPA, 1986), p. 11.

The principles, which are goal-oriented, also provide the framework for the rules, which represent the enforceable provisions of the Code. The rules deal with issues such as independence, integrity, and objectivity; compliance with standards of practice; confidentiality of client information; advertising; and contingent fees and commissions. Later, some of these rules were required to be liberalized because of a consent decree between the AICPA and the Federal Trade Commission that arose from a claim of restraint of fair trade. For example, CPA firms may now accept contingent fees from nonattest clients, and advertising by CPA firms is now an acceptable practice.

The need for interpretations of the Code of Professional Conduct arises when individuals or firms have questions about a particular rule. Ethical rulings are explanations concerning specific factual situations. They have been published in the form of questions and answers. A detailed review of the interpretations and ethical rulings is beyond the scope of this book.

The goal of the Anderson Report and the revised Code of Professional Conduct was to be more responsive to the public's concern by providing:

1. Ethical guidance.
2. Broad positive statements.
3. Specific behavioral rules.
4. Proactive monitoring.
5. Broader rules application.
6. Guidance on dealing with the changing environment.[13]

In summary, the past two decades have brought forward questions from some critics concerning the ethical conduct of professional accountants. The profession has responded by further delineating its responsibilities and by attempting to narrow the expectations gap. However, in spite of its critics, the accounting profession continues to be viewed in a favorable manner. A recent Harris poll found that the public holds accountants in high esteem and above other professions.[14] This favorable view may be partially due to the fact that the accounting profession has proven to be responsive to the external environment over the years. However, the accounting profession must strive to maintain this perception, and the Code of Professional Conduct should be viewed as a starting point in determining the ethical behavior of professional accountants. It may also be necessary to revisit the scope of services issue because this same Harris poll detected some concerns over the variety of services offered by CPA firms to the same client. This and other issues that trouble the public must be resolved in order for accounting to continue to serve its public watchdog function in a manner that is accepted by society.

---

[13] Michael K. Shaub, "Restructuring the Code of Professional Ethics: A Review of the Anderson Committee Report and Its Implications," *Accounting Horizons* (December 1988), pp. 89–97.

[14] Louis Harris, *A Survey of Perceptions, Knowledge and Attitudes Toward CPAs and the Accounting Profession* (New York, Louis Harris and Associates 1986).

International Accounting Standards

The IASC standard that addresses disclosure requirements and ethical responsibilities is *IAS No. 1: "Presentation of Financial Statements."* This statement, which replaced the previous *IAS No. 1*, originally titled "Disclosure of Accounting Policies" (as well as *IAS Nos. 5* and *13*), requires companies to present a statement disclosing each item of income, expense, gain or loss required by other standards to be presented directly in equity and the total of these items. It also requires that the notes to the financial statements present information about the basis of preparation of the financial statements and the specific accounting policies selected, disclose all other information required by IASC standards not presented elsewhere in the financial statements, and provide all other information necessary for a fair presentation.

In its review of *IAS No. 1*, the FASB staff noted that the IASC uses the term *disclosure* to encompass items either in the financial statements or the footnotes. Consequently, an item required by IASC standards to be disclosed can appear in either place. This treatment was seen as possibly complicating intercompany comparisons and financial analysis. However, it was also noted that it is unlikely that any significant differences in the information will be included under the two approaches. In addition, the FASB staff indicated that the IASC's required presentation of changes in equity is similar to that required by *SFAS No. 130* but that some individual items disclosed might differ under the two standards.[15]

Summary

Fair and full disclosure has become increasingly important in financial reporting. In response to changing societal needs, the AICPA, SEC, APB, and FASB have all addressed the question of disclosure. Maintaining ethical conduct has also become increasingly important for the accounting profession. As professionals, accountants are required to maintain the highest ethical standards.

In the readings on the webpage for Chapter 16, the topics of disclosure and ethical responsibility are examined in greater detail.

Cases

• Case 16-1 Two Viewpoints on Accounting Standards

The proponents of neoclassical, marginal economics (see Chapter 2) maintain that mandatory accounting and auditing standards inhibit contracting

---

[15] Financial Accounting Standards Board, *The IASC U.S. Comparison Project: A Report on the Similarities and Differences between IASC Standards and U. S. GAAP*, 2nd ed., Carrie Bloomer (ed.) (Norwalk, CT: Financial Accounting Standards Board, 1999) pp. 63–87.

arrangements and the ability to report on company operations. Opponents of this view argue that market forces alone cannot be relied on to produce the quality information required by society.

Required:
Present arguments to support both viewpoints. What is your opinion? [*Hint:* You may wish to consult Richard Leftwich, "Market Failure Fallacies and Accounting Information," *Journal of Accounting and Economics* (December 1980), pp. 193–221; Steven Johnson, "A Perspective on Solomon's Quest for Credibility in Financial Reporting," *Journal of Accounting and Public Policy* (1988), pp. 137–154; as well as the Solomon and Tinker articles contained on the texts webpage for Chapter 2.]

• Case 16-2 Ethical Dilemma

Barbara Montgomery is a first-year auditor for Coppers and Rose, a large public accounting firm. She has been assigned to the audit of Lakes Brothers, a large clothing retailer with retail outlets throughout the United States. This audit has proved troublesome in the past, and during a staff meeting preceding the audit, Robert Cooley, the supervisor on the audit, indicates: "We are going to be required to work several hours 'off-the-clock' each week until this audit is completed." He also observes that the client is putting a great deal of pressure on the firm to maintain an acceptable level of fees.

Barbara has just been to staff training school, where it was emphasized that not charging a client for hours actually worked is a violation of Coppers and Rose's employment policy, a violation that could cause her to be dismissed. She also knows that only staff personnel are paid overtime and that supervisors are evaluated on successfully completing audits within allowable budgets. Barbara discusses the issue with John Reed, a second-year staff accountant. John says: "Don't worry, if you go along, nobody will find out and Robert will give you a good evaluation." John also indicates his opinion that Robert is very highly regarded by the senior members of the firm and is likely to be promoted to manager in the near future.

Required:
a. Is it ethical for Barbara to work hours and not charge them to the client?
b. Use the six-step approach outlined in this chapter to resolve this ethical dilemma.

• Case 16-3 Type of Disclosure: Various Issues

Lancaster Electronics produces electronic components for sale to manufacturers of radios, television sets, and phonographic systems. In connection with his examination of Lancaster's financial statements for the year ended December 31, 2001, Don Olds, CPA, completed fieldwork two weeks ago. Mr. Olds is now evaluating the significance of the following items prior to preparing his auditor's report. Except as noted, none of these items has been disclosed in the financial statements or footnotes.

Item 1

Recently, Lancaster interrupted its policy of paying cash dividends quarterly to its stockholders. Dividends were paid regularly through 1999, discontinued for all of 2000 to finance equipment for the company's new plant, and resumed in the first quarter of 2001. In the annual report, dividend policy is to be discussed in the president's letter to stockholders.

Item 2

A 10-year loan agreement, which the company entered into three years ago, provides that dividend payments may not exceed net income earned after taxes subsequent to the date of the agreement. The balance of retained earnings at the date of the loan agreement was $298,000. From that date through December 31, 2001, net income after taxes has totaled $360,000, and cash dividends have totaled $130,000. Based on these data, the staff auditor assigned to this review concluded that there was no retained earnings restriction at December 31, 2001.

Item 3

The company's new manufacturing plant building, which cost $600,000 and has an estimated life of 25 years, is leased from the Sixth National Bank at an annual rental of $100,000. The company is obligated to pay property taxes, insurance, and maintenance. At the conclusion of its 10-year noncancelable lease, the company has the option of purchasing the property for $1. In Lancaster's income statement, the rental payment is reported on a separate line.

Item 4

A major electronics firm has introduced a line of products that will compete directly with Lancaster's primary line, which is now being produced in the specially designed new plant. Because of manufacturing innovations, a competitor's line will be of comparable quality but priced 50 percent below Lancaster's line. The competitor announced its new line during the week following completion of fieldwork. Mr. Olds read the announcement in the newspaper and discussed the situation by telephone with Lancaster executives. Lancaster will meet the lower prices that are high enough to cover variable manufacturing and selling expenses but will permit recovery of only a portion of fixed costs.

Required:
For each of the preceding items, discuss any additional disclosures in the financial statements and footnotes that the auditor should recommend to his client. (The cumulative effect of the four items should not be considered.)

• Case 16-4 Preparation of Footnotes

You have completed your audit of Carter Corporation and its consolidated subsidiaries for the year ended December 31, 2001, and are satisfied with the results of your examination. You have examined the financial statements of Carter Corporation for the past three years. The corporation is now preparing its annual report to shareholders. The report will include the consolidated financial statements of Carter Corporation and its subsidiaries and your short-form auditor's report. During your audit, the following matters came to your attention.

1. The Internal Revenue Service is currently examining the corporation's 1999 federal income tax return and is questioning the amount of a deduction claimed by the corporation's domestic subsidiary for a loss sustained in 1998. The examination is still in process, and any additional tax liability is indeterminable at this time. The corporation's tax counsel believes that there will be no substantial additional tax liability.

2. A vice-president who is also a stockholder resigned on December 31, 2001, after an argument with the president. The vice-president is soliciting proxies from stockholders and expects to obtain sufficient proxies to gain control of the board of directors so that a new president will be appointed. The president plans to have a footnote prepared that would include information of the pending proxy fight, management's accomplishments over the years, and an appeal by management for the support of stockholders.

Required:
a. Prepare the footnotes, if any, that you would suggest for the foregoing listed items.
b. State your reasons for not making disclosure by footnote for each of the listed items for which you did not prepare a footnote.

• Case 16-5 Methods of Disclosure

The concept of adequate disclosure continues to be one of the most important issues facing accountants, and disclosure may take various forms.

Required:
a. Discuss the various forms of disclosure available in published financial statements.
b. Discuss the disclosure issues addressed by each of the following sources:
   i. The AICPA's Code of Professional Ethics
   ii. The Securities Act of 1933
   iii. The Securities Exchange Act of 1934
   iv. The Foreign Corrupt Practices Act of 1977

• Case 16-6 The Securities Acts of 1933 and 1934

The Securities Act of 1933 and the Securities Exchange Act of 1934 established guidelines for the disclosures necessary and the protection from fraud when securities are offered to the public for sale.

Required:
a. Discuss the terms *going public* and *being public* as they relate to these pieces of legislation.
b. Regulation S-X requires management to discuss and analyze certain financial conditions and results of operations. What are these items?

• Case 16-7 Code of Professional Conduct

Certified Public Accountants have imposed on themselves a rigorous code of professional conduct

Required:
a. Discuss the reasons for the accounting profession's adopting a code of professional conduct.
b. A rule of professional ethics adopted by CPAs is that a CPA cannot be an officer, director, stockholder, representative, or agent of any corporation engaged in the practice of public accounting, except for the professional corporation form expressly permitted by the AICPA. List the arguments supporting the rule that a CPA's firm cannot be a corporation.

• Case 16-8 Consolidated Reporting: A Case of Ethics

As discussed in Chapter 12, leases that are in-substance purchases of assets should be capitalized—an asset and associated liability should be recorded for the fair value acquired. Mason Enterprises is considering acquiring a machine and has the option to lease or to buy by issuing debt. Mason also has debt covenants that restrict their debt-to-equity ratio to 2:1. The purchase alternative would increase the debt-to-equity precariously close to the restrictive limit and could result in the company's going into default. Also, management bonuses are affected when the debt-to-equity ratio exceeds 1.5:1.

Mason's management is aware that under *SFAS No. 94*, majority-owned subsidiaries must be consolidated. The president, Penny Mason, persuades the board to form a subsidiary that would own 49 percent of the stock. The rest of the stock would be sold to the public. Mason would retain control of the subsidiary by maintaining membership on the board of directors and selling the majority shares in small blocks to a number of investors.

Required
a. What is the economic substance of the lease transaction from the perspective of Mason Enterprises? Discuss.
b. By forming the subsidiary, is Mason Enterprises able to lease the equipment and keep the transaction off their balance sheet?
c. According to the efficient market hypothesis, discussed in Chapter 2, would investors be fooled by the Mason financing strategy? Explain.
d. According to agency theory, discussed in Chapter 2, management may act in its own best interest at the expense of owners. In light of this theory, what are the ethical implications of the Mason financing strategy? Discuss.
e. Does the financing strategy provide financial statements that are representationally faithful and unbiased? Discuss.

• Case 16-9 The Ethics of Accounting Choices

The Flllups Company has been in the business of exploring for oil reserves. During 19x1, $10 million was spent drilling wells that were dry holes.

Under GAAP, Fillups has the option of accounting for these costs by the successful efforts method or the full cost method. Under successful efforts, the $10 million would be expensed once it was determined that the wells were dry. Under full cost, the $10 million would be capitalized. It would not be expensed until the oil from successful wells is extracted and sold.

Fillups decides to use the full cost method because of its positive effect on "the bottom line."

Required:
a.   What are the ethical considerations implied in the rationale for Fillups decision? Explain.
b.   Do you believe that an accounting alternative should be selected solely on the basis of financial statement effects? Discuss.

Room for Debate

• Issue 1

Snappy Corporation enters into a lease agreement with Long Leasing. Long requires that the lease qualify as a sale. Snappy can fill this requirement by either guaranteeing the residual value themselves or having a third party guarantee the residual value. Self-guarantee of the residual value will result in a capital lease to Snappy. The third-party guarantee will allow Snappy to report the lease as an operating lease ("off-balance sheet financing").

Team Debate:
Team 1.   Argue for recording the lease as a capital lease. Your arguments should take into consideration the definitions of relevant elements of financial statements found in *SFAC No. 6*, representational faithfulness, and the substance and form of the lease transaction. In addition, discuss the ethical implications of selecting this alternative as opposed to the operating lease.

Team 2.   Argue for treating the lease as an operating lease. Your arguments should take into consideration the definition of relevant elements of financial statements found in *SFAC No. 6*, representational faithfulness, and the substance and form of the lease transaction. In addition, discuss the ethical implications of selecting this alternative as opposed to the capital lease.

Recommended Additional Readings

Anderson, G. D., and R. C. Ellison. "Restructuring Professional Standards: The Anderson Report." *Journal of Accountancy* (September 1986), pp. 92–104.

Briloff, A. M. "Standards Without Standards/Principles Without Principles/Fairness Without Fairness." *Advances in Accounting* (1986), pp. 25–50.

Brownlee, I. R., and S. D. Young. "The SEC and Mandated Disclosure: At the Crossroads." *Accounting Horizons* (September 1987), pp. 17–24.

Clarkson, Peter M., Jennifer L. Koa, and Gordon D. Richardson. "Evidence That Management Discussion and Analysis (MD&A) Is a Part of a Firm's Overall Disclosure Package." *Contemporary Accounting Research* (Spring 1999), pp. 111–134.

Collins, S. H. "The SEC on Full and Fair Disclosure." *Journal of Accountancy* (January 1989), pp. 79–85.

Handler, Lawrence D. "A Question of Ethics." *Journal of Accountancy* (October 1994) pp. 111–114.

Pava, Moses L., and Marc Epstein. "How Good Is MD&A as an Investment Tool?" *Journal of Accountancy* (March 1993), pp. 51–54.

Preston, Alistair M., David J. Cooper, D. Paul Scarbrough, and Robert C. Chilton. "Changes in the Code of Ethics of the U.S. Accounting Profession, 1917 and 1988: The Continual Quest for Legitimation." *Accounting, Organizations and Society,* Vol. 20, No. 1 (August 1995), pp. 505–546.

Reimers, J. L. "Additional Evidence on the Need for Disclosure Reform." *Accounting Horizons* (March 1992), pp. 36–41.

Shaub, M. K. "Restructuring the Code of Professional Ethics: A Review of the Anderson Committee Report and Its Implications." *Accounting Horizons* (December 1988), pp. 89–97.

Bibliography

Adelberg, Arthur H., and Richard A. Lewis. "Financial Reports Can Be Made More Understandable." *Journal of Accountancy* (June 1980), pp. 44–50.

AICPA. *Restructuring Professional Standards to Achieve Professional Excellence in a Changing Environment.* New York: AICPA, 1986, p. 11.

Anderson, George D. "A Fresh Look at Standards of Professional Conduct." *Journal of Accountancy* (September 1985), pp. 91–92, 95–96, 98, 102, 104–106.

Atiase, Rowland K., Linda S. Bamber, and Robert N. Freeman. "Accounting Disclosures Based on Company Size: Regulations and Capital Market Evidence." *Accounting Horizons* (March 1988), pp. 18–26.

Baker, H. Kent, and John A. Haslem. "Information Needs of Individual Investors." *Journal of Accountancy* (November 1973), pp. 64–69.

Beaver, William H. "Current Trends in Corporate Disclosure." *Journal of Accountancy* (January 1978), pp. 44–52.

Bedford, Norton M. *Extension in Accounting Disclosure.* Englewood Cliffs, NJ: Prentice-Hall, 1973.

Benjamin, James J., and Keith G. Stanga. "Differences in Disclosure Needs of Major Users of Financial Statements." *Accounting and Business Research* (Summer 1977), pp. 187–192.

Benston, George J. "Evaluation of the Securities Exchange Act of 1934." *Financial Executive* (May 1974), pp. 28–36, 40–42.

Benston, George J. "The Value of the SEC's Accounting Disclosure Requirements." *The Accounting Review* (July 1969), pp. 515–532.

Briloff, Abraham M. "Accounting and Society: A Covenant Desecrated." *Critical Perspectives on Accounting* (March 1990), pp. 5–30.

Briloff, Abraham M. *More Debits Than Credits.* New York: Harper & Row, 1976.

Briloff, Abraham M. *The Truth about Corporate Accounting.* New York: Harper & Row, 1981.

Briloff, Abraham M. *Unaccountable Accounting.* New York: Harper & Row, 1972.

Burton, John C. "Ethics in Corporate Financial Disclosure." *Financial Analysts Journal* (January–February 1972), pp. 49–53.

Carey, John L. "Professional Ethics and the Public Interest." *Journal of Accountancy* (November 1956), pp. 38–41.

Carey, John L. *Professional Ethics of Certified Public Accountants.* New York: AICPA, 1965.

Carmichael, D. R. *The Auditor's Reporting Obligation.* New York: AICPA, 1972.

Carmichael, D. R. "Standards for Financial Reporting." *Journal of Accountancy* (May 1979), pp. 76–84.

Casler, Darwin J. *The Evolution of CPA Ethics: A Profile of Professionalism.* Occasional Paper No. 12, Michigan State University: Bureau of Business and Economic Research, 1964.

Chandra, Gyan. "Study of the Consensus on Disclosure among Public Accountants and Security Analysis." *The Accounting Review* (October 1974), pp. 733–742.

Dingell, John. "Accountants Must Clean Up Their Act: Rep. John Dingell Speaks Out." *Management Accounting* (May 1985), pp. 52–55.

Gibbins, M., A. Richardson, and J. Waterhouse. "The Management of Corporate Financial Disclosures: Opportunism, Ritualism, Policies and Processes." *Journal of Accounting Research* (Spring 1990), pp. 121–143.

Groves, Ray J. "Corporate Disclosure in the 1980's." *Financial Executive* (June 1980), pp. 14–19.

Kripke, Homer. "A Search for a Meaningful Securities Disclosure Policy." *The Arthur Andersen Chronicle* (July 1976), pp. 14–32.

Loeb, Stephen S. "A Behavioral Study of CPA Ethics." Ph.D. dissertation, University of Wisconsin, 1970.

Loeb, Stephen S. "Enforcement of the Code of Ethics." *The Accounting Review* (January 1972), pp. 1–9.

Loeb, Stephen E. "Ethical Committees and Consultants in Public Accounting." *Accounting Horizons* (December 1989), pp. 1–10.

Loeb, Stephen E. (ed.). *Ethics in the Accounting Profession.* New York: John Wiley & Sons, 1978.

Loeb, Stephen S. "Teaching Accounting Students Ethics: Some Crucial Issues." *Issues in Accounting Education* (Fall 1988), pp. 316–329.

Longstreth, B. "The SEC's Role in Financial Disclosure." *Journal of Accounting Auditing and Finance* (Winter 1984), pp. 110–122.

Merino, Barbara D., and Marilyn D. Neimark. "Disclosure Regulation and Public Policy: A Sociohistorical Reappraisal." *Journal of Accounting and Public Policy* (1982), pp. 32–57.

Mueller, Willard F. "Corporate Disclosure: The Public's Right to Know." In Alfred Rappaport (ed.), *Corporate Financial Reporting.* Chicago: Commerce Clearing House, 1971, pp. 67–93.

Olson, W. E. *The Accounting Profession: Years of Trial: 1969–1980.* New York: AICPA, 1982.

Pastena, Victor. "Some Evidence on the SEC's System of Continuous Disclosure." *The Accounting Review* (October 1979), pp. 776–783.

Pointer, Larry G., and Richard G. Schroeder. *An Introduction to the Securities and Exchange Commission.* Plano, TX: Business Publications, 1986.

Ruhnka, J., and J. W. Bagby. "Disclosure: Damned If You Do, Damned If You Don't." *Harvard Business Review* (September–October 1986), pp. 35–45.

Singhvi, Surendra S. "Corporate Management's Inclination to Disclose Financial Information." *Financial Analysts Journal* (July–August 1972), pp. 66–73.

Skekel, Ted D. "Management Reports of Financial Statements." *The CPA Journal* (July 1979), pp. 32–37.

Skousen, K. Fred. *An Introduction to the SEC.* 5th ed. Cincinnati: South-Western Publishing Co., 1991.

U.S. Congress. *Accounting and Auditing Practices and Procedures: 95th Congress,* 1st session. Washington, DC: GPO, 1978.

U.S. Congress. *The Accounting Establishment: 95th Congress,* 1st session. Washington, DC: GPO, 1977.

Wallace, R.S.O., and T. E. Cooke. "The Diagnosis and Resolution of Emerging Issues in Corporate Disclosure Practices." *Accounting and Business Research* (Spring 1990), pp. 143–152.

Index

generate cash for short-term needs. The assessment of a company's liquidity was discussed in Chapter 7.

Solvency refers to a company's ability to pay its debts when they become due. Several ratios may be used to evaluate a company's solvency, including the long-term debt to assets ratio, the interest coverage ratio, and the debt service coverage ratio. The long-term debt to assets ratio provides information on the extent to which a company is using financial leverage and its accompanying solvency risk. A high ratio value indicates that a company is using a great deal of financial leverage to acquire its assets and, consequently, has a higher risk of insolvency than a company with a low ratio value. The long-term debt to assets ratio is calculated as:

$$\frac{\text{Long-term debt}}{\text{Total assets}}$$

The calculation of the long-term debt to assets ratio is illustrated for the Kroll-O'Gara Company for 1997 and 1998, whose financial statements are contained in Chapters 4 and 5, and on the text's webpage, as follows:

1997

$$\frac{\$1,532,730 + 2,514,606 + 49,641,484}{\$150,484,480} = 35.7\%$$

1998

$$\frac{\$1,542,588 + 1,625,363 + 39,257,245}{\$248,956,059} = 17.0\%$$

This analysis indicates that the company is not making extensive use of financial leverage and that its risk of insolvency declined substantially during 1998. However, further analysis is warranted. When using this ratio, it is necessary to make adjustments to both the numerator and denominator in order to obtain more reliable results. For example, a company engaging in extensive off-balance sheet financing arrangements may have unrecorded liabilities that need to be considered. Similarly, a company disclosing a large amount of intangible assets may distort the ratios because of the difficulty in determining the reliability of the values of those assets. An analysis of Footnote 9 to Kroll-O'Gara Company's financial statements indicates that the company had approximately $30 million of future operating lease payments due on December 31, 1998. The discounted future value of the amounts comprising this balance should be added to the ratio numerator to obtain a more realistic evaluation of the company's solvency. Similarly, the company's 1998 balance sheet disclosed net intangible assets of $60,988,886 that should be deducted as an adjustment to the denominator. Making these adjustments in 1998 resulted in the long-term debt to assets ratio of approximately 30.0 percent[49]

---

[49] A rough approximation of the discounted present value of the leases was found by taking the average lease payment due over the periods and discounting it back to the present over an average lease life of four years at an assumed interest rate of 8 percent. The analysis of a company's operating leases is discussed in more detail in Chapter 12.

fair market value of the debt satisfied is more clearly evident. An extraordinary gain is recognized for the excess of the recorded liability over the fair market value of the asset transferred. The creditor records a corresponding bad debt loss (not an extraordinary item). In the case of asset exchanges, it is also necessary to record a gain or loss on disposition of the assets to the extent of any difference between the asset's fair market value and its carrying value.

Equity for debt swaps can increase reported income by the amount of the extraordinary gain on debt restructure and by reduced interest expense. Also, debt is removed from the balance sheet and replaced by equity, thereby improving the financial position of the company and its debt-to-equity ratios. For example, in 1990, Financial Corp. of Santa Barbara swapped $50 million of equity for debt and recognized an extraordinary gain of $36.5 million.[47] The common shares issued replaced preferred stock, subordinated debentures, and notes.

Disclosure of Restructuring Agreements

SFAS No. 15 requires the following disclosures by debtors entering into restructuring agreements.

1. A description of the principal changes in terms and/or the major features of settlement for each restructuring agreement.
2. The aggregate gain on debt restructures and the related income tax effect.
3. The per-share amount of the aggregate gain on restructuring net of the related income tax effect.
4. The aggregate gain or loss recognized during the period on transfers of assets.

For creditors subject to the provisions of *SFAS No. 114*, the *SFAS No. 15* requirement that the amount of any commitments to lend additional funds to the debtor still applies. Under *SFAS No. 114*, these creditors are required to disclose

1. The recorded investment balance at the balance sheet date as well as the related total allowance for credit losses.
2. The beginning balance in the allowance account and the changes in it during the period.
3. The creditor's income recognition policy.[48]

Financial Analysis of Long-Term Debt

The financial analysis of a company's long-term debt includes assessing its liquidity, solvency, and financial flexibility, and assessing the risk associated with its use of financial leverage. Liquidity refers to a company's ability to

[47] "Financial Corp. of Santa Barbara's Net Jumps Sevenfold," *Wall Street Journal* (April 24, 1990), Sec. C, p. 22.

[48] SFAC no. 114, op. cit., par. 20.

effect-type adjustment of other comprehensive income are subsequently recognized in earnings on the date on which the forecasted transaction had been projected to occur.

The FASB thus recognizes the emergence of derivative securities and their complexity, and has responded with pronouncements designed to require published financial statements to present a more accurate disclosure of the risks borne by firms using derivative financial instruments. The provisions of *SFAS No. 133* are examined in more detail in an article by Blankley and Schroeder contained on the webpage for Chapter 10.

In addition to the FASB, the SEC also addressed the issue of accounting for derivatives in new required disclosure rules in an amendment to Regulation S-X. This release requires the disclosure of qualitative and quantitative information about market risk by all companies registered with the SEC for annual periods ending after June 15, 1998. Market risk is defined as the risk of loss arising from adverse changes in market rates and prices from such items as interest rates, currency exchange rates, commodity prices, and equity prices. The required disclosures are designed to provide investors with forward-looking information about a company's exposures to market risk, such as the risks associated with changes in interest rates, foreign currency exchange rates, commodity prices, and stock prices. It is anticipated that the information provided will indicate the market risk a company faces and how the company's management views and manages its market risk.

The quantitative information about market risk-sensitive instruments is to be disclosed by using one or more of the following alternatives:

1. *Tabular presentation* of fair value information and contract terms relevant to determining future cash flows, categorized by expected maturity dates;
2. *Sensitivity analysis* expressing the potential loss in future earnings, fair values, or cash flows from selected hypothetical changes in market rates and prices; or
3. *Value at risk* disclosures expressing the potential loss in future earnings, fair values, or cash flows from market movements over a selected period of time and with a selected likelihood of occurrence.

These three alternative methods were allowed because the SEC wanted to allow disclosure requirements about market risk that were flexible enough to accommodate different types of registrants, different degrees of market risk exposure, and alternative methods of measuring market risk

The disclosure of this information is found in several places in a company's annual report, including item 7a of Management's Discussion and Analysis, the summary of significant accounting policies, and the footnotes to the financial statements as illustrated by the Kroll-O'Gara financial statements contained on the text's webpage.

Troubled Debt Restructurings

Corporations occasionally experience difficulty repaying their long-term debt obligations. These difficulties frequently result in arrangements between debtor and creditor that allow the debtor to avoid bankruptcy. For example, in 1976, Continental Investment Corporation satisfied $34 million of the $61 million debt owed to the First National Bank of Boston by transferring all its stock in Investors Mortgage Group, Inc. (a subsidiary) to the bank. Accountants and financial statement users became concerned over the lack of GAAP by which to account for these agreements. Consequently, the FASB began a study of agreements of this type, termed *troubled debt restructurings*. This study focused on three questions: (1) Do certain kinds of troubled debt restructurings require reductions in the carrying amounts of debt? (2) If they do, should the effect of the reduction be reported as current income, deferred to a future period, or reported as contributed capital? (3) Should contingently payable interest on the restructured debt be recognized before it becomes payable?

The issues underlying each of these questions relate to the recognition of liabilities and holding gains. A liability should be recorded at the amount of probable future sacrifice of economic benefits arising from present obligations. A holding gain occurs when the value of the liability decreases. The results of the review of these questions was the release of *SFAS No. 15*, "Accounting by Debtors and Creditors for Troubled Debt Restructurings."[39]

According to *SFAS No. 15*, a troubled debt restructuring occurs when "the creditor for economic or legal reasons related to the debtor's financial difficulties grants a concession to the debtor that it would not otherwise consider."[40] A troubled debt restructuring may include, but is not limited to, one or any combination of the following.

1. *Modification of terms of a debt such as one or a combination of:*
   a. *Reduction ... of the stated interest rate for the remaining original life of the debt.*
   b. *Extension of the maturity date or dates at a stated interest rate lower than the current market rate for new debt with similar risk.*
   c. *Reduction ... of the face amount or maturity amount of the debt as stated in the instrument or other agreement.*
   d. *Reduction ... of accrued interest.*

2. *Issuance or other granting of an equity interest to the creditor by the debtor to satisfy fully or partially a debt unless the equity interest is granted pursuant to existing terms for converting the debt into an equity interest.*

3. *A transfer from the debtor to the creditor of receivables from third parties, real estate, or other assets to satisfy fully or partially a debt.*[41]

---

[39] Financial Accounting Standards Board, *Statements of Financial Accounting Standards No. 15*, "Accounting by Debtors and Creditors for Troubled Debt Restructurings" (Stamford, CT: FASB, 1977), par. 2.

[40] Ibid.

[41] Ibid., par. 5.

reporting standards for derivative financial instruments and similar financial instruments. It requires that an entity recognize all derivatives as either assets or liabilities in the statement of financial position and measure those instruments at fair value. If certain conditions are met, a derivative may be specifically designated as (a) a hedge of the exposure to changes in the fair value of a recognized asset or liability or a firm commitment, (b) a hedge of the exposure to variable cash flows of a forecasted transaction, or (c) a hedge of the foreign currency exposure of a net investment in a foreign operation.

The accounting for changes in the fair value of a derivative (that is, gains and losses) would depend on the intended use of the derivative and the resulting designation.

1. For a derivative designated as a hedge of the exposure to changes in the fair value of a recognized asset or liability or a firm commitment (referred to as a fair value hedge), the gain or loss is recognized in earnings in the period of change together with the offsetting loss or gain on the hedged item. The effect of that accounting is to adjust the basis of the hedged item by the amount of the gain or loss on the hedging derivative to the extent that the gain or loss offsets the loss or gain experienced on the hedged item.

2. For a derivative designated as a hedge of the exposure to variable cash flows of a forecasted transaction (referred to as a cash flow hedge), the gain or loss is reported as a component of other comprehensive income (outside of earnings) and recognized in earnings on the projected date of the forecasted transaction.

3. For a derivative designated as a hedge of the foreign currency exposure of a net investment in a foreign operation, the portion of the change in fair value equivalent to a foreign currency transaction gain or loss is reported in other comprehensive income (outside of earnings) as part of the cumulative translation adjustment; any remaining change in fair value is recognized in earnings.

4. For a derivative not designated as a hedge, the gain or loss is recognized in earnings in the period of change.

At the date of initial application, an entity measures all derivatives at fair value and recognizes them in the statement of financial position as either assets or liabilities. The entity also recognizes offsetting gains and losses on hedged assets, liabilities, and firm commitments by adjusting their carrying amounts at that date. The transition adjustments that result from adopting this proposed statement are reported in net income or other comprehensive income, as appropriate, as the effect of a change in accounting principle and are presented in a manner similar to the cumulative effect of a change in accounting principle. Whether the transition adjustments are reported in net income or other comprehensive income is based on the hedging relationships, if any, that had existed for the related derivatives and were the basis for accounting under generally accepted accounting principles prior to the date of initial application. Transition adjustments reported as a cumulative-

TABLE 10.1 *Types of Derivatives*

Type	Market	Purpose	Type of Contract	Definition
Forward	Over-the-counter	Transfer risk	Negotiated on a case-by-case basis.	Obligates the holder to buy or sell specified amount of currency at a specified price on a specified date in the future
Future	Organized exchange	Transfer risk	Fixed as to face value, period, and point of settlement	Obligates the holder to buy or sell specified amount of currency at a specified price on a specified date in the future
Option	Over-the-counter or organized exchange	Transfer risk	Either negotiated or fixed period	Grants the purchaser the right, but not the obligation, to buy or sell a specific amount of currency at a specified price within a specified period
Swap	Over-the-counter	Transfer risk	Negotiated on a case-by-case basis	Agreement between the parities to make periodic payments to each other during the swap period
Hybrid	Over-the-counter	Transfer risk	Negotiated on a case-by-case	Incorporates various provisions of any or all of the above types.